"Life is full of imperfections. It's these flaws and kinks that can make your life, your memories, your reason for being, or they can be like sand in your shoe that does nothing but irritate. You choose."

Tom Gray

"Pedaling" is not a story about cycling. It is a story of change, a physical and mental transformation of a man named Tom Gray that occurs while riding his bike on a cross country cycling trip with more than forty other adventurous individuals fully supported by CrossRoads Cycling Adventures during the summer of 2004. The transformation during this journey from Los Angeles to Boston has as much to do with shaping his outlook on the future as it does with the miles he travels between these two points. You don't need to be an avid cyclist to enjoy this story; you just need to have the curiosity to follow one man as his life is changed for the better. Along the way you will experience the challenges of cycling, the history and uniqueness of small towns, and the people who inhabit them. You will also learn about the other dreamers turned doers in their pursuit of their own dream. All people referenced within this book are real and quite honestly were a pleasure to know.

ISBN-13: 978-1977982582
ISBN-10: 1977982581

Dedicated to the memory of
Thomas J. Gray, Sr.
1925–1999

"To my dad, my friend who is missed every day, I see you as clearly now as I did when you were here. Thank you for riding with me.

"To my mom, the one who always believed I could do anything I set out to do."

"To my wife Donna and daughters Janel and Nicole, who show me how to live, love and laugh."

"To my granddaughter Olivia Marie, who owns my heart."

"To those who inspired me, rode with me and cheered me on each day, believing in me even when I didn't think I could go on. The successful completion of this coast to coast cycling journey is as much your victory as it is mine."

Pedaling

Tom Gray

My Story

Cycling cross country for me was a significant and enjoyable personal accomplishment. And as if doing the ride wasn't enough of a challenge I wrote and took photographs for the DeLand Beacon, our local Florida newspaper recapping my week by week experience and they were kind enough to print it. When I returned home I was surprised to see my traveling installments covered a half to almost two pages with the photos each week. Sometimes my adventures would be featured in both the mid–week and weekend editions. I also had a small mention and a tickler photo on the front page banner. I was both humbled and proud.

In addition to writing about the trip for the Beacon I also used the time to write daily personal messages to my wife and my two daughters. For my wife I shared my triumphs and failures and how the distance gave me a new perspective on our relationship. For Nicole, my youngest and an avid writer and reader of poetry, I crafted my experience of the day in the medium she enjoys so much. Sometimes quirky, but I thought she would enjoy my experiences in rhyme. Janel, my oldest by sixteen months, challenged me to go learn who I am. Hers was the most difficult daily to write but it was also the most emotional and it was the exclamation point of my adventure. You cannot embark on such a journey and not learn who you are, and sometimes, as in my situation, who you want to be.

With all the writing very little sleep was had during the forty–nine days of travel, but those efforts allowed me to record and share my experience as it unfolded. This is actually four books or diaries of sorts for each of the audiences mentioned earlier. I decided to keep them separate as they were originally crafted so you the reader can enjoy them as you like. I hope you will read all four of the diaries as each contributes something unique to this story.

The personal writings to my wife and daughters were transferred directly from my original notes. My reasoning for this was simple; the words I chose in those moments could not be improved on. Besides my memory of those days will never be as sharp or as clear as it was just hours after stepping off the bike at the end of each day, and I wanted them to feel as if they were in the moment. In publishing this manuscript my wife and daughters will finally get to see the daily messages I prepared for the other two. I hope they laugh at the quirks and feel a deeper connection to each other through my words.

The primary tome was revised to expand on the draft written for the newspaper. The experience remains vivid in my mind and it allowed me to blend in some updated information as I wrote and reflected back to those wonderful days in 2004.

Without the limits of column space I will do my best to describe the adventure at the blistering pace of fourteen miles per hour. I hope you enjoy this story of how a man of forty–five was able to be a seventeen year old boy again, if for only forty–nine days.

Self–Support versus Full–Support

In the purest sense the thought of cycling across America brings about images of lone riders traveling on road bikes weighed down with full panniers—bags mounted on both sides of the front and rear wheels—spare tubes and vital supplies affixed to the bike frame and bars in all the available locations and even more supplies strapped to the top of the rear bike rack and a handle bar bag filled to the brim with road snacks. Water bottles are wedged into their frame mounted cages and maybe the rider has to sport a backpack to contain the last of the necessary items to make a successful crossing. Riders unable to pare down the list of essentials might even attach a towable trailer just to further reduce their chance of success. This is referred to as self–supported cycling.

Each day would be a measure of physical and mental strength in balance with luck and whatever Mother Nature elects to throw into the mix. That's how I envisioned my cross country journey back in my teen years, but three decades later it's not how it played out. I like to think it's because I am smarter now than at seventeen but it's more complex than that. My dream was to ride across America. Not to camp out under the stars each night, wondering when I would bathe next, if I would be rained on, or what I would do if I had a bike failure or even worse, a fall miles away from any assistance. I also didn't want to depend on random acts of kindness by strangers on a daily basis just to move eighty miles down the road each day. I wanted to ride across America on my bike. That's all.

Many others have successfully traversed this country self–supported and some got by with a little help from people they met along the way. A few of those brave souls were kind enough to write about their experience at great length for others to enjoy and in some instances to learn from. Most of what they write about is what happens off the bike and it can be quite entertaining.

I elected a different approach; a nice hot shower and a warm bed each night, a well–planned itinerary and proper support to make sure I only needed to focus on making the pedals go around. This is referred to as fully–supported cycling. My stories may not include close encounters in the night with wildlife or dealing with a sudden rain storm or flash flood while bedded down in a sleeping bag but they do capture the spirit of what happens during the time on the bike along with some "after cycling time" mixed in to add some flavor. So if you were looking for a book on roughing it across America "covered wagon style" I warn you now this is not that story. But if you were looking to get a sense of what it is like to endure day after day on a bike in pursuit of the coast to coast dream, I think you may enjoy reading about my experience.

If you are thinking about dipping your cycling shoes into a cross country adventure I hope my experience provides you with some valuable information in deciding which option is best for you. Keep in mind not all fully supported cycling tours offer the same level of support I enjoyed. At a minimum you should expect someone to chaperon your group and to be responsible for managing the hotel and dining arrangements, provide daily route directions, roadside snacks and mechanical support should it be needed. In addition, the support team should be capable of gaging your performance and to determine if you might be exceeding your physical capabilities before you do. Nothing ruins a cycling trip like "bonking out" because you didn't drink enough water or take in enough electrolytes and cramped up.

Some fully supported tours use a skeleton crew consisting of a tour leader, a person providing roadside snacks (SAG – Support and Gear) and a third person cycling with the group. I was fortunate to have been supported by a larger staff of six to eight people at any given time. This included three support vehicles, all luggage handling delivered to my room each day, fresh fruit and homemade goodies at the SAG stops, experienced mechanics and a highly disciplined staff focused on rider safety and trip enjoyment. I don't think I would have been able to write about my trip if I did not have the level of support I received from CrossRoads Cycling Adventures.

In all fairness I have no direct experience with any other cycling tour groups but I did benefit from the experiences the other riders and staff shared with me. It all depends on the level of service you are looking for unless you are determined to cross the country self–supported. If you do choose to do it on your own I would suggest you have at least one riding partner who shares the same passion.

If you can, write about the trip and share it with others. With the proliferation of blogs today you can post your writing online each day with photos. Your followers can feel like they are right beside you every turn of the pedals, along each mile, through foul weather, up every hill you climb and down every wild descent. You will also enjoy rereading your adventures and reliving the moments of triumph and failure through the photos you collect.

Take pictures of everything and make sure you are in many of them. State signs, people, architecture, roadside junk, animals, the ribbons of asphalt and the landscape; capture it all along the way. You will only have one opportunity to chronical the adventure. Keep the blurry and poorly composed images as well. They all tell a story and will reveal something new to you each time you look at them. Your words and photos will be your record of your once–in–a–lifetime journey into the discovery of you. I promise it will become one of the most important possessions you will have for many years after.

Pre–Ride Journal

As is the case with any training program, most of the days can be pretty repetitive. So I don't bore anyone with the mundane I included only selected entries from my pre–ride journal to give you a feel of what was required, how I was progressing, and more importantly how I was dealing with the coming adventure.

February 17

Getting up this morning to return to the gym after several months was a bit rough. I weighed myself and, to my surprise, I was 197 pounds, about four more than I thought. Inside of me is a 150 pound fit person who I plan to release.

February 27

Today is bike testing day back at Orange Cycle in Orlando. I checked out several bike shops between Daytona and Orlando and this store had the best selection and the people were knowledgeable about their products. I knew very little about the new cycling technology. My last ride was a 1975 ten–speed Raleigh Grand Prix all steel frame bike with steel wheels and friction shifters. In fact, while looking at the new bikes I didn't see any shift levers. Not wanting to show my complete lack of knowledge I tried to figure it out myself but Kirstin, the sales person, was quick to pick up on my fumbling around the bikes. She showed me the new integrated brake/shifter system without making me feel like a complete moron. I quickly yielded to her suggestions and soon my decision was narrowed down to a bright yellow Cannondale and a silver Specialized road bike.

So now it was time to road test each bike to see which one would speak to me. I was amazed at the difference between the two; the frame size and geometry of the components. Neither bike was tuned to my specific fit needs, but with the seat height close, it was good enough to compare them during my around the block rides. I really liked the flashy look of the Cannondale but what it came down to was feel. I felt like the steering was a little too quick on the Cannondale; as if the front wheel could easily get out from under me. I didn't get that impression on the Specialized. Otherwise both were comparable in price and components so I was now leaning toward the more stable riding bike.

Later I would come to learn a simple stem change—moving the handle bars forward or back—could have tamed the sensation of instability. There was so much to learn about current day cycling and not much time to do it. I figured it would be a one–to–two hour ordeal, but it ended up taking the entire day to test the bikes, pick the optional equipment, and have the bike outfitted.

One very important suggestion Kirstin made was for me to get professionally fitted to my new bike. Even the best equipped bike stores can only do limited fittings which include basic seat height and forward to back positioning. This is done to ensure you have your knees properly positioned over the pedals and your leg extension is correct. It's mostly a visual inspection using a piece of string with a weight hanging on the end and an adjustable angular measuring device. It didn't take long to get the basic fitting done.

She said the nearest facility, and the one Orange Cycle referred their customers to, was the USA Triathlon Training Center in Clermont, Florida about twenty miles west of downtown Orlando. For about a hundred dollars I would be precisely measured on a special adjustable bike allowing the information to be recorded and transferred to my new purchase. I figured if they do fittings for the professional riders then I should be able to trust them to get me properly fitted. And it just might help me avoid any alignment issues on the tour; and that

I liked. I seem to recall the only adjustments I used to make was to raise or lower the seat or to possibly tilt the seat nose up or down. Welcome to modern day cycling Tommy!

One additional suggestion I would make about buying a bike has to do with seat size and comfort. More padding and a wider seat may feel fine for a short time but it can cause all kinds of problems on long rides. My bike came with a low end seat so I opted to buy a *Terry Liberator* which was supposed to be a better choice. I would end up using the *Terry* seat to make my cross country cycling trip but I learned years later it was too wide for my bone structure; which explained the chaffing and friction issues I would soon learn about on tour.

Bike stores now have a method for measuring your *sit bones* to size your seat properly. You simply sit on a small piece of special memory foam for thirty seconds and when you get off the staff measures the distance between the two indents your bones made in the foam. And that is how you get sized for a seat. Too wide and your thighs rub against the sides of the seat. Too narrow and you will feel like you are being violated. The last option includes material choice and padding type of which there are many. This part of the fitting you have to do by feel since they don't make a device to measure your padding needs; at least not yet.

My friend and former co-worker Bennett lives close by the bike shop so I called him to share in the excitement. He met me and we grabbed a quick lunch around the corner and then it was back to the bike shop to show him my new wheels. He too was the adventurous type and understood how I was feeling.

After Bennett left the bike shop I was on my own to pay for the wild shopping spree I spent most of the day on. Today it is not just buying the bike; it's the special shoes, bike shorts, pumps, stands, tools, helmets, gloves and on and on until I max out my credit limit or common sense. Nearly two thousand dollars later I was the proud owner of a new aluminum frame high tech Specialized Elite Allez twenty–seven–speed road bike. I loaded everything into my pickup truck and was on my way back home to begin opening the boxes and attaching all of the accessories to my new set of wheels.

February 28 and 29

I had plenty of yard work to keep me busy, so no bike riding for me. You'd think after spending 1,900 dollars on a bike and gear, I'd be riding and leaving the chores for later. Well you'd have thought wrong.

March 3

I quickly learned being off the bike for twenty years made it difficult to adjust to riding in traffic with cars traveling at speed just two feet to my left shoulder. The roads near my house are very quiet and bike friendly but after the first half mile I would need to jump on Kepler Road, a two lane ribbon of asphalt used primarily as a truck route around the east side of DeLand. I would have to travel the equivalent of three city blocks on Kepler until I could drop onto a slightly less busy street. The trick was to wait for an opening in traffic and then pedal like a mad man and hope I could get off the busy road before any cars, or worse, any buses or large trucks try to take back the little bit of roadway I am using. It all sounded good but somehow it fell apart in the execution.

After tooling around town for an hour I had my first close encounter on my new bike. I was partly responsible because I picked a busy time to be on Kepler and there was only a foot of pavement to the right of the solid line. Then it dropped off about two feet into a ditch which didn't provide a cyclist much to work with.

I happened to see in my mirror a school bus using up every bit of its lane as dump trucks and numerous cars were heading in the opposite direction. What got my attention was the large bus mirror extending well beyond the solid line and clearly capable of hitting me in the back of the head. I had about fifty yards to pedal to reach my right turn, but the bus was moving too fast and would be on me before I got there. Crashing into the ditch would have been plan *B* so in that moment I chose to duck down as close to the handlebars as I could. Within seconds the bus mirror zoomed over my head at forty–five miles per hour. Had I been sitting straight up enjoying the ride my story would have a different ending. Likely the ending, or more like my ending, would have come with a sharp blow to the head.

I was rattled to say the least and was questioning my ability to deal with traffic like this riding across the country. After all this was only small town traffic and the cross country trip would entail riding through some of the most congested roadways and cities in America. A little late to get cold feet now so I figured I would have to relearn the cycling and automobile road sharing relationship.

March 6

I learned a valuable lesson today in being prepared and more importantly what happens when you are not. The day started out on the warm side. I was feeling rather strong so I figured I would head across town, then turn north through the quiet Glenwood community known for its divided roadway and mature Oak tree canopy. Since this area was heavily shaded I was not exposed to the heat of the morning as it was building. I continued to DeLeon Springs State Park where you can make your own griddle pancakes at the Old Spanish Sugar Mill built next to the natural sulfur springs known for spewing out twenty million gallons of seventy–two degree water a day.

I stopped briefly at the park entrance to take a drink of Gatorade before leaving the cover of trees and breaking out into the open sun on South Country Road 3. My sights were set on the crossroads town of Barberville, population: 4,586. It's actually nothing more than an intersection of two rural highways anchoring a convenience store, a gas station, and a junk shop selling metal and concrete yard statues and assorted stuff. Most of the residents are spread out across agricultural acreage and are known for growing fern and raising horses.

The ride to Barberville was just another six miles, or twenty–five minutes at my pace, and I was beginning to feel the heat. The plan was to turn back after reaching the Pioneer Settlement for the Arts near Highway 40 but I decided to venture west to the Astor Bridge and cross the St. John's River, the states only northerly flowing waterway, into rural Lake County. I enjoyed the eight mile ride west to the river but I was running out of both water and Gatorade. I also did not prepare any snacks for the ride and my billfold was left at the house. I realized I had exceeded my supplies and was beginning to tire so I turned around.

The air was very still and the radiant heat coming off the road taxed my body. I was running out of energy and beginning to get an uneasy queasy feeling in my gut as I approached County Road 3. I made the right hand turn and then I *bonked!* I stopped, slid off the bike, and immediately threw up. I felt light headed and exhausted so I decided to lie down on the side of the road under a bit of shade from a tree.

I did not let the fire ants bother me as I was too drained to do anything about them. Fire ants, for those who have no experience with them, are extremely aggressive, their sting similar to a bumble bee followed twenty four hours later by a raised white pustule at the site of the attack. The festering wound itches relentlessly and can be painful for days. The ants eventually convinced me it was time to get up, dust off and figure out how to get home. I made my way over to the bike and dug my cell phone out of the bike bag and began making calls.

After nearly fifteen minutes of trying to reach my wife, my brother or one of my daughters, I realized I was on my own twenty miles from home. I was not going to get any help. I figured the sooner I get back on the bike the better. The trek home was slow and I stopped every mile or two for a break. My legs were like mush and my head and stomach hurt. The first goal was to get back to the shade under the trees near the state park but the temperature and stillness of the air negated the benefit I was hoping for. On to Glenwood a few miles down the road.

The rolling hills seemed much steeper and I was covering less and less ground with each stop. Every few miles I would pause and try to reach someone by phone to no avail. After nearly two hours from where I bonked I pulled up to the Stetson University campus and found sanctuary on a bench under a shade tree. I noticed the slightest of a breeze but then realized it was due to the proximity of the bench to the busy Woodland Boulevard. I stayed on the bench for another fifteen minutes before mounting the bike and making the final three mile ride back to the house. It was slow going and when I arrived I leaned my head on the house door for about two minutes before getting the key into the lock and making my way to a glass of water and a soothing shower. I felt dejected but also lucky to have made it home.

I was told you need to experience what it is like to be totally exhausted on the road so you remember to always be prepared. The second lesson is never go farther than the original training plan. I guess it is part of the process and after that day I was always better supplied than my trip required.

March 10

Today I rode indoors on the trainer for one hour, and in the late afternoon I took a spin through Daytona Park Estates, an older poorly planned Florida subdivision of bunker style block cottage houses a mile away from where I lived. It was sunny, but a bit brisk and windy. My goal for the day was to ride for one hour at an average speed of fourteen miles per hour. The final tally for the ride included 16.18 miles covered in one hour and eight minutes, which equates to a solid 14.2 miles per hour.

After a shower and change of clothes I checked my e–mail and read where local cyclists Pat and Vikki Wilcox invited me to ride with them. They live in Lake Mary, a suburban community just north of Orlando and twenty–five miles south along Interstate 4 from DeLand. They would also be joining me on the cross country cycling tour which explained how they got my email address. The reality of the trip continues to sink in. Fortunately for me it sounds like Pat and Vikki are experienced cyclists and based on my training to date I can use all of the pointers they are willing to offer.

March 13

Thanks to the fine hospitality of Pat and Vikki I was riding with their cycling club through the scenic neighborhoods and business areas of Lake Mary. This was definitely a step up in riding for me as I was neither used to the pace nor the experience of riding with a pack of twenty other cyclists. These folks were well conditioned and very competitive. It didn't take long for me to get winded at the pace of more than twenty miles an hour and I was not a fan of riding right on top of someone else's wheel in a pace line. Even more concerning was having someone inches off of my own back wheel making it critical to maintain a very consistent pace.

The benefit of riding in a pace line is the lead rider breaks the wind creating an opportunity for the other riders to be pulled along in their draft. With less of their own effort required to maintain speed those riding behind the leader save valuable energy and can ride much faster than they could on their own without expending any additional effort. Much like the way your car reacts when you move up behind a semi–tractor trailer on the open highway. If everyone takes a turn at the front and rotates every half mile or so there is plenty of time to recover as you drop back in line. While I did not like the close proximity of riding in a pace line it would prove to be a valuable experience in preparing for my cross country trip.

Once we cleared the congested Lake Mary Boulevard and headed north toward a more rural area near Lake Monroe I began to settle into the rhythm of the day. I managed to take my turn at the lead of the pace line and pulled for about a third mile before moving aside allowing the next rider his opportunity. We were passing under continuous expanses of Oak trees and around large fields being worked by farmers for a new growing season. The sound of the wind and cyclist chatter abounded. I was riding five miles an hour over my normal rate and it did not take long before I found myself drifting farther to the rear of the line.

Halfway through the forty mile ride I opted to split off with a group of riders planning to take a slower pace for the loop back to our starting point. I returned to my comfort level and eventually the parking lot at the Lake Mary bike shop where my riding day began. I gained experience in the pace line and was able to spend some time with a fun group of riders. I also learned a little about something called *Butt Butter* and its magical powers.

March 16

Rain, rain, go away. The riding was confined to three hours of indoor pedaling on the trainer, but once the skies cleared I managed to get an hour and a half of actual road riding. I averaged 13.2 miles per hour and covered 20.2 miles.

I also learned lesson one of a three part series. When riding with shoe clips you fall three times before you learn how to unclip and catch yourself. I was coming to a stop and unclipped my right shoe but a sudden shift of balance caused me to fall left landing hard with my weight distributed from hip to shoulder. Then came a *thud* and a *gasp* as I expelled the air from my lungs on impact and created a bit of a show for a car coming up behind me. And wouldn't you know they didn't stop to see if I was okay!

March 18

No riding the trainer today it was all road work! A bit breezy but otherwise a perfect day to ride around the Athens of Florida, otherwise known as DeLand.

I would have ridden for another few hours if I didn't have a doctor's appointment to remove a basal cell growth from my right shoulder. I'll likely be off the bike tomorrow instead of covering the planned forty miles thanks to the minor surgery. Yet another reminder I'll need to purchase a long–sleeved jersey for sun protection on the desert ride.

March 20

A short ride through the south east part of town and I was moving along at reasonable pace when I slowed for an intersection and experienced lesson number two. With my right foot unclipped and just as the wheels were about to stop spinning I rolled over a small twig which was enough to alter my balance and over to the left I fell. This time in front of an audience of four people in a car sitting idle at the stop sign. And just like the first time I fell this car rolled through the intersection without even a hesitation to see if I was okay. Lucky for me the impact wasn't so bad but I need to stop falling on the same shoulder. I finished the day with just over thirty miles covered at a pace of 13.7 miles per hour. Now if I can only get the third fall out of the way before I leave for California!

March 23

I'm down 16.5 pounds and tip the scales at 180.5 pounds. Today was where the rubber met the road. I planned to ride for sixty miles or about twenty miles more than I had ridden at one time. When it was all over, I posted 60.8 miles in five hours, six minutes. This works out to 11.9 miles per hour, not too shabby considering the wind and cold weather conditions.

March 27

It was a bit windy, but I needed to log some riding miles. I set my goal for forty miles for the day and headed off to Deltona via Lake Helen. I was surprised how quickly I was able to get into Deltona riding into the wind most of the way. The sun was bright and I was lucky to ride at thirteen miles per hour into the wind. I figured the good news would be a healthy tail wind to blow me home.

Once getting to Deltona, I was not impressed with the provisions for bicycles. It was either ride on the edge of the white line and risk getting clipped by shoppers looking for the entry to Target or Walmart or ride on the sidewalks—and I don't like to ride on the sidewalks even if they are as wide as a single lane road. Oh, and in Florida it is also illegal to ride on the sidewalks so it really wasn't an option for me.

Deltona is predominantly a bedroom community that transformed from its original retirement community roots planned by the Mackle Brothers in 1962. The walking and cycling trails are limited and the town never quite kept pace with the changing dynamics of its population. Without a balanced concentration of industry to offset the burden on the homeowners, no measureable changes are expected in the near future. Deltona does have excellent soccer fields and parks but it lags behind most other central Florida cities when it comes to walking and cycling pathways. Quality trail systems have proven to boost ecotourism and nearby towns including Clermont, Mount Dora and Eustis have leveraged their investment in trails to generate millions of dollars in additional annual revenue.

April 1

Remembering the recommendation about getting professionally fitted I had previously called the USA Triathlon Training Center in Clermont and scheduled my appoint for today. I met with Adam Baskin, professional bike fitter, exercise physiologist, and cycling coach with degrees in Clinical Exercise Physiology and Exercise Science from two of the largest universities in Florida. Baskin is also recognized as one of top bike fitters in the country. And if that isn't enough, Adam is an accomplished racing cyclist himself. I think this was a wise decision to get fitted by a pro.

Some quick measurements by Adam and the adjustable stationary measuring bike was ready for me to start riding. For thirty minutes I rode while Adam observed my pedaling and made adjustments; lots of adjustments. He also asked me about any discomfort I was having on the bike to which I listed off several. Hot foot, neck pain, elbow and forearm discomfort were the leading candidates but I also got around to mentioning my knee trouble and wrist numbness.

Adam continued measuring and writing and every few minutes he would stop me and make more adjustments to the bike and to my shoes to see how the change affected me. Small changes to the clips on the shoes made a measurable improvement on the sensitivity to hot foot and with each change I was getting closer to a more comfortable and natural riding position.

Adam also asked about my riding expectations and made some very good suggestions on how I should continue training. When we finished he showed me a sheet detailing all of the final fit adjustments and then he went about bringing my bike up to those specifications. With the exception of one detail my bike was exact to the stationary measuring machine. He suggested I replace the eighty–five millimeter stem with one measuring five millimeters shorter to complete the required fit geometry. He also said I should move up from a fifty to a fifty–two centimeter frame the next time I buy one. Interesting to note the shorter stem would cause the same conditions I found a little unnerving on the Cannondale which so happened to be a fifty–two centimeter frame. Go figure. With the spec sheet in hand I could easily restore my bike to the required settings when I unpacked it in California. Now to find a shorter stem for this bike.

April 11

At first light, I was prepping my gear for a day of riding. It was cold and foggy, and I had no idea where I might go, but I was going for an eighty–mile spin. I had to shake off the cobwebs from a few days off the saddle. The ride took me through the quaint little cottage town of Lake Helen, population: 2,808, then on to Deltona, population: 79,749, the largest city in Volusia County. What followed next was a very scenic tour along the northern shores of Lake Monroe through the unincorporated village of Enterprise, which was once the county seat of Volusia County. From there I headed south along county road 415 crossing the narrow St. John's River marshes, past the Gator's Riverside Grill, and into the historic town of Sanford, the county seat of Seminole county, just as the fog was beginning to burn off.

Traffic over the small bridge crossing the St. John's was very tight and no one was giving this rider much room to spare. At the eastern edge of Sanford I turned right heading west on the traffic heavy Highway SR–46 towards Mt. Plymouth, the bright sun warming my back.

The temperature climbed quickly between Sanford and my turn north onto county road 437 in Lake County. I twisted along the asphalt through horse farms and heavy Oak canopies before intersecting with Highway 44 for the final twenty mile push northeast back to DeLand.

Most of the terrain to the St. John's River crossing at Sam Stone Park consisted of mild rolling hills. About three miles shy of the river the elevation changes began to taper off and I was facing a slight afternoon northeasterly headwind. Without any protection from the hot Florida sun I was baking. The heat waves were radiating up from the asphalt blurring and dancing above the roadway. It would be another hour before I could count this ride as done and the sun was going to taunt me all the way.

As I was pedaling along the flats of Lake County just about a hundred yards shy of a slight left hand bend, a car passed by and failed to make the turn without using up the three foot shoulder and a bit of the grass as well. It was one of those moments where I was glad I wasn't just a bit quicker. I figured the driver was busy tuning in a radio station or texting a friend, but either way I could have easily become a hood ornament on his ride if I was just a bit farther up the road. It took just about five and a half hours to cover the eighty–mile trek with only one close call. I would cycle this section of road just one more time for my ninety–mile training ride and then I would have to find safer roads to travel. Mentally I was adjusting to the traffic but I did not want to take any unnecessary risks.

April 18

It's a big day on the bike today. I'm planning to ride a ninety–miler from DeLand into Lake County and back. I ventured out on my familiar northwest route where I would pass through the upper half of DeLand. Block after block of white and pastel painted wooden skewed houses with tin roofs sitting atop of stacked block piers under heavy Oak foliage lined the road. Fifteen minutes later I was rolling through the quaint wooded town of Glenwood and from there it was on to DeLeon Springs before finally arriving in Barberville, where just four weeks earlier I lay sprawled on the ground after losing a battle with heat exhaustion.

As I pedaled by the shaded spot of pavement, I looked it over the same way one would look at the scene of a bad accident. You can't keep from looking but you keep on rolling. Soon it was behind me, fading into the warmth of the morning.

Just over an hour into my ride I pointed my bike due west on Highway 40 and headed toward the river town of Astor in Lake County. After crossing the Astor Bridge, a modern drawbridge built in 1980 and the only hill of any sort since Barberville, I rode deep into Lake County toward the Ocala National Forest. The pavement quickly heated up and I could feel the warmth radiating upward. The air was mostly still but the winds would begin to kick in at a moment's notice.

As I counted off the landmarks sweat began to run down my brow. First up was Astor Park followed by Wild Woods Campground, and then the lakes of Schimmerhorn, Gobbler and Wildcat. My next turn would be a left south onto Highway 19, a nearly dead flat road past the Pinecastle Bombing Range. It would be another eighteen miles before I reach the small city of Umatilla which covers just three square miles and is home to less than 3,500 residents.

The winds were starting to grow slowly out of the east creating a slight cross wind and a much welcome relatively cool breeze. A quick stop at a convenience store for a fresh Gatorade and a snack was in order before pressing on. I was happy forty–five miles of the ride had been covered and I was feeling pretty good. I continued south on Highway 19 headed for the lakeside city of Eustis, population: 17,100, just another ten miles away. The winds continued to increase. I was certain after my turn in Eustis the final thirty–five mile ride east to DeLand would be either straight into a headwind or at best a quarterly headwind. I would also begin to see changes in elevation so having a headwind and hills together were not my idea of the ideal conditions to end a ride. I guess that's why it is called training.

As expected the winds came on strong just in time for me to make the turn in Eustis onto Highway 44. The first ten miles were due east straight into the wind and I could feel my speed react to even the slightest of wind change. As I approached the Seminole State Forest the road took a northeasterly heading and the flats transitioned to mild rolling hills. For the next sixteen miles the winds continued to come at me from the right front and they continued to grow. Since Eustis the wind was picking up the radiant road heat so it was feeling pretty hot and there was not much in the way of either shade or convenience stores to find relief. Even if I did the temperatures would rise and the overall riding conditions would continue to decline. Stopping was not a good idea.

As I approached the Whitehair Bridge to cross back over the St. Johns River into Volusia County the highway bent back to a due east trajectory and it was at this point the hilliest part of the day would be experienced. Stronger headwinds, hot radiant heat combined with big hills by central Florida standards had me dripping in sweat. I had a good pace going and then during one of the longer steady grades just two miles west of DeLand my right knee began to ache. With several small hills to follow I pressed on to the detriment of my knee and my pace. My effort over the last seven miles could best be described as limping home yet I finished the ride of 90.42 miles in six hours, seven minutes for an average of 14.7 miles per hour. Not too shabby but I need to nurse my knee back to where it can handle the distance on consecutive days.

April 19–26

Most of this week was spent recovering from the knee strain. Lesson to self—learn your limits.

April 27

I weighed myself at the gym and bingo! I was down to 170 pounds. How cool is that! Twenty–seven pounds lost since February 17. Ten weeks at nearly three pounds per week. This cycling is really changing me; credit to the diet change as well.

April 28

Crash! I lay flat on my back for several minutes with my head ringing, shoulder aching. It happened so fast. Just moments before I was riding along about a half mile from home on a quick test ride to try out my new eyeglass mounted mirror. I should have left my cell phone at home or in the seat bag but instead I secured it to the bike frame with a rubber band. As a public service announcement, please do not repeat this mistake.

I was moving along at about ten to twelve miles per hour when I noticed my cell phone was about to side out from the rubber band holding it to the top tube connecting the seat post to the handlebars. As I reached for the phone the rubber band broke and it fell to the pavement. Not thinking, I reached down with my right hand to try and grab the phone at the same time I put the squeeze on the left break lever locking the front wheel. This caused the bike to wheel stand and flip me over the handlebars pile driving my head and left shoulder into the pavement. Fortunately at the last moment before planting my face to earth I turned my head to the right allowing the helmet and shoulder to share the impact.

I looked up to the sky on what otherwise was a postcard sunny day in Florida; blue and with just the hint of clouds through the tree canopy above me. It was quiet with no one around except for a few older gentlemen at the end of the next street. The sound of the impact suggested I did some damage but I got up after doing a quick personal inventory and the shoulder seemed to be in the right place and nothing was poking out of the skin. I picked up my phone and got on the bike and rode home. My wife wanted me to go get checked out to make sure I wasn't injured but I refused. I was certain a doctor would tell me I could not go on the cross country ride. And I was going!

I'm not sure if this fall qualified as my third lesson or not but at this point I don't want to fall any more if I can avoid it. Especially on my left shoulder which is still pretty banged up from the two prior falls.

May 1

The bike was packed and shipped, and now I'm anticipating my travel to Los Angeles to get reacquainted with my bike. I would also use the next two weeks to heal my injuries and strains in hopes of being physically healthy and ready to start my seven week eastward journey.

May 5–9

I did some eating the past few days; pasta, cheeses, burgers, chips and dip. Let's not forget the cakes! Returning to my old habits is not very difficult but after making so much progress I have got to pace myself. I need this ride to start soon to avoid gaining my weight back.

Since no one knew what I looked like I decided to get my hair bleached white blonde for the trip. Actually it was L'Oreal 9 ½ NB. It was easier then shaving my head and less permanent and painful than a tattoo. I actually thought it looked pretty cool. I guess I'm unleashing the rebel in me.

Forward

In our youth, we dreamed of the things we wanted to do and places we wanted to go. We talked about careers, relationships and life without considering the preparation, the expense and other hurdles we needed to overcome for us to realize those dreams.

We knew no boundaries; we wanted to be astronauts, doctors, teachers, firefighters, artists, mountain climbers, world travelers, and some of us even wanted to be the president of the United States. We were kids. From grade school through our college years, we had hope for greater things to come.

A few of us were fortunate enough to follow our dreams and live them in our daily lives; while the rest of us let the dreams fade. Periodically, we would reflect back on our plans of youth and wonder if we would ever climb that mountain or be that teacher. We would then have to decide whether to dismiss the dream, forgetting about it completely, or more likely, we would just push it off into the future. "I'll climb that mountain after I retire," we would tell ourselves and then put the dream on hold and go about our daily lives.

Then it happens. The kids move out. You lose your job, or a close friend passes away. You realize time is not on your side, that you are not immortal and your one pass through life is moving so swiftly that today needs to be the day you take your dormant dream out of storage and bring it to life.

At forty–five, all of these events and more happened to me and gave me reason to put my dream of riding a bicycle across America into action. Actually my wife, Donna, revived my cross country cycling aspirations. She told me she found a fully supported bicycle touring company by the name of CrossRoads Cycling Adventures. She insisted I go live the dream before I dive back into another job where I would not be afforded this indulgence. She also told me she'd much rather hear me tell the stories in my retirement years about riding across the country instead of regretting a trip not taken.

My story begins in the early summer of 1976 when I thought I could do something adventurous, crazy, and maybe even a bit scary; at seventeen, I was going to ride across America on my bike. Yes, by bike as in bicycle. Two wheels, a pair of legs and time, lots of time. I read in the local newspaper about one of many bi–centennial celebrations happening at the time included a seventy–six day cross country bicycle ride from New York City to San Francisco, California. Total mileage was somewhere around 3,500 miles so it meant I would only have to ride about fifty miles a day. It sounded pretty easy to me as I was comfortable riding eighty to one hundred miles a day even after mowing the yard and finishing my other chores. You have to understand bicycling was a big deal back in 1976 and getting around the rural central New Jersey area I grew up in was best experienced from high in the saddle and not behind the wheel of a car. It was also easier to mount up and pick up your fellow cyclers as you rode the tarmac.

The idea to join in this cross country cycling endeavor was a joint effort between me and my best friend Jimmy Bishop. We enjoyed riding together but our cycling styles could not have been more different. Jimmy pedaled like a maniac, a natural born spinner, and I was a big ring guy who liked to stand and use my weight to rotate the pedals. Little did I know Jimmy's methods would be very useful in my long distance bicycling farther down the road.

Between the two of us we had a book on biking and camping but other than that we had no clue of what a cross country cycling trip would entail. Unfortunately or fortunately depending on how you look at it, the trip never happened. About two weeks before we were to leave for New York Jimmy told me he was taking a job working in the local grocery store and could not go. I was disappointed because this was something we had talked about for quite a while and I thought it would be within the realm of possibility for us to do.

I had done a few local overnight bike rides sleeping under the trees along the back roads but realistically I was not prepared to do anything like this on my own. I had maybe two hundred dollars to my name and didn't even think about things like spare clothes, parts, tools, a sleeping bag or tent for that matter. The thought of falling off my bike and getting hurt never even entered my mind as something to consider. We were indestructible and little could stop us if we put our mind to it. At least I realized I either could not or should not attempt to do it alone. Had I tried, I would have been lucky to get from New York into Pennsylvania before I was stranded, if I even made it that far. The dream was dashed before it was anything more. It was just a dream. So the boyhood adventure took its place on the shelf where old dreams go, not to be revived or considered again. It was forgotten as a once crazy scheme that only two boys could have thought possible.

I hadn't cycled in more than twenty–five years and I honestly forgot about the silly notion. I couldn't remember telling my wife about it but if I had to venture a guess it would have been while we were dating. After contacting Tracy, the owner of CrossRoads Cycling Adventures, and signing up for the ride I found a job as a building inspector with the stipulation I could take the time off for the ride. The job didn't pay much but they agreed to give me the two months off so I began work as a building inspector while training to do what my body was telling me was crazy at best. Whether it was fate or just a series of unplanned events that led to this cross country adventure I don't know. Looking back on it I can honestly say I don't care how it happened, I'm just glad it did.

So nearly thirty years later, I will live my dream. I guess I already started. For about two months I've been preparing for this adventure. I invited Jimmy to come ride with me and, though he'll be staying back in Atlanta, I'll imagine him riding beside me on the white bike he had thirty years ago.

There will be forty others making the trip for similar reasons. We will ride 3,415 miles averaging eighty miles per day during the fifty days traveling from Manhattan Beach in Los Angeles to Revere Beach in Boston. The trip will span from May 16 to July 3. We will dip our wheels in both oceans, climb mountains, cross deserts, pedal through fifteen states, make some great friendships and climb personal mountains while we watch others do the same.

There will be days where we fall down and we will pick each other up. We will laugh, work, play and, at the end, cry together. It will be the time of our lives. I invite you to come with us as I write about the trip from start to finish.

California Here I Come

Thursday, May 13 (T–minus two days and counting)

It's hard to imagine United Flight 275 would take just over five hours to transport me from Orlando, Florida to Los Angeles, California, but it will take me fifty days to get back to the east coast on my bicycle.

On the flight, I reflected over the past ten weeks preparing for this cross–country, two–wheeled adventure. I thought about how bicycling technology has changed, how highly specialized parts and equipment are now required, and every piece of gear is incredibly expensive.

Twenty years ago, with a pair of well–worn threadbare cutoff denim shorts, straight–laced canvas department store sneakers or if you had a bit of coin and style maybe a pair of Keds or Converse sneakers and your favorite cotton t–shirt, you were ready to ride your bike almost anywhere. Today the standard rider gear includes spandex padded hip hugging shorts, moisture–wicking vented form fitting pocketed synthetic cycling jerseys, clip–on ultralight Velcro secured cycling footwear, fingerless padded specialty gloves, breathable head socks and aero designed safety certified headgear consisting of a foam core with a polycarbonate outer shell; a helmet if I didn't make that clear. And this equipment just covers the rider.

For the bike there's technology—lots of it. Add in computers and GPS devices to track your pedaling cadence, distance traveled, current speed, average speed, max speed, riding time, elevation gain, the grade of the road, the energy you produce and the calories burned plus a slew of other metrics that can be recorded, uploaded, posted to Facebook and Pinterest—which wouldn't actually be available until March 2010—tracked and mapped in real–time by friends and family who think you are out of your mind for sitting on such an invasive seat for a ride around the block let alone venturing from coast to coast.

But wait, there's more! If you are serious about your fitness you also need to have a personal electronic device: a little something called a heart–rate monitor. It consists of two parts, the small computer itself that looks like a Dick Tracy wrist watch you can wear on the wrist—surprised?— or like I prefer, mounted to the handle bars just to the left of the bike stem.

The other part, called a sensor, is a one inch wide slightly curved thin plastic assembly with an elastic strap to secure it around your upper chest so it can pick up the bioelectric impulses generated by the heart; a ticker tracker. A little lick of the two contact patches on the sensor to improve the connection to the skin and you are reading in real time your heart rate and the calculated calories burned based in part on your heart rate, age and weight. It also records a generous set of personal statistics that can be reviewed and later transferred to your personal cycling log at the end of each ride to measure progress.

Managing the heart rate within the proper range can maximize your riding duration and increase your stamina while minimizing the risk of cramping caused by the buildup of lactic acid. This was not on my radar as a teenager but decades later I am very aware of what can happen if I don't leverage the available technology.

Thinking back, as a kid I got cramps from long rides and they sure were painful calf burners but it didn't occur to me how I got them. I never thought throttling back a bit from pedaling like a maniac at the limits of my ability could have avoided the cramps. Cadence, exercise intensity, and aerobic activity were not in my vocabulary either. It was all out, all the time until you dropped. At least back then I recovered quickly.

You learn fast it's the combination of pedal cadence and heart rate that must be managed carefully to get the most out of your body without exceeding its limits. Cadence, the rate at which you are turning the pedals, has much to do with the amount of energy you produce. Lots of spinning generates power more efficiently.

My friend Jimmy Bishop was a spinner and I was a tall gear guy. The contrast between our riding styles was as different as our physicality. He had thin legs and I had the tree trunks. He probably turned 110 rpm's and I

re near 65 rpm. He stayed in the saddle and I stood on the pedals rocking the bike side to side to
_bs. At least that's the way I remember it.

There's a lot of information available on proper training, routines, equipment and techniques on the internet and in books. So if you ride but do not have at least the basic knowledge of proper training practices I recommend you save yourself some pain and start learning.

As you train write down what you accomplish in a journal and over time you will be amazed at how much faster and stronger you become as you increase the riding distance. The day you look back on a fifty–mile ride being easier than the first ten–mile ride you took, I promise you will smile; an ear to ear toothy grin so have your camera ready.

And while I'm on the topic of learning I also suggest you learn a little something about products like Butt Butter, Chamois Cream, and Bag Balm. I'm sure it's age related; either I don't remember the chaffing or I can no longer subject my sit bones to the compressive forces grinding against the seat for hours at a time without a little lubrication.

It's a bit odd at first applying a cold dab of cream especially when you are out on the road, meaning in public with non–cyclists already staring at your odd cycling attire, but when you've lived the options you get over the shyness very quickly. Remember to take care of your bottom; dab early and often.

So before I got a bit derailed on the heart rate and Butt Butter I was describing all of the new accessories in cycling. There is so much that cross country cycling requires you to prepare for and preparation means gear. There are mini–pumps and inflators with spare CO_2 cartridges, extra tubes and foldable tires, tools for spoke adjustments, plastic levers for tire changing, seat bags or other mounted containers to hold the gear, spring loaded clip–in pedals, headlights and taillights, water bottles and cages and aero bars.

Here's a brief list of some of the miscellaneous items you carry in your jersey pockets, bike bags, or hidden in your CamelBak as you ride; Chap Stick, suntan lotion, the aforementioned Bag Balm, triple ointment in case you get a rash, Wet Ones, tissues, eye wetting solution, eyeglass cleaning cloth, Ziploc plastic bags, rubber bands and Band–Aids. Then there's the gum, breath mints, Cliff bars, energy gels, otherwise known as the *Goo*, Nip Chee crackers, a cell phone, pocket camera, your bike tools and a little plastic water pistol. Your contents may vary and mine is actually a short list. For the record no *Goo* was in my bag. Not that there wasn't room, I just didn't like the stuff.

Decades ago when you bought a bike the purchase included everything you needed; a frame, a seat, the handle bars and two wheels. Now when you buy a bike you only get the canvas for which you will paint the fully dressed cycling picture. Nobody rides a bike without personalizing and affixing a very long list of these optional devices. It just doesn't happen anymore. So you can figure the cost of the fully outfitted bike will be from fifty to a full hundred percent more once all of the add–ons are accounted for.

And then there is this relatively new material called carbon; and the new and often more pricy bikes use a lot of it. Your seat post, the front fork; handle bars, maybe a set of add–on aero bars or the entire bicycle frame itself could be made out of carbon. And we like this carbon because it is stiffer than steel and incredibly light weight, which also means it's expensive.

This brings me to something called Zerts; a set of small soft gel inserts molded into the front fork and rear frame on carbon bikes connecting the seat to the rear wheel mount called the seat stay. This nifty little device helps cut down on the vibration and shock your body experiences as the bike rattles over rough terrain.

For me I ride an aluminum frame that seems to transfer the entire bandwidth of road vibrations right up to my butt and both wrists before settling into my jaw. It's what I have to work with so I don't clench my teeth when riding. My saving grace is my bike does have a carbon fork and seat post so there is at least a bit of relief from the irregularities of the road; and it sure beats my old steel frame '75 Raleigh. But alas, it has no Zerts. Maybe someday in the future I can convince myself that I am worthy of an all carbon bike. I think the entry point is in the three thousand dollar range so it will be a stretch. It wasn't long ago that I bought my first car for 200 dollars. *Hmmm*. Time is moving faster than it used too.

You could probably debate the pros and cons about the new gear and technology and whether it is really worth it or even necessary. If it's marketing hype they are doing a great job because I'm buying into it. Maybe a bit reluctantly, but reflecting back on my inventory of bike gear purchased over the past two months I should be on the bike store's Christmas card list.

I'm jumping ahead a bit but when I arrive at the hotel in El Segundo I will meet the folks riding with me from Los Angeles to Boston. At least one rider will be pedaling in a pair of deck sneakers sans the clips and another will sport old style gym shorts from the '70s in place of the form fitted Lycra wearables. And not to spoil the surprise but both riders will do just fine traversing the country albeit not without some heckling from some of their cycling peers because of their non–conformity; doing it their own way and loving it.

I think I covered everything that rolls with the bike except one item I required for the trip, but until a few weeks ago it was completely unknown to me. It's the hydration system; a light weight fabric bag with zippers, straps, clips and a rubber bladder for holding water that is worn like a backpack and because it looks like a camel hump the clever folks in marketing branded it the CamelBak. How original, but how necessary it is on the long rides; and much more convenient then reaching for the water bottles rattling around between your legs on the down tube or seat tube.

The CamelBak has a flexible tube with a bite plug. You clench your teeth on it to open the flow of water. Mine carries two liters and it has a few compartments for stowing the little extras that don't fit anywhere else on the bike. On hot days it is definitely a bit uncomfortable, but the ice I load into it actually cools my back for about thirty minutes into a long ride. I have been told only water should go into it unless I want to spend lots of extra time cleaning the insides of it. Note to self; do not put any Gatorade in the CamelBak!

Back home I have a variety of accessories that don't travel with me but are very useful, and again a bit pricy. You probably noticed those cost comments are becoming a bit of a theme in my writing. The first is the training stand I use in bad weather to ride inside. It converts my bike to something similar to a stationary bike; the rear wheel jacked–up off the ground pressed against a roller containing some magnetic device to increase resistance as I pedal faster and a front wheel chock to raise it up so the bike is level. When I am not riding the bike my trainer is the most expensive kickstand I've ever owned. It's on par with the cost of my old Raleigh Grand Prix I wrote about earlier.

My second indulgence is the mechanics bike maintenance stand which makes servicing the bike so much easier by raising it up instead of me having to bend over to get down to the working end of the bike. If not on the trainer the bike can be found hanging on the mechanics stand ready and waiting for me to take it for a spin.

Then there is the collection of spare chains, chain cleaning and repair tools, torque wrenches, hex wrenches, lubricants, spare seats, various types of mirrors and it goes on and on and on. Why would I have spare seats? Well you will learn when you buy a bike it comes with one, but not necessarily the right one to fit you properly.

The seat is a very important component of the bike and when riding long distance everything must be mated to it properly. Not knowing how to size myself or to quickly determine if the standard equipment is right for me, I had to return to Orange Cycle shortly after to remedy a little disagreement between my rear end and the seat that came with the bike. On the rack was a more appropriate new *Terry* saddle and in short order the technician had it installed and dialed in. Within a few minutes of riding the contact sensitivity issues were put to rest; at least up to now.

Technically the seat is called a saddle because you ride the bike; calling it a seat would suggest you sit on it like a chair; and a chair it surely is not.

Getting ready to ride has changed as much as the equipment. As a kid you either went out to the garage finding your bike leaning against the wall or resting on its kickstand and if not in the garage it was out in the yard laying in the grass or leaning against a tree. If the tires were not flat you hopped on and you were riding. That was the entire process.

Today you spend about fifteen minutes finding all of your cycling apparel and putting it on, then you stop in the kitchen to grab your water bottles, Gatorade and snacks for the ride, and finally you carry your shoes into the garage so you don't mark up the floors. Of course you are carrying all of your other supplies as well; nobody else is going to do it for you. Once in the garage, or a spare bedroom for those having a tighter bond with their cycling equipment and can't come to grips with the bike living in the garage, you strap on your heart rate monitor, slip on your shoes, perform a proper safety check on the bike, air up the tires with the floor pump, check the proper pressure and only then do you put on your head sock, helmet, shoes and riding gloves.

Carefully you wheel your mount outside, click on your lights, adjust the mirror and turn on then zero out all of the electronics so you have accurate data on the ride. Then you push off, clip the first of your two cleats into the pedal until you hear and feel the *click* and with a rotation of the pedals in goes the second and your ride begins. You almost need a checklist to make sure it all happens correctly.

Though biking has become high–tech, the human body remains almost the same; that is, except for the effects of aging. Through my training, I learned my muscles are less forgiving at forty–five than they were at twenty. Old injuries from decades ago present themselves as unwanted guests. The ache in my knee from when I broke it in a 1977 ice hockey incident will be my constant companion—unwanted extra baggage I will try to lose along the way.

I learned through fellow riders Pat and Vikki Wilcox, and through my own errors, cycling training must be done methodically, distance and speed must be carefully increased, and all of your efforts are cumulative.

There were days when I felt so good I exceeded my training plan and I paid the price. I've been totally spent, lying spread–eagle on the ground after forty–five miles of riding and twenty miles from home.

I had planned for a forty–mile ride, but thought I could do sixty–five to seventy miles after riding my first thirty. I didn't have proper food or drink, and I was riding alone. This lack of preparation and not adhering to the plan proved to be a disaster. As embarrassed as I was, I became much better for it.

I've also pushed too hard on a ninety–mile ride, thereby awakening a knee problem which, four weeks later, is still with me.

I have also fallen three times when I couldn't get my feet unclipped from the new style pedals. It's a hopeless feeling, but if you ride you will experience it too; no matter how strong a rider you are.

The good news is I was told you fall three times because of the shoe clips, so I hope I've got them all behind me. Falling for other reasons is still a possibility, and it will likely happen when I'm not paying attention. It's easy to zone out at times on the bike when you are trying to be one with the machine but that runs counter to the whole paying attention to avoid falling paradigm.

Two weeks ago, I was taking a quick test ride to try a new eyeglass mounted mirror. Not more than a half mile from my house I was getting close to the turnaround point and rolling less than ten miles per hour. Looking down I saw my cell phone—which I had just minutes ago rubber banded to the handlebar—start slipping out and then it quickly fell. Back at the house I had a brand new bike mountable cell phone case but it was just a short ride, I wouldn't need it. Actually I didn't need the cell phone either if I had been thinking. In an instant I reached for the phone with my right hand, and at the same time, I touched the front brake lever with my left and ended up going over the front wheel, the bike standing precariously vertical for an instant before gravity pulled me head first into the broken asphalt where I landed solidly on my helmet and left shoulder.

With a *thud* all of the air was expelled from my lungs and my bell well rung. I remember seeing the asphalt surface approaching my face then at the last minute I instinctively turned my head to the right and tucked it into my chest. My entire body hurt and I was extremely dazed as I lay spread–eagle with rocks and twigs jabbing me. I did not move for about a minute fearing something had to be broken. Then I slowly regained my breath, I inventoried my upper body beginning with my fingers, then my hands, and finally my arms. They seemed to move properly so I continued to my feet, then my legs and finally the rest of my body. I sat up and brushed off all of the road stones and grit then I stumbled to my feet.

About a hundred yards away stood a group of three or four people. For a few moments I was more concerned about the possibility they witnessed my awkward aerobatics than I was at checking out my bike. I realized if they saw me tumble they surely would have come to my aid.

I checked over my bike and aside from a broken bar–end mirror, damage to my new extra padded handlebar grips, and some scraps and chips in the clear coat over silver paint on the frame, it was in better shape than I was. I thought my pre–trip fear of getting severely injured had come to pass. Fortunately no broken bones, though the shoulder is still very tender.

When the plane touched down I was jogged out of my daze and back to the present. I had much to do once I arrived at the hotel including the reassembling of my bike. I'm pretty good with mechanical things but I'm still learning the finer points of bike assembly and getting everything reset to where it was back in Florida. As I walked out of the Los Angeles airport I noticed a poster for Boston. A bit ironic I thought and then I smiled exiting to the street in search of the hotel shuttle.

At the hotel I quickly began to unpack and reassemble my bike. I shipped most of my biking gear in the box except for my helmet as Tracy advised. Unfortunately the helmet didn't prove to be the conversation starter on the plane as she suggested. It was probably for the better as I was able to enjoy the flight thinking only about this grand adventure.

In the lobby I met several people including Peter Crowell from New Hampshire. Peter also has a home in Ocala, Florida just about an hour away from my home. This would be the second time he would attempt to ride cross country on his recumbent bike with CrossRoads. Peter was a solidly built, if not stocky man standing just a few inches taller than me. He is a retired pilot, but still keeps his hand in the family sawmill business back in New Hampshire. Unless he tells me otherwise I would guess Peter is about fifty–five years old.

Don Hardin was another man I met today. Like Peter, and most of the other riders, he stands a few inches taller than I do and is in very good shape for a man in his sixties. Don came to the tour from Louisville, Kentucky and like it was for me, this trip has been a dream of his for a long time.

Kathy Stevens, from our destination city of Boston was the first lady I met on the tour. Very outgoing with a great sense of humor, you could tell she was going to be fun to be around. She is about my age and comes from a consulting background which matches closely with my work experience. Being a bit of a class clown myself, I think we will get along just fine.

Then there was Dick Duffey. Finally I meet someone shorter than I am. Dick is not the image you get when you think about cross country cycling. This Irishman from New Hampshire sports a very large belly and walks more like a duck than a marathon runner which, he claims he used to be before taking up cycling. Dick sports a full head of silver hair on his mid–sixty year old head and seems to be quite the joker. I look at Dick and say to myself, "If he can do it I sure can do it!"

The above named cyclists and I, along with a few others, took in dinner at the Olive Garden just a few miles from the hotel and began to share our stories. So it begins the bonding process of this year's cross country group known as XC04. Back to the hotel and it's time for bed. Excited and twenty–five pounds lighter than when I committed to this trip; I'm ready to begin my journey across America.

The Strand

Friday, May 14 (T–minus one day and counting)

We heard about a beach bike path called the Strand which runs for most of the California coast. In the El Segundo area where we were staying, the Strand is a smooth asphalt and concrete ribbon not but ten feet wide frequented by cyclists, joggers, and those on roller blades and skateboards. It meanders through the sand past volleyball courts, barbeque pits, grass patches with park benches and RV camping grounds.

It's a popular attraction for those going somewhere and for others without a specific destination but wanting to take in the sights and to be seen themselves. At several points it exits the sand and gives way to marked areas on parking lots, through marinas and as a parallel lane to the roads through the limited grassy areas. As crowded as Los Angeles is they made it pedestrian and bicyclist friendly. You just needed to know where to find these cycling safe havens to get around.

A ride to the beach would take only about ten minutes from the hotel and it was described as being mostly downhill. So it should be no surprise that on the return trip we would have to work harder to get back to our destination in the heat and likely feeling a bit tired.

Once on the Strand it would be possible to pedal through Venice to the famous Santa Monica Pier fifteen miles to the north. And farther if we so dared, but given the long journey to Boston we were about to begin there was no shortage of cycling mileage to be had. We just needed to stretch out the legs and work off some of the accumulated energy since we last rode our bikes at home before packing and shipping them to Los Angeles.

At about seven in the morning in the hotel hallway near my room Kathy, Don and Dick were preparing their equipment to go for an early morning ride so I hustled to get ready and join them. A quick check of the tires, a scramble for my gloves and helmet and I was in the parking lot to begin the early beachside tour.

It was chilly so I kept my long sleeved black McKenna's Restaurant t–shirt on for the ride. It was one of my favorite non–cycling outfits for riding and it was versatile enough for what the forecast called for. At least it would be great for the outbound trip but for the return trip it could be quite warm in full sun.

This was my first time on the bike in two weeks and I was excited to stretch my legs on a short leisurely ride. The road leading to the beach included four lanes of traffic and it did not have any real accommodations for cyclists. Fortunately the traffic was light and getting to the ocean was without incident. As for the riding being downhill we learned this was not really accurate. It was more of a series of midsized roller coaster hills, each a few blocks long between traffic lights and stop signs. The final stretch was a single long and steep drop a quarter mile in length to the traffic light at the bottom of the descent fronting the ocean.

I remember going down the hill riding the brakes all the way to the beach saying to myself it was going to be a tough one to ride back up. Going down was fast, almost a freefall if you attempted it without brakes. It was a bit sandy and without the knowledge of the traffic and road conditions it paid to be extra cautious. Okay, truth be told it was scary since I hadn't seen a hill like this in all my riding in Florida.

The air was filled with the smell of damp musty salt coming off the surf as it made its way up the beach courtesy of the fine mist carrying it inland as far as it could before settling on the ground and all traces of it were gone. Maybe a block or two was all it was able to muster this morning.

The distinct beach smells were accompanied by the acoustic turbulence of the frothy green waves breaking and dispersing on the beach before retreating back to the sea in preparation for another land assault. It was a continuous series of roaring and crashing, a natural static capable of masking most of the surrounding noises. The muted sea sounds varied in volume and shared the spotlight with the mechanical sounds of traffic moving along the road running parallel to the beach as well as the sounds coming from the people and their pets enjoying the warming of the early morning.

Intermingled with the sounds were the coastal birds, mostly sea gulls who called out warnings to their peers as they navigated the skies over the beach in search of food. There was also the frequent *roar* of the commercial jet passenger planes taking off and landing at Los Angeles International Airport. Our position on the beach just happened to be right in line with and reasonably close to the runways. It was both quiet and noisy at the same time.

Depending on where your focus was it would determine which of the extremes filled your consciousness. I realized once I roll my bike away from the beach toward the interior on Sunday it was an experience that would not be repeated until I reached the eastern shores just outside of Boston, Massachusetts. Seven weeks seemed both long and short at the same time. I returned my attention to navigating across the street and onto the beach path being careful not to collide with anyone or anything.

Once on the Strand we saw other CrossRoads riders approaching from ahead while a few came up from behind to join our group. It seemed like everyone had the same idea about doing a little preparatory riding to make sure they and their bike were ready for our Sunday departure.

Cruising along the Strand you see some very interesting people. Several physically fit speedsters on rollerblades, a few joggers and a wide cast of unique characters including delusional homeless people and those trying to make a fashion statement. I remember one guy wearing a lime green shiny satin dress jacket and a pair of slacks that stood out from the crowd as he rolled by on his blades, but if there was an award for drawing attention it would have to go to the nearly naked man on a beach cruiser bike. Wearing nothing but a skimpy G–string, naked man passed us and for a short while was in front of us through the more crowded sections of the Strand. Two thoughts came to mind; I'd never wear a G–string on a bike and as expensive as living in California can be, don't these people work on Friday?

As we rode through Venice Beach we stopped to get a drink from one of the beachfront stores. It was at this time we learned that foreigners from every part of the globe like the California weather and lifestyle as much as the locals. In just the span of a few minutes I heard Russian, Japanese, an unidentifiable dialect from the somewhere in the Middle East, and a bit of Spanish as well. Not much English being spoken sans the homeless delusional guy who was quickly becoming angry with his invisible friend. What a place.

Kathy was exceptionally quick on her recumbent making it a challenge for the rest of us to keep up. Unlike the upright bikes most people are familiar with, the recumbent bikes are very unique in design positioning the rider in a more reclined position instead of being folded up and over the handle bars. More like a motorcyclist riding a chopper instead of café racer bike if that makes it any clearer to visualize. They look awkward and take some getting used to but those who ride recumbents swear by them; and those of us who get a chance to try one for a brief tour of the parking lot, well, we swear at them. They don't negotiate hills or stops and starts too well but a skilled rider on one of those strange looking creations can make it look reasonably easy.

Once we reached Santa Monica Pier ten miles up the coast we pointed our bikes uphill and inland to check out a shop specializing in sun protection products. After all, we were about to begin a trip featuring a few days in the desert. This was an upscale area where boutiques were more common than chain stores and fashion ranked above function. We reached our destination just a few blocks east, dismounted our bikes and leaned them where we could.

Quality road bikes usually don't come equipped with kickstands nor do they readily accept an aftermarket accessory stand. Strange thing is you either must awkwardly lean the bike against something like a bench, a wall, a post, or a tree as you never seem to stop where a bike rack is stationed and it risks scratching a very expensive bike frame no matter how careful you are. The only other option is to lay the bike down on the ground. Assuming you can find enough space and hope no one trips over it. Actually you do have another option; leave one of the riders outside and have them hold your bike upright for you. There is usually someone in the group who decides to wait outside so give them some purpose and put them to work.

We all walked into the shop to check out the sun gear leaving the bikes in various states of leaning but within view so we could watch them. You never know if the wind might blow or someone walking by might take a liking to your flashy set of wheels.

Inside watching Dick try on the protective clothing was a hoot. After all you don't look good in the stuff; it's puffy, loose fitting and designed for proportionally taller and thinner folks than Duffey. While it may sound like I'm picking on Dick, I'm actually becoming quite fond of him. And you can forget what I said about fashion as it does not apply to the outfit Duffey was sporting.

It occurred to me I bought the same type of sun protective cycling jersey. It's more like a lightweight jacket, similar to a windbreaker with lots of vents built in. It's a Solumbra brand partial zippered cycle shirt right down to the white and yellow coloring. As I said the shirt was more like a jacket and I began to realize I would look just like Duffey did when he was trying on the Sun Precautions gear. Not so funny now come to think of it. Though I could be the next best thing to his twin out in the desert. Okay, that's funny!

With purchases made it was back to the beach for our return ride to the hotel. Past the marina, across the streets and though the human circus on the Strand we made it back to Grand Avenue for our climb to the hotel. Somehow it was steeper than I remembered but at least I was not on a recumbent bike. On the flats and down hills they shine but Kathy was going to struggle on this hill. Fortunately we all made it back to the hotel in one piece and as a group. I did manage to strain my knee which gave me something else to worry about besides my shoulder, which by the way hurt like it was in a vice as I tried to stand up on the bike for the climb back to the hotel.

Late afternoon Don and I did a bit of shopping for fish oil and other remedies we hoped would immediately cure our aches. What a bunch of dreamers we both were. Dinner with Don included my first experience with the Carl's Jr. Hamburger franchise. I must admit it was worth dodging four lanes of traffic to get there. We followed it up with an ice cream on stick before putting an end to our day.

It was getting late and while strolling through the lobby of the hotel I met a tall and fit Englishman from the Bahamas by the name of Tony Hepburn. He was also going on the tour. We talked a bit and I learned Tony was an attorney with some interesting stories to tell. I wondered how a guy from the Bahamas was able to find a place to ride a bicycle at all let alone train for a cross country trip. It turned out I was the first person in the cycling group he had met in Los Angeles after arriving so late. It was good to make his acquaintance and to know yet another one of the riders I would be spending the next fifty days with.

And It Begins

Day 1: Saturday, May 15, Registration Day

Today several of us repeated the ride to the Strand and found the larger crowds on Saturday made it difficult to ride between Venice Beach and Santa Monica. South of Venice it wasn't much different from the day before, but we had to be careful especially where it narrowed down by the marina. At one point we came upon a blonde woman on rollerblades who claimed to be an aspiring singer with a desire to rollerblade across the country. She had no trouble keeping up with us as we sped along the two–mile stretch on the crowded four lane road from the marina back to the Strand. She bent our ears for a while before darting in another direction once we reached the Strand. I can't imagine anyone rollerblading cross country, but then I'm sure others can't believe people would actually attempt to cross it by bike.

At the pier we gathered for our first group photograph; Don, Betty Hayes, Gene Teaney, Don and Helen Reeves and I. Also riding in our group but not in the organized pier photo were Kathy, Vikki, Pat and Gray Pruitt.

The ribbon of concrete blended in with the sand as it meandered through the beach. It was very easy to miss the turns if you were not paying attention. And with several of us riding close together you could not afford a mishap. I tested this theory as I looked away from the path and then realized I could not make the next corner. Being clipped into the pedals I thought I would surely flip over the bars or fall over but as the bike rolled into the sand it quickly sunk down a few inches and then stopped upright as if someone held it in place. Not quite what I was expecting but very thankful for that little quirk. I was able to unclip both feet and dismount the bike without incident. The sudden spike in blood pressure subsided as I returned my bike to the concrete path. Crisis on the Strand averted. Luck was with me today.

As we rode away from the beach up Grand Avenue I saw a bike flag lying on the pavement. It had fallen off the tandem bike as the duo struggled up the hill another fifty yards ahead. As steep as the hill was I knew they would not bother to come back for it. I figured by stopping and picking up the flag it gave me an excuse to rest and earn some good deed points at the same time. I would soon meet Don and Helen Reeves, the owners of the lost flag and one of two tandem riding couples on tour. With the recovered bike flag held firmly across my handlebars, I rode on with the group to our hotel.

Back at the hotel we gathered for bike safety checks, the mounting of our orange safety flags to our bikes, and the process of registration. We finally got to meet the tour workers and some other volunteers who would be seeing us off early the next morning. I was quite impressed with the care and detail demonstrated by the CrossRoads organization. You could tell this wasn't the first time they had managed a group of forty *would be* cross country dreamers. Actually it was forty–eight riders with a few only planning to go a part of the journey with us. I felt some relief and comfort knowing I was in good hands. Like the riders I met earlier, the staff members were from all points across North America.

Tracy Leiner, the leader of this effort from Connecticut is the owner of CrossRoads Cycling. Her short cropped hair and ear–to–ear smile made her easy to spot in the crowd. She was full of energy, well organized and fun to be around.

Trevor Burgis, the Canadian cowboy was in charge of luggage, logistics, and coming up with cool nicknames for everyone. He was also Tracy's right hand man and had been on the tour for the past half dozen years. Trevor was also very personable and outgoing.

Rick Wardell, a quiet yet friendly pharmacist from Wichita Falls, Texas would be our primary mechanic and as I understood he was a very strong rider. His son is keeping the business running for the next two months allowing Rick the opportunity to get away for the tour.

Tom Jelmyer, our other mechanic from San Jose, California used to race professionally and had ridden with some of America's best. He operates his own bike shop called VeloTech in Palo Alto and as I understand it, he lives in an apartment just above the store. Tom has a reputation for fine tuning bikes and people often fly him across the country just to adjust their machines. I'm glad I have such a knowledgeable person at the ready should my bike require any attention.

Margaret Schwartz, hailing from Fort Walton Beach, Florida was the queen of hospitality and would be everyone's mom for the ride. She would be the welcome face we see at our SAG stops offering drinks and snacks to keep our energy levels high.

Clark Dexter, a retired ophthalmologist from Keene, New Hampshire and rider from last year's tour was the person charged with sweeping up the stragglers at the end of each day. I would expect to know Clark pretty well by the end of the trip since we would be rooming together for the next two months.

Larry Potter, Tracy's husband, was also helping on tour. As I understood it Larry was a recent victim of corporate downsizing much like me. After spending several years coming to Los Angeles to help with the tour registration, he was finally getting his chance to be one of the riders.

At our orientation meeting we got a chance to meet more of the riders. It was a high energy meeting with Tracy holding court pumping us up and getting us working as a group with primal yells and clapping. She also led us through the process of introductions and got everyone to share their reasons for choosing to ride across the country. Some of the stories were like mine. They just wanted to do it. Some like Hopper Fulton, who was doing it for the second time in a row, thought it helped save his life after a bout with cancer. You could see that lasting friendships would be made and everyone was going to be changed for the better by this experience.

Then Tracy shared with us two brief but very important stories that would help define the journey we were about to embark on. The first was about the Special Olympics; how could that possibly relate to a cross country cycling trip that a group of professionals were about to begin? And then she opened our eyes with the first story and the beginning of the magic that would be XC04. Steadily she read to us the following news article.

"At the 1996 Special Olympics nine contestants, all physically or mentally challenged, lined up on the starting line for the hundred–yard dash. At the sound of the gun all nine contestants were off, not exactly in a dash, but with the relish to run the race to the end!" She scanned the room locking eyes briefly with the riders.

She continued, "Suddenly one boy tripped and fell; he began to cry. One girl with Downs Syndrome noticed the boy and went back to help. She bent down to kiss his cheek and said 'This will make it better.' With that, the other seven athletes stopped running and went back to the boy who had fallen. In a show of support, all nine athletes linked arms and crossed the finish line together." A chill rolled through me as she continued.

"The crowd came to their feet and their applause went on for five solid minutes." Tracy pursed her lips then smiled, scanning our attentive faces as if to convey the magnitude of this journey; one filled with consuming emotion and capable of transforming individuals, even strangers into a single collective body. One where just like those Olympians she described, we would finish this journey arm–in–arm as one.

Wow, what a powerful message of the human spirit. It was both unexpected and welcoming at the same time. I was moved and motivated. I was where I was supposed to be; in the right place, at the right time, with the right people. This was it. Not knowing how, but over the next seven weeks I would be transformed.

What Tracy said next was not so much a story as it was a quote of inspiration. She read the following words to us:

"Far better to dare mighty things, to win glorious victories, though checkered with defeat, than to take rank with those poor souls who neither enjoy much, nor suffer much, for theirs is a twilight existence that knows neither victory nor defeat. – Theodore Roosevelt April 10, 1899."

We took the first step toward our personal victory. We would suffer, we would enjoy, and we would do it together as one; we were XC04. I couldn't wait for tomorrow so we could get started. After our dinner at the hotel it was off to bed to try to get some sleep before our 5:30 a.m. start. The excitement limited the possibility of sleep and it was somewhere past midnight before my mind finally surrendered and let me drift off.

Day 2: Los Angeles to Riverside (78 miles)

The alarm clock sounded at 5:00 a.m. It would still be dark for another hour or more in Los Angeles but we had to get moving to the hotel lobby for our first cycling day breakfast at quarter to six. Following breakfast we began the daily routine of presenting our two duffel bags containing all of our necessities that would get us to Boston. Each bag was limited to fifteen pounds so there was no room for anything but the essentials. The CrossRoads staff marked specific areas for the bags to be staged near the front door of the hotel. At the appointed time of six thirty, Tracy wheeled the truck in front of the hotel entrance, unlocked and raised the rear rollup door, and then she hopped quickly up into the open box of the truck. From her perch she gave the order to begin the loading process.

While staff quickly organized and stowed our gear Tracy directed us in how the group would assemble and move to the beach. We would have the next fifteen minutes to pump up our tires, take pictures, and make any last minute adjustments to ready ourselves to mount bikes and ride. The excitement was building, our palms were sweating, and everyone was getting antsy. A light drizzle of rain was spitting as we waited.

The last task before rolling out of the hotel, as it would be each day, was to sign the departure sheet. This was one of the first procedural steps I noticed on the tour and it was a product of several years of planning and refining by Tracy and her team. With nearly fifty cyclists on the road you could not be too careful in managing their whereabouts.

We left the hotel at quarter past seven, side by side, twenty–five rows deep, in a slow–paced parade, three miles down to the California coast. It was a sight to behold as all riders were wearing the official XC04 red, white, and blue team jersey. We also had our bike mounted orange pennant flags waving wildly in the breeze as we zoomed along. I was deep in the procession and afforded a good view of my fellow riders. As we encountered traffic lights we would stop, then move as a group as much as possible which added to the parade–like display. At the bottom of Grand Avenue we met the beach and turned south onto the Strand to Manhattan Beach Pier.

The mechanical sounds of moving metal bike parts and rubber tires gripping the concrete were amplified by the volume of riders. Very little chatter was heard so the sound of the surf to our right and pedestrians and vehicular traffic to our left were the only other sounds in our consciousness.

The path we rode was narrow considering our speed and that other cyclists and pedestrians were coming toward us heading north. Patches of sand and puddles of water spotted the concrete and it took extra effort to stay off the wheel of the rider in front and to not make any abrupt changes in speed or position that could disrupt those trailing behind. Concentration would be paramount and so too would be staying on the path itself. It would take us ten minutes to reach our first destination and it would definitely be a test for all riders to get there without issue.

As we arrived at the pier we removed our cycling shoes and socks, draped our bikes over our shoulders, walked down the steps, then carried or wheeled them across the sand and into the surf for the ceremonial dipping of the rear wheel. The tide was out so the walk through the sand to the water was nearly a hundred yards. The sand was soft and loose so it was slow going. While on the beach each rider collected a small film canister of Pacific Coast sand to be ceremoniously sprinkled at each state line for good luck. This was another one of Tracy's cross country tour rituals.

Not everyone dipped their wheel and a few others didn't even venture into the sand. I wanted to experience everything and found myself wet and sandy and glad for it. I didn't think about how the salt water would impact my aluminum wheels and the very fine steel threads which join the spokes to the wheel nipples. Salt water is very corrosive to both of these metals and it would have been wise to rinse off the wheels as soon as I got back on the pier. I didn't.

It was cloudy and a bit cool and most of us were apprehensive about getting started. The smell of sea salt was heavy in the mist and seagulls were busy scavenging in the surf. We climbed up the steps to the pier with our bikes safely resting on our shoulders, wiped our feet, and then put on our socks and shoes. The group, still getting to know each other, was quiet and focused. This was a big day for everyone.

Tracy told us to quickly assemble on the pier for a group photo. This would be the first of many I would anticipate over the coming weeks. Once all of the video and snapshot memories were captured we paired off and pointed our wheels east, heading up the steep grade of Manhattan Beach Boulevard inland toward Riverside.

The climb was taxing yet short and no match for our adrenaline level. In just a few minutes our legs propelled us to higher and flatter ground and into the business district where our heart rates and anxiety levels settled into a more sustainable range.

Traffic on Sunday morning in Los Angeles was light, but it still required all of my attention. Most of the roadway was concrete with cracks, expansion joints, and debris strewn about that could cause a rider to lose control. And in the close proximity of other riders, a slip or a swerve could spell trouble for several people.

Riders began finding cycling partners and conversing as they made their way along Van Ness Avenue. Everyone was anxious about the next seven weeks especially the imminent desert crossings and the mountains we would climb. We also talked about family and our lives back home.

Miles after passing through the older business area the scenery changed to a more residential feel with lots of trees and greenery. Block after block and mile after mile the neighborhoods rolled from one to the next. Stucco and dark wood, '70s style ranch houses set in lush green landscaping with various floral colors dotting the well groomed yards. They were in stark contrast to the multiple lanes of traffic going in either direction. But this was southern California, it's crowded and land is at a premium.

Between the curbing and the roadway we had a tolerable shoulder to ride safely. Most of the morning drivers were respectful of the cyclists but I wasn't sure if courtesy was part of the California culture or if they were just being nice on a Sunday morning. I just hoped it continued throughout the day.

We made it to our first stop at Cerritos Regional Park after riding the first twenty–eight miles from the pier to enjoy the inaugural SAG stop and to see Margaret work her food and energy replenishment magic. The park sat on a large property with ample open space for dog walkers, sports enthusiasts, and those looking to enjoy some quiet under the shade trees. The paved parking area was sufficiently roomy and I rolled up to the white CrossRoads van where several riders had already begun to congregate. Just off the curb and across the sidewalk was a bike rack so I hopped off, wedged the front wheel into a slot, and then removed my gloves and my helmet.

I signed in as per Margaret's instructions, noted the time on the clock, and jotted it down on the clipboard by my name. I needed to wash up and use the restroom so I asked directions and was quickly heading toward a large building across the parking lot. I could see other cyclists exiting the doors so I knew I was in the right place.

The restrooms were located in the Cerritos Community Center fifty yards from our SAG stationed on the north edge of the near empty parking lot. Once I *clicked* and *clacked* my way into the building I had to negotiate around the youth basketball courts to the far side and through a series of doors to find the restrooms. Between all of the kids lining the gymnasium and needing to stay clear of the courts I think we walked much farther inside then we did between the building and the CrossRoads van. I shouldn't complain, the restrooms were adequate and it was interesting to see the future stars of basketball move up and down the courts with their attention on the ball and not on us.

I was back to the group of riders and quickly learning what would become the SAG routine. Light grazing of fresh fruits, cookies, and Gatorade followed by the selecting of a few travel worthy snacks that went right into my cycling jersey pockets. Water and Gatorade were topped off in my containers and I was ready to put on my gloves and helmet, and then be on my way. I checked the tires and made sure my bike bag was zipped closed. Don, Kathy, and a few others were about ready to leave so I pulled my bike out of the rack, straddled the frame, and pointed the front wheel towards the park exit.

It was a quick stop for all and we merged back into the busy Bloomfield Avenue traffic and warmer temperatures as the clouds gave way. After street names like Redondo, San Pedro and Del Amo I thought Bloomfield was very much out of place. The things you have time to ponder on a bicycle.

Traffic continued to build as churches let out and the partiers from the night before came back to life. Heads up riding would be even more important to negotiate the traffic and the directions on the cue sheet which covered six full quadrants to get us to Riverside. The busiest section so far was a half mile of pavement called the Imperial Highway. We crossed over a wide concrete waterway which was part of the Santa Ana River, then under twelve lanes of State Road 91, better known as the Riverside Freeway. It was so wide we did get a bit of shade to cool down but it was a noisy and smelly place to be with the volume of traffic traversing overhead and alongside us on Imperial.

We were riding on the shoulder of this eight–lane engineering wonder avoiding motorists entering and exiting from the Freeway above. *The Where did you appear from?* look on driver's faces would have been funny if I weren't on a bike. It was like I was invisible until I tried to occupy the same piece of roadway. I was not happy to be in this situation.

The next line on the cue sheet called for the quick negotiation of four lanes of traffic while climbing a slight grade, then slipping into one of the two left turning lanes to get onto Santa Ana. Reading it was simple. Doing it was more like a Chinese fire drill.

The first half of East Santa Ana Canyon Road was a four lane divided highway if you don't count the turning lanes at the intersections. Shade trees lined the median and both sides of the roads. Well landscaped houses and businesses were packed densely along the route but there was a dedicated bike lane which helped to make up for the crazy conditions back on Imperial.

It was getting hot; really hot. About two miles into our five mile run on Santa Ana the median, trees, and the bike lane gave way and I was now riding close to and parallel with the busy Riverside Freeway. Climbing was at a slow pace. Large hills and clusters of exposed rock running near vertical several stories above the road stood watch from the right. In some places the rock faces occupied the shoulder making it a very tight passage for cyclists. The light colored rock also reflected the sun and blocked the wind. The carbon dioxide and other noxious fumes, not to mention the intense mechanical road noises, were adding to my stress and discomfort.

Sweat was freely flowing down my brow, from under my helmet, and I could feel it running in other places. My jersey was sticking to my chest and cool beads of sweat were now collecting under my chin strap. *Just like riding in Florida except hillier*, I think to myself. At least the heat was something I was conditioned for. I continued along the hot sections of old asphalt in conditions best described as an oven–like stifling environment. When I did get a brief respite from the climbs I was able to generate a bit of a breeze of my own. It wasn't much and it didn't last long, but at least it was enough to get through the next climb.

Fifty–one miles into the day's ride I coasted downhill and bid good riddance to East Santa Ana, whose name seemed way too nice for the conditions it provided over the last three miles. I had to brake hard for a quick lefthander onto Gypsum Canyon Road leading back under the Freeway for bit of shade, then up a quarter mile stretch into Featherly Park.

Dense clusters of shade trees and decent restroom facilities greeted us in the park where we joined the Santa Ana River Bike Trail for an all too short three–mile break from motor traffic and the radiating road heat. Even shorter was the cover of trees which quickly tapered off after the trail ducked back under Gypsum Canyon Road. We were now riding about fifty yards to the north and parallel to the Freeway. Not as hot but just as noisy as it was on the south side.

I partnered with Don Hardin from Louisville, Ky., and we were quickly becoming friends. It was late in the day and still hot, my legs were feeling the miles and we were climbing a steep grade without much of a breeze after exiting the bike trail. I was climbing a bit faster than Don so I went ahead of him up the hill. It was a tough climb in the traffic with a concrete curb boxing me in against the narrow single lane of cars moving in each direction. I spent most of the way up focusing on the ground directly in front of me thinking about my smart decision to sign up for this tour. The second SAG stop of the day was just shy of the crest on a slight right hand bend and if I didn't lift my head up to look around I would miss the entrance and cross right over the Freeway.

Fortunately CrossRoads clearly marks all turns and SAGs when there is the chance they could be missed by the riders. I saw the orange flag near the gas station and quickly turned into the lot. After parking my bike at the SAG a few minutes had gone by but Don had not arrived. Someone said a rider had passed the stop and I knew what happened. I quickly got back on my bike and raced forward with some snacks. When I caught up with Don he was down the road about five miles, tired and weak, but already being tended to by Lynn Barthel, another CrossRoads rider. His color came back and after a brief rest we continued pedaling on to Riverside.

I told him we would take the next thirteen miles easy, as we had no reason to rush. Just moments later after negotiating a tricky railroad crossing on Magnolia Avenue, he got too close to my bike, clipped my back wheel and tumbled to the roadway. It was a very hard fall for a man twenty years my senior. As much as I knew fatigue was a factor, I felt terrible; our first day of riding and my new riding partner clips my back wheel. I quickly stopped and pulled his bike off of him as two very caring motorists blocked traffic and helped move him to the curb.

I called Tracy to alert her of the situation and the CrossRoads van was there in minutes. Tracy and her team checked Don out, secured his battered bike to the van rack and ushered him into the air–conditioned comfort of the van. As they rode away I knew his dream of crossing the country had ended before it really started. For the next thirteen miles, I rode alone. The palm–lined streets of Riverside with Jacaranda trees in bloom did little to take my mind off the sound of parts breaking, and a friend falling to the ground. I hoped he would be okay but after arriving at the hotel there was little news about Don's condition.

A shower and a change of clothes did little to curb the heat radiating off the sidewalks and parking lot pavement. In fact it seemed hotter at four o'clock with the sky nearly void of clouds than it did at midday. I hope this is not a sign of days to come.

Tomorrow would be another big day of riding as we climb several large mountain ranges and make our way into the California desert. Not much bike maintenance to do but there were two other routines starting in Riverside; washing my riding outfit in the sink and drying them over the air conditioner vents in the room and Route Rap. Before each dinner we would assemble as a group and Tracy or Trevor would discuss the day's ride, what we could expect the following day, and tidbits of information we might find important such as elevation change, historical points of interest and some safety tips. That's Route Rap. After dinner my night of writing would continue until Clark retired, and sometimes longer. My candle was lit at both ends.

Riverside, named for its proximity to the Santa Ana River, was home to one of the more notable auto racing tracks in southern California. The speedway contested major league stock car, Indy car, sports car and drag racing from 1957 until it closed July 2, 1989. In addition to racing, the site was used as a backdrop in several major motion pictures including: *Viva Las Vegas, The Love Bug* and *Grand Prix* as well as television shows such as *Knight Rider, CHiPS* and the *Rockford Files*. Riverside is also the home of the "World's Largest Paper Cup," which is actually made of concrete and stands more than sixty–eight feet tall. The "Dixie Cup" landmark is located on Iowa Street just north of Palmyrita, in front of what was once the Dixie Corporation's manufacturing plant. Yeah, it was news to me too.

Day 3: Riverside to Indio (84 miles)

Target times—this is something new for me and most of the other riders. Not only do you have to pedal the miles, you have to be sure to reach the checkpoints along the way within a specified period of time. This is to insure riders have sufficient daylight to safely reach the hotel on these long desert treks. You also want to reduce exposure in the desert so you don't dehydrate. It is not a pleasant experience. Since I am only an average rider, reducing the amount of time at the SAG and idle time along the road will be important. The last thing I want is to be able to go the distance but run out of time and get scooped up by the support van. My plan will be to ride quickly in the morning, reach the check points on time, and save the social activities and picture taking for later in the day. Sounds easy enough but on the bike distractions come easy.

I learned in the morning Don had injured his shoulder, but fortunately nothing was broken. We crossed our fingers, hoping in a few days he would again mount his bike and continue. In the meantime, Don worked with Margaret on one of the support vans dispensing water, snacks, and encouragement.

After a light breakfast, organizing my gear, and pumping up my bike tires I was ready to go. As riders were about to depart I noticed one of my gloves was missing. I quickly retraced my steps searching the room, all the trash cans between the room and the front of the hotel, the bushes near my bike, and within my pockets and bike bag to no avail. With most of the riders gone I couldn't wait any longer. Rick and Clark were sweeping today and they were the only ones left. I had to get going.

It takes a while to get used to riding with gloves but once you do it's very difficult to ride without them. In the cold morning air they offer some additional warmth and padding to the harsh road conditions.

The ride today took us quickly uphill, through difficult climbs alongside well groomed suburban residential communities, box stores, and strip mall shopping. The lush greenery accented with tall palms complimented the architecture and I noticed the scenery seemed to repeat itself every few miles. It also offered us a bit of distraction from the climbing along the wide and busy roadway.

I did have a bit of good luck after climbing the first long grade when I caught up to Dick Duffey about eight miles into the ride. We stopped to take pictures of each other and then I remembered I helped him with his CamelBak just before leaving the hotel. When I asked him to look inside the pack, there was my glove. I was relieved to find it and quickly put it on to complete my set. Once again we rode blissfully onward, me and Duffey chatting away but clearly at the back of the back.

Nearly two hours into the ride we broke out of the more densely populated area just past a little store as we crossed Redlands Boulevard. Behind us were the gated cluster houses, the green lawns and palms. In front of us were scattered older and more basic bungalow styled houses and sparsely manicured natural greenery. As we rolled along the last stretch of Allesandro Boulevard and into the Moreno Valley the scenery changed again to farming fields with cows and what appeared to be a crop of wheat. I thought this must be the last remnants of rural southern California left.

Off to the right was a small mountain range concealing the largest supply of surface water in the area called Perris Reservoir. And ahead of us was the mountain range that we would skirt around to the south for ten miles through various farms and ranches before we made our way over it into Beaumont. After the earlier climbs we were slowly descending to the base of the mountain range setting ourselves up for another long climb.

So far the ride was relatively light on traffic but as I approached the foot of the mountain and turned right onto Gilman Springs I encountered a measurable increase in truck traffic. I passed Mystic Lake and saw plenty of cattle and horses as the road meandered through the green and fertile pastures.

A light breeze was blowing and a variety of sounds could be heard. It was a concert of nature as the movement of the field grass was adding its own notes; the birds were conversing, and the livestock chiming in with their parts. There were also the mechanical sounds of the bike and traffic but they seemed rather subdued and played a less notable role. Nature was also showing off its variety of smells by way of wildflowers and the distinct bouquet of silage and freshly dropped fertilizer emanating from the cattle farms. After riding through the densely populated areas it was a nice break to experience the wide expanse of working farms.

Pedaling was rather easy as there were a few gentle downward slopes to enjoy. Aside from the trucks it was a very enjoyable if not peaceful ride until we turned onto Route 79N for our climb over the mountain. Tracy warned us that riding up Lamb Canyon this time of the day would be very warm.

In total, we climbed most of the thirty–three miles toward our first SAG stop. On one part of a long and steep six mile highway climb up Lamb Canyon I noticed flies buzzing me. I was riding slowly enough for them to land on me. This was a troubling and difficult section of roadway; the mountainside blocked any hope of a breeze and the sun beat down on the tarmac creating an early morning highway oven baking anything moving slow enough to be caught by flies. I was that thing, the landing pad for those persistent insects.

Today was also the first of several where I would wear my long sleeved sun protection shirt. It helped keep me warm in the cool mornings but it was not so ideal when the temperatures climbed in the afternoon. At least it protected my arms from the sun and had some nifty vented panels to provide cooling. That is if the air was moving. My CamelBak was adding to the heating problem as the water in it warmed up and caused sweat to form across my back where I couldn't get any airflow. I cooked for nearly ninety minutes in the canyon and was glad when I finally began my descent, caught a breeze, and ditched the flies.

At the SAG I noticed I developed my first callous' on my palms from wrestling with the handlebars. This trip was going to test me in many ways and it was only the second day of riding. I also tried to shrug off the pain in my shoulder that was exacerbated by the climbing but it persisted. I began looking forward to riding through the flatter days so I could give it a rest. The question was when I would actually be on flat ground with all of the mountains located within the western third of our route. Not much I could do except pile on the Advil when it got rough.

After the SAG break, we picked up a tailwind and began to travel at incredible speeds. I found myself riding thirty miles an hour across mostly downhill grades, on the brakes to stay below the town of Banning's speed limits prior to entering the I–10 Freeway where the speeds continued. I decided to short cut through the truck weigh station to avoid traffic. I panicked when I saw a set of large gratings at the scale. I immediately went hard on the brakes to slow down but I got there too quickly and ended up trying to hop the bike at speed. Fortunately for me it was a smooth transition and I could have cruised through without any worry.

Then we entered a canyon, home to hundreds or maybe thousands of windmills. The size of these modern windmill machines was incredible. They appeared to be one hundred and fifty feet across the blade tips and mounted on narrow towers standing approximately three hundred feet tall. As windy as it was I was amazed not all of the windmills were operating. I guess they run based on electricity demand and they had plenty of capacity given the wind conditions.

The winds were in our favor, and so strong we zoomed on the flats for fourteen miles without pedaling. This provided just the right conditions to look around and see what interesting landmarks might exist. At the Seminole turn off back under I–10 we passed the Morongo Casino, Resort and Spa which is one of the largest Native American casinos in the United States. It features a twenty–seven–story tall hotel that dominates the San Gorgonio Pass. Then we passed through the tiny town of Cabazon, home to the huge Arrowhead Mountain Springwater water–bottling facility but not much else.

Just across I–10 about a quarter mile east of Cabazon I could see Dinny the Dinosaur and Mr. Rex, two life sized forty–five foot tall steel and concrete sculptures built by Knott's Berry Farm sculptor, Claude Bell back in 1964 to attract customers to his Wheel Inn Café. The dinosaurs even made the big screen when they were featured in the popular 1985 comedy film, *Pee Wee's Big Adventure*. The dinosaurs and the Wheel Inn Café also made a brief appearance in the 1985 music video for Tears for Fears song *Everybody Wants to Rule the World*. You just can't make this stuff up.

Then it was back out into the open desert jumping briefly again onto I–10, which is also known as the Christopher Columbus Transcontinental Highway, before cutting over to Route 111 for our eleven mile stretch to the SAG in Palm Springs. Rocky and uninviting mountains ran to the right of Route 111 and to the left were the endless fields of windmills and small clumps of desert brush. Being so close to the mountainside increased the canyon effect and the winds were even stronger.

I reached thirty–six miles per hour, but others reported speeds over forty. After nearly half an hour of sailing, my feet and nerves were ready for this part of the adventure to end. The dangers of sailing in the wind are the sudden side gusts capable of knocking cyclists off of the roadway into the loose gravel, the guardrail, or even into oncoming traffic; no room for error and no warning. We did experience some side buffeting but never did get the strong side blasts that kept my hands firmly clenched to the grips. As we were about to exit this stretch of highway toward Palm Springs we had to use great care to slow down and a few riders even had to dismount their bikes as we turned our left side into the oncoming wind. It was like nothing I had experienced before.

The skies were partly cloudy yet clear enough to allow us to enjoy the unobstructed views of the mountains rising on both sides of the canyon, the San Bernardino Mountains to the left and the snowcapped peaks on the San Jacinto Mountains in the distance to our right. We arrived in Palm Springs and wondered how such an interesting place could be dropped in the middle of nowhere; a village of unique shops with snow peaks as a backdrop in the California desert.

Ben Dudley, a United Airlines pilot and one of the recumbent riders, was keeping tabs on the wind and temperature conditions by way of either his Garmin or some other device not part of my cross country essentials. He had a direct connection somehow to the high–tech weather reporting system the airline used and no matter where we were he could pin–point our location and gather precise data about it. For now it was a novelty thing but later in the trip this information would be extremely critical to our safety.

While Ben, Kathy, and I were off the bikes at the SAG in downtown Palm Springs, I remember him saying the tailwinds were in the range of forty miles per hour. That explains our speeds through the valley. Then he told us how hot it was; 107 degrees right where we stood, shade temperatures. It was even hotter in the sun and I was surprised at the conditions we could ride in. Now had the wind been in our face it would have been a short day because we probably would have lasted only a little while in a head–on blast furnace. The CrossRoads van might have been packed. We would never know for sure because tailwinds would rule the day.

A quick bite to eat, a bio break, and we were ready to go again before the target departure time of 1:40 p.m. I was riding out of Palm Springs with Kathy and we were sharing our experience of sailing through the canyon. The next twenty–three miles to Indio would not be too difficult. Even though it was hot, we did get a little relief as the afternoon sky was well dressed with light wispy clouds partially blocking out the sun. Clouds increased as we reached Indio but they seemed to transition into more of a haze over the mountains. The reflected light was too bright to tolerate without shades. When we arrived at the edge of town the roadside was covered with drifting sand much like you would find snow drifting in the winter. It was again something new to see.

We took pictures of each other under the Indio sign and I laughed a bit when I read it was the City of Festivals. I found it hard to imagine since this place is in the desert, but the popular Indio festivals include the Riverside County Fair & National Date Festival in February, The Coachella Valley Stagecoach Country Festival in April, and the Indio International Tamale Festival in December. And to think we managed to miss all three of these exciting events.

Indio is also a major destination for golf fanatics with several well maintained quality courses in and around the Coachella Valley. With all the wind and the heat I don't think much play occurs in the hotter summer months making it a good time to enjoy the air conditioning and hit the slots at the Fantasy Springs Resort Casino. If gambling is not your vice you can take in the Coachella Valley History Museum on Miles Avenue or go to the Shields Date Farm to learn how dates are grown and sample a date shake; sounds yummy. And to think my first impression was nothing happens in Indio.

Depending on where you stand in Indio you are somewhere in the neighborhood of fourteen feet below sea level. This would be the lowest point of our trip in many ways. We began to grasp the reality about hotel accommodations and restaurant options. They would get slimmer as we ventured farther off the beaten path and into the wild. The Super 8 Motel in Indo was just a preview.

At Indio Don said he wanted to ride, but he was visibly tired, unable to sleep because of the shoulder pain. Several of us wanted him to rest and recover, as the next few days would be the hardest of the tour. Indio was still very hot, nearly a hundred degrees before dinner. We sat by the pool drying our laundry on the pool deck. We learned quickly, next to riding, laundry would be our biggest challenge.

Dinner that evening was burgers on the grill poolside courtesy of the hotel staff. While the hotel might not be first rate the manager and his team did their best to make us feel special. Most riders turned in early and I was no exception. I made quick work of my evening writing and was in bed before Clark; one of the few times on tour it would happen.

Day 4: Indio to Blythe (102 miles)

Up early for the half mile cycle out of the Super 8 Motel down to a place called Elmer's Pancake House—now known as Sloan's—for breakfast. It's a fast service friendly staffed rustic western style eatery, providing a great breakfast and way too much of it. No way could you eat everything on your plate and expect to make it up the early morning climb that starts just a few miles into the day's ride. They make the best coffee so far; I needed a second cup before pedaling back to the hotel to pack my bags.

Today would be a scorcher as the overnight temperatures dropped down to just seventy degrees. The hardscape parking lot and sidewalks were still radiating heat absorbed the day before and it had already started to warm up by the time I got back to the hotel from Elmer's.

Some of the rider forecasts predicted the highs to be somewhere between 102 and 108 degrees. I haven't experienced temperatures this brutal in many years. According to Clark, last year's tour saw temps even hotter and he told me we were getting off easy. I'm not convinced I should count myself lucky yet. It will still be hot and I'm not sure if I could tell the difference between 105 or 110. Once you get into triple digits with the sun beating on you from above and the pavement radiating the heat back up from below you are literally baking in a convection oven. So back to the room I went to suit up for whatever nature would dish out.

I inserted the cue sheet into the plastic sleeve protector I had attached to the handle bars. This kept the directions within view but the Velcro straps attached to the bars right where I liked to rest my hands. I'm not sure quite how but I need to remedy the attachment to move the straps off the bars and if possible, position the cue sheet a bit farther forward, maybe in front of the bars so I don't have to tuck my head down so far to read them. As it is now the cue sheet is easy to read when straddling over the bike in a stationary position but not so much when pedaling. At times the cue sheet would hang off the left or the right side of the top tube causing it to bind up when I turned but most of the time it would slap against my knee and it became a bit irritating. I'll think about an alternative and make changes when it becomes a priority.

Bags zipped, lotions applied, bike gear readied and I was off to the front of the hotel to join the rest of the riders. The daily ritual included a pre–ride self–check of the bike and hydration fluids followed by a quick topping off of air pressure in the tires. Then at the prescribed time Tracy wheeled the CrossRoads box truck around front so the loading of luggage could begin.

Another part of the daily routine was Tracy announcing the availability of laundry soap. This was like candy to the cyclists. Each rider who planned to do laundry later in the day would take a zip lock baggie or two of the powdered soap so they were prepared to wash their gear. With rider bags limited to fifteen pounds each, Tracy smartly decided it was easier to store the soap on the truck and dole it out as needed than have riders try to carry their own bulk supply. Today I figured a more thorough washing of my gear was in order so I reached into the little soap basket on the back of the truck and scored a pair of baggies. Then I slid them into my luggage bag and waited for the call to present my bags to the back of the truck for loading.

 In our wait riders chatted, joked, checked out each other's rider gear, and asked about biking accessories. It seemed like every day someone had a new gadget of interest. We adjusted straps for each other and made sure to check our own. Tire pumps moved about frantically as did the tubes of sunscreen for the last minute applications of protection before the gloves and helmets were put on. Each day was similar but no two were ever the same.

The baggage loading and stacking was an art of its own and Trevor was becoming known as the *bag master* to us riders. He directed the staging and loading of the bags from his perch four feet above the tarmac, standing just inside the Isuzu truck box with a one hand gripping the rear grab bar to keep steady and the other either clutching a clipboard or free to point and gesture. Bags were grouped on the tarmac and then systematically moved up to the back of the truck. I knew there was a method to the grouping but this early in the tour it was not clear exactly what it was.

I was quickly learning to trust Trevor with my gear since three days in a row I found the bags sitting on the foot of my hotel bed. It was nice to see them in my room without having to carry them there myself. I'm really starting to like this fully supported riding service.

Most mornings Tracy would have an announcement or two about something that either happened the day prior or something we should be prepared for in the day's ride. This morning it was all about the potentially dangerous temperatures, the need to stay hydrated, and to move quickly to get out of the heat as early as possible. It was another day of target times for riding through the desert and an opportunity for Tracy to impress upon us the need to speed or face being swept up by the CrossRoads van.

While Tracy was a veteran of leading cross country tours I couldn't help but notice the look of concern she wore on her face. Not scared mind you, but a look to make sure you listened. I wanted to get through safely so whatever she suggested I was doing. The other riders were also heeding her advice.

Tracy would often invite a rider to be the first to sign out and then joke a bit with them before expanding the banter out to the rest of the group. This was one of the parts of the morning routine I enjoyed the most. You often learned about the struggles other riders had or they liked a certain kind of snack or some other personal preference. Most days she would call riders to sign out based on riding speed; the steady riders going first, followed by the intermediate riders and then the speedsters. Nobody seemed to mind as signing out a group as large as ours still only took about three minutes.

The departure time was well controlled and we learned it was fine–tuned over the years by Tracy. While it was important to leave as early as possible to beat the heat or any expected bad weather, it had to be balanced against the rider's safety which was dictated by their position to the rising sun. Since we were always pointed east the sun needed to be high enough up so the cars coming from behind were able to see us clearly and pass safely. A few riders fussed about wanting to leave earlier than the prescribed time but when you sign up to a tour you abide by their rules. In this case leaving earlier would potentially put a rider in an unsupported situation by riding ahead of the CrossRoads staff. Nobody wanted to be outside the cocoon of support so griping was tempered by common sense.

Rick was wearing his sleeveless *Hotter 'n Hell* riding jersey complete with skull and crossbones graphics. A bad–ass shirt well suited for the rider. Hopefully it wasn't a sign of things to come in the desert. This happened to be Rick's normal cycling attire for the long desert days. I am beginning to tune into little details about the staff and other riders. Maybe it's because I don't have to do much other than cycling and observing what's going on around me.

I slipped into my CamelBak, put on my gloves, clipped my helmet strap, started my heart rate monitor, and reset my bike computers to zero miles. Finally I slid my Harley wraparound shades on and adjusted my small mirror attached to them. It was now my turn to sign out so a quick flip of the pen on the sheet and a sense of urgency I hustled back to my bike to get started. It was a bit of a mad scramble before settling into the long and tedious task of cycling. I thought it was funny yet each day I would repeat the same process. And so would all the other riders.

After six miles of attention to the cue sheets for all the left and right turns within Indio proper we rejoined I–10 eastbound. On the right shoulder of the highway just a mile up the road was a green Caltrans elevation marker indicating I was officially at fourteen feet below sea level. From this point on I would begin an eleven–mile ascent up to the thousand–foot–high desert floor.

The climb wasn't steep, but it was more of an incline than a false flat. In fact once we rejoined I–10 exiting Indio I could see almost the entire climb laid out in a dead straight line. Somewhere near the top it started to bend a bit to the left but I couldn't quite see the crest as the early morning sun rise was still low over the roadway. It would be a grinder taking nearly ninety minutes of steady rhythmic pedaling at about eight miles an hour.

A few riders rode nearby with not much in the way of conversation taking place. I passed a few but mostly I was the one watching others coming up on my left and working their way past me. It didn't bother me much as the climb was not too difficult and I knew I would be faster in the flats and in the afternoon heat.

The shoulder was very generous, maybe six feet wide and it was smooth giving riders plenty of room to pass without veering into the primary traffic lanes. As for safety, the only separation from the two lanes of eastbound traffic was a painted white line and a series of machine cut scallops in the pavement to provide audible and vibratory feedback with any tires attempting to cross it. Whenever a cyclist found their way onto those grooves it tended to be a very unpleasant experience; rattling teeth and shaking the entire body. It also put the fear of falling into your immediate consciousness as well as concern for the wear and tear it was causing to the bike.

On the climb the big rig trucks were struggling to maintain pace. I felt a bit safer when they passed me at slower speeds yet I knew when exiting the high desert they would rocket past in a blur at well over eighty miles an hour.

Up the hills the diesel engines whined as their drivers downshifted to combat the loss of speed. I could hear the trucks close in on me as they approached from the west a quarter mile away. A muffled sound at first but it steadily grew to a loud mechanical roar. With each downshift there was a gasp from the engine as if taking a deep breath followed by a guttural belch of power as the engine RPMs raced. With each truck the turbulent air trapped under the trailer sprayed out grit hitting and sticking to my arms, legs, and bike. I was experiencing a mild sandblasting from bits of road debris. I would accumulate a lot of foreign matter before the riding was done and the thought of a shower was sounding pretty good.

The obnoxious smell of diesel exhaust settled around me as each truck continued their trek to the top. Those carrying heavy loads worked their way down through the gears more aggressively than those in search of new freight to haul. I could taste the sooty diesel from the older trucks and I didn't like it. The tips of my bike mounted water bottles were a magnet for the road grit and soot so I'd have to remember to wipe them off before taking a drink.

At about eight miles up and again at the crest of the climb I stopped to look back and take in the view. I snapped a few photos. It was a panoramic scene of the Coachella Valley with the sun now at my back. Indio was just a small dot in the distance; barely distinguishable from the mostly brown and desolate low desert.

All around me the sameness of the scenery repeated itself. If the few scrub trees and determined wild grass and weeds clinging to life could be removed it would be nothing but dirt, dust and small rocks; almost moon–like.

On both sides of the road the terrain would rise and fall. At times it would elevate into ridges of rocky brown earth running parallel to the highway rising as much as fifty feet above the tarmac. And when the ground dropped below the road surface there were long stretches of weathered square wood posts with a ribbon of dull silver steel guardrails fastened to them to keep motorists in the right of way.

The mounds continued to grow in size the farther up I pedaled and the traffic noise amplified by the geology became a bit menacing. Well maybe not quite menacing, but I didn't feel very comfortable with it playing in my ears. Between the noise, the dirt walls, and the guardrails I had a sense of being boxed in much closer than I would like to be with all of the truck traffic climbing east on I–10. Riding so close to traffic is never easy but the surface was good, the shoulder wide, and the weather clear. I could only hope it continues like this all the way to Boston, though I know it won't.

At the pace I was riding I had plenty of time to scan the details around me. I continued to soak in the views and I took notice of the subtleties of the dry and desolate southwest terrain. The sky was clear with a few wisps of clouds but not a single bird in sight. I noticed the erosion grooves cutting into the dirt; evidence it does occasionally rain here in the desert. At the edge of the road the finest silt–like material collected but was held at bay by the asphalt curbing smartly added when the road was paved.

I saw no wildlife but I'm sure they exist a bit farther away from the man–made intrusions into their territory. Occasionally a truck tire carcass or some type of metal vehicle trash would present itself and require some course adjustment. The big pieces of debris were easy to navigate but it was the smaller items like screws, metal bits, glass shards, and radial tire wire that were difficult to see and inflicted the most damage. I had to be disciplined looking for vehicular danger to my left and obstacles to avoid in front of me while I tried to enjoy the view of nature. All this while paying attention to how I was riding and staying hydrated and nourished. Sounds easy enough and mostly it is, so long as you don't zone out and mentally step away from the riding experience.

I was impressed with the progress I made and decided to snap a few pictures to record the moment. I quickly learned you can never take enough pictures on a ride like this. After all you can't easily go back and snap a shot of what you missed so I made sure not to be in too much of a hurry not to stop. Besides I could use the break for other things like taking a swig of water, a bite of a Clif bar—my favorite bike snack—or to down an energy gel—not my favorite—Tracy kept handy. And if I get the nature call I can find a place to relieve myself.

To this point it was still relatively cool compared to what we would experience later in the day. By my standards I was in full desert gear which consisted of my long sleeve sun jacket, a white head sock to reflect back any of the sunlight finding its way through the slots in my helmet, and SPF fifty on my legs and any other exposed skin. I also had an oversized CamelBak, a rubber bladder holding about sixty–five fluid ounces of water and ice, strapped to my back in addition to the two water bottles I always carried in the bike cages. Several of the riders were wearing arm and leg coolers and Hopper, one of the recumbent riders, was also wearing a full head sock covering his neck and every part of his head except for his eyes and nose. I started to wonder if I was really prepared for these conditions. Concern gave way to worry about how sun exposure in the desert could quickly leave me with painful and unnecessary burns. Riding faster was all I could do now.

On level ground with much of the day's climb complete and a strong tailwind pushing east, I raced mostly alone toward Desert Center. In the distance both north and south of our route were low continuous mountain ranges forming natural boundaries boxing us into the desert floor. Unless I were prepared to climb them the only way out of this place was continuing east on I–10. In cooler weather and with more time to spare I might have taken in the Joshua Tree State Park to the north or the Orocopia Mountains Wilderness Area to the south. Both known for camping, hiking, and rock climbing.

Florida riders Pat and Vikki came up on my left and invited me to be the third wheel in their pace line so we could make better time. I had a brief experience riding with them back in Florida before this trip so with the temperature climbing I quickly agreed to join them. We were soon drafting along at nearly twenty–two miles per hour over the remaining stretch of I–10 to the thirty–two mile mark and our first SAG stop at the Chiriaco Summit rest area.

As we rode wheel to wheel in a tight straight line up I–10 the heat radiating back up from the asphalt intensified and it was beginning to feel like we were in an oven. To cool off I began pouring water from my bike bottles over my head and chest every few miles. Unfortunately relief would seldom last more than ten minutes. It didn't matter if the water from the bottle was hot; it still felt cool as the dry desert air worked its evaporative magic. Even though I was sweating excessively I could not feel it because of the quick evaporation. The only tell–tail signs were the salt streaks looking like lightning bolts on my black cycling shorts. It was a cool design to see but it reminded me how dangerous the desert could be.

In less than an hour in the pace line we angled right at exit 173 for Summit Road crossing back over I–10 and coasted down into the little oasis of Chiriaco Summit complete with shade trees, restrooms, a convenience store, and some other businesses just eighteen miles shy of Desert Center. The trees moved in the breeze and it was noticeably cooler sitting beneath them. It was an opportunity to take off the helmet and gloves, top off the water bottles, and get ready for the next sprint to Desert Center.

A few small birds were living in the trees of the rest area. It was like a prison sanctuary for them; they couldn't escape because they would surely die out in the desert heat without water. I wondered how they got there in the first place. Definitely they would have had to migrate under darkness but here I am riding through when the sun is high in the sky. Would the birds really be any different? And I better mention the tiny mosquito's hanging out in the rest area making pests of themselves by buzzing and taunting us. It was another sign you can't linger for long in the desert.

One of the rest area attractions open to the public is a museum honoring General George Patton and his training complex that was in operation at Desert Center during World War II. The site features tanks and other military equipment and it's just a hundred feet away from the shade of the only trees in the desert area. Inside the museum is an impressive collection of artifacts from World War I to the present day conflicts. The cost to enter is five dollars a person. The tour includes a short movie about General Patton, has displays on WWII nurse memorabilia, and you'll learn about early battle technology like trench warfare. One visitor recommended watching the movie first as it helps to appreciate the artifacts housed in the museum. He said he was humbled at the bravery and sacrifices our Military men and women made in battle. This rather modest museum can be seen in less than two hours and it has knowledgeable staff ready to answer questions. The museum is also free to military veterans.

Behind the Patton museum and running parallel to I–10 is the Chiriaco Summit Airport; nearly a mile of runway and like most of the desert, without any services. At 1,713 feet above sea level we had proof we made it to the high desert. The key now is to get out of it safely.

Riding tailwinds through the desert is definitely the way to cross this void. So far things were not looking so bad for what we were told could be some of the most difficult days on the tour. It was blazing hot, officially it was 106 degrees Fahrenheit in the shade, maybe forty degrees hotter on the asphalt, but at least we did not have headwinds. Fingers crossed I hoped luck would stay with us. Off we trekked toward the feared destination of Desert Center.

Along this section of the ride I began to notice a few lizards; about the only thing that moved in the desert besides cyclist's and a lone vulture eyeing me from above. The flies from yesterday were nowhere in sight and the dirt was beginning to change from a gravely coarse sand mixture to a fine powder. I would learn just how fine the dirt was later in the day.

In less than an hour we rolled into the dirt expanse known as Desert Center; the halfway point between Indio and Blythe. We descended nearly a thousand feet since we stopped at Chiriaco Summit and were now officially at an elevation of 656 feet above sea level. It almost seems pointless to reference sea level in the middle of the desert.

It is hard to imagine that in the middle of nowhere about ninety–five people live year–round in Desert Center. A few abandoned structures and a single café, which strangely has been open twenty–four hours a day, 365 days a year since it opened in 1921, are all to be seen on this patch of gravel and scorched earth plot fifty miles west of Blythe, the next closest town. But I would later learn just 1.5 miles north of this location off of Desert Center Rice Road is the Lake Tamarisk Golf Community.

While I did not see it for myself, a recent Google search revealed the lake, a golf course, and close to a hundred modular homes. Additional Google searches showed several other small clusters of homes, modular and permanent structures, and some industrial activity taking place thirteen miles farther north of Desert Center in Eagle Mountain.

Wikipedia reveals some additional information about Desert Center including: Chuckwalla Valley Raceway, a new 2.68 mile professional grade road racing track built in 2010, is adjacent to the now private airport once publicly operated until closing in 1992. Knowing the elementary and middle school children go to school in Eagle Mountain while the high school students get bussed daily to Blythe emphasized the remoteness of this area for those in school. A failed for–profit prison was also part of Desert Center's recent history. And at Eagle Mountain, Kaiser Steel ran one of the largest open–pit (iron ore) mining operations in the world until it was shut down in the 1980s. The only activity at the mine in recent years has been movie filming. The most notable includes scenes from *Terminator II*, the first 3D movie of the series. Apparently the Desert is not as desolate as I first thought.

Off the back of the truck riders could replenish their ice, top off their water and stock up on some snacks before embarking on the next leg of the ride. My shorts still sporting the salt streaks from perspiring looked like they added a few new flash bolts. Like a piece of art in process. Still cool and I thought I might try to find shorts with a similar design printed on them after the tour concludes. Or maybe not as I would look like a profusely sweating cyclist.

I heard other riders talking about seeing a roadrunner earlier in the ride. Not the '70s vintage classic car which would appeal to me but the fast little desert bird. My knowledge of the roadrunner was formed by the Warner Brothers Looney Tunes cartoons I enjoyed as a kid. That little blue bird could run like a rocket to keep out of the Coyote's reach. And in the pseudo–Latin cartoon speak he was known as *acceleratii incredibus, velocitus tremenjus, hot–roddicus supersonicus, batoutahelius* or one of several other hilarious names. In my mind he was poking out his tongue saying, *Beep, beep!* The heat of the desert is creating mirages in my mind. Anyway they said he was little, brown, and fast, and he didn't make a sound.

Out of Desert Center and the gravel lot back under the highway and up the ramp I went. I continued to zip along I–10 toward the final SAG for a quick stop near mile eighty–two but this time I was riding solo trailing another rider by two hundred yards. From the south I watched a dirt devil cross the road just behind the rider and for a moment I thought he might get caught up in it. A few moments after the devil crossed the highway it lost its organization and disappeared. Moments later, another dirt devil came up behind me from the right and swept me up. Immediately, I was consumed by dust, nothing but brown could I see so I closed my eyes and held on tight. My bike jumped left, then back, right and forward, as if someone pushed me about. It lasted just two to three seconds and it was over. I never saw it coming.

With eyes partially closed I braked to a stop to regroup from the event, and noticed I was covered from head to toe like a cinnamon doughnut. I poured the hot water from my bottles on my head and chest to cool down and to try to remove some of the dirt, but all I got was mud. My ears were coated with a fine grit as was my nose, mouth and every other possible opening. The grit had even found its way into my bike shorts creating some new problems.

With more dust devils twisting in the area and the heat continuing to sap my strength I quickly got moving to the SAG. A quick refill of my water bottles and another shot of extra strength green Gatorade and I was heading down the ramp and back onto I–10 for the twenty mile push to the hotel.

In the desert you need to protect your body from dehydration and loss of electrolytes from sweating. Since sweat evaporates so fast you remain dry and have little warning of how quickly you are losing fluids. That is why CrossRoads serves up the Gatorade in a rather thick, some say chewy blend. They know riders get so busy pedaling and doing whatever else they do on the bike they forget to take a drink every few minutes. The only variation from day to day was the flavor which a few riders affectionately referred to as "nasty" and "tolerable."

Tracy knows a rider can't get through the desert sections on only one bottle of water so she encourages riders to fill at least one with the Gatorade. That way, like it or not, you would have to take in the nutrients you were giving up to the desert heat between SAG stops. Most riders also followed Tracy's advice to supplement their routine in the desert with electrolyte tablets. It could have been the subtle reminders of riders who failed to sufficiently hydrate and replace electrolytes in the desert and eventually ended up in the hospital replenishing via an IV. Or maybe it was just common sense guiding them. I learned to live with the regiment as it promised a better chance of crossing safely to Boston. One thing we did realize was after a few days of this concoction we were more motivated to get out of the desert.

When I exited Interstate 10 toward Blythe I rolled down a hill and to my amazement I saw a valley of green. Blythe had a supply of water, and vegetation and life were abundant! I saw and heard birds that could not have survived out in the desert wild. Water was the only thing needed to turn this parched earth into a place fit for the more fragile living things. The fields of green also provided a noticeable respite from the desert heat and I was glad to ride between two wide farmed fields entering Blythe.

Once in town the heat increased rapidly as the vegetation gave way to more asphalt and concrete and buildings. The thermometer peaked at 106 degrees for the day. Less than it could have been, but hot enough for the rubber on my cycling shoes to be tacky on the hot hotel asphalt parking lot. I guess it could have been chewing gum fragments, but that wouldn't help with my story.

This was my first century ride and I averaged a solid 15.4 miles per hour. I thought about Betty Hays, a member of our group who, at fifty–seven, was making her second attempt at the cross–country ride. It was last year, eighty–two miles into this ride to Blythe where she fell and dislocated her shoulder. When I arrived at Blythe, I saw Betty smiling at the hotel. She made it! And so did I. It was time for a shower to wash away the sins of the day. Then it was first aid for my bike, a search for post cards, route rap, dinner at the Towne Square Café, and journaling. And since we were overnighting at the Holiday Inn Express I could use that to be an expert in anything I chose. *Beep, beep!*

Day 5: Blythe to Wickenburg, Arizona. (115 miles)

The excitement of our first state line crossing had everyone pumped up for today's ride. But my excitement was tempered by the fatigue I was feeling from the last three days of riding and today would be my second century ride in two days. I had never ridden two centuries before let alone two back to back. To make it even more concerning I had never ridden farther than I did yesterday except for under ideal conditions when I was sixteen. Good reasons to be apprehensive about what could happen.

On a more positive note I did not have any saddle issues like others were talking about and I was thankful to have been introduced to Chamois Cream by Pat and Vikki. For those of you who do not know what I am talking about, think something the consistency of soft butter or a heavy sunscreen cream. Chamois Cream, Butt Butter, and Bag Balm are just a few of the branded products used to lube your undercarriage; the contact points of your sit bones and the bike seat. It's kind of messy to apply and a bit odd to get used to; especially when you cannot find a private place for a refresh. There is nothing like palming a mound of lard down your pants along a busy roadside to attract attention. Anyway you get used to it. The key is to apply often, not too much where it oozes out of your shorts but enough to have an even film giving your bottom some relief. If you let the friction and sweat and heat get a rash going you might find yourself off the bike until you recover. And as a cautionary public service announcement; too much will have you slipping around on the seat and potentially barred from local businesses for slipping around too much on theirs!

In keeping with the routine I suited up in my desert gear, lathered on the sun screen, and presented my bags to the front of the hotel. No laundry soap for me today. Tires pumped and out into the morning traffic, me and the rest of the forty or so riders headed to our first state line crossing. Even though I was a bit nervous I was still excited for the day. We had covered just shy of three hundred miles through California by the time we crossed the border into Arizona.

Groups of riders gathered at the official Arizona sign for our first state line photo shoot and to sprinkle a pinch of the Pacific beach sand we collected from Manhattan Beach. The logic for sprinkling the sand at each state line was to bring us good luck and protection from flat tires. Hokey to some, but I don't want to chance a flat so I sprinkled as directed. This part of I–10 was exceptionally busy and a long climb started immediately after we departed the border crossing.

With six miles under our belts and the mercury already in the low seventies we would continue to climb for the next twenty–two miles. For the third day we were again working under target times; most of the riders where getting used to the drill and what was necessary to avoid being swept up.

The cue sheets were sectioned off into quadrants. Depending on the complexities of the route it might cover a single side of the paper or it might continue on to the back side. It had nothing to do with the actual mileage and in the early part of our crossing we could easily go twenty–five miles or more between turns. I liked the days when instructions were plentiful and constant attention was required to avoid getting lost. It seems like you were make lots of progress; at least on paper.

The reason for the quadrants was to allow riders to fold the sheets small enough so they could fix them to their handle bars for easy directional reference of the section of the ride they were experiencing. Most riders had cue sheet holders; a simple clip or a nifty waterproof clear plastic holder with Velcro straps for attachment to the bars. I had the ladder device and it worked well except it would wave in the breeze and rub against my knees. I eventually had to move it forward on the bike by attaching the straps to the shifter cables. No longer in my way but now it was behind the small T–bar mount holding my two CatEye computers. I just couldn't find my way to happiness with the whole cue sheet mounting situation. At least it gave my mind something to do other than count minutes and hundredths of miles covered for the day.

My mind wonders onto the little things about bike technology. Something as simple as the cue sheet holder can occupy my brain for thirty minutes or more. All of the options available, the complex, the pricey, the stylish designs, but in the end all they do is hold up a piece of paper so you can read the instructions easily while riding.

A simple "Chip Clip" used to keep snacks fresh seemed to be the most reliable and effective method of securing the sheets. And did I mention cheap? You can get a multi–pack of various sizes at the dollar store for, ah, a dollar! The only tricky part is how you mount the clip to the bars. This is where the engineer in me comes out to play. Good ole electrical tape was the most effective and it bested rubber bands by a mile. You could use rubber bands for a day or two at the most, and then they would quickly deteriorate in the sun and fail leaving your cue sheet back on the roadway behind you. Backtracking for a downed cue sheet was not on the list of things to do while on a cross country cycling journey.

The only real drawback to the clip was rain. Without proper protection the instructions would bleed out and you could be left with a soggy sheet of nothing but smeared remnants of a route. So I usually reverted back to my plastic holder when rain was in the forecast and I would have to stop to carefully pull out the sheet and reorient it as I crossed into another quadrant. I tried doing this while riding but the results included a few near falls, cue sheets haphazardly inserted that could not be properly read, and a few cue sheets dancing behind me in busy traffic after I dropped them. Stopping to flip the cue sheets actually saved time and aggravation.

Twenty–three miles into the ride I saw the first of many Dairy Queens promised by Tracy. Unfortunately it wasn't even nine in the morning and the thought of having ice cream that early with another ninety miles to ride seemed to be out of the question. There would be plenty more and I planned to look over the cue sheets later at the hotel so I'd know when the next one comes up.

Focusing back on the road I found myself exiting I–10 for the less traveled Route 60E that would deliver us to Wickenburg. Just shy of forty miles for the day the first SAG stop was dead ahead in Brenda; a little town with not much to mention except an old rustic store, an RV Park, and a few houses dotting the neighboring properties. A sign indicated more than six hundred people live here but they must be pretty well scattered about. At least we found some shade on the store porch at the Brenda Country Store. It was a weathered wooden structure surrounded by a gravel and dirt lot, fitting right into the image of the rural southwest. We had to be out of the store parking lot by eleven forty–five to avoid the dreaded sweep. We still had almost eighty miles yet to cover before we would arrive in Wickenburg.

The second desert day was much different, hillier, with more vegetation, but still very much a desert. It was hot and felt about ninety–five degrees or more. The wind pounded us on our right side, and at times offered brief tailwinds. As we rolled through the changing terrain Saguaro cactus became more plentiful and seemed to be growing in size. New types of vegetation and small squatty trees covered with bright green foliage became the norm and so did other signs of life.

Just to the east of Brenda we rode through Bear Hills, an outcropping of stone that crossed Route 60E and rose up approximately seven hundred feet above the road. It was a gradual rise not a canyon so most riders would have likely dismissed it as another named mound of rock. This area was full of mines including the Shamrock Mine less than a mile off the right on the back side of Bear Hills. This is but one of 1,439 documented mines within the state of Arizona for those counting.

After fifty–two miles and feeling the effects of the heat, I rolled through the unincorporated town of Hope. A few rundown, near–abandoned buildings at the crossroads of nowhere; actually the forked intersection of Arizona 72 and Route 60E. Forty years of dust and dirt caked the windows of the buildings and the few forgotten cars left suspended in time somewhere around 1960. As for the town name, it was inspired by the community's hope for increased business after merchants visited the town. It didn't look like it improved their situation.

I pedaled out of the town on a slight but straight incline and saw a spirit–crushing sign, "You Are Now Beyond Hope." Talk about a downer when you didn't need one. And what kind of demented mind would put up such a sign? Then it came to me; a sad soul with nothing to do, no way out of town, and a brush and some paint. I hated him already. Only a guy could do that. I was ready to quit. But I guess that was instant karma getting back at me for dissing the town.

I'd been riding alone most of the day and needed some encouragement, and this sign was not it. I pressed on slowly making my way up a slight grade following the highway as it bent left and right around a few mounds of earth and rock known as Granite Wash Pass cutting through the western fringes of the Harcuvar Mountains. It must have been too much trouble to remove the rocks so the road could run true.

Immediately to my left was Winchester Peak, part of the ridge I was winding through. With the peak at 2,700 feet above sea level it was only about nine hundred feet above and less than a mile north of my location. Not like I had any intentions of climbing it but I needed something to do to get my mind off of the grind of the day. Directly between me and Winchester Peak was Black Cat Mine. I bet the mine had some stories buried in it. Too bad I couldn't explore, but then again I might never make it out of the desert if I did. To the right was another smaller mountain called Pyramid Peak. It was just a rock pile at two miles out. I guess it is so flat out here that anything more than a hundred feet above grade is considered a peak.

Very few cars had passed by since jumping off of I–10 so when I saw a white truck and a sign that read "Welcome CrossRoads Riders to Charlie's Oasis" with a smiling character waving a water bottle, I thought it might be a mirage. But he kept on waving and as I drew near he was as real as the desert heat. And I was happy to stop for a drink. I found the encouragement I needed at mile fifty–eight.

I was refreshed and revived by the cool bottle of water Charlie handed me. It went down fast and burned cold. For a moment I forgot how much I was toasting in the sun. It was a well needed and much appreciated break. Charlie was a pretty cool guy who had made the crossing last year. He took the day to drive up from Phoenix to pay it forward to the XC04 riders and without his kindness I would have struggled. Actually I still struggled but for a few minutes in the desert in the company of Charlie I put the discomfort on hold.

Onward I rolled through a little town called Salome where the population was teetering on 1,670 residents with 1,176 housing units officially recognized by the county of La Paz. A total of 27.4 square miles of land with no signs of surface water explained the arid conditions and the lack of anything green. Since I had just been at Charlie's little piece of roadside heaven I didn't stop at the store in Salone noted on my cue sheet. Besides I had only ridden three miles since the Oasis and it was less than five miles more to the second SAG in Wenden.

I was now riding through what was known as the McMullen Valley. It stretched from Charlie's roadside stand to just east of Aguila. To the north seven miles were the Harcuvar Mountains measuring about five miles wide, twenty–five miles in length, featuring four peaks in the range including Harcuvar, ECC, ECP and Smith Peaks in the order I would ride past them. Smith Peak, the nearest to Aguila, was the tallest at 5,242 feet with Harcuvar Peak coming in at 4,618 feet.

To the south was another mountain range called the Harquahala Mountains. This range started in Salome and disappeared near Aguila. It topped out at 5,105 feet and included Socorro and Twin Peaks. Information about local geography and the details of the little towns was easy to find online or from the myriad of brochures found in the hotel lobbies and country stores. I was getting a bit of a headache from all of the geography so it was time to find something else to ponder.

On I went in search of the SAG, water, and more people. After about twenty minutes of riding nearly straight east I arrived to find the only good thing in Wenden; the SAG and knowing I actually dropped about fourteen feet in elevation.

This town was much smaller than Salome with a population of just 556 residents. My guess is most of them were there against their will. It was a dive even by desert conditions but how does one escape from such a void without a place to go?

I should give them credit for having at least one two story building by the road tall enough we could get a slice of shade to stand in even if for only a few minutes. With the sun high in the clear sky and no porches to find refuge, leaning close to the old building was the only option. There was not enough room to sit and stay in the shade and riders had to take turns to get out of the sun. And when I said close to the road I'm talking about six feet from building to asphalt at most. With all this wide open space you'd think there would be more distance from traffic to buildings. Any hope of finding lakes, ponds, or even a puddle will have to continue east of Wenden; very far to the east I'm thinking.

From the shade I saw old weathered structures that hadn't seen paint or maintenance in years. The sandy brown/tan grit washed onto the road making the usable surface narrower and the shoulder, where you could find it, less safe for the skinny bicycle tires to find traction. Traffic continued to be sparse so there would be little objection to favoring the middle of the east bound lane to avoid the sand as needed. It was time to check the bike tires for glass fragments and bits of wire, apply a little seat lubricant, and put on the gloves. Every five minutes standing here I fall another mile behind.

Margaret reminded us to depart without haste. She booted us out of her SAG. Target times were in effect and all riders would have to move on before quarter past two to stay out of the vans. I was safely inside the target time but no reason to push it. Margaret might just sweep me up to show me she can. So I guess mingling with the locals, if I could find them, would be out of the question. And I so wanted to ask someone why they stay here. The mystery remains unanswered.

With sixty–six miles in the mirror I was looking at the cue sheet to see what turns come next. Hold the applause. There were no turns; nothing but more of Route 60E with the sun now directly overhead. Hot, hot, hot and getting even hotter. The well–worn two lane road was less than ideal with lots of desert crushed stone mixed in with the old tar to bind it all together.

I felt lots of vibration causing my wrists to ache and the bike to make some grunts of its own as it chattered across the washboard road. Well it might not have been quite that bad because I could almost fall asleep on the bike with the monotonous scenery and laser straight road if I could just figure out how to keep my balance.

The heat waves rising up from the road ahead distorted the distance; a mirage–like effect as it is known. I didn't see any islands or anything unusual in the distance but it did play tricks on my mind about the heat. To the right was a stretch of land that looked like it might have been farmed earlier this year but it was dry and without any vegetation. To the left it was wild and natural, mostly sand and rock with little mounds of dry brush. In the distance on both sides the range of rocks stood above the flats. This was the view I was to enjoy for the next hour. Maybe I'll start looking at my digital displays for entertainment. *Oh look, my pulse is up and I'm pedaling at less than fourteen miles an hour!*

I continued pointed in the same direction for another twenty–three miles and another ninety minutes later I was arriving at SAG number three. I was now working on hour number four on this road and was anxious to get off it. The bottoms of my feet were radiating from hot foot; the right one being the worst. It's a sensation like an open flame being held directly under the bottom of your foot where it is in contact with the pedal. It flares up quickly and then as soon as you unclip from the pedal it goes away; very strange and very irritating. I would fidget around with the clips moving them forward and back each evening as needed to try to suppress the problem. As for now, out here in the desert, I have to live with the aggravation.

According to my cue sheet I would have to go *off route* if I really wanted to exit Route 60E. Aguila, with a handful of buildings and cars looked like it had been trapped in the 1950s, yet another small crossroads between destinations. Surprisingly it is home to about 750 people that enjoy a newly built public library just a block off Route 60E on 50023 N 514th Ave. Even though the town is small they have enough vision to follow the same street numbering system as Phoenix just in case an economic boom comes to town.

The major economic activities include cantaloupe farming and formerly included mining. So it must have been a cantaloupe patch I saw back toward Wenden. For entertainment there is the Coyote Flats Café which scored a four out of five rating by a single reviewer on tripadvisor.com. The chili and the burgers with all the fix n's come highly recommended but your pets have to stay outside. The reviewer did reference it as the only option for miles so maybe that factored into the rating. And if you want to call it a day, get off the bike and forget about going all the way to Wickenburg. There is the Burro Jim Motel right next door to the Café. And did I mention some quiet time reading at the library?

Margaret is on the clock again with 4:20 as the hard stop. She continued refreshing the table of snacks as the riders descended on her fine display like locusts. She was also chasing off anyone who lingered too long. Working the SAG may look easy but it takes quite an effort to prepare and operate with our crowd. She always had fresh bananas and quite often strawberries and grapes. Grazing at the SAG was always a treat.

I noticed Kathy was sitting on the sidewalk in the shade with her hands on her knees, her left one wrapped in a leg brace and not looking like she wanted to remount her bike. Nobody did once they stopped. It had been a long day and more to go. Since Kathy rode a recumbent bike she was able to wear a pair of nifty riding sandals. They looked much more comfortable than the shoes I had on. I would have gladly tried anything to give my feet some air. A few other riders including Jim Aubert and Tom Kahrl started to stretch as if preparing to exit Margaret's little paradise. You could call it rider posturing to see if they could get anyone else to follow.

Enough dawdling, it was time to return to cycling mode and tackle the final twenty–six miles to Wickenburg. As we left Aguila it was up to 100.4 degrees making it the hottest part of our day. The scenery does begin to change as more fine grassy scrub growth appears along the roadside. It looks like it's more prominent where there may be some source of water, possibly runoff from the fields, but it is still dry and brown. And who knows how long it has been there.

The terrain is becoming hilly which doesn't take much of a change as most of the McMullen Valley was extremely flat. The road however continues on an unfavorable uphill slope all the way to the outskirts of the city. At the same location the small mountain ridges begin to close in. Off to our left is the Black Mountain range rising up to 5,049 feet. From this point on into town we are rewarded with a cyclist friendly descent out of the open desert and into Wickenburg. Tired and covered in dust we are finally getting a favorable change of scenery.

On the way into town we pass the municipal airport and more houses than we had seen across the entire day's ride. There are more than 5,100 people living in the town which was originally founded in 1863. Wickenburg was named after Austrian, Henry Wickenburg, an early prospector who discovered the Vulture Mine from which more than thirty million dollars' worth of gold was recovered. From 1863 to 1942 the mine produced three hundred forty thousand ounces of gold and two hundred sixty thousand ounces of silver. The mine is located about seventeen miles to the southwest of town and it offers two hour, dirt path, guided walking tours at the site. The tour costs ten dollars a person and is one of the best opportunities to see the remaining buildings, structures, and tools from that era.

Wickenburg is also the Dude Ranch Capital of the World and it certainly has that flavor. The town's main drag was aptly called Wickenburg Way; just a local name for the Route 60E Highway. The street was sprinkled with other historic structures including the Eller General Store, built in 1864, the Pastime Pool Hall, circa 1893, the Saguaro Theatre completed in 1948, and the WW Bass House which opened in 1908.

Wickenburg's largest employer is the Remuda Ranch, the nation's largest eating disorder treatment facility which was once a popular Dude Ranch. The facility has treated more than ten thousand patients since opening in 1990. And even though the Remuda Ranch no longer feeds the cowboy appetite those folks looking to try on their own set of chaps and ride a horse or clean the tack room can satisfy their inner cowboy at one of three unique ranches right in Wickenburg—Rancho de los Caballeros, Kay El Bar Ranch and the Flying E Dude Ranch. *Can I get a Yee–haw?*

We stayed at the Best Western Rancho Grande, one of the few motels on the tour which provided each guest room direct access to the parking lot. It's a funky cluster of old mish mashed buildings, some with post rails to lean your bike and old style porches complete with areas to sit and stare out across the courtyard parking lot to watch other riders stroll around or clean their bike. The main buildings most of the CrossRoads riders stayed in faced a common parking lot and gave a modern day feel to the concept of circled wagons. It was like no other on the trip. Wickenburg also has some very healthy palm trees in the downtown district. Something we haven't seen since Palm Springs

I wiped down my bike and checked all of the moving parts to make sure it would be ready for our day of climbing to Prescott in the morning. No glass or wires in my tires today and the drive train seemed to be working flawlessly. Some of the other riders have to make adjustments, or have Rick make the adjustments for them, to get the shifting smooth and ready for the mountains. For the day I logged 117 miles so either I swerved enough to gain two extra miles or I have an issue with my bike computers. Right now it doesn't matter. I made it to Wickenburg. Even if it took me eight hours twenty-eight minutes averaging 13.7 miles per hour, I damn sure made it!

It was still very hot in the late afternoon so I made time for a quick shower before route rap to wash off the day of dust and sweat. With the briefing on the ride to Prescott complete and a recap of the long day's ride to Wickenburg, we left the hotel and headed a few blocks down the main drag for a family style spaghetti and chicken dinner at the Golden Nugget. Not a fancy place, and the food definitely not like mom would make it, but after a long day of riding it went down quick.

After eating my fill of spaghetti I decided to do a bit of looking around the town. It didn't take long to be over the town tour, maybe a block or so heading away from the hotel, and then I thought I'd about seen it all—or at least all I wanted to see—and decided to head back and rest. Truth is my feet decided I'd seen it all and they were obviously now in charge.

In the three block walk I think I captured the essence of what a western town was about. I tried to imagine how it would have been fifty or a hundred years ago and I kept coming back to the same conclusion; it would be just like it is except the cars and pavement would be replaced with horses and dirt. That's it. This place was stuck in time.

After missing the first DQ of the tour I decided to see how many Dairy Queens would be on our route and when the next opportunity to enjoy a soft serve swirl would come. According to tomorrow's cue sheet when we ride into Prescott we will pass a Dairy Queen just a half mile shy of the Springhill Suites. Now there's the motivation needed to pedal the fifty–nine miles through the Bradshaw Mountains!

While flipping through the rest of the cue sheets I counted twenty–four DQ's and on a few days we could expect to ride past two of them. These exceptional ice cream days would occur on our rides to Holbrook, Guymon, and Niles. And there would be no reason not to pull a Dairy Queen double header if we were so inclined. Why not, with all of the calories we were burning we didn't have to worry about packing on the pounds.

And for Country music fans here's a little Dairy Queen trivia for you. Which singer songwriter met his future wife in a Dairy Queen? That would be Alan Jackson in his home state of Georgia. Yeah, I didn't know either.

The night ended for me with at least an hour of writing post cards and gathering my thoughts from the day in my journals. I think I fell asleep somewhere in the middle of writing. And it wouldn't be the last time.

Day 6: Wickenburg to Prescott (59 miles)

The morning routine commenced with a few minor changes. It was breakfast back at the Golden Nugget where we stood outside on the porch next to the life sized wooden Caballero waiting for the place to open. With the shorter distance I thought I could enjoy more breakfast, including a cup of coffee, which was more than I felt I could handle through the desert. I was also back in my patriotic cycling jersey and out of the long sleeved sun shirt which felt pretty good even in the cool morning air.

Before we departed the hotel it was already fifty–six degrees. It was definitely going to be warm climbing the mountains once the sun was higher up in the sky. The high eighties or even ninety degrees would not be out of the realm of possibilities.

The last bit of business was to apply sun screen and pump up the tires on my bike. I like to run with one hundred pounds per square inch (psi) in the front and 110 psi in the rear since the back tire carries the majority of my riding weight. Other riders liked to pump up their tires to as much as 120 psi front and rear but once you get to about ninety to one hundred psi I don't think you get much more than the risk of blowing out a weak tire and tube combination. And when one blows it sounds like a gun being fired and it can startle you even if it only happens in the parking lot.

Quality tires and tubes can handle as much as 125 psi but I have never tested their limits. The skinnier the road tire and the heavier the rider the more air pressure is needed to retain the proper shape of the tire in contact with the ground. Too little and you risk damage to the wheel sets and increased rolling resistance. Too much and the ride becomes harsh and the tire potentially has less grip. My bike is equipped with 700x23's which are fairly narrow and with my weight require the upper end of the air pressure to hold form.

In the past skinnier tires were believed to provide less rolling resistance but there are some new studies suggesting a slightly wider tire actually has less. The wider tire also requires less air, provides a wider contact patch for better grip and a cushier ride. This could potentially be the Holy Grail of bike tires providing comfort, safety, and better speed in a single package. If this turns out to be true I will be moving to the 700x25's. I will certainly appreciate the benefits when zooming down the steep descents but for now I am going to have to trust my skinny tires to get me safely off the mountains and down the road.

As we were preparing to depart I spoke to Don about his condition. His doctor advised him to go home and recover, so this was the last we would see of our friend for a while. He gave me his Arizona flag, a camera and some other supplies, but I was tearing up, knowing he would not be going with us. He promised if he recovered in time, he would rejoin the tour. Truth be told, he will ride all the way with me in spirit.

Sign—out begins and the riders exit the still sleeping town of Wickenburg. We turned off the main drag making a right onto Tegner Street and passed by the Desert Caballeros Western Museum. This place is rated as the second best museum in the entire southwest and it features an excellent collection of southwestern art in water colors, oils, and bronze. I am always impressed how gems like this find themselves in such hideaway places.

From Tracy's route rap session explaining the day's ride I knew today was going to be a challenge with all the climbing through the mountains, but I was not prepared for what I was about to undertake. It would be one of those milestone days where I would be tested not just physically but also mentally. And it would be how I dealt with the mental challenge that would determine the outcome of my day and possibly the entire trip.

Climbing was something I did when I was in my teens but after being off the bike for more than twenty years my only recent training was in the heat on flat ground. The desert was tough but at least I felt like I was somewhat prepared for it.

Exiting Wickenburg the roads were straight, narrow, and busy in the morning with more traffic than you would imagine for a place seemingly in the middle of nowhere. Gravely soil with limited scrub brush, sparse desert trees, cactus, and a few clumps of grass lined the pavement. The road was rough in texture and colored in brown tones showing off the native rock used in its construction. Conditions were right for flat tires today.

After leaving the town proper we were on rural Highway 93 before we transitioned onto Arizona 89, the Old White Spar Highway that would take us all the way to Prescott. Off to my right a sign advised the Wickenburg Ranch Golf Course was just over the hill and out of our view. As we rode over several rolling hills most of the riders stayed single file and well separated hugging the shoulder so as to not aggravate the local motorists. I got the impression they didn't like cyclists anyway as a few honked horns and gestured as they gunned their engines and accelerated by.

This was also Yavapai Indian Country and in the early days of Wickenburg the Indians would stage raids to kill the settlers and to break their resolve to stay. It almost worked but with the combined forces of the Arizona territorial militia and US Army the settlers hung on, Wickenburg remained an orderly town, and the Yavapai were driven back to their reservation which had been moved farther from town and reduced in size so they could be better managed.

I find it to be rather unsettling to think about people as being *managed*. It suggests they are like criminals with less rights and privileges to move freely about. But if you are going to be raiding and killing your behavior can't be tolerated for long. Our history about the settling of the west is marred with many incidents of injustice and much of the sacrifices made were borne by the Native Americans. History just seems to record it mostly from the perspective of the settlers, the eventual winners in what was known as the taming of the west.

Off to the right about six miles out my morning workout was now in full view. Soon I would be heading east and up the mountains that from a distance appeared rather small and pastel purple in color. As I continued to get closer to the mountain I learned they were neither small nor purple.

It was about a sixteen miles of pedaling mostly up slight grades from Wickenburg to the Congress Trading Post marking the bend in the road where I would begin to see the mountain climb head on. The town of Congress was off to the left where about 1,700 people were most likely busy starting their day; maybe having a cup of coffee before heading outside, but likely not planning anything like I have scheduled for the day. With an hour of riding and nearly a thousand feet of elevation gain behind me I decided to stop at the trading post before climbing up to Yarnell.

The Congress Trading Post houses a unique collection of antique guns, along with swords and Civil War uniforms, all in the basement of a little building standing alone in the desert. The proprietor, I believe he said his name was Ed Gregory, told us the collection is worth something north of half a million dollars. The only thought I could come up with was if I were him, I'd sell it all and move to a better location. But then I don't really get the whole *out in the sticks* western solitude mindset anyway.

The *Post* is a real western style single story saloon–type structure with deteriorating earth tone siding and an inviting porch beckoning you to take a seat on an old chair next to the bearded Mr. Gregory and leave your two wheeled steed leaning on the post. There was no indication it was anything more than an old structure with no stories to tell. Like the shell of an oyster hiding it's pearl, except for a small hand painted wooden sign hanging over the porch with the words: "Trading Post – Congress, Arizona."

Several riders stopped to look around inside. It was much larger than it appeared from the front of the building. There were lots of old tables and display cases containing a variety of artifacts and other interesting items from around the area. We scanned them, took a few pictures, including one of Bob Cordes pointing out something interesting on a table, and headed back out the door. The really good stuff was in the collection downstairs.

The trading post opened in 1895 and aside from the corrugated porch roof and the swamp cooler precariously perched upon a questionable support stand; it probably hasn't changed much since. The transition from Highway 89 to the trading post porch is nothing but fifty feet of level loose gravel so returning to the road can be a bit sketchy for my narrow tires.

Much like the rest of this area vegetation was in short supply except for a rather healthy five foot tall collection of prickly cacti and something that looks like a snake plant just off the right front of the porch. A couple of questionable outbuildings and few personal artifacts, known in more populated areas as junk, were scattered around the building as a personal artistic expression of the property owner. He is definitely in the right place.

Out of Congress there is a slight descent followed by what appears to be a longer, more gradual drop toward the base of the mountain. A road sign said it was nine miles to Yarnell. Unfortunately it is only an illusion; a false flat that plays with your mind making you feel weak and frustrated. At mile marker 269 I crossed the dry bed of Martinez Creek and headed to the junctions of 62 and 109; Hillside to the left and Stanton to the right. I continued straight on 89 and about a mile farther the right lane became two. I was definitely climbing now.

Slowly at about six miles an hour I make my way through the false flat toward the steep right hand bend that puts me parallel with the mountain and officially on to the grinding and strenuous part of the ride. Little did I know this would be just a teaser to what would come later. The lanes of traffic separated just as the road turned sharply right. There would be no oncoming traffic; the terrain could not allow it.

My eight–mile climb up the face of the Colorado Plateau, two thousand feet up the Weaver Mountains to Yarnell Pass is the biggest challenge of the tour yet. My left shoulder still aching from my pre–trip fall and my right knee not yet recovered from the strains of the past few days were cause for concern. I need the strength of my upper body to pull on the bars to increase the efficiency of my slower pedaling when climbing. And it is even more important when I need to get up off the saddle and stand for the steepest climbs. Trying to compensate by using only my right shoulder was not the solution and it only caused me to be more unstable jerking the handlebars erratically to a point of almost falling over.

The pain in my shoulder just above the pectoral muscle and below the socket would keep me in the saddle and grunting with pain. Neither cursing nor tears would make the situation better but the more I pressed on the more of both were coming out of me. I was riding solo which compounded the mental stress. I was trying to occupy my mind with anything except the pain, the frustration of the steep grade and the rising temperatures. As other riders passed by with little visible effort and quickly disappeared around the next turn I sank farther into thought about how I could not climb this mountain; that the trip was a mistake. That it shouldn't be this hard and that I can't do it because I'm injured. It was becoming very easy to justify stopping and waiting for one of the CrossRoads vans to come by and scoop me up for the ride up to Yarnell Pass and maybe even all the way to the hotel in Prescott. The inner *quitter* was taking hold of me and it got worse as riders twenty years my senior continued to ride by me on my slow three–mile–per–hour climb.

Since I had my CamelBak on I would drink from it while climbing to avoid the awkwardness of one handed riding that goes with drinking from a bottle. The disadvantage of the CamelBak was it felt awfully heaving on my back. The straps were digging in as I squirmed around making it even more uncomfortable. I could feel the sweat starting to form between my back and the CamelBak which is unpleasant at best.

I stopped several times during the climb to rest, drink Gatorade from my bottle, take in the breathtaking scenery, and snap some photos. The views continued to get better the farther I climbed which helped my attitude. The sights back down the mountain toward Wickenburg were more like the perspective you would expect out of an airplane window. I was now a few miles out and three thousand feet above the town I left earlier this morning. I made sure I soaked in my accomplishment as I was now nearly five miles into the climb. *Only three more miles to go,* I said to myself. It felt good to stop. Not just to rest but to listen to the sounds, or lack of sounds on the mountain. At times the only noise was the wind, maybe the rustling of the dried vegetation but no animals, no mechanical sounds emanating from my bike or other noises coming from me. No cars or planes or other people. It was very quiet.

Not wanting to be last to the top I pressed on. Each time mounting the bike proved a bit of a challenge as I had to quickly engage the shoe cleats into the pedal clips and start pedaling before doing a comical but painful *dead man's fall* maneuver. I executed the fall a few times but fortunately not on this day. Once clipped in the first few rotations of the pedals seemed easy and just when you begin to wonder what is so hard about climbing it comes back to you. Then the process of overcoming the mental challenge begins again.

The only good thing I can think of about being passed by other cyclists on a mountain climb is it forces you to keep the cries of frustration to yourself. I didn't want anyone to know how bad I thought I was suffering. And when I really looked at the situation, other than the physical baggage I was dealing with, my suffering was a matter of perspective. It was a mental hurdle, one I could be overcome. I may be a vacuum of positive thinking but as long as I could stop for a break when I wanted it would be okay. I can do this. Just focus on something other than the grinding of the climb. And suck it up!

Most of the road is a divided highway with the descending lane about one to two hundred feet higher up the rugged mountain. Lots of switchbacks and dangerously tight curves keep the speed limit for motorists at thirty–five miles per hour. To the drivers I probably look more like a stationary object and with all of my bright clothing I'm pretty visible and feel as safe as I can expect to be. I had the opportunity to check out the fine set of guardrails skirting the road and was sure they would be sufficient to keep me from flying off the mountain. They also provided a nice place to sit during my many rest breaks on the way up. I only hope they are as plentiful and as well constructed on the down side.

Much like the false flats the blind turns around the large rugged rock outcroppings suggested I was near the peak. But each time I round the bend I find another section of mountain that continues on farther upward until it too disappears behind yet another bend. This continues all the way up to the top of the mountain and it is frustrating to say the least.

I rode part of the remaining section of highway with Fred Miercort, and having his company helped me focus on conversation and being more positive, I felt Fred was in the same situation. Well, if he was he kept it to himself. Fred had about twenty years on me but he gave me hope. When I am his age I will still be able to do things like this; whether they will be considered smart things remains open for debate.

Fred and his younger Brother Roger decided to do the tour together and most days they could be found keeping each other company. Today Roger was one of those riders who passed me earlier in the climb. I would see him hopefully at the top of the mountain if he decides to wait for Fred. Around the final left hand bend Clark was hollering encouragement from the crest of the hill. I was now in sight of Yarnell Pass and I was going to make it. The worst was now over. Or at least I thought so. It was getting warmer and the sun was now becoming a factor in the ride.

After a quick break at the SAG to freshen up, relieve myself, and get my heartrate in check, I rolled through Yarnell past an old train museum, several rustic houses, shacks, and sheds. The roadway began to drop sharply into a valley. The descents were frighteningly quick with sudden crosswinds upsetting the bike causing me to clench tightly to the handlebars and hope for the best as I applied the brakes to drop my speed back down below thirty miles per hour. The road seemed to narrow, rock walls closing in, and the shoulder drop–off became more pronounced and treacherous as I passed through a constricted chasm before the terrain began to level out into more of a cyclist friendly experience. My biggest worry through this area was dealing with traffic, but motorists were scarce, and those I did encounter gave plenty of room.

As a teenager I loved a speedy descent but not now. I know from experience the pain that comes with a fall at such speeds. I am more at ease on the flats or on the climbs. I'm no longer the daredevil rider I was at fifteen.

The view was breathtaking and the adrenaline rush from the free fall ride only added to it. Over the next six miles the scenery changed to more rolling hills with field grass and trees. In the valley were a few equestrian farms. I stopped along the road at a fenced pasture of several horses. While I got out my camera a beautiful light brown stallion came over to check me out and pose for a picture. He probably thought I had food.

There were a few steep but more enjoyable descents matched with some equally challenging climbs before the terrain changed once more in a place aptly named Skull Valley. Strength sapping false flats took me through the fields to the base of the Bradshaw Mountain Range, which separates Wilhoit from Prescott.

Crosswinds and a few headwind gusts kept the pace slow and annoying as I made my way to my next destination; a small old country store in Wilhoit. A few other riders arrived and we struck up a conversation with the young lady working the counter. Her name was Carmen and we asked her about life in the small community and specifically what keeps people there instead of leaving for a bigger city. She said most stay because they enjoy the quiet that can't be found anyplace else. Carmen said a few years earlier she had traveled as a roadie with her boyfriend's band but could not deal with the bigger cities and came back to Wilhoit. I was surprised by her comments because people in their mid to late twenties tend to prefer life in the big city.

Houses, trailers, and RV's sparsely dot the landscape and you can imagine at night it can be a very quiet and remote place to be. Less than seven hundred people make the western side of the Bradshaw range home compared to more than forty thousand living just to the east in Prescott.

Outside the store a few riders gathered at a picnic table near a shade tree. My bike was leaning against the tree so I walked over and joined in the conversation. It was warm and the conversation was about the remaining part of the ride and what to do in Prescott when we get there. Everyone was upbeat, but tired. Climbing can extract as much out of a rider as the long miles in the hot flats. By the notes on our cue sheets we knew more climbing remained ahead of us.

The last eighteen miles were steep grades, full of false flats and summits and places where people with an affinity for rocks would really enjoy. Excavation for the original road left several expanses of fractured dull red and gray rock formations standing as much as twenty feet high. The rock colors continued into the dirt and broken gravel doing their best to provide an anchor point for some very determined plants. Large woody roots branching out into smaller tentacles found every crack and crevice in the rock faces, holding on where there was no soil. It was a tough place for even a small tree to survive especially along the edge of the rock ridges. With limited water it was likely these trees and brush were much older than they appear.

In areas where erosion had been severe the sides of the road resembled scaled down versions of the Grand Canyon walls; visible layers of hardened deposits tapering outward to wider dirt bases that spilled onto the edge of the road. A few white desert flowers were fit enough to bloom in the road margins leaving a very delicate fragrance blending with the smell of dirt and traces of pine. A palette of green vegetation contrasted with the earthy tones of the rock and sediment. At every ridge, the foliage changed, getting thicker and greener and more alive with animal activity. It was the beauty of the high desert within arm's reach.

The sun was blazing directly above and the climbs were tough. Sweat rolled freely about my forehead and into my eyes. Drips steadily fell from my chin and forearms. I was moist all over from my body trying to stay cool. The air was stagnant, hot, and dry. There was no breeze aside the one I could create riding and my shoulder and knee were having their fill of it all. I had been climbing for miles and I was looking forward to a very welcome and long descent.

At one point I thought I reached the peak. It sure looked like the top and as I raced down for a long distance I allowed my body to relax and cool off in my own speedy breeze. Suddenly the road leveled off, then bent sharply upward. Without braking I rolled to a quick stop and realized I was in trouble. I was deep in the middle of the mountain range and in every direction I looked I was forced to crane my neck to see out of the rocky bowl. Worst of all I had to face yet another steep incline that disappeared around a corner fifty yards ahead. And in one of my many mental moments during this crossing, I thought I was facing defeat again.

The climb in front of me was like a wall, at least in my mind, which was now working at an increasingly faster pace to get my attention so I might recognize and heed the words it played over and over. If I would listen, if I would concede then maybe, just maybe my lips would repeat those words, *I quit!* and it would be so.

I was fighting it but slipping closer to submission with every rotation of the pedals. Slower and slower the crank turned until I was moving so slow I now had to focus my efforts on balancing to avoid spilling over onto the pavement. My gloves soaked in sweat slipped around easily on the handle bars. I was beyond uncomfortable. Either quit or continue but falling was not an acceptable option right now. I actually can't conceive a time when it would ever be an option; at least not by choice or by plan.

The energy and desire flowed out of me as I began to consider the easy way out. The voice, persistently chiding me that it was time to give in, that I did well but my time had come, to concede to the reality that it was just too hard to do. I started buying into the thought of giving up. I would not quit, no not me, but I could give up. There was a difference and in my mind it was a big difference. Like a person hopelessly alone at sea who just stops treading water. They don't chose to drown they just stop swimming.

Somewhere in my consciousness I was getting the mental pat on the back, the towel ready to be tossed into the ring. I made it this far which is pretty damn good, but could I really expect myself to do it all; every mile? Alone and losing the fight to the quitter inside me. I could flag down one of the CrossRoads vans and be at the hotel in Prescott and start fresh tomorrow. No harm in that. Then I stopped.

I got off my bike and leaned over, my left arm on the bars and the other on the seat. Sweat running off of me began to create little wet spots on the road. I was head down ready to concede the day. I'm not sure what I was expecting but the van never came. I waited for several minutes but it never came. Neither did any riders. Fortunately for me no one was around to witness my struggles. I was going to have to deal with this on my own.

There were tears, lots of self–pity, and a salty gritty undesirable taste in my mouth. It was defeat I tasted; bitter and unpleasant. Aside from my shoulder and knee, off the bike I felt physically okay, which was in direct conflict with the way my mind was making me feel while on the bike. If I were so unable why did I feel okay? It was a mental obstacle I had to negotiate.

But I felt like I had already conceded. I got off the darn bike! But did I really quit? I'm not in a van. I'm okay and the bike is able. Through the tears I will admit to no one something was happening. I was beginning to get angry about my situation. This was a good thing. I was beginning to fight. *Why can't I do this? It's only a hill. I'll ride some and stop and do it again. At least until the van comes by.* Another punch from the quitter landed square on the jaw.

But I got back up, took a look around, and stepped over the crossbar and clipped my right foot in the pedal. I pushed off, clipped in my other foot and I was going up. I was not done. I did not quit!

At the bottom of the descent after all of the struggles inside me I found just enough desire to keep going. My body was able and my confidence, still shaky, was slowing coming back. I may not achieve my dream of pedaling all the way across this country but today on this hill is not where I will concede. I am not a quitter. Not today. I stopped part way up and snapped a picture looking back down the mountain. I wiped my forearm across my face and a trace of a smile emerged. A few words of defiance followed and I set off once again.

Nobody cares if I make it all the way, no one will remember nor ask me about it months or years after and that's fine. But I care, and I will continue to care long after. I need this one important personal victory to remind myself I can do the hard things if I want to. After being laid off from a job I was pretty good at I needed a confidence boost. A reminder I can do what most can't. My reasons to climb are my strength and with each turn of the pedals I am getting closer to that dream I had so long ago. It is with me still and always will be. Any tears that may fall from here into Prescott will be happy ones.

Whenever I stopped I could hear nothing but the wind and an occasional bird. It was beautiful and peaceful; my hardest ride so far. I pressed on, and to my surprise I rounded a corner and across a gorge about two hundred feet higher up on the road maybe fifteen minutes away was the CrossRoads van. The climb was steep but finally I could see I was not alone on the mountain. Margaret cheered me on and I pedaled like I was a small boy heading home after a day of playing. For a moment I forgot all about my struggles just a few miles back. I handed her my camera and she captured a picture of me with the days climb to my back. I felt like a winner. I was a winner. In that photo I was confident and strong. And that is how I will remember the day.

I continued riding and just beyond mile marker 305 at the end of a guardrail and just in front of a large rock mound covered with small brush I stopped at the sign marking 6,100 feet, the top of the mountain. In the back of my mind I thought, *Could there be another climb?* A few others coasted to a stop and we took a few minutes to swap cameras and take pictures of each other. It's amazing how different cameras can be when all they need to do is point and click.

Equally amazing is that you can ride for more than an hour in these mountains without seeing another cyclist until you stop. That's when they usually appear. The views to the right of the road were of a deep sweeping valley full of pine and greenery nestled between the mountain I was on and another range about two miles away to the southeast. There was not much room between the traffic lane and the guardrail; two feet of gravel beyond the painted stripe at best. Any hint of a riding shoulder was gone, but we did have two lanes of traffic going each way for passing because of our location at the top of the mountain. I guess we can consider this extra lane ours. The ground dropped off very steeply beyond the guardrail so it was a bit tight with more than just a few riders and their bikes.

About a mile farther down Route 89A and just before descending into Prescott—which was quite an exhilarating experience—was a wooden sign touting some of the city's historical highlights and current features. Prescott is home to Embry Riddle Aeronautical University which has a twin campus in Daytona Beach, Florida not far from where I live. It also mentioned the Smoki people, white citizens who attempt to preserve Indian culture and ceremonials. It mentioned several other facts about Prescott including the welcome greeting, "Stay and enjoy our cool climate and warm hospitality" which about this time I think we all could look forward to.

There was one unsettling thing found at the sign; the charred remains of a mature pine forest covering hundreds of acres. A fire must have swept through some time the year before as the lower grass and smaller bushes were already green. Most of the tall pines were burnt beyond recovery. They may not have even been salvageable as lumber. It was a sad scene but nature was in recovery mode and in a few years new trees would again take hold.

Dropping down into Prescott was more like a friendly slalom course of wide twisty roads with decent pavement. After two miles of burnt forest it gave way to a dense cluster of tall, healthy pine trees. Through this stretch I hit my top speed for the day at just a tick over 34.1 miles per hour. Another photo opportunity presented itself at the official Prescott sign letting us know we were entering the town limits. I stopped long enough to snap a single photo of the sign and continued on. The road flattened out and it got pretty rough with potholes and wide cracks demanding my full attention. There was one last small hill to climb along with a few traffic signals to negotiate and motorists to steer clear of before the final few blocks down to the Springhill Suites on East Sheldon Street. According to a digital outdoor sign it was seventy–eight degrees in the downtown; perfect conditions to end a ride and get off the bike. I made it. A day full of many highs and lows but in the end I checked it off as a victory; a very personal victory.

Prescott is nothing like the western side of the Bradshaw Range as it is full of dense and lush greenery of all types, beautiful lawns and landscaping tying in nicely with some interesting historical architecture. At an elevation of 5,300 feet and its proximity to the Bradshaw Range it provides Prescott with a unique four season climate coupled with a small town atmosphere.

The city began as Camp Whipple in 1863 but one year later it was officially founded as Prescott. The first official rodeo was held on July 4, 1888 in Prescott, and is renowned far and wide as "The World's Oldest Rodeo." Plenty of fine dining and things to do, but for me, I need to ready my bike and this rider for another day of mountain climbing.

Tonight would be a *free night* for dinner meaning riders would be responsible for their restaurant selection and paying for their meal. After several days of planned group meals it was nice to explore. Prescott has no shortage of good places to eat, most within walking distance of the hotel. It was also laundry day so I hustled to get the chore finished as quickly as possible. While most hotels do offer laundry facilities, having to share with nearly fifty cyclists needing to do wash can be a taxing proposition. Sometimes it is better to find a Laundromat. Tonight the *lords of laundry* were with me and I was done within an hour using the hotel facilities.

I would capture the highs and lows for the day in my notebook. Performance–wise I averaged an embarrassing 9.6 miles per hour. I was in the seat six hours thirteen minutes completing every inch of those 60.27 miles. I nearly broke, but somewhere deep in the mountains I found the will and the strength to keep pedaling. Thankfully the CrossRoads van never found me when I was ready to give in. I'd like to think Margaret or Tracy were watching from around the corner, wanting to cheer me on but knowing I needed to turn the day around on my own. Just pedal, just pedal, that's what I needed to do and that is just what I did. My day ended on a high note. *I can do this—I can do this!*

Day 7: Prescott to Cottonwood (44 miles)

After yesterday's poor performance on the climbs I realized I needed to check my cassette ratio; the range of gear teeth available that determine how fast I can turns the pedals. It seems like climbing is more work for me than it looks for others. When you are struggling up a hill you have time to think about stuff like gear ratios. And I could certainly use more than what is available on the bike. I was counting the number of times I would turn the cranks compared to other riders and in most cases they were spinning more than I was. This could only mean two things. They had the same gear and were climbing faster, which I could obviously tell if they disappeared quickly around the next corner, or two, they were running a larger rear cassette gear than I had. The larger the rear gear the more pedal revolutions required to cover the same distance, but it also means it requires less effort due to the improved mechanical advantage. I made a point to stay at the same pace as other riders and I realized I was right on option two, at least for a few riders. They did indeed have a better gear for climbing.

From what I could estimate the ratio was six turns of my pedal to seven of theirs. This was roughly a fifteen percent advantage so with me running a 25T (tooth) cassette they had something between a 28T and a 30T gear. This morning I would give anything to have the better climbing gear but it was not going to happen. I was going to have to climb with what I came on tour with.

Logic would suggest that with twenty–seven speeds to choose from one of them would be the *Easy Climb* gear. As a kid I was able to go in the taller gears and climb over just about anything. Now I can't find a gear low enough to get up these hills. And yes, I understand over time I will get stronger and will be much more adept at climbing in a moderate gear but I don't know if I have much time left; at least not between here and Boston.

All this mind–work spent on cassettes and bike gearing is making me hungry so I got out of bed, put on my street clothes and drifted down the steps to get something for breakfast in the hotel lobby.

I started the day feeling a bit off, but once on my bike I forgot about my ills and focused on staying warm. It was cold the first few miles. Temperatures dipped to thirty–eight degrees overnight so it would take a while to get my body comfortable. My hands quickly numbed over in the wind and my cheeks were flush and tight. The air going down my throat burned. It was raw and the faster I moved the more biting it became.

Through rough construction and roads full of potholes, we exited Prescott in rush–hour traffic. A mix of fast descents in traffic snaking through winding roads countered by short climbs and strong side winds that slowed our progress as we pedaled the thirteen miles toward Mingus Mountain. The roads leading to the western base of Mingus included Arizona State Highway 89, the Pioneer Parkway, which was quite wide but left you fully exposed to the whims of the wind. This five mile section of roadway offered us a blend of gradual climbs and descents with a great view all around as we made our way above the surrounding terrain. Behind us, Prescott and the Bradshaw range along with our memories of our first extreme day of climbing on the tour.

Now filling our view were the Black Hills. They consisted of several individual mountains including Hickey, Woodchute, and St. Mathews to our left and Crater, Kendall Peak, and Goat Peak to the right. Mingus stood straight ahead. We were riding at an elevation of 5,100 feet through the Prescott Valley and exchanged the wide and busy highway for a two lane narrow continuance of State Route 89A that would take us up Mingus. I paced my way for the first few miles through areas of field grass containing few if any trees. Exposure to the wind was adding to the difficulty of my efforts to move through the false flats.

I passed by the Yavapai County Fairgrounds where they held horse races and other western styled entertainment and the two small rural housing developments of Coyote Crest and Mingus West. Beyond these clusters of civilization there stood nothing but ranchland until the serious climbing would start.

This section of rural roadway was in relatively good shape and it offered a fairly generous shoulder to ride on. Not a bike lane but it was close. After crossing over a cattle guard I was unofficially at the base of the mountain with only five miles to go to reach the summit picnic area where our only SAG of the day would be found. So far so good after all I had climbed nine hundred feet up out of Prescott and only needed to gain another thousand feet of elevation. Of course I'd have to climb it in one–fifth the distance.

The terrain changed quickly as did the vegetation. Scrubby pine, short bushy trees, and sagebrush increased in density and the wide shoulder disappeared into a single painted line separating us from traffic and the sloping gravel tapering off into the brush. Pedaling was getting harder, I dropped speed and then into lower gears one at a time. It would not be long before I was in my lowest gear and settling in for the long ascent at four miles an hour. What seemed like such a short distance was no longer measured in miles. It became tenths and then the next landmark just yards ahead. A few riders were near me but I was lost in my own world thinking about each turn of the pedals. The summit was now about one hour and fifteen minutes away and it didn't seem like I was getting any closer.

During the climb there would be very brief respites of flat or even a slight downhill allowing me to get out of the bottom gear and the little chain ring attached to the pedal crank affectionately named the *Granny Gear*. The constant changing of gears takes concentration and at times can be problematic. Shifting on the climbs needs to be executed carefully and waiting too long to downshift can cause excessive stress on the drive system. It can be noisy, giving the impression something is out of alignment. In more extreme situations a chain can drop off or even bind up between the frame and the crank. A very bad situation if you are firmly clipped into your pedals.

Riders tend to believe their problems are with the bike. They seldom own up to it being the person pedaling when they struggle on the climbs or toss a chain because of improper shifting. No matter the reason, at the end of a climbing day Rick is a very busy mechanic.

My shifters performed well with crisp and quiet changes between gears when I was changing just one increment at a time. It was not so quiet when I was forcing it to make up for my inept decisions. On one section of a generous downhill grade, the biggest during the climb to the summit, I was moving along at a very good pace somewhere north of sixteen miles per hour when I tried to change the front gear and tossed the chain to the inside of the granny gear. I was not able to pedal to keep my momentum on the next uphill section and would be coming to an abrupt stop. I quickly unclipped my shoes and waited for the bike to stop rolling. Several riders passed me at speed leaving me less than happy with my bike.

I was riding without my CamelBak today so the stop gave me a reason to take a long pull of water from my bottle. It was no longer cold. I chased it down with some Gatorade out of the other bottle and took another electrolyte tablet to fend off any cramping. It was warming up so I quickly wiped my brow, put the chain back on and was ready to mount up. I was fortunate the chain did not bind up with the frame. At least one rider had it happen and he could not free the chain from under the gear studs without help from a more experienced rider.

The grade of the road continued to increase and the ground immediately to the right edge of the rough pavement dropped off more aggressively as I progressed upward. The road was transitioning from gentle curves to sharper turns. It would eventually give way to several switchbacks leaving me blind to traffic in both directions. The lack of visibility to motorists concerned me. I could hear a car coming but they would not see me until they were within a hundred feet or less.

The roadway cut into the mountain exposing large rock expanses of various colors just feet off the left side shoulder. Falling rocks and bits of broken stone added to the hazards and it kept me on my toes as I continued to climb. On my right the drop off was so steep I was eye level with the tops of even modest sized trees. I was glad guardrails were in place and well–constructed to keep me from going over the edge but they also could prevent me from taking evasive action should a driver not see me. I didn't want to get trapped between a car and a guardrail. With all of the trucks running the mountain road between Prescott and Cottonwood I was also very attentive to their sounds moving in both directions.

This was a tough climb but it was also quite beautiful. The trees were tall and plentiful, the birds and small animals could be heard moving about, and the winds offered its own pleasant sound as well as a bit of the mountain fresh smell of pine. With just a few clouds dotting the blue sky I could see clearly through the mountains and across the valleys. I stopped and took pictures along the climb to help break it up. Looking through the camera lens back down the route brought a smile of accomplishment to what I had done. There would be many pictures to enjoy after the tour.

Around some of the tightest turns the speed limit dipped to fifteen miles per hour. Not like I could hit such speeds on the climb but going down the other side would likely provide me with speeding opportunities. Higher up the climb some of the rails, mostly in the turns, were severely dented, rusted, and damaged indicating several drivers would have gone over the edge had they not been in place.

Along at least one stretch of roadway an old stacked stone and masonry wall replaced the guardrail keeping drivers safe from a near vertical drop. The stone wall was showing signs of impact damage as well with large cracks and missing mortar. I stopped to take a few pictures and made sure not to lean on the wall just in case.

Several sections of road were extremely crowned; the middle being several feet higher than the edges making it odd to look at and harder to negotiate on the bike. At least one left handed turn was banked high like a racetrack. As I rode along the guardrail the ground directly beneath me was at least six feet higher than it was on the opposite side of the road. I was riding the edge of a testy banking and it had to be in this turn, a blind, steep, and tight turn that traffic from both directions would arrive at the same time as I did. I could have done without the loose gravel which was the only piece of the road available to me, but the cars passed simultaneously and it was over in seconds. Being clipped into the pedals makes you so much more vulnerable in these situations. Following a quick adrenaline rush and some strong bar clenching I was able to breathe and continue upward.

Then I rounded a tight right hander and passed a sign a half mile from the park at the top of Mingus. I was getting close and the legs were getting tired. My shoulder was still giving me trouble but it was not yet screaming and it blended into the chorus of aches I was about to overcome on the climb up Mingus.

Still in my lowest gear I rode on at a blistering five miles an hour. Actually the only blistering happening was on the palms of my hands from pulling on the bars. My attitude about the mountains had improved, thanks to Clark. Instead of focusing on the climb, I pictured the view at the top; the harder the climb, the sweeter the image in my mind. It worked. The guardrails ended, I was nearing the top. And there it was, the Elevation marker standing in the left shoulder. I had reached the peak at 7,023 feet. Kathy Stevens arrived on her recumbent seconds later thanks to a courtesy push over the crest by Lynn. We captured the moment in a single snapshot. Two cyclists in their team jerseys smiling at the camera with a firm grip on the sign so as to not let it get away.

Just under my orange cycling safety flag was the small American flag I planned to travel with all the way to Boston. For the moment I felt like the explorer claiming the mountain for his country. It felt that good. I also had my Three Stooges finger puppets rubber–banded to the pole and they had been watching my back since Los Angeles. The boys and I had plans for a safe crossing and who knows what would come after finding the Atlantic. A few other riders joined us at the sign so we took their pictures before crossing the road to cheer for Tom and Andreana Kahrl, one of the tandem riding couples, as they made their way to the summit. We cheered for other riders as well before we moved up the road a few hundred feet to the SAG. Lynn even went part way down a few times more to give riders a push, including the tandem of Helen and Don Reeves. It was a team effort captured on film.

We were now standing in a brisk wind at the peak trading stories and laughing while we enjoyed Margaret's spread of cycling snacks, fresh fruit, and more Gatorade. I had a piece of banana as I always do at the SAGs and then grabbed a granola bar to go with my Gatorade. I might have even grabbed an Oreo cookie or three before departing for the final seventeen mile stretch to Cottonwood.

As we climbed most of the mountain I recalled the winds were either weak or completely blocked by the tall trees and protected coves making it comfortable to ride in the fifty to sixty degree mid–morning temperatures in the sunlight. But once we reached the peak they were strong and it felt much cooler. In Cottonwood it would be much hotter.

I wanted to share the moment with friends back home so I pulled my cell phone out of the bike bag, waited for it to light up, and found I had no coverage. I didn't often pull out my phone during the day so I was not sure if by chance this was the first time I had no signal. Then it occurred to me. I'm riding in the wilderness; about as out there as you can get and still be on a paved road. This wasn't the last time I would see the dreaded red slash indicating I was *off the grid* and on my own.

Exiting the rest area was a sign showing an image of a truck pointed down a steep grade indicating it would be like this for the next twelve miles. I figured it would be all downhill but the first quick drop was met with a steep uphill that my legs were neither ready for nor happy to see. I went from the big ring to my granny gear as quickly as the bike would allow.

I was not a fan of the high speed downhill's where you could accelerate from zero to thirty plus in seconds. The speeds if left unchecked can exceed fifty or more and a fall at speed can be catastrophic. I topped out at about thirty–six miles per hour before I decided it was enough for this cyclist.

Riding the brakes becomes a necessity for heavier riders like me and the stress on the hands clamping down on the brake levers takes away from your ability to properly control the bike. If you manage to keep the brakes on for a long descent you can glaze them over making them less effective and in extreme instances you can cause a tire or rim failure.

The tight turns are sharp even for a bicycle and the road surface had tire grooves worn into them from the weight of the cars braking hard approaching and through the turns. The corners were also steeply banked creating conditions where you picked a groove or a rut to go in approaching the corner and you stayed in it until you were completely through the turn. Sometimes the best line was in the middle of the lane where the rut was not as extreme but you also had to contend with traffic and some drivers who frequented the road were not afraid to exceed the corning speed limits. They also didn't give you any room to safely ride.

In most sections of this downhill slalom I was exceeding the limit by nearly twice the posted speed and then I would brake very hard through the turn to keep control. I had to stop often to give my hands and my nerves a break. If I were a teenager I would have loved the high speeds on this part of the ride but being older, wiser, and slower to recover I was looking for flat land to come to me.

The descent was scary and quick but it did afford views even more spectacular than those on the climb. Of course they were best enjoyed by stopping at the few pull–off areas along the route. The best place to stop is just about a mile uphill from Jerome where a large parking lot was built for people to comfortably take in the view. Looking back up the mountain I retraced my route and marveled at the elevation where I was just minutes before.

After two thousand feet of spiraling down the treacherous and twisting grade, past the remains of rock slides the size of cars, views of mining remnants, and the mechanical scars cut into the rocks, we stopped in the hillside town of Jerome for lunch. We rolled down the main street of town and found the famed English Kitchen on 119 Jerome Avenue, the oldest eating establishment in Arizona dating back to 1899. We enjoyed great food, great bike stories, and a view of the red rocks of Sedona fifty miles across the valley.

The town is precariously perched on the ridges and cliffs edge halfway up the mountain overlooking Cottonwood. Most of the buildings have been in existence for more than a century and while tired and worn they are home to just over four hundred residents. It's hard to imagine this town founded in 1876 was once the fourth largest in all of Arizona. Getting up and down the mountain is risky even in the best conditions. I could not imagine driving these roads in the snow, the rain or even in the dark.

Jerome offers some interesting shops featuring southwestern art and jewelry, Native American made blankets, leather goods, and dream catchers along with the standard fare of Knick knacks, t–shirts, and postcards to suit anyone's desires. As for restaurants the choices were plentiful—Alice's Restaurant, the Mile High Grill & Inn, Belgian Jeannie's Bordello Pizzeria, the Flat Iron Café, and the Haunted Hamburger. For a cold beer Paul & Jerry's Saloon and the Spirit Inn at the Connor Hotel were conveniently located right on Main Street. This was definitely a tourist destination.

As for scenic tours in Jerome there is the Gold King Mine Ghost Town a mile up Perkinsville Road past the Jerome Fire Department, the Jerome Historic State Park, featuring the Douglas Mansion, built in 1916 by a family of influential mining entrepreneurs, and the Tuzigoot Indian Ruins. After eating way too much for lunch I was able to walk around and look into a few art galleries and stores but I passed on the other diversions. It was such a short day I could have easily visited all three of the sites and probably should have. When you are on a trip like this you owe it to yourself to take in as much of the local flavor as possible. The history is rich and your personal experience will be as well. As I learned on earlier days of the trip there are a lot of hidden gems scattered across our route worth seeing.

The last eleven miles into Cottonwood we raced down 1,500 feet of elevation drop on narrow, winding roads with steep drop–offs just feet from the road and, at times, no guardrails. The crosswinds were very unpredictable, and most riders were on the brakes during much of the descent. I found myself getting blown half way out into the lane by just a single unexpected gust of wind. Riders became vulnerable to these occurrences when the roadway broke out of the rock gorges and were raised above the surrounding terrain on a few fast and straight sections. It was white–knuckle scary to me and a thrill for many of the other braver riders.

It's interesting to note the tandem and recumbent bikes had trouble on the climbs, but were quick on the descents and the flats. The last few miles to the hotel was more rolling and gentler terrain. I was actually happy to pedal after the speedy descents earlier in the day. Tonight we stay at our second Super 8 motel on the tour. Cottonwood is not a big city making our choices limited. It is only about a fourth of the population as Prescott which is likely attributed to the climate. Cottonwood is much hotter and more of an arid desert than on the west side of Mingus Mountain. I will be doing laundry tonight, drying my clothes on the railings and after route rap it will be all I can eat at the Sizzler.

Day 8: Cottonwood to Flagstaff (46 miles)

Up early we headed for breakfast at Randall's, a little family owned restaurant just down the street from the motel. Today would be another short but very busy day climbing in the mountains so breakfast needed to be sufficient to power me up the hills, but no so much that I got sluggish. Mornings on tour always start out quiet, but after a few cyclists gather around food the conversations get pretty active as stories are traded. I spoke with Tom and Andreana Kahrl from West Falmouth, Massachusetts. They are riding one of the tandems and raising money for charity. Before arriving in Los Angeles, they had already raised twenty–five thousand dollars. We eventually label Tom and Randi *The Kids* as they rode so care free each and every day; always smiling and always together on and off the tandem.

It's been a week since I read a newspaper or saw much besides the Weather Channel. I had no idea what was going on outside our tour. I conceded that unless something major happens it was not worth trying to stay up on the news. It was nice to peel off that layer of my normal routine. Besides most news was centered on disasters, acts of aggression, and other negative events that led to worry about things beyond my control. On tour I was just another step closer to the carefree boy who rode around the back roads of central New Jersey thirty years earlier.

The morning temperatures were in the low sixties, but had climbed to the mid–seventies by the afternoon. The first stretch out of the hotel on Route 89A gave us some really smooth and long downhill runs where speed was easy to come by but well within the fun range. Even in traffic I was grinning through the morning chill until I had to start working my way up out of the outskirts of Cottonwood. The hospitality of the town was now behind me. It would be thirteen miles of gentle climbs and descents with a few false flats mixed in to try and confuse me. My legs were numb almost like jelly and I was wondering how I would climb Oak Creek Canyon later in the day.

Not to get too far ahead of myself I shifted focus back on the highway in front of me. Following a rather friendly descent around a gentle right hand bend I came to the first major climb of the day. It was a 1.2–mile seven–percent grade which I surprised myself by pedaling over without much difficulty. I did have the CrossRoads staff cheering me and the other riders on from their position at the bottom of the climb. I'm not sure if it is the motivation of the cheering or the fear of looking like a weak cyclist that propels me forward but I guess it really doesn't matter so long as I get over the hills.

From here I sailed on toward Sedona with Vikki, Bob Cordes and a few other riders. The mountain rocks were quite the sight to see as they appeared to glow in brilliant orange and red when illuminated by the early morning sun. As we worked our way closer a few riders were stopped ahead on the flats about two miles shy of town. How appropriate; it was another flat tire party on the flats and with a quick offer to help we were all waved off. Apparently they were about finished with the repairs and our stopping would only be a distraction. Anyway, it's always best to offer help as it is good karma to keep you in favor with the tire Gods.

Sedona, named after Sedona Arabella Miller Schnebly (1877–1950), the wife of the city's first postmaster, straddles the counties of Coconino and Yavapai and is home to more than ten thousand residents. Its main attraction is its array of red sandstone formations known as the Schnebly Hill Formation, a thick layer of red to orange–colored sandstone found only in the Sedona vicinity. The sandstone, a member of the Supai Group, was deposited during the Permian Period. And for those counting that was between 252.2 to 298.9 million years ago.

The red rocks form a popular backdrop for many activities, ranging from spiritual pursuits to the hundreds of hiking and mountain biking trails. Aside from the sheer beauty of the rocky scenery Sedona is a major destination for art lovers of all genres. Home to several musical events—the Bluegrass Festival, Jazz on the Rocks Festival, and Chamber Music Sedona—it demonstrates the variety of tastes and interests of Sedona's residents and visitors alike. Sedona is also home to the oldest arts center in Northern Arizona, the Sedona Art Center founded in 1958. The town hosts the Sedona International Film Festival, the Annual Sedona Marathon, and it has been home to a nonprofit poetry network called NORAZ. Sedona is also a destination for spiritualist's who seek out the *spiritual vortices* purported to be concentrated in the Sedona area at Bell Rock, Airport Mesa, Cathedral Rock, and Boynton Canyon.

Even in a town of this modest size Sedona is home to several diverse higher learning institutions. Yavapai College's Sedona Center for Arts & Technology includes the Sedona Film School offering certificates in independent film making, the Business Partnership Program, the Osher Lifelong Learning Institute (OLLI), and the University of Arizona Mini Med School are the most notable. The Osher program is probably the most interesting because of its focus on noncredit courses with no assignments or grades to *seasoned* adults over age fifty. This program created by philanthropist Bernard Osher in 2001 offers classes at over 120 universities and colleges in forty–nine states and the District of Columbia.

Some riders stopped at the Sedona Sweet Arts Bakery while others, including me, pressed on to the Pink Java Café in the tourist strip of Sedona about three miles farther up. From the café we were afforded a fantastic view across Oak Creek through Bear Wallow Canyon and on to Munds Mountain to the east. Coffee and pastry tasted much better on the outdoor deck. The view was definitely a factor. For riders looking to satisfy their extremely sweet or salty palette Sedona has two places that might answer the call—The Sedona Fudge Company and Buck Thornton's World of Jerky. Both located on the left just a bit east of the Pink Java

Café. Satisfied and back on the bike I passed by Jeep Tours, Sedona Motion Picture Museum, Sedona Crystal Vortex, and the Psychic Center of Sedona; just a few of the businesses lining Route 89A.

The road exiting Sedona was busy and narrow affording us little room to ride. Small tree branches and bushes extended out over the guardrail and it was difficult to tell how they might affect the bike should I try to ride through them. The smart thing to do was move into the traffic lane but timing with traffic was critical. At times the guardrail was nonexistent alleviating the boxed–in feeling riding so close to the cars, trucks, and monstrous RVs but we never had more than a foot of usable road before it dropped off into gravel and dirt. Dangerous is the best way to describe this passage to the top of Oak Creek Canyon twelve miles ahead; dangerous yet exhilarating at the same time.

Winding through the rocky range zipping past the Red Rock Lodge around blind turns taking in the breathtaking scenery as our hearts raced. Sweating, breathing hard with a tight grip on the bars a narrow but short gorge closed in on both sides of the roadway only to reveal the expansive arched Midgley Bridge that crossed over Wilson Canyon straight ahead. The signs on the bridge said "No Walking" and any hint of a shoulder was gone. We had a painted white line covered with gravel and it was clear bikes and cars on this bridge would not mix. I raced as quickly as I could only to be greeted on the other side by a gravel shoulder beyond the stripe masquerading as a firm patch of asphalt and a four foot high chain link fence another two feet farther out. Had I misjudged the shoulder and tried to ride on it I would have slid and likely fallen.

Motorists probably thought I was hogging the road by not riding on the shoulder where they thought I belonged. But they could not see the difference in road surfaces that a cyclist cannot afford to misread. The line of cars behind me was growing and the drivers were getting daring in their passing. All I could think about was pedaling faster and that they would be gone soon. Tour buses were traveling in both directions and they didn't seem shy about speeding over the narrow roads either. But so far so good and everyone in front of me was still pedaling. It will be okay and someday it will make for a good story to tell.

Every so often I would notice a new sound. Not quite mechanical but not natural either. It would come and go in a rhythmic fashion. Sometimes it begins as a very minute sound that is hard to detect and at other times it's loud enough to immediately grip my attention. My tire was picking up small stone fragments! If I ignored the ticking and continued riding without removing the shards I was at risk of getting a flat. A quick stop for checking and cleaning the tires and I was back on my way. This was an everyday occurrence on the bike and you learned to interpret the sounds quickly.

The offensive smell of diesel exhaust came and went but it was no match for the smell of the greenery that was becoming even more abundant as we descended closer to the water in Oak Creek. It seemed as if buses were coming toward me at a rate of one a minute but maybe that's a bit of a time stretch. In either case it was a very popular tourist area. The foliage enveloped the road and we were quickly riding under a canopy of lush shade trees. You could feel the temperature change moving through the shaded parts of the route. It felt good to get some shade but the evaporating sweat made me tense with brief body shivers. In the sun it was only seventy–four degrees, nearly perfect cycling conditions given the amount of physical effort required through this section of the day.

We still had the guardrail, a painted line for a shoulder, and traffic to contend with but it was a visual treat. I hurried past Rainbow Trout Farm, the Oak Creek Visitors Center, and then the Indian Gardens Trading Post and Deli noted on our cue sheet. There was also a historical marker across from the trading post but I rode right by it and haven't a clue what it said. Someday I'll make a point to stop at the sign. That is if I am ever riding my bike through this part of the country again.

Oak Creek Canyon is known for its peaches and apples and several businesses and even a roadside truck advertised them for sale. Around another bend and past a falling rocks sign and then it came into view just as Tracy indicated on the cue sheet. Dairy Queen! It was still early and I just had a cup of coffee a few miles back in Sedona so I made the untypical decision to forego the treats at Dairy Queen, which by the way would have been a twisty soft serve cone. Chocolate and Vanilla, why choose just one?

Two miles up we passed Slide Rock State Park. So tempting to stop and take a cold ride down a rock slide in chilly water. If it only were at the end of the route it might have happened. Maybe someone else will give it a go and fill us in on their side trip adventure. Continuing through the tree canopy we encountered rock walls just feet off the right side of the road reaching four stories high. This was an amazing trail running so close to Oak Creek you could hear the water washing over the rocks. Massive pines and shade trees replaced the rock walls and we were now deep into the forest. Anticipation was building and I found it interesting that in this out of the way place I would still see houses scattered along the route. The scenery replayed itself over and over between deep woods and shear rock walls along a near constant upward sloping road. We were climbing.

Finally we reached the base of Oak Creek Canyon's steep climb. In front of us was a mountain of rock two thousand feet tall, and as we crossed over a small creek bridge, the climb began. It was very steep, zig–zagging up the edge, one switchback after another. On the right hand turns the shoulder felt like it was almost vertical. This was tough climbing.

The most concerning part of the climb was making a sharp right turn and having a tour bus attempt to pass me from behind. The long buses negotiating the canyon's narrow and sharp turns where I was riding would win every time. I just prayed the rear wheels wouldn't run me over. I was lucky on all corners of the entire climb. Each time a bus passed me it was either on a straight section or a left hand corner. In the first few switchbacks one bus got close but I stopped on the straight and let it go. I'm sure I would have lost the challenge if I forced the issue. Neither my body nor bike would register to the driver as I get pressed into the pavement. I'd be no different than a bug, except I'd leave a bigger mark behind.

At each pass up the mountain, I could stop and look back down to see where I had been just minutes ago. In fact I could see as many as four or more bands of roadway zig–zagging up to where I stood. It was an amazing view and seeing other riders slowly climbing their way up was inspiring.

It was a difficult climb, but the view kept getting better. Then I cut back to the right for the final pass, and saw where Kim Simoni and Tom Jelmyer, had written all of our names on the road in chalk. Motivation to pedal harder I thought. I took a photo of my name and quickly got back on the bike to finish the climb. A thousand feet ahead, then five hundred, then I turned into the scenic stop to rest, chat, and look back down into the valley.

Hot, sticky, and sweaty I cracked a smile and stopped to talk to Vikki about our latest victory. My shoulder pain, at least for the moment was not raising a fuss and I was able to enjoy the moment. Other riders quickly converged on the SAG, then over to the lookout point for a canyon photo. I was awed by nature's beauty and the climb we had just made. The image was as sweet as the one I had kept in my mind.

While the climb was tough for me—Kim, Gary Decker, Paul Kvam and Hopper Fulton went back down to climb the mountain again. Kim actually did the climb three times! They must have figured the rest day in Flagstaff would allow for plenty of recovery from their climbing spree. I was happy doing it just one time and saving my energy for the rest of the ride. Training in Florida did not prepare me for this type of terrain.

Pictures were taken, water bottles were refilled, and a few snacks at the SAG were consumed. Maybe a granola bar or two was stuffed into my jersey for the final eleven miles through the pines to Flagstaff.

We finished the day's ride and the first full week on tour tired yet satisfied. We deserved a day off. Before showering and cleaning up I washed my bike and made sure it was ready for use again on the near century ride to Holbrook on Monday.

After dinner we celebrated Barbara Bransky's sixty–fifth and Clark Dexter's sixty–third birthdays. Following the party, Pat, Vikki, Gray Pruitt, Kathy, and I went to the Lowell Observatory for some stargazing. The Saturday night sky was clear but it was also cold at our elevation of 7,260 feet. We opted to take in the planetarium show and learned the significance of this historic site. Lowell was where the first evidence of the expanding universe was revealed. It was also where Clyde Tombaugh carefully scanned the skies through the powerful telescope and discovered the planet Pluto on February 18, 1930. Unfortunately in a controversial decision two years after I visited the observatory, scientists would redefine the requirements to earn planetary status and Pluto no longer qualified. It was now in a new category defined as a *Dwarf Planet*. At least it was still discovered from the Lowell Observatory, planet or not.

I was impressed with the rather crude mechanics of the dome covering the telescope. It actually rotated on several sets of automobile tires and wheels. Some of the wheels still have hubcaps on them! The dome itself was made of wood and remained in very good shape for its age. Not very large or very fancy but it was effective. The telescope was a bit more technical featuring a twenty–four inch Alvan Clarke and Sons refracting lens system built in 1896.

It was an interesting and educational evening and because they are only open Wednesday, Friday, and Saturday nights in May, we were lucky to have the opportunity to visit. It was an excellent find at just five dollars per adult with discounted rates for students and seniors. Lowell Observatory remains a private, non–profit astronomical research institution to this day and is located just outside and overlooking the historic downtown district at 1400 West Mars Hill Road; a very fitting address for an observatory.

The next day was a day to rest, do laundry, go sightseeing, and write letters. I also got a call from Don. He was in therapy, feeling better, but he had separated his shoulder. He said he would likely see us when we pass through Indianapolis. And so ends our first week of riding.

Day 9: Flagstaff (Rest Day)

Sitting here in Flagstaff, Arizona, our first rest day since starting our tour, I'm reflecting back on our ride beginning at Manhattan Beach, just outside Los Angeles, seven days ago.

We are forty–eight riders and six staff members, mostly strangers, but with common goals capable of molding us into friends, community, and by the tour's end, a cycling family. We are pioneers, adventurers, fund–raisers and medical miracles. All good people I hope you will come to know over the next few weeks.

By the numbers, we covered 526 miles during this first week and climbed nineteen thousand feet of mountain ranges. We were as low as fourteen feet below sea level in Indio, California, and as high as 7,023 above sea level on Mingus Mountain. Our average age is fifty–seven; we range from forty–one to sixty–nine. But the story is not the numbers; it is the people, their goals, their challenges, and their accomplishments.

Flagstaff with a population of more than sixty thousand residents is the county seat of Coconino County and home to Northern Arizona University, Lowell Observatory, the United States Geological Survey Station, and the U.S. Naval Observatory. Several companies including Walgreens and Nestle Purina operate distribution hubs in the city. Flagstaff is also a center for medical device manufacturing as the city is home to W.L. Gore and Associates, the makers of Gor–Tex.

Flagstaff is named after a Ponderosa Pine, stripped of its bark and branches to make a flagpole to raise the American flag. This was done by a scouting party from Boston, known as the *Second Boston Party* to celebrate the United States Centennial on July 4, 1876. Located at seven thousand feet above sea level, Flagstaff is considered a high elevation semi–desert; though the abundance of trees and the year round snow on the distant mountain make it hard to believe. It also borders the western edge of the largest contiguous Ponderosa Pine forest in the continental United States.

Visible to the north of Flagstaff are the San Francisco Peaks. Agassiz Peak at 12,356 feet is the second tallest in Arizona and Freemont Peak, the pointy one on the right, is the third tallest in the state topping out at 11,969 feet. Humphrey's Peak, the tallest in the range is not visible from Flagstaff. These snow–capped mountains are the remains of an old stratovolcano, made up of many layers of lava and ash piled up as the volcano violently erupted over the years. Formed over an extremely long period, from 2.8 million to two hundred thousand years ago, this mountain would have looked much different than it does today. It is speculated that a single peak reaching sixteen thousand feet in height was the victim of either a large sideways eruption, glacial erosion, or both carving out the northeastern side of the mountain forming the five peaks as they exist today. An aquifer within the caldera supplies much of Flagstaff's water. The mountain itself is located within the Coconino National Forest and is a popular site for outdoor recreation including hiking, biking, and skiing.

Beyond the San Francisco Peaks lies Sunset Crater, the youngest in a string of cinder cone volcanos dating back to A.D. 1085. Sunset stands 1,120 feet above the surrounding grade and tops out at an elevation of 8,042 feet. For tourists there is a one mile self–guided loop trail located at the base of the crater but hiking to the summit is no longer permitted. The hiking trail skirts the substantial Bonito Lava Flow; a hardened coal black textured mass snaking across the forest floor. The lava flow also created an ice cave or tube, but after a partial collapse it was closed to the public. The trail once providing access to the summit and crater was closed in 1973 because of excessive erosion caused by hikers. The entire mound is nothing but loose rock; a massive pile of volcanic gravel with no binding material to support foot traffic. A visitor center is located near the park entrance, fifteen miles north of Flagstaff on Highway 89.

Flagstaff's proximity to the Grand Canyon National Park, Oak Creek Canyon, Meteor Crater, the famed Route 66, and skiing at the Arizona Snowbowl insures a robust and diverse tourist industry. The town also offers great western style architecture, art galleries, and dining for all palettes. Many cyclists can afford the carbs and calories of a well–crafted beer and for those folks you can find Beaver Street, Mother Road, Flagstaff, Lumberyard, and many other brewing companies all within a three block section of the historic downtown near the Amtrak Station. More if you venture out farther. As for places to eat you can order lunch or dinner in any of these breweries or check out one of the many dozen other local eateries. I found a great place for pizza for lunch and in the afternoon I walked over to Walmart for some traveling supplies and relaxed the rest of the day until dinner.

After staying in the Super 8 motel in Cottonwood it was nice to be in a bigger, more inviting hotel for our rest day. The Comfort Inn had a rustic character and a very nice two story common area lounge complete with a large stone fireplace and the gratuitous buck head mounted above the mantle. Lots of windows and cozy seating made it the focal point for hanging out with the other riders. Breakfast tomorrow will be across the street at a local place called Coco's.

Day 10: Flagstaff to Holbrook (96 miles)

Today we were blessed with perfect cycling weather; overcast skies and morning temperatures in the low fifties. Several riders including Pat and Vikki were wearing their legwarmers so I was beginning to question my shorts–only clothing selection for the day. My concern didn't last long as my legs quickly warmed up once I started pedaling.

We joined the famous Route 66 through town passing several interesting vintage brick and wood sided buildings, most with ornate wood trim details and a few with southwestern style signs bearing the name and type of business within. Some of the structures had wooden porches and overhangs, others plain in comparison but they continued for several blocks drawing my attention away from the traffic moving past just a few feet across the white line to my left. This was the heart of Flagstaff. Surrounding these few blocks were more modern and generic structures lacking the character of the core district. I continued to switch my focus from watching the road to taking in the last impressions of the Flagstaff architecture and what little culture I could extract from the views. Better judgement said I needed to look ahead as the procession of bikers would be turning soon.

Our cycling parade continued to stretch out as we approached the historic Flagstaff Amtrak train station. It was once the Atchison, Topeka, Santa Fe Railway depot for all you train buffs following along. The station was built in 1926 in what was called the Arts and Crafts style architecture mixing brick, stone, exposed beams, stucco walls, and multiple steep pitched shingle roofs. Several brick clad chimneys protruded from the roof and it looked like the building had been recently refurbished. The station, which also serves as a visitors welcome center, has many similarities to photos I had seen in books about Swiss architecture. It was very appealing and fitting for its surroundings of cafés, boutiques, and other specialty shops in downtown Flagstaff.

Alongside the station was an older solid–red sandstone freight depot built in 1886 by the Atlantic and Pacific Railroad. Both structures are part of the Railroad Addition Historic District and stand exactly 6,902 feet above sea level. *Whoo! Whoo!*

A few right and left turns just past the train station to stay on Route 66 and we were soon free of the Monday morning commuter traffic several miles beyond town. Route 66 may have romantic connotations but this section of it was in desperate need of repair. The road was a combination of concrete and asphalt full of holes, riddled with cracks, and it was rough on a bike. It did have a shoulder sufficiently wide enough to keep us away from the cars, which though fewer, were moving along much faster than they were a few miles back.

On a shallow but steady climb the road improved. Asphalt replaced the concrete and guardrails now separated us from the sloping ground on the side of the road. The shoulder was ample and smooth and I was now pretty happy. Riding parallel with Interstate 40 to the right I began to feel the wind behind me blowing from the west; a tailwind to help on this near century trek along I–40 to Holbrook.

I rode with Betty Hayes and together we traveled swiftly along somewhere between twenty and twenty–five miles per hour. About forty miles into the ride, we passed Meteor Crater, the best–preserved and first proven meteorite–impact site on planet Earth. The crater measures nearly a mile across and more than 550 feet deep. It's quite spectacular—having seen it on a previous visit to the Flagstaff area—but we would not be stopping there today. For those who did stop at the site it added ten extra miles to their trip as the crater is located five miles south off of I–40. Add in the time to look around and it will tack on about two to three more hours to your day. And if you didn't catch it the first time, we would be riding just shy of one hundred miles for the day.

At the pace Betty and I were riding we would be in the saddle between five to seven hours. Considering the chance of wind shift, overcast skies that could turn wet, and sweaty bike shorts, I don't think it would be a good decision to detour. Maybe on a shorter day there would be better opportunities to go off route and do a little discovery riding. I'm confident most of the other riders will be thinking along the same lines as I am.

Interstate 40 was littered with radial–tire debris, broken glass, and rusty metal bits left behind by the volume of cars and trucks and other assorted vehicles traveling eastbound. Cleanup in the wide open is either not a priority or they get more than their fair share along this stretch of roadway. The accumulation of debris formed visible piles in the safety shoulder that could be seen more than a hundred feet ahead. This provided ample time to dodge around the hazards. But it was the rogue pieces of debris, those smallest of wires and bits, alone on the tarmac and nearly invisible to the rider that could find their way into the tire. Damage would come quick; a tire would go flat within a mile of the puncture. Many of the CrossRoads riders would be delayed to make repairs, changing a tube if lucky, and replacing the tire as well if they were not. It was an interruption of more than five minutes, a mile of distance lost on the road. It was to be avoided at all cost.

Now if there is a positive coming from a flat tire it would be this; assuming it is not your tire, you have a chance to stop with the flat tire rider, you can check your tires for debris, and catch a breather until their repairs are made. If you are a real friend you'd get off your bike and help your buddy. That is after you performed your own safety check. Nothing is worse than pulling away from a flat tire stop and finding you have a tire going down unless you didn't help them out and they ride off as you slow to fix your tire in solitude. Karma can be so unforgiving.

On this day, Pat and Vikki, the first couple I met prior to the tour, were among those who would succumb to the dreaded flat tire decease. Pat was pretty generous at helping others if they had a flat and he was on duty helping Vikki through this ordeal. He was skilled and efficient at the process and could have you going in less than two minutes stop to start. For most riders they would need more time to complete the repairs. My takeaway from this was to always offer help, and if someone is struggling, do the work for them. I would become proficient at changing tubes by learning on their bike.

Even for those skilled at making the repairs, a typical quick stop to fix the tire still demands at least five minutes of time. It includes the inspection of the tire to find the bit of wire, or sometimes glass that pierced the tube, removing the wheel, pulling out the damaged tube, inspecting the inside of the tire carcass, installing a new tube, filling it with air, and inspecting the readied wheel before putting it back on the bike. That's a lot of work within three hundred seconds and in those precious minutes your fellow riders have moved down the road nearly two miles at the speeds we were traveling today.

And if you think you can catch back up to them consider this. It would likely take an hour or more riding two miles an hour faster than those ahead if you even have a chance to be riding with them again. Unless they linger on route or get a flat or have some other problem. And do you really think you can amp up your pedaling to close a two–mile gap? If you answer Yes, than I'd ask you why you weren't riding at that pace before. You'd have to be riding the *Goo* train for that kind of power boost. Idle time on the shoulder quickly puts you behind. But hey, maybe another rider will come along and provide the company you need.

To avoid flats some riders opt to ride a more durable tire like a Continental Ultra Gatorskin brand at about a thirty–five dollar premium per wheel. These tires have an increased thickness of rubber in the contact area and the sidewalls are more rugged. But even these tires are no match for the very small and sharp wire used in most radial truck and car tires.

When a bike is equipped with these robust tires even a skilled tire changer cannot remove or install a new Gatorskin without the aid of the plastic pry bars, or tire levers as they are more appropriately named. And tire levers in the hands of an unskilled operator are nothing more than an opportunity to pinch the new replacement tube. And a pinch almost always leads to a flat. I don't think the benefits of these tires outweigh the problems they cause. In most instances checking your tires thoroughly each time you stop will prove more effective.

There are other devices cyclists use to try to improve their odds against getting flats and they work with various results. Tire liners are a thin piece of plastic or other flexible material like Kevlar that are inserted inside the tire and acts as a shield between it and the tube. Liners add rolling weight; they increase the difficulty of properly changing the tire and will cost you between twelve and twenty–four dollars per wheel. Some even come with a one hundred percent guarantee but it doesn't do you much good if you get a flat out in the desert along I–40.

I have also watched novice riders using liners with Gatorskin tires in hopes of avoiding flats. One such rider could not remove the tire even with the proper tire levers. Then they could not figure out how to remove and install the liners. They punctured two replacement tubes with the tire levers and after the fourth tube was successfully installed they had another flat not fifty yards away because they did not get the culprit wire out of the tire carcass in the first place.

I came up on this rider struggling to change the newest flat and got them back on the road. Not because I'm an expert in the process, but I do follow the basic steps and I'm very careful not to pinch the tube. I also learned that I like neither the liners nor the Gatorskins. So my takeaway is this; even with all of these preventative measures he still got flats and he needed to be capable of doing the repairs. To add insult to injury this guy had spent an extra sixty dollars per wheel to try and avoid having the problem. Learning the process would be a good investment as we have many miles yet to go over the next six weeks of riding.

I mentioned the tire levers and there are several different kinds. I use the flat plastic set of three, each measuring about six inches long and bent at a slight angle on each end. To look at them with the body horizontal the left end would bend up and the right end down. Both ends are curved and free of sharp edges reducing the risk of a tube puncture. They can still do damage if not used properly.

The trick to using tire levers is to hook one end under the tire bead and use the rim as the pivot point while applying pressure to the other end of the lever. As you push down, the tire bead passes the rim giving you room to insert a second lever. With both in place you carefully move them apart along the rim and the tire bead gradually works its way off the rim. Some people use the third lever but as you get proficient at the process two is more than adequate to get the job done. If this isn't clear then maybe you need to see it done to understand the process.

Most riders have this same compact set of levers but at least one rider on the tour had a nifty kit with another tool; one resembling a lever with a long extension to hook on the axle. You follow the same process except you extend the lever end and lap it over the axle. This gives you a pivot point to apply more leverage and it affords better control as you slide the lever around the rim. I think this would be the hot ticket for those riding on the Gatorskins.

Rick, our mechanic, uses heavy tubes in the desert and he swears by them. I think this is a good way to go and your premium for each wheel is only about three dollars. I never used them but according to Rick they buy you a little more time as it takes longer for the wires to poke through the thicker tube. So if you check your tires every time you stop you may benefit from them.

The last item is a product called Slime. Peter Crowell used it in his tires and he said it eliminated his flats. Slime is uncured glue coating the inside of the tube and when punctured it bleeds out though the hole and dries thus sealing the tire. You can buy tubes with Slime already in them for a five dollar per tube premium or purchase Slime in a bottle starting with an eight ounce size for about six dollars. Very cheap, very effective, environmentally friendly, and not allowed on CrossRoads tours. The problem with Slime is it can potentially get into the tour bike pumps and gum up the heads. If you use your own pump then enjoy. Like most new technologies, tour groups like CrossRoads have to be careful to fully research products that may have an impact on the entire group. Slime is still an unknown with Peter as its only evangelist.

I stopped several times during the day to help fellow riders and each time I inspected my own tires I found bits of wire. As many as six or more very short pieces, less than a quarter inch long, just starting to work their way into the tire rubber and if left unchecked, to the tube. There is no pre–flat warning unless you are lucky enough to pick up a long piece of wire and you hear it slap around the wheel or the bike frame each time the wheel rotates. And that is the exception.

I have fairly good tire changing skills and with more practice I can be even better. Few people will turn down my offer to change their tire so I use the opportunity to gain experience. Easily within three to five minutes tops. At least once I did it in less than two. I can complete the entire process removing and reinstalling the tires without any tools. I have even managed to do this with a slightly used Gatorskin tire one time, but never since. I ended up with nasty callous blisters to remind me why I avoid these tires on my own bike. It also took me fifteen minutes of grunting and wresting to get it off. I don't recall how long it took to get back on but I think it was even longer. Learn how to use the levers properly and save yourself some grief.

Whenever you stop take a minute to spin each wheel and lay your gloved palm over the moving tread. If a wire is in the tire you should feel it. Then look at the tire tread as you spin the wheel again looking for rocks, glass, or cuts in the tire. This inspection is quick and reliable to avoid flats.

But when you do have a flat I cannot stress enough the importance of a thorough tire carcass inspection when it is off the wheel. The wire usually burrows down below the tread surface and pokes through to the inside at an odd angle making it difficult to feel as you slide your fingertips carefully inside the entire circumference. Fair warning, when you do feel the wire it will be like the stab of a thorn and nobody likes that. Glass can also get embedded into the tire and cause flats. The last thing you want to do is skimp on this process only to get it back together and have another flat within minutes.

I will bring my tire and tube sermon to a close by telling you what I use; regular tires, standard tubes, no liners and no Slime. Check tires often and avoid debris as best you can. *And everybody said Amen!*

We arrived at the SAG to the warm reception of the CrossRoads staff at a rest area along I–40 just two miles beyond Meteor Crater. Since we were making good time and the cue sheet indicated our second SAG just thirty–five miles farther down the road we lingered a bit to talk with other riders, refuel, and check our tires. No surprise I had several potential flats in the making. I carefully removed the wire bits and looked over the general condition of my tires. They were showing signs of wear, lots of small cuts in the tread and a few in the sidewalls. I even found a piece of glass in the tread so I pried out like a pearl from an oyster shell with my pocket knife. Not recommended for those who haven't mastered the skill.

The ride to this point had been excellent given the favorable winds. We enjoyed the mostly flat and gentle rolling terrain that provided us an unobstructed view back to the San Francisco Peaks from as far as thirty miles east of Flagstaff.

The landscape varied between moon–like rocks and dirt to thinly covered and parched grasslands but you could see the trend was moving toward the more barren and lifeless. Other mountains could be seen to the north and south but they remained at such a distance that they appeared a soft pastel range of blues and purples. We also crossed a few flat bridges traversing dry riverbeds and washouts and there were a handful of recessed shallow basins close to the road but aside from these features the ground was mostly level.

Between Meteor Crater and the rest area there were several rock formations ranging between ten to thirty feet in height scattered about both sides of the highway. The rocks were predominantly red in color; dull, flat, and dusty in tone. The dirt and gravel covering most of the ground offered the same hues. I didn't study much about rocks in school so you'll only get a limited geology lesson from me.

While the tailwind was great our speeds coupled with the abundance of debris on the shoulder would not allow us to take focus away from the road for more than a brief moment. Truck traffic was heavy and their speeds produced a huge outward gust and then a suction effect pulling us toward them as they passed. You wanted to stay as far right on the shoulder as possible to minimize the turbulence the large trucks created. Often the debris piles I mentioned earlier demanded the deliberate drifting into the traffic lane to avoid them. I was constantly scanning ahead and mapping a safe route to travel.

The highway had a wide shoulder measuring about six feet across but a series of ground–in recessed rumble strips narrowed it up about two feet along the painted line. The remaining width was a minefield of road litter; failed tires, shrapnel of wire, metal parts and pieces of hardware like screws and rivets and bits of asphalt gravel were in such quantity I wondered if they ever cleaned the roads. And the farther away from the traffic lane I moved the worse it got. Constantly swerving and looking behind in the mirror was the rule and it prevented riders from getting close enough to hold a conversation. Tailwinds tend to provide a more quiet environment so it was unfortunate to not be able to pass the time chatting.

About twenty miles later we exited I–40 for the historic Route 66 highway. Thoughts of Corvettes and other automobiles from the '50s came to mind as I headed into Winslow. The name created an impression much larger than reality but after riding past nothing for miles it was good to finally arrive somewhere; it might as well be Winslow.

Approaching North Kinsley Avenue, I could hear the '70s Eagles' lyrics: *Standing on the corner in Winslow, Arizona, such a fine sight to see* .... A bronze statue and some wall murals mark the location; it's Winslow's main claim to fame. I put my cycling helmet on the statue's head and posed for a picture. In the roadway right at the intersection of North Kinsley and Second Street where we stopped to take pictures was a huge painted Route 66 emblem. It was a very nice touch and easily visible on Google Maps if you want to check it out.

The town is home to the Winslow Theatre, Old Trails History Museum, some Indian themed wall murals, and surprisingly more than 9,500 people. Winslow is also home to the 9–11 Remembrance Gardens, a memorial honoring those who lost their lives during the September 11th attacks. The memorial was constructed using two beams recovered from the wreckage of the World trade Center towers in New York City. And here I thought all the debris ended up on Staten Island or in landfills in New Jersey.

Winslow offers an array of dining options. Aside from the chain restaurants you can find several varieties of food including Mexican, Chinese, and even Vietnamese. For the record I did not try any of them. I'm just giving you the facts I learned later on.

The city was founded as a railroad town in 1882 by the Atlantic and Pacific Railroad Company as a main division point for the Southwest United States. It remains a railroad town to this day serviced by the Burlington Northern Santa Fe line. Winslow lies in the Little Colorado River Valley in the scenic splendor of Northern Arizona's high desert plains. It's ideally located as a border community to the Navajo and Hopi Reservations. The Farmer's Almanac even rated it as one of the top ten *Best Weather Cities* in the United States. You may not agree but somebody at Farmer's is making the claim.

Exiting town the DQ was holding court so Betty and I stopped in for a quick ice cream to get us the next fifteen miles to the SAG. I had a soft–serve swirl.

We passed through mostly flat plains and made a stop at the Jackrabbit Trading Post seventy–five miles into the trip. It's a must to get your picture taken on the giant saddled rabbit statue in the parking lot. I did.

Little Izzy, a young girl about six, was there offering us drinks and encouragement. Her parents own the trading post and they keep her home from school on the day CrossRoads comes through. It's a big day for Izzy when so many people on bikes pass through and stop at the post. It's likely more people stopped by today than any other during the week. Tracy commented she first saw Izzy as a baby and hasn't missed seeing her every year since.

There is nothing around the trading post and few cars pass by it on Route 66. It's hard to imagine it was once one of the bigger thriving attractions along the old highway before Route 66 was decertified and replaced by I–40 when it was completed in the 1980s. Billboards for the Jackrabbit Trading Post once existed as far away as Chicago. Each sign had the silhouette of a jackrabbit and the distance from the sign to the trading post. In front of the post is a sign with the words, "HERE IT IS" and the side of the building has a twelve foot rabbit painted on it. The Post is a piece of living history on Route 66 and it is still a destination for many enthusiasts. I bought several postcards and looked around at the unique novelty items for sale in what was one of the last holdouts of a passing era.

Hollywood paid tribute to the Jackrabbit when in 2006 the animated film *Cars* had the trading post's "HERE IT IS" signage depicted with a Model T Ford in place of the jackrabbit and *Lizzie*—a 1923 Ford—as the store's proprietor. I hoped for Izzy and the Jaquez family the Jackrabbit got a boost from the movie and remains a roadside attraction. I revisited the Jackrabbit in the spring of 2013 when I made my second crossing and was happy to see it was still in operation just off exit 269 of I–40.

Betty and I detoured through Joseph City five miles beyond the trading post and on into Holbrook another fifteen miles farther up I–40. Holbrook was another railroad town named after the first engineer of the Atlantic and Pacific Railroad and it became the county seat of Navajo County in 1895. It was known as the town too tough for women or churches.

Near the old Santa Fe Railroad Depot was a road fronted by restaurants, bakeries, and a Chinese laundry. There were drug stores, a mercantile, and even a trading post. Along with these businesses Holbrook became a place to practice the holy trinity of Wild West pursuits: gambling, prostitution, and gun fighting. In the early years the town was untamed and the risk of dying by violence was one in ten. That all changed on September 4, 1887 when Commodore Perry Owens, the sheriff of Holbrook, dubbed *Saint George with a six–shooter,* made it known law and order had finally come to the territory. When the day ended the cattle rustling Blevins Gang were mostly dead and for nearly ten years after the sheriff would maintain peace in Holbrook.

Through Holbrook Route 66 is called Hopi Drive and it runs right past the historic Wigwam Motel which is a surreal visual experience pulled right out of the past. I stopped to take a few photos of the hotel with the vintage '50s and '60s cars in the gravel lot. I counted two Studebakers, a '55 Oldsmobile, a '49 Ford and a couple of Chevrolets amongst their collection. Built in 1950, the Wigwam Motel is listed in the National Register of Historic Places. I believe this is the only place in the country where motel rooms are shaped like individual teepees. It was like a postcard scene from days gone by. And to prove it I bought a postcard in case my pictures didn't come out.

A half mile ahead is the corner where we turn left on Navajo toward the hotel but if you detour to the right and down a block past the A&W you will see a group of dinosaur sculptures in front of the Indian Rock Shop. A few of the statues stand twenty–five to thirty feet tall and are brightly painted making them hard to miss.

One block farther south is Central Avenue just across the railroad tracks. The street sign indicates it's more colorful and notorious name; Bucket of Blood Street. It was named the sixth wackiest street name according to a 2006 poll by Car Connection website. On the south east extent of this street is the old Terrill's Cottage Saloon. This place gained fame and earned its place on the list of notorious gun battles of the west. As a result of a simple poker game that ended in a drunken brawl and murder the saloon will forever be known as the Bucket of Blood.

The story starts with Grat Dalton, a member of the notorious Dalton Gang, and a gambler named George Bell playing poker with two other men at the Cottage in 1886. An argument over a deal of cards ended with Dalton firing his forty–five killing the two men. The dead lay side by side on the saloon floor while Dalton and Bell fled. After the bodies were removed people said the floor where the men died looked like a bucket of blood had been spilled.

Dalton managed to avoid arrest for the shooting but his day would come. Six months later in Coffeyville, Kansas his luck ran out. He was shot and killed along with three other members of the Dalton Gang following a botched bank robbery attempt.

If you stay on route North onto Navajo immediately on your left is a brilliant western themed wall mural painted on the south side of a building. After being involved on a wall mural project in Belvedere, Illinois back in 1997, I always marvel at the site of large scale murals designed to attract tourism to the smaller towns. A good mural can tell a story about the town, its history, and the people who live there. The combined beauty of paint, time, and talent put to good use.

A few blocks farther up the street another Dairy Queen waited for the riders just two miles shy of the Days Inn where we would hold out for the night. Aside from the flat tires, this was a safe and enjoyable ride. I averaged a stellar 17.3 miles an hour and limited my seat time to five hours thirty–one minutes.

At dinner no one talked about stopping at Meteor Crater. I take it as confirmation no one did. We left Denny's and watched the sun set quietly in brilliant shades of red and yellow under the fading blue to black sky over the mountains of Flagstaff some ninety miles away. And to think here in this town 125 years ago it was anything but quiet.

Based on the next couple of cue sheets lower daily mileage, we will be doing a lot of climbing. I hope things continue to get better with my shoulder and the legs get stronger since they both had an easy day today.

Tomorrow, we ride to Gallop, New Mexico, to celebrate our second state–line crossing. Gallop is known as the heart of the Indian southwest and we will likely see many examples of authentic Native American culture.

Day 11: Holbrook to Gallop, New Mexico (90 miles)

The alarm goes off early and the daily routine begins. Clark sits up in his bed and opens the morning with some conversation about the weather, the winds, and how to prepare for the day. After showering and putting on our gear he continues sharing his thoughts about the day's ride. He doesn't reveal details about the terrain or the difficulty of the ride because the weather conditions really dictate the experience. A tailwind today in the cool air would be a completely different experience from a hot day facing strong headwinds. Road conditions could easily change; new pavement or construction, traffic and rain are just a few of the other variables included in what determines the ride.

And then there is the human memory variable. How is it possible to recall all of the twists and turns and climbs on more than eighty miles of roads and condense it all into a simple commentary about what to expect? At best you get just a brief series of highlights to formulate a riding strategy. It would not be unusual to recall a single big hill within the last twenty miles of a ride only to retrace your route a year later and find there were actually a half–dozen climbs and all were as tough as the single climb you remembered. Following this ride I would make the crossing three more times and prove that to myself. How would you feel if as a rider you were told to expect a single climb only to be completely worn out after the first and then having to deal with five unexpected additional hills? Not too happy I would guess.

Each rider is different as well so if Clark told me it was an easy day for him it might seem hard to me. He rides in New Hampshire and I ride in Florida. And to me a highway overpass is a big climb. The best advice that can be given to someone on the day of a ride is to just pedal. Take your time, don't stress about what might be. It can be done under even the most extreme conditions. Just pedal.

The riding is mostly mental unless you have physical issues preventing you from moving forward. Looking back on each day's comments I really appreciated the way Clark advised me. He is a good coach and a mentor from whom I would learn much about cross country cycling.

Often on tour riders would ask Tracy for route specifics; mostly about the climbs. She would usually describe the route as consisting of mostly gentle terrain and never yielded from this description for reasons mentioned earlier. There is no benefit to knowing the details that cannot be guaranteed. Just pedal.

It looks like another desert day to ride with my white and yellow sun shirt to fend off the sun. I'm not sure why they call it a shirt. It is more like a pullover windbreaker with zippers and side vents. You wouldn't really want to wear it without a cycling jersey or a liner shirt underneath. I think I'll just refer to it as my riding jacket and leave it at that.

Hot coffee and a small breakfast at Denny's gets the day started. I'm filled up; my bags are packed and the bike is readied per the usual routine. Tracy told us to expect lots of road debris again today so I am getting my mind focused on making plenty of stops; to help others of course. Conditions today mirrored those on our ride to Holbrook. It was cool, the road straight and it was very windy—fortunately it was a tailwind—and the skies were overcast.

The first six miles out of Holbrook had us on a northeasterly trajectory before the pavement bent slightly more to the east aligning with the winds at our backs. I rode alone most of the day on Interstate 40, but stopped to help every time someone had a flat. Flat–tire parties, we call them, and I figured if I helped, maybe the flat–tire gods would spare me. Today I had none. I was getting lots of experience changing tires and my times were dropping quickly. I think my best was just under two minutes which to me is quite sufficient. The stops afforded a few minutes to talk in normal volume to others; something not really possible when scurrying down the highway with the wind zooming noisily past your ears.

The noise reminds me to come up with a device capable of diverting the air away from my ears; a shield or a spoiler that doesn't cover my ears but lets me cut out the obnoxious rush of wind. I can cup my ear with a hand and the noise is gone so maybe something along those lines is what I need to do. If successful it would be a hot item for other riders. And maybe a business opportunity in the making if it is really good and really cheap.

Most of the impromptu roadside discussions involved expectations for the rest of the route, finding a semi–private place for a bio break, concerns about running out of tubes, and explanations on how a camera worked so pictures could be taken. It would have been pretty convenient if everyone had the same cameras but what fun would that be? We also commented on our less than sporty attire and appearances just before setting off down the road. That's why they call them flat–tire parties.

I moved along quite effortlessly which was like another day of rest on the bike. I had time to look around and take in the wide open desert landscape. The clouds stayed with us for most of the morning so it remained bright and sunglasses were a mandatory part of the riding outfit. Truck traffic was steady, noisy, and moving at least the posted seventy–five mile per hour speed limit. Occasionally I was peppered with fine sand and grit propelled by the truck's self–generated gust of turbulence. Most times it was harmless unless it got past my glasses and into my eyes. I stopped a few times to get the irritant out of my eyes but that was it. No lasting issues or eye problems.

I noticed even in the cooler riding conditions the road grit found its way onto my exposed skin, especially my legs. It was like a thin film of nastiness; sand, dirt, bug parts, fragments of things once living now dried out like jerky and pulverized into a fine powder. The the ring of filth accumulated at the top of my fancy cycling socks as if the thickness of fabric formed a shelf for the debris to accumulate. The thought of what I must be carrying with me was getting a bit disturbing and it continued to deteriorate from there. That is until I found some purpose in the distance; something else to focus on.

I fixed my sights down the road, the pavement narrowing, the white and yellow painted stripes converging until they disappeared into a single point. And as the distance increases the colors took on a more blue–gray tint. It's the same illusion causing mountains in the distance to have a bluish–purple cast to them. They really aren't the color you see, but then again it is what you see from a distance.

The same is true for the size of objects. To the eye they become smaller and their movement slower. You can reach out and almost pinch a semi–truck between your fingers from half a mile away, which by the way is a fun thing to do on foot but not so much when you are riding a bike. The point is these observations lead to ideas and ponderings that can have a field day in your mind and it doesn't hurt to play along, analyze the environmental minutia, and then discard it.

These moments can entertain you as you grind away on the pedals for minutes and then for miles if you have nothing better to think about. And if anyone asks you can tell them you are practicing for your next role in life as a physicist. Let them think you are closer to crazy so they have something to ponder as you pedal toward the convergence in the distance. You'll be too busy to care what they think.

And I almost forgot about sounds. The farther away a sound originates the quieter it will be but if the sounding object is in motion the direction of travel adds to the magic. Trains coming toward you or trucks moving away; everyone has experienced this thing they call the *Doppler Effect*. They probably just didn't know what it was called. Before I apply some additional focus on my route I'll share this little nugget that may be on the test at the end of this book. As objects move toward you the sound waves they create are being compressed and produce a higher pitch tone than when the object is moving away from you. And thanks to good timing or for drawing the short straw, Austrian Christopher Doppler will always be remembered by me whenever I see a little boy quickly turning his head from left to right—or vice versa—as he screams out *YEEEEEE–ooooooooow!*

We passed by small roads that crossed I–40. There were few if any buildings at the intersections or much of anything else besides a line of wooden power poles and a few old signs pointing us toward businesses probably long since gone. Everything exposed to the elements was weathered and worn; wood dried and bleached of color, paint faded and powdered revealing the brush strokes from prior decades.

I did see a few random cellular towers so I was hoping that in the event of an emergency I might actually be able to call someone. Not sure who that someone might have been out here between the mile markers. I didn't bother to stop and pull out my phone to give it a try. I'd hate to know with any certainty that I was truly on my own.

I kept looking to the left and the right of the highway to see if I could discover anything unusual or exciting. *Billboards!* Someone got a really good deal on land for signage as the number of billboards seemed to increase and then disappear like the ebb and flow of the ocean as you neared a crossroad. Shortly after seeing a sign for Exit 303 advertising a place called The Rock Factory that sold petrified wood I saw to my right a *T–Rex* running around near a bunch of painted Indian Tee Pee's. Actually it was a posed statue but at a quick glance it looked like it was in mid stride. It turned out this was the Painted Desert Indian Center and there were at least a dozen Tee Pees and a few other T–Rex statues in front of the building vying for the attention of tourists coming down the road. It was a weird mix of the Wild West meets Jurassic Park. For me to go there I would have to exit and swing back about a quarter mile in the opposite direction on a partly dirt road. It wasn't going to happen for me or any of the other cyclists. Not today.

At the same exit just past the ramp to the left of the highway was a most unusual site. High on top of a fifty foot rock ridge was a yellow school bus and a sign for a place called Stewart's. A hundred yards farther was another T–Rex standing next to an old four door Chevy Chevette. I wondered where they got that dinosaur of a car. The big reptiles were a popular item out here in nowhere land. Then I saw a huge sign reading "METEORITES/GOLD NUGGETS" in front of a white and blue building brandishing the name Stewart's on the front along with lots of other words describing the things they have. This must be the Rock Factory I saw promoted on the big billboard farther back on the highway. On top of the building was big Pterodactyl looming over the front parking lot with two more Chevettes and another one of these vehicular tin cans just around the left side of the building. Years ago I owned one of these clunkers; a 1981 two–tone maroon and beige two door model. If they had a postcard of those old cars it would have been worth stopping.

With no room for souvenirs I pedaled on past this roadside diversion and continued scanning the terrain for other interesting items. There was a fenced in area with more odd animal statues, a sign for feeding ostriches, an abandoned building, and what looks to be a cowboy on a mutant horse farther up the ridgeline.

Ten minutes farther down I–40, just off the left side of the road, I noticed a twenty foot long home–built lizard on a dirt ridge. It has spikes on its back and looks like it is howling at the passing cars. The only other thing around is a pair of square boulders that might be old petrified trees, but I really can't be sure. There were no signs and no exit to go check it out. I did see a few trees to the left and some very low almost unnoticeable mountain ranges in the distance.

At mile marker 307 there was a sign informing me that should I have access to an AM radio I could tune into 1610 and get the latest news on the Petrified Forest. How much could it have possibly changed in the last five or ten thousand years? On the left I spotted a wood–framed house but it was too far away for me to see if it was lived in.

A bit farther down the highway, a road came up on the right and ran parallel to I–40 until it made a hard ninety–degree right turn and went off into the distance. It was at this bend in the road where I saw a shanty shack combined with an old mobile home. The building was worn and rusted and looked like it was a junk heap but the grounds around it suggested someone actually calls the place home. They even have a guest suite, a tow behind trailer oddly positioned on a berm behind the shack. *Reservations for none please!*

Just past mile marker 308—you can tell I'm bored when updates come every mile—there were another slew of billboards advertising places in and closer to Gallop. In the order I passed them they were Richardson's Trading Company at Exit 16, the El Rancho Motel at Exit 22, Comfort Suites at Exit 26, USA RV Park at Exit 16, and the Navajo Trading Center at Exit 325. I was starting to notice my landmarks were reduced to mile markers. Those little green signs are easy to miss but they seem to be the most prominent thing aside from billboards, the continuous overcast sky, and the almost unchanging terrain.

We crossed washes and basins like yesterday where the road was lined with metal guardrails. One was named Wildhorse Wash but there were no horses or anything else in it. The shoulders were narrower and often more ragged than on the other side of Holbrook but they still were not terrible. They were smooth enough to not rattle my teeth zipping happily toward anyplace with people.

We passed the Petrified Forest at Exit 311. I didn't realize a permit is needed to camp overnight in the Petrified Forest but it's designated as a wilderness area by the government. I should be happy a permit is all they required to pitch a tent, roll out a sleeping bag, or just doze off in the dirt. In the park there is a hotel called the Painted Desert Inn and several places designated for camping, picnicking, and hiking. Along the highway there wasn't much other than rocks and sparse clumps of grass, and maybe a bit of sagebrush. I saw a single broken tree on the ground. We crossed another dry wash and then the Dead River at marker 316 which actually had some muddy water in it.

At Exit 320 was the first of two SAGs for the day. I pedaled up the ramp and was greeted at the top by Tracy and Margaret. I stopped on the edge of a dirt road which seamlessly transitioned into the wide open expanse of more dirt with little covering it. Great views in all directions but there wasn't much in the way of shade or protection from the wind if conditions deteriorated.

I signed in, loaded up on snacks, and today I ate a whole banana. Then I chased it all down with Gatorade, refilled my bottles, checked my tires, and found a bit of privacy to relieve myself before getting back on the bike. I am so glad not to be a woman out here in the open dealing with nature calls but the ladies seemed to cope just fine.

Still riding a tailwind sailing down the ramp onto the highway, then immediately having a downhill section of road was a double bonus. Speeding right along until I reached the Navajo Exit 325 where on the cue sheet it indicated there was a store. A few small trees clustered around the Navajo Trading Post and alongside was a road with a cattle guard, a device we would learn more about later in the trip. The most important thing to remember is to cross them carefully when on the bike. I stopped with Betty and a couple of other riders taking the opportunity to use a proper rest room and to wash my hands. You really begin to appreciate sanitary conditions when you don't have them available.

The tint of the water running down the drain made it clear to me the dust I was collecting on the ride was indeed layering up; on my legs, hands, arms, on my face, and even in my ears. I could feel the grit when I pursed my lips. I could taste it in my mouth, and I could smell it each time I took a breath. It would definitely be a day for a deep cleaning. My bike and my gear were not spared either so laundry and a thorough bike wash would be part of my post ride activities.

As I continued riding I could see the distant mountains coming into view. To the southeast the terrain was lower than the roadway. A quarter mile off to the right, the tracks of the Burlington Northern Santa Fe Railroad connecting Holbrook to Gallop ran parallel to the highway. We would be riding right along the tracks almost all the way to our destination. I began to pay better attention to the trains as they rumbled by. They crossed the flats in both directions at least every ten minutes. All were long freight trains made up of as many as a hundred box, tanker, flatbed, open hopper, and specialty container carrying cars pulled by at least two to four diesel locomotives. When I stopped to take a few photos I counted one train consisting of two diesel engines pulling 102 full coal hopper cars and then a second train had six diesels engines pulling and two pushing a total of 120 full coal hopper cars. The second train must have been nearly a mile and a half long.

Trains are interesting to listen to as they move in the distance. They produce subtle sounds of metal–on–metal grinding and scraping, whining and clanking of the couplers pushing and pulling one another and the flexing of their frames all forming a chorus riding on the low frequency droning of the massive weight of its load as it compresses the roadbed beneath the rails. The occasional burst of an air horn and the clacking sound of the wheels on the rails let you know without a doubt it is a train. Even above the wind noise and the vehicle traffic the sound of the train comes through. It is as distinct as the sound of the ocean or a waterfall.

At Exit 333 several riders decided to stop for lunch but as usual I had my fill of proper snacks at the SAG and didn't like to be delayed nor weighed down with a more heavy meal. I declined and kept riding. As I rode by on the highway I noticed the restaurant sign for the Chieftain Inn mounted fifty feet up on a big monopole. It sported the head of an Indian chief in full headdress resembling the Indian Motorcycle logo. Easily seen by west bound traffic but as I was heading east the view was blocked by the overpass crossover so I couldn't see the sign until I was past the exit and it is too late to do anything about it. For me it was just an observation as I had committed to keep going.

The scenery which was relatively unchanged for fifty miles was suddenly different; small trees and mini–mountains dotted the north side of the highway and just beyond the railroad tracks now less than two hundred yards to the right of the highway were several small flat top ridges. Smaller trees and scrub brush increased along both sides of the four lane highway and by the time I crossed over Querino Road the highway was traversing wide rocky washes, open expanses of gorges, and cutting through large rock ridges and hills. The road was no longer flat and cycling became a transition from riding easily with a tailwind to intervals of climbing and descending. The rail line detoured away from us and trains could neither be seen nor heard. I was all by myself pedaling and wondering what I would see next.

Fortunately I still had the wind at my back and the shoulder of the road was improving. The highway carved its way through several low ridgelines leaving vertical jagged walls soaring up forty to fifty feet on either side of the eastbound lanes. I could only see the westbound traffic through sections where the road broke out of the rocky hills. Had this been a hot day riders would have cooked in these mini–canyons.

For five miles the roadway rolled up and over the rocky terrain but as I continued it became less aggressive, the stone edges a bit softened with more scrub growth covering the rocks. The westbound lanes were now mostly in view. I saw signs for Fort Courage, a site made famous by the TV show *F–Troop* which aired on Television from 1965 to 1967 so I decided to have a look. I figured I was climbing up this section of highway anyway so what would it matter to take a steeper route up the exit ramp. I had fond memories of watching Larry Storch, the bumbling Corporal Randolph Agarn with the sideways, misshapen Stetson hat and yellow bandana on the show but this side excursion was both a bust and a disappointment. If you have any intentions of visiting Fort Courage while in Arizona, I'd recommend you drive right by. The view of the fort looks the same from the highway anyway. They do have a trading post there so it you need a drink or something else it would be worth stopping. The next nearest conveniences are three miles east and seven miles west.

I crossed back over the highway and then climbed the on–ramp until I was back on the shoulder for the three mile hop to Indian City and SAG number two. Looking down the road I was imaging where I would be if I didn't stop at Fort Courage. With the exception of a slight bend to the left midway to Exit 351 for Allentown, I held the bars straight and climbed most of the distance. There were eight billboards along the last mile of highway to the exit advertising Indian blankets for $4.99 and up, snacks and sandwiches, souvenirs, t–shirts and ice cream, Navajo Pottery, Indian Jewelry forty to fifty percent off, Clean Restrooms, Tacos, and again Clean Restrooms. I am guessing it's the clean restrooms which they are focusing on to differentiate their establishment from the other trading posts. I think it's an excellent marketing move. That is as long as they are really clean. I had to use the men's room so I will do my own evaluation and report back.

In this stretch of road I had to dodge half sections of truck tires and I was reminded that getting a flat tire was a real possibility today. At the Indian City Trading Post I rolled through the rough gravel parking lot and found a section of wooden fence to lean my bike. So I wouldn't forget I went right to my tires to begin the detailed inspection for wires and glass. Only a single small wire which appeared to have just started the process of working its way into the front tire was found and quickly removed. Then it was into the *Post* to check on the restrooms. For this part of the country they scored an *A+* in restroom readiness and overall cleanliness. There really is truth in advertising.

I decided to browse the gift shop for postcards and found plenty to choose from. The prices were favorable so I picked up several cards for just a dollar. After being in the wind and hearing little but road noises I found myself lulled into a happy place by the sounds coming from an Indian flute. Much like the music that tamed the Tasmanian Devil in the *Bugs Bunny* cartoons I was pretty sure I wasn't going to do anything crazy as long as the flute music continued. They were selling hand–carved six–hole flutes with tiny little carved animals perched on top. I passed. I might buy a CD of the Navajo flute music when I get home to avoid having to lug it around. And I can't play it on the tour anyway. I restocked and re–lubricated with Gatorade and as I mounted up my bike it occurred to me I forgot to check out the Indian blankets to see what you could actually get for $4.99. Maybe just a handkerchief, but what do I know. I wasn't going back inside. Besides, the blankets I was close to in the trading post smelled a bit like musty burlap.

From Indian City I rode into New Mexico with Kathy Stevens so we could take pictures of each other at the state line. At mile marker 357 while enjoying a very nice long descent I noticed the railroad tracks had now found their way back to I–40. Train watching had resumed and I was now close enough to see the details of the engines and hear their low powerful rumble along the tracks once more.

As we approached the New Mexico border, some very interesting rock formations presented themselves and a photo stop needed to happen. One of the massive rock structures resembles a long running Mesa that is tabletop flat with vertical walls dropping down about a hundred feet or more before tapering out to a wider base. And the other was more dome shaped, closer to a semi–circle than anything else. Both formations are similar in color to dry unfired red pottery and have various crevasses, holes, and naturally carved–out cavernous sections disbursed across their entire vertical surface.

Two great examples of these rocky protrusions were seen on the north side of I–40, the dome shaped formation about a half mile before Exit 359 for Grants Road and the Mesa immediately after the exit. On the Mesa stood a variety of goats and other animal statues mixed in with various Knick knacks mounted on the side of the rock ledges to attract attention for the shops below. Tacky, wacky, but I enjoyed looking at the crazy things people do to draw attention.

Then we were back on our bikes for a quick half–mile scoot to the border crossing photo area. The sign was sufficiently far enough off the road providing plenty of room and safety away from traffic. I posed like I was a bullfighter holding an imaginary red blanket to the bull under the New Mexico sign. I should have checked out the blankets at Indian City when I had the chance. So after a dorky pose the small containers of Pacific beach sand were retrieved from our saddle bags and just a pinch of the magic granules were sprinkled as prescribed around the legs of the state sign.

New Mexico wants to make sure you remember coming into their state as the sign is both big and a very bright yellow. The whole Native American thing is really working for me; the music, the bold logo on the sign, and even their state motto, *The Land of Enchantment* is kind of cool. I did see Arizona's sign facing the other way but I already had a picture of the one entering the state from California so I wasn't looking go back for another. Besides it was smaller than the New Mexico sign and not as impressive.

New Mexico has since updated the signage replacing the Native American logo with two chili peppers. I wonder if they had complaints about the sign not being politically correct. If they had a vote I would want to bring back the old design, but I'm just a rider passing through and I don't get to vote in the state.

After crossing the border, the final sixteen miles of this ride were between two towering rock walls measuring two to three hundred feet high at times and spread about a mile apart. I believe they were the Torrivio Mesa's North and South which both top out at an elevation of just less than 7,050 feet. This canyon helped increase our tailwind and ensure our speedy arrival in Gallop. With the exception of some rather tense and congested sections of roadway undergoing repairs near a bridge crossing one of the many dry riverbeds we were pretty safe riding on the I–40 shoulder.

A few riders came through closer to the late afternoon rush hour and had to vie for their space in the only open lane crossing the hundred–yard–long bridge. Factor in the construction trucks, the men, and all of the materials they were moving around in the closed lane, and at times poking into the other lane, and you could understand why they said it was a very heads up section of riding. No casualties were reported and no damage other than a rash of flat tires put a dent into an otherwise perfect day on the bike.

For two days in a row now I had a great tailwind experience through reasonably gentle terrain; and another low impact day for my shoulder making it much more enjoyable. It was probably as close as I would get to resting while on my bike. I don't think my shoulder bothered me except for a few short climbs where I got out of the saddle and tossed the bike from side to side to muscle my way up a climb. Hardly necessary but sometimes it feels good just to do it. I averaged a respectable 15.6 miles per hour which meant I was only on the seat for five hours forty–seven minutes over the 90.47 miles covered. Tomorrow we continue in the same direction, but the weather conditions are beginning to concern all of us. How long can we ride this tailwind? Should the wind come at us from the east, it will cut our speeds in half, making it a very long day; even if it's only sixty–eight miles to Grants.

I think it is safe to say most riders hope and pray it goes–and blows—in our favor. Maybe a little Navajo flute music and chanting will help. I should put a little war paint on the Three Stooges for tomorrow's ride to taunt the wind. Maybe I'm just asking for trouble.

After cleaning the bike and checking the tires I showered off the accumulated layer of grit before settling into the writing of postcards and making my journals entries. Then I did a little research on Gallop and learned the following tidbits of information. There are ninety–six restaurants in Gallop and we are eating at the Ranch Kitchen. Gallop has two thousand hotel rooms and we are occupying about two and a half percent of them. In addition there are twenty thousand people, forty churches for thirty–one denominations, twenty–three public parks, four museums, and just for kids they have a place called the *Playground of Dreams*. I grew up with jungle gyms, monkey bars and concrete pipes in the sand. I'm not sure what they have but to me, I had the playground of dreams.

On a more serious note Gallop is the undisputed fountainhead for original, authentic Indian arts and crafts. The Navajo are widely regarded for their remarkable achievements in wool, with Navajo rugs and blankets sought by collectors and museums throughout the world. The Zuni noted for their exceptionally fine jewelry, the Hopi, noted for their distinctive pottery, and the Acoma and Laguna people, each with their own unique pottery traditions. According to the Visitors Bureau the best way to enjoy Gallop is on foot in the twelve–block downtown area bordered by Route 66/Main Street (north), Hill Avenue (south), Fourth Street (west), and First Street (east). Most of the trading posts and galleries are located within this area.

No laundry for me today, just a quick hand wash of my biking clothes, so I was clear until route rap which came quickly. It also ended quickly as Tracy only had two quadrants on tomorrows cue sheet to describe. In the bottom of quadrant two was my highlight of the route; another Dairy Queen at mile 62.4. She did remind us to move our clocks forward since we crossed into the Mountain Time Zone when we rode into New

Mexico. Had Arizona observed Daylight Savings Time like most states the time change would have happened one state line sooner. The time change is yet another sign of progress on our trek to Boston. Just two time zones to go; we are oh so close.

Following route rap it was an unmemorable dinner at the Ranch Kitchen and their specialty is southwestern cooking, imagine that. Don't ask me what I ate; I've already forgotten. Lucky us we will be there again for breakfast. I may just check out the breakfast offering in the hotel lobby if they have one.

At the end of the day just as we turn in for the night Clark reads from his journal the day's ride he experienced a year earlier. The conditions are much different, more challenging with higher temperatures and less favorable winds. He describes his difficulties which surprise me because he is such a strong rider and in the end he reaches his destination by following his own advice to just pedal. It reminds me of the closing moments of the TV show *"The Waltons"* – Goodnight John–boy!

Day 12: Gallop to Grants (69 miles)

There was nothing to eat at the hotel so breakfast was at the Ranch Kitchen. It may have been Déjà vu but it was a quick event and soon I was back at the hotel getting my arm and legwarmers out in preparation for the ride. Smart riders were raiding their rooms of the disposable shower caps to keep their heads warm. They work great but heat up quick. I remember Lynn was quite happy to have a warm head as she was pumping up her tires.

When it gets cold I feel it in my chest and hands. Even when I am wearing multiple layers like I am today; a liner shirt, a cycling jersey, and my sun jacket nothing stops the cold air from blowing through to my chest. Since I am wearing most of what I brought with me including my arm and leg warmers I have only two realistic options; wear a plastic trash bag or put a piece of cardboard in between my shirts to break the wind. I didn't find a trash bag and I wanted something easy to remove as it warmed up so I opted for the cardboard. A simple piece of cardboard the size of a standard writing pad is plenty to block the wind from your chest and keep your core temperature up. I probably should have taped it to my shirt but even with it moving around a bit I was satisfied with how well it worked.

My cycling gloves are the fingerless type, so a few days earlier back in Flagstaff I made a point to pick up a pair of cheap cloth work gloves at the local Walmart. I think they were something like $1.88 so I bought two pair. They fit right over my cycling gloves and still allow me enough feel for the bars to ride. Just getting my skin out of the direct wind was a big improvement.

I made a few other adjustments to my outfit before I was ready to ride. First I pulled the sides of my head sweat over the tips of my ears. I would have preferred one of those nifty headbands, but I didn't think about that when I bought the gloves. Next I put the disposable shower cap from the hotel on and tied a bandana around my neck. All zippers in the jersey and jacket were snugged up to my neck; I put on a little chap stick, and was as ready as I could be. The only thing I could have possibly added was a pullover ski mask, yet another item not at my disposal.

We left Gallop at quarter past seven under overcast skies with a twenty mile per hour tailwind and temperatures in the low forties. It felt colder and I thought I could see some frost in the shadows on the ground. My breath was fogging in the air and my nose was running. The wind on my cheeks was raw and taking a deep breath burned. Well maybe not quite that bad. I wasn't breathing hard yet.

Starting from an elevation of 6,515 feet we would be climbing throughout the day. Out of the hotel pointed east on Route 66 we passed the Gallop Municipal Airport on the right and the Burlington Northern Santa Fe rail yard on the left. We then skirted the old downtown district, the Gallup Cultural Center and the Southwest Indian Center before coming to one of the more unique landmarks in Gallop, the El Rancho Hotel.

While it doesn't look like that big of a deal the fancy sign says it is the home of the movie stars. At least it used to be. The *El Rancho* was linked to Hollywood and the movie industry until the mid–'60s. Ronald Reagan, John Wayne, Katherine Hepburn, Spencer Tracy, Errol Flynn, Kirk Douglas, Gregory Peck, Rita Hayworth, and Humphrey Bogart are only a few of the film stars who stayed at the hotel while making movies in the vicinity. We took in the view of the hotel while we waited for the light at Ford Drive to turn green and then off we went making our way out of town toward Red Rocks State Park.

The cool morning actually went well with our climb along Route 66 past rock walls exposed after the roads were cut into the hillside in an attempt to level the pavement. Maybe thirty to forty feet high at some points affording a view of the various layers of sediment accumulated over the millions of years to form the rocks. Tan, red and gray sediment in varying textures made for interesting roadside scenery to our right. And we were supposed to be looking at the red rocks on the other side of the road.

My legs warmed up after an hour of pedaling. The route crossed another cattle guard and it had a big crack in it as indicated on the cue. These crossings are designed to allow traffic to drive over but prevent cattle from crossing the road. They are made up of rails or pipes laid perpendicular to the road with a few inches of space between them. Should cattle attempt to walk over them their hoofs will slip in between the rails catching their leg and then the animal will quickly stop and pull back. At least that's how they are supposed to work. The most common is the rail which looks like a small gage train track. This is what we were dealing with at the crossing.

The crack mentioned on the cue sheet meant the rail was not continuous from shoulder to shoulder and for narrow bike tires like ours it creates a slot where the wheel can drop down and get caught. So you avoid the cracks to avoid serious injury. This crossing had several cracks and deserved our full concentration. Had it been wet it would have been even more dangerous.

Route 66 crosses over and joins I–40 East ending our ride on a rather lightly used roadway. I took a moment to stop on the overpass to take in the views of I–40 and to make a few adjustments. Off came the shower cap and the warmers. My ears were out of the head sock and the cloth gloves were put in my bike bag. It was officially nice biking weather as the sun was moving higher into the cerulean blue sky. A long pull of Gatorade and another of water out of my second bottle and I was ready to go again.

We were going to play in traffic with the tractor trailers running eastbound freight above the seventy–five mile per hour speed limit on a shoulder that was narrow, rough, and full of road trash. Not all of the trucks, or cars for that matter, respected the painted stripe. I was hugging the edge of the asphalt as close to the twelve to fourteen inch drop off as I dare leaving me about three feet off the line. While I didn't get nicked by the traffic I was awfully close to a few.

The need to stay focused on the road edge was intense while keeping a keen ear tuned to any vehicles crossing into the rumble zone. When I would hear the tires vibrate on the rumble grooves I would know they were within a foot of my left shoulder. I was also busy glancing in my eyeglass mounted mirror to get a visual whenever I thought I could pry my eyes from the road in front of me. A few times the rumble warning went off and I tensed up until it passed; definitely white–knuckle moments for this shoulder cyclist.

A few riders made some pretty bold and rather stupid decisions by choosing to ride in the traffic lane to avoid the rough shoulder and the radial tire debris. They failed to grasp the concept that if the traffic was coming behind them two abreast they dramatically increased the risk of an accident. There were lots of honking horns and pissed–off drivers but fortunately no accidents and no injuries. Luck was riding with them and they had no clue how close a few trucks came to hitting them. I watched from the shoulder as one close call after another played out in front of me. Fortunately the truckers were able to safely brake and move over just enough to avoid the riders and allow them to continue on their eastward trek. They probably thought the truckers were honking in a friendly gesture. There was a gesture all right; just not so much a friendly one.

We had a tailwind helping us up but the stress of riding in the shoulder along the highway didn't leave much time to think about the climb itself. It really wasn't that bad. It was just a long highway climb. Had it been hot, had we not had the tailwind, or had it been raining, this would not have been such a good stretch of road to be riding on a bike.

We climbed along I–40 for eleven miles until we exited the highway back onto Route 66 for our only SAG of the day at the Indian Village store. We had reached the famous Continental Divide and according to the wooden sign along Route 66 we were now at 7,245 feet above sea level. On the west side of the Continental Divide, all waters flow toward the Pacific Ocean and, on its east side, they flow to either the Atlantic Ocean or the Gulf of Mexico. We may not be halfway across the United States, but according to the water flows, it's all downhill from here.

It seemed like a substantial accomplishment for our group of riders. The climb to this point was well worth the effort, as the scenery and the views were some of the best on our tour. The rock textures were impressive and their scale immense. The colors of the greenery were equally amazing; deep, dark, and thick.

At the SAG Clark did his best *Groucho Marx* impression, complete with the trademark glasses, fake nose, and bushy mustache. His sense of humor and entertainment skills was enjoyed by all. This was the midpoint of our ride for the day. The rest of the route was described to us as being gentle and rolling terrain. We still had a favorable wind so we scored another great day in the saddle.

The typical SAG routine was replayed; riders checking time and signing in, snacks of all types spread out on a small folding table complete with a red and white plastic table cloth, water and Gatorade coolers in the back of the Crossroads van servicing the riders, and a rotation of riders going in and out of the little store to use the restroom. Add to this the photo opportunity of the Continental Divide sign in front of the Indian Village store all decked out with way too many gaudy signs of its own. It was visually stimulating for sure. Riders checked tires for foreign debris and then mounted up and headed back to the road.

At the SAG there was a really upbeat vibe going on amongst the riders. And why not, we had a string of perfect days riding with tailwinds and good weather. How could it get any better than this? As a thank you courtesy for using the restroom I bought a few postcards from the store. They had a few Indian themed ones which I really enjoyed but my favorite was of a cactus flowering in the moonlight.

We topped off our fluids and checked our tires then turned east back on Route 66. I was really beginning to like this road and it now afforded us a long gradual descent out and away from the Interstate. The Burlington Northern Santa Fe rail lines were now on our left and trains were again in plain sight. Train lovers will find the stretch between Gallop and Grants to be of much interest. Approximately every ten minutes the Burlington Northern Santa Fe locomotives would pull a line of tankers and boxcars along the tracks, with the mesas and green fields as a backdrop.

Most trains had several locomotives pulling a hundred or more cars. I was impressed at just how busy two sets of tracks could be. To show that nothing is perfect, the rail lines left a pile of mangled box cars—each empty weighing in at sixty–three thousand pounds—that had derailed near the road for the curious to photograph. Others would speculate on just how they met their fate. For a few miles we rolled over winding roads littered with old buildings; some abandoned and others in various states of disrepair.

From this point, we had twenty miles to Grants, but sudden strong head winds, and a pair of Dairy Queen Restaurants, would slow our progress. Even though they were separated by just about eight miles, I used both DQ opportunities to get out of the wind with hopes it would settle down before getting back on the bike. I struck out on both stops but not before enjoying some fine soft serve. Leaving DQ number two it was flat and slow for the five mile crawl to the hotel. With the exception of a climb or two to clear an overpass it was mostly uneventful. Traffic which was rather thin coming into Grants was getting heavier. As a few people said jokingly in the morning we would "Gallop to Grants" and we did.

After pulling into the Best Western Inn on Santa Fe Avenue I gave my bike a quick visual check and then a proper cleaning. The hotel management was a bit picky about having bikes inside on the carpets and they required us to carry them to our room because they thought we would leave tracks. I think they failed to notice the rugs in the common area were not in the best of shape and after cleaning the bike it didn't leave behind any tracks. But it is their hotel and they did let us keep our bikes in our rooms. The hotel also was quite unique; it had a huge multistory courtyard contained within the big square of rooms running around the perimeter. I so wanted to ride my bike in the courtyard past the indoor pool and into my room in the back of the hotel. I'm not sure if it was the wide open courtyard or the front desk directing us to carry the bikes. Maybe it was both.

After sorting out everything at the hotel several of us descended on Walmart for supplies and photo processing. I'm beginning to think this bike trip is becoming the "Walmarts across America tour." I also noticed it's not just the Walmart that is the same in each town, it's also the shoppers. The rather large lady with the way–to–tight spandex pants and the man with the beer gut peeking out from under his Dale Sr. t–shirt were a bit too familiar. I've seen them both and their rag–tag family members in Walmarts going back to California. I wonder if they are on some kind of parallel tour I don't know about.

After doing a little research, I found Grants is home to the New Mexico Museum of Mining. The museum is situated over a former uranium mine and features Indian artifacts, geological exhibits and a simulated uranium mine. Former miners, turned tour guides, provide demonstrations of how the mine was run. The word uranium stuck in my mind. It was enough to keep me away and find alternative entertainment.

By mid–afternoon, the temperature had reached a warm seventy–six degrees. The only business remaining for the day was two days' worth of laundry. Easy said; easy done. Route rap was in the lobby followed by a really nice dinner spread put on by the hotel. It was a massive meal featuring my favorite, spaghetti and other dishes with plenty of sides and bread. The feast was quickly followed by dessert. I felt a few pounds heavier but quite content. Breakfast will be in the same place and my guess is it will be another fine meal.

It quieted down quickly after dinner and I had a few quick words with Trevor before retiring to my room for some postcard and journaling duties. I happily recorded my day on the bike covering 69.01 miles in four hours fifty–five minutes averaging fourteen miles an hour. Clark came in much later after finishing his end–of–day chores. He shared his journal entry from last year's ride and then it was lights out bringing the day to a close. Rise, ride, relax was becoming the core routine on this tour. All I had to do was ride and do my laundry. Like it was when I was twelve; except for the laundry part.

Day 13: Grants to Albuquerque (79 miles)

Sunrise in Grants revealed heavy cloud cover and temperatures in the low forties. There were isolated showers predicted for the Albuquerque area, and we thought our string of perfect weather days may be at risk. It was also another day to bundle up to keep warm; and hopefully dry. With the cloth gloves over my hands all of my fingers were content.

I've ridden in the cold back in north central Florida while training without gloves. Winters in Florida are damp making the cold even more intense. Once your fingers get cold they stiffen up to the curve of the bars and then they start to hurt. I have to peel the fingers open which is no treat at all. Then I need to warm them up. I'm not sure if everyone is affected the same way or if a case of frostbite during my last winter living in New Jersey back in 1981 is the cause. I really don't care why I just know I do not like riding with cold hands.

If I didn't have full fingered gloves I would have to get creative to keep my fingers warm. The most effective way is to get them out of the brisk moving air; to make fists and hide them behind the bars. Instead of wrapping them around the bars I lay then on top, maybe a bit behind, and hook my thumbs under the handle bars to hold on. It's more like leaning on the bars but it helps. I will try a variety of hand positions and move them frequently to reduce the stiffness and the burn from the cold air. My next hand position is leaning my fists against the brake hoods but it's not as safe. I don't have as much control and my grip is, well, there is no grip. What I can't do is put my hands in my pockets. Not even one at a time. I have decent balance and can ride without my hands on the bars but if I put even one hand in a pocket I would not be able to get it out in time to protect myself in a fall. But today I have warm gloves so I don't have to do much handlebar jockeying nor do I have to spend much energy thinking about cold hands.

We backtracked up Route 117 a half mile crossing over the Burlington Northern Santa Fe tracks and at the bottom of the overpass we turned right onto a secondary road toward the southeast. In just a few hundred yards we were out of town and in the weeds. Five miles farther out we crossed back over the rail line on our approach to I–40. We picked up the frontage road SR–124/Route 66 just before the interstate and made our way through wide valleys containing fields of volcanic formations—large black, brown, and red rocks pocked with gas–formed holes called the Zuni–Bandera volcanic field that was part of the Bandera Crater lava flows ten thousand years ago. Purple flowers lined the roadway and horses grazed in the fields of sparse grass.

More cattle guards and rough roads were on the menu and they would be jarring and punishing my wrists until better roads were found. At one point we made a sharp turn through a short tunnel under I–40 that was dark, narrow, and full of ruts and pot holes. It was difficult to find a clean line through. Then we ran parallel to I–40, happy we were not on it because of the traffic, but not really liking the rough roads we were on either.

At several points the route would cross back over I–40 and then diverge out into nature. The roads were hilly and the landscape filled with little shacks and fenced pastures with animals providing lots of visual enjoyment. Between the road and a high ridge several horses grazed quietly in the field just west of Paraje, a little village claiming 669 residents. We crossed over State Road 22 and Paraje was just a memory of a few scattered houses and wire fences. We were hugging the low mountains to our left while the valley extended outward to our right. It was mostly exposed rocks and red and brown soil close to a gravel consistency. Vegetation was sparse, but where it existed I saw green clumps of desert brush. We were still just shy of six thousand feet above sea level as we bounded around up the hills and down some exciting descents. Rogue dogs chased a few riders on a flat section of road but none were successful in doing anything other than make a rider pedal faster.

Coming into Laguna the road expanded into a divided four lane. Fewer than four hundred people lived in the village but it was considered large enough for its own post office. This area is home to the Laguna Pueblo, a Native American tribe of the Pueblo people in west–central New Mexico. As remote and rural as the area is the Laguna people value intellectual activity and education, and because of a scholarship program there are many well educated Lagunas. Uranium mining on Pueblo of Laguna land has contributed to this scholarship program as well as to skilled labor learning among Laguna members. Lagunas and other Pueblos enjoy baseball and like many Pueblos, the Laguna people are skilled in pottery.

With thirty miles behind us we turned into the SAG for a well–deserved break. It would be another twenty–five miles before we would stop again so the line for the restrooms was pretty long. I took the opportunity to liberally apply lubricant to my sit bones and for a few minutes I was again walking around a bit awkwardly until I got used to the fresh application. Every time you reapply it is the same experience. Somebody should design a pair of shorts capable of automatically dispenses the right amount of lube when needed. Your hands wouldn't get greasy and your snacks wouldn't taste funny.

Exiting the SAG we would be getting back on I–40 and I was having mixed feelings about rejoining the highway. I can only hope the shoulders are friendlier to cyclists than what we experienced yesterday.

The hills turned more chiseled, and large cube–shaped boulders of red became more pronounced. As we entered the Interstate we were running east on a long descent with unpredictable and strong winds blowing across the roadway. The road turned south for a stretch to clear a rocky pass and then it returned to a due–east trajectory as we broke out into wide open terrain. The wind danced around, sometimes with us and at times against us, but with the rolling terrain and the scenery we had plenty to think about besides dwelling on the wind. And fortunately we were afforded a decent shoulder on which to play.

Since I started training back in Florida I have been wearing a heart rate monitor. This allows me to know how well my body is dealing with the environment and how much I am working it. I seem to be getting better at interpreting how I feel without having to look at the heart rate monitor but I have gotten so used to it I am almost out of uniform if I get on the bike without it. It's most useful under hot conditions and when climbing and we will be doing plenty of that out here in the west.

The heart rate monitor has two parts, an adjustable band consisting of an inch wide plastic strap with small internal sensors and the receiver which looks like a digital wrist watch. The band and strap assembly fits around the trunk of your body just below the pectoral muscles with the plastic curved portion containing the sensors in contact with your chest. The receiver can either be worn on the wrist or, as I prefer, mounted on the handlebar right next to the stem using a nifty little companion bracket. This steals a bit of my handle bar grip position and also interferes with aero bars. Fortunately for me my bike does not have the aero bars so it's not much of an inconvenience for me to utilize the bar mount option.

When I am riding I can see my heart rate, calories burned and a little beating heart icon letting me know I'm still alive. At the end of the ride I can press a button and review my total calories burned, average, minimum, and maximum heart rate, total time of the ride, and the time I was within my target heart rate range. All this helps me to train and condition myself safely and efficiently.

All I did for twenty miles was pedal. I was watching the twin bike computer displays mounted in front of my handle bars to track my riding stats. On the left I had my cadence, which let me know how fast I was pedaling and the distance traveled. The one on the right tracked my speed and the elapsed time of the ride. If that wasn't enough I could push a button and see my max speed and average speed but those really only mattered when I was writing them down in my journal at the end of a ride.

My objective was to pedal at a cadence of seventy–eight to eighty–four rpms. That seemed to work best for my heart rate and overall long distance endurance. I also liked to ride in the smallest rear gear as possible while maintaining the cadence. This was usually in the range of fourteen to eighteen miles per hour and all of these numbers had to be balanced with my heart rate staying in the mid–140s range. If I exceeded that for more than an hour I would begin cramping from lactic acid build up in my legs. And my day on the bike would come to an abrupt end. The longer I ride the better my stamina and riding strength. The heart rate monitor also tracked calories burned which gave me an indication of how much I would need to eat to replace my energy stores for the next day. I had beautiful scenery around me and all sorts of technical information on my displays to occupy me as I road down the long straight sections of highway.

At one point on the trip one of the doctors said he was sorry I was wearing a heart rate monitor. He thought I had heart trouble. I thanked him for caring, smiled, and went on about my business. I laughed a bit and figured it was just like me not knowing about Chamois Cream. There is so much to learn about long distance cycling but I'm at least getting on the job training.

A few miles shy of the second SAG I began a pretty taxing climb. My heart rate ramped up and the downshifting continued until I found my rhythm and settled in at the lowly pace of seven miles an hour. What are you gonna do? Just pedal. And I did pedal even after I reached the crest and sped down the other side of the mountain. I pushed the pedals hard for the better part of a mile cruising at thirty miles an hour. It felt good to have the wind in my face knowing I was getting another break and this time the SAG was at a Dairy Queen at a major travel plaza.

It was almost like the oasis in the middle of nowhere; lush green turf, plenty of landscaping, and some shade trees. I found a place under a tree with several other riders for some much needed banter while consuming more of Margaret's treats. Fig Newton's, some fruit, a few gulps of Gatorade, and I can't remember what else as it was a bit of a feeding frenzy. I took half a banana and a honey oats granola bar for my pocket and topped off my fluids. The plaza was both big and busy. The restrooms earned a big thumbs–up for cleanliness and capacity and I found a few postcards for scribbling notes about my ride to friends and family.

When exiting the SAG I rejoined the I–40 and began climbing a five mile stretch before settling into the fifteen–mile trek on a high plateau that would deposit me to the outskirts of Albuquerque. While climbing along the shoulder I was moving slow enough to finally notice how lush by desert standards the valley was. It was boasting an abundance of green thin blades of field grass and a rich bouquet of yellow flowers in full bloom. The smell of pollen filled the air while traffic did it's best to tickle my senses with diesel fumes and the smell of burning rubber.

The trucks were struggling up the steep incline and somehow I felt a bit of comfort knowing I was not the only one on the road grinding my way at a pace I didn't enjoy. Every so often one of the truck drivers would wait too long to downshift and the truck would scream out in mechanical pain giving me reason to crack a smile. Exactly why I don't know, but I smiled anyway.

I did stop to take a few photos and the farther I climbed the more intense and impressive the colors of the wildflowers behind me appeared. I learned this was an unusually lush year because of early spring rains. The norm would have been brown fields with no flowers at all. Just another example of how something as simple as a bit of rain can completely change the riding experience from one year to the next. Mixed in the flowering fields were several rocky mounds which appeared to be void of any vegetation. I guess that is what the rest of the area normally looks like. Good thing I capture the images in film because these subtle details could easily be forgotten.

The skies began to clear as the sun warmed the countryside to a pleasant seventy–five degrees. As we approached the city, I realized it was quite large; a total of seventeen exits off of Interstate 40 led to the city. Albuquerque sits down in the valley, and all of its beauty is evident as you descend the last two miles into its core.

High crosswinds made a fast–glide into the city unsafe, so I worked the brakes hard to stay below twenty–two miles per hour. The first phase of the descent I encountered mostly dirt cross streets, fields of wild brush and not much else. As I began to enter the city proper, cross streets with stop lights and multi–lanes of traffic became the norm and my progress slowed.

With plenty of buses, trucks, and cars to negotiate just feet to my left I wasn't able to do much in the way of scouting out the area businesses and side streets while I was in motion. But when I did stop at a light I craned my neck and quickly studied the billboards and signage to get a pulse of what the city has to offer. There were lots of small independently operated repair shops, assorted service businesses, and plenty of colorful, predominantly Mexican eateries identified by roughly painted and weathered signs but serving plenty of customers.

Farther into town, the more predictable chain franchises began to displace the independents. It was obvious the cost of real estate helped decide who was located where. And until I was deep into where the historic architecture and bold southwestern colors would be in full display, the chain stores did little to identify what part of the country I was in. It was a ubiquitous blend of repetitive visual indifference. But the roads seemed to be better so I guess I should be thankful after riding on the broken gravel strewn shoulder farther out of the city.

One of the crossroads was Unser Boulevard, named after the famous Indy–car–racing Unser family who make their home in Albuquerque. The Unser's are quite the celebrities of the community having earned the naming rights to such a busy stretch of roadway. To my knowledge there are no Unser's racing in any of the major series but in Albuquerque the Unser family still draws a following at the racing museum bearing the family name. You can find it closer to the downtown district just off of Montano Road. The museum is open daily and ticket prices top out at just ten bucks for adults, six for seniors and veterans, while kids under sixteen are free.

I grew up watching the Brothers, Al and Bobby, take their share of wins and championships in the Indy Car Series including multiple wins each at the famous *Brickyard* before turning the reigns over to the next generation of racing Unser's. Later I cheered for *Little Al* who followed in his famous father's and uncle's footsteps starting first in sprint cars on the dirt before making it all the way to top of Indy Car and NASCAR stock car racing. The family also dominated the races at Pikes Peak in Colorado since an Unser first tackled the formidable mountain on a motorcycle back in 1915.

What a rush of information all because of a sign bearing the name "Unser Boulevard" and thirty seconds of wait time for the light to turn green in my favor. The museum presents the history about racing and the Unser family along with a grand display of several original sprint cars, Indy cars, and other rare memorabilia. I wished I had the time to visit the museum on this trip but I will be back to Albuquerque to check it out and enjoy some of the unique art galleries and small restaurants I made note of.

Back in traffic pedaling at a brisk pace, I was watching out for cars turning right and those entering my lane from the side streets. It was all business until the next light but according to my cue sheet I was just blocks away from the muddy waters of the Rio Grande. The road continued to descend slightly toward the center of town and I was no longer able to see the bowl shape of the valley. I was deep into it. I could only see the mountains that formed a ring around Albuquerque's perimeter.

To the right of the road just at the approach where the bridge crosses the Rio Grande River stood a southwestern style stucco sign bearing the Route 66 emblem and the name of the famous river. Painted in terracotta and turquoise colors standing more than twenty feet tall the sign resembled a winged totem pole. It was quite a sight; and another photo opportunity for Betty, Lynn, and I to add to our trip's photo album.

We crossed the tree–lined muddy–brown Rio Grande, and then we headed toward *Old Town* anticipating we would take in some traditional adobe–style architecture. A few blocks later we passed a freshly mowed lawn, and it was the first time in two weeks I remembered having such an experience. It was a good day for riding; the pungent sweet grassy smell stayed with me for several blocks.

A quick left turn onto Rio Grande Boulevard and my bike was successfully across the busy traffic of Route 66 and officially into the historic town core. The colors and the rugged architecture did not disappoint. This was the real deal, rustic round timbers protruding just under the roof lines and smooth plaster walls supporting some rather interesting wood doors and window planters. I committed the views to memory because I did not want to stop in the narrow and tight traffic to take a photograph.

Betty and Lynn were just ahead of me and farther up I could see at least another CrossRoads rider. After traversing Mountain Road, then making the final right onto Indian School Road it was a straight three–mile shot all the way to the hotel where we would happily put our bikes up for the night. With mostly tail winds, clear skies, and favorable temperatures, the bikes saw light duty and were in need of nothing more than a basic wipe–down and chain cleaning. In other words it was a good day for the bikes as well.

The CrossRoads team was busy at the truck with their end–of–day prep work in full swing; restocking the SAG supplies for the vans, inventorying tubes and tires, checking and double checking the to–do lists, wiping down the vehicles which seemed to be impeccably spotless even before they rubbed them down. Tracy, Clark, and Margaret were cheerfully offering their congratulations to the riders as they rolled into the hotel parking lot. Tracy was more vocal and if you were lucky enough to get a big "Yo! Yo! Yo!" or an ear piercing two–fingered whistle you'd smile wide enough to chap your parched lips. Well worth it and nothing Chap Stick couldn't remedy afterwards.

For the record this was the typical scene at every hotel and the staff of CrossRoads was proving to be as predictable as the sun itself coming up each day. I was getting accustomed to the consistency and assurance of my routine. I really liked my role as a bike rider being cared for by people who truly loved what they do.

Rick was tending to a few adjustments on rider bikes at his work stand before he would put his own Lite Speed up for some TLC. I would make sure I parked my bike near Rick so I could watch and learn while I cleaned off the day's grime from my machine. His bike and his equipment always looked new and I quickly learned if I take just a little time each day to maintain my bike it would not only look like new, it would ride like new. Rick was an excellent mechanic and a strong cyclist.

I didn't stay on the hot parking lot for long. The temperature was near the peak of eighty–one degrees but the heat radiating from the dark asphalt surface made it feel much hotter. A dry bake for anything not smart enough to move. Since there wasn't much in the way of shade I continued with my usual routine of a quick bike inspection and cleaning followed by a hot shower for the rider. It was always a hot shower. Then I changed into one of my limited street outfits and began poking around the lobby. I felt like a new man; fully refreshed and gritless.

Before we left Los Angeles the riders were aware not everyone was cycling all the way to Boston. Today was the day we would say goodbye to the first group exiting the tour.

At the hotel several of us chatted about an early tour departure and how hard it would be to leave after bonding so quickly with our group of like–minded adventurers. I'm glad I was not one of the folks leaving. It would feel like unfinished business even though I don't really know the goals for each of my friends. And they were friends, not just riders. I like the way I subconsciously made the distinction. We are just two weeks into this epic journey and just like Tracy told us back in Los Angeles, we would become one. I'm not sure if we had achieved *oneness* in its entirety but we were either very close or at least pretty far down the path.

Later in the evening, a few riders would be leaving the tour. As much as we wanted them to continue with us, their plans were for just two weeks of cycling in the southwest. They would ride with us in spirit from here to Boston. Informally several remaining riders exchanged words with those leaving. I'm sure those discussions involved the days riding together and the fun and camaraderie they shared.

While they conversed Rick was busy disassembling their bikes and packing them for shipment home. With the same care he unpacked and assembled the bikes in Los Angeles, four boxes were quickly packed and readied for either Fed–Ex pick up or for the ride to the airport with its owner in the morning. Yet another part of the CrossRoads attention to detail and a reason to be glad I was traveling under their care.

We gathered at Applebee's which was adjacent to the AmeriSuites hotel for our evening dinner. Hungry and full of energy we bid farewell to Scott, Maryann, Bud and Rick. This was the end of their XC04 ride and for the rest of us we would ride out of Albuquerque a little empty and a little sad. Kathy sang *Happy Trails* and we all enjoyed a good laugh. We will surely miss their company.

I closed the evening with a flat tire party, starting in Phil and Barbara's room, before migrating up to Betty's on the next floor to patch her tire. Earlier in the day Barb found a great bakery near the hotel and we enjoyed a wonderful Danish ring. It was sticky, sweet, and a perfect way to top off a great meal from earlier in the evening. I enjoyed the time shared with this trio and I made myself useful by peeling off the tires and switching out tubes to get their tires prepared for the next day's ride. I rode around and with Barb and Phil over the past two weeks but this was the first time I really had the opportunity to share more in–depth and personal conversation. We talked about family and careers and goals and dreams. We connected and without realizing it, the time we shared that evening in Albuquerque would be one of the highlights of my entire trip.

Back to my room and a quick scribbling of journal entries and it was lights out. It had been a long and exciting day both riding and socializing with the group. I averaged sixteen miles per hour covering 79.07 miles in four hours fifty–five minutes. Not a bad day at all. Tomorrow we make our way to Santa Fe where we will enjoy our second rest day of the tour. I am happy, excited, and optimistic about the ride and about my future. I am learning much about myself through this experience. It is so much more than just a bike ride.

Day 14: Albuquerque to Santa Fe (67 miles)

We headed east out of Albuquerque as Ken Gregor's bike–mounted CD–player filled the air with the voice of Frank Sinatra and his moving rendition of God Bless America. Bike mounted is probably not an appropriate word to describe how it was fixed to his bike; it was more like hanging loosely, dangling and swinging from the cross bar. As the volume oscillated up and down it draped a pleasant vale of song over the mechanical sounds of the early morning stop and go traffic.

I continued along the busy thoroughfare avoiding the massive transit buses stopping for passengers at nearly every major intersection. The smell of diesel exhaust in the cool air was in contrast to the beauty of the new morning sky complete with bright, nearly blinding sunrays emanating from the direction my bike was pointed. It was the start of another day filled with adventure and anticipation on the bike. The forecast for the day would see the mercury climb from a low of fifty–nine degrees up to a rather warm eighty–five degrees, maybe more, if the skies stay clear.

Sometimes in good company and at other times left only with my imagination to draw focus from the efforts of pedaling; a day very different yet much the same. Ken and Sinatra slowly faded behind me and I turned my focus to the locals entering the crosswalks, cars pulling on and off the pavement, and the weather–worn road surface full of cracks, road debris and potholes. I noticed my exit from town was mostly up a very slight grade, but it would be nothing like the climbs to come.

Ten miles out of town, we finally began climbing the Sandia Mountains, which rise sharply to an attention getting 10,378 feet. Fortunately for us we would cross the mountain at a much lower elevation, much closer to 6,600 feet above sea level.

Since I was not going to the top of the Sandia Peak I could not witness the panoramic views of the eleven thousand square miles of New Mexico desert, canyons, and lush forests that made up the Cibola National Forest in person, but I trust the brochures describing the views, which are best seen from the 2.7 mile sky tram, were accurate.

Maybe the next time I come to the *Duke City* I will drive up to Sandia Peaks and see for myself the beauty of the Rio Grande Valley and the *Land of Enchantment*.

Origins of the name "Duke City"

In the early 1700s, King Philip of Spain granted a group of Spanish colonist's permission to start a new city along the banks of the Rio Grande. The colony's governor, Francisco Cuervo y Valdez wrote a letter to the Duke of Albuerquerque in Spain, reporting the new settlement and its name: the Villa de Alburquerque. They had named their new city after the Duke. Over the years the middle "r" was dropped from the city's name but the reference to the "Duke City" remains to this day.

Riding at the speed of sound—the sound of bones creaking, muscles straining, and the *tink, tink, tink,* that can only be described as the cry of a precision road bike operating at its least efficient and slowest pace, I inched my way upward. That's how it felt to me. It was worse for a few others and for those cyclists accustomed to the terrain it was a pleasant workout. On such climbs I get a flavor for how well I ride compared to others. Fast riders come up from behind often with ease as they quickly dispense with me and are out of sight after just a few bends in the road. Slower riders who took advantage of an earlier departure from the hotel quickly come into view. Slowly they grow in size as I get closer. I easily recognize them a hundred yards out by their body motion, bike details, and their cycling outfits. Then I bypass them in much the same manner as the fast riders did to me. Other than seeing folks stopped along the road or pairing off with one or more riders this is the only time I come close to the other cyclists.

You have to be careful when it comes to maintaining your own comfortable pace. If you try to keep up with a faster rider you might exhaust yourself and if you back off to the pace of a slower rider you risk exceeding your seat–time and that can lead to all kinds of problems between you and the bike. Stopping on a climb is also tempting but just a few minutes off the bike cannot be recovered even if you were only moving along at a slow pace.

Remembering to drink in the thin dry air is also very important. Once you get behind the hydration curve you put your day and possibly the next day's ride at risk. It's much better to error on the side of too much drinking just to be sure. And making frequent roadside stops to find a tree, a sign, or some other privacy prop becomes a whole new adventure not featured in the cross country cycling brochures!

It was a healthy climb out of Albuquerque, which is situated at five thousand feet above sea level, and I was pleased with my morning efforts. *So far so good*, I thought. Cycling at these elevations is even more difficult for those accustomed to riding closer to sea level where the air is more dense and it is easier to get a full breathe of air. My preparatory rides in central Florida never exceeded 120 feet above sea level. So for me it had been a week of riding in thin air and I was looking forward to exiting New Mexico in a few days and reaching lower and friendlier elevations.

Each of the individual climbs up the mountain offered a small respite from pedaling but it was the final climb to our first unofficial rest stop that provided the biggest challenge and the greatest thrill in a long and very fast descent. An unofficial rest stop is really an opportunity for Tracy and the CrossRoads staff to park by the roadside and watch us to make sure we all make it up the climbs.

I was nearly fourteen minutes into my disciplined rhythmic ascent crawling at barely four miles per hour in the lowest gear the bike could offer when I crested the peak. Expecting an enjoyable downhill rest I relaxed and lightened my grip of the bars. In moments I was accelerating as if I were in free–fall. Dodging drainage grates in the middle of the traffic lane at speeds approaching forty miles per hour kept the grip on the bars tight and eyes wide open. I was more winded from the excitement of the exhilarating glide then I was from climbing. It was only minutes but it seemed to last much longer.

Another small climb, then it was time for a welcome break and some enthusiastic cheering from Margaret and the CrossRoads team waiting for us at a well–placed convenience store. A glacier blue Gatorade and a little package of Ritz Cheese Crackers to fill the personal fuel tank signaled it was time to go.

After the morning climb and a break at the crest we began a gentler and spirited descent through rolling terrain full of rocks and piñon trees along the Turquoise Trail Scenic Byway, otherwise known as Route 14 North. The road was reasonably smooth offering up only a mild but steady vibration up through the front fork and bars before it transferred into my wrists. I could feel it in my seat as well but it was nothing I needed to be concerned about today.

The contrast of the blue sky against the greenery was an inspiring sight. It was easy to see the beauty within this part of the country. I savored the next forty minutes covering just a tick over eleven miles especially the last long speedy drop into our official SAG at the Golden General Merchandise Store. Like most of the transitions off the road we had to be extremely careful navigating the gravel. Unclipping from the pedals and keeping the bike pointed straight were essential to staying upright. Even at a walking pace dumping over into the gravel would amount to grinding your flesh on a cheese grater. Bad enough you suffer the immediate pain but skin cuts and abrasions can present plenty of problems for several days after.

I realize some readers may be so focused on the cycling experience that the local history and facts about the places I pass through may be of little importance, even a distraction from their reading enjoyment. If my writing is too historically weighted, if it has too many comments about non–cycling topics, or my attempts to paint in words a picture of the people and their communities is dialing back your interest I must warn you; it's going to become even more informative.

Woven into my days on the bike are nuggets of information describing the people, the places, and events covering the rich and interesting tale of their existence. This is the story of our country, much of it I find truly amazing and compelling to write about happens to be in the west; the wide open and wild parts of the country I know little about. Without the history I would deny myself the complete and proper recording of this cross country experience.

As the reader you do have a choice. You can begin skimming through and reengage when you see me talking about pedaling and gear changes and brisk descents. But if you stay with me, if you read all of what I have labored over to put into words, I promise it will add color to an otherwise monotone single dimensional story of a biking experience that moves only from point *A* to point *B*. It will bring my story life and it will help you to be in the moment, on the bike, one rotation of the pedals at a time, as you and I breathe in the air and enjoy the silence masking the great events from days gone by. If I do my job well you will hear my words and not simply read them on paper. You will engage your imagination and you will see what I have seen. I ask you to trust me, and to enjoy as I did.

Other than a single store there is not much besides nature itself for miles around Golden. Well a few secluded houses maybe, but no commerce or town hub. Quite a contrast to its past as Golden was once a bustling and lively place. It gained notoriety as the site of the first gold rush west of the Mississippi back in 1825. It was actually Placer gold prospectors first discovered on Tuerto Creek on the southwest side of the Ortiz Mountains. With gold came the people, then the San Francisco Catholic Church was built around 1830, and as the new gold–mining district grew several saloons, businesses, a school, and even a stock exchange would be built. In 1880 a post office would open but the gold was soon starting to dwindle. By the end of 1892 the mining was finished and ranching became the mainstay of the local economy.

In 1918 the Golden General Merchandise Store was opened by Ernest Ricon. In the '60s a man named Henderson married Ricon's daughter and they took over the store. It remains the last continuously operating business in the area and it is referred to by the locals as the Henderson General Store.

As the population shriveled the post office closed in 1928 and it officially was on its way to ghost town status. For years afterwards, many abandoned buildings remained, tumbling down between its few remaining occupied structures. Vandalism also took its toll on the town and its remaining structures, but a few crumbling ruins still provide excellent photo opportunities. The San Francisco Catholic Church, which was restored by historian and author, Fray Angelico Chavez, in 1960, while he was the padre of the St. Joseph Church in Los Cerrillos, is Golden's most photographed building. Across the highway, west of the church are the ruins and remnants of the old mining days.

Though I could see no signs of it from the small patch of shade I found at the store, Golden is said to be experiencing a small rebirth as new residents settle in building new homes and restoring others viable enough to be rehabilitated.

I was officially half way and this would be the last support stop until I rolled into Santa Fe. I made sure to top off my bottles and fill my pockets with treats to complete the ride. Carefully out of the gravel lot on to the roadway, my shoes now fully clipped into the pedals, I left the SAG behind. Route 14 continued up a long climb past a large stand of distinctly brown and thin piñon trees. They were the victims of bark beetle blight, which was on the rise due to the extended drought conditions in the area. Drought also prevents new trees from taking their place.

We continued our climb to 7,500 feet, winding through rocky peaks covered in loose rocks and sparse brush, through the mineral rich Ortiz Mountains before we descended the steep mile grade into the town of Madrid. The quality of the road dwindled significantly the more I descended. My lane was full of large potholes and patches sending shocks up through the front wheel and into my hands and forearms. It was an excessive amount of punishment for the bike and coupled with the speed made it very unsafe to continue without braking to slow down to a more reasonable pace.

The road was narrow and not bike friendly with traffic. Fortunately there were very few vehicles trying to pass. Off to either side the mostly rocky terrain was littered with shanty shacks and old box cars pieced together with sheets of corrugated tin and scrap metal. The dominant color was rust. Whoever the builders, they were a resourceful and crafty lot. It would be safe to say they did not have a home owners association in this little community just a hundred yards or so out of Madrid. I took a few pictures because I wasn't sure I would be able to accurately describe what I saw in words. It bordered on third world construction, if it was even that good.

Madrid is an interesting place with a deep and detailed history worth exploring. It was a former company owned coal–mining town originally known as Coal Gulch and it came into existence in the early 1800s. The area had a very unique geology where a combination of hard (anthracite) and soft (bituminous) coal lay in seams side by side. This rare phenomenon had been found in only two other mines in the world. To extract the coal workers would toil in shafts as deep as 2,500 feet below the rocky surface.

When the Santa Fe Railroad became a customer in the early 1900s, Madrid began to grow, reaching a population of four thousand in the 1930s. As more workers were required to support the expanding coal needs of local customers and the U.S. government, housing was in short supply. To accommodate the growing population the mining company bought framed houses from as far away as Kansas, and then disassembled, shipped, and reassembled them along the crude dirt streets. Residents had access to elementary and high schools, a fully equipped hospital, a company store, and an employee's club. The club was an employee funded effort created to support community causes and all employees were required to participate in town events such as the Fourth of July parade celebrations and the now famous Christmas light displays.

At Christmas time, Madrid's Christmas light celebration powered by the mine's generators was so brilliant in the 1930s it encouraged airline pilots to detour over Madrid so passengers could witness it. Over one hundred fifty thousand lights lit up the ball field, the town, and the hillsides with Christmas scenes, using five hundred thousand watts of electricity costing more than fifty thousand dollars. Life Magazine featured a story about the event and over a hundred thousand people came to enjoy the animated displays, the Ferris wheel, merry–go–round, and other rides set up on the ballpark. During the 1930s Madrid was called the *City of Lights* for the extravagant use of electricity during depression times. Artists from the Santa Fe area helped and each year there were even greater displays than the years before. The first lighting was 1922 and the last occurring in 1944 when wartime restrictions forced an end of the celebration.

The company town would also gain notoriety for its minor–league baseball games played at Oscar Huber Ballpark, named after the owner of the Madrid Mine. The Madrid Miners, New Mexico's only Class *AA* minor league team, played against the black–bearded House of David team. The Miners won many pennants playing in the Central New Mexico Baseball League with team players who were also coal–company employees. Of course many were hired after they fell short of making the major leagues and held only token jobs at the mine.

Built by Huber in the 1920s, the Madrid field was the first ballpark west of the Mississippi River to have lights. It had an electric scoreboard also powered by the mine generators. He envisioned the field as a place where his miners could play at night after working the mines. Not much has changed in the last eighty years; the field remains a flat grassless diamond revealing very little about its storied past and the men who played there. Rumors suggest Thomas Edison came to Madrid to help design the lighting system for the ballpark while working on projects in the nearby town of Cerrillos. It's also alleged Babe Ruth once visited the field but no evidence could be found to support this claim.

In 1950 demand for coal waned and the mine closed just four years later. The ballpark deteriorated and the players moved on to other jobs. Madrid became a ghost town. Joe Huber, Oscar's son, would offer the town for sale on June 17, 1954 through an ad in the Wall Street Journal. For the paltry sum of two hundred fifty thousand dollars everything in the town could be purchased; two hundred houses, grade and high school, power house, general store, tavern, machine shop, mineral rights, and 9000 acres which were further described as offering an excellent climate in a fine industrial location. No one bought the town.

In the early 1970s, artists and craftspeople arrived and converted the old company stores and houses into quality shops and galleries. The US Census in the year 2000 pegged the town population at 149.

Madrid has a mining museum and an original tavern called The Mine Shaft, which has one of the largest wall displays of dollar bills I've ever seen. A fire inspector might classify the place as a fire hazard with most of the walls and ceiling papered in what is claimed to be a million dollars of U.S. *Greenbacks*. The waitress said everyday more dollars get added to the display and if I'd like to have my dollar tacked up she'd be happy to take it off my hands. I think the estimate is excessive but the display was pretty darned impressive nonetheless. The food and the service weren't bad either.

Another interesting fact about Madrid had to do with the water supply. Until the 1970s all of the water had to be trucked in. It was an expensive and troubling proposition until the few people living in Madrid decided to form a Water Cooperative and to dig a well so they could manage the water supply on their own. The Cooperative bought the existing water rights from Huber for a dollar and for another dollar they bought the town roads and the ballpark. Eventually a landowner's association was established and they set about cleaning up the town and embracing the reality they lived on top of a coal mine. It would be a ghost town no more.

Madrid has more recently found its way into the limelight when Touchstone Films produced the 2007 movie *Wild Hogs* that showcased the town and featured actors Tim Allen, John Travolta, Martin Lawrence, and William H. Macy.

Beyond Madrid, farther uphill we pedaled, to the town of Cerrillos. This town, with its dirt streets, was once seriously considered for the capital of New Mexico, but today serves as nothing more than a reminder of the old west.

The Cerrillos mining district was once the source of turquoise and lead used for jewelry and pottery-making by the Indians.

The rich and full history lesson of this area concludes with a few more brief facts about Cerrillos. The town started in 1880 as a mining community when the railroad came through the Galisteo River Valley. Cerrillos supported the mining district to the North. In total there are over two thousand Territorial mines in the hills producing Gold, Copper, Silver, Galena, Turquoise, Manganese, and Iron. Mining of Cerrillos Turquoise began around 900 A.D. and it was traded far and wide.

After just a few miles of climbs and entertaining descents winding through more piñon trees and rock filled mountains, we finally broke free into more open terrain. Over the next six miles the roadside would transition from huge pock-marked rock formations the size of small buildings to rolling open plains leading us all the way into Santa Fe. It was very hot, but the wind, which had been in our face through the Cerrillos Historic Park area, reversed direction and helped push the tired riders.

Just eleven miles shy of town we passed a large prison off to our right. It was the New Mexico State Penitentiary, a men's maximum-security prison facility. I was happy to view it from a distance and I believe my cadence increased slightly as I left the prison behind me. I continued pedaling along Route 14 North toward Santa Fe until a familiar sign caught my attention. It was a historic Route 66 sign. I had been riding on the old Route 66 since turning onto Route 14 way back near Albuquerque. *I'm get 'n my kicks,* I smiled to myself.

The last stretch was a curving highway climb continuing all the way to the hotel. Just ahead was the official Santa Fe city limit sign and I stopped with Betty to pose for a picture. I was now at an elevation of seven thousand feet standing on a dusty patch of nearly lifeless ground straddling my bike frame and smiling; my ride was almost over.

The Three Stooges finger puppets still secured to the bike flag pole would be due a washing and some earned time off the bike on the rest day. My shoes were covered with dust but I was happy I decided to wear my bright yellow jersey as it made me extremely visible against the dull tans of the landscape. I pushed off and rolled down the wide concrete sidewalk until I was able to use a side street to get back on the main road. The hotel was now within a mile, maybe two at most.

Minutes later I reached the hotel parking lot, dismounted my bike, and walked into the lobby. For the first time I really focused on the United States map that traveled the tour with us. It was about four feet wide and showed our planned route in a light pink tone and the sections we completed were darkened with a black marker line. Each day might yield an extension of a half to maybe more than an inch but it never seemed to align with the effort I felt after stepping off the bike at the end of the ride. Looking at it now, not for today's effort but seeing the length of the line from the Pacific Ocean to Santa Fe I began to sense the impact of what we had done.

We had traveled more than 918 miles in two weeks; a huge accomplishment by any standards. Other riders came in and seemed to ponder the same thing. We were gaining momentum and about one quarter of the way to Boston. It put a little spring into my step as I signed in and picked up my room key and then headed up to my room to shower and plan out my laundry strategy. If I could get the housekeeping chores out of the way I could spend tomorrow as a real tourist.

With both me and the bike cleaned and laundry completed at the Laundromat next to the hotel, I reflected back, thinking about all of the interesting stories and historical references I took in today. Some found on historical markers, others found in signage on old buildings, promotional fliers nailed to walls, restaurant menus, printed glossies stocked in lobby display racks, newspapers, and in conversations with the local people. A few were the result of my curiosity after cleaning up at the hotel and using their guest computer to do a little internet research on the areas I had been through. Each tidbit seemed to connect to another and the story of the day required all of its parts.

I made my journal entries noting the distance of 68.17 miles, five hours twenty–eight minutes of seat time at an average of 12.4 miles an hour and a maximum speed of 36.4 screaming miles per hour. Then I set out to find postcards to convey the story of Santa Fe. So far I was crafty enough to find a postcard for each town we overnighted at. It was just one of many little victories that made me smile.

Next to the hotel just past the Laundromat was a southwestern junk shop full of pottery and rusting metal welded sculptures. There were huge sundials torched out of sheet metal and twisted rebar formed into the shape of animals. There were lots of interesting yard art but no postcards to be found. I decided to walk farther up the street a block or two but still no sign of any business selling postcards. I decided to defer the postcard hunt until tomorrow. I convinced myself I would find the right cards in the historic downtown. I was sure of it.

On the way back to the hotel I noticed a sign describing the use of pecan shells as landscape mulch. Sure enough below the sign along the median and the sidewalk was a wide patch of nothing but shells. I almost mistook the shells for pea gravel but this was a smooth mass of pecan shells. The more I looked the more widely used the shells were. Apparently they provide great weed control and they don't absorb the heat like the rocks and gravel. It seems to be the perfect material for the application. And at least in the few blocks around the hotel it was a pretty popular choice.

A free night in Santa Fe means Mexican food would be on the menu. I met up with a group of about eight riders in the lobby and we walked a few blocks to an authentic Mexican restaurant. It was nothing like the Chili's or other Americanized chains claiming to offer Mexican food. It was different and much better. The food was spicy hot and a bit foreign to look at. I tried the green salsa for the first time and I liked it. It went well poured over what was a burrito–like main dish I ordered by pointing at a diner's plate on the neighboring table. If I could read Spanish I would have known what it was. A large unsweet tea chased down the main dish complete with refried beans and chips. It was very salty, but very good.

We hung out for quite a while at the restaurant before we made room for other patrons. More than a few beers were enjoyed and I held the spicy burn off with plenty of tea. Everyone was going downtown tomorrow to take in the historic city but we couldn't agree on a time. Fortunately the city has a robust transit system with a bus stop right in front of our hotel. About every twenty minutes a bus loops through and makes the fifteen–minute run to what the locals call *The Plaza;* the heart of downtown Santa Fe.

Full from dinner and our cycling conversation it was time to call it a night. The group made its way back to the hotel crossing only a few side streets along the way. I was back in my hotel room and settled in about twenty minutes before Clark returned. He had gone out with the CrossRoads staff for a much earned dinner as well; Mexican, after all it was Santa Fe.

Before turning in for the night Clark and I talked about the first two weeks of the tour and about plans for tomorrow's rest day. For Clark it would be a day of work, washing and prepping the vehicles, icing up the coolers and filling them with water and Gatorade. If he has any energy or time after he would likely play tourist like the rest of us.

Day 15: Santa Fe (Rest Day)

After more than nine hundred miles of cycling, we were able to enjoy a day of rest in Santa Fe. I opted to use the city bus system to get to Old Santa Fe and found it to be both rider–friendly and very affordable at just two dollars for a day pass.

Within fifteen minutes, we were strolling around Southwestern–style adobe buildings full of art galleries, jewelry shops, and sidewalk artist displays. The terra–cotta buildings trimmed with dark–stained carved wood details were framed by a colorful variety of native trees and flowers.

The weather was perfect, with clear blue skies, temperatures in the low 70s, and breezy. We visited the public library to access e–mail, and through the courtesy of some of the locals, we were able to find some of the best attractions. I snapped many pictures of the streetscapes and tried to find just the right images and angles to capture the essence of the old town. Every building surrounding the Santa Fe Plaza—a beautiful family friendly tree–lined park—was worthy of remembering in film; if not for the brilliant adobe and timber design for the interesting signage and business names they brandished.

We made sure to swap cameras, capturing ourselves on film, so we had proof we were actually there. No matter which street or business I looked in, I saw a cyclist from the group. It was no surprise Duffey, Big Mike, and a few others were found in the Haagen–Dazs ice cream parlor on East San Francisco Street. I saw Gordon and Betty, Paul, and the Kahrl's; Randi and Tom scouting out the handmade wares offered for sale by the street vendors and in the authentic southwestern shops. Everyone was enjoying themselves and putting plenty of mileage on their sneakers, except for Kathy and Peter who were getting around in their sandals.

I love regional art and make a point to explore as many of the art shows, galleries, and working studios as I can find. Santa Fe is an art lovers dream with some very impressive options that unfortunately cannot all be appreciated in a single day. I had to work fast and choose my galleries wisely. I know what I would be doing the rest of the day and I had gone rogue to pursue my indulgence. I toured the New Mexico Museum of Art and was impressed with the scale and variety of the paintings featuring the Native American culture, the buffalo and wild horses, and of course the dramatic rocky landscapes.

I am drawn to the paintings and it didn't matter the medium; oils, acrylics, or water colors. Even some monotone ink drawings fit into my preference of art. In the working galleries I watched portrait artists create and even broadened my focus to enjoy the work of a bronze sculptor as he intensely scraped the clay of his model. Quality art is not only visual it has a way of moving you to feel the calm of the solitude in a sunset landscape or the struggle of the massive buffalo as they attempt to evade the hunters. I stood at some paintings for minutes breathing in the scenes before me. Then I would have to quickly move on to the next piece where I would be equally moved.

In most places the visual experience was accompanied by the soft and airy notes of flute music. Spiritual, soulful, a feeling of sorrow, a story, a hymn, a calling, it came from speakers but it felt as if it were radiating from the art, the walls, the floor, and the ceiling. As if it was coming from nowhere and everywhere at the same time. It could have been coming from within me. The music was like none I had experienced before. No words yet it spoke. No religious tones yet I felt I was in a sacred place. The paintings came to life with the music and I was drawn deeper into the experience. I became connected spiritually to what I saw through what I heard. It was beautiful in a way I had not known music to be. A rush of a story filled my mind as I looked at the art, as if it told the details behind the images, the struggles of the wild animals, the landscape as seen through the eyes of the native America Indian in full headdress upright on his horse as he surveyed the horizon. I was no longer looking as an observer. I was placed into the scenes through the sounds of the Indian flute. It washes over me gently, warmly, lovingly. It stirs my soul and the music of Santa Fe claims a piece of me. I close my eyes and I feel relaxed and at peace.

In one working studio and gallery combo I found an artist who focused on painting stone and adobe walls with vibrantly painted wooden doors in fire reds and bold blues. You might think the artist was rather limiting in their focus but her work was fresh and unique and very striking. All of this art chasing and walking around was making me hungry so I headed back onto the plaza and met up with Kathy and we headed off to enjoy a fine coffee and hot chocolate at the Burrito Company Café on Washington Avenue. We sat outside and enjoyed an outdoor Native American sidewalk sale and craft display on West Palace across from the plaza.

In this place called the Palace of the Governors the Native American crafters would display their handmade crafts on authentic woolen blankets. If you are looking for authentic Native American jewelry or crafts, I would recommend you check with the street vendors, who are also the artists. Their passion and ability to describe their products enhance the shopping experience, and you will often pay a fraction of what the stores ask for similar items. They also get the benefit of every dollar you spend; a win–win transaction in my book. I enjoyed talking to the artists and knowing the markings on the backs of the jewelry were their own initials. There is a sense of connection with the art and the artist I value.

As a teenager I had a simple silver cross that I had lost and I was never able to find a suitable replacement. While crouching down to better look at the handmade jewelry I found a silver cross just over an inch tall, hand formed and worked with a hammer. It was perfect. I spoke to the lady who made it and for the small sum of twelve dollars it became mine. She gave me her card and assured me if it gave me any problem she would repair it and make it right. I appreciated her standing behind her work but there was nothing to fail on the cross. The only thought I had was I might lose it and would need to call for another.

I put the cross and the chain around my neck and let it hang there aside the only piece of jewelry I wear; a keepsake from my father. The two swing freely in front of my heart as if they were connected in some way.

I returned to the small shops and galleries to take in what art I could before my time would come to board the bus back to the hotel. There was so much to see. It was all impressive but I needed to go. I would miss out on other points of interest including St. Francis Cathedral, constructed by Bishop Jean Baptiste Larny in 1869. At least I enjoyed the art and walked amongst the craftsmen and craftswomen at the Palace of the Governors and I talked at length with them about their work. I will cherish those conversations.

While waiting for the bus I read the Palace of the Governors was constructed in 1610 making it the oldest continuously used public building in the United States. I also learned Santa Fe is home to the oldest house in the United States, built by the Pueblo Indians out of "Puddled" adobe more than eight hundred years ago. And then there are these factoids; Santa Fe—meaning "holy faith" in Spanish—is the oldest capital city in the United States and with a population pressing sixty–eight thousand it boasts a total of twenty–three parks of various sizes and types. I just needed a few more days to experience it all. Santa Fe is an art–lover's paradise; it is also one of the most historically rich cities in our great country.

We closed the day enjoying another fine dinner in the company of friends. It was a night full of laughter and the sharing of stories about Santa Fe and its charm. We were optimistic and excited about the next few days of riding as we descend out of the mountains and into new terrain at much lower elevations. It would be flatter and the air would be more oxygen rich. Breathing would be much easier and we would fatigue less. We left the restaurant for the short stroll back to the hotel where final riding preparations and sleep awaited us. The highest elevation on tour lay before us, but we are rested and ready.

Day 16: Santa Fe to Las Vegas (72 miles)

Today I awoke to breakfast at the Village Inn and a six quadrant cue sheet full of cracked cattle guards and warnings of dogs. Walking to the restaurant gave us a taste of the day's weather; it was cold. To be more precise it was starting out with cloudless skies, temperatures struggling to reach the 40s, and it was very windy.

I debated wearing my jacket and leg warmers for the ride but it was a short one sided discussion. I was going to wear them both. If it warmed up they would easily come off. I wasn't going to chance it staying cold and me be on the bike without the extra layer of protection. The high for the day in Las Vegas was forecasted to be eighty degrees. So there was some expectation my legs would see at least a bit of sunshine, maybe even before noon.

I just wasn't too sure about the forecast. I only watched the weather report on the television the night before and it likely could change. We exited the hotel and made a series of left turns working our way east along Rodeo Road. The majority of the population was north, just to our left. We road parallel to I–25N and then turned south onto Old Pecos Trail to continue stalking the Interstate.

The roads were a series of inclined rollers and the riders were beginning to spread out as they warmed up. Traffic continued to be light along this two lane road allowing us to focus on more important matters, like the temperature and staying warm. I was hoping the temperatures would start to rise to a more comfortable level or at least for the wind to die down a bit.

After a few miles on the Pecos we joined the Interstate and continued climbing through the mountains. Shaggy Peak was off to our left and the mountains were growing ever larger with each mile we forged upward. Somewhere along this stretch of I–24N we reached the highest elevation of the ride. We had peaked out at 7,575 feet above sea level; a mile and a half above my normal riding elevation and the air contained only about seventy–five percent of the oxygen I was accustomed to back in Florida. It made my breathing more labored and I felt like I could not get enough air. Not like I was being unreasonably deprived of oxygen but I did notice the extra effort in pedaling.

The roadway swung around to the left taking the path of least resistance and we were now tracking to the northeast through a natural valley towards Glorieta Pass. The mountains closed in and the details of their geology were now in plain sight. Their formation must have been quite an event; lots of fractures in the exposed rock and only limited vegetation to hide it. Fortunately for us the mountain had a break in it preventing the necessity to take a more direct and steep route over it.

Traffic raced by as we oscillated between periods of reasonable speeds and slow crawls. The shoulder of the road where we were restricted was now drawing mixed reviews. Most of the pavement was decent but in several sections, especially in the first few miles of the Interstate, it had clumps of grass pushing up through the cracks in the surface and bits of loose gravel that would kick out from the tires as I rolled over them.

The conditions improved as we rode, the surface became more consistent and smooth but we still had just enough room for a single rider to pass thanks to a wide imprint of continuous grooves designed to startle drowsy motorists should they stray onto the shoulder. A modern version of the rumble strips if you will. At best we had two feet to work with; just a few inches more than the width of our handlebars. We also had another new obstacle to deal with as we rounded the first curve; a guardrail. No longer were we afforded the opportunity to take our chances with the loose ground beyond the shoulder to evade cars, dodge debris or moving animals. We were boxed in between the rails and the traffic. Should there be any debris in our narrow lane our options would be few.

In the wide open we took the wind from whatever direction it decided to hit us. As we trekked to the south it was decidedly at our backs; a very pleasurable and welcome wind. But as we worked our way through the valley toward Glorieta Pass it was mostly a twenty to thirty mile per hour crosswind and at times a partial head wind. It could easily push me into the guardrail or the warning strips. Contact with the rails would be the worst possible scenario.

Even though the wind seemed lost at times, it always found us and slapped us about so we did not forget it was there. It was still brisk and even in the mid–morning it was decidedly cooler than we were expecting. Having my leg warmers and jacket on was a good decision.

During a long descent facing a quarterly head wind from my left I found a large debris field, a tire carcass off of a tractor trailer in my path. I was moving at about twenty miles per hour and had to either stop very quickly or jump over the warning strips and into the traffic lane.

On a downhill you never ever want to scrub speed and stopping is only a measure of last resort because you never know how hard it will be to regain the momentum. I could see a break in the traffic so I made the split decision to take the lane.

The shock and vibration as I skimmed the warning strips sent a wave of pulsing tremors through the wheels and into my hands and seat. Accompanying the vibration was the loud and distinct fast paced mechanical growling sound that let other riders know I had ventured into the danger zone. It was more violent than it would appear and without a firm grip a rider could cross the bars, pancake the front wheel, and kiss the pavement. Potentially one of the most dangerous and damaging fall a rider could have without involving another obstacle.

My grip was tight, my wheel straight and true. I crossed safely into the motor lane without incident. I checked my eyeglass mounted mirror to gauge the time available to stay in the lane. I was happy to see there were no cars within my field of view. Carefully I scanned the shoulder for a safe place to transition back across the warning strips. It was a textbook execution and I barely lost any speed through the entire process. I heard the two quick mechanical growls of a rider behind me safely executing the same maneuver.

So on I pedaled toward Glorieta Pass and a bend in the road where I would find more favorable winds. As I rode I noticed the terrain changed again, the mountains receded and the vegetation became more abundant with larger trees near the roadway. I had climbed much higher into the range and the ground was no longer soaring up on both sides of the road. I was also happy to see the guardrail come to an end.

Unfortunately, the temperature remained cool until about noon, and other riders who did not dress appropriately suffered through the entire morning. Betty borrowed a pair of arm warmers to put over her legs and then used a trash bag as a jacket to keep her upper body warm. It wasn't stylish but it worked.

When riding in cold temperatures, it is important to retain body heat any way you can. Most of the day, we rode at an elevation of seven thousand to 7,500 feet, which greatly reduces your stamina, heart–rate control and your ability to catch your breath. As well as we did today, we should be very well prepared for days when we ride closer to sea level.

On the last descent before exiting the Interstate for Pecos, I was within a hundred feet of several riders strung out into a single file line traveling above twenty–six miles per hour. With only two feet between the deeply cut warning strips and the guardrail we had to be extremely careful. The crosswinds caused the bikes to dance between the two obstacles without warning, making it mentally as well as physically taxing. We also had to contend with broken glass, radial–tire debris, and other discarded materials on the highway shoulder all while listening for approaching vehicles from behind.

When descending under crosswind conditions, hands fatigue from heavy braking, and shoulders and forearms tense against the jarring road surface and buffeting winds. It will be good to get beyond the steep grades and high winds; the sooner the better.

At the top of the exit ramp we veered left, and then made a quick right after crossing the Interstate below. The CrossRoads van awaited us with Margaret bundled up in her heavy jacket smiling and cheering us on. We had been on the bike for just less than two hours and it was still cold. A few riders were chatting with Margaret and I pulled into the gravel lot with several others. It was an opportunity to take a quick drink and eat half a granola bar before setting off again.

Pecos National Monument was just eight miles farther so I figured I would ride until then before stopping for a bio break. Just in case there was also a store four miles up but I wasn't sure if they had facilities available. Off the Interstate the road became a more intimate and scenic ride complete with plenty of graceful downhill grades and an abundance of lush green trees and fields of long grass covering both sides of the two lane rural road. Modest houses with fenced yards and small gardens dotted the road along with a few rural mailboxes that stood like metal soldiers awaiting their delivery. I crossed the first of several cattle guards without incident and returned my focus back to enjoying the scenery.

On a downhill we passed a historical marker off to the right describing a battlefield event; the Battle of Glorieta Pass. On this ground Confederate and Union soldiers fought and died in one of the most significant yet little known confrontations during the American Civil War. For three days beginning on March 26, 1862 the Confederate soldiers battled for control of the New Mexico Territory with the intent of pushing back the Union troops to gain control of Fort Union, twenty miles north of our destination town; Las Vegas. If successful they would have forced the Union soldiers to retreat back into Colorado Territory.

The Confederates held the advantage until their critical supply train was destroyed. Without sufficient food and supplies the Confederates were forced to retreat from a sure victory. The Union was handed the victory in what history will remember as the *Gettysburg of the West*.

In 1993 the congressionally appointed Civil War Sites Advisory Commission designated the site as one of ten Priority One (class *A*) battlefields; a designation reserved for principal strategic operations having a direct impact on the course of the war. Considering the commission reviewed more than 10,500 actions this site ranks right with Gettysburg and Antietam.

Through the cool air under intermittent shade of dense stands of trees I kept rolling quickly along New Mexico 50. On my left were several exposed rock expanses maybe 150 feet in length. It appeared the rock was cut away to make room for the road to pass through. At its highest point the rocks stood twenty or more feet above the roadway with many full grown trees perched above.

There was a bit of a shoulder and traffic was limited allowing riders to cluster and converse. The downhill grade continued and the miles were ticking right along. The lush trees faded into the background and the high desert–like terrain consisting of exposed rock and earth with small gangly bushes and scrubs became the norm. It was a quick transition as the road continued winding down until it deposits us at Griego's Market, the store indicated on our cue sheet. More riders were waiting there and the store did have a working restroom. A welcome break but a line formed quickly. Proper etiquette was to buy something if you use the restrooms of a business. I think a candy bar or a granola bar should cover it.

After a steep and speedy descent through the town of Pecos the road abruptly ended at a stop sign at the bottom of a hill. Our cue sheet instructed us to turn right for a gradual two–mile climb to the Pecos National Monument. I was riding in the vicinity of Lynn and a few others and it seemed everyone wanted to at least stop at the visitor center to learn a bit about the monument. I stopped at the entrance and took a few photographs including one of Lynn on her bike, the mountains forming a beautiful backdrop as I looked back to the northwest. Then Lynn and I pedaled to catch up with Greg, Kathy, and the others at the visitor center.

We were in the Sangre de Cristo Mountains in the midst of piñon, juniper, and ponderosa pine woodlands. The remains of an Indian Pueblo stands at the top of the ridge just a few hundred yards beyond the welcome center, a reminder of those who once controlled the trade route through the Pecos Valley. It was the gateway to the plains. This was shaping up to be the most interesting stop of the day. After reading the history inside the welcome center we decided to take the thirty–minute walk to see the ruins for ourselves.

Along the trail we kept a watchful eye out for snakes as recommended by the trail signs. Soon we were standing amongst the impressive adobe remains. Several markers continued to tell the story about the site and I learned this was once a center of power and influence from A.D. 1450–1550. In its heyday the main structure stood four to five stories tall, with few openings in the outer wall and a large open courtyard in the center. The lower levels were used primarily for food storage, and the upper levels served as living space for two thousand Pecos Pueblo Indians. As we surveyed the remains there was nothing more than three feet high except for a few walls of the church.

This village commanded the trade path between Pueblo farmers of the Rio Grande and hunting tribes of the Buffalo Plains. The Pecos Indians were the middlemen, transmitters and partakers of the goods and cultures of the very different people on either side of the mountains.

In later years, the Spaniards would come to occupy the region, living and working with the Pecos Indians. The remains of a mission complex completed in 1717 sit on the site of the First Mission Church, originally constructed in the early 1600s to the south of the Pueblo. We traded cameras, posed for pictures and captured a bunch of film and digital memories. Pecos National Historic Park was well worth visiting but we had another forty miles of riding to get to our destination. It was time to get back to the welcome center, get on our bikes and ride on out to Route 63 toward Las Vegas.

A few miles down the road we were on a short downhill grade leading us to a quick right hand turn under I–25N. Cattle guard number two, this one with a big crack, would challenge our concentration and attempt to snag a wheel just before the turn. As we came out of the shaded tunnel yet another cattle guard was waiting for us. Everyone around me navigated the crossings without issues; three down and four more to go. Luck and focus would keep our bikes upright over the guards. As I rolled up to the stop sign marking Route 34 I flipped the cue sheet and was reminded about the dog warnings. This is pretty rural and wild so I imagined the dogs would be large and scrappy. Maybe a shepherd mixed with an *ankle–biter* breed.

I turned left on to Route 34 and continued to scan the roadside for potential canine trouble. Over the next mile or so I passed several worthy opponents but fortunately for me they were properly fenced–in nearer to the house than to the road. The dogs barked and put on an aggressive display but the fence would keep them in check.

I kept an eye out over my left shoulder just in case they found an escape route under or through the fence. A few hundred yards ahead on the right were several young hounds stirred up and now fully attentive thanks to my barking friends from the corral. Fortunately for me they only caught a glimpse as I passed and was now two hundred feet beyond their yard. They didn't show much motivation running only about fifty feet before realizing I was no longer a viable target. Not knowing if I would encounter any other dogs I kept watch of the road and the yards. I took nothing for granted.

For the next ten miles I had a roller coaster of a ride as Route 34 paralleled the Interstate. Several large stair–steppers gave me the opportunity to cut loose on the bike and hit speeds near forty miles per hour. The lane was narrow, the traffic light, and the wind was just unpredictable enough to make the hair on the back of my neck stand up as my bike screamed down the steep drops. I strained to keep control of the bars and the wheel straight. With each jolt of the front wheel as it encounters a dip or patched hole I cringed. I knew the carbon fork was strong but I had yet to assign it my full faith and trust. I held my breath through the drops and then squealed and laughed as I reached the safety of the flats. Then another drop would come and it would cycle through all over again. I was scared but wanted to keep on speeding down the hills, eyes wide open and white knuckles choking the bars. Unfortunately for me the descents didn't last and I found myself shifting through the gears to spin my way up several long grades.

On the climbs I watched my heart rate and breathing go up. I was working but unfortunately for me, not very efficiently. Getting out of the saddle was more of a mental advantage than it was at providing any physical benefit. After standing for a portion of a climb I learned to stay put in the seat. Even if I had to drop to the lowest gear, sitting was still the best way to go. I was no longer seventeen so I had to shake the notion of what I used to be able to do on a bike. At least I can remember when I could. But when I do stand on a climb, I like to toss the bike side to side like the pros. It felt really sweet even if it only lasted a few seconds. I imagined it looked impressive too—at least in my own mind.

Even with the wind I could feel the heat beginning to radiate off the road. It was warming up and the jacket and leg warmers would be going into my bike bag when I arrive at the SAG. They did their job and they earned their time off. I just wished I could stow myself into the bag and let someone else pedal the rest of the day for me.

Before I knew it I was at the SAG at a place called the El Alto Bar. This little piece of paradise more closely resembled an abandoned junk yard. An old '40s panel truck with the rear doors wide open was the hangout for a gang of goats. These little climbers stood on whatever they could; cars, stumps, rocks—a cyclist if you let them. The goats were scavenging for food and Margaret's table was an opportunity to graze. They never got close enough to enjoy the spoils. Too many riders beat them to it. They did however come over to me while I was sitting on the ground removing my leg warmers and putting my shoes back on. I thought they were just curious until one started licking my legs. It must have been the salt. Clark snapped a picture of the scene and I remember it would live on my refrigerator back home for quite a while. It makes me laugh to think about it even today.

As per usual SAG etiquette, the gloves came off, hands were cleaned, and then grazing at the SAG could commence. I ate a whole banana and drank my share of Gatorade. I ate a few of those mini blueberry muffins and a few grapes and strawberries. I have no idea where Margaret found such good fresh fruit out here in the middle of the wilderness but she did it.

I did manage to find the restroom in the shack of a building. I remember going into the back door which looked like a candidate for the TV show *Hoarders*. Inside there was a bar, a few patrons, and a server behind the counter. The restroom was located just around the corner and it was befitting for the environment it was in. I tried not to touch anything.

Back outside I finished the SAG ritual by topping off my bottles and putting on my head sock, helmet, shades, and riding gloves. It was time to get moving, but before I pushed off I checked the cue sheet and saw we would climb to the hotel. I thought we were already doing a fair bit of climbing. I was expecting to work even harder now.

Out of the gravel lot leaving the goats and their junk field behind me, I eased back into the pedals and clipped in. A short climb brought me to a crossover and back to the north side of the Interstate. The bridge was framed with a pair of cattle guards number four and five which were expertly navigated and left behind without a thought. It was getting warm, the sun now high in the sky. Little did I know I would soon be pining to be back on the Interstate. For the next fifteen miles I pedaled up and over the elevation extremes of this lost highway.

The Interstate was relatively smooth and flat. The problem was I was not on it. Route 34 was old, pocked with holes, cracks, a few patches, and hot tar spots. There was also loose gravel scattered across the surface to make it more uncomfortable. This was my playground for most of the remaining ride to Las Vegas. Strong crosswinds, heat, and steep hills all conspiring to slow me down.

The Interstate pavement was new and the designers had the mind to level it out as best possible instead of conforming to the natural contours of the terrain. Over any given mile of road the Interstate would either run slightly up or down while the road I was on was as erratic as could be; endless steep climbs with matching drops. The contrast between the two roads was quite striking.

What I wouldn't give to be back on the Interstate right now. I would only have to cross a small barbed wire fence, scramble down a steep hill across a ditch, and back up to the roadway. *Should be easy, I just might do it*, I thought. But then I would crest the hill and put all my attention into accelerating through the gears and speeding toward the bottom to carry as much momentum up the other side as possible. Then I would be challenged to quickly move through the gears before coming to an abrupt stop. Gravity is so unforgiving.

Two of the more memorable moments through this section included the dead animal carcass I barely missed just shy of one of the steep crests. It was one of the few times I was happy to inhale the stench of the dead. I was breathing heavily looking down at the road surface just feet ahead of my front wheel oblivious to most everything else. The fowl odor caused me to jerk my head back in time to see the road kill and I inched by it without contact. It was likely a black–tailed prairie dog. Not a highlight but a memorable moment none the less.

The second moment came on an exceptionally steep descent as I broke out into the open revealing a near vertical drop off the left edge of the road spilling into a deep gorge sixty feet below. There was no guardrail and I began to feel like I was at risk of careening over the edge. The sensation was as if I were riding on the edge when in fact I was nearly ten feet away from it. My mind was trying to tell me I was in great peril when I surmised it was probably my uneasiness with heights. Riding at speed just compounded the sensation.

The thrill of the descent was at risk of losing out to the agony of the climb. As the day wore on I was wearing out. My legs were tired and the fun meter had been pegged. I was also beginning to tire of the craggy rocky brown scenery. A change was in order and it would be coming soon.

Eight miles shy of town I was finally out of the oscillating ribbon of road. I was on a pleasingly fast and long but shallow descent enabling me to speed with some confidence of control. This was my reward for the last fifteen miles. And I earned it.

Ben Dudley, another one of the recumbent riders, passed me and was quickly getting smaller in my view. He was in his element in the flats and downhill's but the climbs were a struggle for him as well as for the tandems. So far the hills had been a struggle for me too.

We had a pair of tandems and five recumbent bikes on tour and each one was unique in design. The tandems while being heavy and long were able to be disassembled quite easily and fit into a custom bike box just a bit larger than a standard bike box. Handy when you needed to travel with the bigger bike.

With the exception of Kathy's recumbent most of them looked like small wheeled stingray–styled choppers I rode as a kid. Sleek, speedy, and just plain cool. A few had wind screens and the others took the breeze right in the face like the rest of us. And somehow the bikes seemed to fit the personality of the rider's themselves. Until coming on this tour I would not have guessed there were so many unique bikes. The variety would keep the mechanics on their toes.

I would need to cross over the Interstate once again so near the bottom of the descent I had to scrub off the speed and prepare to turn and cross the final set of cattle guards framing the overpass. With the cattle guards behind me I dropped down another gentle descent on to the frontage road and was now on a good piece of pavement level with the Interstate, I would begin a gradual incline putting my legs back to work for a few more miles.

I kept telling myself it was almost over. The only problem is my mind decides the ride is over before I get there leaving my tired legs to figure it out on their own. And the legs don't do so well without the brain running interference or providing thoughts of encouragement.

For the final time I crossed over I–25N and carefully followed the cue sheet to avoid going off route. I guess this also helped to keep my brain engaged, not allowing it to dwell on the other inputs my body was sending to it.

I rolled past the Dairy Queen which was highly unusual for me. It wasn't too spectacular anyway as it looked like the seating was mostly located outside in the parking lot. I was tired and planned to stop only at the hotel where I could step off the bike for more than a brief few minutes. Through town I worked my way up a short incline and eventually transitioned to a gentle downhill exiting the congested core. At the less populated edge of town I found the hotel. The Days Inn was nothing fancy, but for this rider it was a welcome sight. After five hours five minutes covering 74.48 miles and averaging 14.6 miles per hour it was welcome indeed.

Las Vegas was established in 1835 after a group of settlers received a land grant from the Mexican government. The town was laid out with a central plaza surrounded by buildings serving as fortifications in the event of an attack. This was commonly referred to as traditional Spanish Colonial style. The town prospered as a popular stop on the Santa Fe Trail. During the Mexican–American War in 1846, Stephen Kearny delivered an address in the plaza claiming New Mexico for the United States.

When the railroad came to Las Vegas in 1880 the town boomed, quickly becoming one of the largest cities in the American Southwest. It also brought with it the lawlessness and notorious types including the likes of Jesse James, Billy the Kid, Wyatt Earp, and Handsome Harry the Dancehall Rustler. Historian Ralph Emerson Twitchell once said, "Without exception there was no town which harbored a more disreputable gang of desperadoes and outlaws than did Las Vegas."

At the turn–of–the–century Las Vegas had all of the modern features including electric street cars, the Duncan Opera House, a library, and a grand hotel. In the mid–'50s the railroad industry declined and the population remained relatively unchanged ever since at just over 14,400 residents.

For a town the size of Las Vegas it's surprising they have more than nine hundred buildings listed on the National Register of Historic Places. Many are deteriorating while others have been restored or are awaiting restoration. Probably one of the most notable restored structures is the Plaza Hotel, built in 1881. This hotel was the site of the first reunion of Teddy Roosevelt's Rough Riders in 1899.

Las Vegas has also been the setting for many Hollywood films and television series beginning with the silent westerns to the iconic 1969 film, *Easy Rider*, starring Peter Fonda and Dennis Hopper. A few other notable movies filmed in Las Vegas were *Red Dawn*, *Wyatt Earp*, featuring Kevin Costner, the *Astronaut Farmer*, *Wild Hogs*, and *No Country for Old Men*. The versatility of the terrain and the town enabled Las Vegas to be a stand–in for scenes in Kansas, Wyoming, and Mexico.

After wiping down the bike, showering, and doing a bit of *Sink Laundry* it was time for Route Rap. We were in the rather strangely decorated lobby; a cross between southwestern style comfort and a taxidermist museum. I think I saw a Jackalope somewhere high on one of the ledges amongst the dream catchers, Indian wool blankets, western themed paintings, and a few other articles you would expect to find in this part of the country.

We listened to Tracy talk about the day's ride; she praised a few for their tenacity and others for keeping their humor or stopping to partake in a flat–tire party for a fellow rider. Tracy saw everything out on the road and we benefited from her keen observational skills. Most riders didn't even know she was watching, but she was—watching everyone one of us.

Besides the basic Route Rap agenda, which was a brief walk–through of the cue sheet for the following day's ride, Tracy could often find some nugget of rider news to share; someone's birthday, an anniversary, a special achievement or it might include something as simple as a presentation of a favorite candy bar to one of the riders. She involved the entire group in these little moments and turned them into lasting memories.

I was impressed at not only her attention to detail but her depth of caring for her riders. She studied and learned much about all of us as well a she learned the route and the adventure touring business. Every day was another lesson, an example of how to operate a successful business, exceeding customer expectations, and developing a network of lasting friends. Tracy could succeed at any business because of her exceptional people skills. She loved to make your day memorable and to be the best at what she does. And even at this early stage of our journey I think it is fair to say she is the best I have seen across my personal and professional endeavors.

Tracy would use the meeting time to reenergize the group and to share with us cautionary details that would prove useful on our eastward migration. At times she would remind us of proper trip etiquette like, "Don't leave each day without signing out," or "If your bags are too heavy send some stuff home!" It was never boring at Route Rap and everyone enjoyed her. On occasion she would let Trevor handle Route Rap but not tonight, not in Las Vegas.

The highlight of her Route Rap presentation to the riders was a date with the *Wall*, a very steep climb cut into a rock cliff. I was hoping the hype of the climb exceeded reality but according to Tracy it would last a full three quarters of a mile. Even if it were a beast to climb I could manage for that distance. I'm sure I could. I hope so. Tomorrow's ride to Tucumcari is a long century and we will climb another three to four thousand feet like we did today. Wind will also be a factor across the open plains.

Dinner would be across the gravel lot and down about half a block at a place called Pino's. It had to be the proximity to the hotel because it sure wasn't the food that brought us there. We ate family style on overcooked spaghetti pasta bathed in a water–thin pasta sauce; or more accurately a pasta soup. Surprisingly we all ate our fill. The day had taken its toll on us and our bodies seemed to recognize adequate carbs, even if our palettes thought differently. Disappointment crossed my mind when it occurred to me this could very well be the best food the town has to offer. We would be back for breakfast in the morning to see if they could master that meal. I was neither excited nor looking forward to returning to Pino's. Not tomorrow, not ever.

Back at the hotel room I worked on my post cards and journaling while having the usual pillow talk with Clark. From what he read to me about his trip the year before, the ride to Tucumcari can be real tough. It was hot last year and tomorrow's forecast is predicted to be hot as well. The saving grace for me is we will drop out of the high elevations of Las Vegas—6,424 to 6,533 feet depending on where you are standing—and get to something a bit more agreeable with this rider. Pink Floyd echoed in my ear as I drifted off…..*All in all it's just a brick in the wall.*

Day 17: Las Vegas to Tucumcari (110 miles)

Pino's managed to serve up another uneventful meal. I was cold and still a bit tired so I looked for the safest options and downed some whole grain carbs, a bit of scrambled eggs, and coffee. Not quite what I was hoping for but it would have to get me through the day. The walk back to the hotel in the brisk morning air helped to elevate my attentiveness after the coffee kick–starter.

We started out today's ride in cool temperatures, clear skies, and barely a breeze. This would be our second–longest day so far, and pacing ourselves would be very important. We would cover 110 miles beginning with rolling grassy prairie and transitioning into desert–like conditions for the last seventy miles of the day.

We started out by backtracking through town on Grand Avenue, eventually finding our way onto Route 104 were we would continue up and over I–25N. There was a troubling note on our cue sheet advising there were no rest rooms or services for 75.9 miles. We were heading into the unknown, the three SAGs our only support for the day. I also found it interesting how I could ignore the cue sheet for most of the day. Our travels would continue on Route 104 all the way to the hotel in Tucumcari.

It didn't take long and we were winding our way up hill to a sweeping view of Las Vegas in what was now taking on the look of a shallow valley. The buildings were beginning to run together forming a continuous mass of blended shades of white and gray. The distance was stealing away the building's actual colors; it does the same thing to the mountains giving them a more purple–gray tone instead of the true green of their vegetation.

The entire group was staying a bit tighter together this morning. It was probably a mix of the cold and the climbing right out of the hotel, but I would also believe the distance of the ride gave reason to set a comfortable if not slower pace. I found it interesting not a single tree or mountain could be seen across the prairie. In fact, the tallest objects besides horses and cows were the power poles and a lone cellular tower. Riders commented on the huddling cows by the tower, but we could not think of a reason why. Maybe they feel more secure next to a taller object like a little kid clinging to the leg of a parent. They sure were not going to tell us.

The road meandered over the rolling hills dropping us briefly between the high points limiting our views. On the top of the crests we could see much farther, but the land still intersected with the soft blue cloudless sky in a distant blur. Maybe it was the absence of the trees, but something made the landscape seem artificial, almost unnatural. I couldn't quite figure it out but then again I'd never been here before so I might be trying to impose my own sense of normal onto the landscape.

Sparse field grass, it could have been wild wheat, made up most of the vegetation. Along the roadside weeds could be seen squeaking out a minimal existence in the dry loose soil. Most of the fields were framed in barbed wire or other field fencing. The metal strands appeared aged with rusty brown hues, the wooden posts tired and weathered. Gates were rare as were roadways or drives angling out into the grazing fields. Farm buildings and other structures were few and those I could see were set back as much as a half mile from the road.

Over the next few miles the structures grew in number and moved progressively closer to the road. A small animal barn, a basic single story box of a house, a storage building, each revealing their details and allowing us to speculate on what life in this part of the world is like. A failing roof on an old barn, the weathered gray of old wood plank siding telling a story of abandonment and a lack of either the resources or the desire to fix it. A quick stop to capture the images with my camera and I was back on my way.

As we progressed along the route the overall condition of the buildings seemed to improve. There were now at least one or two structures per mile and a definite shift from out–buildings to houses was evident. A definite sign the population density was on the rise.

We entered a transitional zone full of elevation changes and an increase in large rock formations. In the middle of this area we descended into a deep valley full of short but broad–branched trees and rocky soil with little grass. To our right we could see a deeper and more erratic series of valleys and gorges with even more tree–like vegetation. Farther in the background were the southern reaches of the Rocky Mountains. On our left the gentle rolling plains played out to the horizon; the grass thicker and more friendly to the grazing livestock. The road shoulder was mostly loose gravel but traffic was light affording us the opportunity to use the entire lane; sometimes more.

We climbed out of the depression and back into the familiar prairie grass on more level ground. We had actually skirted to the north of the rugged terrain and continued tracking in a southeasterly direction. A gentle right hand bend complete with fenced fields on both sides led us another quarter mile farther where we came along a mobile home and several rustic farm structures right up against the road; this was Laguna Huerfana. We had reached the SAG. As I prepared to turn off into the dirt I saw Tracy maybe a hundred feet in front of me holding a sign with the big bold words, "1,000 Miles!" This was a definite treat. We had accomplished quite a milestone and Tracy was squealing and hollering to make sure we knew it.

Looking around the SAG I noticed lots of riders smiling and of course gorging on the treats laid out on the small folding table. In some respects it was like any other SAG but we were reminded by Tracy strict target times were in force and we needed to exit by ten. I took a photo looking back down the road and could see another rider in a yellow jersey. They were just a dot in the distance but it made the scene all the more impressive.

The ground was extremely flat; the valley to the south was completely out of view but in the distance again were the flat topped Rockies, colored dull blue–purple just above the distant horizon. Nothing but weeds and patches of dried grass mixed in with clumps of green and exposed rocky soil surrounded the SAG. There were no tall trees for miles except for those planted by the farmer to provide shade to the house. There were several of the stunted short and bushy trees maybe ten feet tall scattered about the fields to break up the grassy areas.

Wooden cattle corrals were adjacent to the low and weathered barn but all of the cattle were across the street. They were shiny black, few in number, and secured behind a wire fence to keep them off the roadway.

The sky transitioned from a medium blue to an almost white as it met the horizon. Where the road vanished you could just make out the slightest of a distant mountain range. Power poles stood unchallenged as the tallest features above the landscape; flat with no means of resisting a wind.

Out of the SAG the Rockies to the right continued to grow in size and the details of the valley in between were being revealed. About a mile farther the road turned ninety degrees to the left and I began to pick up speed. Small ranches consisting of dilapidated barns, wind vanes, and mobile homes became more frequent; several within western neighborly range of each other. I could no longer see the mountains as I continued the gradual descent along a straight road, stair–stepping down the visible ridges. The stunted trees swarmed around the road and became densely packed in the fields. It looked as if I was in a valley but the road continued to drop.

There were rocks as big as pillows intermittently scattered along the recesses sloping away from the roadway. I started to slow so I began to pedal harder. I was on a series of shallow inclines and descents riding about fourteen miles an hour. Just the right conditions to observe my surroundings.

Still descending the road bent off to the right. I passed a sign for Trujillo, and then an old adobe brick constructed set of barns to the right of the road. I suspected they were abandoned as some of the metal and wood roof framing were missing or had collapsed.

Ahead and to the left I could see the heavily forested area beginning to mount up. The terrain was actively changing even at the slow speeds observed from a bike. Signs with squiggly lines and other warnings let me know the straight road had officially ended.

On my right stood a pair of interesting houses built less than fifty feet off the road. They featured lush green but small lawns very much out of place for the rural standard. Both yards were framed with ornate metal arches patterned after wagon wheels between stone columns forming quite the impressive fence. This was the town of Trujillo. Don't blink; it's that small and hardly deserving of a sign. Maybe the descendants of the town's namesake live in the fancy little houses.

Trujillo was about thirty miles from Las Vegas, and I wondered what their life was like living in such a remote area. If someone was around, I might have asked. Then I saw the diamond shaped sign with the symbol for a steep descent; the box truck sliding off a triangle warning me about what I was going to experience for the next three miles. I was descending from 6,500 feet and it was beginning to drop quickly. To me this was a mountain but to the locals this road down was known as Corazon Hill.

The large hill to my left had grown to more than sixty feet above me. A guardrail appeared on my right along with a series of warning signs with arrows pointing left, one spelled out "Falling Rocks" followed by more left arrows. The road continued to bend left and I was beginning to see what was beyond the hill; little snippets of the mountains and the valley below.

Trujillo must spend all of its money on signage because the cattle guard even had one. Well, one in print and another showing the silhouette of a cow. The right side of the landscape dropped off quickly and I was now even with the tree tops. To my left the gentle mound had transformed into a sheer rock wall standing forty feet tall complete with full sized trees that towered menacingly over my head.

On the right a sign with the graphical image of a mountain dumping rocks on a car came into view. I get it. If you don't ride off the edge you risk getting hit on the head or crushed by rocks.

Then I saw the cattle guard. It was a dangerous and rough monstrosity, the asphalt stopped inches short of the metal grading and it had a long slotted opening running parallel with the road about three feet from the white stripe which was my lane. The crack was wide enough for a narrow road bike wheel to fall through and I'm sure it was looking to catch a rider. Should a cyclist hit the crack just right it would likely flip them straight over the handle bars. Disheartening to know this would likely be the best case scenario. The cattle guard ran about a foot beyond the road and then it was boxed in with a rust colored vertical pipe standing a foot above the grade. You could hardly see it but if you hit it with your pedal or wheel it would likely be the worst case scenario for you. D–A–N–G–E–R–O–U–S! I would roll slowly and cautiously over the metal cattle guard with both shoes unclipped from the pedals just in case.

A hundred yards past the cattle guard was a humungous bolder maybe twenty feet across each dimension precariously perched above on the forty–five degree incline ten feet off the road. It looked like it could slide off with just a push, maybe the weight of a small bird landing on it. The gorge to my right was full of trees and had not yet fully revealed its depth. I was picking up speed quickly and riding the brakes to maintain control. The dust on the rims caused them to squeal before they grabbed.

I wasn't kidding when I said the white stripe was my bike lane. To the right was loose gravel and then if I was lucky a decent guardrail. At times the guardrail was only a foot off the white line leaving me precious little room to operate. The main road was only two lanes and very narrow so sharing the road would be non–negotiable. I would need to take the lane at times or pull off to the side of the road and hug the guardrail if I had more than a foot of shoulder.

Motorists would have to understand. I hope they will understand. And trucks, well I hope I don't encounter any. I guess the only positive was the signs said it would last for three miles. The mountain descent did have several wider areas separating the road from the guardrail however they were nothing but loose gravel and didn't always have the guardrail or at least a good one. They did however give me a place to take photos and to catch my breath.

We descended the high prairie through part of the Rocky Mountains. The roads were steep, but the views of the desert floor more than a thousand feet below were amazing. In the distance the colors were muted tones and without detail.

Aside from the mechanical sounds emanating from the bike all I could hear was the pinch of sand and pebbles exiting from between my tires and the road. Of course there was the wash of wind racing past my ears, which I could only abate by turning my head sideways. Of course when I stopped I was able to hear the quiet of this remote area. The sound of the wind blowing the sparse grasses or a lone bird chirping was the best nature could offer.

Occasionally a lone truck would whine and rumble as it struggled and shifted gears climbing the mountain road farther ahead of my position. A few times I could see the truck a mile or more away much farther down the valley. A little dot of movement growing larger as it approached and then disappeared behind the mountain folds. The sound carries quite a distance and as it ascended out of the valley it was hard to tell from what direction it came.

The steep windy grades permitted thrilling speeds to be achieved if you were able to grip the bars and avoid the brakes. Some of the riders said they were going more than forty–six miles per hour down the mountain, but I stayed well below the posted speed limit of twenty–five to thirty miles per hour. The thought of falling off my bike at speed was enough to keep me under control.

At several points along the rapid descent there were sections of guardrail where the ground beneath was so eroded the vertical opening between the rail and the ground was more than three feet tall. Considering the near vertical drops beyond the guardrail, thoughts of falling off the bike and sliding underneath the rail to my demise seemed more plausible than they should. Some of the rails were severely damaged from past impacts and a few of the support posts were almost completely exposed due to erosion. So now I'm beginning to doubt the ability of the guardrail to keep me on the mountain should I crash into the steel strip. These are not the thoughts a cyclist should have while trying to enjoy a scenic descent; not at all.

I stopped a few times to get off the bike and shoot some photos. At least I picked a safe section with adequate guardrails and a few feet of visible earth on the other side. There's no reason to give fate an opportunity to trip me up.

I managed to capture an interesting scene across a gorge maybe 1,500 feet away. The mountain was steep; maybe a forty degree incline of scrub brush covering about half the brown rocks and dirt. Jutting out almost level to me was a unique rock formation. It looked like a section of a concrete highway; a flat surface with a shear vertical walls dropping off fifteen to forty feet farther down the mountain. It ran about a mile or more laterally and then disappeared into the mountainside in both directions. The right side formed an arch like a bridge. It was but a single odd formation on the entire hillside and it surely has a proper geological description for this layer of rock appearing so different from the rest. I just didn't know what it is.

I panned my camera around to look directly through the mountain pass to capture a view of the valley below. It was miles out in front of me and it was now possible to see the flat table top surfaces of the distant mountains. Both sides were level, the left range showing off the road I was riding on cut deep into its side maybe another half mile away and several hundred feet below. The section of road I was looking at had no shoulder and I could only hope it had a railing. So far on my descent I passed sections void of guardrails for a hundred feet or more. Obviously they are either short on funds or figure if you can't descend without the guardrails maybe you shouldn't ride the roads.

I was not comfortable on the road at all. My hands were fatiguing from the strangle–hold I had on the bars, the rough surface sent shocks up through my entire body and my head was bouncing around so much it was hard to focus. I had to remember to keep my mouth open to avoid rattling my teeth. And I held my breath way too long and then gasped like I had just surfaced from a long underwater swim. *When is this ride off the mountain going to end?* Obviously it would not end soon enough for me.

Over the first mile and a half I had given up five hundred feet of elevation. This is about the length of one and a half football fields. The grade averaged about 6.3 percent but a few sections were much steeper.

The corners were sharp and I was blind to oncoming traffic for left turns. The few cars approaching from behind seemed to pass in the faster sections or where the railing was non–existent; as if I didn't have enough going on with the road and the missing or deficient guardrails. In the turns the roads were rutted from the braking of heavy trucks. Loose gravel was everywhere and I could feel it shooting out from under my tires and at times it caused the bike to slide without warning.

I did not like riding so close to the guardrail and not being able to see the bottom below. All I could see is the valley way below rolling out away from the steep drop off. I was also concerned about the rocky walls to my left. They were eighty feet tall at points with nearly vertical faces of fractured rocks and an abundance of loose material, rocks, and boulders perched on top. There was abundant evidence of rock slides on the road and the uphill shoulder. Would I have enough time to react if a rock came down or would it just knock me out and over the rail? I hope I don't have to learn the answer first hand.

The road continued to wind around the mountain ledge until I could see the valley floor coming to me. I was beginning to feel some relief. A few more turns and hard braking; the road was still very steep and the descent fast.

Then I noticed I was not getting any closer to the bottom. The valley floor was not flat; it was dropping right along with me. I had much more elevation to give up and I was now in a section lacking a place to pull off. I had just given my hands a rest and immediately I was flirting with speeds in excess of thirty miles an hour.

Then I saw the second cattle guard on a very quick stretch of the road. I was hard on the brakes, the rims squealing with contempt, but I was able to rein the speed in and get safely across the guard without issue. The tension rolled through my body like a wave from my hands, into my core, and finally exiting through my legs to the pedals as if it were electricity looking to find ground. This cattle guard was marginally better than the first, but then again I zipped past it much faster than the first one. I released the brakes and accelerated, trying to balance between resting my hands and speed control. I passed a sign indicating seventy–one miles to Tucumcari.

The descent varied in pitch and it snaked in and out of the contours of the mountain. At times I thought I reached the bottom only to round another bend and find more drops. Then the guardrail ended and I was beginning to see I was just yards above the terrain to my right. I was near the bottom and my hands and the brakes were finally able to relax. After several miles of working my hands, my legs were going back into service. I would begin to question my lack of appreciation for the down hills. I would have plenty of time to think about it as I pedaled the rest of the distance to Tucumcari.

Coming down the mountain I was so focused on controlling my bike I hardly noticed the others riding near me. I know they were there but the level of concentration required caused me to tune out a lot. I know Greg, Betty, and Lynn were in front of me and I could see them dotting the road in the lower portion of the descent but I don't think I was looking much beyond twenty yards in front of my wheel on the steeper sections except to sneak a peek over the edge down into the distant valley.

I was now onto the valley floor 1,200 feet below the town of Trujillo. It was a quick descent on a very straight section of Route 104. For the next six miles the road would be reasonably level and straight.

It was ninety–five degrees in the valley and the winds were strong. Both would prove to be a challenge. I quickly moved away from the mountain and was surrounded by miles of the dry desert floor full of rocks and exposed soil, patches of wild grass, and small scrub trees.

In the distance were more mountains. Some standing alone while others formed more of a chain. They were visible in every direction with just a few clear gaps between. Some of the mountains were truncated with low flat tops while others retained more pointed and erratic profiles. It was quite a contrast to the western side of the Rocky Mountains. I was wet with sweat which caused me to drink my water and Gatorade at an accelerated rate.

Without warning the climbing began and sweat was now rolling off my brow. I was working and so were the others around me. Greg was about fifty yards up front with Betty and Lynn just behind. Gray trailed behind me and we pretty much moved as a herd through the terrain. There were other riders several hundred yards ahead and behind but it was not possible to tell who they were. If we came upon a rider with troubles we would stop. We believed the other riders would do the same for us.

Just beyond the mile forty–four marker, in what was basically the middle of nowhere, was a sign for Trementina and a Post Office. The road was unpaved and I could see no buildings for quite a distance. It turns out Trementina is an unincorporated community whose name is Spanish for turpentine. The name was in reference to the pitch of the pinyon pine which was used by Spanish Americans as a folk medicine and as a substitute for chewing gum. It was so sparsely populated and many of the buildings were abandoned giving it the look of a ghost town. Nothing to see and no reason to stop, we pushed on toward the second SAG.

A few steel buildings dotted the landscape as we approached a turn to the south. Off to our right was a DOT supply yard with mounds of gravel and stacked sections of large silver corrugated pipe. It seemed strange for it to be in the wide open instead of closer to where the materials would be used. I hadn't crossed a ditch so I couldn't even guess where the pipe would be used.

A minute later we were rolling into the SAG at a small rest area. A modest protective awning sheltered a single picnic table where we would be dining on peanut butter and jelly sandwiches. It would prove to be a protein rich fuel stop for our bodies and a chance to refill our CamelBak and water bottles.

Since there were no restrooms you couldn't be too shy about making a nature call. By this point in the trip it wasn't a big of a deal for most riders, provided you could find an obstruction or enough distance from the group. This area was a bit restrictive because a barbed wire fence ran right behind the awning, not allowing much in the way of privacy by trekking off into the field. Fortunately the CrossRoads truck was strategically parked and riders afforded each other the courtesy of a bit of privacy. You give and take.

At the rest area was a wooden sign just like the one found at the Continental Divide. It was the Official Scenic Historic Marker for the Canadian Escarpment and it contained the following information:

Prominent landform of northeastern New Mexico that extends for almost 100 miles between Las Vegas and Clayton. From this point, the grasslands of the High Plains reach northwestward to the foot of the Southern Rocky Mountains which rise to elevations of more than 13,000 feet. Elevation here is 6,300 feet.

We had climbed 1,100 feet since we first set our wheels on the valley floor. Now I know why I was working and sweating so hard to get to this point. That's quite a bit of climbing in twelve miles.

It had been a long day so far and the heat was raising our concern for the next sixty miles. Besides the distance we had the *Wall* to contend with twenty miles farther up the road. No time to waste. Tracy or Margaret would be closing the SAG at eleven forty–five as per the target time limit noted on our cue sheets. A quick application of sunscreen and I was off with the group consisting of Lynn, Gray, Betty and Gary. Kathy and Peter on their recumbent bikes along with and Helen and Don Reeves on their tandem zoomed past. So did several others but we were solidly in the middle of the group. We had a long way to go and today would not be a good day to race.

My group took turns leading allowing those in tow to get a bit of rest. Lynn and Gary had the aero bars allowing them to tuck in tighter, creating a lower and narrower profile to slice through the air more efficiently. Gray still had fenders on his bike so he was clearly the least aero efficient rider. He made up for it with his cycling strength and never was a cause for the group to slow.

We talked as we rode and since traffic was almost non–existent we rode in two–by–two formation whenever it was safe. Our riding conversations were both retrospective and about the remaining miles. The *Wall* was a huge part of the conversation. We had been assured it would be a challenge but discussing it seemed to take the edge off. It was only seven–tenths of a mile anyway. We also shared ideas for getting more comfortable, spinning versus grinding in a high gear, and the condition of our seats. It seemed several riders were getting a little raw in the saddle.

I was continuing to have hot foot issues from the prior day's ride. With so many miles to go today I was trying various methods to reel in the foot pain. Since it was mostly my right foot I would unclip it and pedal with my toe or the ball of my foot; anything to get off the pressure point. I tried pedaling with the left foot only while the right foot dangled but it was a futile attempt to meet my needs. Not to mention it was just dumb. I would eventually reach down and loosen the shoe to find some relief. Better, but not quite the result I hoped for. I tried to focus on my heart rate, cadence, and staying in formation.

Both sides of the valley were boxed in with a continuous flat–topped rocky range maybe a hundred to 150 feet tall. We were much closer to the rocks on our right and could see wire fencing running along and up the steep inclines. We passed a lone mailbox to our left, directly across from a gravel drive that disappeared into the foot of the mountain. I had forgotten people really do live this far out in the wilderness. If not for the paved road it would have looked as it did hundreds of years earlier.

We rolled through some enjoyable descents and began to ride parallel with a rugged mountain to our right. It was more of a single standalone formation as we got right up to it. Full of mammoth sized boulders and loose earth it seemed much larger than it was. As we came around to the far side of the formation we saw the object of our conversations; seventy miles into the ride, we came to the *Wall*.

It was a three–quarter–mile–long cut straight up the face of a mountain with about a nine percent grade. Red rock walls lined both sides and no wind made its way through the channel making for even more grueling conditions. The horizontal sediment lines in the rock walls accentuated the angle of the incline as they disappeared into the ground along the pavement. It was steep, my pedals turned slowly, and I was out of gear options. All I could do was grunt it out. Even my bike was making grinding noises as if to protest the climb.

Betty and Greg managed to tough it out making it all the way to the top without stopping. I could not quite make it all the way without sending my heart rate right off the chart so I stopped about midway up to catch my breath. I wiped my sweaty hands off on my jersey and hopped off the bike. I also used the moment to snap a few pictures as it would seem the conditions I would eventually describe to other people might not be so believable.

At the top I stopped again so we could all gather as a team. The view back down the mountain was incredible. We were now at the top and the valley below seemed distant and small. A picture was all I needed as proof I was finally on the top. It felt good and the well–earned Gatorade went down easy.

It took quite a bit of energy to take on the *Wall* and win. The heat, the stillness, and the radiant thermals coming up off the road were taxing. Greg's charge up the *Wall* about wiped him out for the remaining forty miles. I was pretty used up but I was going to manage with what little I had in my reserves.

The rest of the day we climbed giant stair–stepped hills and fought the wind. We did enjoy some very interesting and vibrant red rock formations and patches of small wild flowers as we rode. Had I been riding solo this would have been very lonely and mentally challenging. Even if we did not speak it was comfort enough to know there were others with me.

I continued trying to remedy my hotfoot, I caught glimpses of Greg stretched out on his aero bars as if he were splayed out on the ground while I chatted with the others. I could also hear everyone breathing and the mechanical sounds of shifting up and down through the gears from all the bikes. Not all were shifting crisply. It had been a hard day for the bikes as well. Rick who was riding sweep would likely have a long day fixing and tuning bikes for the following day's ride to Dalhart. This was real work on the bike but we were knocking down the miles.

Finally the third SAG came into view at a store with restrooms. It was good to have working plumbing and privacy. The mood at the SAG was a bit more subdued. Everyone was tired and looking forward to stepping off the bike for the day. But today was quite an accomplishment; one I will not soon forget. Margaret did her best to raise us up and get us down the road. I grabbed a granola bar and a banana and was set for the last thirty miles.

The final stretch was a continuation of rolling climbs. I fell in line behind Lynn who trailed Gary and Gray. Betty would ride beside me at times so we chatted to pass the time. We were averaging just shy of fifteen miles an hour, which I thought was impressive given the conditions and the terrain. The sky remained cloud free allowing the sun to drive the temperatures higher. Without sunglasses it would have been very hard on the eyes as well.

I wore a pair of black prescription sunglasses in a sporty wraparound Harley–Davidson branded frame complete with flame graphics. With the frame in near contact with my skin around my eyes, ample dust protection was provided. They also eliminate any chance of glaring sunlight getting to backside of the dark gray lens.

The only issue I had with the shades; they were a single focus lens correcting my vision for distance. Great for looking down the road but useless when it came to looking at the instructions on the cue sheet or reading my digital computer displays. I made due by tilting my head up slightly, squinting, and looking under the bottom edge of the frames. Sometimes I had to take a hand off the bars to lift them up but not so much it caused any concern. Things were blurry but still legible.

These shades were ideal for cycling and they also were a conversation starter off the bike. I remember back in Florida a few months before the trip a construction supervisor noticed them and asked if I was a cycle rider. Yes. Yes I was. I rode bikes, just not the bikes he was thinking about.

I could see a rider about a half mile ahead with fifteen miles to go but there would be no way our group could catch them. I'm sure others behind us thought the same thing. I don't recall anyone else passing us before the hotel. The fast riders were already gone so there would be no feelings of defeat in the final miles.

With my focus on the hotfoot I did not think much about the squirming I was doing on the seat. My tail had enough and it was beginning to tell me so. I stood up a few times where I could and repositioned on the seat to settle things down. I would need to address both of these issues tonight so tomorrow would be a more comfortable ride.

A few miles outside of Tucumcari I stopped to take a picture of a sign marking the elevation at 4,085 feet with the tag line *Tree City USA*. I thought for sure someone made a mistake because there were not many trees to be seen. Low raggedy bushes yes, but trees, seriously? Then I noticed a smaller line of text "Arbor Day Foundation – 2 Years" so maybe it was part of a tree planting project. Either way it got my attention.

Farther ahead I could see a huge white letter *T* on the side of the mountain overlooking the man–made structures forming the town of Tucumcari. As it turns out this mountain is special, it has its own story, a legend if you will, and later in the evening I would come to know it in detail. When I pencil in my journal entries before turning in for the night, I'll make sure to include the Legend of Tucumcari Mountain so it doesn't disappear from my experience.

We were on the cusp of completing 110 miles in a day. It was our third official century of the tour. After seven and a half hours of desert riding, we arrived in Tucumcari.

As we crossed Main Street we were just minutes from our destination. The final left turn across a patch of loose gravel into the lot at the MicroTel Inn was the last bit of precaution I would have to take before I unclipped from the pedals and rolled to a stop. The lot outside the hotel was nothing short of plain; just a dusty dry gravel and partially paved expanse fitting right in with the other business lots.

As I stood stationary over my bike I proceeded with my now normal end–of–ride routine of unclipping my helmet strap, checking the ride stats on my Cat Eye computers, then peeling off my fingerless cycling gloves. Next I would chat up the ride with those around me, wipe the sweat off my brow, lean my bike against the building, and walk into the hotel lobby to sign–in making the day's ride official. It was officially hot and I was officially drained.

I finished with a solid average speed of 14.67 miles per hour. I could finally put up the bike and shower the road dust and sweat off my body. I would even do a bit of sink laundry. Just stepping off the bike renewed me. After cleaning up I would feel like a new man. I'd settle for just a cleaner me in street clothes.

I gave some thought to addressing my hot foot issues and the best options I could come up with were to double up the socks, add a pair of those Dr. Scholl's insert pads, or play with the positioning of the shoe cleats to move the pressure point and hope to find a comfortable balance. I decided to play around with the cleats and ended up having to do some shoe sole carving with the blade on my multi–tool to get to where I thought the cleats needed to be. Tomorrow I could test out the changes and if it needs to be further adjusted it would only take a few minutes of sitting idle along the roadside.

Having to deal with saddle issues is a real challenge and even describing it can be most embarrassing. But one thing you learn when distance cycling with a group like CrossRoads is you shed those barriers of shyness and self–consciousness and do what is necessary. Sometimes it means finding a bush—or another cyclist—for cover to relieve yourself in the desert or it may entail standing around at a SAG reaching down your shorts to apply another soothing layer of butt cream while conversing with fellow riders. And to think this happens within the first few days of the ride. Go figure.

And you ask what more acts of embarrassment could possibly happen to stun those not familiar with life on the bike? So setting pride and embarrassment aside I'm going to crack the vault and unleash one more of those secrets for those following along. Feel free to laugh, gasp, or skip a few paragraphs to the word "SAFE" if you choose. I'm writing it anyway. After all when I'm old and forgetting more than I do now maybe someone will read this book to me and I can be reminded of all those embarrassing things I did and laugh again until I cry happy tears knowing I did live a bit like a rebel when I was able. Of course this rebel always wore a helmet.

When you have saddle issues you can feel around your backside to check for ride ending blisters but anything less requires a visual inspection to assess the damage. Like a doctor you need to diagnose and prepare a treatment game plan. Ah but how do you get a good look at the landscape? Maybe pull off your bike mirror and aim around. A good idea if you think about it. The helmet or eyeglass mirror is likely too small but a decent sized bar–end mirror would be priceless. Unfortunately I never thought about this option until after the tour so I looked elsewhere. No pun intended.

Good thing for hotels with those narrow but tall mirrors running from the floor toward the ceiling. My inspection option was in plain sight hanging right on the wall allowing me a full view. Even before I put the words out there you are beginning to get the visual. A visual that makes you clench your eyes tight and hope for nothing but darkness. Then you peek and continue to read and find your fears are my reality. *Boo!*

There is nothing that would make a mother more proud then seeing you bent over, legs spread, naked looking back over your shoulder and smiling at her as if she is ready to take your picture. Unfortunately it only works when you are a toddler. At forty–five my mom would have a heart attack if I posed like that. This is not one of those proud moments to record in a photo album, nor should it be experienced with your roommate present.

So on this day I had plenty of room light and was able to inspect the situation. Once I got over my odd contorted reflection and the thought some rogue camera could be hidden in the room forever remanding my image to some internet joke site, I found my issue was just a moderate condition of seat rash. No blisters, no broken skin, no flaking, and fortunately the damage appeared to be limited to just two small patches right on my sit bones; those being the pressure points on the skin between the seat and the lower bone of my hip sockets.

The cure for this little demon was a good dry–off and a generous layer of triple–ointment antibiotic gel. Keep it cool and dry and by morning it would hopefully be fine. I would need to have a happy bottom to avoid any compounding of the problem which could lead to blisters, time off the bike, or both. I'm quickly learning Clark was right when he said it's your butt that gets you across the country and not your legs.

My final comments about undercarriage inspection are this; too much body hair, too little sun exposure, and a real appreciation for the unsightly job proctologist's have. If you stayed with me I promise this is as bad as it gets. If you smiled or laughed, then it was worth the effort and embarrassment to write it down.

"SAFE!" Good thing you skipped those paragraphs about the saddle issues. You wanted to read about cycling cross country anyway and didn't need to be exposed to such off–track nonsense. You see I'm tuned into what you like so enjoy as I finish up the day in Tucumcari.

Our treat for the day was dinner at "K–Bob's Steak House, Home of the Salad Wagon." This regional chain served up some good food in a rustic western style atmosphere. And the salad bar was in fact set into an authentic wooden wheeled pioneer style wagon. They even have something for the regulars called the K–Bob's Reward Program if you like that sort of customer loyalty thing.

The owners of K–Bob's were a young couple; hard working and very polite, doing whatever needed to be done to help our large group have a good dining experience. Our group by itself could fill a smaller eatery and overwhelm its staff. Even getting drinks out quickly for a group of forty plus is a challenge. We had our own reserved area and as per usual glasses of ice water and extra pitchers of water were at the ready on the table for us.

A quick round of the tables to get our main dish ordered up and we were turned loose on the salad bar where we could begin grazing. Nobody left without having their fill of the wagon's surplus and I myself took a few trips as all that goodness could not fit on a single plate.

Time passed quickly and our orders began to arrive. The main attraction for K–Bob's was steak cooked anyway you like. And if you don't like steak they had fish and chicken to satisfy just about anybody. I enjoyed the chicken–fried chicken breast with country gravy and left just enough room to sample the all you can eat soft serve ice cream. It was a treat and a feat to eat!

Tucumcari is built on deep red dirt approaching the color of cranberry sauce. I've never seen soil like this before. Eastern red clay cannot even compare. The things you notice walking around a new town.

Tucumcari is home to a dinosaur museum located within the Mesaland's Community College and the main draw is a forty foot long skeleton of a Torvosaurus, which is a rare carnivore relative of Tyrannosaurus Rex. The Museum's focus is on the Mesozoic period, which is also known as *The Age of Dinosaurs*. The Mesozoic is comprised of the Triassic, Jurassic, and Cretaceous periods just in case you need to know this bit of trivia.

For those who enjoy local history there is the Tucumcari Historical Museum located on 416 South Adams. They also have a Facebook page revealing quite a bit of the early goings on in the town. The early photos reveal art–deco style signage and some pretty diverse businesses including a broom manufacturing company, a cotton gin, wool scouring company, feed lots, and a Coca–Cola bottling plant. If you are a fan of the historic Route 66 then the Blue Swallow Motel might be on your list to see. It's a quirky little motel with garages to park in making it a rather unique place to stay.

After taking in the sites it was a short wobble back to the MicroTel Inn. I was officially done exploring and it was time to set my sites on the next day's ride. As I looked over tomorrow's cue sheet with directions to Dalhart, Texas I noticed we would have an encore dining performance at K–Bob's as it was our breakfast destination. I had mixed feeling about it. The food was great but if I eat too much of it I will be a slug on the bike. And I don't do self–moderation very well.

Tonight is our last in New Mexico, as we will cross into Texas tomorrow. Looking back, I must say it's a very beautiful state, offering a variety of scenery and rich history. For many reasons Santa Fe will be my favorite, but I would be happy to ride again through any part of it.

More New Mexico postcards with short sentences and various destination addresses were written and my journals filled with news of the day. I readied my cycling gear for the morning and then it was time for another part of the daily routine to begin.

Clark opens his journal and reads to me his trip of the day. His story was better than mine; much more adversity and more hours in the saddle. It was much hotter and windier. As much as I thought my day was tough, I was reminded again how strong a rider Clark is and how fortunate I am to have him coaching and encouraging me. My success each day is in part his victory, but as my roommate he has to listen to my struggles every night. As I get stronger and more confident in my ability to ride all the way to Boston, hopefully those struggles will be replaced with excitement and anticipation of each day's ride. With the journal entries complete and our conversations concluded it was lights out and I was off in a deep sleep.

Legend of Tucumcari Mountain

The origin of this myth began when Apache Chief Wautonomah, who lived on the mountain with his tribe, was near death and concerned about his successor. His two finest braves, Tonopah and Tocom, were rivals and sworn enemies, and both were vying for the love of Princess Kari, the chief's daughter.

Kari's heart secretly belonged to her true love, Prince Tocom. The chief arranged a knife battle to the death between Tonopah and Tocom; the winner to be the new chief and the husband of Princess Kari.

The fight raged, and Tonopah's knife mortally wounded Tocom. Kari, overcome with sorrow and rage, seized a knife and killed Tonopah, and then took her own life. The Apache chief, grief–stricken by his losses, buried the knife into his own heart, crying out loud in agony "Tocom–Kari." The town and mountain still bear the name of Tucumcari; the legend lives on.

Day 18: Tucumcari to Dalhart, Texas (96 miles)

The day started early and after scanning my gear I headed over to K–Bob's for breakfast. It was just a short walk of a few hundred feet across the gravel and asphalt lot but in the early morning coolness it felt very refreshing, if not tingly.

Breakfast was buffet style so it was a quick event. Something for everyone's palate could be found but a cyclist has to consume food with the highest energy value and not the heavy comfort foods. Seeing a spread like K–Bob's makes me wish I were driving a car instead of riding a bike. So much goodness, so much I wanted to enjoy.

I did see the owner again and had the opportunity to learn she was also a recording artist and local radio personality. How cool is that? And I couldn't help but notice even after working dinner the night before, in the early morning hustle to keep everyone's cups filled with coffee she was still full of energy and her smile, it was relentless if not infectious.

What a pleasure it was to get to share some conversation as she paused briefly from her maneuvers around the dining area. She was good people and very proud of her little corner of the world. In the lobby near the register I found a display of her CD's so I bought one for my daughter and had it autographed. Another unique souvenir for my coast to coast journey was now in hand.

Then it was back across the parking lot from the restaurant, which just happens to be collocated with the large truck stop, to the hotel to begin readying my bags and riding gear. Out in front of the hotel it was still a bit cool after the mercury bottomed out at fifty–six degrees Fahrenheit through the night. It was expected to get up to the low nineties by mid–afternoon in Tucumcari but Dalhart, which was nearly a hundred miles to the northeast, should have more favorable temperatures. Overall we would do some mild climbing before finishing at about a hundred feet below our current elevation.

After the morning ritual of tire pumping, bag loading, and signing out we exited the hotel backtracking a mile and a half toward Main Street where we would exit east out of town. Skies were clear, the air crisp and fresh, and just the wisps of clouds thin overhead blending into the almost white horizon sky. For the first few miles I mingled with other riders paying careful attention to the cracks and loose gravel on the well–worn streets. Big Mike and Duffey were going about their usual conversations as I passed them and it wasn't long before the tandem of Don and Helen came scooting by with several others in their draft. There were riders moving forward while others drifted back within the group, conversations passing up and down the line.

I found myself again riding with Betty, Lynn, Gary, and Gray. I assumed a cadence that quickly warmed my legs. We angled to the northeast on Route 54 toward the town of Logan. Not long after the low slung recumbent carrying Peter Crowell joined up with us momentarily before continuing on with the faster moving group of Kim Simoni, Gordon Kniefel, and Gene Teaney. For the most part groups formed and then disbursed without orchestration. It was an interesting dynamic to experience.

In the cool morning air my nose would begin to run and today was no exception. You don't have many options when riding a bike unless you stop so I would attempt to manage the situation in the following order; one, with my right hand I would pinch my nose and in a single motion flick the wet stream to the side of the road. This worked the best but not an option if you were riding alongside other cyclists.

My second option might be a bit odd but since I do my own laundry it's my prerogative. I cross an arm in front of my face and wipe my nose onto my forearm or jersey sleeve. I told you it was odd, okay maybe even a bit gross.

The last option is to use the back of my right glove to wipe the flow. I wash my gloves every night too so you do whatever works best, not necessarily the most socially acceptable. And you might be surprised to learn many cyclists do the same thing. Welcome to the world of distance cycling.

The thing you don't do is purge your nasal store while both hands are on the bars. You just can't control the spray and it sticks to the bike frame. And these bikes are too expensive and too revered to just go and blow your nose all over them. Besides by the end of the day it would be a *booger* to get off the frame when you clean it up after the day's ride. There you go, pun intended.

Paul Kvam, a rider out of Atlanta, and I began riding together in this part of the tour and we would usually be found in the same proximity from here on into Boston. We seemed to share the same humor and we both picked up on the Choice Hotel's commercial playing on the radio and TV featuring Johnny Cash singing, *I've been everywhere!* It was fitting and each time we would ride near each other we would shout to the other, "Hey, where you've been?" and the response would roll right into a line of Johnny's song. Yeah that was fun and it never got old. It seemed to define the trip as I could say without hesitation, *I've been everywhere!*

Along this rather flat and boring twenty mile stretch to the town of Logan we bantered about and watched the long freight trains rumble by just off to our right. Paul had the idea to get some action shots of us riding so we made the rather awkward camera exchanges without stopping and took turns posing for the camera with the occasional train as a backdrop. The complexity of what we were doing was compounded by the fact we were still riding amongst a few other cyclists. Great pictures came of our efforts and since nobody crashed it was well worth the effort.

About a mile outside of Logan the road descended down toward a dirt and rock lined ravine through which the Canadian River slowly passes through. The bridge spanned less than five hundred feet and remained level over the river about fifty feet below the road surface. The water level was maybe a foot or two deep but there were a variety of dense tall weeds standing twenty feet or so away from the water indicating it normally is much higher.

I was afforded an unobstructed view of the bottom because the river runs parallel with the left side of the highway and after crossing under it takes a full 180–degree turn and runs back along the right side for a thousand feet. It was in this area the rail line diverged away from the highway to the right and we would not be close to the tracks again until we arrived in Logan.

Unfortunately for the riders the generously wide shoulder crossing the bridge was on the other side. We found ourselves rushing across the bridge to reduce the time spent playing with the trucks and cars that seemed to increase in number without explanation. Single file crossing over the bridge happened in just under twenty–five seconds but it seemed much longer. The adrenaline was high and it sure helped to climb up the steepest incline of the morning, a slight left hand bend into Logan. The town was a dozen blocks long and most of it was on our left. A few businesses including a restaurant and a store servicing the population of just over a thousand were at our disposal if we needed to replenish our fluids or use the restrooms. I scanned the cue sheet and it was only four more miles to the SAG so I kept going. Within a half mile we cleared the town and started a climb over a concrete arched bridge to get us across to the other side of the train tracks. At least the downhill was nice.

We arrived at the SAG which was nothing more than a wide paved area on the left of the dead straight section of highway but it had Margaret and snacks so I was pretty happy and excited as usual. We were being conditioned to spot white vans and when we saw one on the side of the road we would be drawn to it smiling with a little extra spring in our pedaling. It meant Gatorade, snacks, and encouragement. It also kept us going.

There were a few trees providing a bit of privacy for those needing to answer nature's call. Since we had gotten accustomed to our rather public arrangements most folks took the opportunity to give back to nature. I walked the thirty yards through the field grass toward the train tracks, prepared to relieve myself, and was greeted by another freight train. I smiled and doubted I would cross paths with the engineer again so I didn't worry about what he might have thought and kept on about my business. He probably got a good laugh; I know I did. I applied another layer of butt lube as I was beginning to feel a little burn from the first thirty miles of riding.

After enjoying some cyclist banter, fresh strawberries, and a healthy cross section of other delights I topped off my bottles to get going down the road toward Dalhart. I still had sixty–five more miles to ride and the wind was picking up and starting to move around. I sailed off with a group so I could occupy the time chatting on the long flat stretches. To this point my hotfoot was in check but it was still a bit premature to say if it was the cleat adjustments or just the time off of the bike. More riding should give me a better idea about the change.

The favorable weather we enjoyed since California has finally hit a speed bump. It was still sunny with moderate temperatures but we lost favor with the wind. We rode the remainder of the day into what seemed to be a twenty to thirty mile per hour alternating crosswind headwind. Not only was it shaving about three to six miles an hour off my speed, it was also taking away any opportunity to coast on the downhill's and flats. Without relief on the downhill's it felt like I was climbing a good portion of the day. And with the extra effort the issues lingering from the prior day were beginning to demand more attention.

I slogged along much like the others applying more effort than I had grown accustomed to using on such gentle terrain. I remembered in my training rides back in Florida the wind could be more of a challenge than the hills and this day was reinforcing what I learned. Slow and steady, the conversations had died down and I found myself riding almost solo with a bit of a gap between me and the other riders.

Twenty miles out of the SAG I rolled into the town of Nara Visa, population: 112. To my right I passed the sketchy Morning Stars Motel, a U.S. Post Office, and several abandoned wood–framed houses, masonry structures, and vintage gas stations. Then six short blocks later I rolled right out of it. The town had a Main Street and it was just a block north of my position, Route 54, or Bell Street as it is known to the locals. Main was an unpaved road and ran just shy of four blocks. I was unimpressed.

Not much of anything happening in Nara Visa; not even a stray dog running around looking for a cyclist to chase. As I crossed North 5th Street to my left was a field of junk cars and written on several rustic signs and car windshields was the warm welcome, "Keep Out!" This friendly attitude might explain why Nara Visa is all but a modern day ghost town.

I did take the time to look up a bit of history on Nara Visa and in its hey–day, which was somewhere between 1910 and 1920, there was a school, four churches, eight saloons, and at least three dance halls. Along with a variety of businesses including butcher shops, drug stores, general merchandise stores, auto shops, hotels, a bank, and a barber shop it was a place with everything going for it except a future.

Just before I was clear of the town I passed a relatively large brick building on the right of the road. It was the Nara Visa Community Center. It seemed so out of place yet it left an impression on me as to why it would have been built at all. I continued searching until I had the answer. It was the town school; kindergarten through senior high. It closed in 1968 and gained life as the Community Center where it hosts numerous events and is home to the town's museum. Activities in the building, which is listed on both the national and state historic registers, are diverse. Weddings, parties, and an annual gathering of well–known cowboy poets like Buck Ramsey and Andy Wilkinson now take place where the children of Nara Visa were once schooled.

The town is not without its notable residents. John Wilson, president of Tandy Corporation, is a Nara Visa native and returns yearly to visit relatives and friends. Every town has a story. This one just required a bit more work to find it.

Five miles ahead I would cross into Texas; another state and another opportunity to sprinkle sand. Each state crossing brings with it a level of anticipation, another check in the box, one step closer to Boston, but it also is a reminder this trip is finite, it will end and moments like a state line crossing are to be celebrated, photographed, and talked about. With that in mind it is important to reach the border with other riders. And our arrival into Texas would be no different.

I rolled in with Betty Hayes as Greg, Gray, and a few others were waiting at the border. Actually it was just past the border marked by the standard unimpressive metal highway signage. Riders were parked near a marker better suited for a state like Texas. It was a large concrete slab shaped in the likeness of the state with tall engraved letters "T E X A S." It had a few chips and pockmarks from some errant bullets likely left by local rowdies after enjoying a few tall ones. This was a sign to be photographed! It was large, heavy, immobile, nearly indestructible, and a magnet for all the riders. It had the grit and edginess that can only be found in the middle of the northwestern wilds of Texas. A very memorable sign that likely will not be bested by any of the remaining border crossings.

I clicked off several pictures of others as they returned the favor for me. Pictures of me posing in front of this sign are some of my favorites from the trip. They remind me of the toughness of the day, but more importantly of the satisfaction radiating from my smile, as permanent as the monument I was leaning on. I made it to Texas! And I was continuing east.

The scenery along the way was finally constant, desert vegetation with lots of rocks and dirt. Just a few trees dotted the landscape. There were random areas along the rail line completely void of vegetation; sand dunes in Texas. These features gave me reason to think about the fragility of the area. A lack of rain, enough exposed earth, and it could be the Dust Bowl all over again. It was a place that required a strong will to stay. I'm only interested in passing through. The Texan's of this little corner of the state will have no challenge from me.

I did enjoy the passing of two freight trains, and as I reached the outer limits of Dalhart, I saw several commercial cattle feeding farms with thousands of acres of corrals to fatten up a sea of cows numbering in the hundreds of thousands. The largest feedlot was XIT Feeders and from what I could see their claim to fame was cow patty mounds measuring more than eight feet high and sturdy enough to support a small herd of clueless cows. It is an unofficial record that likely will go unchallenged.

You could smell the feedlots from miles away; pungent, sour, like rotting grass. And it's something the Dalhart Chamber of Commerce should not include in any of their promotional campaigns.

Once I reached the feed lots they continued for much longer than my interest in them. The smell was strong, the flies were a nagging bother, and there was no shade. It was hot and dusty. I had to keep my mouth shut the last hour to Dalhart as the wind seemed to blow the flies and dirt into it every time it was open. Not the place for an enthusiastic banter of conversation.

And the views at the feedlots were also a bit of a downer. Cows standing and staring at you, maybe they knew what was happening, maybe they wanted someone to open the gate, to let them run. Maybe they knew there was really nowhere to run if they got out. At least there was feed and water as they stood and fattened for the market.

Somehow I felt like they knew that I knew. Weird, the thoughts you have on the bike in the heat and the dust and the stink. I'm not sure if a shower will wash away what I saw in their eyes. And then my thoughts go to, *two all–beef patties, special sauce, lettuce, cheese, pickles, onions, on a sesame seed bun!* Where did that come from?

The temperature, which had risen quickly in the morning, continued to bake the landscape. It was hovering in the mid–nineties. The final push into Dalhart presented us with a half mile incline as if we were climbing out of the frying pan that was the day. In town the roads flattened out. With just a few traffic intersections to negotiate we were angling into the Days Inn parking lot and under the entrance canopy; finally some shade and relief from the elements.

Sitting at the hotel I had a chance to recall the day. It took just over seven–and–a–half hours to complete the ride averaging a dismal 12.7 miles an hour. My reward was a bad case of hotfoot and saddle sores. The last twenty to thirty miles were a real challenge, but I made it, everyone made it. Even some of the stronger riders were whipped from the day's conditions.

For most of the day I rode again with Betty and we survived what might have been the most difficult riding day either of us has encountered over the past three weeks. I'm soaking my feet in the indoor pool, thinking about our state–line crossing into Texas this morning and the next two states we will cross into over the next two days. It won't be long before we reach Topeka, Kansas, the halfway point of our trip.

Dinner for the night was Pizza Hut, rather ironic in the middle of cattle country but I don't think anyone minded the selection. Morning would come early as we turned the clocks forward, yet another indication we were progressing east. Breakfast would be at the Sands, which I can only guess is a local eatery. After dinner I was back to the regular routine of finding local postcards and recording the day in my journals.

It seems Dalhart is more than a dusty collection of feedlots sitting at just under four thousand feet of elevation. Dalhart, home to more than seven thousand people, was at the center of the Dust Bowl during the 1930s and thrived early due to its proximity to a railroad junction. It has a rather interesting attraction called the XIT Historical Museum featuring an extensive collection of ranching equipment, cultural exhibits, extensive photo archives, an art gallery, and historical records and documents. The museum is free and open most days to the public.

The downtown streets are brick paved which adds some charm to the rather small and isolated city. Another point of interest but easy to miss on the way into town is the Empty Saddle Monument at the crossroads of Dalhart—U.S. Highways 87, 385, and 54—which honors the memory of the cowboys of the now defunct XIT Ranch.

The economy is centered on agribusiness, including farming, ranching, feedlots, and pig farming. They do make the most out of their patch of dirt. There are no lakes or other standing water so they depend on the rain and the few wells afforded to the community.

The heat never relented until well after sundown and tomorrow's forecast is for more of the same. The good news; we only ride 72 miles. I can still taste the dust and a faint smell of the feedlots lingers. Too bad I missed the right turn on Railroad Street to the Dairy Queen when I rolled into town.

Day 19: Dalhart to Guymon, Oklahoma. (72 miles)

The Sands is a local family eatery just up the street from the Days Inn towards the center of Dalhart; nothing fancy, basic breakfast food, coffee, juice, and fruit in an older, well–worn establishment. The staff, as pleasant as can be expected for a morning shift, made sure the coffee cups were full, the food hot, and the biker crowd got out as quickly as possible. Was it the desire to impress or to get the strange group of spandex and bandana wearing two wheeled travelers out of their establishment? Does it matter? I'm tempted but I'm not even going to ask, though part of this trip is to engage and learn. Maybe cyclist's come through this town every day. Nope. Still not gonna ask.

Up and out of the rustic eatery I went with a few other refueled riders. Through the mini lobby past postings of second hand items for sale, day work opportunities, and a mishmash of other notices tacked and taped to the wall, I pushed through the exit door and onto the well–used sidewalk. Just a few feet past the building the sidewalk ended dumping us onto the sand and gravel expanses running parallel to the roadway. I'm not really sure if they were parking lots or just patches of land unable to grow grass, but the sound of us stepping through the gravel was quite noticeable as it mixed with the morning noise of cars and trucks increasing in number on the roadway just twenty feet away.

And somehow walking on these shoulders I manage to pick up tiny pebbles that worked their way down into my sneakers. In just a few steps they get the best of me. I can't walk to the hotel with nuggets pressuring the bottom of my foot and another wedged between my toes so I prop up against a power pole to do a quick removal and shake of the sneaker. Out drops the little offenders back into dirt. They always look much smaller than they feel.

The few blocks walk back to the hotel got the settling of my breakfast started. I actually ate a bit heavier this morning given the mileage was less than we had been riding. I needed to build up my stores for the long ride into Kansas the following day. It was a good thing my body knew to increase the food intake without depending on the brain because it was way too early to be paying attention to such matters. Sometimes getting a pair of matching socks can be a challenge. And judging from the appearance of my co–riders I'm not alone on this.

My riding gear was prepped the night before but since I have a little OCD in my DNA I was compelled to check it again. Obsessive–Compulsive Disorder is what it is commonly called but to be precise it is known as Arithmomania—A mental disorder. Go figure.

I'd like to think about it as being prepared. I count things like steps on the sidewalk and I check, check, and recheck things I know are correct and don't need to be checked, but I do it anyway. I like even numbers when I'm counting even though my real favorite number is seven. I'm like the person who counts their steps between cracks, not quite *Rain Man* but I think you get the picture. Maybe I am that guy. If you don't do it yourself you know someone who does. Enjoy their quirkiness or embrace your own.

With my pre–ride room readiness routine complete it was time to bring my gear downstairs. Like many hotels we visited the Days Inn did not have an elevator. Rooming on the second floor required either two trips to bring down your bags and bike or a bit of creativity to do it in one trip. It was interesting to see how people negotiated their own situation. Some were challenged right at exit from their room as all of the hotels we stayed at were equipped with an auto–close mechanism.

With bags balanced on the bike a rider would get halfway out and then get clamped between the door and the door frame. Sometimes the bags would fall, the door would close with some stuff coming to rest on the inside of the room and the rider now in the hallway, left scrambling to hold the bike upright as other items scatter. No one was immune, not even me. The smartest thing was to make more than one trip but early in the morning you try to avoid repeated trips up and down the stairs. Which actually seems funny because we would be riding out in the heat for hours and an extra trip up and down only took a few minutes at most.

The recumbent and the tandem riders were always given preference to rooms on the first floor and with the size of our group, especially out in these small towns, we took most of the rooms in the hotels. I didn't mind and it made it easier to figure out where riders could be found. The recumbent crew of Peter, Hopper, Gary, Kathy and Ben along with the tandem riders of Don, Helen, Tom and Randi made up one sixth of our group which I thought was pretty large. On the few occasions they were in rooms above the first floor it was a real challenge to see how they negotiated the elevators, stairs, and the fire doors. And every rider was willing to pitch in to hold a door especially as the train–of–a–bike tandem needed to pass through. I never did hear anyone have an issue with the first floor preferences for these non–standard bikes. That told me quite a bit about the kind of people I was on tour with.

So after I pulled off another successful single trip from my room to the lobby I worked my way out the door and found a place to lean my bike, then dropped my bags on the cool concrete. The tire pumps were all in use so I took note of the pecking order and found my place in the queue behind Betty. Tires didn't really need to be pumped everyday but I did it anyway; one hundred psi in the front and one–ten in the rear. My tires were designed for up to 125 psi but the higher the pressure the harsher the ride. Each rider had to find the right balance because too little air pressure increases the rolling resistance. As a rule of thumb the lighter the rider the less air pressure is required to keep the tire from flattening out against the road.

The pumps Tracy provided each day were pro grade and it only took a few pumps to top off the tire pressure. My narrow tires used a smaller air stem called a Presta valve. Unlike a regular Schrader valve found on a car tire, this smaller valve required a tiny little knurled nut to be backed out to ready the valve for mating with the pump. Forgetting to do this would mean no air could get into the tire and if I unscrewed it too much the delicate valve assembly could get bent when attached to the pump head. Easy to do and to remember once I did it a few times but this is the first bike I owned with this Presta system. When finished with the pump the nut needed to be tightened and then I always screwed on the little plastic protective cap to keep the dirt of out the stem.

Waiting in anticipation for either Tracy or Trevor to wheel the CrossRoads truck under the hotel canopy, I engage in conversation with Ken Pope, Bob Cordes and others. There is some talk about the big ride to Dodge City on Thursday but mostly the focus is on the state crossing into Oklahoma. This is Don and Helen Reeves territory and sometime during the day it might be worthwhile to seek their council on what can be expected in the *Sooner* state.

The truck rolls into position and the show is about to start. Tracy takes her perch up on the back of the box truck; her orders are quick and well–rehearsed. She lays down the final words of wisdom and warnings and then before starting the luggage loading process, Tracy gives the last call for laundry soap, checks the wall–mounted clock and only then does she commence with the loading process.

In just a few minutes the precision and efficiency of the process leads right to the moment when Tracy calls forward the first person to sign out. Her reasons may be random or to acknowledge a birthday or some other event but she always had something fresh each day. Today it was the birthday boy's turn. "Step up Frank Campbell!" or something similar Tracy said. Cheers and a good send off for Frank and she points and calls names for the rest of us to sign out and get moving down the road.

I don't think this part of the daily routine will ever get stale. My turn comes so I step to the back of the truck, I note the time and scribble my name on the sheet and head to my bike to mount up, clip in, and reset my onboard computers to capture the stats for the day. And in an instant the pre–morning jitters are released; another adventure into a new state begins.

Out of the hotel I crossed traffic hooking left onto Route 54 east. I guess asking for a strong tail wind was a bit much, but today, cooler temperatures and overcast skies prevailed. There was only a hint of head winds until we were about ten miles shy of the Oklahoma border. It was a day to recover and also to prepare for tomorrow's 124 mile ride to Dodge City, Kansas.

I find it hard to believe after spending a week in New Mexico, that Texas and Oklahoma would only be our hosts for a day each. Between Dalhart, Texas, and Guymon, Oklahoma, there is little to see other than the thirty foot tall cowboy statue in Conlen, Texas, a few grain elevators, long trains moving cattle to the left of the highway, and rolling hills, which turned almost flat as we crossed into Oklahoma.

The road heading east had seen better days. The bumps, cracks, and holes effortlessly transferred their irregularities into harsh vibrations and jolting impacts up through my front wheel, through the handle bars, and into my hands. The shocks continued upward until finding refuge in my shoulders. My still tender left shoulder did not appreciate the road humor.

Not to be excluded the rear wheel took a measure of the impacts sending them through the seat post to my tailbone and rattling my spine before doing the same to my teeth. I guess I'm glad my front fork and seat post are both made of carbon and supposedly reduce the vibrations, but the rigid aluminum frame does not. I am beginning to wonder if an all carbon framed bike could provide comfort through these rough conditions.

Aside from the bigger impacts the constant vibration of the washboard surface takes a toll on your wrists. If you don't move your hands around the handle bars often and occasionally remove them completely to shake out the stress they will quickly go numb. Not only is this uncomfortable, it is also makes for dangerous cycling conditions and could lead to long term wrist damage.

Route 54 had its share of truck traffic; grain haulers and open cattle transporters were among the most common. Having the big trucks passing by added to the discomfort of the ride and left cyclist's looking for a clean and safe piece of shoulder to steer clear of the thirty ton land trains. The shoulder measured from a few feet to as much as six feet wide but a variety of rumble strip grooves cut into the road surface and the generous smattering of gravel and truck tire debris quickly reclaimed much of the usable areas. My eyes are darting about checking for approaching traffic in my eyeglass mirror, and then refocused forward quickly scanning for a clear line to avoid the debris.

At times the trucks would form up in a tight line of four or more and when they would pass by I would get a strong blast of air pushing me to the right and forward immediately increasing my speed by a few miles per hour. In contrast a group of trucks approaching from the opposite direction create a more impactful force. Like a smack in the face, complete with stinging sand and dust. At times I felt like I was almost stopped in my cycling tracks. And regardless of direction if the trailers are hauling livestock the smell rolls off and lingers like an invisible stench cloud.

Just twenty miles into the ride a row of large grain elevators began to grow on the left side of the roadway. They were visible from miles away looking like a large gray and white mass of something man made. Within a half mile the details begin to appear and as I got within a hundred yards or so I realize just how imposing these large structures are. Massive assemblies of engineered concrete silos, metal appendages, piping, and conveyors, with corporate logos affixed to them. Not more than fifty feet off the left side of the road trucks line up to receive their fill of the stored grains. The mechanical whining noise of industrial equipment is pretty extreme but fortunately localized enough that after passing the structures it quickly fades into the background leaving only the rush of the wind, road traffic, and the grinding of sand between my bike tires and the road.

These grain elevators are the giants of Middle America and mark the centers of commerce for the little towns dotting the landscape. In Conlen, Texas they had a roadside attraction, a giant cowboy statue watching over the motor traffic crisscrossing at his feet on Route 54. Wearing a hundred gallon hat and a belt buckle with the name *Tex* this quick–draw gun touting figure looks more like law enforcement than a bad guy. But you can make up any story you'd like.

After more than an hour of riding Conlen was a good place to stop. A quick check of the mirror, an inspection of the shoulder to find a safe exit point into the sand and gravel lot, and I roll to a stop at the base of this artificial Texas giant's feet. Laughing to myself he is less than knee high to the immense grain elevators towering across the street but he is the biggest cowboy around.

It's hard to take a decent picture of this cowboy statue and even harder to get one of me with it. I thought I would have to settle for a picture standing by his boot and then another one from a hundred feet away with *Tex* standing alone, but the camaraderie of the group kicked in, cameras exchanged and pictures snapped.

Duffey and I posed for a quick shot and our images were digitally captured as proof of our visit. Me in my bright yellow jersey and strapped on CamelBak. Dick in his CrossRoads colors, shoulders straight as if he were standing at attention. We were wheel to wheel, our long shadows falling to the west, smiles on our faces under the pale blue and misty clouded sky. The benefits of riding with others I concluded.

For a brief moment I think about the riders racing to be first to the hotel. I bet a few of them either didn't stop or didn't have a companion to snap their picture to mark the moment. It's not like you get the opportunity like this every day; unless you live in Conlen. Yupp, someone in Boston will surely ask if anyone can send them a picture of *Tex*. I just know it!

Ten miles farther up the road is the only SAG of the day. I figured I would be there in about forty minutes so I put my head down and resumed pedaling amongst the truck traffic until I crossed the railroad tracks into the town of Stratford. Our SAG was at the Dairy Queen so it would give me reason for an early morning ice cream and access to a real bathroom. Some of the riders were applying lotion, others were applying seat lube to gain some comfort for the next forty miles to Guyman.

Stratford was a boom town compared to some of the other little crossroads marked by the grain elevators. It had a few gas stations, convenience stores, restaurants, and people wandering around. Centered at the intersection of Route 54 and Highway 15 Stratford is home to nearly two thousand residents and is the

Pheasant Capital of Texas. On an old block building entering the town was a sign, "Welcome to Stratford, home of God, grass and grit." Yeah man, this is west Texas!

Twenty miles farther down the road we would arrive at the border crossing into Oklahoma. A group of us left the SAG and rejoined Route 54 in the direction we had been heading since exiting the hotel parking lot. This was definitely not a day needing much of a cue sheet to find our destination. In fact it would only require two turns about two miles shy of the hotel to get us safely there.

I figured the half a banana and cliff bar I put in my pocket at the SAG would give me something to munch on as I got hungry. I didn't eat much at the SAG except for a bit of a banana, some berries, and an energy bar. I was careful to top off my bottles with both water and Gatorade. I learned you never pass up the opportunity to fill up especially when another forty miles of riding remains.

In small groups we rode only to reassemble in number as we stopped at the Oklahoma border just shy of a town called Texhoma, Texas. We posed for pictures and sprinkled Pacific beach sand for luck. It was ironic the first county in Oklahoma we entered was called Texas County. The state sign was big, standard issue DOT construction sitting off to the right of the highway in a treeless expanse of the state whose name is derived from the Choctaw words *Okla* and *Humma,* meaning "red people." I'm still trying to understand why this wide open relatively flat and treeless part of the country appeals to so many. It is so different than what I am familiar with back on the east coast.

Back on our bikes down the highway we pressed on the quarter mile until we crossed Route 95 in Texhoma. The town actually straddles both Texas and Oklahoma and like Dalhart it is a ranching and livestock center built along the Rock Island railway line. The town is unique not only because it sits in two states but the educational system is supported by a cooperative effort between the two. Kindergarten through fourth grade attends school in Texas and fifth through twelfth grade attends school in Oklahoma. It's also the only city or town in Oklahoma qualifying for instate tuition in either state for high school grads looking to go to college. With a population of just over nine hundred it is neither a big nor a growing city. In the '50s the population tripled to almost 1,500 but during the following decade it dwindled back down to the level it sits at today.

Before this part of the country was opened to settlers it was known as "No Man's Land" and with few notable people hailing from this part of the country combined with the limited historical sites and absence of growth it would appear it can still lay claim to the early moniker. My apologies go out to anyone living here who may think differently. With the exception of crossing route 95 I did not stop in the town.

Exiting Texhoma the temperature climbed into the eighties, the sun broke out from behind the haze, and the wind shifted to what could best be described as a twenty mile an hour head wind. Our speed was dropping quickly and it was a struggle compared to what we experienced earlier in the day. It was becoming hard work and the conversations dropped way off.

Betty and Gray were riding in my proximity and in an effort to improve our progress we joined about ten more experienced cyclists in a pace line riding very close together in a single column. The point of a pace line is to conserve energy, but the pace was more than most could maintain. Gordon, Kim, Gene, Jan, Pat and Vikki made up the core riders and at times the tandems and recumbent riders would join in.

About four riders dropped off before I did, and while I appreciated the speed, I was not very comfortable riding in close quarters, unable to do anything but focus on the wheel directly in front of me. And when you are close enough to see the salt stains and fraying threads in your leading rider's shorts you begin to make other rather astonishing observations. Like your speed is not really constant and you struggle to maintain any semblance of a straight line. Riding alone I thought consistency in speed and a laser line trajectory were the norm requiring no real attention to maintain. I was wrong. When I ride within inches of another cyclist's wheel I realize I'm as jerky and erratic as a circus clown on a two wheeler. Well maybe not quite so bad, but there is no room for error and no reset button to get you out of trouble when you are sandwiched in a pack of riders with tires so close the air between them begins to whistle and handle bar to rider hip contact is not out of the question.

This lack of consistency is what really challenges your will to ride on someone's wheel and when two riders are out of sync the gap between them expands and contracts several inches in a split second. The erratic nature of cycling and the need for your full and constant concentration makes riding in longer pace lines an even more risky venture. In an instant, a single touch of two wheels can put the entire group down on the pavement. No warning just the sound of rubber to rubber friction followed by the ping popping of spokes, scraping of metal and the guttural grunts and *Oh Shit's!* coming out of mouths before the breaking of glass, bodies impacting the road surface, bike parts scattering in all directions, the sound of air being forced out of tired lungs, and then the equally sudden quiet right after. While in the pace line I could gain about two miles per hour, but I didn't like the down side risk. And I feared I would miss out on what was around me even more.

If I crossed the country with nothing but the view of someone else's rear wheel, what have I gained? I would rather look around and take it all in than be confined by the pace line. It also seemed those who favored the pace line saw fewer sites, took fewer pictures, and arrived at the hotel much before the rest. They were opting for speed to the finish and not so much the enjoyment of the journey—unless they measured enjoyment in speed alone. I stopped often and snapped plenty of pictures of the sites and the other riders. It was working well for me.

For twenty miles I worked hard pedaling to maintain anything near twelve miles an hour. At times my progress was much slower and I continued to ride in the proximity of others but for the most part I was alone. Conversation was replaced with looking about and thinking of the miles ahead, counting them down by the tenths as I looked at the bike computers to get an instant update of my progress. This is when cycling is not much fun. The mental challenge is getting into the excitement of the surroundings and out of the counting mode. But with a headwind, heat, and rather bland unchanging scenery it's a challenge for this boy.

The state motto of Oklahoma is *Labor omnia vincit*—Labor Conquers All Things and today I would need to abide by their saying to get me through. How appropriate their motto. I just wished it was more on the lines of "Sit back and enjoy the tailwinds!" Keep pedaling and keep an eye ahead and an ear out for the cars and trucks coming from behind.

The town of Guymon with its hundred–year–old brick–lined streets was a welcome sight. It was huge in comparison to the little crossroad towns I passed through earlier in the day. There are more than eleven thousand people who live in this part of Texas County. It was incorporated back in 1901, six years before Oklahoma gained statehood. It looks and feels like a real town with history and diversity in employment opportunities. It feels alive.

More than twenty percent of the city's population works at a large double–shift pork processing plant handling about eighteen thousand hogs a day. While pork processing may be the largest employer in the city they also have manufacturing operations producing agricultural equipment and storage tanks. Guymon manages oil and gas wells and is an agricultural trade center for wheat, cattle, and dairy. The Oklahoma Panhandle State University is just eleven miles southwest of town and Guymon Municipal Airport once had regularly scheduled air service.

As for entertainment there is the eighteen hole, par seventy–one Sunset Hills golf course, Thompson Park featuring the thirty–two acre Sunset Hills Lake stocked for fishing all year round, and No Man's Land Rifle and Pistol Club with a fifty–station handgun and rifle range. There is also the Guymon Pioneer Days Rodeo which has been an annual event each May since the 1930s. It's the fifth Largest Outdoor Rodeo in the country.

There are also a few historically designated sites including the Texas County Courthouse which is on the National Register of Historical Places and three archaeological sites located nearby. To keep informed there is the Guymon Daily Herald newspaper and three local radio stations. Not too shabby for this part of the country.

Guymon sits at an elevation of 3,123 feet so without knowing it I actually enjoyed about an eight hundred foot decrease in elevation; lucky me. As I continue eastward I will lose elevation and the air will continue to become denser with oxygen making it easier for me to ride and breath. I'm more comfortable with flat terrain at sea level but I'm starting to adapt.

I was pleasantly surprised to hear music as I rolled through each intersection. The town had installed speakers on each traffic–light pole in an effort to lift people's spirits, according to a pamphlet I read. After a day of nothing but wind and truck noise, it sure lifted mine. Come to think of it, other than an amusement park or a few patio restaurants, I can't think of another place with outdoor music like this.

At the end of a long ride several of the cyclist's enjoy a cool beer to replenish the calorie burn. If you want something stronger you won't find it in Guymon as Texas County is a dry one. No hard liquor for twenty–five miles. I don't think there will be many in the group upset by this.

I gladly made the final two turns to get to the Ambassador Inn. I did the quick check and cleaning of my bike before I stripped down in my room to shower and hand wash my riding clothes. I can't get over how renewed I feel once I get the road dust off and my regular shorts and a t–shirt on.

Since my street clothes options are limited I usually put on either my grey or dark blue CrossRoads shirt and try to coordinate with my black or tan cargo shorts. A pair of white New Balance sneakers and cycling socks and my outfit is complete. *Easy–peasy* as Tracy says.

I was ready to hunt postcards and do a bit of discovery in Guymon until I realized there wasn't much within walking distance and I'd already seem the town as a rode in. A quick and close scouting around the general area of the hotel proved sufficient to complete my quest. I wasn't up to hiking around for too long nor was I interested in getting back on my bike until the morning. I found a set of black and white photo postcards circa 1900 depicting the downtown of Guymon. If you ignore the old cars and the black and white contrast it looked about the same as it did when I rolled through not two hours earlier.

It was hot standing in the sun. I heard another rider say it was nearly ninety degrees. I was starting to sweat so I headed into the shade of the lobby to pick up whatever miscellaneous local information I could use to tell the story of Guymon. Every hotel we stayed at had a rack of flyers, maps, brochures of various attractions, apartment rentals, and real estate magazines. And it was amazing after a while how similar all of the racks full of brochures began to look.

With the local literature in hand it was back to the air conditioned room to start writing postcards, journals and the daily installment for the DeLand Beacon. I was making progress but I have no idea how it would look in the newspaper back home. No matter, I just start writing it down and I'll leave it to someone else to decide where to trim my words to fit the space. I made sure to include the 73.8 miles covered in four hours fifty–nine minutes giving me a solid 14.6 average speed for the day.

An hour later I put the pencil down and washed out the water bottles again and set them to dry. Then I rearranged my damp cycling clothes I had draped over the air conditioning unit and the back of a chair to catch as much of the benefit possible to dry them out. Today's cycling outfit needs to dry completely, like it does every other day, so I can pack it into my duffel bag. The last riding prep chore was to ready my cycling gear for tomorrow's ride so I could be organized when I get up.

We celebrated Frank's birthday today with ice cream and cake at the Ambassador Inn. I hope as he blew out the candles he wished for tail winds tomorrow.

Day 20: Guymon to Dodge City, Kansas. (124 miles)

Written on a wall at the Ambassador Inn, Guyman Oklahoma June 3, 2004 – *Far better to dare mighty things, to win glorious victories, though checkered with defeat, than to take rank with those poor souls who neither enjoy much, nor suffer much, for theirs is a twilight existence that knows neither victory nor defeat.* – *Theodore Roosevelt April 10, 1899.*

Today I will know victory as I ride to Dodge City, Kansas 124 miles away. It will be a test of endurance and a challenge to overcome the weather. It started late last night when thunderstorms rolled in and tornado warnings were issued. The hotel staff took us to the basement fallout shelter for a drill, and we feared we would be in that room again before the night was over. At least they had a disco ball hanging from the ceiling.

I remember saying to myself, *So here we were on the eve of our longest ride; could we go the distance? Will it rain, will the start be delayed?*

It was a long night, but we awoke to clearing skies and barely a breeze. It was quieter at breakfast than prior days. The mileage of today's ride clearly had everyone's attention. This is the first year Tracy had opted to pull a double–day of riding, skipping the normal stop at Liberal and continuing all the way to Dodge City. Her logic was sound. The ride to Liberal with a tailwind would be short at just under two hours. Adding another eighty miles would be about five more hours. It was about the same distance we covered when we crossed the desert from Blythe to Wickenburg. And that was a hot day with a thousand feet more of climbing. The payoff was a full day off the bike in Dodge City; an extra rest day to do some looking around. We could do this.

The ride to Dodge City also had other semblances to the desert rides; target times, CamelBaks, and three SAGs. I would need to exit the SAG before the target time or else I'd be swept up by the Crossroads crew. Nothing like a little added pressure to keep things interesting. All I needed were a few mechanical issues, maybe some headwinds and I'd be at risk.

I thought back to Clark's pep talk the night prior. He said I could make it to Dodge City. He believed I was physically able but it would be decided in my mind before I ever got on the bike. Believe you can't and you won't. Believe you can, and you will. I trusted Clark this far so my mind says I can. I'm nervous, unsure, but I can do this. I will do this. I'm not getting into a van today, nor will I on any other day.

I headed out at 7:00 a.m. rolling at about fifteen miles per hour. If I could keep this pace, my seat time would be eight hours. And eight hours is about the longest I had spent in the saddle ever. I was unsure what to expect if I took much longer to get the job done.

The sun was bright and in my face like most other clear mornings. Slowly it began to warm me, the rays beaming across the landscape as I pedaled; my efforts adding to the warming effect. Sounds filled my ears. The air felt cool on my arms and legs. I breathed in the coolness and my nose immediately became wet. This is what it feels like to be alive; to have your senses on full alert. Excitement, fear, unknowns, and success waited. It wasn't to be found at the end of the day but through the entire day's journey. It was one turn of the pedal, one mile, one landmark, and one moment with friends at a time. Breathe in, breathe out, and know this is how lives change. And the changes come in ways we don't control nor fully understand.

Guyman disappeared in my rear view and I pedaled toward a new destination. It would be another day of firsts. I wiped the wet from my nose on the back of my left glove and snorted out the rest. There is no modesty in cross country cycling. Just don't pick your nose.

My legs were just getting warmed up as I rolled east on US–54 past Optima; a little blip off the right side of the highway on the way to Hooker. Though you wouldn't know it by appearance Optima is considered a town. Wikipedia says they have approximately three hundred residents. To me it was little more than a handful of well–worn single–wide's and several large rolled hay bales. Even at bike speed I passed it by in less than a minute. Well, maybe a bit more but it was quick. I could imagine Leslie Nielsen seeing Optima and saying his line from the movie *The Naked Gun,* "Nothing to see here!" It was flat, almost treeless and not a person to be found walking around.

To the left was a grain storage and transfer station just beyond the Union Pacific rail line. As a boy I loved trains. My dad bought me one for Christmas when I was way too young to appreciate it but it planted the seed for the big iron machines that remains today.

And for the other train and history buffs out there, the Union Pacific Railroad is the last major U.S. rail system whose name has never changed. With all the consolidations and acquisitions that's quite impressive. The Union Pacific story dates back to 1862 when it was chartered to build the nation's first transcontinental rail line westward from Omaha, Nebraska. Construction began in 1865, and it was completed on May 10, 1869. Their shield–shaped emblem dating back to 1886 and the bright yellow colors going back to the 1930s are still worn by their passenger cars and locomotives. As they move along the tracks the rumble in the air and through the ground are like nothing else on earth. We would likely see several fully loaded trains as long as we run close to the tracks.

The grain complex consisted of a single tall rectangular earthy–toned elevator structure reaching more than ten stories skyward. It had several exhaust stacks and structural framework rising above it and piping connected to more than a half dozen silvery round metal storage tanks measuring half its height. The tanks were arranged in a single row and the piping and conveyors intersected with their cone shaped tops. Lesser metal appendages were connected to the main structure including what appeared to be a covered garage where the trucks would drive through to accept their load of grain. Oddly the structure was not really close to the rail line so they must use trucks to fill up the storage tanks.

Beyond the grain station was the unobstructed horizon; green–brown earth converging with the endless blue of the sky. Aside from the slight visible dips and rises in the road it was as flat as the desert. If you continued east to the end of US–54 you would end up in western Illinois. Change directions and El Paso, Texas would be the end of the line. *I better keep the other riders in sight,* I thought to myself.

Twenty miles out our group rolled into a little anomaly called Hooker, Oklahoma. This was a place with a bit of spunk and personality. I saw a sign, "Hooker, OK, Home of the Hooker Horny Toads," which happened to be an American Legion baseball team. Beyond the sign was a little metal building, almost the size of a two–car garage. It was the Hooker Oklahoma Chamber of Commerce and Gift Shop. I had to stop and so did a few others. Inside the building was a series of spirited t–shirts with quotes like "Hooker OK, a destination not a vocation", and "Once a Horny Toad, Always a Horn Toad!" and they were being sold by blue–haired church–going ladies in their '60s and '70s. They really embraced the town name and were not about to shy away from the novelty of it. Shirts were running nearly twenty bucks a pop and everyone needed at least two of them. Aware of the target times I was in and out in five minutes with plenty to laugh about with the other new "Hooker Patrons" over the next few hours.

And just like that we were twenty miles into the ride with only a hundred more to go. I continued pedaling in the company of many other riders. We moved around talking at times, drafting and conserving energy when needed but I tried not to get too caught up in the pace line action. Instead I shared brief conversations in an effort to pass the time. Pat and Vikki, were up ahead, Gary Decker cruised alongside with Peter Crowell, both on their low slung recumbents offering advice and support, as Phil and Barbara, Ron, Jim, Carol, and Geoff moved in and out of the group. Riders would come from behind and join in and others would drop back to mingle. Paul, Greg, Betty, Gray, and Kathy were the ones I remember most through this stretch. We rode close to the same pace and were fairly predictable in how we altered our riding.

In the pace line I noticed a lot about the riders in front of me. For a stretch I rode within a few feet of Betty's rear wheel and watched her fluid smooth pedaling with little shifting of her upper body. Her hands were loosely gripping the top of the bars and her forward motion was consistent staying less than six feet off the rear wheel of Gray. I tried to mimic her riding but I tended to get more erratic the more I concentrated on riding. I had to let my body manage the bike while my mind made sure I didn't run into Betty.

I craned my head and leaned to the right so I could look up the entire line. I was number seven for the moment. Orange flags attached to white fiberglass poles affixed to the rear of each bike were fluttering in the wind we created. I saw blue, orange, yellow, and even a few CrossRoads jerseys fitted to riders on Treks, Cannondales, and some highly custom bikes. Betty wore her CamelBak but most of the others relied on their bottles to stay hydrated. I could feel the draft and the benefit it provided but I was uncomfortable with the added pressure of staying in sync with others. I would eventually drop off enough to lose the aerodynamic benefit of the draft but still close enough to chat. Now if I only had my iPod and earbuds so I could find a tune to groove with like my training rides back in Florida.

The scenery changed as I rode. I saw rolling seas of bronze wheat fields and corn planted in quarter–mile circles, huge rotating water systems like never–ending suspension bridges stretching above. Center Pivot Irrigation systems is what they were actually called.

The wind evoked a rustling sound out of the fields which was actually quite loud considering there were no other noises for it to compete with. The rubbing of the corn leaves had a woody and thrashing sound and it reminded me of running through the cornfields as a boy back in New Jersey. It would ebb and flow with the wind waving the fields and it provided a bit of entertainment and distraction as I pedaled.

The first SAG was in Tyrone; nearly thirty miles down and only ten more to go if our destination was Liberal, which it wasn't. I still had ninety plus miles of pedaling to reach Dodge City. I need to think about something else and not dwell on the remaining mileage this early in the ride.

Margaret reminded everyone to sign in and wash their hands before reaching into the food baskets. And use the tongs she provided to avoid fingering all the food. With hands clean I topped off with Gatorade and water, popped a few tasty items into my cycling jersey, and then ate my normal half of a banana chasing it down with two cups of Gatorade. I grazed a bit on some berries and bite sized cakes before taking a few minutes to talk about the day. Miles and wind were the topics of discussion.

Applying sunscreen and chassis lube were common at the SAGs and I made sure I had plenty of the slippery stuff in place to keep my contact points with the seat happy. With each application the coolness of the lube reminds me how nice it would be to warm it up before reaching down my shorts to glob it on. But you do get over the cold shock about as quickly as you do the embarrassment of reaching down your pants in public. And for those innocent people who happen upon us as we conduct our SAG business we are not perverts just because several of us have our hands down our pants as we socialize.

Riders had to hustle out of the SAG by nine fifty and though I had plenty of time I didn't want to burn it up early. I grabbed another banana half from the table and popped it into my pocket. Then I did a quick tire check, put on my gloves and helmet and returned to US–54 eastbound with the majority of the cycling herd.

Five miles ahead of us was the Kansas state line. It would be yet another opportunity for photos, the sand sprinkling ritual, and entry into our sixth state. At nine thirty in the morning Gray, Kathy, and I, along with a few others made it to the big blue "Welcome to Kansas" sign featuring the state flower, a bright yellow wild sunflower. So here we stand in Kansas, the thirty–fourth US state that joined the union back in 1861. We did the photo shuffling and the rest of the dance then quickly got back on our bikes and pedaled into Liberal. US–54 was locally known as West Pancake Boulevard. It was also known as the Yellow Brick Road from the *Wizard of Oz* fame.

We passed signs offering directions to visit Dorothy's House and the Mid–American Air Museum. Both are worth the visit but it wouldn't happen today. The Air Museum has the fifth largest collection of civil and military aircraft in the United States and it was just a half mile off to the left.

Liberal sits at an elevation of 2,835 feet and is home to more than twenty thousand people. It boasts four newspapers, nine radio stations, and a television station. Their highly successful semi–pro baseball team called The Liberal Bee Jays, have won five national championships, thirteen state championships, and have sent 165 players to the major leagues.

As for job opportunities the beef industry which includes ranches, feed lots, and packing plants is Liberal's largest source of employment. I'd be fine working on a ranch as it has the romantic cowboy thing going for it, but the feed lots and packing houses are much too far down the food processing chain for me to mess with.

We had a long way yet to go so we made our way through the two miles which was Liberal proper and exited back to the emptiness of the wide open. There was a small plateau on the left side of the highway. It seemed out of place but it turned out to be part of the local landfill. Kansas was still flat.

Grasslands and crop circles covered the landscape. Jack rabbits darted through the grass, cows were grazing, and horses with their newborns were moving about the fields. If you become numb to the scenery you can count telephone poles. They had one every few hundred feet.

At the end of each day it was important to do a bit of research about the area covered in the ride so I could provide some color to my writing besides the hard core bike stuff. Then I would insert it where it makes sense, hoping when I read my account years from now I can better appreciate the entirety of the experience. And if others read it that's great and I hope you enjoy it, but my writing is intended for a small audience. No best seller expectations here.

In my discovery I learned the state motto of Kansas is *Ad Astra Per Aspera* which is Latin for "to the stars with difficulties" or roughly "A rough road leads to the stars." I guess they are right. The roads are favoring the rough side and I would expect in the wide open at night the darkness would provide for perfect stargazing.

As for rainbows, they would only play in my mind. Here in the wide open it is possible to dream without interruption and to listen to music stored deep in the recesses of your mind. I channeled Israel "IZ" Kamakawiwo'ole and turned the volume all the way up on *Somewhere over the rainbow*. It's one of the most beautiful songs sung by the most unlikely of singers; soulful, simple, and my favorite. For uncounted miles I played it over and over pinching my eyes to release the tears behind my shades. A smile frozen on my face; a memory I'll remember always.

Beyond Liberal, the sun warmed up, and so did the winds. Strong and steady side winds from the southeast and an occasional head wind had riders working hard all day.

The scenery was consistent throughout the day. I saw more rolling fields of corn, grains, grazing fields, a few scattered trees, but fewer grain structures except for one brief break just fifteen miles beyond Liberal. In an area called Arkalon Park was a shallow depression where the Cimarron River crossed under US–54. It looked completely dry but it was fairly wide suggesting it floods in abundance. I didn't realize over the last few miles the elevation dropped but I did feel it when I had to pedal a bit harder to climb out of the shallow bowl.

SAG two at the E–Z Stop came and went in Plains at mile sixty–four and I was well out in front of the 12:50 p.m. target time. Plains was another town built around massive concrete grain silos that dominated the view at the southeast corner of town. A quick photo or two to capture it seemed appropriate. The town gained notoriety for having the widest main street in the country measuring in at 155 feet five inches. I didn't know there was even a competition. I'm sure somewhere it probably includes the fact most of it is cobble stone.

US–54 took a turn due east and I was now seeing the wind almost head on. Speeds dropped quite a bit and this was a good time to find a partner to pair up with. I was still in the proximity of Gray, Betty, Greg, and Lynn so we leaned on each other for the remaining miles to Meade. The flatlands became more irregular with distinct hills and drops. We crossed a few more shallow depressions as the topology continued to change. We were crossing hills and the rolling countryside was now becoming craggier with sharper cuts and depressions.

In Meade we exited US–54 turning south onto Pearlette Street to find the Dalton Gang Hideout. It was another one of those stops you just have to do because you are there. Besides they had no less than three signs on the highway marking the turn to the hideout so it must be something to see right? It was only four blocks off route and it had clean restrooms so thanks to the Dalton Gang for making it a convenient stop for us.

The hideout is actually a small white clapboard house with a few other small structures on the property. There's also a short tunnel connecting the house to a barn some ninety–five feet away that was supposedly used by the Dalton Gang to evade those who pursued them. More photos and back on the bike for the push to SAG number three.

The road bent to the left putting us back on a northeast trajectory with the wind off our right side and out of our face. I pedaled at a more respectable pace through Fowler and into Minneola for the last SAG of the day but my thoughts of being off the bike within eight hours had been erased.

Feeling the fatigue I rolled to a stop at the Corner Store and made my way to the CrossRoads van for replenishment. I had cleared the century mark and was blessed with the best possible scenario to cover the final twenty–four miles to Dodge City. Exiting the SAG the route turned north and I rode a tailwind for the next twenty miles. It was fun and fast and in an hour I stood with Betty by the Dodge City sign getting our picture taken.

Next to the city limit sign was a smaller one declaring Dodge City as Tree City USA. I thought it was odd for Dodge to part of the Tree City USA program when there were so few trees. I later learned the name is well deserved because of the state's dedication to managing urban and community forests. They plant nearly ten thousand trees a year and maintain another fifty thousand. Go Kansas!

Entering Dodge City on North Second Avenue we crossed the Arkansas River. Not much of a river but more of a very wide flat bottom channel with raised banks lined with fence posts and cattle wire to keep people and animals out. Aside from a dirt single lane service road the river bottom was a lush green. Its depth was capable of holding back a dozen feet of water across a width close to five hundred feet. To see it flooded, now that would be a sight to experience.

A quarter mile beyond the Arkansas River I turned left onto West Wyatt Earp Boulevard for the last mile to the Comfort Inn, I could finally step off the bike and call this ride complete. Betty led the way and I trailed a few lengths behind. We passed the Boot Hill Museum on the right and a massive grain elevator farther up on the left. Relieved and safe we completed another significant ride on our way to Boston.

I covered 124 miles in eight hours forty–three minutes the hard way, and the reward is a day of rest in Dodge City, Kansas. I learned others did not fare as well. Vikki, one of the strongest and most seasoned riders, had a bout with the saddle that put her out early; her plan to ride every mile from LA to Boston was dashed. She was one of few I thought would never have trouble because of the miles she rode back in Florida. But no matter how prepared or experienced you are it only takes a few minutes of imperfection to get the best of you. All you can do is rest and recover and go after it another day. It also makes me question the need to pedal every mile. There is so much more to this trip than just sitting on the narrow seat.

It's a free dinner night which means Mexican for me and then maybe a stop at the Dairy Queen for chocolate soft serve ice cream. Then tomorrow a tour of the town, a search for postcards, then catch up on letters to home, laundry, write my installment for the DeLand Beacon, and enjoy good company. A busy rest day it will be. But first I need to clean this bike and shower off the grit and grime of the day. I'm a little tender in the private area but that's to be expected after nearly nine hours in these shorts. I can't wait to see Clark and celebrate today's ride.

So let's recap the day, I spent the morning with a couple of Hookers, traveled some rough roads in headwinds, laid low in the Dalton Gang Hideout, and cycled farther than I've ever done before. I averaged 14.2 miles per hour and topped the speed chart at a decent 25.8. Welcome to Kansas!

Day 21: Dodge City (Rest Day)

I learned from Clark where his inspiration came from in his pep talk he gave me two days prior. It was a quote from a pretty reliable source and it goes like this. – *Whether you believe you can do a thing or not, you are right.* – *Henry Ford*

In the morning I grabbed breakfast and struck up a conversation with a few people in the Comfort Inn lobby. Two ladies were traveling nurses. One had signed on for a thirteen–week stint at one of the local hospitals and they talked about the large Hispanic population, how they dealt with it, and the difficulties they faced with Spanish speaking patients. Both were looking forward to finishing up and moving on to another contract in some other city. Someone from the media was talking to a few of the riders as I chatted with others from our group. After a few minutes I headed out to explore the town.

Dodge City has a rich history, a diverse population, and a wide range of entertainment opportunities. Downtown I found Boot Hill Cemetery and Museum, historic Fort Dodge, and I was even close enough to step out on the Santa Fe train tracks if I dared to. Dodge City was also a hideout for the notorious Dalton Brothers. They were the infamous outlaws who robbed banks and trains in the region; the hell raisers of their day along with the likes of Jesse James and his gang.

I walked to the historic area around the Boot Hill Museum but they do have a trolley service providing an informative tour about the city. The narrative includes the rooms and locations used in the filming of the *Gun Smoke* TV series. On a sidewalk near Boot Hill I found a bronze plaque and Dennis Weaver's signature and hand prints in the cement. Dennis is one of the few living cast members from the series and folks may also remember him from the popular and more recent TV show, *McCloud*. He signed the concrete just a year earlier on May 25, 2003. And if you are into trivia, do you remember the name of his character on *Gunsmoke*? For those playing at home the answer is *Chester*.

Almost eighty percent of those living in Dodge City are of Spanish/Hispanic descent and nearly half do not speak English. This is not what I expected. Even though Dodge City is within 120 miles of Texas it seems like it's much farther north for such a cultural mix. This is southwestern Kansas so I need to realign my expectations. Touring around town I saw some interesting and even some quirky stuff. Dodge City did not disappoint. On a side street I took a picture of a law firm sign. Not just any law firm, it was the "Frigon Law Firm" sign. Now if I can only find the one for Dewey, Cheetum, and Howe.

Between the hotel and downtown there was an expansive grain silo complex along the rail line. A mile east of North 2nd Avenue where we came into town stood yet another pair of towering silo structures near a rail yard. Beyond the yard was the National Beef processing plant; definitely not on my tour plan for the day.

The Boot Hill Museum is located on the original site of the Boot Hill Cemetery where they have daily gunfight reenactments on Front Street with the period correct wooden buildings as a backdrop. You can belly up to the bar at the Long Branch Saloon for an ice cold sarsaparilla or a Budweiser, which by the way was the original beer served back at the Long Branch in the 1870s. It came in from St. Louis via the Santa Fe railway. Beer, trains, gunslingers, oh my!

Want to dress up as a character from the old west and take home a souvenir to remember the moment and impress your friends? Then an old time photo at the Boot Hill is just what you need. Looking for a place to get hitched or have a blow–out party? Why not do it at the Boot Hill? Seriously you can get married here. A shotgun wedding would be fitting. Maybe dress up the entire wedding party in period correct outfits. Definitely a story to tell the kids! Of course they have a gift shop, a restaurant, and an ice cream parlor. Would you expect anything less?

And about the name Boot Hill Cemetery, it came about because so many people were buried there with their boot on. It was only used for six years from 1872–78. So much history right here in the middle of southwestern Kansas. All you have to do is look for it—and did I mention the Teachers Hall of Fame? It's a real place located at 603 5th Ave, Dodge City. Look it up. Who comes up with this stuff?

On my way back to the hotel I saw a race car parked in a gas station parking lot. Of course I had to take a closer look and talk to the young kid standing by the car. It turned out he was racing that night at the track I passed the day before just two miles south of town. The gas station was one of his sponsors and he was there doing his promoting thing. So of course I had to find a way to get to the track to watch. I could walk if needed or take a cab but I was blessed by another rider who rented a car for the day and they let me borrow it for the evening.

Back at the hotel I looked up the track to get their phone number and proceeded to call their office. I talked with a lady in their marketing group. I mentioned I announced stock car races back in Florida and she invited me to come out as their guest. It kept getting better; a car, a free ticket, a hot night at the races.

So I did my quick sink laundry and in–room scatter drying, prepped my gear for the next day, and finished my postcards and writing before getting something to eat. After dinner I ventured out to the Dodge City Raceway Park to witness the opening night of sprint cars and late model stock cars on their new three–eighths mile dirt speedway.

What a show place it was. The city had gambled thirteen million dollars to create another source of tourism for the town and from what I could see it will pay off. The entire facility matches the amenities of a major league baseball park or even a NASCAR cup series host track. There was a high banked dirt track circling a smaller pavement track making it a highly versatile facility. The raceway had an outstanding lighting system capable of turning night into day and the seating was comfortable, affording a clear view of all the action. Unfortunately the hot temperatures brought with it an evening thunderstorm washing out the program after just a few preliminary events had been run. I never did get to see the boy I met at the gas station race his car.

It was a good solo outing for me even though it rained out. I was able to get back to the hotel to catch the local news which featured a story about some crazy bikers pedaling across the country. The reporter interviewed Tom and Randie Kahrl, part of our cycling group raising money for charity. How cool is that? I saw them speaking with the news crew earlier in the day but I was thinking it had something to do with a newspaper story. Tom and Randie were crossing the country on a tandem bike, a bicycle build for two just in case you weren't sure. It was cute to watch them on TV. They are good people with a compelling story to tell. It was nice to see the local station thought so too and gave them time to showcase their charity.

And so ends our third rest day. I wonder what Great Bend holds for me tomorrow.

Day 22: Dodge City to Great Bend (89 miles)

It's the first thing that goes on in the morning and the last to come off at night. It's a keepsake, just a simple silver disk, not much larger than a dime. Its shape is irregular, with the impression of my father's thumb print inscribed with "POPPY 1925–1999" on the opposite side. It hangs on a length of chain around my neck just over my heart. As it touches my skin I feel a connection to him. I've had dad's keepsake since shortly after he passed in the early morning hours of December 26, 1999. At times I find myself holding the silver rubbing my thumb to his print just as I remember holding his hand in the twilight, rubbing it softly as he slipped away from cancer and became whole once more. I wear no other jewelry, no rings, no watches, nothing except this memory.

The weather forecast called for violent thunderstorms including hail and the potential for tornadoes by late afternoon. I feel like I may be holding the lucky lottery ticket for today's weather. With the warning message received the goal for the day will be to move as swiftly as possible to the city of Great Bend. Sounds so easy for the weatherman to say, he doesn't have to pedal for six hours in whatever conditions Mother Nature decides to put in front of us, or behind or over us for that matter. That's my job, and the job of more than three dozen others waking up to his joyful news in their rooms scattered about this hotel. In my viewing experience the weatherman is usually wrong, and that's okay. Today I really hope he is wrong.

So I roll out of bed and then I realize at this point in my cross country adventure I can pretty much ready myself for riding in my sleep. Sometimes my body finds it difficult to shake the night's cobwebs off when the alarm clock sounds but today I'm pretty alert and ready to get this day in motion.

I shower, dress, and take my bike down the stairs and out the door to the Golden Corral for breakfast just a mile back towards downtown on West Wyatt Earp Boulevard. In less than five minutes I'm seated at a table with some other strange looking spandex wearing early risers. At least I fit in. Weird. Not that I fit in it's just some of the other riders push the strange meter in their choice of outfits. Like old granny outlaws weird. Coffee calls so I gladly hold out my cup for a full pour from the nice lady with the thermal pot of full strength brew. No decaf for me.

With some chatter and coffee to wash down the ample breakfast I was warm and filled. I pushed my way from the table, stepped outside, and mounted my bike to retrace the route back to the Comfort Inn. As I carry my bike up the stairs and back to my room the thought of crawling under the covers tempts me. It passes as soon as the door opens and Clark's gear is already out of the room. I breathe out asking myself, *How does he do it?*

I methodically collect my personal items, stow everything going directly to the next hotel into my two duffels, and the rest I either hang off the bike bars or put into my jersey pockets. Then back down the steps to the staging area right out in front of the lobby doors.

I do all of the proper things with my bags, then I take my place in the pump queue to top off the air in the tires. The remaining minutes tick by to the chatter of riders as we wait for the official call to sign–out and begin riding.

Temperatures hovered around sixty degrees under lightly clouded skies with only a trace of wind coming out of the south. Cool by cycling standards but it would be fine once we were riding.

The morning exit routine for riders who do it every day is not such a big deal but to those who unexpectedly catch us in action it could be anything from humorous to disturbing. I can just imagine the conversations they tell. "Martha! Martha! Look out the window. That guy on the bike is wearing puffy underwear and his bike has no seat! Good Lord! There are more of them! Is that a contamination suit? Stanley lock the door!" In your mind you can see it too. I knew you could.

As Trevor and his team load the bags on the truck Tracy gives the departure orders. She makes each day special for someone by calling a rider's name to be the first to sign out. Then she calls the order of riders which is usually the more casual paced, followed by the steady, and then the speedy riders. It makes sense as it tends to tighten the group up a few miles out from the hotel. After that the faster riders begin to open the gap.

So off we go heading back towards downtown Dodge City and a half mile in we make the left north onto Fourteenth Avenue and immediately up a damn hill. Why is there always a hill when we start? At least there was only a hint of a breeze and fortunately it was behind us.

As I pedaled I could feel my legs compete with my digestive activities. It would be a while before my legs get the proper support so I settled in and did my best to maintain the pace of those around me. Duffey was nearby working his pedals with his knees pointing decidedly outward and almost perpendicular to the direction he was traveling. Like a big guy on a bike too small. But he looked like that every day and managed to get along just fine. I'm not exactly the model example of the ideal cyclist either so I better focus on my own riding and on the road.

In just over two miles we made the turn onto the wider and much busier US–50 Bypass heading east and almost immediately I could feel the wind coming from my right. Over the next few miles the wind picked up and it moved around from the south until it was right in my face. It might have only been blowing at ten miles an hour but it sapped my strength and cut my speed.

All the riders reacted knowing they are much better riding together in headwinds. We began to form natural groups. I was with Kathy, Betty, Greg, and a few others. I also saw other groups forming into a mixed bag of formal pace lines and clustered groupings of a more social nature. We crossed Avenue P and left Dodge City behind us trading buildings and humanity for green fields.

A few miles later we passed the Dodge City Municipal Airport. We couldn't actually see the airport but the large round orange balls hanging on the power wires alongside the highway gave us proof it was there.

Traffic was light, the shoulder wide and smooth, and only the customary rumble cuts in the asphalt to separate us from traffic. The cuts were just about a foot inside the shoulder of the white line leaving us at least five feet of clear riding space. It was possible to pass other riders safely without having to venture into traffic but I would not make a habit of riding side by side for anything more than to pass a slower rider.

I much preferred the rumble cuts instead of the reflectors. I think they provide a better warning for vehicles drifting onto the shoulder and that gives me a bit more time to react if needed. At the edge of the pavement the ground sloped down into a shallow ditch providing a reasonable exit to safety. I just hope I never hear the rumble and have to commit myself to exit. Being aware, I hope, is the extent of my actions for this trip.

Aside from the tree line along the edge of the airport property there was nothing but green fields as far as I could see. The grasses waved in the breeze, I could hear the wind shift as it sync'd up with the bending of the greenery. Actually it would be quite relaxing if I didn't have to pedal to keep forward motion.

Hopper was battling a cold and was not up to full strength so Betty and I decided to ride with him to block the side winds. He tucked in close to my left and slightly behind to take full advantage of my shielding. Betty would take point adding to the protective cover and every mile or so she would drop back to catch a break herself.

I hadn't talked to Hopper much so far. I don't think he spoke much to anyone but he was struggling and I wasn't so there we were, three riders now separated from the rest. One recumbent rider cloaked in full sun protection from head to toe with only a small circular patch around his mouth, nose, and eyes exposed to the elements. This was in stark contrast to Betty and I with our arms and legs freely collecting the sun.

We didn't speak much as we rode but having the added responsibility kept me from focusing on the odometer and other digital readouts that only served to disappoint me with less than desired progress reports. It was a nice change of pace having the opportunity to ride with Hopper and it got me away from thinking only about the elements and my personal challenges. I knew Hopper made the crossing the year before so I was interested in talking with him later at the hotel when we were off the bikes.

Over the next hour the road curved to the northeast and then a bit further into the ride the winds increased but to our benefit they also shifted from the east to south giving us a bit of a tailwind bump. I could now begin enjoying the land waves and the new found speed. The temperature was on its way up and it had already crossed seventy–five degrees on the way to a high of ninety.

Past Spearville and the grain towers to the right there is nothing but green fields and large modern windmills as far as I can see. The road continued smooth and flat. We stayed in formation and clicked off miles at an enjoyable pace. Periodically I'd look left and check on Hopper. Each time I saw the same look of fatigue, the tell–tale signs of a cold, and his determined focus to stay in the sweet spot of my wake to take full advantage of the draft. He was like a bird in formation; never too close and never too far off my position. Straight and steady according to the moves Betty and I made. There was trust, respect, security, and even a bit of comfort. Days down the road Hopper would surely return the favor if needed.

The SAG was just ten miles ahead at a convenience store in Offerle, population hovering just over two hundred. We would stop, refresh, and get back on the road as a set of three. It was working for us so far and I sure didn't want to miss out on our good fortune of a healthy tailwind. I'd like to think it was Hopper's doing.

The windmills continued long after Spearville. I was in awe of the massive white structures. Large, slender, round towers maybe two hundred feet tall with three blades each extending a hundred feet from their axis. They were so far from the road it was actually hard to gage their size but I'd read up on the engineering of these structures long before making this trip. They also stood much taller than the grain towers and I could eyeball their proportions to the other buildings so I was pretty confident in my estimates.

About three miles ahead I begin to make out the white boxy structure of a grain tower. Offerle was just ahead. Our route had taken us parallel to the rail line but the train traffic had been particularly quiet today. At times the rails were only fifty feet away so a train riding in our direction would provide quite a sensation.

The grain tower rose up to our right and the CrossRoads van was visible on the left in the Offerle Country Store parking lot. We were thirty miles into the ride with only another fifty–five to go to reach Great Bend. What started out as an uncertain day was shaping up to be a very good one. Betty, Hopper and I made the turn into the lot taking care not to slide in the loose gravel, and then we stepped off the bikes.

I went about the normal SAG routine, replenishing water in the CamelBak, snacking, taking advantage of the restrooms and checking the bike tires for glass bits, radial tire wire, and cuts. Everything was in order so after checking out the large western wall mural on the Offerle Taco restaurant and flipping our cue sheets, it was time to continue on.

Hopper didn't bolt out as he easily could have. He was much faster on his recumbent than anyone on an upright. I think he enjoyed the company and the opportunity to conserve his energy. So off we went back on US 50E with sights set for our next turn 7.2 miles ahead onto US–56E toward Larned.

On the way we passed the cross roads of US–50E and 50th Avenue otherwise known as Ardell. It was nothing but two rusting abandoned metal train service buildings and a small single story bunk house. We never broke our stride. Our pace continued to increase as we crossed over the twenty mile per hour mark and eventually settled in at a solid twenty three plus. That's nearly half again my normal pace when riding solo without any wind.

We rounded a slight left bend past a house sitting amongst some trees, then exactly where it said on the cue sheet was our right hand turn onto US–56E. A few hundred feet later we had arrived in a place called Kinsley, or as it is more famously known, Midway USA. From here San Francisco and New York City are the same distance; 1,561 miles each way to be exact.

It took a moment to sink in. We were half way across America. It said as much on the large sign so we got off the bikes and posed for pictures, me in my solid bright yellow jersey, Betty in her bright blue colors, and Hopper in his dress whites. He was the one in the contamination suit I mentioned at breakfast. Actually he was very cautious about skin cancer and was smarter than the rest of us.

We didn't take the time to visit the Sod House and Museum located on the back of the property even though it's free to the public, but we did go over to the old locomotive sitting just off of US–56E behind the Midway sign. It was a 3400 Pacific 4–6–2 built between 1919 and 1924 by the Baldwin Locomotive Works; one of only fifty built. Most were used until 1950 when they started to be retired. Except for this engine most were gone by 1955, which means they were likely scrapped. AT&SF 3423 was operated by the Atchison, Topeka and Santa Fe Railway, better known as the Santa Fe Line before it was taken out of service and moved to its current home. As for the Sod House I learned inside the museum building is a 1957 replica of the type of sod house common in the area back in the 1800s.

After a few minutes and some pulls of water we mounted our bikes and were back on the road to our second SAG of the day at Downey Park just past the town of Garfield. Miles before we reached Garfield the grain towers gave its location away. It took us only twelve minutes to cover the four miles to town as we were gliding effortlessly along compared to our earlier pace.

Named after James A. Garfield, the twentieth President of the United States, Garfield is home to less than 190 people and it covers an area of less than .54 square miles. Surprisingly it has a City Hall, a library, and a Post Office established in 1873. After only twenty–two miles from the last SAG it was nice to have another restroom break and some quick snacks.

The three of us were back on the road and aside from some care to negotiate a rough railroad crossing at mile sixty–two we would have an arrow straight shot all the way to Great Bend. Along the way we would pass through Larned, population: 4,100, with a thriving historic downtown district and the home of the Central States Scouting Museum.

As we approached the town of Pawnee Rock, Betty and I told Hopper we were going to detour off route to check out the historical marker on the right side of the road and then over to the Pawnee Rock monument itself. He was going to continue on to the Great Bend so we slowed as Hopper accelerated. It was amazing how quickly he disappeared and I could only assume he was clocking over thirty before he was gone. I was sure he rode at our pace as a way of saying thank you for helping him earlier in the day. I thought it was pretty cool.

The historical marker described the Pawnee Rock landmark as the midpoint of the Santa Fe Trail between Missouri and New Mexico. It continued on detailing the brave people who followed the trail in search of something better than what they had back east. I snapped a photo of the sign; we rode to town and made the left onto North Center Street to see the monument for ourselves.

The town of Pawnee Rock has a small population of somewhere near 240 and it has been in decline for the past twenty–five years. The sandstone rock the town is named for is also known as the "Citadel of the Prairie."

Located a quarter mile north of US–56E the rock offered a high vantage point nearly a century ago for the Indians to watch travelers as they crossed the wide open country. This made it one of the most dangerous spots on the Santa Fe Trail. The view from Pawnee Rock is impressive. I could see the city of Great Bend fifteen miles away to the east and the tree lined Arkansas River three miles south.

A plaque on the rock had a quote from Private Jacob S. Robinson dated July 8, 1846 that gave context to what I would have seen if I had been here a hundred years earlier.

"The buffalo herds marched in rows while others grazed freely. Their numbers were so great that the distant hills to the north and east turned black."

Looking east it was hard to imagine such a herd could be possible but I trust his record of the day was accurate. I just wished I had the opportunity to see it for myself. There was a second monument honoring those who traveled the trail. It read—In honor of the brave men and women who passing over the old Santa Fe Trail, endured the hardships of frontier life, and blazed the path of civilization for posterity.

After fifteen minutes taking pictures and soaking in the views Betty and I rode down the mound and back through the little town of Pawnee Rock making the left turn east onto US–56E for the final fourteen miles. The tailwind kicked in and we were at the Super 8 Motel in less than forty–five minutes.

Unlike most hotels we have stayed at the Super 8 was set back from the road, tucked in behind other commercial operations and flanked to the left by some rather modest private homes and close to a rail line at the rear. It did have an indoor pool and Jacuzzi for those looking to get wet.

Upon arriving in Great Bend the temperature had reached ninety degrees and it was very humid. Storm clouds formed to the east but the violent weather predicted earlier in the day never materialized.

My bike required only a gentle wipe down and then I put it up for the night and proceeded to shower and do laundry. Dinner was at Perkins as would be our breakfast tomorrow. I caught up with Hopper at dinner and he thanked me for the day's ride. He said he doesn't ride with many people but he said I'd be welcome any time. Kind words from a man who says few. The rest of the evening was routine and when writing my thoughts for the day I made the following notes about Great Bend:

- It has a population of more than 15,500 with a total land area covering 10.71 square miles sitting at an elevation of 1,850 feet above sea level
- Home to the Kansas Oil and Gas Museum
- The first nationwide NHRA sponsored drag racing event called "The Nationals" was held in 1955 at the Great Bend Municipal Airport
- Jack Kilby, a graduate of Great Bend High School, inventor of the semiconductor, and the 2000 Nobel Prize Laureate in Physics is from Great Bend
- The city airport was used for B–29 bomber training in World War II.

I recorded the mileage and my average speed for the day at 89.16 and 15.7 respectively. Somewhere I reached 24.2 miles per hour. I'd like to think it was a solid five hours thirty–nine minutes of riding mixed in with some sightseeing. It's not a race and I did have some help the last two thirds of the day thanks to the wind and my riding partners. And that was my day. Good riding, good company, a good dinner, and one happy cyclist who had a perfect day in the saddle. Fingers crossed many more follow.

Day 23: Great Bend to McPherson (64 miles)

With short mileage today riders get to enjoy another delayed departure from the hotel. The added hour of sleep is welcomed by most, but a few riders have a hard time venturing away from their cross country routine. Their alarms ring early and they find themselves dressed, packed, and sitting idle waiting to get on the road. Me, I used the extra hour last night to write. Clark manages to tolerate it and since he gets up early to handle his staff duties I'm not far behind him starting my day.

Our schedule was clear, breakfast at seven thirty, luggage loading at eight fifteen, and then we roll out of Great Bend at eight thirty sharp. At least that's what was on my cue sheet. We only had two quadrants on the cue to navigate saving the third quadrant for hotel and other details at our destination town.

These vital instructions were yet another example of the precision and detail Tracy labored to complete prior to tour. Every critical turn, every point of interest, every cattle guard and tricky railroad crossing called out precisely, with distance measured in tenths of miles and in feet where needed. Her attention to detail ensured I would enjoy the experience instead of trying to figure out where I am and what I needed to pay attention to. One of many little things adding up to the big thing that makes CrossRoads the right decision for my journey.

It's day twenty–three and like all those behind me—and those yet to come—it's unique. I find it exhilarating to think about it in this way. In the middle of Kansas, part of a nomadic group, passing through the lives of the locals living and working in the small towns, streets lined with predominantly white framed houses conservatively trimmed in pastel shades and anchored to their plots with white picket fences and well–groomed landscape.

Flowers bold and fragrant offering a rainbow of color, trees blooming with new spring growth, the earthy yet slightly sour smell of fresh cut lawns, a hint of dust and a cool breeze washing over the warming asphalt; bees darting about. The air has weight to it and a subtle taste of freshness. Mixed breeds big and small barking from behind protective fences as a warning to the two–wheeled intruders they're on duty. It's hard to say if the fences keep them in or strangers out. From their calls most dogs want to play while others have plans of a different kind.

Over the next few blocks the palette transitions to brick and stone commercial buildings, then metal and concrete grain silos, bricked streets marking the town square, rail crossings cutting diagonally across the roadway, and signs of all types and sizes until it gives way completely to greenery. In my mind a visual symphony of the man–made with nature's backdrop of greens and browns tying it all together under an ever changing sky of pale blue and clouds. Each day is unique. Each bird that flies by and every person I see marks it as such. As I imagine it in my mind so it shall be as I ride. All I need to do is observe, engage, and pedal. I can't wait to get the day started!

A shorter day on the bike calls for a fitting breakfast so I stepped up the calorie consumption. Extra coffee, extra bacon, a pancake, and a few other things I've forgotten about to go with the normal eggs and assorted sides Perkins is known for. With forty–five minutes to eat and report to the lobby with my luggage I was more about shoveling food and gulping the coffee than socializing. Riders did talk, and we did laugh about things that happened in our first half of the trip. And like most mornings we sprinkled in a few predictions of what was yet to come. Would we be right in our forecasts? Maybe, but we'd find out for sure over the next few weeks.

Nobody mentioned being disturbed in the night by trains at breakfast. I guess the tracks running just feet off the back of the hotel see sporadic use at best but more likely no trains travel them anymore. Trains or not, I slept so deeply I didn't hear any rumbles.

There is a feeling I recall from middle school, maybe even high school, the optimism of what is to be and the excitement of it unfolding. At this moment I don't feel my age. I feel like a boy and it makes me smile. Could riding my bike be the elusive fountain of youth so many have longed to find? I'm sure it isn't, but in this moment it gives me hope and it nurtures my soul. It takes me back to the happiest times in my life; the simplest where time was abundant and I felt connected to my surroundings without my mind troubled with thoughts that steal away the pleasure. A boy on his bike; two wheels in contact with the ground, feet pedaling and hands steering the bars in whatever direction my mind takes it. Heaven; it must be this way when I get to heaven.

And so the unique day marking this twenty–third start begins in a crushed stone and pavement lot amongst friends. The distance through the lot before joining West 10th Street gave me ample time to safely clip into the pedals and make the usual body adjustments.

Each day was like a new introduction of your sit bones to the saddle. You ease into it until all of your weight is distributed between the butt and the bars. Some days you go heavy forward on your arms and other days your bottom doesn't argue. Today I am heavy in the saddle which is a good thing. I was getting a bit stiff in the wrists the past few days and this would allow my hands and arms a break without having to affect my balance. I'd also get to practice one of my favorite positions; riding hands–free straight up on the seat with my hands hanging down at my sides. It didn't happen often and it wasn't something I did without being fully attentive because things could go wrong really fast. It was still a fun throwback to the days of the kid on the old ten–speed.

The first few turns on the cue sheet had us move quickly off the busy undivided four–lane of West 10th Street buzzing with commercial activities and continuing east on Broadway just a few blocks north. A few miles later we would return to West 10th Street and continue out of town.

Logic would suggest it'd be easier to stay on 10th right out of the hotel but then we would have missed the peaceful ride on Broadway. Offering a single lane of divided traffic, beautifully landscaped medians and what I'd like to think of as a super wide bike lane and not empty curbside parking, Broadway was a joy. I rode past well–maintained mature yet modest wood frame houses, an abundance of large leafy shade trees in the medians and yards, lawns green and cut making it clear these folks were proud of their homesteads. A few lights held riders up for cross traffic and it afforded me a brief opportunity to chit–chat, take a pull of water, and adjust my gear or the boys. The boys being the Three Stooges finger puppets I had riding on my flag pole since Los Angeles.

The last few blocks of Broadway were a transition from landscaped medians and homes to commercial businesses and pavement running curb to curb. The cue sheet showed a right onto the 281 By–Pass which was also Main Street in the downtown proper. This five block stretch would close the loop back to 10th and put us on a trajectory to Ellenwood a little over nine miles east on US–56.

On Main Street, Betty and I passed the Barton County Courthouse positioned in the middle of a two–block park–like square. The impressive four–story off–white brick building with arched windows was set back sixty feet surrounded by ample grassy areas flanking the structure and crisscrossed with sidewalks. Had it not been across the traffic lanes we might have taken the opportunity to explore the grounds and take photographs.

If you ride past the courthouse today you'll see a memorial featuring three larger than life bronze statues; an adult and two small children in front of the building. To the left of the memorial a sturdy pole where the stars and stripes were proudly waving thirty feet up. This is the *Gift,* at Kilby Plaza dedicated to Jack Kilby, inventor of the semi–conductor, winner of the 2000 Nobel Prize in Physics, and native of Great Bend. The statues depict Kilby handing a microchip to a boy while a girl points to the stars and readies herself to receive the microchip so she can share it with the world. Kilby was a prolific inventor with more than sixty patents to his credit. Besides the semi–conductor, he also co–invented the pocket calculator and thermal printer. And not to be left out, Chet Cale, a *Great Bender* himself is the artist who created the sculpture. Though the memorial was not on the courthouse grounds when I pedaled past in 2004 I would be remiss if I didn't include it for those who may follow in my tire tracks.

I did learn a bit of the area history. Barton County was organized May 16, 1872 and it was named after Clara Barton, the Civil war nurse and founder of the American Red Cross. As for Great Bend, well it got its name because the town was built at the spot where the Arkansas River bends in the middle of the state; simple right? These are just a few more reasons why I should ride across the country again.

Within minutes we were free of the commercial zone and well into the green. We crossed Walnut Creek, one of the tributaries to the Arkansas River that rambled just out of our view to the right amongst the trees. If it were fall or winter we may have been able to see it. Thinking back we did cross over it as we rode into Dodge City a few days ago. US–56 ran close to due east absent of major cross roads except for KS–156 which forked off to the northeast just past Fort Zarah Park. Besides KS–156 it was only secondary side streets that intersected with the highway and dissolved into the distance.

Winds have been slight since leaving the hotel, mostly from the west providing the slightest of tail winds peppered with an occasional shift from the north. Temperatures started in the mid–sixties but are expected to rise into the mid–nineties, nearly ten degrees above the average for this time of year. Humidity will be high getting to the upper eighties by the late afternoon. For now it's very comfortable and I plan to enjoy the ride. So far so good.

Patches of tree clusters dot both sides of the road. The pavement narrowed to a single lane each way leaving a generous and smooth shoulder to pedal safely away from traffic. The carved–in rumbles that would alert us to errant vehicles stayed true and well within the shoulder side of the white line. Riding conditions were good and I was able to let my mind wander.

I am like a cloud, slowly moving across the road which is my sky. And as I do I am transformed, reshaped and renewed. You may see in me dedication, or struggle, fear or joy, but you will see something in me for sure.

I may disappear from my sky at the end of the day but in the morning I will return with the sun, inspired and slowly moving like an artist's brush across the canvas, transforming through the day, better than I was before.

Day dreaming, when riding allows it, is one of my favorite experiences. I can mentally go places while my body moves with the mechanical advantage the bike affords. Sometimes they are the same place but the best trips have two destinations; one for the body and one for the soul. I don't drift off like I'm sleeping but I do let the parts of my brain not critical to safe cycling wonder. It's like listening to the radio in the car, and I'm sure everyone has had those moments when they realize a few miles had passed and they wonder how they got where they are. And if it's just me did I ever reveal a bit of truth I can't take back.

To my left and right, a few old rusty mechanical oil wells called *Pump Jacks* are scattered along the roadside and in the fields see–sawing their way through the day and night pumping oil. In a slow and steady motion like a musician's metronome keeping time, keeping the rhythm, up and down, up and down, counter weight turning, a trace of mechanical noise blending in with the wind moving past my ears. No storage containers are visible. I wonder if they are buried under ground or if the jacks are connected by pipes to storage tanks located farther away.

Most pump jacks extract less than ten barrels of oil a day but they continue to operate because at such low levels they would not be able to restart. Those that can be restarted are turned *On* and *Off* depending on the cost to extract the oil. Pump when you can make a dollar and let it sit in the ground if you can't. It's really that simple.

I don't know much about old oil wells but it's a basic piston pump driven by an electric motor forcing the oil out of the ground. Most have large heavy flywheels or counterbalances a few feet in diameter rotated by the motor. Connected to the massive wheels are metal beams attached near the outer diameter and the other end to the large pump arm that converts the rotational motion into a linear force down the well. The piston pumps just a few feet vertically into the ground but it is enough to bring up the crude.

It turns out that ever since Kinsley I have been riding through very productive gas and oil reserves well hidden beneath the fields. I see nothing but fertile ground sitting atop the buried gold. I wonder who thought to even look for oil here, or anywhere for that matter.

The rail line came back to greet us running parallel and less than a hundred feet to our right, the tracks slightly elevated on the crushed rock bed. Between the road and the rails a slight grassy depression gave a clear view should we be treated to a long–haul train.

Not much traffic today as we ride into Ellinwood but we do give up our shoulder as it converts into a secondary traffic lane at the town's welcome sign. Tall weathered concrete grain elevators stand to the right of the road, a long train of various colored open and closed grain cars sits idle on the rails. To my left the earth–tone colored brick Methodist Church and a block farther up a metal four–legged water tower with "Ellinwood" painted in big bold letters. Under the steel tower is the supporting equipment surrounded by chain linked fencing securing the Ellinwood Power Plant.

A hundred yards ahead the buildings encroach on the road. To the right a metal building, grayed, drab in color, made of overlapped corrugated metal siding and roof panels, the patina of rust on the edges and where secured by nails. It stood eight feet to my right with only gravel separating it from the roadway. On the left a more pleasant white building, the Ellinwood Emporium that leads the eye down the brick paved Main Street. In fact most of the streets I could see were paved in brick.

So before I mention how this town came about I'm going to talk about the coolest thing this town could have possibly ever experienced. Back in 1973 the rock band Kansas rented the Ellinwood Opera House to perform for a New York record executive. As a way to draw a crowd and impress the executive they offered free beer and charged only a quarter for admission. It worked. There were 526 people in attendance and their performance ended in a record deal. And as they say in show business, the rest is history. As for the Opera

House, it's dust in the wind. It would have been one of my preferred stops if it still existed but it was demolished leaving only the memories. Carry on my wayward son!

Ellenwood, population: 2,140, was first staked out in 1872 when it was certain the railroad would be completed nearby. It's founding was not unlike the other towns across the Midwest. The town named after Santa Fe railroad civil engineer Colonel John Ellinwood was incorporated in 1878. It became a fast growing community attracting descendants of southern German/Austrians thanks to a creative marketing campaign launched in Illinois. During the late 1890s Ellinwood was a social and cultural center and it continues to show its distinct German heritage in its architecture and brick streets.

What makes this town unique is that two cities, one above ground and one below ground, are built there. I assumed the underground was built for safety but it was actually built to provide a more private place for the cowboys of the west to conduct business and pleasure. From approximately 1887 to the early 1920s you could wash off the dirt from the Santa Fe Trail in a metal bath tub at William Young's Bath House. You could get a drink at one of the eleven saloons, get your horse and wagon repairs done at Tom Drake's Harness Shop, a hair cut in the barber shop, deposit money in the bank, or find some companionship in one of the brothels, all out of public view. It was a network of underground passage tunnels connecting much of the downtown building basements. Today you can see a portion of the tunnel that has been restored revealing a "men–only" barbershop and bath. It was not open on Sunday so I had to learn about the underground by looking it up on the internet. It's still some interesting history for an old train town.

When you bicycle through a town you owe it to yourself to learn about what you have seen. Better still if you plan a trip like this make sure you study the route as best you can in advance to learn about the places worth more of your time and then make the effort to explore. You will likely never get a chance to do it a second time. At the very least, talk to people in these pass–through towns. They are pretty darn interesting. They have dreams to do things and they will definitely be interested in hearing about your journey. Consider it a community service to motivate others to life changing pursuits like you are doing, will be doing, or should be doing. And if you haven't pondered a life changing event this is your, "Get off your ass notice!"

Even at this point in the trip I wish I took more time to talk to at least one person each day. Going forward I'll ask a person in line at the convenience store why they like the town, the guy behind the counter at the sandwich shop if he always lived here, the seniors sitting at a table when I stop to each lunch if they play bingo or cards. These conversations enrich the journey and create unshakeable memories of the trip. I'll take time for the kid who says "Mister why are you wearing those funny shorts?" or the burly bearded leather clad bikers outside the ice cream shop to compare our mounts and helmets. The ride is for the body and these connections are for the soul. It is life changing and I expect until my maker takes away the memories these will be the ones I go to when I need to be happy. Easy–peasy said the Queen bee.

Exiting Ellinwood we did recover our riding shoulder but as we crossed from Barton to Rice County it was only about half as wide. I got spoiled having six feet of lane to ride but it's still a good smooth patch of road so I'll enjoy what I have and make the best of it.

At twenty–four miles into the ride I saw a billboard for First Bank. "Welcome to Chase," was on both sides of the sign which made me laugh. It was such a small town it didn't warrant a second sign, one on each end of town. Technically Chase was not on US–56 but off to the north so maybe they figured they'd save a few dollars with this sign. Less than five hundred feet from the sign was the green road department sign pointing left for Chase and the actual turn looked more like a driveway than the main street into town. Blink once and Chase is in your mirror. I blinked twice and I kept following Betty east.

The riding seemed rather easy, but not just because we were having slight favorable side and tailwinds. We were giving up elevation which means it has been downhill since Great Bend. Technically we started at 1,850 feet of elevation this morning and by the time we reach Lyons two hours later we were at 1,680. That's 170 feet or the height of a fifteen story building. We did have rolling hills but it was way more down than up. This was pretty significant considering Kansas is visually flat.

Through this portion of the ride I experienced some of the most enjoyable and beautiful scenery so far on tour. Rolling hills dressed in bands of golden wheat, knee high green corn, and fresh tilled brown soil providing a sharp contrast to the blue skies. The kid was coming back and the adult was pushed to the background. I felt energized and a bit snappy on the bike.

Lyons was a bigger town as evidenced by the Lyons Rice County Airport just west of town. That's not to say you could fly commercial out of the airport unless you consider a Piper Cub a commercial flight. The shoulder also widened a bit making conditions better.

Lyons was founded in 1870 as Atlanta but was founded again six years later as Lyons, named after Freeman J. Lyons. I have no idea what Freeman did or who he was and Google was no help at all. The town was incorporated in 1880, the same year the railroad was built through it.

Lyons feels much bigger than the population of 3,730 would suggest but it is tightly packed into a one and a quarter mile square surrounded by fields. You either live in the town of Lyons or you are grazing on the plains. There is no 'burb to this happening place.

The usual suspects of Pizza Hut, Wendy's, and Sonic Drive–In provide a familiar welcome. They are conveniently located on the south side just in case I want to get something before the SAG—but I won't. I'm a SAG man, spoiled by Margaret since day one, so I'm not going to stop. But if I did I'd want to taste the local cuisine, maybe El Potrillo where the vegetarian menu is highly praised or Scrambled Sam's for the cob smoked bacon and pancakes. And if I were hungry, really hungry, I could try both places and roll slow the last thirty miles to McPherson.

For those seeking to refuel their spiritual tank in Lyons you have plenty of options too. I passed Faith Bible Church, First United Methodist, and the Church of the Nazarene while pedaling the mile along Main Street. If I were curious enough to venture off of the main route I could find Grace Lutheran, the Church of Christ, First Presbyterian, First Christian, St. Mark's Episcopal, and First Baptist Church. And if you seek spirits in a bottle you'll find them at both the east and west ends of the Main Street. I'm not sure if it is by coincidence or divine province but the spirits and spiritual centers are within steps of each other.

At mile 31.9 I stop at East Avenue to take a photo of the Civil war monument standing in front of the Rice County Courthouse. A tall angular pillar of stone, topped by a soldier standing, both hands firmly gripping the barrel of his musket, wood stock planted by his feet. The words, "Lest We Forget" scribed into the base. The monument likely looks as it did back in 1918 when it was erected. The four–story courthouse of brick with arched details and a soaring clock tower set into a landscape of green grass and mature shade trees served as a fitting backdrop. The SAG was just two blocks ahead and when the light turned green I pedaled on to my destination.

Workman Park is just a small two acre oasis behind a convenience store but it offers shaded picnic tables, green grass to relax on, and a compliment of playground equipment put to good use by several riders. For a few minutes I could imagine the years rolling back as feet pointed high into the air, legs pumping driving the swings ever higher. Riders were having fun and I was enjoying the doughy snacks and fresh fruit found on the red and white checkered folding tables. SAG heaven. I chatted, topped off my water bottles, and made sure to have a few swigs of Gatorade before finding the restroom and then Betty so we could roll on the last two hours to McPherson.

On the fringe of town a half mile south of US–56 where it bends to the northeast there is mining operation, one of only three underground salt mines in Kansas. Operations began here in 1890, when the Western Salt Company put down its first shaft a thousand feet into the earth. Working in shifts miners use explosives, heavy equipment, and conveyors to extract their portion of the state's three million tons of salt each year. Like oil and gas, salt is just another hidden treasure in this part of Kansas.

Severe thunder storm warnings were in effect for the afternoon, which kept us motivated, but nothing ever materialized. Temperatures quickly rose from the low seventies to the nineties and the humidity was approaching ninety percent.

We pedaled past clusters of evergreens and humble homes adrift in the expanse of green. Miles later I saw gas fields on the right, dozens of grassless pads with pipes protruding from the ground. Some pipes connected to small white painted tanks and others bending back into the earth without explanation. There were metal control panels protected by tin roofs twenty paces from each protruding pipe. And at each panel a post with a service light. Wells were spaced nearly four hundred feet apart in a grid parallel to the road. This was Mitchell, Kansas and it was very flat in every direction.

US–56 remained fairly straight; fields of corn, grains, and wild grasses continued right and left to the horizon and every so often a lone shade tree, maybe a cluster of trees, were anchored to the ground. There were a few muddy creeks intersecting the road but they would disappear quickly into the grass.

A large installation of tall cylindrical tanks and complex interconnecting pipes occupied several acres of land to the north. It was some sort of processing facility, or weigh station for the raw gas coming from the wells. I don't think it was a refinery. There were no vent pipes spewing burning waste like the refineries I remember seeing in Newark, New Jersey. To the far right of the property was one very large, squatty storage tank with Williams Energy Services painted in large letters. Behind the Williams tank were a trio of chimney stacks and numerous steel buildings dispersed amongst the maze of pipes. The complex was quite a contrast to its surroundings so Betty and I stopped for photos.

Two miles farther and we rolled through Conway, a substantial gas field with hundreds of wells and a rail side piping complex used to load tank cars for transport to other locations. Conway is home to a large underground refined petroleum storage facility. The storage consists of large caverns carved into the underlying salt beds with a holding capacity of over four million barrels used for gasoline, propane, and other refined petroleum products. Approximately thirty percent of the propane stored in the United States is held in the storage facility here in Conway. As I ride through Kansas I am equally amazed by what I don't see as much as what I do.

The remaining miles to McPherson I enjoy the car–wide shoulder, smooth and free of road litter. To my left the rail line hugs the road and occasionally crosses over wooden timber supports to give passage to the creeks below. Betty leads but it is a causal pace as we begin to enter the outer edges of town. And then the rhythm of the ride changes as it always does where rural meets urban.

The energy of traffic, now four lanes wide, amps up my attention and I focus on the sliver of shoulder afforded to me. I follow Betty across a set of railroad tracks and pause for a few traffic lights as we continue through the heart of McPherson and cross over Main Street. Brick buildings, an abundance of shade trees, and then the older two–story painted wood houses scroll by as if a mirror image of my departure from Great Bend earlier this morning. The familiar is comforting and it has a good vibe to it.

Then a slight but long grade takes us out of town and over the main rail line. The effort to climb was not without reward, an equally long descent is our invitation to coast to the bottom and beyond. Like many days on tour we find ourselves riding through and nearly exiting town before arriving at the hotel. When you are drained it can break your spirit but on the plus side you don't have to tack on those miles the next morning. It would be cool to stay in the heart of a town but in end you stay where the lodging is. And in McPherson it is across the tracks east of town in the box store district.

At 63.5 miles we make the right onto Champlin Road then angle left to the Days Inn. We are home once more, at least for the next sixteen hours. To make a great day even better, Betty's husband, Sonny, surprised her at the hotel. It was good to see her excited and the riders present enjoyed it too.

A quick wipe down of the bike, then I checked in at the front desk and pick up the key card. The rest is all rote as I strip down, shower, and get back into street clothes. My afternoon is a blur of chatting, writing, prepping for tomorrow, and then dinner. Tonight we dine at Montana Mike's just across the highway. I'm thinking steak, fries, and a big glass of unsweet tea.

The town of McPherson sits at an elevation of 1,496 feet. It was founded in 1872 and named after General James Birdseye McPherson, the highest ranking union officer killed in the Civil War. The community celebrates its Scottish heritage with a Scottish festival the fourth weekend of September.

Census reports show more than 13,500 people reside in McPherson where the median family income is just under forty–nine thousand dollars. Women slightly outnumber men and there is less than five percent minority representation in the community.

Points of interest would include the McPherson Opera House and the Mid–Kansas Model Railroad Exhibit which is one of Kansas' largest model railroad layouts featuring more than 1,250 feet of N and HO gauge track.

The city has two colleges including Central Christian and McPherson, a four–year liberal arts college. McPherson College offers the only four–year Bachelor of Science degree in Automotive Restoration Technology in the United States. The program focuses on the complete restoration of valuable, classic, and antique automobiles built from 1886 to 1970. The program offers several scholarships including the Fred Duesenberg Memorial Scholarship endowed by comedian and car collector Jay Leno. If I were to go to school for a new career I think I would find myself right here in the automotive restoration program at McPherson.

I recorded 65.22 miles in four hours fifteen minutes averaging 15.2 miles an hour. It was a good day to play. Lights out tomorrow will be here quickly.

Day 24: McPherson to Abilene (62 miles)

Two days in a row our departure time would shift one hour and all of my prerequisite activities would adjust as well. Breakfast would have us back at Montana Mike's for what I planned to be a heavy carb load. Eggs, pancakes, bacon, fresh fruit, hash browns of course, and coffee, at least two cups, maybe three.

Riding sixty miles is a four hour endeavor at best in favorable conditions and that is just what we expected to be served after this filling meal. The day breaks down into an hour of warming up the legs followed by a second hour of getting into the rhythm of the day before taking a break. And when we stop maybe a normal SAG snack, maybe something special Margaret has not yet revealed. Then two hours of what seems like afterschool play through the countryside to carry us to our destination. I imagine it to be such an easy day after all the challenging days I rode to this point. It will be a joy to ride, a joy to experience the sights, the sounds, and the memories as we continue our journey east.

With breakfast behind us we scurry across Route 56 toward the hotel. Traffic is light and we safely assemble for our eight thirty departure with our bikes, bags, and gear as per the daily routine. Tires pumped, gloves secured, and helmets on, computers and heartrate monitors are zeroed out, or synchronized to record the day.

The group banter is alive. I hear Peter Crowell's New England tones and a chorus of other rich voices I have come to enjoy. I see the smiles on the faces I am coming to know and hold as special. I see the possibilities of the day. I see Big Mike and Duffey, the big, the small, those two in such contrast. Trevor and Tracy stand on the lip of the box truck directing traffic and offering encouragement as we build up to the moment of departure. First the slow riders roll, then my group, and last the speed demons join us on the road.

I love all of the mornings but I love days like this the most. We are blessed with sunny skies, maybe a few clouds moving hastily across the blue, winds blowing out of the south holding steady just below twenty miles an hour, and temperatures already in the low seventies. It's a bit sticky but comfortable. The early news report called for seventy percent humidity and no rain to dampen the day.

We would ride due east for twenty miles, then due north the remaining forty. A strong side wind would lead to a tailwind that could only be rivaled by our experience back in Palm Springs.

As I looked east on Route 56 just past the crossover at I–135—the highway running north and south connecting the Kansas cities of Salina and Wichita—I see riders tilted right, nowhere near perpendicular to the road surface. The force of the wind demands riders to lean aggressively into it to maintain balance and a true line on the road shoulder. I realized I'm doing exactly the same thing without even thinking about it. The marvel of the human body making such adjustments without the need for conscious thought is impressive. Much like breathing and blinking I can only assume. So on we pedal tacking like sails on small boats leaning into the invisible wind.

There are few trees to provide protection from the forces coming from the south. The terrain is slight with not much more than a few shallow rolls in the road mimicking the contours of our surroundings. The proper pavement afforded to us is narrow, maybe three feet at best. We are lucky considering the opposite side of the road has but half the width of shoulder available.

If we were traveling in the opposite direction, as a few self–contained solo riders we crossed paths with chose to do, it would be a difficult day on the bike. Thinking back to my original dream of riding east to west creates visions of much pain and struggle, even for a more youthful lad; if there were any romantic sparks to the notion they are now dosed, fully extinguished, and put to rest. I find comfort in knowing CrossRoads rides toward the east. I know most other tours do as well and it is because of the wind and the weather that makes it the logical choice. It's the safe choice.

I ride close enough to others I can hear their chatter. There are conversations about home and family, the day, the wind, tired legs and achy bottoms. Laughter above all cuts through and it's contagious. On days where there is little struggle there is much room for joy. I share in the conversation with Betty and she says what she says on most days, "I don't feel strong today so don't leave me behind." What I find so funny is on most days she finishes solidly ahead of me.

Sometimes the other riders ask Betty where she left me because we are found riding together so often. We don't ride together because we are the same age or the same size or have much in common. We do so because we ride the same pace. Most of the groups form and change partners throughout the tour for similar reasons. All riders get stronger, some faster, a few like to change pace, to relax and take in the views and the history, others like to change the conversation and shift between groups to fill that need. It's music, changing cords and notes and tempo. It's a mixing and blending to reach the right consistency, a balance, a fit, or a feeling. Cascading along the miles it flows without a plan, no script to guide it or to control it. Free.

My circle of cycle mates changes but Betty and I are the core. Kathy, Greg, Gray, Paul, Lynn, and a few others rotate in and out but most of the time we are a small pod of riders when I am not riding alone. As a group we may merge with Ken and Gayle, or the Aubert's, Jim and Carol, or the Bransky's, Phil and Barbara whom I adore. Then there are the faces that pass us forward and back throughout the day. Gary and Ben and Hopper on their recumbents, Geoff and Frank, Ron, Scott, Maryann, and Gordon trying to stick to Kim's wheel, Pat leading a pace line with Vikki and Gene and Jan, the tandems of Don and Helen Reeves and Randie and Tom Kahrl. And not to be left out are Rich and Mike, the riding buddies Ken and Bob, Tony from the Bahamas, Brother's Miercort, Roger and Fred, Larry, the two Peter's, Rosner and Crowell, Bud, Ed, John, Duffey, Big Mike, and Don and Miguel who exited the tour way to early. We are XC04. We always will be.

We tack like sail boats bouncing against the wind for twenty miles through rich farmland and fields of golden wheat, milo, and soybeans green and strong. We roll past Jim's Motor Machine and Hungry Man's Café in Galva, population just under eight hundred and growing.

Off to our right telephone poles stand like tick marks spaced equally apart and available to measure progress. The poles vanish into the distant road and as I ride they begin to appear on the opposite side as if they had suddenly jumped across to the left. Why I even notice this I cannot say. It must be the pace that allows such fine observation.

This is still oil and gas territory though we do not see the well heads and storage tanks so common yesterday. Maybe there is a tank or two a hundred yards off the road but not the large gas fields and huge complexes of piping and valves hiding behind secure chain link fencing.

As the wind gusts I can see the riders in succession briefly twitch to a more upright position as if a great finger dragged along a piano keyboard of cyclists. The wind plays us like a music scale but I hear only the rush of the wind and rider banter and my bike tires trying to sing from contact with the pavement.

Then out of the noise of the wind buffeting the right side of my head I hear the soothing sounds of the flute from Santa Fe emanating from within. The timbre resonates and moves in time with the ebbs and flows of the grass. It replaces the wind and the banter and it soothes my mind and my soul. It would take me to another place if I were released from the gusts trying to disrupt me. And I would go if it were possible. Off to a dream–like diversion of the mind while the body continues to push away at the pedals to move me forward.

A sign for Canton High School stands by the side of the road. Another reads Canton–Gateway to Maxwell Wildlife Refuge. Metal buildings stand in groups hundreds of yards to the left. Various sized and shaped structures, silos and grain elevators mark the working part of Canton. A pole sign with the words "Happy Trails" stands in front of a nondescript doublewide market with tiny windows, walls covered in black and white postings for beer and cigarettes, a single door to enter. A half–circle metal building stands off to the left, a shed, fencing, and a few small signs dot the landscape. Each fixture scrolls by like in a slow motion movie.

I cross through deserted intersections absent of signal lights. Stop signs and yield signs are the only controls and even they may not be necessary. Open country. Wide open country. It goes on until the curve of the earth consumes it. Few live here. Few cars or trucks travel the roads. If you wanted to drop off the radar this would be the place to do it.

Canton, population hovering near 790 becomes a dot in the mirror. Sadly what I saw was just the fringe of what Canton is or might be. I saw no town, just the signs and distant agricultural buildings. But Canton should not be footnoted for the traces of rust stained metal and the single crossroad I passed through. It is more than that. So I did a little digging and found some good to say about this place. Maybe even something I'd be proud of if I lived there. Canton does claim three attractions, one with community roots, one of great national importance, and one down right kooky.

Canton is home to the annual McPherson county fair held here at the fairgrounds since 1948. Everyone, even those from the city can appreciate the county fair. It's about 4–H ribbons, Future Farmers of America, showing prize pumpkins and livestock, and honey jars, pecan and shoefly pie, quilts and wooden toys, old farm equipment on display, model railroads, displays of all types for all types, tractor pulls, hog calling, clog dancing, the food stands and beer gardens, elephant ears, fried dough with powdered sugar, corndogs, and friends you haven't seen in a while. And I left out the pickers picking on string instruments of all types; the older the better. That's the county fair in Canton and everywhere else they assemble across the country; a community at its best.

Six miles north of Canton is the Maxwell Wildlife Refuge. This tract of land totaling 2,254 acres owned and managed by the Kansas Department of Wildlife and Parks was established in 1859 by John Gault Maxwell so future generations could experience Kansas as it was in the 1800s prior to settlement. The refuge is a preserved natural prairie, comprising rolling hills, creeks, springs, and beautiful prairie grasses and wildflowers. It's home to two hundred head of bison and fifty elk all roaming freely. It's the only place in Kansas where the magnificent bison can be seen in this habitat.

It's hard to imagine at one time nearly three million bison freely roamed the North American landscape from the Appalachians to the Rockies, from the Gulf Coast to Alaska. It's even harder to imagine by 1889 through a loss of habitat and unregulated shooting they would number only 1,091.

I can envision a future trip through here, maybe a diversion off US–56 at Canton onto 27th Avenue up to the refuge to see the bison grazing on the grasses of bluestem and Indian, switch grass, and side oats as they meander lazily near the water. Then I'd continue north to Roxbury to the first paved road east toward Route 15 where I could continue the directions outlined in the cue sheet to Abilene. That's what I think I might do.

What most will remember about Canton if anything at all is the quirks. Someone back in 1956 had the bright idea to paint the two water towers as a tourist attraction; one painted red with the word *HOT* and the other blue labeled *COLD*. And that someone was Mrs. M.D. Fisher, a local real estate agent. There was nothing special about the tanks and both actually held ambient temperature water. And I don't think anyone outside the town even noticed.

Years after my XC04 tour, Canton would be the punchline to a Stephen Colbert skit as part of his satirical news show on Comedy Central. Colbert would later apologize and then turn his attention on every other Canton in the country. His poke likely did more to get Canton, Kansas attention than anything else including the hot and cold water towers.

The road bends right and then corrects itself and realigns to the east. The telephone poles switch sides of the road with no explanation. In the distance a grain elevator white and massive is visible halfway to the horizon. The largest incline has been the manmade one forming the overpass as we exited McPherson. Before us lies the bulk of the eleven hundred feet of climbing. When will it come? Will we even notice it?

Without warning the road shoulder widens and gives ample clearance from passing cars. I managed to bounce over the rumbles and rattled my teeth and shook my arms and for a moment all of my attention was drawn toward righting my error. The shock quickly gone, I checked my mirror, happy to see I was not drifting into the path of a rider attempting to pass. No one was close; I saw only a few small figures on bikes maybe a hundred or more feet behind. The images a bit blurred because of the vibration of the mirror and my taking just a quick look without letting my eyes come to a full focus.

As I rolled past the sign for Lehigh on the far left corner of Route 56 and Highway 168 I saw what appeared to be a herd of cows down in the grass. But as I came to the intersection I saw it was a cemetery and what I thought were cows were the cast shadows of individual tombstones. Cattle posts with wire strung between enclosed the football field sized rectangular plot with white painted posts and rails marking each of the four corners, an entry arbor of white, the name Lehigh hand–formed in metal letters above the open gates. Only the east end held markers for those who have moved on; modest at best, better described as sparse, few markers more than three feet in stature, most hugged the ground. Stones lined up like soldiers each with a unique story, carved with their earthly names as they were known to those who loved them. I felt in awe as I rolled past, a respect for those on both sides of the ground. I felt neither sadness nor joy in the moment but I felt something. I don't remember if I stopped pedaling or if I kept my legs in motion.

The sound of birds, flute music, and the wind under the blue skies of central Kansas completed the canvas. I heard no one speak until we were past.

I looked to the east at the horizon where the blue and green collide, the pavement, the telephone poles, and the riders ahead all moving toward a single vanishing point where the colors become a blurred mix of greys.

I pedaled past a water tower standing guard over the roadway and then Route 15, locally known as Santa Fe Avenue, comes into view. I bank left allowing the wind to increase its effect pushing me through the sweeping turn. I track behind a dozen giddy cyclists, colorful jerseys aligning into a single column, the wind squarely at our backs. One or two riders pull out of line and form up in pairs as traffic allows. Our speed increases yet the effort to pedal trails off. We ride effortlessly despite the slight incline visible in the road ahead. Kids, that's what we are in the moment. Happy, giddy, laughing kids on bikes absent of worry and free of care for the next forty miles north to Abilene.

Along the way the road cut through a stand of trees and a wide flat concrete overpass carried us across French Creek. Ahead we would cross more water including Silver Creek and the much larger North Cottonwood River. Each crossing was much the same, the trees congregated around the precious water, flat and wide concrete platforms supported the road, a slight dip could be felt at the transition of pavement and concrete.

With the wind at our backs it offered little audible turbulence opening up our ears to more interesting sounds. Those coming from the bike, the mechanical movement of gears and chains, pedals in need of oil, tires squeezing out the road grit trapped between rubber and asphalt, creaking of the handle bars as I shift my weight forward and back. There was the sound of my jersey fluttering in the air and a bug, buzzing through my personal space. My breathing and the occasional pops and clicks coming from my moving joints added to the mix. The grass rustled rather loudly as it bent under the pressure of the strong breeze. The dried golden wheat fields were the loudest. "On your left" calls a rider looking to pass and I hear similar mechanical sounds from their mount as they move near and then shrink the farther ahead they advance.

The smell of fresh cut fields, the aroma of roadside wild flowers, and the smell of tar coming up off the road surface added to my own scent. The air remained crisp and fresh and my lungs drew it in with long full pulls.

My bottles had warmed yet they were still refreshing. I had to remind myself to drink often and alternate between Gatorade and water to maintain a balance of hydration and the necessary electrolytes. Cramping, nausea, and lightheadedness were always a threat to riders not staying current with their fluids. I know it all too well from my training rides in Florida. Soon I would be at the SAG so I could use up what I had without fear of being without fluids. And the refills would be cold and mixed with ice, sufficient to carry me the last thirty miles.

While pleasant sounds and smells were abundant, it was the visual images of the golden wheat, the green corn and soy bean fields swaying to wind as if they were a sea on land. I could see the wind move through the fields like white caps moving on waves of water. Along the roadside wild flowers exploding in bright colors of pink and white and yellow complimented the massive fields. It was as if we were riding through a living canvas of color the entire day.

I saw a sign for Tampa in the shape of a covered wagon. Tampa, Florida came to mind but the sign said it was four miles ahead. It wasn't the town I was thinking of; not even close.

The morning traffic remained light allowing me to move off the narrow road shoulder and into the lane. To the right a slight drop from the pavement to gravel sloping off into a grassy ditch before it sloped up and out into the fields twenty feet beyond. Few fences were needed and few were seen.

Another white structure came into view. As it got bigger it transformed into a grain elevator, then I saw the storage tanks and out buildings. Signs for a railroad crossing at mile 30.4 carefully noted as slick on the cue sheet was just ahead. I checked my mirror and looked for traffic ahead to so I could cross the angled tracks squarely. I slowed twenty feet out and cut left toward the centerline and completed the maneuver. I moved right and pedaled through a shallow drop and then up the other side. It was barely noticeable.

A few modest houses on both sides surrounded by clusters of shade trees led me to the Red Barn Café where a small pavilion at Durham Park would provide us the only SAG stop of the day. Topped off with food and fluids, a stop in the restroom, and Betty and I were on our way.

For two miles the shade trees clustered to the right provided cover for a creek, but beyond this water feature trees were sparse. The wind pushed us effortlessly up rolling hills at more than twenty miles per hour. On the flats I could stand and broaden my shoulders and catch even more of a push. At one point I was gliding at a thrilling thirty miles per hour. In the quiet distant birds sang, dried wheat rustled, tires hummed, and voices carried clearly.

We rode past Elmo crossing over West Branch Turkey Creek and continued nearly an hour before coming to the blinking light at 1400 Avenue. In the last seven miles to town the dips in the road became more pronounced, the terrain more varied with cattle grazing. We managed to scale the elevations without resistance. I tried my best to communicate with the cows but they just looked without interest as I sped by.

Just past a gentle right hand bend on a slight downgrade a concrete drive meanders up to a house of size sitting up on a hill. In the center of a circular grass courtyard stood a statue of a large eagle, wings fully spread. It must have been bronze and nearly twenty feet from wing tip to tip. A telephoto lens would be needed to capture it in any detail. And only a person of means could have commissioned such a grand structure.

The glide north continued across the Smoky Hill River, a wide muddy lowland about five hundred feet across, but only fielding a hundred foot wide flow. It was the largest water crossing in the ride but it had the usual concrete structure less than twenty feet above and large trees congregating along its rocky banks.

Abilene was in site, first a few houses, then a large metal industrial building. There was farm equipment filling the expansive lot, John Deere green was the dominant color. The buildings continued like dominos on my right, dressed in shades of tan and white, all with large rollup doors, tractor trailers, utility trucks, rolls of wire, and various construction materials scattered about. Two lanes of traffic flowed in either direction requiring heightened rider attention. To the left a small RV Park, then white framed houses from the mid–century with green fields in the background.

A "Welcome to Abilene" sign provided a proper greeting along with American flags proudly waving from front porches, businesses, and telephone poles. At the intersection of Southeast 5th Street and South Buckeye Avenue I carefully rolled over what I hoped was the last set of tracks for the day. On my left was a large white and stone building, the Greyhound Hall of Fame. Across the street I would find a park–like setting where the Dwight D. Eisenhower Presidential Library and Museum could be found. I would visit these and many other sites on tomorrow's rest day.

The twenty to twenty–five mile per hour winds from the south would continue pushing the remaining riders into town and maybe beyond if they didn't brake for the hotel. Stopping to take in the sights and to pause for traffic, the temperature felt every bit of the ninety degrees reported. My legs felt strong as they should. Thanks to the glorious tailwind it was the easiest 1,100 feet of climbing I can remember.

The last mile through town gave us plenty to enjoy. The Abilene Smokey Valley Excursion Rail Road had a sign welcoming the CrossRoads' riders. We passed through a classic western town of square brick and painted structures, colorful awnings over the entries, more railroad tracks to tip toe over, amazing historic mansions lining the main throughway, and the always present grain towers lurking just blocks away. At Northeast 4th Street a ten foot tall pixelated black and white image of Eisenhower's bust graced the wall of the Central Auto Supply building. There were small businesses of local flavor, stone churches, and magnificent shade trees filling the spaces between houses nestled on groomed plots. People returned a wave and a smile from the sidewalk. Then the feeling of belonging rippled through me. Abilene. I cannot wait to see what you have for me to discover.

Betty and I pause for the lights but as we reached the 1600 block of town it's clear we have seen most of it and are now broaching the northern outskirts. It's not industrial like the south side of town, this is more commercial; the ALCO grocery, the fueling plazas, the Country Mart, the Holm Chevrolet Dealership, and

Dollar General. On the left a low two story brick building just before going under I–70 is the Best Western. We have arrived.

The evening routine was much like those before. It was a free night so after cleaning bikes and bodies, we ventured off in search of dinner. I don't recall the name of the local grill, I think it was the M & R, but it was a small place just two blocks from the Best Western. The Mexican food was somewhere between chain and authentic but I enjoyed it. It went well with the beers and the talk about what we would see tomorrow. I think the beer may have been the reason why I'm not sure about the name.

Laundry is 1.5 miles away and it will be my priority before doing anything else tomorrow. After laundry I can search for postcards, take in the sites, and then close the day with journaling. Tomorrow is also day twenty–five, the official mid–point in days of this forty–nine day adventure. What's crazy is counting tomorrow we will have had four rest days in the first half and only two remaining for the next twenty–four days; one in Champaign, Illinois and the last in Erie, Pennsylvania. That just doesn't sound like enough. And the thought of this trip being over in just three more weeks seems so unfathomable. We have something like 1,800 more miles to go! That's crazy talk.

I finished the day covering 63.53 miles in three hours forty–six minutes averaging 16.8 miles an hour. My computer also recorded a top speed of 32.3 miles per hour, which happened on one of the downhills racing along Route 15.

Day 25: Abilene (Rest Day)

Rest days provide the freedom to roam around in cargo shorts and my unfashionably white New Balance sneakers. And today is a perfect day to wear the embroidered CrossRoads t–shirts. It will be a tough choice as both the navy blue and black are my favorites.

I've been asked more than once about CrossRoads, and nearly as many times I'm asked if it's some type of religious group. The question is usually asked with some reserve, as if maybe they want to know if I'm part of a cult. It's actually funny because what I am doing is cult–like. I'm a nomadic oddly dressed traveler following a charismatic leader who provides for all my needs as I and my fellow riders spend most of our day pedaling in silence staring miles ahead. Maybe I should tell people it really is a cult and I'm looking for an escape then wait for a response. Alright, maybe that's not such a good idea.

When I left the hotel it was in the low eighties, the humidity still manageable, and the sun was reflecting off the asphalt and concrete making it even warmer. By late afternoon it would be in the nineties and according to the local weather report it would be sunny, maybe a passing cloud or two and definitely no rain. Winds were pushing twenty with gusts to thirty and it was steady from the south meaning the ride back toward town would offer up a chance to taste the hot headwinds.

Full from breakfast I made good on my first mission of the day. Laundry is not my favorite activity but having a good book to read or a notebook to write in makes it less of a chore. Today I would be writing. My notebook was nothing fancy; a small eighty page ruled white wire bound slightly bigger than my hand. Portable and forgiving as I write my notes in pencil and then make numerous corrections to keep my hand printed letters clearly legible and my thoughts in order.

Each week I would tear out the written pages, clip them together, and pair them with a disposable camera full of photos taken on my ride. Then I'd mail the collection as a care package to Margery Dykes back at the DeLand Beacon Newsroom. She would faithfully retype each of my entries and select the photos to appear in the paper each week, actually twice a week, once in the mid–week edition and a bigger spread in the weekend publication. I would use the laundry time to capture the fun I had yesterday riding into Abilene and later I would write about what I see today. I would also find the post office to mail my journal pages covering the events from Dalhart to McPherson.

In less than two hours I was back on the bike, clothes folded and stowed in my carry bag and headed to the hotel. I dropped the laundry at the room, applied a quick dab of sunscreen, and was ready to go against the wind once more; a proper investigation of the town was waiting.

Kirby House was the first stop. Several riders were there enjoying gourmet coffees; others strolled through the restaurant enjoying the restored 1885 architecture and history contained within its walls. Someone described the feeling they got from the Kirby House as if stepping off a steam train a hundred years ago. It was an amazing example of architectural artistry.

I had a full day planned beginning with a visit to the Dickinson County Library to catch up on e–mails. I checked in, found an available computer station, and quickly began exercising the keyboard. As I worked my way through the inbox it occurred to me how easy and immediate it is to communicate compared to the late '80s. Yet on this trip I was straddling technology sending emails to some and postal letters to others. Both were comfortable for different reasons.

Recording my adventure seems a bit archaic by today's standards. The use of iPads to capture both photos and text and blogs to publish it all makes it possible to share the experience quickly and with little effort. You could even FaceTime with people back home and if you dare you could strap them, in the digital sense, right onto the bike if you wanted. Garmin's with their GPS tracking capability made sure riders are never lost to their followers, no matter how many wrong turns the cyclist may make during the day.

But somewhere in the written words of lead on paper, stamped envelopes transported by the postal service to be retyped and finally printed in a small town local paper that requires two folds opened to enjoy, there is a romantic element making it all worth doing. I enjoy the art and craft of hand lettering and composing thoughts clearly as to avoid the use of an eraser.

As I type now I find it too easy to roll back my words, reorder the sentences, cutting and pasting with little thought until I see my words scrolled in paragraphs across the screen. Handwritten requires commitment, and discipline, and even confidence. I enjoy getting it right first, legible, and leaving behind a smudge on both hand and paper; after days of writing a callous forms on my left thumb and middle finger. A reminder of the miles of lead I put to paper.

I sent emails to home and to friends and family who are following me. I read well wishes and emails of life back in Florida. When I was caught up I logged off in search of postcards. I'd find them at the Greyhound Hall of Fame and surely at the Eisenhower Museum.

It was convenient to ride my bike into town but each time I ventured indoors I had to secure it to a post or a bench. Abilene appears to be extremely safe but I could not complete my ride without my bike. I made sure I was mindful about safeguarding the frame and wheels with the cable and lock I brought with me.

Rolling through the streets I found something of interest I wanted to explore on North Broadway. It was the Fashion Museum, a unique showcase for the extensive historical clothing collection of the Dickinson County Historical Society. It was here I learned the history of fashion from the 1870s to the 1980s. The collection of period clothing from the turn of the century I found most impressive and in like–new condition. The cost and craftsmanship of these garments ensured they would be maintained and handed down for generations, at least until the fashions and personal taste would change. Who would have guessed this would impress me?

Most of the dresses were bulky and heavy. A faint musty scent revealing their age was evident as well. I don't think these garments would be appropriate in today's heat but in the cooler time of year, even in the winter they would get their use. In my mind I imagined the effort it would take to get into these outfits. The thought of putting on a layer of armor, actually several layers is the best description I can muster. And at the end of a day removing the clothing must have brought much relief.

I saw no equivalents to shorts or t–shirts in this period. They may have existed but maybe they weren't thought of as something to preserve. I didn't pay much attention to clothes from the later periods because they weren't much different than what we wear today. The turn of the century was a pretty outlandish time for women's dress design and I'm glad I spent the few dollars and took the tour. I'm equally glad I wasn't a female who had to live through that period.

Back on the street I called my friend Kathy in Florida. She was at work in her cubical scheduling a software release and as we talked she commented about how much more interesting my day was than hers. She always called me *Graymatter* and wished she was on this adventure out in the fresh air. I said I'd continue to send postcards to the office documenting the journey with bits of interest and wit tossed in. She said while there were several doubters in what I was doing, she wasn't the only one who wanted to tag along. I came away from the call feeling lucky, if not blessed, by the misfortune of lost employment, the start of a series of events leading me to this intersection of North Broadway and Northwest 3rd Street in Abilene, Kansas on a sunny Tuesday morning.

My next stop was the Greyhound Hall of Fame I passed entering town yesterday. As I walked into the entry doors of the Hall I saw a commemorative plaque noting its opening in 1973. As I moved farther in I saw paintings, artifacts, and statues of these sleek race–bred canines. I introduced myself to a kind gentleman, a volunteer by the name of George Clark. George provided me with a treasure trove of information about the Hall, the hounds, and the history of Greyhound racing.

The first dog track opened in Tulsa, Oklahoma in 1921 and today more than fifty tracks are in existence. I've been to two in Florida including the Palm Beach and the Daytona Beach Kennel Clubs. The racing is exciting and unpredictable but I'm not a fan of the betting element involved.

I also learned Abilene remains a hotbed for breeding, raising, and preparing the *Grey's* for competition. Only the fastest make it to the tracks and for those who do their careers are often short as those of any high performance athlete. When they retire they join the Greyhounds who never reached canine stardom in the hopes of a happy life with an adopted family.

The Hall of Fame is also home to three retired ambassador Greyhounds including "Shige," who met me at the door. The *Grey's* are friendly, calm and quiet. Nearly eighteen thousand a year are adopted in America after their racing career comes to an end. It's easy to fall in love with these beautiful creatures but they can't travel with me on the bike. And that's a good thing because I wanted to take "Shige" back home to Florida with me to let her run with my herding dog "Lady." I can only imagine how they would run together.

My last visit before lunch was the Eisenhower Center. This college–like campus includes a visitor's center with a theatre, a museum, the Eisenhower Library, his boyhood home, the "Ike" statue and "The Place of Meditation." The Place of Meditation is the final resting place for Dwight, his wife Mamie, and their first born son, Doud Dwight Eisenhower. From the outside it looks like a small Chapel but inside it is a unique memorial to a very important American and President. On the property was the actual house where Eisenhower lived in Abilene for about twelve years with his parents and five brothers before going off to West Point in 1911 at the age of twenty. It was a very basic mid–American wooden white structure of two stories that was small for a family of seven.

Eisenhower would become a decorated military general and in 1953 running as a Republican against Adlai Stevenson he would win in a landslide, and then begin the first of his two terms as the 34th President of the United States. America liked Ike. He authorized the forming of NASA, the massive jobs program with the Interstate Highway System, and the establishment of a strong science education program. His popularity in and out of office earned him respect and consideration as one of the greatest U. S. Presidents.

To experience the museum properly would take hours. I enjoyed studying the wall murals, the theatre experience, and all of the period artifacts throughout the expansive complex. I highly recommend walking through the display of old TV shows and the auto and military vehicle display. They have an electric car that even in its day could rival the performance of those built just a decade ago. All of the exhibits are well organized and cared for.

If your time is short visit the Place of Meditation first. Then make your way to the large bronze statue in the center of the complex before moving on to the museum and Eisenhower's childhood home. If time allows take in the library, walk the grounds, and return to the museum to finish your visit. It is the only Presidential stop on the cycling tour and the experience cannot be overstated.

I sat in the central courtyard on a stone wall just to the left of the bronze statue of Eisenhower, his likeness clad in full military attire. In the walkway at the base of the statue the words "Champion of Peace" and around his likeness five large stars. Eisenhower was one of just four Americans to earn the five star rank alongside his colleagues Generals George C. Marshall, Douglas MacArthur, and Omar N. Bradley. All of these distinguished men served proudly in the United States Army. In the warmth of the sun I imagined the guts and grit Eisenhower must have displayed on the battlefield yet in this place it radiated peace and a calm that was comforting.

I opened the bag of brochures I collected and items purchased that would help me recall the day in proper detail. The postcards were many and I decided to start writing them out. There were postcards of all types, some from the Greyhound Hall of Fame and others from the Eisenhower Museum. Each one selected with a specific person in mind; humor for some, a serious postcard for others. I found Greyhounds in paintings, the splendid architecture of the Kirby House, views of downtown Abilene, and expansive fields with hay rolls and tractors, the Abilene train station, and the historic homes, sunflowers against blue skies, and so many others.

I would write dozens of cards but the most important went to my wife. Every day a new card, every day it was a new challenge to find one. Abilene was easy but in places like Holbrook and Cottonwood it was not. Each card a message crafted for the person who would receive it. To my mom, my daughters, my sisters and brothers, to aunts and uncles, cousins, nieces and nephews, friends, and coworkers past and present, every one unique, words penned just for them. It was as much a part of the cross country adventure as pedaling the bike. I would draw pictures on a few and mention embarrassing moments on others. Some brought tears to my eyes as I wrote them. They would never quite know what it was like for me because words on a postcard just could not describe the emotion, the sense of accomplish, and the awe I felt in what was happening with and around me. Years later the emotion remains raw enough that by closing my eyes I can feel the sun on that day, the breeze across the complex, and the words as I put them to paper.

I often wondered what people would do with the cards. Would they save them? Would the ones going to an office be shared, maybe posted on the wall? I know the ones going to my sister and brother in law's restaurant in New Smyrna Beach were going on their wall. It would become a weekly endeavor to post the card and move the little bike on the map of the United States they had hung up. Patrons who didn't know me followed along. For seven weeks it became a thing. A boy riding his bike and people were actually paying attention. I've always been proud of my family but in this I am especially proud of my Sister Janet and her husband, my Brother Mike. I hope they hoist a beer to celebrate when I make it to Boston.

I found my way back to my bike I've dubbed the *Silver Streak* and released her from the restraints and rode off past St. Andrews, across the railroad tracks, past the county jail stopping at the post office on the corner of Buckeye and 3rd. With the few dozen postcards and the package for Margery safely conveyed to the postal clerk I left in search of a late lunch. Then I'm going to hang out at the hotel, review the brochures I collected, and write about the day and of Abilene.

Founded in 1857, Dickinson County once a place inhabited by Native Americans grew with the westward expansion of the railroad. In 1860 Abilene was named a city and today it has a population of more than 6,650. For the past fifteen years it has been growing a half a percent each year. As for the name, it had a unique story having originated from a Bible passage (Luke 3:1) meaning *city of the plains*. It is said the Bible was open to a random page and the first name pointed to was the one chosen. There is supposedly a marker on the property of the Lebold Mansion describing this tale but I did not pursue it.

The Lebold Mansion has its own unique history. It was built in 1880 by Conrad Lebold, one of the town's early developers and bankers from 1869 to 1889. The structure stands over a stone cellar called the Hershey dugout where it provided shelter for early settlers prior to the construction of the twenty–three room house. The mansion was open to the public when I rode through but today it is a private residence, restored to its original glory but unfortunately no longer open for tours.

Abilene is in Dickinson County which lies in the Flint Hills region of the Great Plains. The city is serviced by two railroads including the Kansas Pacific line of the Union Pacific Railroad running east to west and the Burlington Northern Santa Fe Railway which enters from the east and exits to the north. There is a small municipal airport located to the southwest and I–70 runs east west a few hundred yards north of the Best Western. The town has a single newspaper with an interesting name; it's called the Abilene Reflector–Chronical. You likely won't find another by that name anywhere else.

The town became a thriving community once the Kansas Pacific Rail Road put in a side switch and rail yard for loading cattle cars. By 1867, less than eight years after the city was named, Abilene became known as the first *cow town* of the west. And to this day Abilene remains a cattle yard town with services for loading grain and other crops. Most any part of town is close to the stated elevation of 1,155 feet above sea level. It's pretty flat.

Attractions are few but significant with the Greyhound Hall of Fame and the Eisenhower Museum and Library being the largest draws. Visitors will also find Eisenhower Park, which is home to the largest rodeo spur, a riding arena, baseball fields, and fairgrounds.

Historic homes include the Seelye Mansion on Buckeye that is open to the public and the LeBold Mansion west of downtown on North Vine across from the rambling Mud Creek. Besides these two fine architectural houses, there is Kirby House that should not be missed. Throughout the city you'll find other homes worth seeing and photographing. The town is well designed with most streets running east to west and north to south. There is a sense of pride in Abilene in how the people care for their property, by their display of the American flags throughout the town, and the kind and courteous nature they demonstrated in the cafés and businesses I visited. I enjoyed and very much liked the town, which is surprising for this east–coaster.

There is one more interesting bit of history for Abilene and its sheriff worth telling. Town marshal Tom "Bear River" Smith was initially successful policing Abilene, often using only his bare hands to keep the peace. He survived two assassination attempts before he was murdered and decapitated on November 2, 1870. Smith wounded one of his two attackers during the shootout before he died, and both suspects received life in prison for the offense. In April 1871 Wild Bill Hickok replaced Smith as the marshal in Abilene but his time was short–lived. While standing off a crowd during a street brawl, gambler Phil Coe took two shots at Hickok, who returned fire, killing Coe, but then accidentally shot his friend and deputy, Mike Williams, who was coming to his aid. Hickok lost his job two months later in December.

And that is how I ended the day writing about Abilene. Tomorrow I ride a full 105 miles to Topeka. It will be the last stop in Kansas before I cross over into Missouri, the seventh state on this trip. Time to turn off the light and call it a night.

An Ode to Johnny Cash

Somewhere in the middle of our travels Paul Kvam and I started singing an old Johnny Cash song that was used to promote one of the hotel chains in their TV and radio advertisements. For days we would banter back and forth whenever we were riding near each other. If you don't remember the song here are a few of the lines so you can get the feel for what we had playing in our heads. It fit our cross country cycling trip perfectly. After all…we'd been everywhere…or at least it felt like we had been.

I've Been Everywhere lyrics
Songwriters: Geoffrey Mack & Michael J. Faubion

I was totin' my pack along the dusty Winnemucca road
When along came a semi with a high and canvas covered load
If you're going to Winnemucca, mack, with me you can ride
So I climbed into the cab and then I settled down inside
He asked me if I'd seen a road with so much dust and sand
And I said, "Listen, I've traveled every road in this here land"

I've been everywhere, man
I've been everywhere, man
Across the deserts bare, man
I've breathed the mountain air, man
Of travel I've had my share, man
I've been everywhere
I've been everywhere

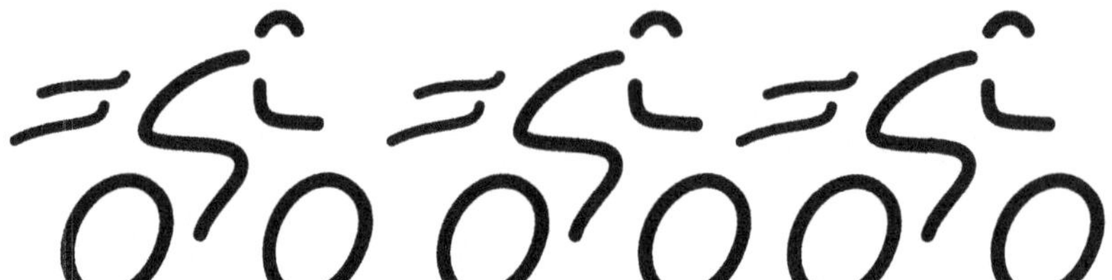

My Four Bikes

Blue Bike, Green Bike, Old Bike, New Bike.

Every boy I knew had a bike. I was fortunate to have four. Not all at the same time, but the right bike at the right time. My first was not a looker. It was not even a boy's bike. It was a small wheel Schwinn girl's bike painted a metallic medium blue with its share of chips, scratches, and rust on the frame. Blue was an odd color for a girl's bike at the time. The chain guard was gone, pedals well–worn black hard rubber, and from where it came from before this elementary school boy got it is anybody' guess. It was a neighborhood hand–me–down for sure.

The frame had two *S* shaped bars connecting the front fork to the upright seat tube at the pedals. It was easy *On* and *Off* and I exited the bike often dumping it onto the ground without much worry when I was focused on something else. Most of the original parts were replaced. The handle bars were the original high risers with yellow and black striped Esso tiger hand grips, the seat was a short leopard print banana style seat. Not the kind with the sissy bar; just a simple seat post mount barely big enough to sit on. The fenders were long gone and soon so were the original tires. In their place would come a strange combination of rubber. The front sported a lightly treaded blue tire and the back, a bright orange drag slick.

The bike was fast because the rider made it go. I learned to jump ramps, squeal the rear tire on hot tar patches, and do wheelies. It was my freedom ride in the neighborhood.

Eventually I outgrew the blue bike and graduated to my first new ride; the green machine from Sears, Roebuck and Company. This one was a Christmas present when I was in seventh grade. It was a twenty–seven inch full size bike with chrome fenders, a big bulbous headlight, a bike rack behind the seat, hand brakes, and five speeds to choose from. Mom and dad spent about sixty dollars for the bike which at the time was almost half of my dad's weekly take home pay. I didn't know it at the time how lucky of a boy I was.

The big bike expanded my travels. No longer limited to riding within two miles of home, I could now ride nearly six miles each way to middle school up and down big hills, on fresh chip–sealed asphalt and oiled down dirt roads. It was also fast, and weather permitting I chose the bike over the school bus. Together we would ride a spring and another full year to Readington Middle School, and it would eventually take me all the way to high school about another five miles in the other direction.

In between it would carry me on my first long distance bike trip. Not measured in miles but in time. I strapped a sleeping bag to the bike rack one warm summer Saturday just after dinner. I told my mom I was going for an overnight with Ray down the street. I wasn't. I was going solo on an adventure to ride until I either got tired or found a cool place to roll out the sleeping bag. I rode about five miles before turning onto Craig Road, a rolling stretch of freshly oiled dirt cut through farm fields, and just past the muddy pond on the right I decided the stand of trees running parallel to it would make for good cover.

I enjoyed the quiet of the late evening and star gazing into the night. I was out of sight from the road and safe. Back before the days of cell phones, reliable portable radios, and child abductors. The biggest threats of the camping experience were the mosquitos and the two hound dogs that found me in the morning. As it warmed up I made the ride back home knowing I was now an experienced overnight cyclist–camper.

I would eventually work my way up to some long distance riding, at least for one event. It was a cold windy spring day and my Sister Kathryn and I had signed up for a charity bike–a–thon. We were sponsored by the mile and on this day I was able to complete fifty–six miles in total riding through the rural New Jersey countryside. Kathryn did not put in as many miles but she stayed the entire day with me and did an excellent job raising money on a less than capable bike. It was one of the things I enjoyed doing most with my sister besides artwork. I really liked this big wheeled bike and it would be my faithful mode of transportation until I was introduced to my first ten speed; the Tour de France steel frame bike.

I got this well–worn racing bike from a neighbor down the street the summer before high school. I remember because I crashed it days before I started freshman year and it put me in the hospital. This story is worth telling from the beginning so I'll back up a bit. It was a clear Saturday in September on a Labor Day weekend. I was on a dirt road prepared and ready for chip–seal when I was challenged to a race. A neighbor on a motorcycle said he would race me down the road which was loaded with shale fragments and I figured I could beat him. I thought I could beat anybody. I didn't care if they were on a pedal bike or a motor bike.

I took off like a shot and I could hear the motorcycle rev up as I accelerated down the dirt hill. The pedals turned faster as I advanced. I could hear the roar of the motorcycle closing in, it was gaining on me. As I reached the turn in the road the bolt in the headset securing the handlebars snapped, the bars went left, the front wheel went right, and I sailed straight as the bike collapsed into the road. I face–planted at speed and was knocked out.

My buddy Jimmy Bishop was there when I came out of the fog. So was Mr. Bishop. I was out long enough for Jimmy to ride home about a quarter mile to get his dad. I remember their car, blood on my shirt, and lots of pain in my face. They scooped me up and took me home about a half mile away.

In the bathroom mirror I saw nasty road rash on my left cheek, and a deep cut over my left eye with a piece of shale still sticking in my forehead. I looked awful, I was covered in blood, and when my dad saw me he made the quick decision to take me to the emergency room. Jimmy came with us and made jokes about the situation. When they draped me with the sterile covers I couldn't see much except for the big needle Jimmy described right before the nurse jammed it in my head to numb me up for stitches. Did that ever hurt! I could feel the pull of the stitching thread through my skin as the doctor patched me up. I wondered how I would look going to my first day of high school in just a few days. I was a mess and my first day at school I looked like hell.

I eventually healed and I would fix this bike and together we would have more crashes and some good times before we parted. It was on this bike I built my hefty thigh muscles climbing hills and expanding my range. The green Sears cruiser became my Brother Jerry's ride.

This French bike was my old bike. I put tires and handgrip tape on the bars; I sanded the frame and painted it a pale powder blue with a spray can. I managed to get overspray on my Sister Janet's new car and everyone thought it was a sticky residue from riding too close to a molasses truck—true story. It took me a while to realize it was my doing from spraying the bike in the garage while her car was parked inside. I never did say I was sorry to her.

The bike had a chipped tooth on the smallest rear gear which would only skip the chain if I were standing or applying lots of force. The pedals would jerk forward about three quarters of an inch with each skip. Not a problem during a leisurely ride but when I was climbing hills or trying to speed down the flats it would click forward and threaten to spin the chain right off. It never did though. I could have avoided the problem by using the next larger rear gear but I liked to apply force and not pedal so fast like my friend Jimmy, who was a natural spinner.

I raced this bike twice. The first time I entered a race it was a tour through Flemington put on by the local bike club. I was racing in the age's fifteen to seventeen category and like I said, I had never entered an organized race before. I thought I would win. I had always been the one to beat in my neighborhood so I had the confidence to get the job done.

On this day it was wet, cold, and gloomy. At the starting line it was clear I didn't look like the other riders. They had leather toe clips and I didn't. They wore spandex and I wore cut–offs. They had the little short billed cycling caps and I had only shoulder length hair. They sported logos on their jerseys and I wore a blank t–shirt.

With the starting line at the courthouse and a two lap route covering a big square through most of the downtown I was anxious to get going. The gun sounded and I was quickest to go. I didn't have to clip into the straps and was more than fifteen yards ahead by the time we reached the first left hand turn onto Maple Avenue. The road was broken concrete and cobble stone bricks so I put out my left foot to catch the bike just in case the tire slid but it never wavered. A few riders behind me lost control and slammed into the curb. More than one was tossed onto the hay bales placed on the corner to provide crowd protection.

I quickly got the pressure to the pedals and rocketed downhill toward Broad Street and another left hand turn which would take me west up the long uphill backstretch toward Pennsylvania Avenue. I kept looking back and saw I was pulling away from the next two riders. Maybe thirty yards or more and then another thirty back to the rest of the riders.

I crossed Penn Ave and continued to increase my margin. I was making the chain skip over the broken tooth but I was still faster. I thought it was easy to be riding so strong and my chances of winning were good. The road kinked to the right and I was now on a downhill stretch toward a sharp left hander onto New Jersey Avenue which would take me a long block back to East Main on past the Flemington Presbyterian Church, the triangle intersection by the Veteran's Memorial, and back into the business district of the downtown center.

With the first lap nearly complete I looked left at the Union Hotel and to the right at the old Flemington Courthouse, where on February 13, 1935 Bruno Richard Hauptmann was found guilty of the kidnapping and murder of Charles Lindbergh's son in what was known as the *Trial of the Century*. I was still leading and by an even greater margin. I crushed the pedals as hard as I could and angled into the turn onto Maple making sure not to hit the curb on my wide sweeping arc. I was safely through the slippery transition onto Broad Street, off the seat pedaling as hard as I could on the rough incline.

Just a half a lap to go and I was still in control. Then I took a glance back behind me and saw the two riders tightly aligned and gaining. I pedaled harder but they kept coming. Fifty yards was a big gap but they were closing in and I was beginning to think it would be a race to the finish. I was still leading on the downhill turn onto New Jersey Avenue and albeit by a lesser margin onto East Main. I was maybe fifty feet ahead as I approached the Veteran's Memorial for the final four block sprint.

I thought I had the race until the last stretch when the first of the two riders eased past on my right. He looked relaxed and smooth and the second rider not yet in my periphery could be heard working the pedals just behind me. At the finish line the second rider edged me out by just a few feet. It was my first race against real cyclists and even though I wanted to win I recognized I was out classed by both man and machine. I would never race another competitive contest like this again and I was okay with that.

My prize for the day was a new hard leather saddle worth fifteen dollars from Pete's Bike Shop. Just what I needed, a hard seat to sit on.

Through the summer I would ride with Jimmy Bishop all over the area. Our most adventurous ride was to Ringing Rocks County Park just across the Delaware River about twenty–five miles away. We would do this ride in the afternoon after mowing the lawn. It was about four hours of riding on busy highway shoulders in the heat and we loved it. A round trip would easily log us fifty to sixty miles and we were still fresh afterwards.

These rides with Jimmy would prepare me for a long day of riding, my longest actually. It was a Saturday morning and I entered a long distance race put on by the high school. Actually it was a timed event of eight hours. The object was to see how far you could go in a set amount of time. The course ran from Hunterdon Central High School to the Thomas J. Lipton manufacturing plant parking lot which was a four mile loop. Not counting the fourteen mile round trip from home I managed to record twenty–eight laps or 112 miles. Not bad considering I arrived thirty minutes late and was so far ahead I stopped thirty minutes before the time ended. That was an average of sixteen miles an hour with a skipping chain. I remember during the laps I was told to slow down by the event staff thinking I would run out of energy, but I didn't. I just kept on pushing the pedals making the chain slip. I found a rhythm that worked and I beat the next person by more than a full lap even though I gave up an hour of riding. I knew he couldn't catch me else I would have kept on riding. This I could do. And it was on this bike I dreamed of riding cross country—New York to San Francisco—for the 1976 Bi–centennial. Me and Jimmy. I had a book on cycling and camping across country and I thought we could do it. But we never did. We got busy with jobs and girls and somewhere we lost the dream. It was so far forgotten I would not attempt another marathon ride for twenty–five years.

In my first year of college I got the new bike. Not brand new but new to me. It was a 1975 Raleigh Grand Prix, white with baby blue accents. It was perfect. It was the bike I saw on display at Pete's but it was out of my price range. By chance Cortland Eble, a high school classmate who also worked at the bike shop owned it, but didn't ride it much. He needed cash and I had it. I paid 180 dollars for a bike worth easily another seventy more.

I wish this bike's story was a good one but it was short and full of neglect. I rode it a few times, got busy with school, a few moves, and after college I landed in Orlando, Florida and I didn't feel comfortable riding it in the urban traffic. Somewhere in the mid–'90s the bike got swept up in a garage clean–up effort while I was away on business. I had less than two hundred miles on it and other than being twenty years old it was not even broken in. I couldn't be mad about my wife's decision, but I thought someday I would clean it up and start riding. It would be another ten years before I owned another road bike.

Each bike in their own way shaped my interest and love for cycling. I felt completely free and in control on these machines and I couldn't imagine growing up without them. They took me places, they allowed me to share experiences with friends, and I would not trade them to avoid all of the cuts and scrapes and injuries we experienced together. I would never have guessed they would prepare me for my next riding phase as an adult. A much older man with the spirit of a boy and a soon to be discovered bike number five.

The Joy and the Agony

Everything has a balance. For every up there is a down, for every gain there is a loss, and in cycling this universal rule holds true.

Joy

There are many reasons why I enjoy bicycling. There is the connection between my physical investment in moving forward and the rewarding breeze in my face. The harder I pedal the faster the breeze. I control the reward. Seeing the world at a pace I can consume it is another. Connected directly with the environment; feeling, hearing, and smelling my surroundings and at times catching a bug in my mouth and tasting it too. It's a dimension beyond riding as a car passenger, windows up, air conditioning on, separated from the bumpy road and wind turbulence by engineered systems that sanitize and separate you from what is beyond the glass. To bicycle is to become part of the world, all the good and the bad it offers. Some may describe it as a Zen–like experience. To me it is pure joy.

Agony

But riding does not come without cost. If you ride you fall and at the end of the fall there is the final event; a crash. There is no such thing as a soft landing. There may be impacts that are less painful and end with fewer injuries, but all crashes are hard and they are always painful. On the bike there are three categories of crashing; contact with a vehicle, contact with other riders, and a solo fall. I include contact with dogs or wild animals within the solo category.

I've experienced two occasions being brushed by a moving vehicle and fortunately I avoided the fall. Once is rare, but to avoid a fall twice I must have an Angel riding with me.

I've touched wheels with my friend Don and watched him hit the pavement hard on our first day of riding to Riverside. Again I was fortunate, but Don fell, he impacted the ground with a chilling thud as his bike shed pieces. Force equals mass times acceleration, or in this case deceleration. No matter the numbers the damage to the body is real. Broken bones, lacerations, bruises, internal injuries, and even death can come at the end of a fall. We know it, but we don't dwell on it. It's worth the risk. Don dislocated his shoulder but worst of all his adventure ended that day.

I've crashed solo for many reasons; unforeseen road conditions, an inattentive driver, mechanical failure, and of my own carelessness. In those falls I don't think I ever broke any bones, at least none were visibly broken. I may have broken my thumb and a pinky because they hurt like hell for a long time. I have been knocked out, I've been scrubbed raw by gravel in a continuous ribbon of red from my left wrist to my left ankle and I was cut open to the bone on my right thumb. As a teenager I even had a piece of shale wedged up under my skin just above my left eye that required stitches. It was the only time I received medical care for a bicycle fall.

I suffered a severe shoulder injury just before leaving on this trip, but I also knew if I went to a doctor this ride would have never taken place. It was my biggest adversary and concern climbing in the mountains and it would take more than a year for me to be able to sleep through the night because of the lingering pain. It still gives me trouble years later. I suspect I tore it up but I'll never really know.

As for the full length body rash, it took me months to heal as it was in delicate areas that needed to move and twist, not to mention the worst part was on my hip and restricted by the *Tighty Whities* I wore. Showering was a painful reminder every day of the fall as were the change of dressings.

Anatomy of a fall

The rash crash happened during a thirty mile ride, I was on the return loop less than ten miles from home, the weather was perfect, a slight breeze, sunny skies, and close to eighty degrees. I tried a new street and was crushing the pedals; my speed was faster than eighteen miles an hour on a slight downhill grade. I could see a turn ahead but what I couldn't see was the gravel hidden by a dark patch of shade cast over the road by a cluster of Oak trees.

The instant I heard the front tire begin to slide across the gravel I knew what was going to happen. Snap. I was down on my side still clipped into the pedals. My left arm was fully extended and dragging behind me, I instinctively pulled my right hand behind my head to keep it from bouncing on the pavement. Midways through the twenty–five foot slide I separated from the bike and watched it continue bouncing another twenty feet until it caught the grass. In those brief moments I could feel the asphalt scraping off my flesh, the sound of gravel scraping against the metal bike, parts breaking, audible sounds coming from my mouth as the air was forced out, and then the silence. It was so still, so quiet.

I lay on my back not moving. I felt both pain and numbness, and then the sharp stinging took over—all over. It might have been fifteen seconds or more before I tried to move. I started blinking and then began an inventory of my body starting with my head. My neck turned left and right, it was okay. I did manage to hit the helmet pretty hard before my hand was under my neck. My right thumb knuckle just as it exited the glove was cut to the bone and bleeding. I flexed my fingers and they seemed to respond. The rest of the pain was on my left. My new jersey, and a good set of cycling shorts offered little protection as they shredded on impact. My side looked like raw hamburger. Bits of gravel, sand, dirt, and sweat were mixed into the damaged areas and it hurt to move. I had to know if I was broken so through the stinging pain I moved arms and legs. Then I stood up and did a more thorough inspection. No broken bones but it was bad. I looked like a truck ran me over. I walked over to the bike and sat down in the grass and began the slow and painful process of picking out and brushing off the foreign matter. There was a lot of blood and I don't do well when it's splattered all over me.

I was alone except for an old man standing a hundred feet away watering his lawn with a garden hose. He just stared at me, didn't move or say a word. This is a typical reaction from people when you crash so don't expect any help from the bystanders.

I had no towel or bandages so I could do little else except examine my bike. Two weeks earlier I had new bar tape installed. Now the left wrapping was ruined and dangling. My bike mirror was in pieces and was lying on the grass. The side of the seat padding was ripped and would need replacement. No other damage beyond scrapes and paint chips. I got on the bike and rode home. I don't remember if anyone stared at me as I crossed through town. I was only concerned about pedaling. My body was stiffening up and the stinging persisted. I would not enjoy undressing or the first shower. It would be weeks before I could get back on the bike. I think I scared my wife too.

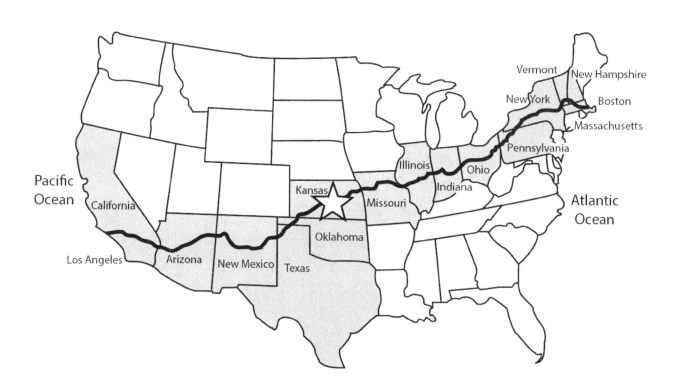

Pacific
Ocean

California

Los Angeles

Arizona

New Mexico

Texas

Oklahoma

Kansas

Missouri

Illinois

Indiana

Ohio

New York

Pennsylvania

Vermont

New Hampshire

Boston

Massachusetts

Atlantic
Ocean

Half Way

Day 26: Abilene to Topeka (107 miles)

The alarm clock sounded early ending what was a sound sleep. I fumbled in the dark to silence the buzzer and then lay back on the bed for my eyes to adjust. I stretched some of the kinks out of my shoulders and tried to resist committing to forward motion. Routine kicked in and I began the preparatory tasks of washing and dressing, applying carriage lube, folding my sleeping gear, packing toiletries, and making sure all of my personal items were accounted for and stowed in the proper bags. Unpacking and repacking the same stuff every twenty four hours; it should be easy after nearly four weeks but it isn't.

My minor OCD issues cause me to perform extra room scans and accounting before I can accept all is in order and I can relax. I'm not sure why I tense up over a single misplaced item but I do. Strangely it's never the important stuff like my cross or dad's thumb print medallion. No it's more like the plastic case with half a dozen Q–tips or an almost finished tube of toothpaste that has me checking two to three times extra as I conduct my departing room sweep. I'd say it would be funny to watch, and likely boring, as I go through the motions, but from my perspective humorous it is not.

Maybe if I intentionally left something behind I'd laugh at my quirks and move past the anxious chill it casts over me. Maybe it would make it worse; a crapshoot for sure but the shadow of *worse* looms larger than the alternative. It's like checking a box on a list and then rechecking that I checked the box on the list a few more times as if I weren't sure I'd get it right the first few times. Frustrating, it can be tiring, and it steals fun out of my life. I find it odd that while I can admire others who don't obsess over the mundane I also feel a bit stressed they don't. It's maddening.

Time to begin the day. I pulled back the curtain, looked out the window to find a less than spectacular view. It was overcast, the sky was spitting, the concrete sidewalks darkened by the moisture. Morning had all the makings of a soggy start on the bike. I would either enjoy or endure the conditions but I could not avoid what was outside. There would be enough moisture on the asphalt to create a spray off the front tire lifting bits of road grime and dead matter and transferring it onto my legs, shoes, and the lower part of my bike. The spray from the rear tire would be abated by the rack mounted bike bag but I'm certain some of that disgusting goo would find its way onto my CamelBak, and possibly the back of my neck. And if it should turn into a hard rain the spray could be right in my face. I'll remember to keep my mouth closed.

In conditions like this it's wise to use the hydration system and not the conventional water bottles. Frame mounted bottles sit low in the spray path making them a perfect canvas for wet road grime. And if you do attempt to drink from them you'll have to avoid the nastiness of the grit and bacteria that can make you sick. Tracy mentioned the wet country roads can deliver bits of manure, worm guts, and specks of roadkill right to the mouth piece on the water bottle so think about those things before reaching down without looking as you ready yourself for a long pull of refreshing water.

Winds were out of the south fluttering around ten miles an hour and the temperature was just above seventy degrees. The dampness passed right through my riding outfit making it feel much cooler.

Tracy sent us out in the usual fashion pointed back toward town and into the wind. Our route would be mostly east but there would be several miles of headwinds early in the morning as the cue sheet steered us beyond Abilene and to the south. With any luck the wind would die down, shift to our backs, or remain unchanged. The thought of it shifting into my face for more than a few miles was not appealing. For the day, temperatures would rise into the low eighties and I would confront 2,400 feet of climbing as I pedaled the 107 miles to Topeka. By the end of the day, XC04 would officially be halfway to Boston.

Bike–friendly weather it was not and it didn't take long for the water to soak through my jersey and for my feet to be sloshing around in my waterlogged shoes. In spite of this, today felt special. The trees in Abilene looked greener, the air smelled fresher as the procession of cyclists carefully negotiated the left turn onto West 1st Street. For the next five miles we were pointed east, a healthy side wind pushing from our right. Yes, today would be special. I prayed it would be safe too.

The buildings of Abilene began to fade behind us, the grain elevators became smaller, their details disappeared, and plowed and planted flat fields with properties defined by stands of trees dominated the landscape ahead. At South East 4th Street we carefully negotiated the angled train tracks coming from our right without incident. About two hundred yards to our left the tracks curved back toward our direction and remained parallel with the road until we found our way onto State Road 43. Our loose pack of riders passed a lone stubby red round silo sans the top dome in the middle of a green field. It was one typically found near a barn so I figured the structure either burned down or was torn down but the silo, possibly made of concrete, was not so easy to erase.

On KS–43 South we crossed over a narrow section of the Smokey Hill River and on into Enterprise, Kansas, population: 843 and home to the first kindergarten in the state. It took all of six blocks to see the entire town but in those blocks were proud buildings of brick and limestone, two clearly marked with the date 1878 stood to our left. Across the street the Dickinson County Bank, the R–Bar, a tiny United States Post Office, and an assortment of small, but charming freestanding businesses lined the road before giving way to modest homes with welcoming front porches. It was a smaller version of Abilene for sure.

Railroad crossings marked both our entrance and exit to Enterprise. We managed to navigate back into the headwinds for the next several miles. Along the route we passed the small Mt. Hope Cemetery standing alone in a field, the single entrance marked by stone pillars and fenced with white capped posts connected by heavy looped chain. It was a bit more than a modest place of rest, no church around.

My legs were finally beginning to warm up after nearly an hour of riding. I was in the company of other riders but not much chatter was going on. I think everyone was a bit taken by the change in weather and the longer distance. If you asked, some riders would have preferred another rest day in Abilene. There were no bursts of excitement for reaching the halfway point as of yet. Maybe it would come later. For now it is all business about pedaling into the wind and wet.

KS–43, locally known as Mink Road, intersected with a railroad crossing Tracy called out as extreme on the cue sheet. More than extreme it was the narrowest angle crossing I had ever been on. The ideal crossing is perpendicular to the road and the total crossing is less than ten feet. This intersection was so skewed crossing gates would have been nearly 250 feet apart. I estimated the intersecting angle measured less than twenty degrees at most. The only safe way to negotiate this set of tracks was either to walk the bike or to pedal to the left road shoulder and then cut back to the right almost ninety degrees to the road. I walked because it was wet. Only in the rural areas could such a crossing be considered acceptable or even possible.

The road began to heave and drop, not much but enough to see a change in the terrain. In all directions the flat ground was transforming into mounds and small hills, the land equivalent of an ocean swell. The terrain changes were still shallow but very much like what I encountered just before rolling into Abilene. Pedaling was not much of a challenge except for the wind that was still in my face stealing about two miles per hour off my pace.

The route turned left fifteen miles into the ride. Relief from the headwinds for now but I was still cold from the front wheel spray on my legs. My nose was a wet stream causing me to blow it frequently and at times I rubbed the flow onto the back of my hand. This is a common occurrence in cycling, but more extreme in the cold wet weather. My gloves were streaked and so was my right forearm. I would win no style points nor be greeted by strangers with a hearty handshake.

I continued on KS–43 through the town of Navarre, the name is French for plains. The town consisted of a few well–worn basic houses and a commercial grain complex of two elevators straddling the north–south Santa Fe rail line, part of the North Central Kansas Co–Op.

While not much to see this little bit of civilization amongst the plains has a story to tell. Like most Midwestern towns Navarre was founded with a church and school. In 1869 the Navarre Church of the Brethren gave birth to this town and would be a cornerstone of the community for nearly 150 years. The church held its last "Homecoming Service" in August 2001, after which the church bell was donated to the Navarre cemetery two blocks southwest of town. They had a post office too and it had a good run of nearly a hundred years spanning February 7, 1884 until its doors were closed and operations discontinued on September 3, 1971.

I'm not sure how a town really disappears but Navarre never recovered from a fire that destroyed much of the town in 1939. They lost the Helstab Hardware store, Hussey lumberyard, the Larsen Creamery, the town hall, and the Larsen house. Between 1917 and 1929 other fires took the original Brethren Church, the school, a telephone building, and the Navarre hotel. The combination of poor heating systems and a lack of proper firefighting equipment and water were the cause and the response from the community was to not rebuild.

I pedaled past 3rd, 2nd, and 1st Streets then crossed over the railroad tracks. Navarre was now behind me, I aimed the *Silver Streak* east toward Woodbine. As I rode through the open fields I wondered, *Will Navarre be completely gone in ten or twenty years?* That's anyone's guess. I'd like to think it will be reborn but it's too far from anything else to be even slightly probable. The stories and struggles of Navarre and other rural Kansas towns can be found by searching on Lost Kansas Communities. Another good read about Navarre was written by Adam Coup, *"The Town That Refused To Give Up."* Coup provides a vibrant account of the forming of Navarre, the people who lived and worked there through the early 1900s, and the names of the people and the businesses that gave it life.

I feel this is as much a part of the experience as the pedaling; to know something about the journey through time for these markers along my journey to Boston. It's like the thread of my trip and that of the other riders are being woven into the threads of the towns and landmarks to create a symbolic fabric unique to the XC04 experience. Is it a romantic notion? You bet it is.

After crossing two creeks and pedaling another six miles I arrived in Woodbine, population: 191. The entire town was to my right. Mostly gravel roads, a few houses, and of course grain elevators. Near the houses were large propane tanks for heating, a few strands of wire connected to old wooden posts masquerading as a yard fence, and random cars parked in the unkempt grass. No sidewalks to be found. And no one was trying to impress their neighbors.

Woodbine was all of nine blocks west to east with the Co–Op right in the middle. At one time it was home to four churches; a Lutheran, a Baptist, and an English and a German Methodist. Founded in 1871 it was home to a high school and lower grades until 1962 and 1979 respectively as they were absorbed by the Rural Vista school district. The town has seen an increase in the Latin population from less than one percent in 2000 to nearly ten percent today. The per capita income is just over twelve thousand dollars and more than sixteen percent of the population lives below the poverty line. Nobody famous can be traced back to Woodbine and much like earlier towns I was ejected back into the wilds where farming dominated the landscape.

The road shoulder remained minimal with bits of gravel or non–existent at all. Traffic was light, but then again I was between crossroad towns well removed from interstates and main thoroughfares. Ditches with rocks and water, posts connected by wire, and a line of power poles were the only constants. A few no passing signs and an occasional old farm windmill dotted my route. I would have added a straight road to the constants but then just past Lyons Creek a sign with *S* curves forty–five mile miles per hour ahead caught my attention. As I rounded the first bend a very large mound of green grass presented itself to my left. I was struggling up a steep incline cutting through a passage of green on both sides. Kansas was no longer flat. I worked up the hills and enjoyed the gravity boast on the back sides.

A sign for Junction City and Herington let me know I was approaching the next milestone on my cue sheet. I slowed with a few other riders at SR–77 and then continued on with Betty in front of me and a few others farther ahead. In my mirror I could see riders stopping at the crossroads and then regaining momentum. It was a good time to adjust, take a pull of water, or maybe grab a snack. On a long ride like today all of the stops need to be deliberate and efficient.

The rolling hills had protrusions of rocks and instead of just rolling over the topology the roads cut into the ground in an attempt to flatten it out. I could see beyond the riders in front of me as many as four shallow rollers in the dead straight pavement ahead. On the steeper descents I picked up speed, every exhilarating glide was earned.

The road bent around the larger hills and across yet another creek. Where it was flat the road was straight and true. Fences became more prevalent and so did the houses. I was surprised to see sidewalks at the corner of 6th Street and West Harris, the road I'd been on for miles. My impression was tempered because the sidewalks only ran for a hundred feet or so before they disappeared into the grass and brush. Still they were sidewalks in the middle of farm country. We turned right on 6th and negotiated the rough double tracks on West MacKenzie Street, the main drag heading into White City.

I rolled to a stop at the first SAG. Target times were in effect for the day and riders had to exit the SAG by ten thirty to avoid the sweep. I had plenty of time as did everyone else. You could replay the conversation, the grazing of snacks, the banter, and the encouragement from the staff. It was familiar and comfortable to have such a routine even when the weather and riding conditions were anything but. I had completed one third of the miles, I felt good, the drizzle had tapered off into a mist, and I really enjoyed the scenery the morning offered. I'm excited about the rest of the ride but I believe most of the climbing lies ahead. I'm sure of it.

White City with its cobblestone main street and sidewalks has the flavor of a modern day western town. Framing the downtown are boxy turn–of–the–century two–story structures of brick and limestone, crowding both sides of the street, several with garage doors and painted fronts without signage. Mixed in amongst the old buildings are the newer structures of steel, smaller in scale filling voids likely left behind by demolished buildings. There is no consistency of look or flow. The word *haphazard* comes to mind.

As I moved through town the buildings leaned in and then backed away. Random porches cover the sidewalks, crossroads mostly gravel and dirt. Some of the buildings made of wood with the square flat fronts extending to the height of a second floor capture the look of the mid–1800s. I imagine gunslingers and lawmen would be comfortable as they looked east and west along MacKenzie, but today there is almost no one to be seen. It is almost a ghost town.

In the space where commerce should be thriving much of White City is empty and most in a state of disrepair. There are clues to suggest in its day White City stood strong and proud. I wondered what happened and if people might someday return and rebuild her. It has the look of a town familiar to me back in Florida; a town called Cassadaga, but with a western vibe yearning to be kept alive.

The town sits at an elevation of 1,470 feet which means since Woodbine I'd gained 220 feet of elevation. Though it's small, the town is bigger than anything since Enterprise. It boasts a population of 558 and has been growing albeit slowly for the past four years.

White City was founded in 1871 by a group from Chicago and named after F. C. White, Superintendent of the Neosho division of the Katy Railroad. Naming towns after railroad executives was quite common in that era. It was almost named Swedeland or New Chicago as so many *Swedes* from Chicago settled there.

There is a bank, a service station, an auto repair shop, and a Christian and United Methodist Church. White City is also home to a public library, and two parks—Centennial and Katy. According to their website, White

City is close to larger cities and boasts several reservoirs and lakes nearby making it a destination for fishing, hunting, and raising a family. Access to colleges and having a healthy agricultural base are also mentioned but there is a stark contrast between what they are promoting and what I see. I like it, but I don't think I could live here. Not now anyway.

Of interest to the ladies might be that the men outnumber women but only slightly. The per capita income is almost fifteen thousand dollars with about seven percent of the population living below the poverty line. The school includes kindergarten through high school and they are known as the White City Huskies.

A few dedicated people have researched and recorded the history of small towns in Kansas and if you want to understand why they struggle to remain viable you should start with the story about White City by Brooke Hollis titled *A Sketch of White City, Kansas: A Colorful Past*. It's a short but informative read including cyclonic calamity, bed and breakfast occupancy rates, the loss of the Beech Aircraft Company, the closing of the Delevan Air Force Base, and much more.

Full, fueled, and with an empty bladder I leave the SAG with my small band of riders. The rough cobblestones gave way to decent pavement marked with recently painted lines, but no proper shoulder. The terrain was constant; fields of green, various crops and textures, wire strung between short wood poles of various size, the drop off from pavement to the dirt and gravel shoulder leading to a grass ditch. I listened to the wind mix with my breathing and the mechanical sounds of the bike. I took it all in. The pace was not too fast and my heartrate held steady below 130 beats per minute.

Traffic consisted mostly of cyclists and the occasional farm tractor or car. "On your left" was a common phrase breaking the silence as riders approached to pass. The road was again straight with visible ripples in the ribbon of pavement.

The sky still overcast with a low cloud ceiling delivered a drip or drop every so often that went mostly unnoticed. The temperature still hovering at seventy degrees continued to provide enjoyable cycling conditions.

When the road crossed creeks or dry beds the safety rails would appear and guide us across the concrete surface. It seemed every crossing was concrete. The guardrails raised my attention and I checked for vehicles as I approached. It was far better to be passed without a guardrail limiting my options. They made each crossing feel very constricting and it was something I did not like.

Our route passed the small stockyard pens of the Diamond L Ranch, the road curved left and right through the elevation changes, and horses watered behind fences along the many creeks. Ahead a stand of dense trees marked a turn north; a tailwind waited for us. Over the three miles toward Dwight I pedaled with ease over the rolling hills thanks to the wind at my back.

There was no sign welcoming us to Dwight, just a green highway sign pointing right toward Eskridge, our next destination on the cue sheet. At the intersection near the edge of Dwight each rider in line banked right to stay on SR–4E; two–wheeled ducks I thought. As I prepared to turn at the cottage with the white picket fence I finally saw in the shadow of a large tree just beyond the corner the green Dwight City Limit sign. Having a population of just over three hundred must have qualified the town for such a marker.

Our path was again due east, then north for a mile as we rode the tailwinds before returning to our eastward flight. This section of road took us through the Flint Hills, through more aggressive rolling terrain, exposed rock, and the best part of the day. It was beautiful. We rode through cuts in the terrain with stone walls just feet off the pavement. Tan and gray, some hints of red in the layers of crumbling rocks. Bits of stone piled like gravel at the bottom of the cut spilled toward the road. Wire fencing ran along the top to keep the cattle from falling down to the road.

Weeds tried to gain a foothold in the cracks and some of the cuts were as much as two stories tall. The dramatic change in scenery stole away any focus on the effort to pedal though we had to work harder, much harder than we did earlier. Yet, it was worth it even as the sky began to spit more drops down on us.

I didn't care much for leading so I followed Betty and Greg, Lynn, and Gray through rolling hills of emerald–green grass with buffalo, cows, and horses grazing. In one field, a pair of donkeys and a few ponies wandered amongst several horses with their colts. The contrast of the green landscape to the misty gray sky created an artificial environment as if it were a movie set. Like there was nothing beyond the hills, a self–contained world of some sort. I never had this sensation before and it may have been caused by the rolls of green void of trees where ground reached up and contacted the sky. It was a new and a bit magical of an experience. It fit my image of Ireland or Scotland, two places I have never been to in person. The heavy wet air also absorbed the sound playing in the imaginary set I envisioned. I felt like an extra in someone else's film; relaxing visuals to experience and a very peaceful morning of cycling.

Blind curves on uphill climbs revealed panoramic views at their crests and rewarded riders with a burst of downhill speed. Trees favored the lower areas, probably a good indicator of where water could be found. A few farm buildings and stockyards dotted the route but most of the interest was in the wide open as the animals grazed as if they were in the wild. From the top of the hills you could see for miles and at times I stopped for a quick photo and then rejoined the rest.

As we maneuvered the hills I noticed our direction was constantly changing; east then north, then southeast. There was no shortcut through these hills and the wind would seem to dance around from or right to our back and then almost in our face. Looking at a map later I would learn through this area we would ride two legs of an equilateral triangle first northeast followed by southeast; each leg approximately two miles long. The missing leg was the due east route which was blocked by a very large and rocky hill.

Miles later on our right a wall of stone stepping up in two lifts each about twenty feet high ran parallel with the road. As we climbed out of the depression and reached the apex of the hill I saw an unexpected site. Lake Wabaunsee, a popular local vacation destination about a mile across, revealed itself just beyond the wall. The water was moving as the wind tried to make waves. I imagine it would be beautiful under clear sunny skies but there would be none of those today.

Riders stopped across the street at the Lakeside store and then continued on to the SAG. The next five miles were far gentler then what we had covered the last twenty miles, but it was not flat.

We entered Eskridge, a town of 569 people and shrinking. In 1910 the population peaked at 797 and it has steadily declined ever since. The demographics are very much like those in Woodbine with a very low average income and a high rate of poverty. By all measures it's a place to be from.

The story of Eskridge is both interesting and dark. It started like most other Midwestern towns founded by Colonel Ephraim Sanford in 1886 when the railroad came through. After platting out the town Sanford allowed Charles V. Eskridge, an Emporia, Kansas journalist and politician, to buy the first lot and have the town named after him. Eskridge served in both houses of the legislature and was elected as lieutenant governor under Governor James M. Harvey in 1869. If anyone was famous it was Eskridge.

I turned right on Main Street and a few blocks later a left into a small tree covered park where the SAG was in operation. A few riders had been through here more than forty–five minutes earlier. I knew because we all sign in at the SAG when we arrive. I'm not sure of the hurry to get to Topeka other than limiting the contact time between rear and seat. And I wonder how you find time to take in the scenery and capture the moments in pictures if you are heads down staring at the road just above your front tire. I want to take it all in and imprint what I see and feel into the deep recesses of my mind. I don't want to lose these memories and I want as many pictures as backup in the event I do.

I topped off my water and lifted a few snacks for farther down the road. Two hours of riding are in front of me and the sky is still spitting. The winds remain steady out of the south at ten plus. As I mount my bike I look at my legs. They are carrying bits and pieces of things I would rather not think about. Crusty, speckled, with sand and matter I dare not identify. I need a shower as soon as I arrive at the hotel, and so does everyone else. I clip into my pedals one foot at a time and roll back onto Main Street. My feet still wet but closer to damp then soggy. I'm sure the bottoms of my feet are prunes full of wrinkles and almost a blue white. I'll need to dry my shoes for tomorrow and give the toes a little TLC later.

As I exited Eskridge I couldn't help but notice the similarities to White City; few people, many vacant storefronts downtown, and sadness for those who live here. It looked like a town going out of business and the only thing remaining was to roll up the streets and put them in the back of the moving truck and drive away. All my years have been in places of prosperity and growth. I don't know if I could be happy here. No, I'm pretty sure I can't, but it does make me appreciate the places I lived and where I live today.

I mentioned the dark side of Eskridge. Actually it's not unique to this town; it's shared with seven hundred other places throughout the United States and recorded in history. The shadow over Eskridge began in 1943. German and Italian prisoners of World War II were brought to Kansas and other Midwest states to address the labor shortage caused by American men serving in the war effort. Internment camps were set up throughout the region including the one west of Eskridge at Lake Wabaunsee.

Prisoners worked, were housed, fed, and even paid a stipend of eighty cents per day. While their treatment may seem harsh it was the same compensation, rations, and housing afforded to our men in uniform. It was considered better than the conditions many of these captives would have expected back in their country as a civilian. The money they took back also helped fuel their post war economic recovery. Many returned to America after the war in search of a better life. I consider it a dark past because there is nothing about war that is not dark.

For the next hour I pedaled in a stair–stepped north and east pattern through rolling country. The skies overcast and wet. We crossed Mission Creek and rolled right into the unincorporated community of Dover, Kansas. While it may look like a sleepy intersection of K–4 Highway and 57th Street today, Dover was once much more. Settlers first arrived in 1856 and in 1860 it was founded after the town of Dover, New Hampshire.

During its peak years, Dover had a match factory, a wagon making business, two grist mills, two blacksmiths, an inn and stage coach station, livery stable, general store, and three cheese factories. When looking at output figures, two of the largest cheese factories in the United States were in Dover. The Stone House Cheese Factory, built between 1856 and 1865 still stands today. The stone 1878 Sage Inn & Stage Coach Station, and the general store built in 1900 also survive.

The general store known as Somerset Hall was built by Alfred Sage, a native of Somersetshire, Bristol, England. Sage was also appointed the first postmaster of Dover in 1862. The first floor of Somerset Hall was a general store and later a café.

According to the cue sheet the Dover Grocery occupied the Somerset Hall. And for pie lovers this is a must stop. Norma Grubb bakes some mighty fine pies. How good? Well a few years after I rode through, on November 16, 2008 to be exact, Norma appeared on the nationally syndicated Good Morning America program as one of four finalists in the "Country's Best Pie" competition. One week later Norma's coconut cream pie was voted the best. Norma was eighty–eight years old at the time and claimed to have baked 8,963 pies. Had I known what I was missing I would have stopped instead of turning left and continuing on toward Topeka.

If you are cycling through Dover use caution and show consideration for the motorists sharing the road. It seems there is a rift between the local residents and cyclists. It stems from the frequent use of the K–4

Highway by a group of Topeka cyclists who have made it difficult for motorists to pass them along the narrow and twisty highway. The cyclists also frequent the café as one of their stops. This is a popular spot for the locals too.

As you cycle make sure to ride safe, in a single column and preferably with plenty of space in between you and your fellow riders. It would be asking for trouble to ride two or more wide and to hold up traffic unless a dangerous situation would be created if you didn't. If you cycle often you know what I'm talking about. There is a time and a place to "take the lane" such as narrow bridges and construction zones. Don't mess with the cars. They always win.

You may also notice works of anti–bicycle art along the highway near Dover. A local man named Blodget gets the credit for his efforts.

The north and east stair step route continued all the way to the outskirts of Topeka. It never warmed up and we had *On* and *Off* rain until reaching the hotel. Topeka was busy, the last three miles riding along the undivided four lanes of traffic without a shoulder or bike lane. As if the pressure of late afternoon traffic wasn't enough, I noticed the edge of the road had a solid eight–inch curb preventing any thoughts of getting away from a car that looked too close in the mirror. I could have given in to the honks and aggressive drivers by hopping onto the wide sidewalk, but most states and local regulations consider bikes as vehicles making it against the law to ride the sidewalks. Even if the drivers thought I belonged there I was staying in the street.

I rolled down a shallow descent to the light on Wanamaker with riders in front and behind. On the green our procession turned left single file, staying as close to the edge of the road as possible except for the last foot of concrete which was separated from the lane by a continuous and deep gap in the concrete. This put me two feet into traffic as I was more afraid of getting a wheel caught in the groove and falling into the lane then contact with a car. I pounded through potholes and patches, I slipped past dangerous storm drains with metal grates reaching out to the lane, but I stayed upright and in minutes it was over. I'd endured the hairiest part of the ride in those last twenty minutes. I hated to end on a stressful note and I wanted to remember the day for the scenic adventure it was.

After eight hours of riding in the rain, I was finally halfway to Boston. It was a good day and I averaged more than 13.4 miles an hour including stops. My computer recorded 106.77 total miles covered in seven hours fifty–five minutes with a maximum speed of thirty–three miles per hour. I dismounted and parked my bike against the exterior wall of the Days Inn. I took a quick look at my bike and at my legs; filthy. That's all I could say. I began cleaning my bike, chatting with others doing the same, and watching as more of the group angled into the lot and coasted to a stop. One of the CrossRoads vans rolled in and Margaret parked it next to the big white Isuzu box truck to begin restocking for tomorrow's ride to St. Joseph, Missouri.

CrossRoads operated like clockwork; every day without fail. Trevor was his usual self, wrapped with a smile and his keen Canadian whit. He joked and laughed as he worked in the back of the truck and he called out with encouragement as the weary dismounted. He always got a smile out of them too.

I accomplished another century ride. It was number five for the trip. Tailwinds were favorable and I didn't fall off the bike. My streak of no flats continued though my tires were looking shabby from the rough roads. I would have much to say about the ride in my writing later but first I had to get a shower and back in street clothes.

Before dinner and route rap I crossed the four lanes to the Walmart Supercenter. The people inside looked like the same Walmart shoppers I saw a few days earlier. Maybe it was the unfit in the outrageously overstretched bright pink and lime green spandex. Maybe it was the kids running lose or the pot–bellied folks wandering around as if in a trance. It was familiar but not in a desirable way. Walmart does attract some interesting people. And I guess it would include the likes of people on bikes looking for a fresh supply of ointments and creams to heal tender areas below the beltline.

During the day we negotiated several rough railroad crossings. Some of the tracks were skewed to the road and riders had to steer their mounts to cross perpendicular to avoid slipping and spilling off the bike. Not everyone crossed the tracks without falling. There were skinned knees and bruised egos for those with an audience. Until someone slips on the tracks and takes a fall they seem to pay little heed to the cautionary notes Tracy so carefully detailed on the cue sheets. As for me, I fell enough times during my Florida training rides to not respect the crossings. They had my full attention and I either crossed them slowing at a right angle or I got off the bike and walked across them. There is no shame in being safe.

Dinner would follow route rap at the Timberline Grill. In the morning breakfast would be at Denny's which sat right in front of the hotel. I was tired so I took the opportunity for a rare and brief nap. Clark arrived at the room but left quickly to do staff stuff. I'd see him a bit later just before route rap.

The city of Topeka is home to more than one hundred twenty–six thousand people. If you include the immediate suburban surroundings the number gets pretty close to a quarter million. The metro area has produced its share of memorable people including actress Annette Bening, who happens to be my age, the rock band Kansas, including its founding member Kerry Livgren, the journalist Bill Kurtis, Katrina Leskanich, lead singer of Katrina and the Waves, and artist Peter Max Lawrence. Not the original Peter Max, but he was named after the iconic pop artist and has his own painting style.

From a historical perspective Topeka is home to the first African–American kindergarten west of the Mississippi River. It also became home to Oliver Brown, the named plaintiff in *Brown v. Board of Education*, a landmark United States Supreme Court case responsible for eliminating the standard of "separate but equal," and requiring racial integration in American public schools. That decision occurred more than fifty years ago on May 17, 1954.

Topeka has two newspapers including the Topeka–Capital Journal and the Topeka Metro News and several radio and television stations. While there are no professional sports teams, fans can cheer for the Topeka Golden Giants collegiate baseball team, a wooden bat league, or the Topeka RoadRunners of the North American Hockey League.

There are plenty of educational places to go including the Topeka Zoo, famous for having the first indoor rain forest and for being the birthplace of the first golden eagle chick hatched in captivity. I won't have time to navigate the city beyond tomorrow's cue sheet but if I'm ever back this way I'd like to hear the crack of the wooden bat and see the hustle on the diamond.

Topeka didn't make the list for unusually named places but you'd have to wonder when the best they could do was pick a name that means "A good place to dig potatoes." It's a Kansa–Osage Indian term and it was first recorded in 1826. The city was platted in 1854 and chartered as a city three years later. I could cite other interesting points but it's time to put the pencil down and turn off the lights on Topeka. I'm half way to Boston; the end and the beginning of my journey.

Day 27: Topeka to St. Joseph, Missouri. (87 miles)

It was rise and shine at the usual hour and by this point of the tour the morning routine of gearing up was nearly automatic. The only variables would be the weather and where we would eat.

Breakfast was just across the parking lot at the Denny's franchise and I was expecting our swarm of bikers to tax their daily routine. Feeding a troop of fifty in thirty minutes or less wasn't likely but there was incentive on both sides of the table to get us in and out as quickly as possible. Rider's complicated the effort with way too many customized orders; extra jelly, no butter, syrup on the side, potatoes cooked separate from the meats and on it went. CrossRoads staff advised the manager the night before with the time and headcount but somehow Denny's still managed to short staff the breakfast shift further compounding the situation. I kept it simple and was out quick, others returned to the hotel with coffee breath and complaints. This was not unusual on tour.

Today was shaping up to be a soggy ride, but the weather shifted, the rains let up, and not much more than a drizzle escorted us out of Topeka. It would be a day unlike any so far and likely any day yet to come. Exiting the Days Inn we made a series of right turns, three in fact within the first eight tenths of a mile. This was followed by a series of left–right–left turns over the next five miles all under the intense traffic pressure that was the Topeka morning rush hour.

With the last left turn onto South Kansas Avenue I headed toward the large concrete bridge to cross over to the north side of the Kansas River. No shoulder for safety and no relief from the traffic. It may have been only a few hundred yards but it seemed much longer before I dropped off of the bridge and back onto surface streets.

The loosely grouped tour riders would be pressured by traffic for the next mile until crossing into the more residential area on the north side of the river, but not until pedaling through the busy NE Morse Street intersection, past the Quincy Elementary School, and finally rounding the left hand bend around Garfield Park before making the right hand turn onto North Kansas Avenue. Our route took us over Soldier Creek and then the neighborhood transitioned back to more industrial and retail space as the route came up on US–24E.

Nine miles in and I am wide awake, senses finely tuned into whatever the day will bring. I veered south onto the shoulder of US–24E and within a hundred feet the highway divided with two lanes traveling each direction separated by a thirty foot wide swatch of grass. Running parallel to my right was a paved frontage road servicing a flower market, a gun & pawn shop, an animal hospital, and an RV Center amongst other businesses. The frontage road would have provided safer travel but unfortunately it ran out after less than the length of a few city blocks.

I would continue to ride on the busy thoroughfare for another three miles dodging bits of road debris and wavering cracks running in all directions in the well–worn asphalt. At least the shoulder was generous at six feet across less the carved–in rumble strips claiming a foot of usable surface just to my side of the painted line.

I settled in, checked the cue sheet, and kept pedaling alone. The nearest rider in front, maybe fifty yards ahead, and in my mirror I could see a pair of riders about the same distance behind. Traffic was busy but less intense than in Topeka proper.

I was exposed to a blend of vehicle traffic noise, random sounds from the local businesses, a bit of wind buffeting my ears, and my bike casting off mechanical noises. Bits of rock pitched out randomly from under the tires creating a rubbery pinging sound and the chain added its own soundtrack as it forced its way around the gears and through the guide mechanisms.

I believe there was even a faint ticking sound with each turn of the crank but it was buried under the rest of the chorus. I'd have to focus really hard to detect the source. Could it be the left pedal brushing a slightly askew bike pump? It's done it several times before. Maybe it was one of the computer sensors slightly out of place making random contact with spinning parts. I've had that happen too. I would continue to listen as I rode the shoulder and would check for the source when exiting the highway a short distance ahead.

I pedaled across concrete bridges traversing a few gullies and again over Soldier Creek, but this time the water was much wider and deserving of the name. The road bent gently left then right as I approached the exit for SR–4E. To my right and down low was a railway line running parallel to a narrow stand of trees. Beyond the trees were acres of farmed fields reaching all the way back to the Kansas River nearly a half a mile away. To the left of the highway I could see only trees; lots and lots of trees. Thick clusters, each tree full of leaves, dark in color, maybe Oaks or something similar. It's hard to tell one green leafy tree from another unless you are looking at Birch, Willow, or an evergreen. The rest look like big green leafy trees to me.

The exit dropped down a slight grade bringing me to a full stop and a chance to check the source of the ticking sound coming from the crank. It turned out the Velcro strap securing the bike pump was loose and the pump handle was making ever so slight contact with the left pedal arm as it reached the high point of each revolution. Problem solved. I turned left onto SR–4E and according to the cue sheet I was heading toward Valley Falls. That sounds like a good place to ride to so I pedaled.

Ahead of me was rural country consisting of slight grades and rolling descents, easy cycling conditions on a shoulder not more than the width of my handlebars. To my right the ground dropped off a few inches to gravel and dirt. It was three to four feet wide before transitioning into a weed filled grass depression—a ditch—another few feet down. Tracy would describe it as gentle sloping terrain for a ditch so I'm going to give it the same review. Aside from the random signs and small posts the grassy shoulder was a safe route to bail out if I'm put in harm's way by traffic. Away from the road the ground varies. In places it continues to slope downward into fields and woods where the maintenance crews dare not mow and in other places it angles up to transition to higher ground. There may be posts strung with barbed wire, trees, clusters of thorny brush and wild flowers, but it looked soft and safe from my seat.

To motorists the gravel shoulder looks like pavement and I'm sure they question why bicycles don't use the wide patch instead of hugging the white line on the proper road. From the saddle it also looks like it could be smooth pavement, just lighter in color, but by careful observation or a quick drop onto the gravel will tell you differently. I sampled the gravel once in this stretch and that was enough to keep me on more firm ground. Luckily I was going slow and was able to hop the front wheel back onto the asphalt.

The road continued on much the same through grazing fields, stands of trees, past a few large homes set way back, intersecting occasionally with roads going in different directions. There was no one around me, no one behind, and no rider in front. I was free to see, to smell, to listen and to drift as I rode north and east depending on the whims of the road. The weather was right, traffic was accommodating, and I was enjoying a peaceful day creating my own breeze. The only thing I needed to do was check my mirror, look ahead, and keep moving. Simple stuff; wash, rinse, and repeat.

Pedaling along the busy highway shoulder less than an hour into the morning ride my body found its rhythm. My heart rate was steady, my breathing was paced and relaxed, and the mechanics of my locomotion no longer required the full attention of my mind. I was no longer erratically scanning my handlebar mounted digital readouts to determine my heart rate, speed or cadence every few seconds. I no longer felt compelled to watch the tenths of miles tick away.

My body had achieved a Zen state, acting as if it was on autopilot and the feedback of information became a direct connection between the physical and some lower level of brain function. No need to strain to read my two computer displays and Polar heart rate monitor, no need to process the visual information into performance measures, and no mental mathematical brain gymnastics required. It was as if the task had been passed to someone else to handle; and I was fine with that. So much more efficient, less stressful and it was freeing my consciousness to dream with my eyes wide open.

I was on the bike physically but mentally I was not so sure. Maybe I was hovering over it or watching my progress from a vantage point I can neither describe nor understand. This happened without warning or plan or effort on my part. I couldn't have willed myself into such a state but nevertheless I was there. It was good in a way that almost defies description. Like the feeling of peace you have at the moment you wake after a restful sleep. Like floating in water neither too cold nor too hot, numb barely feeling but aware.

Road noise, wind, the metallic tones emanating from my bike were all lost in a cloud of softer sounds that spoke more of wide open country void of any roads, machines or other unnatural devices. Without meddling or monitoring my body had things in order and I continued to advance along the route toward my next destination; a SAG stop some sixteen miles ahead. I could have taken a moment to stop to relieve myself but I neither wanted nor felt it urgent enough. I could make it to the SAG.

I remember scanning the roadway in front of me casually and smoothly shifting left then right soaking in the foliage and rolling terrain. It was as if my eyes could taste the images. I could surely smell the sweet sour hint of cut grass, the wood and the pollen; smells reminiscent of my early cycling days growing up in the rolling farmlands of central New Jersey. What wind I could hear was not a noisy turbulence passing my ears but a soft wash of a breeze moving through tall grass; rhythmic and soothing. The edges of my view were softened, a bit fuzzy and traffic seemed to nearly vanish as the last of the early morning rush hour turbulence moved on. My narrow piece of asphalt to the right of the worn painted stripe seemed plenty wide and I had no inclination to plant my tires on the very edge to distance myself from the traffic. It was as if I was enveloped within a blanket of protection; invisible, flexible, and secure.

I was enjoying my solo ride listening to the breeze and a hint of music emanating deep from within. Everything was in balance as my mind adjusted from classic rock to easy listening to country. I was in my own world until I was joined by another rider who came up on my left and slowed to my speed. I presumed I was riding my normal rate but that information was no longer within my charge.

His bike was vastly different than mine; it didn't have the multitude of fancy gears, computers, or other accessories deemed necessary for distance cycling. His was a basic machine, a single speed with spots of rust on the frame and on the chrome bars, knobby fat well–worn tires and a large welded wire basket behind his tractor wide spring loaded seat. He wore no special cycling gear and no helmet yet he rode effortlessly and smoothly along my flank in the traffic lane. His bike was suited for the slow paced crushed shell roads I'd last seen him riding on back in Florida. It had been more than four years since I last saw my dad pedal his oversized three–wheeler to the mailbox at the end of the quarter mile long road and back to the house where he and my mom lived. I was a witness to his riding from my own home just across the street on many occasions. Sometimes I would see him on days when I would return from work, catching a glimpse of dad at the mailbox or just as he would make the left turn into his driveway. I never rode with him before but today I have been given a gift to do just that in the middle of nowhere Kansas.

We talked at length about things I cannot recall but we didn't talk about his cancer, or how much he was missed or anything like that. We talked as we always did when working side by side in his workshop or out in my yard taking down trees or building sheds. I was cut from the same cloth as he was. He gave me the gift and appreciation of working with my hands. He gave me a target of how to be a good man; no flash, no fanfare he was a quiet humble hardworking person. He was my dad. As we continued down the highway I remember looking at him and noticing the scenery was a bit blurred, maybe a bit of glare too but I also remember seeing the same when I looked off to my right. I was relaxed in his company and felt as I did years before the first symptoms of prostate cancer slowed him down. Over the miles we covered much and I was able to share with him what had happened in my life, but he already knew.

Then as swiftly as he rode up we reached a point in our ride where our routes would diverge. There was no turn or fork in the road but he drifted to the left as I continued straight along my path. The sound of traffic and the wind and bike noise filled my ears as a multitude of cars and trucks zipped past in close proximity. Just two hundred yards shy of the SAG on a slight right hand descent my autopilot has returned control. I was fully focused on safely angling across the highway to the convenience store parking lot where Margaret was set up and cyclists were congregating. I brought my bike to a stop, dismounted, and trekked into the store to find a restroom. Then I stepped back outside, blended in with the group and enjoyed the SAG buffet of fresh fruit, cakes, energy bars, and Gatorade.

I can't explain why on this morning of all mornings so far into the tour I would experience such an event. I cannot find the words. Nor do I think it is necessary to ensure anyone else grasps what happened today. I am simply recording the events that happened and I don't ask for agreement or acceptance from anyone else. It just is as I wrote it. This was a gift of time from my dad to me; a gift that somehow he was able to transcend the after and the now. It does not require understanding it simply requires faith in what cannot be comprehended in our juvenile minds. "How real was it? Was I dreaming?" Some will say it couldn't happen but it was as real as the scar over my left eyebrow and I was fully aware, in tune, and focused. My eyes were open, I saw the landscape roll by, not some imaginary landscape but this specific section of road with all of the hills and turns that can be confirmed on the cue sheets. In the years since I have retraced this section of road three more times. If it were a dream I welcome an explanation as to how I was able to safely cover an hour's ride without remembering any traffic or road hazards in some dream state.

I did not share this with the other riders or with the staff. I could not explain it and I was so emotionally charged it would have come out all confusing if I tried. Even now I cannot find the words to convey the event even to myself. Sometimes feelings have no place in words.

Looking back on this day more than thirteen years later it remains clear and vivid in my mind; a very special moment in my crossing that would not be repeated. It was the last time I saw and spoke with my dad. I realize he was deceased more than four years so I have no explanation of the possibilities of such matters. They just happen. It did happen. And I am glad he chose to seek me out for whatever reason at that moment. I am glad he was without a trace of cancer and I am certain he rides on some shell rock road everyday on the other side of this life. And I feel the next time I ride with him it will not be in this world. For now I'll assume he has my back when I ride and I will be safe under the watchful eye of my father.

And except for the words on this page it has been neither shared with nor told to anyone. It remains a very private and emotional event in my life; one of faith, of hope, and one of comfort. I spent enough time in the parking lot and it was time to roll. I pondered the idea of dad joining me farther down the road but it was clearly not based on what I wanted. If I were to ride in the company of others the rest of the day it would be my fellow XC04 friends. I put on my gloves, adjusted my helmet strap, and clipped my right foot into the pedal. Then I pushed off and quickly clipped in my left shoe as I exited the parking lot and rejoined the route continuing on the short downhill and into the eastern limits of Kansas. Tears did fall. Happy tears.

To my left is the town of Valley Falls, population: 1,191 and falling. Women outnumber men by ten percent and the city employs just two people to run its daily business; a city administrator and a part–time clerk. Welcome to the big city of Valley Falls, originally known as Grasshopper Falls. The town has a single elementary school and a high school so if you root for the home team you'll pull for the Dragons and wear black and gold. And if you are curious, a professional baseball player named Fred March was born in Valley Falls in 1924.

Three quarters of an hour later SR–4E unceremoniously turned into SR–59N. The only evidence of the road change—aside from the DOT sign—was the Jefferson County Middle School sitting on the inside of the graceful left hand bend in the road. I was skirting past the east side of Nortonville, a town that barely covered six blocks square, when this identity change event occurred.

The middle school marked the eastern extent of town which measured less than half a square mile and was home to just over 620 people. According to Wikipedia the only notable details are the elevation at 1,165 feet, the fact Nortonville follows Central Standard Time, and that the town sits at the northern most edge of Jefferson County. The town was platted in 1873 and named after L. Norton Jr., a railroad employee so there's a little nugget of train trivia for my railroad friends to keep them turning the pages.

The first post office was established in May of the same year and there is no evidence anyone famous or infamous hails from Nortonville.

I did notice in a google map search Nortonville is home to three churches including the Nortonville United Methodist Church and the St. Matthews Lutheran Church that compete for souls near the intersection of

Norton Avenue and Elm Street which is almost in the center of town. Norton United is an old white clapboard structure modest in size and St. Matthews is a more modern brick structure and is by far the largest. A few blocks away on the north eastern fringe is St. Joseph's Church, a classic red brick house of worship, on the corner of N. Sycamore and 206th Streets. No house of worship is more than five blocks walk even if you get lost on the way.

The town does have a proper Main Street business district covering the essentials—Kendall State Bank, a bar called "The Hop," Noll's Wood Shed, a barber shop, York Heating & Air Conditioning, and the Mainstreet Restaurant all within a single block. Around the corner you'll find the Knights of Columbus, a public library, a post office, and a few other businesses. The big deal in Nortonville is Mid–West Fertilizer, Inc. and if you believe the tag line on their sign, "They keep things growing!"

Behind me I leave the town of Nortonville, Kansas. Maybe next time I pedal this way I'll detour left onto Nemaha Road which becomes 189th Road before it concedes to the name of Railroad Street as it enters the condensed downtown proper. I'll have to remember to make the turn just less than a mile before SR–4E ends. But then again it is a dirt and gravel road so maybe I'll save myself the trouble, the added mile, and a chance of flats and stay on the pavement.

The scenery shifts more to farm fields including new corn standing knee high and a variety of grains. It could be wheat, could be hay, but my field savvy is right there with my ability to identify trees. Farmers plow it and plant it and I just ride by and look at it. Then I put up the bike for the night, get out my pad and pencil, and write about it.

The corn does make the most noise of all the planted fields when it is driven by the wind but today the fields are not talking above a whisper. The plants do wave and move about resembling the motion of open water. The wind slowly stirs the corn, folding and turning the leaves creating a contrast of green shades that seem to rise and fall like a green sea. It's captivating to watch, and the rhythms and movement create a calming effect as you look on. Riding the road along the dancing fields gives the illusion of sailing my bike across an expansive ocean of green. Aye, aye captain, time to set eyes back on the road.

I continue riding past Cummings seeing nothing but corn all around and a small blue sign for their Methodist Church. The elevation has dropped nearly two hundred feed since Nortonville so I'm not complaining about the terrain. It's working in my favor.

The view is consistent except for a high voltage electric line crossing the road from my right flank, popping out of the trees and continuing forward and to the left until the towers disappear behind more trees within the rolling terrain. Miles ahead I see off to the left and down in a shallow valley a power tower, then another. They begin to angle toward the road becoming taller as they approached. Up ahead I see a building of some sort and it looks like the road and the power lines will converge at the structure. I pass a house off to my left as the distant structure comes into view. A mile or so out it is massive, a large rectangle laying on its side with a single protrusion pointing upward and offset to the right. The road is dead flat, the power towers are now parallel with the road and there is nothing but acres and acres of corn to my right.

The structure is as tall as the power towers. The protrusion extending upward doubles its height and I can now see it is some type of grain storage facility. At a quarter mile away I can see a series of rail cars exiting from behind a bank of trees stretching all the way to the structure. I assumed they were open hopper cars used to transport the grain from the storage structure. Behind the rail cars and the tracks the building has a lower but very long steel extension. There are other structures including a round squatty silo much smaller in size but still very large. Piping and structural framing painted mostly white cross over the tracks in several places and appear to be the filling tubes and supports for moving the grain to the train cars.

I finally reach the closest point to the site and I stop to take in the view. Concrete and steel make up the massive structure whose bulk is close to one hundred feet tall and the smaller extension, a narrow tower reaching up yet another hundred feet sits on top. It could be bigger but I'm more than three hundred feet away so I can't be sure. At least it's the biggest thing I have seen since I left Topeka and in this relatively flat terrain it is quite a formidable site.

According to the information I have this area is called Parnell, named after James L. Parnell, a member of the 13th Kansas Militia Infantry Regiment who was killed in the Civil War. They had a post office in Parnell which opened in 1883. It closed forty years later.

Just past the grain storage site the power line jumped back across the road and angled off to the right in the direction of the next big town of Atchison. I was pedaling north east with an ever increasing shift toward the east as I pressed on. I passed by a few private homes with well–groomed lawns and ponds along the way. I did notice the elevation changes on both sides of the road becoming more dramatic.

Around a graceful right hand bend the sides of the road dropped off more aggressively and safety rails which I hadn't seen for many miles became more commonplace. On the left side of the road were a small creek and another storage facility of some type with a series of concrete silos running the length of several football fields. It was much longer but not as tall as the one I saw in Parnell.

To the right I saw more houses but they were modest and mixed in among a few modular homes. Beyond the facility older homes and small businesses lined both sides of the road. The speed limit dropped from sixty–five to fifty–five miles per hour and the trees were condensing closer to the pavement. A DOT sign with a camper trailer graphic indicated Warnock Lake was somewhere off to the right. Ahead an abandoned service station, junk cars, and shipping containers blended in with the declining neighborhood. As I approached the city limit sign for Atchison an old charter bus and a collection of industrial and construction equipment lay rusting on the ground and in the process of being reclaimed by nature. Welcome to Atchison!

The guardrails returned, the road crossed another creek, and traffic picked up. Metal silos accumulated on the left while old brick buildings strung out to the right. The structures were getting closer to the road and I felt like I was being guided into a narrow pass. The roadway had widened to two lanes each direction to service the truck traffic but the shoulder was gone. Within two feet of the road edge telephone poles, brick steps leading to businesses, and trees were now a concern. The power lines crossed the road yet again and this time the leg of one of the towers was only eight feet at best off the left side of the road with no protective railing as a barrier. I don't want to be around when a large truck takes the tower out and drops the high voltage lines in the road.

I crossed through the light at 14th and George Street continuing on SR–59, the undivided two lanes of traffic flowing each way. Before the light the road transitioned into a dirt and grass shoulder providing an option to exit if a car threatened to occupy my pedaling space. After the light a concrete curb lined the road making sure I would be kept close to the lane of traffic. To make it more of a challenge Atchison had storm drains extending into the lane. At least the speed limit was reduced to thirty–five miles per hour so I guess I should just enjoy the experience and keep my eyes open.

Then the signs all pointing to the left—Atchison Rail Museum, Visitor Information Center, Cray Historical Home, Muchnic Art Gallery, Birth Place of Amelia Earhart, Reisner Park, LFM Park, Historic Home District, and Independence Park. And so you don't think there was a left–only conspiracy, signs pointed to the right for Bromley Park, Warnock Lake, Emelia Earhart Earthwork, International Forest of Friendship, and if needed, *H* for a hospital.

Approaching the major intersection of KS–7, US–73, & KS–192 also locally referred to as 10th Street, I brought my mount to a stop. With both feet planted firmly I began checking the cue sheet as I was about to flip to the third quadrant and begin hunting down the Dairy Queen at mile marker 57.7. If I turned left I'd head to Troy and right would take me to Leavenworth. I'm forging ahead on SR–59 because it tells me it goes to St. Joseph, Missouri.

More signs—Right to Jackson Park, left to Shopping and Business District, the Benedictine Bottoms Widelife Area, and the Benedictine College.

The speed limit dropped down to thirty miles per hour, the second lane tapered off, and I could see more silos standing just a few hundred yards to the left of SR–59N. Passing through 6th Street the buildings right up against the road formed a narrow brick canyon as I made my way toward the bridge to cross the Missouri River. This old primer colored steel truss two–lane bridge completed in 1938 was scheduled for replacement with a new, more modern concrete decked arched steel span that would be dedicated to the memory of Amelia Earhart as was the original span.

But the new bridge was still a few years off so today I would have to endure the rough road surface as I rattled across between the three foot tall ornamental safety railing to my right and the continuous flow of traffic skirting closely by on my left. I would ride through this massive erector set for nearly half a mile and both my pedaling and my heartrate seemed to increase the entire distance until I was able to get some assistance from gravity as I arched over the crest of the bridge and started my gradual drop toward Missouri. I made it safely across as did all the other riders and the back side of the bridge dropping into Missouri afforded a nice coasting opportunity and a chance for a brief respite from pedaling.

When the new bridge opens late 2012 it would have provisions for two additional lanes and a healthy ten foot wide shoulder. A much improved smooth road surface and ample room for those on foot and riding bikes. It would also be elevated much higher than the old road deck to overcome the challenges experienced by floodwaters in the past. Crossroad riders would experience the thrill of riding the old bridge through the tour of 2012. The old span would officially be decommissioned and finally demolished with explosive charges on October 9, 2013.

Somehow I missed the Dairy Queen which was supposed to be on my right about half a mile before the river. It was the only DQ opportunity I would have on the day but given the congestion along this stretch of the ride I was better off forging on to the next SAG four miles ahead.

Once clear of the river I was in Winthrop, Missouri. This dot on the map was nothing but a few fuel stops, convenience stores, and service type businesses along the board flat road. The commercial operations would soon give way to open expanses of farmable fields stretching out in all directions. The road shoulder was wide but in poor condition and in minutes I rolled up to the official Missouri State Line sign. I guess they decided it should go where it is convenient to stop for photos and not right on the border itself. The sign was not as impressive as most of the state signs but I was chalking it up to SR–59N not being one of the marquee entry points into the state.

Through Kansas and on into Missouri we had a slight tail wind and temperatures in the seventies for most of the day. It was a fun ride. The scenery was much like the previous day, with rolling hills of corn and grassy fields complete with cows and horses.

As riders stopped at the second SAG the talk was about the contrasts between Kansas and our early experience in Missouri. Most agreed when we exited Kansas we said goodbye to the best bike–friendly roads we've known on the trip and started on the worst in Missouri. Missouri road shoulders were narrow, full of holes and strewn with glass. Many riders experienced flats, and a few had words with some less–than–courteous drivers.

We will spend the next three days in Missouri, and I hope the *Show Me State* residents show some kindness and courtesy to those biking across this beautiful state.

For the next ten miles we rode along the Burlington Northern and Santa Fe rail lines watching trains lumber by on our right, some with full loads of open hopper cars and round tankers. Most were very long but there were a few others traveling faster and lighter with a similar mix of rolling stock. The farm fields to our left were varied and plentiful; most with corn blanketing thousands of acres in a deep green hue. Behind the trains were small hills, the first we'd seen since entering the state. They were covered in dense trees and were maybe sixty feet above the tops of the passing trains.

The view remained unchanged until the road began to rise up where it would cross over to the right of the rail line. The ragged shoulder I had on the flats evaporated at the base of the overpass and created a bit of tension between me and the cars trying to negotiate past in both directions through the tight confines. At least one driver gunned his engine and forced his way past as I dropped through the gears to offset my slowing pace on the climb. "Nice to share the road with you too!" or something similar was what I interpreted by the driver's actions which were emphasized by the close proximity of his fender to my handlebars as he zoomed by. The Show Me State drivers could show a little courtesy.

At the top of the concrete bridge a long train was passing underneath me generating the typical rumble and clatter of a fully loaded mile long train. The ground vibrated and I could now see into the open hopper cars. They were full of black coal and not grain I assumed earlier.

The effort spent riding up earned me a pedal free glide down the other side until I was back on flat ground, with a returning albeit a crappy shoulder. I noticed my side of the road did not have the rumble strips. Not sure if it was a good thing or a bad thing, but I still noticed it. The other side of the two lane road did have the grooves carved into it so at least half the job was done.

Cornfields were on my right and a buffer of trees intermittently blocked my view to the left where the trains and more corn were known to be. I kept pedaling and settled into a cadence of seventy–two to seventy–five rpms. Pedaling at this rate for me seems optimal. If I pedaled faster I would needlessly raise my heartrate and waste energy. If I pedaled slower it increased the force I had to exert on the pedals and strained my knees.

You can compensate by adjusting your speed and changing the gears to find the ideal combination for the conditions you are riding. It all happens naturally. You don't need to think about it too much to find your right pace. Your knees and your heartrate will provide the clues to find your optimal cadence. As a starting point set a target for the speed you want to ride and then find the gear combination that feels most comfortable where you can maintain the rate. There's no magic to it but you do need to have the proper information by way of your bike computer to track cadence, speed, and heartrate.

When I was a teenager I preferred to stand on the pedals and spin them at a slower rate. That was before I had bad knees and noticeably less leg strength. Many of the XC04 riders are spinners. They turn the pedals eighty to one hundred times a minute which seems to work best for them. I also noticed the thinner the rider the faster their cadence. Not always but I believe there is a correlation. Skinny long legs seemed to like a faster cadence. The important thing is you have to do what works best for your body; a pace that can be sustained for the entire day's ride. Go find your groove!

Well lucky me the rumble strips have found their way to my side of the road. The Bargain Barn Flea Market and the mini storage units to the right are my first clues I'm getting closer to town. I pass by a couple of farms, I see silver metal corrugated grain silos, and an odd looking tractor with the huge tires on all corners, big plastic tanks mounted above the frame, and extendable pivoting arms to spray the crops with either pesticides or fertilizer. The tractor looks like a big mechanical bug and when rolling on the road it looks high enough that I could almost ride under it if I ducked down. Not like I would try it, just making the observation.

The speed limit has dropped down to forty–five miles per hour further confirming the end of the wide open section of my ride. A Quick Stop convenience store, a couple of houses and a few commercial businesses sit just off to the right. I pass another speed limit sign now restricting traffic to thirty miles per hour. My cue sheet says I'll be making a right turn onto Alabama Street. I'm paying better attention to the small street signs so I don't miss it. Valley, Eureka, a no name street, there it is, Alabama RT–752 East! I angle onto the narrow two–lane, the shoulder is gravel for a bit but it is then replaced with a sidewalk so I've got a painted line and six inches before I brush the curb. I'm sure I'll make drivers mad but I'm taking the lane; at least a few feet of it.

It's an older neighborhood, wooden framed houses mostly white of modest size sit within twenty feet of the road, but they are clean, reasonably maintained, and offer a welcome to town that seems oddly quaint and inviting.

Eight miles to go and I make the turn onto South West Parkway, a narrow divided uphill road similar to a golf cart trail through a country club. The pavement winds through the campus of Benton High School past several brick buildings and a few homes. Shortly past the main structures the lanes blend back together and I continue through a series of climbs and tight switchbacks in a park–like setting.

I drop the gears to keep my cadence up as I quickly lose speed until I reach the crest and begin dropping down the other side. The turns are tighter and I am rewarded with exhilarating acceleration through some long but shallow wooded drops. I continue over a concrete overpass traversing a rail line and Garfield Avenue before I speed past a community park complete with several baseball fields and the St. Joseph Bode Ice Arena. In the flats I resume pedaling through cross streets, then the western fringe of the Fairfield Golf Course.

In short order I am deposited deeper into established and much older neighborhoods, a mix of large single and multi–story homes with grand front porches and ornate wood and stone details that require a dedication of effort to keep in proper shape. Several homes have large retaining walls of stone or block separating the sidewalk from their respective house perched a half a story above.

 I'm climbing steadily and eventually the residential area gives way to proper businesses. A CVS pharmacy on the right anchors several smaller local operations and within a few blocks as I near the left hand turn to Woodbine Road the scenery reverts back to a more residential flavor. I time the oncoming traffic and make the turn. I'm now dancing the last few miles with four lanes of traffic, no shoulder, and a concrete curb to keep me in play.

Woodbine is a straight line of rolling hills with heavy afternoon traffic. And I'm not feeling the love from the impatient drivers trying to make their way by. Working hard to keep speed on the final incline, I see an Applebee's on the right and just beyond is the light for my final right onto Fredrick Avenue. In the last few blocks as I cross over I–29, I see the Drury Inn, and prepare to turn left across traffic. A wide center turn lane affords me the opportunity to wait for oncoming traffic to clear and I quickly dart across. A short pedal through the Conoco fuel station lot and I'm up the drive and coasting to a stop at the front of the hotel.

A few riders were talking and checking their bikes as others slowly trickled in. Soon Rick would have his repair area set up but I doubt many bikes would need adjustments. It was a good ride, tense at times, but free of mechanical issues and body aches. I covered 86.34 miles in five hours forty–three minutes with a respectable average speed of fifteen miles an hour. The computer indicated that I peaked at twenty–nine miles an hour and I can only guess that was on the scenic South West Parkway.

A quick check of my bike, some conversation exchanged with a few riders by the entry, and I was inside heading to the front counter to pick up my room key. The rest of the post ride routine went according to plan, my riding outfit was spread out to dry, and I was grit free and back in my cargo shorts and CrossRoads t–shirt.

Finally a bit of time before route rap to learn about St. Joseph, Missouri. It was founded in 1843 by Joseph Robidoux, a fur trader and owner of the Blacksnake Hills trading post. Because of its proximity to the Missouri River and being a popular supply point for those heading farther west, the trading post became highly successful and eventually grew into what is now known as St. Joseph. Today it is the sixth largest city in the state with a population of just over seventy–five thousand.

Tourist points of interest include the Pony Express museum, the prestigious Wyeth–Tootle Mansion, built in 1879, where one of the country's finest Native American collections is kept, and the house where Jesse

James was gunned down on April 3, 1882, at the age of thirty–four. Jesse was shot to death by Bob Ford, a member of his gang, to collect a ten thousand dollar reward offered by Governor Crittenden.

Tonight is a free dinner night and there's a barbeque joint called Bandana's off the back corner of the hotel which looks promising. After route rap and enjoying the complementary drinks and snacks at the Drury I'll see if anyone else wants to walk over for ribs or maybe some pulled pork. I have to say the Drury is one of the nicest hotels we've stayed at and according to the information Tracy provided this won't be the last one on our way to Boston.

Tomorrow it's another eighty–six mile day as we ride to Chillicothe. Maybe I'll do some real laundry instead of sink rinsing my cycling gear.

Day 28: St. Joseph to Chillicothe (87 miles)

The best hotel by far on this trip has to be the Drury Inn. It's a quirky name for a hotel chain and one I never heard of until riding into St. Joseph. I think it's a toss–up between the hospitality, the good food, and the clean and well–appointed rooms that appeal to me. Then again it could be the free beer. Who am I kidding? Anyway, in a few days we will be back in a Drury Inn for a two–day stay in Champaign, Illinois. That's right; our traveling circus can debate the reasons for why this chain is going to be a success. Over several beers of course!

After completing my pre–breakfast readiness I was down in the lobby to begin my carb loading and trying once again to slay my caffeine demon. Coffee is one of those things I have a hard time identifying exactly why I drink it. It doesn't really taste good, so it must be the warmth or the social comfort that drives me to drink it. It certainly can't be the addictive quality some say it has. Nope it isn't that. But I think I'll have another cup.

Today I'll climb about 2,800 feet, the most since riding to Tucumcari eleven days ago. Tucumcari, that part of the ride feels like it happened months back, not just a week and a half ago. New Mexico, Texas, Oklahoma, and Kansas have disappeared into my mirror and now I'm in Missouri. There has been some serious progress made by my bike and I. And just past half way it will be more about counting down instead of adding up the miles.

My bike and I make quite a team. Together we will arrive in Boston and put wheels and feet into the salty Atlantic Ocean. We'll celebrate the end of this pedaling odyssey and we'll both appreciate some time off. We might even toss the three stooges into the waves for good measure; after all, they earned it too. When we get home we'll separate for a bit, maybe just a week or two, and then we'll get reacquainted and begin more casual riding. No more century rides in the immediate future, not even a fifty. I think two hours should become the norm. Yeah, a two–hour ride sounds about right.

If you find it odd talking about a bike as if it has some personal qualities remember I spent a lot of time in intimate contact or at least constant contact for several weeks with that narrow seat. Even with the padding on both seat and shorts we managed to aggravate each other; not all the time, but enough.

The Atlantic Ocean; I find the image of stepping into the wet sand, the pungent smell of sour salty air and seaweed hard to comprehend. Where I am this morning, standing in the lobby of this hotel in St. Joe, I've got to believe it is possible. That anything is possible if you just start on the journey and keep looking ahead.

Outside it's seventy–five degrees and overcast. It's sticky and from the slight haze in the air the humidity must be pretty high. All of the riders are in their official Crossroads jerseys which makes us look like a well–defined, maybe even an organized troop, not just a collection of individual riders. I imagine people driving past us are thinking we're in a race or part of something big. We are the later for sure.

I pumped my tires to the usual one hundred psi in the front and 110 in the back. That's a lot of pressure but most of my weight is in the rear; my rear as evidenced by the bulging contact patch between tire and ground.

In my bike bag I locate a few fresh rubber bands and secure Moe, Larry, and Curly to the flagpole. I might need to do this again as the bands quickly become stretched and brittle in the sun. Not one of them seems to appreciate the upgrade so I turn them to the back so they can watch traffic as it sneaks up on me. Nyuck, nyuck, nyuck.

The wind continues to blow steady out of the south at a solid ten plus and it will be to our right most of the way. It might rain at some point and if temperatures reach the mid–eighties as predicted I would appreciate a good shower; nothing heavy or thunderous, but just enough to take the edge off. I'll sweat out the coffee and whatever toxins I may have in me before Chillicothe. Of that I am certain.

Our group rolls out from under the portico at the hotel entrance and day twenty–eight is officially on the road for the next eight–six miles. In small groups we scurry across the bulk of Fredrick Avenue and find our place in the right lane heading east. It's busy and the four lanes of traffic are not cutting us any slack. My right knee pops and grinds, my bike makes ticking sounds too. I'm not quite mated to the seat properly so I begin moving around trying to find a good compromise. Eventually I give up. I'm going to have to make a more deliberate adjustment the first time I stop.

Betty and Greg ride immediately in front of me. The other riders all in matching jerseys are no longer so easy to identify. Riders normally have a favorite jersey you can identify them by; for Greg it is red and Betty blue. Me, I'm in bright yellow every chance I get. I want to be seen and short of anything Day–Glo, yellow is the color.

Not a mile down the road SR–6E drops a lane in either direction and we get a five foot wide shoulder to ride on. In that space the usual rumble cuts steal the left half of the lane but the pavement is reasonably smooth even with the cracks and bits of broken stone. The road continues with a slight downgrade and across a flat concrete bridge, the sign says 102 River. It looked like a flood zone but sure enough as we neared the end of the crossing a river did run beneath. We made a similar crossing over the Platte River and then without warning we ran out of good shoulder. There was pavement but it narrowed and was broken up except for the part with the rumble cuts. That part remained.

Looking at the two quadrant cue sheet I noticed we will remain on this road for the next sixty miles. Through this early stretch the road was mostly flat, the ground on both sides wet and fertile, and I imaged this area being mostly under water in the rainy season. And it didn't appear it would take much to get there. A slight climb, a bend to the right, then a similar downhill and we were tacking left to get back on the easterly course.

As we pressed on our shoulder narrowed until we were graced with a single painted white line with maybe half a foot of asphalt before it dropped down into a gravel and dirt runoff. It meant we would take the lane out of necessity.

Not an hour in we came to a stop sign and our first instruction on the cue sheet. We crossed and hooked left picking up a tailwind. The climbing began. It was gradual at first, but eventually the ground heaved and dropped, the road satisfied to ride the contour. As the terrain became more extreme the road no longer followed. We pedaled through cuts creating embankments on both sides and through the drops the road was built up to find a balance as true as reasonably possible.

Betty was maintaining a good pace; Greg stayed low and favored his aero bars. Gray with his fenders and flaps moved up and down the group taking pictures and video. Every so often Gray would speed up until he disappeared only to materialize on the side of the road a mile up with his small video camera in hand capturing all of the riders as we rolled by. With all of the photos and video being taken our group will have quite a collection come Boston.

I'm in the zone; I feel good, my heartrate is between 125 and 140. I got comfortable in the seat and I adjusted gears so I could maintain a cadence near eighty. My shoulder still not recovered from the fall back in Florida was tender but gave me no trouble. My wrists demanded attention and they were aching from the vibrations. I moved around the bars frequently switching my grips from the hoods to tight on the stem. I would alternate taking my hands off the bars to shake them out; then I would try a different grip at the extents of the main bar where it curves toward the hoods. Relief was always temporary. Without thought my grip would always tighten, my hands would ache again, and the cycle repeated itself. At least I wasn't having issues with hot foot.

Up ahead was the Finish Line, a convenience store Tracy had marked on the cue. A few of our group stopped, their bikes leaning against the front of the store. My detachment kept pedaling since it was only another 15 miles to Maysville, the home of long distance cycling.

Guardrails appeared on the left side of a right sweeping turn. We were climbing and it was getting to be more of a challenge to keep pace. Some of the faster riders who stopped at the convenience store closed in and passed us. Peter and Gary on their recumbents were among the group of nearly six other riders and in a matter of seconds they had pulled back in front and all but disappeared. To see those two leaning back like they were in a recliner was a contradiction to the speed they reach pedaling. They were nearly two miles an hour faster on the flats without any sign of effort. They were pedaling and working, it just didn't look like they required the amount of effort I did to maintain speed.

I remember each time they passed, Gary would smile and Peter would say something in his New Ham–shah drawl making even the mundane comments entertaining. To Peter's credit, most of the time he said something funny. He was loud and had a strong opinion of how things should be, but he was a kind and very friendly person once you got a chance to know him. I loved his talk about Slime, the green goo he put in his tires to prevent flats. He swore by the stuff and would go round and round with Tracy about the benefits of Slime. Tracy would have none of it. If you use Slime you don't use her tire pumps. No exception. It became a bit of a comic routine. He tested Tracy but this was his second time riding with her and she was a good sport. I know she liked him. She knew Peter well; better than she knew the rest of us. And she seemed to know us pretty well.

On a straight uphill grade we approached Maysville, population: 1,172 and would assemble all of the riders in front of the brick Maysville School just a few blocks shy of our downtown destination. Maysville was one of the larger rural towns we rode through but it was different in many ways. First the population was almost all White. I don't mean it in a derogatory way; it was a fact 98.6 percent of the population was White. Native Americans accounted for one third of a percent; that's only three people, and all other races had less than half of that representation. Poverty and income were also a problem for Maysville. The per capita income was the least of any town I remember at 11,871 dollars. This put almost seventeen percent of the population below the poverty line. The town had little to offer other than a close–knit neighborly community that would welcome us as one of their own according to Tracy. We would see soon.

With all of the riders accounted for Tracy took control and began to prepare the group of more than forty eager riders for what was about to happen. She told us about Maysville, what we would see, how we would feel, and the joy we were about to experience. She was just shy of preaching, her ever–present smile turning even the doubters. She told us about the previous seven years where this small town in DeKalb County would greet Crossroads. They would now greet us, and cheer for us, and then feed us peanut–butter–and–homemade–preserves sandwiches, and lemonade. There would be homemade cinnamon rolls too. "You need to personally thank Marilyn, 'The strawberry preserve lady' and her Brother Buck for getting up in the middle of the night to begin preparing the cinnamon treats," she said. Then she pulled back the smile and told us our annual visit was a big deal, one of the better things that happen in this town every year and we need to do our part and ride proud into town. Then she smiled, gave us a side glance, and I think she said, "Chop, chop!" which meant get moving.

We assembled in two columns, and with our red–white–and–blue CrossRoads jerseys on, we paraded down the main street to the cheers and applause of the residents. I was a few rows back in the right lane and Kathy Stevens was to my left on her recumbent. It was as Tracy described. We were treated like family returning home after a long absence. Pictures were taken, handshakes and hugs shared, friends made, and tears of joy everywhere. It was as if I were home but in a place unlike home. Their hospitality overshadowed any concerns we may have had about the people of Missouri. Those we met were genuinely happy for us and we were happy for them. We ate and drank and told stories outside the Historical Society building.

I spoke with Emma Newkirk, a volunteer with the historical society, and I could not help but notice her care and concern for the heritage of Maysville and DeKalb County. She said our annual visit is very important to the town as it has created lasting friendships through e–mail and letters between the residents and the visiting riders. We posed for pictures, me in my patriot colors and Emma proud as a Mother on her son's graduation day in her pale blue blouse. The memories made in that short time remain precious and alive today.

On display in the historical society building's second floor are the photos from every high school graduation class and newspaper articles of every soldier lost in war. They love and remember their own and I couldn't exit that building without a strong feeling of community pride.

Maysville is also home to long distance cycling; actually home to the first person to ride cross country from San Francisco to Boston in 1884 and later around the world finishing in late 1886; his name, Thomas Stevens. As much as it is a challenge for me to pedal across the country it is nothing like what Stevens experienced. He rode a fifty–inch Columbia Standard high wheel bike, also known as a *Penny Farthing* bicycle. He traveled mostly on dirt roads, on the shoulder of rail lines, and any place else he could find a route. He rode alone with only a spare shirt, pair of socks, a jacket, and a revolver. Stevens was described as being slight in build, wearing a blue flannel shirt over blue overalls tucked into his socks at the knees. A handlebar mustache was also standard issue just as you would imagine. He is the ultimate self–supported distance cyclist, many, many levels above the likes of me and my fellow riders. I can only imagine the struggles he had and the satisfaction he experienced over those miles. And instead of traffic Stevens would contend with herds of cattle and other wild animals.

Fortunately Stevens wrote about his travels in his two volume book, *Around the World on a Bicycle*. It became a best seller and is available online. I read excerpts from the first book and I was taken by his incredible ability to describe what he saw. His writing is poetry and literary magic that draws you in. In those sentences I could see what Stevens saw. I could feel what he felt. I was right there crossing the mountains and forcing my way through the muddy roads in the pouring rain. His account is truly inspiring.

Tracy met Stevens' grand–nephew, Carl in Maysville back in 1997 and she even rode his high wheeler. They keep one in the historical society building on the ground floor along with copies of the books Stevens wrote. I plan someday to buy the set and read his adventures from cover to cover.

Before leaving, I put another sandwich in my pocket and had my picture taken with Emma and her husband, Gene. I believe a little bit of Maysville will stay with me long after this trip is over. I smiled, waved, and went back to climbing hills en route to Chillicothe.

A search on the internet will reveal little about Maysville other than it was founded in 1845 and the DeKalb County Courthouse is listed in the National Register of Historic Places. It's a place you must experience in person, preferably on a bicycle because they showed us the love today.

For the next fifty–five miles I would be entertained riding and enjoying the rather large rolling climbs and drops that define this part of the country. In all I would spend the better part of six hours riding the coasters down and straining up each hill to reload for the next trip to the bottom. The glides were fast, always too short, and I stood often because that is how I remember it as a boy. I'm not sure how many hills I climbed, but I'd guess it was somewhere between one hundred and 150. It was a day for climbers and a day of survival for the flatlanders. I was more of the later and each climb made my association ever more clear.

Just a few miles outside of Maysville I passed an old tour bus on the right side of the road with "Ray Charles and his Band" painted on the side. "What a Wonderful World" began playing in my mind and a big smile crossed my face. Before you music historians jump all over me I know Ray never recorded the song, it was Louis Armstrong whose rendition came to mind. It's really the only version of the song that should have been recorded. Why it came to mind instead of Ray's classic "Georgia on my Mind" I can only guess. I love both of these songs and the men who sang them rank among my favorite performers. On the news that evening I learned Ray Charles passed away one day earlier. I believe now Louis was welcoming Ray's arrival into heaven in the most fitting way he could; from one wonderful world into another. Lucky for me heaven has no limits to its reach. I heard only joy, there was no sadness in those moments pedaling through the rolling hills and winding roads just outside of Maysville, Missouri on a most beautiful Friday, June 11, 2004. What a wonderful world.

Things started to change quickly. It was hot. I was cutting through water quickly and sweating it out continuously. It was every bit of eighty–five degrees and even with the overcast skies the heat radiated through the helmet and to my scalp. My headband held back the moisture but it couldn't stop the beads that formed just over my brows. The salt stung as it rolled into my eyes. I'd reach a finger behind my shades to wipe it away.

My forearms were wet, the beads accumulated and gravity and the wind channeled the drops until they fell from my elbows. I was also dripping under my jersey from my pits down my sides, my jersey clinging to my back under the weight of the CamelBak, and sweat rolled down into the crack of my butt. My shorts were wet and I was in need of a change. I stopped often to drink Gatorade from my bottle. I could take a pull of water anytime from the hose dangling from my CamelBak. Taking pictures was always a good excuse. I lubed my undercarriage as a preventative measure and then I pedaled on.

Since Maysville I was riding solo. I needed a bit of alone time to stop at my leisure, and because Betty was faster on the climbs than I am. It doesn't bother me. I have nearly twice the weight to lug up the climbs and physics clearly shows the effort is proportional to the mass being moved. I rode over Lost Creek and Eastman's Branch before arriving in Weatherby, population: 117. With all of the climbing I'm surprised I'm only 879 feet above sea level. Weatherby has been in existence since 1885 and has a post office which has been in continuous operation since 1886. The town struggles, the demographics are extreme, and it beats Maysville in all categories challenging a community. In towns with so few people and a population changing every year, who updates the head count on the green signs at the edge of town?

I pedaled on, crossing marshy areas and eventually passing over I–35. To my left I saw a sign in front of a small dirt track. It was I–35 Speedway. I detoured off route and had a look at the track. It was void of any activity and after a few minutes of looking over the fence I was back on SR–6E. I turned south onto US–69 then left at the next intersection. Soon I found my way into Altamont. I take back what I said about Weatherby. Altamont has almost twenty–nine percent of the 212 residents living below the poverty line. They did score points for having a water tower and a store so I stopped to flip my cue sheet to the second quadrant.

The shoulder improved as SR–6E took me past Gallatin and over Grand River. I crossed the creeks of Big Muddy, Brush, and Thompson in quick succession and there I found my turn at V on the right, a big shade tree in the middle of a cornfield marked the turn. This part of Missouri uses letters to designate roads instead of proper names. Maybe it saves on lettering costs. Regardless, it is easy to remember a single letter.

Safely back on a quiet rural road I made a quick stop for a nature call and joined the rest of the group at the last SAG of the day. It was another routine stop with sixty–three miles down and twenty–three to go. I was back in the company of Betty and she would remain mostly within my view for the final stretch to Chillicothe.

Out of the SAG I passed over Clear Creek then rolled into Lock Springs, population: sixty–three and a new winner on the poverty meter. A town in name only, Lock Springs topped the charts with thirty–seven percent of the population living below the poverty line. It was fitting that the town, what's left of it, has a row of brick buildings that have all but collapsed. One was a bank, another was the fire station. Across the street the only maintained structures included a grain storage facility, all of corrugated silver. Dotted around the curve a few run down homes and single wide trailers showed signs of life. It was eerie to ride through here in the day. At night it would be out of the question.

Around a sharp bend in the road and to my left was a stone marker. It was out of place for what I had just passed through, but it warranted a stop. I hopped off the bike and walked over to read the inscription. It was dedicated to Jerry Litton, a member of the US House of Representatives. The inscription said Lock Springs was his birthplace and his boyhood home. He was on earth from 1937 until 1976. Besides the dates defining his life was one of the most profound statements I have read since Teddy Roosevelt's moving passage back in Guyman, Oklahoma. This inscription immediately became my favorite. It read, *"Happy are those who dream dreams and are ready to pay the price to make them come true."* These are the words of Leon Joseph Suenens, Cardinal and Archbishop of Mechelen–Brussel, serving the Roman Catholic Church. I think this describes all of the XC04 riders, those who came before, and those who have yet to realize this adventure will be their destiny.

I seemed to be noticing the small creeks today. It might have been the pace, I might have been a bit tired of looking at my computer displays, or it might be the signs were right at eye level and difficult to miss. After leaving Lock Springs I crossed over Penitentiary, Indian, and Bachelor Creeks. There were several other unnamed creeks I crossed over. Too many to count and maybe they just ran out of green signs and letters. I'm sure those named creeks have a story to tell if you could find a local who would share it. Especially the one called Penitentiary.

The remaining sixteen miles to the hotel included many steep climbs. The terrain demanded I use the granny gear more than I'd like and my progress dipped below five miles an hour before I reached the top only to find temporary relief. Then I would repeat the process losing count of how many hills I climbed. I'm sure my memory will remember only a few and I'll find more good in the day than bad.

When my forward motion was slowed on the climbs my riding style would no longer be straight and true. I'd weave slightly into the lane and on the really steep sections I would veer several feet toward the double yellow stripes. I kept an eye in my mirror and made sure I didn't twist the bars to the left when traffic approached from behind. If I had a proper shoulder away from the traffic lane it would not be a concern but to my right was crumbled asphalt at best and unsettling ditches at worst. A few inches of white striping marking the edge of the road would be as good as it gets for miles. The ditches were more common on the climbs and descents likely caused by natural erosion. It's just an observation.

Sweat dripped from my entire body and I was getting tired. I was leaving droplets of perspiration on the crossbar and my grips were becoming wet from my palms. In the early afternoon temperatures had peaked somewhere near eighty–five, the southern breeze was fading. In the open flatter sections I found a bit of the wind but in the climbs with dense stands of shade trees lining the road it became still and stuffy. Baking might be appropriate as I grunted out the steeper inclines.

I did not enjoy being surprised by oncoming traffic that could not be heard until appearing over the crest and almost on me. Fortunately the car counts were low and truck traffic, except for the smaller box trucks, could be counted on a single hand.

Betty was moving farther ahead with each climb, but on the flats and descents I'd reclaim only half what I lost. She was gradually becoming smaller and had no intention of slowing for me. It made me think about her standard morning comment about how she didn't feel strong and for me not to leave her behind. I think it might be a psychological game; tell me you're feeling weak then smoke me on the climbs until I feel beaten. It worked some days but I got used to Betty's riding and knew in the afternoons I shouldn't expect her to linger. I'd always see her at the hotel.

I passed other riders squatting in the bush or stopped for some other reason. Most of the faster riders were in front of me and I'd guess by the headcount at the last SAG maybe a dozen were still behind. Somewhere along a flatter section of pavement a CrossRoads van passed by but I wasn't sure who was driving. It didn't matter; they beeped the horn and kept moving up the line of riders making sure everyone was safe. It was quiet except for the scrubbing of my tire against the road as I twisted the bars coupled with the straining of the drive train under my weight against the pedals. Maybe even a hint of chain misalignment sprinkled in to see if I was paying attention.

I passed over unnamed creeks and pedaled through cornfields standing behind small white signs clustered in groups and spaced about ten rows apart. The signs offered a warning; they actually said something close to "DANGER, Genetically Modified Organisms." Not the expected text I thought I would find posted at the edge of a cornfield.

Genetically Modified Organisms (GMO's) are re-engineered bio products resistant to bugs and disease making it unnecessary to apply pesticides. Sounds like it should be healthier but some may argue this point. My conspiracy mind thought it would be a great cover to keep people from picking the ears of corn but it could be a legitimate warning. I wasn't looking to steal corn so I focused on the curves and hills ahead.

The terrain was flattening and the shoulder appeared more favorable in the distance but it turned out to be only a three foot wide ribbon of gravel a few shades lighter than the asphalt. The pavement I was riding on was at most six inches to the right of the white line putting me at least a foot into the road. To motorists it looked like I was infringing on their lane for no reason. Their focus did not account for the fact the loose gravel was not compatible with the skinny tires on which I traveled. Some would honk but it was not the friendly honk I would hear from the CrossRoads vans. It was more deliberate, more aggressive, and held long past my position. At least they didn't throw anything at me. I had enough of that in my training rides back in Florida.

Past junction *Y* a yellow sign with a bike symbol and the words, "Share the Road" made me wonder if the suggestion was intended for the drivers or the bicyclists. I assumed it was for the drivers but some cyclists struggle with respecting the motorists. That leads to shorter tempers and guilt by association. After all if you are in a car you must be in a hurry, unlike on a bike where you are just tooling around with no schedule or destination.

I rolled through a wide sweeping turn crossing a marshy flat leading to a narrow but long bridge over Thompson River. Miles were winding down so it shouldn't take long to reach SR–65S, my last turn before the hotel. It was through this section I felt a bit sluggish and my speed reflected it. It might be the slightest of inclines but after the bigger hills it was not possible to tell for sure. All I could do was keep pedaling. Betty and at least one other rider were still in sight. Then I saw the ground begin to rise up yet again. I was not done climbing. It seemed like much longer than the few minutes it must have been before SR–190 relaxed, giving me a shallow descent followed by an equally friendly climb. A water tower was in view, reduced speed signs, a blue hospital marker, and other reference points let me know the turn I was seeking was just ahead.

I rode the four–lane for the next three miles. Part of the distance I enjoyed a friendly shoulder but eventually it gave way to a concrete curb putting me back in the lane. Traffic was picking up but it was manageable, buildings clustered tighter as I entered what must be the business center. I was getting a bit of that last stretch energy but it was tempered by a series of stop lights impeding my progress.

As I rolled up to Calhoun Street I saw to my right the first of several murals; it was a big wave breaking on the surf. Strange to find this wall painting in Missouri but immediately following were several extraordinary themed murals telling the story of the area. Train murals, streetscapes from the 1920s, nearly two dozen murals in all. Most were twenty feet tall by eighty feet or more in length. One was well over a hundred feet long.

Ten years earlier I had the opportunity to participate in the painting of mural in a town called Belvidere, Illinois, some seventy miles west of Chicago. These projects create a bump in tourism and instill a level of pride within the community. Whoever was running this project in Chillicothe was doing a fantastic job.

To my left on the corner of Webster Street, probably the most important mural of all, the one declaring Chillicothe the "Home of Sliced Bread." In 1928 in downtown Chillicothe, Missouri an Iowa inventor by the name of Otto Rohwedder had his new bread slicing machine put in service at the Chillicothe Bakery. This marked the first time sliced bread was offered for sale anywhere in the world; true story.

I saw riders stopped at the mural so I detoured over and we took turns photographing each other before we completed what had been a good day on the bike. It was not easy, I covered eighty–seven miles in just over six hours of pedaling or a tick shy of 14.5 miles per hour, but it was a good day. No, it was a great day thanks to the kind souls in Maysville.

I still had water in my CamelBak and Gatorade in my bottle. It doesn't do me any good if I don't drink it. I need to be better at using what provisions I ride with, even if it means taking it in way before I get thirsty. Carrying the dead weight as I roll into the hotel does me no good at all. And if I drink every drop I could find more en route.

After getting cleaned up and doing a little touring around the immediate area, which included a stop at the Dairy Queen right next to the hotel, we enjoyed a picnic style dinner put on by the manager of the Best Western. It was burgers and fixings by the pool.

Everyone has been conditioned to pay attention to the weather because it determines much about the riding experience, the challenges, and our enjoyment. At eight in the evening it was still more than eighty degrees with winds from the south at just under ten. Rain is expected sometime in the early morning hours but it should move through before we ride to Kirksville. Tonight I'll listen to the air conditioner hum in this mid–northern Missouri town of nearly 9,200 people and hopefully wake up to dry conditions in the morning.

Day 29: Chillicothe to Kirksville (75 miles)

One of the best corporate tag lines I've seen is, "We love you and we need you at the Golden Corral," and that is exactly where we would be having breakfast this morning. Buffet style of course. Having to feed nearly fifty people at a time is a challenge for any restaurant. Ordering individually for a group like ours could take a server as much as twenty minutes, and on several evenings in crowded restaurants we dined in, it took even longer. We've proven to be an impatient lot with pretty demanding eating requirements. I would go as far as to say some of us are picky; not to be difficult, but to make sure a specific diet regiment is followed. Not me, I eat whatever is served. I can be happy with almost anything hot, cold, or in between. And when it comes to capturing the details of our wants the writing is often longer than the note pad the server carries. It's a challenge best addressed by a fully loaded buffet arrangement with pitchers of water, coffee, and juice waiting on the table. Welcome to the Golden Corral.

Twice during the early–morning hours, severe thunderstorms passed through Chillicothe. I know because they were loud enough to wake even a heavy sleeper like me. Over the past few weeks we've managed to ride in wind and rain, but lightning would keep us off the road. By six o'clock the storms had moved past, and only overcast skies remained.

Gear stowed, tires pumped, and one by one we signed the sheet and marked the time according to the official CrossRoads clock hanging inside the back of the truck. Cautiously I rolled down the Best Western side drive into traffic. It was nearly seventy degrees and winds were slight. It was a welcome relief from yesterday's heat, but if the clouds move off temperatures could be expected to reach the low, maybe even the mid–eighties.

The pavement was wet, puddles marked the low spots, but there was little spray coming off the tires. Our group made a few quick jogs to get on SR–36 heading east and then we set our sights on the exit for Brookfield.

For the next twenty–four miles I would ride this four lane divided highway amongst the string of cyclists diving under a trio of train overpasses, past the Chillicothe Municipal Airport marked by a pedestal mounted jet fighter at the entrance, through the middle of Pershing State Park, and across more than a dozen flat concrete bridges over small waterways.

At the start of each bridge was a green DOT sign marking the water crossing and at my slow pace I was able to read the names on all of them. In order they were the creeks of Blackwell, Leeper, and then Circle. Grand River, the widest waterway so far, came next followed by the creeks of Muddy, Center, Little Parson, Parsons, and Hickory. Each time I saw the guardrails and the road shoulder closing in ahead I knew I would be crossing another waterway. The length of the bridge provided a clue if it would be a creek or a river. That is until sixteen miles into the ride when I crossed the widest body of water oddly named Higgins Ditch.

The name made absolutely no sense to me. A ditch is the smallest of drainage features and in my mind it is reserved for describing a feature on the side of the road. They require no name, as they are a ditch, a trench, a shallow depression running along the right of way. Somehow, someway, midway between Meadville and Laclede someone named this thing a ditch, Higgins Ditch. Maybe it was mismarked. Maybe it was a sign shop joke no one noticed and the sign was installed, or maybe something in the name is significant. I don't know but I've got time to think about it as I pedal.

Higgins Ditch, located on the western edge of Pershing State Park, turns out to be a canal, a manmade feature described as a point of interest for tourists. It is also considered one of the top–ten canals in Linn County. The history behind the name remains a mystery though it may possibly trace back to a state Supreme Justice named Andrew Jackson Higgins.

This area of north–central Missouri is known as the Lower Grand River Watershed consisting of numerous waterways and marshy wetlands. Ostrich fern and the endangered Eastern Massasauga Rattlesnake seek refuge in its low elevation wetlands. The surface water supports the drinking water supply from Meadville to Brookfield but it is not without its issues. Water quality problems, including the presence of E. coli contaminating the water coupled with drought conditions are an ongoing community concern. Even swimming in the water is prohibited when the bacteria levels exceed the prescribed healthy limits.

Over the remaining miles along SR–36E I had a few more creeks to cross including Locust, a second pass at Muddy, then Turkey, and finally Little Turkey. If I recall I crossed over a Big Muddy River yesterday on the way to Lock Springs. Maybe they ran out of names to use, or it might be the name Muddy was just too appropriate for both river and creek not to use it.

It wasn't only bridge signs I saw along the way to Kirksville. I saw speed limit signs, stop signs, yields, center lane turns, signs with town names and distance, church signs, business signs, billboards, signs for the Rotary, Kiwanis, and the Lions, water towers with big letters, mile markers, real estate signs, right lane ends, signs on wheels, street signs, route signs, road closed, keep out, for sale, headlights on when wipers required, county signs, deer crossings, danger signs, warning signs, adopted road signs, cemetery signs, city limits, population signs, school zones, wood carved signs, school bus stops, school crossings, do not enter, yellow signs with curved arrows, signs of hope, one way, pole mounted signs, faded signs, broken signs, junction signs, hand–made roadside memorials, folding signs, railroad crossings, illuminated, temporary, hand painted, and signs on walls, buildings, and barns. "Sign, sign, everywhere a sign."

Trucks pulling trailers, car doors painted, branding and words, mobile billboards. Signs, signs, signs! Some were bright and flashy, others boring and plain. Rigid block letters and bold flowing script, hand painted, vinyl, plastic, and metal, icons, logos, national brands and mom and pops; every conceivable sign. It is a story of what we value, on display not more than a hundred feet from my bicycle seat. They interrupted the scenery but I enjoyed the distraction of reading all I could. Observing, seeing, and taking in every bit of the view along the 3,400 miles includes the signs almost as much as the natural scenery. I just happen to like signs. I should, I've been painting them since 1975. Signs are a form of art and expression as much as a medium for communications. Signs tell me where I've been and where I am going. "Tell me, have you seen the sign?"

The benefit of riding the main roads are many including better maintenance, a more level road, and a defined shoulder as wide as a traffic lane. On this section of road it was even wider. I just hope it stays this way. Highways are not without their issues and four lanes means lots more traffic. It will require attention in the mirror to look for passing riders and when dodging debris ahead. It will also be noisier but I can tune it out if I focus.

As generous as the shoulder was it did have the familiar rumble cuts, cracks, tire debris and vehicular hardware. All the tire threatening features I have been trying to avoid since leaving Los Angeles. I'd say I've been pretty successful so far since I've not had to fix any flats. I noticed this highway does have a level and safe run–off into the grass should it be necessary to take extreme measures to avoid a car, or even a truck, if one strays into the shoulder where I'm riding.

My safe run–off option would disappear each time I came to a bridge crossing water. The shoulder would narrow to the width of my bike and I would be crowded between the fast moving traffic and the metal guardrails. A very uncomfortable feeling that would last until I cleared the final section of guardrail and grass returned to the edge of the asphalt. I rode faster through these narrow channels and my pulse accelerated.

Out in the fields between Laclede and Brookfield every Labor Day weekend they hold a hot air balloon festival named the "Great Pershing Balloon Derby." What started in 1977 has turned out to be a three–day festival drawing balloonists from as far away as Florida and the Pacific Northwest. Named in honor of General John J. Pershing, a native of Laclede, this balloon derby has been recognized as one of the longest running continually sanctioned ballooning events in America by the Balloon Federation of America. More than forty–five balloons compete each year in front of a crowd estimated at over fourteen thousand. I've been to many balloon events and I can imagine the colorfully large balloons filling the blue skies over the wide open fields as the pilots unleash the hot gases creating a roar of the burn as they climb. Today the fields are quiet, nothing but clouds filling the skies.

By the time I reached the exit for Brookfield, population: 4,678, the roads were dry, skies still overcast, but there were signs it would clear off. Beyond Brookfield the roads remained friendly for a few miles except for the absence of a solid shoulder along SR–11N. I had six inches of asphalt to the right of the stripe before it ran off into loose gravel and weeds. My saving grace was light morning traffic on the backroads allowing me to enjoy the quiet as I pedaled along.

A turn north and the ditches got deeper, the terrain more disturbed. Somewhere in front of me were a string of 148 rollers I would have to overcome as part of my 2,800 feet of climbing. Tracy described the features much the same as the humps on a roller coaster track. The first would be a slow climb followed by a mad rush of exhilaration as I scramble through the gears to build enough speed to stay in the top gear and muscle up and over the next hill and down the other side. If I do it right, I can string together a series of hills. If I ran out of steam on the climb it would be an even crazier effort to drop down into the lower gears to save myself by spinning. It sounds like child's play and it is. We are all big kids at heart regardless of age and we will have a chance to let the inner child show what they can do on the rollers.

I worked my way up several steep climbs thinking I had started the run of rollers but the next hill seemed much too far away. I did enjoy the downhills but the road quickly leveled and began climbing again. On a straight section of road I noticed I could see several humps, like a dark gray serpent's back sticking out of the sea of grass. Three maybe four hilltops visible, with each new hill the downside became steeper. The next hill that followed was closer to the one before it.

I couldn't see beyond the peaks when I got down between the hills. It was getting hot and it was quiet. The sudden sound of a car breaching the crests was startling. They just appeared as if by magic.

To my left and right the landscape looked like it had been gouged by a giant's rake creating chasms of green running perpendicular to the road. The planted fields were crooked and skewed at such odd angles I wondered how a farmer dare run a tractor over the land without fear of tipping over. As I continued the hills became closer and more extreme.

And then at the crest of one hill the other side just dropped off. It dipped so steeply it looked more like a cliff than a road. Telephone poles and their wires followed; they disappeared and then reappeared on the far side of the gorge in front of me. As I rolled over the peak I was almost in free–fall. I couldn't shift fast enough, my gears and chain rattling, the bike shaking, my wrists pounding from the rough road. I was falling and flying at the same time. I crossed forty miles an hour in a few yards. I reached top gear still pedaling downward and then as Tracy described it I was upended climbing a wall, forcing all of my body weight against the pedals searching for power to get to the top. My speed scrubbed off so fast it felt like a parachute or the hand of a giant got a hold of me and slowed me down. I was well short of the top and it was clearly too late to downshift so I unclipped and prepared to stop. Had I waited a few seconds longer my progress would have stopped and I would have toppled over. It was humbling to think that all of the weight I carry could not transfer the power I needed to climb the next hill.

I stepped off the bike and looked around. Betty was over the hill and I was maybe sixty feet or more from the top. The hilltops stood forty to sixty feet above the trough; five stories of ups and downs in a very short distance. I turned around to look back at the road I just descended and it was a wall; a dramatic drop off propelling me to such speeds only to turn me over to a mirror image that stole the speed right back. I took a pull of water and made a quick change of gears as I held the back wheel off the road and I was ready to finish this climb in the granny gear. I did not claim victory over this hill but I was ready to do it again.

At the top of each hill I would look across the ribbon of asphalt in front of me. I saw as many as six crests in a straight line, the telephone poles, trees, and fields rippling in sync with the road surface. The sun finally broke out from behind the clouds and it heated the road. The hot surface radiated blurred waves I could see dancing in the distance, my brow dripped of sweat and I thundered down the other side.

Several times I was sure I would not make the top so I dropped gears at the bottom and coasted as far as I could until my speed slowed to match the gears. I climbed up slowly reaching the top only to repeat the process. I saw nothing from the bottom except walls. No breeze could find its way into the abyss. The view from the top couldn't have been any different. At times I saw Big Mike and Duffey on the hills behind me. I saw other riders as they crossed the peaks in front. I chatted with riders on the peaks and raced down into the gorges in their company. We were working our tails off, we struggled, yet we continued.

And then I had a perfect string of hills, the preceding one larger than the next. I raced down and ran out of gear, but I pushed with everything I had and climbed up. Finally I had the momentum, just enough of it, to cross the apex and shoot down the other side still in high gear. Three maybe four hills in succession I finally did it. I made it to the top and rolled over just like the coasters in the amusement parks.

I never counted how many hills or where they officially started. I trust the number 148 was a good estimate; the hills quickly sapped me of my strength. I would size up the hills from the top, and then I'd race down the ones I thought I could make and stay in high gear where I could. The ones I thought would be too tough I'd be ready to downshift.

As the day wore on my assessments got shakier. I was stranded in high gear on hills I thought I could master. Each time I would unclip and safely dismount. The ones I rolled over gave me just a little extra momentum to attack the next. It felt great when it happened and even though it was difficult it gave me reason to smile.

On my dashes to the bottom there were a few times where my chain came off. Sometimes it jammed. There was nothing I could do except coast to a stop, replace the chain and resume the slow climb back out of the hole. If the chain jumped off during a climb it was always problematic. It happened when the front derailleur misaligned because of incompatibility with the rear cog or I either under or over shot the guide when pulling the levers. Even though it was considered a twenty–seven–speed bike it was not designed for riding with the chain crossing the most extreme combinations. Under load on a climb a severely misaligned chain does its best to stay on the gears but the force from the pedals often causes it to walk right off. It would suddenly freewheel or jam the crank freezing it in position. If I were barely moving I wouldn't even get to choose the side to fall on. There is just enough time to realize what is about to happen and then it is over. I was fortunate the few times it happened to be rolling just fast enough to unclip and catch myself. It still sent a brief chill through my body as if to say, "Next time!"

From the tops of many hills I tried to capture the extremes of the terrain with my camera but photos could not fully capture what it looked like from the seat of the bike. Riders in the distance popped up and disappeared in the hills ahead. The same was happening behind me.

My legs were feeling the punishment and a long overdue SAG stop at mile fifty was just ahead. I rounded a bend and enjoyed a long gradual downhill that took me all the way to the CrossRoads van, Margaret entertaining the group of riders. Sandwiches and the usual compliment of snacks would fuel us for the final twenty–five miles to Kirksville.

I could see everyone was both tired and entertained by the rolling hills; maybe not everyone. The tandems of Randie and Tom Kahrl and Helen and Don Reeves didn't have the luxury of stopping on the climbs. Their bikes were also significantly heavier and harder to maneuver with the extra few feet of length. Where I could swerve perpendicular to the road they could not. But they made it; they toughed it out.

The recumbents also struggled because their reclined position did not take advantage of their body weight like the upright bikes leverage gravity to help force the pedals to turn the crank. Ben and Kathy rode near me so I saw them struggle. Hopper, Gary, and Peter were all ahead of me and were at the SAG with almost everyone else when I arrived.

I topped off my fluids, had a sandwich, and grazed on the offerings of the checkerboard table. A half a banana and some cakey treats finished the stop. Then I was busy yapping and storytelling about how I slayed the dragon. Funny we all had basically the same story to tell.

Most of us had to be told to leave the SAG. It was a very social stop and we had much to talk about but the longer we stayed the less capable we would be to continue. That's the funny thing about biking. Once you stop your body quickly adapts to the more sedentary activity and resists your attempts to get back on the bike. I think it begins the process of recovery. Wait too long and your legs turn to jelly and your day on the bike is over. The ideal is to be off the bike just long enough to refuel and give your butt a few minutes without the pressure of the seat wedged against it. The sweet spot seems to be somewhere in the ten to fifteen minute range.

Exiting the SAG the downhill ride continued. My legs were a bit mushy so I coasted for a distance and when it was time to begin climbing again they were not prepared. The climbs would be steep but nothing like the rollers we had leading to the SAG. In the valleys it was still. There would be no breeze unless I was fully exposed near the peaks. It was eight–five degrees, the wind, when it mattered, came from behind at barely five miles an hour out of the south. It didn't help nor hurt.

I pedaled up quarter mile long inclines only to level off then climb again. There were farms and ponds, wide expanses of green fields planted with corn and other crops. Cattle roamed in other fields and shade trees clustered together in the wet areas. Large forest tracts lined the horizon. It was very pretty country that saw few afternoon water crossings until I reached the Chariton River ten miles shy of my destination. The bridge was much longer and thankfully it had a dedicated shoulder to ride on. What was odd is before and after the bridge there was no more than a foot of shoulder.

I would climb and descend through wooded areas, the road stair–stepping up and down. Cars would pass; I could see Betty ahead with Greg and others. Behind me a faster rider would close the gap, call out, "On your left," and continue on by. Some would slow and converse, others were on a mission to end the day. I was happy to enjoy the more accommodating terrain now that my legs had rejoined the effort.

In an area of trees and blind corners I passed the Sugar Creek Conservation Area, a 2,536 acre forest that is part of the Sugar Creek State Forest. I continued past ranch homes with their expansive mowed lawns and a few small ponds just off the side of the road. Fir trees absent from my view for the entire day were now part of the scenery. On my right was a post rail fence painted white running along the road. Behind the fence set way back was an impressive two story house sitting in close proximity to a large pond. Ahead of me three more shallow rollers and a generous stand of fir trees as much as twenty feet tall running for a half mile or more on the right side of the road. They were a wind break, blocking the breeze coming from the south.

There would be more white fences and fancy houses, barns and fresh cut fields, and lawns in the final miles. The road began to tip up and down more aggressively and the shoulder was only the painted line.

Ahead the sign to Kirksville came into view; less than two miles to the Holiday Inn Express. All I needed to do was make the left turn at the stop sign and cross the road on SR–63N. I could do that.

I rode up a long slow incline and through a dip to climb the final stretch to Franklin Street. Through the intersection I pedaled, looping to my right, and then I paused to make a safe crossing. As the light changed I rolled across the divided highway and from there it was all downhill to the hotel.

At the Holiday Inn riders were wiping down their bikes, filling out repair tickets for Rick and Tom J. and continuing their stories from the SAG. As I spoke with several riders I could hear Peter having conversations with others. It's that New Ham–shah tone I'd grown fond of since the first night we shared dinner back in Los Angeles. I talked with Kathy as Dick and Big Mike coasted in and then I started my bike check and cleaning before signing in and getting my room key. My computer recalled 75.33 miles, five hours twenty–one minutes, an average speed of fourteen miles an hour and a maximum speed of 38.1. I love modern day technology.

It was very humid, very hot, and very sunny. I would need a shower to wash away the sweat and the excitement of the day. It was another unique experience for the boy and I know he enjoyed it.

We would eat at the Ponderosa Steakhouse tonight. I will be fueling up for tomorrow as we face another round of the rollers and cross the two thousand mile mark in this trip.

At dinner the conversation will be about friends and family, the day's ride, and tomorrow's challenges. We will laugh and we will joke and we will remember. For me I will remember today for the sensation of falling down the hills, accelerating so quickly, being a bit afraid but mostly excited, and then humbled by the sudden loss of speed when the road rose back up to challenge me. The road won most of the time but I got my due. I was able to roll over about a dozen, maybe a few more. The rest I had to climb with tired legs.

The times I rolled over the hills, one after another in high gear, was the best. Standing on the pedals, forcing everything I had into the climb knowing I would crest the top—what a rush. It was as if knowing success was about to be realized felt much better than the accomplishment itself. Those are the memories from today that will get me through tomorrow and tomorrow's tomorrow. It will be the joy I feel years from now. I believe it to be true. I need it to be true. This journey has not been easy but it has been a blessing. It continues to change me. That fear in my gut no one sees is shrinking away. The voice that says I cannot is being replaced with the one that screams I can. That is the change in me.

I entered the town from the south side and never did see Kirksville proper. The town was laid out in 1841 on a forty–one acre site and incorporated in 1857. It would go on to become the county seat of Adair County.

Kirksville has a population of 17,193, the number of people who live below the poverty line is just under thirty–one percent, and for every hundred women there are only 82.5 men. Guys having trouble getting a date should consider moving here.

Higher education options are many in Kirksville. The town is home to Truman State University, a public liberal arts and science institution, with more than six thousand students. The Moberly Area Community College operates a branch campus offering associate degree programs in Nursing, Early Childhood, Graphic Arts, Computer Information Technology, and Drafting Design Technology along with transfer degree programs. The A.T. Still University of Health Sciences, which happens to be the world's first osteopathic medical school, founded in 1892 by Dr. Andrew Taylor Still, trains osteopathic doctors in drug–free non–invasive holistic medicine focusing on total body health.

Notable people from Kirksville include Academy Award–winning actress, Geraldine Page and John Wimber, the keyboardist for The Righteous Brothers. The city is home to a single television station, seven radio stations, and three newspapers including the *Kirksville Daily Express*, and the *Index* and *The Monitor* both produced by the Truman State University students.

There's a bit of American Civil War history here too. The Battle of Kirksville fought August 6–9, 1862 saw the Union troops led by John McNeil force Confederate volunteers under Joseph Porter to vacate the city. It was reported 150 to two hundred died and as many as four hundred were wounded in the confrontation.

The body and the brain have had enough. It is time to close the notebook for the night and start all over again tomorrow.

Day 30: Kirksville to Quincy, Illinois (74 miles)

It was cool and clear this morning as we made our way to the Country Kitchen for breakfast. From the hotel it was about a quarter mile walk mostly through a grassy inclined field. The route was a bit steep in parts and the wet grass quickly dampened my sneakers as they picked up bits of loose grass. It was the same walk we had the night before for dinner. We occupied most of the restaurant and enjoyed the banter and comradery we developed over the past four weeks. From the thrashing of utensils and plates I'd say everyone enjoyed breakfast as well.

Today I would achieve another milestone on this trip; I would eclipse two thousand miles of pedaling. Our group would also ride into our seventh state and cross the Mississippi River. The morning table conversation focused more on the good than the troubles anyone was having. Moods seemed to follow the weather and road conditions. Give us a tailwind and comfortable temperatures with a clear sky and our world is good. Raining, cold, too hot, headwinds, or bad roads and we complain. Just like kids. We are just like kids.

We left breakfast in a group like we had arrived. This time gravity was in our favor as we slid and jogged hurriedly down the damp grassy field toward the hotel. We crossed the road and into the hotel parking lot to begin the pre–riding routine. In thirty minutes Kirksville will be just another footnote in this journey.

On exit from the hotel we immediately climbed up the road parallel to the grassy hill we traversed for breakfast. It was sixty–three degrees, a ten mile an hour breeze coming from the south southwest would play to our favor. I was cold but figured I'd warm up with the weather pretty quickly. The forecast called for clear skies and afternoon temperatures in low eighties. We had about 1,300 feet of climbing; most of it would come early. Considering the distance is the same as yesterday but with half the climbing I think it will be a good day on the bike; even a bad day on the bike beats being at work.

The single file procession of riders stacked up at the light at the top of the hill. It was a bit of a mad rush when the light turned green as several riders tried to move to the front of the pack as if it were a race. I just wanted to clear the intersection at SR–63 and get moving along the quieter Route 6E. Some riders are more like kids than others and traffic light stops bring out the child.

It didn't take long to settle in. I pedaled through rolling rural Missouri amongst established farms, past lovely ranch homes, some with white painted post and plank fences framing well–manicured lawns and patches of interesting color. I saw fields growing freely with thorn bushes and wild flowers and open pasture land behind field fencing; cows and horses somewhere just out of sight. I enjoyed the random color of the wild flowers; white, yellow, purple, and pale blues. Each color a different type of flower, some in clusters and others thinly spread as if trying not to draw attention. But they do. A color in a sea of green stands out even at a distance from the road.

The breeze was slight but it gave motion to the tall grass. Patterns formed as the air moved through the fields. Subtle as they were they did not go unnoticed. There was even a trace of sound above the noises coming from the line of cyclists.

Riders announced when passing, others chatted about in a continuation of breakfast conversation. I was right at home with Betty a few lengths in front of me as she trailed Paul and Geoff and another twenty happy riders in front of them. In my mirror it was much the same. I was dead in the middle of more than forty riders. There was a lot of movement. Riders passed me from behind and I passed others. I was not in a hurry, just trying to find my morning legs like everyone else.

For miles the scenery rolled by at fifteen miles an hour, ever changing yet consistent as if there were some type of pattern; fields, farms, ranch houses, and mailboxes guarding gravel drives repeating over and over. The road was straight. Telephone poles lined the two–lanes but had trouble committing to a side. Sometimes the poles with their electric and phone wires strung between them crossed over the road and other times they occupied both sides. Looking about the landscape kept me from staring at my digital displays that always moved too slowly.

If the ride had a mood it would be easy. If it had a song it would be the Commodores, Easy Like Sunday Morning, which it was. My legs turned the pedals in a comfortable cadence. I did not have to think about the mechanics of motion. It was all very fluid like the gentle motion of water; rolling and swaying and calm.

The painted line dividing traffic was also non–committal. It would be a double solid yellow then alternate with a hash mark to the left then after a stint of double solids it would flip to the right. At the edge of the road a continuous white stripe of paint separated asphalt from gravel where it dropped down a few inches. In some areas the gravel had been infiltrated with weeds and wild grass making it all but invisible. Where field fencing ran close to the road tall wild thorn bushes and grass clustered. Amongst the randomness, flowers would find a place to thrive. Occasionally I would see a pond, a few scattered evergreen trees, and a concentration of shade trees identify low wet areas, maybe even a small stream.

Sections of road would be in great shape and then a crack or a broken piece of pavement would momentarily shake the bike. I'd briefly be jarred out my rhythm but in a few pedal strokes I'd find it once more. Darker patches of asphalt where the tar was coming to the surface accumulated in the areas where vehicle tires applied the most force. It was smoother, more worn in the tracks, but this is also where the broken bits could be found. Traffic would be light for the next ten miles so there was no pressure and no stress other than the daily battle I'd have finding comfort on the bike.

My normal repertoire of riding body issues included shoulder aches, numbness and pain in my wrists tired from the excessive forward weight I put on the bars, and hot foot. It's a condition my feet often get after twenty miles of pedaling and the only way to relieve it is to unclip the offending foot from the pedal. It's usually my right foot for reasons I do not know. What I do know is I spent lots of time fidgeting with the shoe cleats at the hotels to find a compromising positon to relieve the stress. I even cut away some of the soles to gain more adjustment, but I'd get only marginal benefit. My feet seem to swell more with the continuous riding so a slightly larger shoe might also be part of the solution. I was told by other riders I should replace the mountain bike style clips with the more rigid *Look* clips that distribute the pressure over more of the shoe and across more of my foot. So new shoes and clips at somewhere near three hundred dollars may be the longer term solution but for now I have to work with what I brought. Pain be damned.

I have other pains when I ride my bike but not as often and not as intense. I get sensitive in my bottom which as long as it remains in check is just a nuisance. Sometimes it takes getting up off the saddle every mile or repositioning to find a better contact point. When immediate attention is required and the obvious tactics fail I can't hesitate. If I do I will lose the battle quickly and my butt will come up off the seat until I deal with it. A drop of the shorts and a healthy dab of undercarriage lube is often enough to get back in the saddle and finish the ride. A rash or worse and I could be sidelined. You have to remember the ass is in charge of the ride and no matter how much you think you can, it is not possible to ride long distance standing up.

I also get a sore neck from carrying this heavy weight on my shoulders. The only remedy is to keep turning and rotating my head to stay loose. When I ride with my head forward fixed on the horizon using only my eyes to scan the view ahead I stiffen up quickly. I tend to do this when I have a headwind or when I'm riding on a long flat boring section of road like those I trained on back in central Florida. Come to think of it, I do the same thing whenever I engage a pace line. Yet another reason not to ride so close to someone's back wheel.

Today I was having only wrist issues which I tried to address by riding one–handed where I could and no–hands when I thought it was safe enough. When I pull even one hand off the bars I realize how much forward weight I have when I ride. I remember as a teenager most of my weight was right over the seat and I could remove my hands from the bars without shifting my body. Even after the thousands of miles I've been on this bike I still search for the proper fit and balance. Maybe I always will. And maybe it's why I own three different bike seats and a box of miscellaneous accessories; each believed to be a solution to the quest for biking comfort.

I talked with those around me but the conversations tended to be short. If a rider was faster they kept moving up the line and conversation was limited to a sentence or two. I'd call out to Betty having a conversation with the back of her head. It was awkward but effective. The roads were not conducive to riding side by side and if you watch people paired up they tend to swerve together and sometimes they crash. Riding single file with a few lengths in between is much safer for everyone even if the conversational aspects are lacking.

I pedaled past low billboards advertising local businesses. I spotted vintage farm implements rusting away in the fields and witnessed the road change from asphalt to concrete without reason. I passed a horse pulling a turn of the century wagon complete with wood spoked wheels, two women in the seat, and four small children riding behind. Their black head coverings revealed they were not married, the solid blue outfits confirm they were Amish. The horse was a chestnut brown, the mane and tail solid black.

Around the bend I found the town of Brashear, population: 284. It marked the first opportunity to stop at a convenience store. In the parking lot, Trevor and his box truck full of luggage was parked. T–Rev was watching riders pass and talking to those who stopped.

Five miles and a few turns later we crossed a train overpass and skirted the southern extremes of Hurdland and its 203 inhabitants. The term, "Nothing to see here folks" came to mind but it does have a small claim to fame. The Hurdland July 4th celebration is the oldest annual Independence Day celebration in northeast Missouri and one of the oldest in the state. The two–day festival first held in 1873 features live music, games and contests, talent shows, and a large fireworks display.

Betty and I reached an awkward stop sign at a curved intersection and the mileage aligned with the cue sheet. We were making a left and rolling across South Fork South Fabius River on our way into a town called Edina. Though it didn't look like it Edina had just over 1,200 residents. What I saw entering town were steel commercial buildings, a hardware store, gas station, and a hodgepodge of other small businesses, some with signage and others not. The owners likely assumed customers knew they were there so signs were an unnecessary expense. I thought I'd seen all of Edina but then I started climbing a hill. It didn't look steep but it was taxing my legs. Riders in front of me were bunched up suggesting they were getting up the hill slowly as well.

As I crested the top I saw a blinking light and more of the town. On Lafayette and South Main I found its center. The Edina Double Square Historic District encompasses thirty–seven buildings built between 1865 and 1945. It includes two distinct architectural styles; Italianate and Streamline Moderne. The Italianate style originated around 1802 oddly enough in Britain by a man named John Nash. The design draws heavily from the sixteenth–century Italian Renaissance architecture featuring arched windows, bracketed cornices, and protruding towers. Streamline Moderne, or Art Moderne, is a later iteration of the Art Deco style and design that emerged in the 1930s. It emphasizes curved forms, long horizontal lines, and even nautical elements. Both styles are unusual and even more unusual is they can be found here together in Edina.

Besides the architectural discovery I spotted a water tower bearing the town name and a downtown park in the center of the Square full of shade trees with crisscrossed sidewalks in front of what appeared to be the main public building, possibly the city hall or court house. Edina has good bones, but that's all it was. This town has no skin, no meat on it. I was troubled by the high vacancy of the downtown shops. More than half were empty, even the architecture looked sad.

The Edina Double Square Historic District is listed in the National Register of Historic Places but I sense this is nothing more than a paper headstone for a place deserving not just be remembered, but to be alive and revitalized. I can imagine a future with people walking around, music playing in the evening air, restaurants and shops full of customers, courteous conversation, people coming from a distance to enjoy Edina. What I saw was not that. What I saw was yet another piece of America rusting and crumbling away, a past soon to be forgotten, but I found it and put it to paper so it can be shared. I will pass through this town again and I hope when I do it has moved closer to the vision I wish for it. Hope, prosperity, a thriving future built around its architecture and the beautiful Square.

First platted in 1839 the community was named after the Scottish city of Edinburg. The post office bearing the same name has been in continuous operation since 1850. Much like Kirksville, women outnumber men five to four with a fifth of the population living below the poverty line. Growing up on the east coast I did not see continuous community decline and poverty. As I see it on this trip I have to ask, "If we are all so blessed to live in the greatest country in the world, why do I see so many towns shrinking, the declining communities, and the masses of people living below the poverty line? And what are we going to do about it?"

The heartland is more than a landmass separating the coasts. It is the land that feeds us, the frontier of our potential, the glue that binds us and keeps us together. Having passed through it on these narrow ribbons of roads, having experienced it at such a slow pace, a pace only by bike or by foot could afford, it is now a part of me and I am a part of it. The dirt and dust cling to me and my sweat is left for payment. It cannot be unseen but it can be remembered. Even these concerning moments are my memories. I am better for seeing Edina.

The town covers roughly ten by fifteen blocks and I saw just the south east corner. The line of riders ahead rolled down a slight slope past an old quirky motel plucked right out of a scene from a '60s movie, a few framed houses and older structures, and large political signs in one yard but not much more. This town sitting at an elevation of 814 feet released its grip on the riders as we crossed the North Fork South Fabius River and headed off to the east with fifty miles yet to cover. I find it interesting the entire town is tucked in between the north and south branch of the same river.

Less than nine miles ahead in Knox City would be our only SAG stop of the day. A city instead of a town, it suggests something bigger. In forty minutes I will know.

Along the way the terrain continued to roll along in smooth waves, the road a bit flatter. Corn was a staple crop in this area with fields of maturing stalks standing more than four feet tall; the tops level as if trimmed by a barber. In cut grass pastures large rolls of hay, some standing and others on their side, waited for farmhands to bring them to the barn for storage. A water tower stood a quarter mile off to the north in the middle of corn. Clusters of trees surrounded by tall grass formed at the boundaries between road and fields.

A green tractor pulling a dull red farming implement passed going west, one of those high–wheeled machines with big plastic liquid tanks and lattice work of folded arms and spray applicators crossed the road and into a field just a few power poles ahead. I didn't like to share the road with the spray rigs. Every time I saw one in the mirror it looked as if it were a huge spider intent on rolling right over me. I'd find the edge of the road and pedal fast. Then I'd duck down just a bit as I heard them close in and pass me by. They always seemed larger and more menacing in the mirror.

Somewhere along the way the white stripe ended; the grass now in direct contact with the charcoal gray asphalt. Even the gravel had disappeared as I rolled into Knox City. A well–worn sidewalk appeared on the left, then a small brick building. In the familiar aluminum letters that mark most of the post offices in America it read—United States Post Office Knox City, Missouri 63446. It was the temporary location for yet another CrossRoads SAG.

Tracy was hosting and Clark was assisting. My roommate was pretty good at the routine; chatting it up with the riders, making sure they remembered to sign in and wash their hands. It was another magnificent spread and some new treats of fresh local berries. It would not last long so I grabbed a cut banana and coffee cake, and then chased them down with Gatorade and water. It was pretty warm in the direct sun so I rounded up Betty and we rejoined a few others back on the road. Knox City turned out to have a population of only 219. I was expecting more but the cue sheet did say no bathrooms so it was a bit risky to get my hopes up. I don't think this was the original post office but Knox City did have one in operation since 1873, a year after the city was first platted.

Old dilapidated buildings with junk strewn about gave way to basic wood structures, some with pealed paint exposing the raw wood beneath and others surprisingly well cared for. In a few short blocks we passed the green DOT sign indicating LaBelle was five miles straight ahead. Not three blocks later the road took a slight bend to the right and we were surrounded by corn.

The white stripe at the edge of the road returned and it brought with it a generous eighteen inches of properly paved shoulder. In the dead arrow straight sections I could see a mile or more ahead, the road dipping and bulging skyward. If this is the climbing for the day it is surely welcome. I can see traffic, what little there is, way before it is on me. I'm enjoying it much better than yesterday's surprise of cars breaching a peak right in front of me without warning.

Rolling into LaBelle I could see just beyond the handcrafted wooden monument sign the silver corrugated metal grain storage tanks and support framework. Closer in, the three concrete grain elevators grew in stature until they dominated the landscape just fifty feet south of Route 6. A long barrel shaped metal building led me to the vacant heart of LaBelle. To the right of State Street were twenty single–story store fronts but only three with signs of activity. To my left nothing but grass and dirt parking and a few lamp posts. I'm surprised the poverty rate isn't more than the twenty–nine percent I was able to discover. Other than the nice sign this town needs work, and businesses to fill the vacancies.

At the corner of *K* and State Street, stood a white two story wooden structure with a graveyard of old bicycles piled outside. Other bikes were clearly visible through the windows. The old commercial buildings quickly gave way to mostly white framed houses and a few weathered single–wide trailers before returning us back to the open countryside.

I would never have guessed 665 people live within these few blocks, or that it could support four churches including the Assembly of God, the First Baptist Church, the First Christian Church, and the Mt. Olive Baptist Church. Clearly agriculture dominates the economy and the mainstay is the grain elevator facility on the western edge of town.

In the quiet I pedaled along, riders strung out ahead and behind; plenty of time to mentally wander back to my hotel room before the day started. On my rest day in Santa Fe, a simple silver cross found me. It reminded me of my dad so I decided to loop the chain that held it around my neck. Afraid the fragile chain would break, I added the cross to the sturdy chain holding my dad's finger print medallion; much better. Safely I ride with God and my father. It's more than bits of silver, much more. Without a thought my fingers find the silver as the chain falls loose from the confines of my jersey. I hold both metal and memories, and it brings a smile. Then I tuck them back safely against my skin and draw the zipper up a notch and continue pedaling. Few would notice, and fewer still would notice the tears forming behind my shades. All happy tears remembering a life well lived. This is for you dad.

I road through Lewistown, population: 571, which seemed much more appealing and better kept than the town of LaBelle. Then I was rambling through rolling fields, a pond to the right, wildflowers reaching to the sun, a water tower letting me know I was in Cougar Country. It was one of the best days on the bike; the climbing slight, a tailwind played at our backs all day, and temperatures were aided by the periodic passing of scattered clouds. I enjoyed the brief interludes of town and country, the brick and white framed structures alternating with the expansive green of corn, natural fields, and shade trees.

I stopped at Johnny's in Ewing for a bio break and to get another fresh Gatorade. It had been twenty miles since our SAG and I had another twenty to go. Ewing had a grain elevator and a water tower to service the 461 residents, but it also was the boyhood home to a Mr. James Earl Ray. If his name sounds a bit familiar it should be. He was a convicted murderer who assassinated the celebrated civil rights leader, Martin Luther King Jr. on April 4, 1968 in Memphis, Tennessee.

Ray was convicted on his 41st birthday after entering a guilty plea to avoid the death penalty. Sentenced to ninety–nine years for his crime, Ray died in prison in 1998 from an infection caused by hepatitis C. A 60–acre farm in Ewing was his home from the time he was seven until he was sixteen. Those who knew Ray knew him by the name Raynes, an alias his father assumed after he fled from Alton, Illinois where he tried to pass a bad check. Who would have guessed such a troubled soul could come from this quiet town?

A few miles ahead the town of Durham; I smiled as I rode past the American flag whipping in the breeze. A white church completed the backdrop amidst a deep lawn and a stand of trees. Aside from a few curves the road was true and the view enjoyable. There were more challenging climbs than I saw earlier in the day but each provided a descent as my reward. The final downhill with a bit of the tailwind pushed us to the truck stop just shy of Route 24. After a quick stop Betty led the way and we were within ten miles of our destination.

In the last few miles before crossing the Mississippi River into Illinois, I thought back on the past couple of days spent in Missouri. Coming into the state, we didn't have the best of roads, weather, nor did we get favorable treatment from some of the motorists. After the first day, the roads improved the scenery of rolling hills and farmlands left us in awe, and the experience we had in the small towns such as Maysville made for positive memories. "The Show Me State" is one of the most beautiful places we visited. The struggles up the hills will fade fast, but the images of green fields full of horses and cows will remain clear.

The wide shoulder of the concrete divided highway scored with expansion joins every ten feet created a rhythmic vibration as I rolled across. Patches of rumble cuts roughly three feet wide by four feet long occupied the left half of the shoulder in intervals of fifty to sixty feet. They created a visual rhythm all their own. The important thing was not to run over them as they would send a sharp pulse of vibration through the wheels and into the wrists and bottom that would cause my teeth to rattle.

The runoff area was level with the road. The mowed grass extended to a shallow retention ditch connected to the occasional storm drain and corrugated pipes buried under an access road. It smelled freshly cut. It was a smell that would elude us once we left Los Angeles until we reached Kansas. It was the smell of the Midwest and my early days in the northeast. It was familiar and it reminded me of being a kid. As a boy in the farming area of central New Jersey I spent most of my time outside and the sour scent of cut grass was one of those smells I could not mistake for anything else. It came with blue sky sunny days, a gentle breeze, and running barefoot feeling the cool ground and the warm blades between my toes.

A fresh cut field of grass can be the time machine connected to those deep memories; for a second or for as long as you wish to enjoy them. I'd have flashbacks but sometimes I dwelled in those memories for much longer. The body was able to maintain control of the bike while I drifted and somehow I always remained in tune with the surrounding traffic.

Over the last stretch of Highway 24 the elevation dropped slightly, the divided highway came together forming a single strip of concrete more than seventy feet wide. Each direction of traffic consisted of two lanes and a shoulder. Separating traffic was a shared lane for turning marked by solid painted yellow lines. The road had leveled out into an expansive flat area occupied by massive fields of corn. In the distance a tree line, likely the higher ground of Illinois a few miles ahead, came into view. No bridge yet in sight, only a few farm structures scattered about. There were a few highway service depots; a gas station and convenience store, a cluster of auto auctions, and used car lots. I even saw one of those parachute–styled ultralight aircraft fly over the highway and land in a grass field. Let me add that to my bucket list of things to do.

During an earlier stop I took the disposable camera out of my bike bag and moved it to my rear jersey pocket. I wanted to capture a photo when I cross the Mississippi and thought I might not have a chance to retrieve it at the bridge. I've taken photos at other bridge crossings and most didn't afford a place to stop because of the narrow roadway leading up to and over the bridges. I'd be ready if it were possible to take the shot.

A slight bend to the left and a manmade incline leading over a rail line caused me to pedal with more effort. To the south a large train yard with blue and silver passenger cars moving toward my direction. Off the spurs were assorted box cars and flats loaded with trailers and equipment. It was the Burlington Northern Santa Fe facility; not very big, just a small yard to reconfigure trains and likely to load and unload the bounty of used cars. As I crested the tracks a pair of diesels pulling a long line of rust colored fully loaded coal hoppers exited beneath me toward the train yard. The rumble and vibration of the massive train moving could be both heard and felt right through my tires and the noise of the passing traffic.

On the downhill continuing toward the flats I could see a go–kart track, another convenience store and truck stop on the left and a low marshy looking area to the right. Straight ahead a cluster of trees, the road separated and I could see a dull boxy structure maybe a half mile ahead. In the wooded area the road remained flat and the ground on both sides dropped away. A guardrail boxed me in with traffic and my pedaling accelerated. I passed signs prohibiting cigarette bootlegging and the official .08 alcohol limit for the state of Illinois. Not like there was a place to turn around if I were in violation of either.

Then as the river came into view the safety of the road shoulder was stolen from me. All traffic was funneled between the narrow confines of dulled silver and rusting rails not twenty–five feet apart. There was a faded stripe on the right side of the road but it was a waste of paint. If you touched the stripe with your tire you would have already collided with the guardrail. I followed Betty as the muddy river drifted southward just a few feet below us. We had taken the right lane and not to the satisfaction of passing cars. The bridge was still a quarter mile away so we were hammering the pedals across the tarmac as if in a sprint.

I glanced quickly to the right and left to take in the view. I had never seen nor crossed the Mississippi River and it was impressive. Huge barges were like little toys in the massively wide river. They were moving slowly and created almost no wake. To the north was the Bayview Bridge, a more modern cable–stayed design that handled the westward flow of traffic crossing the river from Quincy into Missouri. Near the mid–section were two *H* shaped towers reaching two hundred feet up with cables fanning out from the top and connecting to the bridge deck. It was very delicate in appearance but structurally capable of carrying the traffic. Trees lined both sides of the river.

As the eastbound roadway started a shallow incline up to the bridge it required more effort to maintain speed. I was uncomfortable between the guardrails and having to share the space with large trucks. The cars created enough tension but at least I was close to eye level with their drivers.

The details of the bridge became clearer as we approached. It looked like two massive verticals of steel interconnected by a series of smaller diagonal braces tying the sides together. My Uncle Bill, who at one time was a bridge designer for Harris Steel, would know much about this bridge. He may have even studied it when he was in college. It was a truss bridge twenty–seven feet wide, less than 1,200 feet long, and built in 1928. The entire span across the river measured 3,510 feet in length, nearly three quarters of a mile, or five minutes of traffic induced stress.

We pedaled right into the throat of the bridge with jaws opening a full fourteen feet high to traffic. I followed Betty staying in the center of the right lane to force traffic to use the left. There would be no way we could risk sharing the lane with traffic. We had to take it all until we were safely across the Quincy Memorial Bridge.

Six stories below us the river was busy at work. Barges carrying raw materials were being pushed and pulled by tugs up and down the river. Other vessels close to the embankment loading or fueling. On the south side of the bridge was a pair of cylindrical steel structures with piping extending over a barge. An extension pipe ran down to an opening in the hull. It was a grain loading operation in process. Farther down the banking were several off duty tugs nosed in and tied to the docks. Floating in the middle of the expanse, several barges connected together were being maneuvered by a single tug. I saw similar configurations to the left and right, but the movement was slow and purposeful. There was no recreational traffic to be seen.

Wrapping all around us the dull blue metal structure resembling an erector set that seemed more delicate then on my approach. It cast interesting angular shadows on the road and across Betty as she zoomed forward thirty feet in front of me. I reached into my pocket and retrieved the disposable camera. It was already set to take a picture so I carefully pointed it forward and snapped a shot of Betty as I steered with my left hand. Not wanting to risk dropping the camera, or crashing while advancing the frame for the next shot, I decided to put it back into my pocket. I think it was a wise move and I hoped I captured a good photo for Betty and for my next installment of the cross country article I would send to the DeLand Beacon.

Betty's orange flag fluttered from the pole, the stars and bars waved as well. She was in her favorite blue cycling jersey and had her small CamelBak strapped to her back. Even though she is from Phoenix she seems to have tanned up quite a bit on this ride. I know I have too. My legs are browner than I've ever seen them, the back of my hands clearly more golden then where my cycling gloves protect them. As the bridge shadows move past I can see the reason why Betty outpaces me on the hills. It's those well–developed calf muscles she has turning the pedals. Dare I say I hope mine look that good when I'm fifty–six?

The exit out of the bridge was in sight. I could see buildings jutting out of the greenery on the Quincy side, the sky blue tapering off to an almost white horizon. Some buildings brick, others of concrete, structures extending on pilings over the water and large multi–story buildings stood on the top of the hill. A metal skeleton structure supporting high voltage transmission lines was the last obstacle to ride under before I could see the big green and white welcome sign with "Illinois" in bold four foot tall letters.

The sign was at the edge of a concrete retaining wall so it did not allow much room for photos. We parked our bikes in a patch of grass just beyond the sign and took turns posing under it while holding the railing. The person taking the photo would have to watch traffic coming off the bridge, time it such that they could run about fifty feet back against traffic, turn and snap a photo, and run back without causing a wreck. It wasn't as hard as it sounded and after pedaling across the bridge, running a hundred feet in the awkward cycling shoes was almost a non–event.

Other riders exited the bridge and wanted to be photographed as well. Included were the usual suspects of Big Mike, Duffey, and Geoff. Others too but I can't recall their names. This created a bit of commotion as we traded cameras and repeated the posing and the mad scramble to get the photographer in position and safely back to the sign. I think I did the scramble at least three or four times before there was a break in the riders exiting the bridge. When we do the state line crossing routine we tend to get so focused on the activities we forget all the participants. And that's why we take the photos. This state line crossing just happened to be the least accommodating of the seven we've made because of the confined space and the absence of a safe place for a photographer to take the picture. Maybe that's what also makes it memorable.

We cover the final miles to the Comfort Inn by way of Maine, 36th and Broadway. The street names more fitting for New York City, but the architecture and the landscaping of the grand homes along the route are every bit as impressive. I love architecture and know quite a bit about landscaping. There were no shortcuts in the care provided to these lovely properties. Block after block, bigger and bigger homes, mansions some of them, all multi–story, fancy stonework with spires and turrets, detailed windows and grand porches. The most notable is the Newcomb–Stillwell Mansion completed in 1891 and now home to the Quincy Museum. It features the Richardson Romanesque Revival architecture style incorporating the heavy arches and massive stone exteriors with ornamental carvings. The light colored Berea Sandstone quarried from the Cleveland, Ohio area and transported six hundred miles to the site was specified by the Boston architect Henry Hobson Richardson, one of the most popular U.S. architects in the late 1800s. The museum is open from one to five Tuesday through Sunday requiring only a nominal donation. They even have a dinosaur display.

Quincy, also known as the "Gem City" is home to 40,473 people. The city's population is more diverse than what I have seen over the past week with a racial makeup of ninety percent White, and nearly six percent African American. Latinos account for just less than two percent of the total. It may be the size of the city that welcomes diversity or the more urban industrialized environment and less of an agriculturally centric one.

The 160 acres on which Quincy was founded was purchased for sixty dollars by a man named John Wood sometime around 1819. The original community name, Bluffs, was changed in 1925 to Quincy in honor of

John Quincy Adams, the sixth President of the United States. Quincy is the county seat of Adams County which was also named in honor of the President.

The city is served by two hospitals, several colleges and universities, a small regional airport, two daily Amtrak trains to Chicago, and its residents enjoy a variety of outdoor cultural festivals and events. The cost of living in Quincy is well below the national average including the cost of food and utilities. Commute times, high school graduation rates, household income, and home ownership rates make Quincy one of the top small cities to raise a family. What it has when you pedal through it is a welcoming vibe.

Tonight is a free dinner night so I have a choice to make. I'll stay close to the hotel, maybe walk up to the Pizza Hut I passed on the corner of 36th and Broadway. I'll see where others are going and then decide. I'll have a free night from laundry as well since the hotel has no machines. I could take advantage of the indoor pool, I could write in my journals. I could do anything I want after I clean my bike and get out of these clothes.

My bike computer displayed an average speed of 17.14 miles an hour over 75.95 miles with four hours twenty–six minutes of seat time. Even my top speed of 34.7 miles per hour was impressive.

I am now in Illinois, the eighth state of fifteen on this tour. I crossed the two thousand mile mark but I have no idea exactly where it happened. I think I was either daydreaming of too busy looking around the countryside. Maybe it was early when I passed Trevor in Brashear or maybe it was at the post office in Knox City. I know I did it and it is behind me. I can now look ahead to tomorrow's ride. It will be a long one covering 107 miles to the city of Springfield. There will be about 1,900 feet of climbing. Weather, especially the wind and potential for rain will play into the ride. I'll ask for riding advice from Clark when he finishes his staff duties and if I'm lucky his experience from last year will be of comfort.

Day 31: Quincy to Springfield (107 miles)

The words for today are "keep moving." It's amazing how much ground you lose by stopping even for just a few minutes. Some riders stop at every store, marker, or interesting point along the way. Some make multiple nature stops and a few riders stop just because others do. On a hundred–mile ride, frequent stops can put you twenty miles behind the group. I learned to take pictures and to eat and drink at speed; which I continue to relearn is a relative term. I try to keep the necessary stops as short as possible, and that helps to limit the fatigue in these hefty legs I was gifted with; again a relative term.

The other reason to keep moving on a long ride is weather. We started out with a storm cloud over us that kept the wind direction changing. The threat of rain and lightning also was a factor, and our plan was to outrun it if we could and hope stable tail winds waited for us. On a bicycle you really don't outrun a storm; you barely outrun anything except foot traffic and baby strollers, but it sounds at least like there exists the possibility to affect your situation. When cycling, the weather determines if you are left alone or if you are overrun. That is the reality on the bike. I don't like it and I'm sure nobody does but to think or say different would be foolish. And we don't want to wear that label. Not even in black spandex shorts, puffy shirts and shoes clicking on the pavement like we are tap dancers.

It was a damp sixty–five degrees when we rolled our bikes out the front door of the Comfort Inn through the rather compact lobby and into the empty Monday morning parking lot. Some overnight stays afford us a rather generous lobby where we can stage our bikes while finishing our morning hotel breakfast buffets, but today we were not so lucky. This morning we fueled up at the Village Inn which does its best to measure up to an IHOP. Some folks complained a bit about the food and service but you have to keep it in perspective. It was coffee and bland snack cakes under a heat lamp back at the hotel if we were lucky. Maybe a few English muffins or bread put out much earlier in the morning were also part of their enticing spread. With that point of reference I'll offer a tip of the hat to the Village Inn servers who hustled on my behalf to fill my coffee cup more than once and sent me off with a warm and filling breakfast. *Thank you ladies!*

I was dressed to stay warm in my long sleeved sun shirt, which as I have described before is more like a pullover windbreaker with a zipper that only goes down half way to my belly. It's quite the universal necessity suited for both cool and extremely hot temperatures. And today I would work both ends of its useful range. A mix of pastel yellow and white panels with numerous vents in the rear areas under my arms and a triple set of pockets across the back, it was a cyclist's equivalent of the handyman's tool belt. When loaded down with snacks, tubes, and lube it gave the appearance of droopy drawers under the shirt if you know what I mean. I'm definitely not making any fashion statements in this outfit. It's all about utility and comfort, for which it scores high marks.

Out of Quincy heading east on Broadway Street, as Route 104 is known inside the city, we cross over interstate Highway 172 not two miles from the Comfort Inn. Two lanes of divided traffic heading each direction, the road shoulder is both wide and smooth. It's a forgiving route, one perfect for getting me into the morning routine; turning my legs into something more like power pistons than jelly stalks as the pedals go around all while my lungs learn to cope with the body's demand for more oxygen.

Beyond I–172 the trees and open fields are abundant. The urban environment of chain stores and other businesses seemed to dramatically end right where the roadways intersected. Slight but gradual climbs and descents take us farther into the more rural countryside and I take note of the sights. Tucked into the right side of my view along one of the downhill grades not fifteen minutes into my ride is Quincy Raceways; a little bull ring of a race track I would surely stop to check out if I wasn't pressed for time. The Midwest is riddled with these automotive playgrounds and on most weekend nights they draw a rabid crowd of cheering fans. As the raceway signs fade behind me I am left to wonder what type of racing they have there. It looks like a little track, a circle track for sure, but the sign said Raceway's which would imply more than one.

Another twenty minutes of pedaling and the trees give way to flatter fields of wild grass, farmer's fields of early corn, and to my left across the divided highway, mowed expanses leading to a dozen buildings of various sizes at the Quincy Regional Airport. In front of the mostly metal structures stood an old white single story wooden bungalow styled house maybe sixty years old. It was somehow incorporated into the airport operations, maybe as an office for some of the desk workers. No fences or barriers of any kind separated the roadway from the airport property which I thought was a bit odd considering all of the post 911 travel and security regulations. I was warmed up and moving at my normal pace, but with the skies overcast and the wind dancing around I needed to step it up.

I didn't see any planes flying around nor did I hear them taxiing on the ground. The thought of the weather came to mind and the fact it was still rather early on a Monday morning. As regional airports go I learned this one supported a mix of general aviation, airlines, air taxis and military flights. It had a lighted wind indicator but no onsite air traffic control tower. Aside from the structures it was just three long ribbons of asphalt and concrete each equipped with runway edge lights crisscrossing each other on a patch of land they called Baldwin Field.

Commercial airline service would not officially start until the spring of 2005 and when it did it would only account for about two thousand passenger boarding's a year. And to no surprise it required hefty subsidies for the airlines to establish flights in and out of Quincy. Carriers and destinations would change frequently and over a period of years it would see regional providers for American, United, Trans World Express, Mesa, and Great Lakes connecting to places such as Decatur, Chicago Midway, Kirksville and smaller airports in Missouri and Iowa.

The bulk of the airport activities were the single engine private planes accounting for almost twenty three thousand annual aircraft operations; the term used to describe take–offs and landings. That's about sixty–one events a day. Less than fifty planes and a few small jets and helicopters are stationed at Quincy and I was past the 1,101 acre facility in just minutes. Officially the airport identified as UIN is at 769 feet above sea level in Gilmer Township, a small district contained within Adams County, Illinois for those of you propeller heads following along. And I say that with all due respect to one of my traveling partners, Ben Dudley, a retired United Airlines pilot who hails from Edwardsville, Illinois just two hours south of here by car. Ben is also our on–tour weatherman and one of four recumbent riders.

Up ahead Illinois 104 narrowed down from the divided highway into a two lane country road. It was all about the connection between Quincy and the airport. The shoulder seemed to narrow but the cut–in rumble grooves were no longer present. Their absence seemed to even out the usable biking lane. Nothing but corn fields in all directions, wooden power poles running parallel to the pavement to my right and a John Deere Tractor store across the traffic lanes on my left. This was definitely out in the country.

The shifting wind fluttered the corn making a rustling sound that moved around in sync with the breeze. That and the constant rush of noise past my ears created as I propelled myself forward were the primary sounds I heard. Truck and car traffic was limited, no birds, no animals, no mechanical inputs of any kind besides those made between my tires and the road and an occasional metal to metal contact caused by shifting gears and the tension change in my shifting cables.

Up ahead was a bend in the road, a sweeping right turn at the crossroads of County Road 1900 where a sign pointed to the left for Columbus and a place called Siloam Springs State Park. I passed through the intersection marked by a small white cottage house on my right and continued on I–104 which was now identified as Main Street. I was heading into the village of Liberty, Illinois; population hovering around five hundred. This area is home to hearty blue–collar workers whose ancestry traces back to German, English and Irish roots. In fact more than thirty–five percent of the employed work in blue–collar occupations compared to the national average of just fewer than twenty–five percent. Settled in 1822 and covering only a tick more than a third of a square mile the heart of the downtown measures less than five by ten blocks.

Fortunately for me a Country Market Express convenience store marked the outer edge of town giving me an opportunity to step off the bike and unfold after just fifteen miles of pedaling. I still had to cover another ninety–two miles and adhere to the CrossRoads target times that were in force. There would be no services for the next eighteen miles, a clue I was going even deeper into the wild. I was in the company of other riders who chose to stop at the store to restock and to use proper restroom facilities. I took my turn in line and enjoyed a bit of warmth while I waited.

Today's cue sheet was a single sided four quadrant set of directions listing a Dairy Queen at mile sixty–nine, a McDonalds at 104 and a few destination notes about having an indoor pool and a Jacuzzi but no on–property laundry. The nearest one was a half mile away so it would be a quick rinse of my outfit in the sink tonight. There was also a reference to Springfield being the site of the old state capital and the home of Abe Lincoln. So I got my tidbit of history for the day in early. I wondered if anyone will be touring the town to check out the sights after finishing this marathon ride.

As I continued scanning the cue sheet I realized I would be in the first quadrant for another two hours. No need to get excited about flipping it over just yet. Then I noticed restrooms were listed as possible for the SAG. Possible, as in alternative facilities may need to be planned for. If it remains rural I suspect trees or a field of corn will suffice but I do prefer the more modern accommodations. As you continue into the crossing you find you don't worry about what the other riders think, they have to deal with the same accommodations. What matters is how the rest of the world views you as they drive by. You don't want to give them the impression cyclist's stop wherever they want and pee on someone's property indiscriminately do you? No, we don't want that.

I checked to make sure the Velcro straps of the cue sheet holder were secure and my rear carrier bike bag was zipped shut. I looked at the finger puppet Three Stooges I had rubber banded to the bike flag pole and while Moe, Larry, and Curly were a bit weathered from the journey they still had my back. I'd have to consider replacing the rubber bands at some point so they don't fall off. They have been a conversation starter on this ride and with the boys behind me I guess you could say I was never alone.

I stayed just about five minutes, chatted a bit with Betty, Greg, and others, then got back on my bike. I noticed as we left the store riders were a bit more grouped. Kim Simoni from Sebastopol, a small city in Sonoma county California and Gordon Kniefel from Gold Hill, Oregon were part of a small group that would usually finish the day's ride early. Big Mike and Duffey were making a group and I was part of one anchored by Betty, Lynn, Greg, and Gray. The recumbent and tandem riders were pretty strong through this stretch of the tour so they joined groups for more social reasons. The rest of us took turns leading and following and as others passed by we moved from group to group according to our pace and interests. It was a very dynamic forming, norming, and reforming social process all happening on two wheels in our eastwardly migration.

For a short distance we had sidewalks and a few larger buildings to our left. We passed a brick church and a ball field and on our right we saw a house or two and then a long stretch of nothing but corn fields. It seemed like a few minutes of riding before we actually entered the center of Liberty. A few houses, a white framed church on the right, then sidewalks on both sides of the street presented themselves as we continued to the heart of the village. We found the downtown to be of rural standards; a few brick two story buildings including the First National Bank, a water tower bearing the village name, a post office, and a few more houses before it gave way to fields and farmland on a left hand sweeper. In my rearview was Liberty and I was now on a mission to get to the SAG and depart by the target time of 10:40 a.m. Easily doable as it was not quite half past eight. I figured I would reach my destination by ten.

The route continued to stair step east and south as we clicked off the miles in the rolling terrain. There were white painted lines along IL–104 but they marked the edge of the pavement with about six inches to the right before dropping off into the gravel. This was hardly a bike lane which meant we were in the right of way of moving traffic. The road was decent but worn; cracks and broken chunks of pavement intruded into the stripes giving fair warning for riders to stay to the left of the paint.

About half the distance we pedaled in the open exposed to the wind, which at times pushed and pulled and prodded us from the sides. There were also stretches where the wind was blocked as we rode through corridors of tall shade trees standing like soldiers beyond the ditches on both sides of the road. I liked the trees but if the wind was just right it could channel through them forming a nasty headwind. I just pedaled and chatted a bit with the other riders, making sure to keep pace, to watch my cadence, and change gears as needed to keep a steady motion on the bike.

I kept checking my mileage counter and was beginning to anticipate our next stop. Just another mile or so and we should see some indicators such as orange painted marks on the road that we've seen before or maybe an orange flag poked into the ground just off the shoulder. On a long straight stretch of road that was ever so inclined we broke out of the trees. To our right was another field, but this one had a parking lot, a building and the CrossRoads van sitting in it. We arrived and it was just about ten; right on time.

As we pulled into our first SAG stop of the day at the John Wood Community College Agricultural Education Center we got word there had been a collision and several riders were down. All of this was happening behind us, not more than two miles back on a rather narrow rural road running through farmland lined with wet ditches and shaded by trees. Speculation about the incident ran high. The Crossroads staff was at their best relaying information, moving vehicles, and getting aid where it needed to be. Within minutes word came that most of the damage was limited to severe abrasions, scrapes to the bikes, and a few bruised egos. All riders were en route and heading to the SAG. I felt a sigh of relief as even a low speed fall on a bike can result in severe injuries.

We did have restrooms thanks to the administrative staff at the school that were kind enough to allow us the use of their facilities. I found my way to the men's room and took my turn rearranging and reapplying some comfort to my bottom. On my way out I spotted a drinking fountain and took the opportunity to enjoy a bit of cold water. I never quite understood why the bathrooms were always designed to be at the furthest point away from the front doors. Maybe it's to discourage use but it sure reminds me of our first SAG in Cerritos on day one riding to Riverside, California.

The lady at the front desk, bless her Midwestern heart, seemed to be entertained by our attire; all of us in spandex shorts, form–fitted jerseys with pockets loaded down like they were full of potatoes in the back, and our shoes clicking and clacking on the terrazzo floors. Blue jeans and plaid shirts in combination with either sneakers or work boots were the norm around here. Earthy colors like greens and browns were not in our cycling wardrobe and Day–Glo pinks, yellows, and greens were definitely not a part of theirs.

After a quick topping off of fluids, some fresh fruit and pastries, I needed to get back on the road. I put a carrot cake Clif bar, a pack of cheese crackers, and half a banana in the back pockets of my cycling jersey and pushed off from the parking lot back onto the road. I'd learn the crash details later in the day, but I can assure you I'm glad I wasn't involved.

Every time you stop for more than five minutes your body seems to forget how to operate the bike. The primary offenders are the legs. They seem to go to mush, some call them oatmeal legs, but for me I just want them turning the pedals at fifteen miles an hour. My shoulder pain still lingers, in fact it bothers me every day I ride but what's the point in dwelling on it. It'll probably hurt until long after I finish in Boston which is now becoming less abstract of a concept.

Finishing in Boston? Wow, that's a pretty weighty thought, but in twenty days I'm going to have to deal with the reality of ending this adventure. Will I be at the end or will I be at the beginning? What happens if I don't want to let it end? Is that my choice? Do I turn and go back the other way? Will my rear end challenge my mind and call it done or will the whole of my being allow me ride to on? Do I somehow ignore the entire experience and just pack my gear in the van and drive off like it's some mundane event on some same old unmemorable day? I know that isn't possible. That's not what this is and that's not what it's about. Will I be enlightened as to my purpose? Will I break down in both victory and the loss of reaching the end? I don't have a clue. But when I get to Boston, or more accurately when I step onto the beach of Revere and wash myself in the waters of the Atlantic, I know—I know I will not be the same as I was before. I'm already not the same as I was. I am excited and afraid at the same time, but I welcome everything that lies before me.

I root for the average guy in me to make a mark in life, for it to mean something if only to myself. I want to know that I lived life if for just a few weeks in a most unconventional manner making others take notice, possibly be amused, or if in the slimmest of hopes they may actually envy what I am doing. Envy not to be like me, but for themselves to live just a bit of their own life outside their box, where it is uncertain and scary and maybe even a little unsafe. By doing so they will know what I'm feeling in this moment, right now as I pedal along this narrow rural road in Illinois, eyes welling up in tears in the gravity of the entire experience. I am the luckiest person on the planet and I don't want to ever forget the gift I am living. So many people helped me; some don't even realize how they motivated me. In less than three weeks I will reach yet another crossroads, the fork in the road that is Boston.

My speed picks up and I'm dropping quickly down a steep grade. Rumble strips dead ahead, the intersection of SR–107 lies at the bottom of the hill. My eyes blurry I grip the bars even tighter as I vibrate over the first set of those disruptive lines of asphalt. I break free of the tree line and green fields consume my view in all directions.

A hundred yards ahead and just shy of the intersection is another set of rumble strips. I look left, and then right in rapid succession. As I get within a hundred feet of the crossroads my bike rattles the last set of bumps sending a shock through my body. I see the stop sign but I don't want to brake and lose my momentum. On SR–107 a tandem dump truck is approaching from the right, downshifting and roaring as it slows for the four–way stop. It's clear left so I make a rash decision to sail right through the intersection. The adrenaline is high, the airbrakes blast, the friction of metal on metal brings the truck to a stop at the painted white line, and I continue pedaling, bolting right past it at what feels like thirty miles an hour. I wasn't sure of the speed because I was afraid to look down at the computer readouts. I'm riding alone so I didn't involve anyone else in my questionable choice not to stop. Had I been with others I doubt I would have been so reckless. The boy inside me belts out a yell of sheer joy echoing across the fields. I'm alive and I'm living life!

Eventually the excitement wanes and I'm back into a rhythm of riding along at just less than fifteen miles per hour. Chambersburg lies just a few miles ahead and I begin to wonder about the river crossing a few miles beyond the town. The cue sheet said it was a narrow bridge, but I'm not sure by what standards. I'll be there soon enough so for now I concentrate on the road ahead and the occasional traffic coming from behind.

The road shoulder is no more than two feet wide but it's in relatively good shape. There's a twenty foot wide strip of wild grass containing a shallow depression to hold the water runoff and if needed, it looks to be a safe place to land to avoid a collision. These are the things to consider when riding alone in unknown territory.

Farther out are the endless fields planted by the local farmers; corn and what looks like soybeans are the dominant crop here. Clusters of trees line the fields and an occasional section of guard rail lies just a few feet off the pavement wherever the ground drops more than a few feet below grade. The speed limit signs draw a slight smirk; fifty–five miles per hour, I wish.

I find myself rocking side to side as I search to find a bit more comfort on my seat. I look in my mirror and see no one behind me so I'm free to recall songs and sing to entertain myself; most of the time I sing in silence, and for good reason. In my mind I have excellent tone and if I sing aloud it affects my breathing and heartrate. I also suspect if I sing amongst a group of riders I would soon find myself pedaling in solitude. I'll keep this in mind when I don't want any company.

There are times on the bike when I do get bored and having computers instantly report my progress can remind me of just how slow the riding can be. One display is reporting back in increments of 0.01 miles, or 52.8 feet per click. If you watch the mileage it's like watching a pot of water boil. Unfortunately I'm a victim of the gage monitoring but I do mix it up with soaking in the roadside views and breathing in the occasional aroma of aged road kill.

As the miles click by and I begin to roll faster down another tree lined grade, a sign for Chambersburg comes into view. Gravity continues to accelerate me downward and the wind noise gets pretty annoying, but it does feel good not to pedal and the breeze feels pretty refreshing too. Though still cool, the air is beginning to move off the low of sixty–five and is expected to head toward the mid–eighties by midday. A curb appears at the road edge and then a series of metal guardrails just off either side guide me into the town proper. There's a white church on the right corner and a well–weathered wooded structure on the left as I zip through another intersection across Main Street; this time without a stop sign to impede my progress. I'm cruising along just shy of the posted speed limit of thirty–five miles per hour as I pass a few houses and abandoned structures before I exit the three blocks defining Chambersburg.

The land beyond is flat and the breeze has its way without the trees to interfere. I pass another green DOT sign letting me know Meredosia is six miles farther. I have been riding for forty miles and have another sixty–seven to go. I need to make time where I can.

The road offers a slight bend to the right and in the distance I can see the bridge described in the cue sheet. It stands above the landscape and it's quite large making my approach seem slower than it probably is. It's still overcast but the sky is beginning to show signs of change for the better.

I see small figures ahead of me; too small to be cars and moving as if they are either on foot or on bike. I decide to push harder to see if I can close the gap. The fields appear wet, maybe a bit swampy; ahead I see a few trees between me and the bridge. Another half mile and I can now identify the images before me; they are indeed cyclists but they are too far ahead to assign names.

The bridge continues to come into focus, the dark distant greys take on a blue tone and the details of a massive truss bridge are revealed. Impressive, and I'm still a ways from it. The riders ahead of me reach the bridge and then they are lost in the lines of structure and cast shadows. I pedal on.

Several hundred yards from the bridge I now see the climb leading to the river crossing. Guardrails tucked in tight, no shoulder, and as promised a narrow crossing was just minutes away. A tractor trailer rumbles past me and begins its approach. I was stressed by the thought of crossing such a bridge with trucks and cars, so I got up on the pedals and willed my way faster than my body preferred.

My angst was balanced with the engineering beauty of this bright blue complex bridge looking more like a massive *Erector Set* than anything else. Shaped beams, flat plates, and gussets all held together with thousands of palm sized rivets and dressed in bright blue paint; a most uncommon color for a bridge. And as I rolled onto the structure itself I was fortunate the traffic timing was in my favor. This allowed me the opportunity to look up and soak in the product of men who designed and built this amazing wonder. I'd guess the top of the bridge reached more than sixty feet above the road surface. My Uncle Bill was one of those bridge designers back in New Jersey and I wondered if his designs at the old Harris Steel Company were on the scale of this structure.

As much as the bridge itself impressed my engineering mind the view of the brown water from the crest was worth the climb. Tugs slowly moving large barges north and south on the Illinois River could be seen on both sides. About a quarter mile south was a structure resembling a power plant of some type and a large pipe extended outward from the east bank on a set of steel and concrete pilings twenty feet about the water. I could only guess what it was used for.

A fast drop off the bridge and I was amongst a collection of two story brick buildings which comprised my welcome to the Village of Meredosia, population hovering around eleven hundred residents. This western corner of Illinois is home to the Meredosia National Wildlife Refuge, and in the 1800s it was originally referred to as *Marais d'Osier*, which is French for willow swamp. And for fishing enthusiasts Meredosia is known as the catfishing capital of Illinois and home to the Asian Carp. To me it was just a dot on the map along an old muddy river.

The road flattened out and in just a few blocks I saw on the left my destination, Casey's General Store. A collection of cyclists were hanging out enjoying chocolate milk, Gatorade, snack cakes, and other treats so I checked traffic and leaned left into the parking lot under the shade of the gas pump canopy. My stop was brief. I felt like I should be in the company of other riders for a while.

I pulled out with Betty and a few others and we rode in proximity of each other for the next twenty–five miles through Bethel, Chapin, and then along the southern fringes of Jacksonville. Conversation was light but it felt reassuring to be in their company. We rode sections of wide open highway through residential neighborhoods and light commercial business districts, each offering their own unique cycling challenges and distractions.

When we turned onto the two–mile stretch of Morton Avenue, a very congested four lane undivided highway along a highly popular commercial district with no dedicated bike lane, my heart rate jumped. This was by far the most intense part of my day's ride. I was concerned for myself and those around me. I pedaled way above my pay grade and had to be mindful of passing cars. I imagined drivers thinking they were safely past, and then turning in front of me to enter department store parking lots. I also was keeping a keen eye on those poking the nose of their cars out of the lots to make sure they saw me coming.

Single file fifty feet or so between us we leaned right one after another and made the turn onto Lincoln Street. I could finally breathe and I sensed the others did too as the pace dropped back to a more normal cadence. Lincoln didn't offer us a lane but with only a single lane of traffic each way it was much more manageable. A half mile later we regrouped at a stop sign and prepared to make a left across traffic onto Michigan Avenue. After the urban stretch I was caught off guard by the red barns and a silo marking a farm on the corner. There was even a vintage early 1900s metal wheeled steam powered tractor in the field so I made the turn, stopped quickly, and snapped a few photos. It turned out the farm was actually the Prairie Land Heritage Museum.

Sixty–nine miles into our ride after enjoying views of corn, a water tower, and a quiet mile of residential sprawl we rolled up to the stop light at Main Street and made our way into the left turn lane. At the green we jogged left onto Main Street, then immediately made the right into Dairy Queen, our second SAG of the day. The target time for departing the second SAG was 1:50 p.m. We arrived in plenty of time but with less than forty miles remaining many riders were lingering longer than they usually would. There were more than twenty of the nearly forty riders filling the lot and a few more spilled into the eatery. Bikes were leaning on every available tree, post, wall, dumpster, or just resting left side down on the asphalt. This was protocol to avoid bending the sensitive derailleur assembly; the odd looking appendage that shifts the rear gears. Margaret set up under the only tree in the back of the lot and had a fine spread for us to enjoy.

After signing in I hung around for about fifteen minutes. I watched riders arrive and others depart before Margaret started to send my group down the road. My legs were tired and standing around only made leaving more difficult. I topped off my fluids, pocketed a few snacks, and was ready to go. The skies had finally cleared but the wind would remain with us all the way to Springfield. There would be no coasting and no tail winds today. It was much warmer than it was just an hour ago.

A group of six riders, consisting of Greg, Geoff, Gayle, Ken, Betty and I, left together and worked our way back onto the busy Morton Avenue. As we broke free of Route 104 we formed a pace line, like a train onto Old Route 54, to cut down on the wind resistance. Our route was nearly due east with a few short stretches favoring a northeasterly direction. The wind was coming out of the north which meant we were buffeted from our left side for nearly twenty five miles.

We rolled through Arnold and Alexander on the way to New Berlin for a quick stop at another convenience store. Then we continued on through Bates and according to the last cue sheet instruction in the third quadrant we were hunting for a right turn onto Van Deren 94.1 miles from where we started this morning. The entire distance from Arnold to Curran we rode parallel to an east–west rail line. I don't recall much train traffic but for this part of the ride I was not noticing a whole lot besides the bike wheel directly in front of me and the rear end of the rider hunched over the bike it was attached to.

Hotfoot was adding to the challenge and I did my best to apply the tricks I learned earlier in the tour to manage it. Unfortunately there would be little managing to be done. I had exceeded the nerve's limits and to say it nicely, my foot was voicing its disapproval of the ride. I would occasionally pull my right foot out of the pedal clip and ride with the ball of my foot centered on the pedal. It made for a very awkward motion and my foot slipped around on the pedal making it hard to get much power out of the right leg. I also had to be careful because in the pace line I couldn't afford to be erratic with my speed. One rider described hotfoot as feeling like a blowtorch was pointed up from under the pedal and today I tend to agree. I will need to make adjustments to the cleats when I get to the hotel because my foot will not accept another day like this.

Greg was our leader most of the way, and he helped us get through some tough riding. In the last ten miles, he dropped back in line, as he was physically drained.

When we found Van Deren we got a brief respite from the wind and actually had it at our backs. This was quickly remedied when we turned east onto Spaulding Orchard Road. Six miles of rolling hills and wind kept us in the seat. I dropped back alongside of Greg to make sure he was okay, but like the trouper he is he stayed low and extended on his aero bars and kept on pedaling. With his eyes hidden beneath his dark sunglasses there was no telling what they might be saying if they could talk. And as far as talking was concerned there was almost none of it to be heard as we began to spread out a bit more from each other.

We were no longer in a pace line and we were no longer a group. At Route 4 we had to stop and wait for the traffic light to turn green. Quiet ruled over the riders, each with one foot on the pavement and the other clipped in balancing carefully, breathing heavily, tired and used up.

Just five miles from the end of our ride we turned north onto South Second Street and straight into the wind. Our pace, which had slowed since Curran, dropped a few miles an hour more. Even a slight breeze has a major impact on riding speed and today it was much more than a breeze. As we slogged it out for nearly three miles on Second I think everyone was feeling the discomfort I was experiencing. The hot air was in our face and the pavement radiated even more heat back up to us under direct sun. I was grinding my thighs against the seat and feeling the wear. As much as I could benefit from some chamois cream I thought if I stopped I would not want to get back on the bike. Finally we crossed into a densely populated area entering Springfield. The trees and the houses helped to break the wind and as we snaked along St. Joseph Street, I–55, and Stephenson Drive, we hugged the road shoulder in the late afternoon traffic with the wind now back on our left. Just two miles more and we will make our next turn.

As we sat at the light waiting for the green to turn left onto Aldof Lane we needed to roll just a tenth mile more. It wasn't quick and it wasn't pretty, but we made it. After more than seven hours seventeen minutes riding and 108 miles behind us, we were glad to see the Hampton Inn hotel. It was our sixth day in a row on the bike, and we are looking forward to a day of rest after another riding day tomorrow. Factoring in the unfriendly wind, averaging 14.8 miles per hour for a century ride was not a disappointment. I even reached a respectable top speed of 30.6 miles an hour somewhere on the tarmac, but don't ask me where.

The first order of business after a ride like today is to check the bike for any mechanical ills, then wipe it down to show it proper respect. There was just a little dust and some road dirt in the crevices and some film of oil on the drive train that needed to be addressed. When I was finished the cassette shined new and the chain could no longer leave an imprint on my leg. Any sign of a rider sweating over the bike or spilling fluids had vanished. She was once again a pretty ride.

I treated myself to a hot shower, a little application of triple ointment to my sensitive parts, and then I gave my wearable cycling gear a quick rinse in the sink. The room was quickly filled with my damp laundry over the chair backs and on the air conditioning unit. I only needed to get it dry enough so it could pack into my bag in the morning. It would be properly washed on the rest day in Champaign.

I set out tomorrow's riding gear and went through my bike bag to see if I could lighten the load of things I really didn't need. As usual nothing was removed but I had to go through the motions. Next on the list was to find postcards, write them out, fill in my journals, and find out what happened in today's crash. So with a plan in place I was out of the room feeling much better than I was a few hours before.

Springfield was home to Abraham Lincoln and it's the state capital of Illinois. That much I learned from Tracy's cue sheet comments. It's also the sixth most populated city in the state with nearly one hundred twelve thousand residents. Founded April 10, 1821 sitting in the flat plains at an elevation of 558 feet makes for hot summers and cold winters. I can definitely vouch for the heat as it warmed up to an uncomfortable eighty–six degrees. This part of the Midwest is also prone to violent summer storms and tornadoes. Lucky for us storms aren't on the radar for the next twenty–four hours.

As for historic sites there is the Old State Capital, Lincoln's Tomb, and Lincoln's Presidential Library and Museum. For those who appreciate architecture the Dana–Thomas House in Springfield is among the best preserved and most complete of Frank Lloyd Wright's early "Prairie" houses dating back to 1902. There are many more notable points of historic importance but these make for a good short–list of the "Must See" tourist destinations.

For entertainment Springfield is home to Knight's Action Park, the largest amusement park in the area which also boasts the only remaining drive–in movie theatre in Springfield, the Route 66 Twin Drive–In. The city has a rich baseball history and is currently home to the Springfield Sliders, which is part of the Prospect League, a collegiate summer league featuring players from North America and other points around the globe.

When it comes to higher learning there are many options to choose from. Springfield is home to three universities including the University of Illinois at Springfield, Benedictine University at Springfield, and Robert Morris University. And then there is the international cultural aspect that can't be overlooked. Springfield has five sister cities across the world including Astaneh–ye Ashrafiyeh (Iran), Villach (Austria), Killarney (Ireland), San Pedro (Mexico) and Ashikaga (Japan).

Springfield also lays claim to a few interesting fun food facts. Locals claim the corn dog on a stick was invented in Springfield under the name "Cozy Dog" but the assertion is still subject to debate. There is a Cozy Dog Drive–In about a half mile north of Stevenson on I–55 which claims to be the historic counter–serve corn dog joint. If I do find my way through Springfield again I'm going to make a point to check it out. Another foodie claim to fame not in dispute is the origin of the horseshoe sandwich. Little known anywhere outside of Springfield, this delight is an open–faced sandwich consisting of thick–sliced toasted bread, a hamburger patty, French Fries and a secret cheese sauce. Take away the French Fries and it is close enough to what they call a patty melt on the east coast.

The first drive through window in America is still operating in Springfield at the Maid–Rite Sandwich Shop. The store in Springfield is one of nearly seventy locations of the restaurant chain founded in the 1926. You can find it west of Interstate 55 on Highway 97, or more precisely at 118 North Pasfield Street.

The city is also known for Chili, which they spell as *Chilli*. The misspelling has been attributed to a sign error dating back to 1909 at a place called the Dew Chilli Parlor. Others say it was purposefully misspelled to represent the "Ill" in the word Illinois. In 1993 the state legislature adopted a resolution proclaiming Springfield the "Chilli Capital of the Civilized World."

I was not planning to venture far in the late afternoon and unfortunately everything of interest was beyond walking distance. I'd have to make due with a trip to a nearby store for the postcards and a review of the hotel lobby attraction flyers to get a feel for what I was missing. In Champaign I plan to take the day to explore and mingle with the people of Illinois.

Outside the Hampton Inn I caught up with Pat and his road rash. It was pretty nasty stuff; think raw ground beef wrapped in gauze covering large patches on his arms and legs. He was pretty sore from the fall and would be hurting even more come morning. He told me he got into the rear wheel of another rider while tucked in close, his front wheel jerked one way and he vaulted the other.

It happens in an instant and the rider behind is always the loser. Others got caught up in the carnage with bodies going in all directions bouncing hard against the tarmac, riders yelling and bikes grinding to a stop. Knees, elbows, forearms, and legs were involuntarily offered up in sacrifice. With soft flesh against the road there was no doubt about who would come out on the short end of the confrontation.

Fortunately no one tried to catch their fall with a stiff arm to the road. This often results in more damaging injuries like broken wrists, elbows, and even worse, a broken collar bone. The fact no one pounded their head against the road and got knocked out was a real surprise. And based on the account of the event all riders involved were by all measures extremely lucky. Whatever their faith it is time to put in a little knee time and say a few prayers. I forgot to ask much about the others involved but I figured they would be the ones limping or bandaged when we regrouped in the morning to head out to Champaign.

One thing I noticed with Pat was he shaved his legs. I'll keep an eye on his healing to see if there is any benefit in the event of road rash aside from the less painful bandage removal. And he had plenty of bandages on his extremities to deal with.

I was able to complete all my writing before dinner. Usually I end up writing late into the night while trying not to disturb Clark as he sleeps. He was a good sport but I needed to make sure I did not overstep his room rights. As long as the day was my writing would be trimmed down to the essentials. I would fill in the details on my rest day. Letters to my daughters today included: *tired, tender hide,* and *feet catching fire.* Imagine that.

The postcards were dropped at the front desk as I joined the group heading over to the Maverick Steakhouse. I was physically tired but very hungry and I was not shy about cleaning my plate. Lots of beef was consumed along with a pile of loaded baked potatoes, salads, and glasses and glasses of water, tea, and sodas. I'm sure the staff was glad we came in but even more so when we left. Our group is like a swarm of locusts; way too many arriving at one time and they leave very little behind for anyone else.

I get the complexities of trying to serve a small army like ours but not all of the riders are open to the realities involved when fifty people arrive at the same time and back up the kitchen. And it doesn't help when many want substitutions, special attention to how their food is handled, and if their salad needs to come out before or with their meals or if the dressing needs to be on it or on the side. My upbringing in a family of nine trained me for such realities.

After good food and much banter about the day it was time to go back to the hotel and call it a night. I chatted with Clark for a while and finally settled in. All riders would continue on tomorrow and the only thing in short supply would be band aids. According to the cue sheet from today's ride breakfast would be at Bob Evans. Very good comfort food but I have to remember to use a little self–control if I'm going to be able to get back on the bike and ride. Finally the alarm is set and the lights go out. Day thirty–one on the XC04 tour comes to a close and morning will come fast.

Day 32: Springfield to Champaign (87 miles)

We left the hotel expecting a relatively short day on the bike. After all it was twenty miles shorter than yesterday's ride so it wasn't a stretch to think of it as being shorter. It was cooler than the day prior, somewhere in the upper sixties and overcast. It was supposed to reach eighty degrees in the afternoon so I would layer up with a liner shirt and my cycling jersey. Since rain was not expected until after lunch, I would take my rain jacket with me but keep it in my bike bag.

Pat and Vikki had a guest riding with them today; their daughter. She's an avid cyclist and appropriately employed with the Trek bike company. This also explains Pat and Vikki's allegiance to the brand yet after seeing their collection of high end Trek's I'm leaning more toward obsession than allegiance. Like most joining riders she was given the proper introduction in the morning and some instruction about safety since she knew only her parents riding styles. It was always a treat to have new people join the tour even if for only a day or two. And yes, she was riding a Trek as well.

It was a bit breezy but not a problem to getting down the road. The wind was on my left out of the north. It created a hint of a tailwind at times blended in with a side wind. In the distance to my left I saw a large storm cell that appeared almost out of nowhere an hour into the ride. I kept glancing over as it grew darker and more defined. It was full of turbulence and it was reshaping itself into a nasty form. The top of the clouds appeared to flatten and I could make out a definite edge to the system as it pushed against what I assumed was a warmer front. I had seen these clouds featured on the Weather Channel before and they were usually pursued by daredevil storm chasers.

The clouds continued to move east, parallel to our route. The temperature began to drop and I knew we were going to get rain early. As the sporadic rain began to fall the storm changed course and was now on a trajectory to cross my path within minutes. Without much of a thought I pulled off to the side of the road, hopped from my bike, and quickly rummaged through my bike bag to find the camera.

When I pointed it toward the north and focused in on the storm I could make out a well–defined anvil shape, deep purple gray on the bottom and bright white on top. The top of the cloud blended into the overcast of the sky making it difficult to see where one ended and the other began. A downpour of rain could be seen emanating from the bottom of the cloud soaking a line of mature trees not more than three quarters of a mile away. I had a clear view across the flat ground with nothing but a set of railroad tracks separating me from the storm. Adjacent to the tracks was a lone railroad traffic pole, the only other thing standing upright in my view.

I quickly closed the camera, returned it to the bike bag, zipped it closed, and remounted the bike. This might possibly be the only picture I take today. Storms like this are impressive to see but I am ill–equipped to try to evade one on my bike. I indexed the gears, stepped up the pace, and blended in with a few riders who were, until this point, hundreds of yards behind me. Everyone was moving a little faster now.

As if on cue the CrossRoads vans were canvassing the string of riders, lights flashing, horn squealing, and staff advising us to seek shelter. This was the first time we were in an emergency situation and I could tell the storm was going to be bad. I felt a chill roll through my body; not one driven by cold, but by the fear of the coming storm. There was urgency in the warning so I got up on the pedals and pushed, but to where I was not sure. I was not going to be caught out in this storm, flashing with bolts of lightning and possibly hail and winds that could—well I just pedaled harder.

There was nothing but grassy fields, patches of clustered trees, and a few scattered ranch style houses maybe a hundred yards off the pavement to provide protection. Along the road was a ditch and smaller trees but I was not seeing it as an option, at least not yet. Riders were scattered more than a mile apart and fortunately I was near enough to several. No matter what, I would not be alone. The raindrops increased and the pavement was beginning to darken with moisture. My eyes were scanning; my mind racing and I could hear my breathing rushed and deep.

I was heading to a more dense line of trees paralleling the road when one of the white CrossRoads vans stopped in the middle of the pavement maybe two hundred yards ahead. Riders were detouring off the road to the left. They disappeared behind the trees as the rain began to fall heavily and the winds whipped strong. As I got closer I could hear the orders coming from the staff; "Go to the barn, seek shelter in the barn!" From first warning to finally seeing the big steel building just off the left of the road I had traveled only a half mile. In those minutes the weather had pounced on us. I followed the other riders up the short gravel incline right into the open barn.

It was a massive building used for storing farm equipment and grain. Fortunately, the barn was mostly empty and large enough to accommodate all the riders. More importantly it was right where we needed it to be. With the rain coming down in sheets, lightning and wind roared just outside our safe place. A few riders did not make it to the barn but the staff confirmed they found shelter about a mile away.

When we first arrived at the barn Tracy was quick to get the riders inside and then bring in the caravan vehicles before shutting the huge doors. The two vans and the box truck were safely inside shedding their share of collected rain like metal ducks, leaving ever growing puddles of water on the concrete floor. The cavernous structure was nearly empty except for a lone forty–foot trailer used to carry grain. I was parked fifty feet into the barn. I stayed close by the trailer thinking if the roof and walls got torn away by the winds or more likely a direct hit from a tornado, I could dive underneath the multi–ton piece of equipment for protection. At least I had a Plan *B*. In hindsight I would have been sucked out into the swirl and deposited half a mile away like I'd seen in news reports of other tornado disasters. But I was ready for Plan *B* to go in motion.

Popularity can rise and wane within a group according to many factors. Today it would be the connection to precise weather tracking data that had Ben mobbed by the pack of riders eager to know what was happening outside the confines of our steel shelter. As bad as the wind and rain were there were no tornadoes in our immediate location. Constant updates through the howling and hurricane force winds alleviated us from what could have been hours of serious panic and anxiety. We were still anxious and concerned so it was good to have Ben with us for more than just his jokes and good company.

The rain was cold and horizontal with dense and enormous drops. We took turns peeking out the barn doors from time to time to get a visual on the outside conditions. Across the gravel lot, maybe sixty feet away stood a dull–silver, lightly rusted metal silo, a towable grain conveyor, and a few other pieces of large farming equipment. Taking my turn to peer out through the narrow gap in the large doors I could see they were barely visible. Most of the time all anyone could be see was the whitish blinding spray of water as if coming from a hundred fire hoses around and over the barn toward the silo. Had the rain been pounding straight onto the large doors we would not have been able to look outside.

The barn had no other windows or doors anywhere within the nearly eighty by more than two hundred foot dimensions. It was a twenty foot high metal drum sitting on a cold concrete slab. The lack of insulation under the roof created a perfect amplifier for the conditions outside. With the rain continuously and relentlessly beating the roof and sidewalls of the barn like a percussion instrument, we were slowly becoming numb to hearing anything or anyone. It was as if a tremendous marching band was doing its best to wake the dead or at least make us deaf. The volume was extreme, it was the sound of Niagara Falls and industrial mechanical sounds combined. Lips were moving but unless they were yelling you didn't hear an audible word. It would drone on and then there would be a brief but noticeable respite; then a full on pounding all over again.

The wind howled like a screaming locomotive and it was making us go a bit stir crazy. I was sure of it because the look on the other rider's faces matched the way I was feeling. I tensed even more each time the winds amped up. I jumped at the crack of thunder.

I was not sure if it was the wind or an emergency siren warning us about imminent danger, a possible tornado? Ben continued to provide updates and slowly the news would telegraph through to the entire body of hostages held by the storm. No tornadoes, not yet anyway.

The building was cold, so cold and we were soaked to the bone, dripping and sloshing in our cycling shoes. The cold of the rain was transferring through the metal of the structure and I could detect the slightest of air movement as the cold tried to occupy the little warmth still in my body. I was beginning to shiver and so were the others. This was not going well. I wondered, no I worried, what were we going to do?

Tracy stayed on top of the situation as best could be expected. How can you plan for this type of event? You do the best you can but you can never fully prepare for everything. The worst part for Tracy and the staff was the few riders scattered about, sheltered elsewhere, temporarily outside her care. I was worried about them too, but the reports coming in indicated they were safe.

No one questioned Tracy about the actions taken. She found a perfect place for nearly fifty people and three support vehicles to wait out the storm. I could not imagine what it would have been like to be stuck, alone, or at best with one or two other riders in a ditch quickly filling with water as bolts of lightning jolted the ground every few seconds. As bad as things were we avoided a true nightmarish experience.

With all the tornadoes in this area, I was sure we were going to experience one for ourselves. It never happened. Ben's reports contained only severe storm cells but no cyclonic activity.

Then the first cell passed, we opened the barn doors slightly for a better view. The wind was still pushing rain over the top and sides of the barn but no longer so full of water and power. This allowed us brief glimpses of the flow of the air during the stronger sustained winds. I remember the worst looking like the smoke testing in a wind tunnel where the air flow is fully visible. It was safe enough to step outside; first a few riders and then I followed. More ventured out too, but we quickly realized the calm was relative. It was still very windy and rainy. We returned to the dark and cold building just as a second storm cell moved in. We endured another long round of thunder and the pounding of rain and wind.

Knowing we would be captive for a while Tracy opened the van; an impromptu SAG was put in motion. Eating and drinking helped take our minds off of the storm. We were now off the bike for more than two hours after covering just fifteen miles. The cold and the time off the bike was not a recipe for success.

Whenever you bicycle–ride, it is important to minimize the breaks to avoid what we call *oatmeal legs*. Our long delay in the barn had everyone feeling like they rode sixty miles instead of fifteen. How could I ride more than seventy miles after such a cool down? I shivered again. I started to move around a lot to get warm. My shoes were still wet but no longer dripping. My clothes were damp having given up most of the water collected in the rain. Slowly I was beating the cold.

The second storm cell packed much less of a punch and it finally moved through. After three hours since the start of the chaos, we were cleared to ride, albeit in a light rain with a head wind. I decided to give my rain jacket a go since it was still raining and I was still cold. Before departing the barn our stranded riders came to us. A few had found sanctuary on the porch of a small house back up the road and the others, who were ahead of us, found shelter in a clump of trees. Everyone was safe and together again. There would be many interesting stories later in the day from the riders who weathered the storm in a more direct and intimate way. I was happy to listen and glad it was not my story to tell.

The next seventy miles were very tough. We tried to stay warm in a *pissy* drizzle that kept the roads wet enough to generate a thin spray off our tires. In the spray were bits of road grit, dirt, bug parts, worm guts, remnants of road kill, and animal poop. With each rotation of the wheel the swilling garbage was being layered onto my bike frame, my water bottles, and me. My legs were disgustingly coated in debris I would never allow to adhere to my body under normal circumstances. There was no *normal* here. Dare I say it was pretty crappy?

While the disgusting stuff sprayed up from the road the steady rain kept affecting my vision. I had smartly protected my bike computers with plastic sandwich bags secured with rubber bands before departing the hotel, but now they were coated with little droplets I needed to constantly wipe off in order to read mileage and other information of lesser importance given the riding conditions. It was also getting directly into my eyes and on my glasses making it hard to see the faults in the road surface. It was quite risky to poke a wet dirty finger into my eye in an attempt to see a bit better. At least I was kept occupied until I reached the old store in Chestnut; especially as I navigated the rough and slick railroad tracks a hundred yards shy of stepping off the bike.

I was happy to have a real roof over my head again, even for a few minutes. I shivered a bit; made my way across the old wooden floors to the restroom for a much needed bio break, then I cleaned my glasses. Through the clear glasses I could see my legs looked even less sanitary. No point trying to clean them up, more *road goo* waited just outside the door. I could only guess what the person behind the counter thought as I bought a warm drink as a courtesy for using the restroom. And they saw many riders before me and several more after so I'm sure they had an opinion. They must think we were out of our minds!

Reluctantly I stepped outside, rearranged the bags over the computers and set off toward the Dairy Queen a dozen miles down the road. In the cold the DQ did not seem so appealing but they would have some heat. And it would be dry inside.

My rain jacket did its job shedding water but it was creating problems of its own. Ingenious by design the jacket fits into a travel bag about the size of an adult's fist. The outside is bright yellow affording good visibility and it's plastic coated, allowing it to shed water freely.

Being plastic over a Tyvek fiber it has tiny holes to let the excess body heat out. And therein was the problem. The jacket does not breathe sufficiently to maintain any balance in body temperature. It didn't take long to start sweating inside the jacket to a point where sweat accumulated and was rolling around in the sleeves. This is both uncomfortable and gross. I got so hot I had to open the zipper. Then I was cold in the chest but still had sweat rolling in my sleeves.

If the holes were bigger or if the temperatures were a lot lower maybe it would work. But in these conditions and with the temperature and more importantly the humidity on the rise, I was fighting a losing battle. For miles I struggled with the decision to take off the jacket. I even stopped a few times to pull open the elastic around my wrists to pour out the sweat. I finally had enough and the jacket came off at an intersection before I reached the Dairy Queen. Now I was cold all over but I was not swimming in sweat. I think I picked the least of the evils.

Several sections of road were either under construction or severely deteriorated, adding to the effort and my discomfort. There was one section of extremely unbearable road and it created a safety issue for many riders. The eastbound lane we were riding on had been ground down by a large specialized machine. This created a texture ideal for bonding new asphalt but it caused a ride so rough on a bike it was best described as bone–jarring.

The shock was coming up through the wheels and into the aluminum frame which by design was rigid for strength, but offered no shock absorbing qualities. My wrists took the shock from the front wheel and sent it right on up my arms. The back wheel was kind enough to send its share of the shock load up through the seat to my spine and into my jaw causing my teeth to chatter. I had found the resonant frequency of my body and I was being rattled apart. As much as I wanted this to be over the faster I rode the worse it got. I had no choice but to slow down.

It was still raining so the visibility issues were stacked on top of the fantastic road conditions. The opposite side of the road was paved, smooth, and a thing of beauty. One rider had had enough and made a choice to get off the washboard. It was Hopper on his recumbent all wrapped up in his sun protective whites. Like the Sheik on a bike he bolted. While I understood the move to go to the better piece of road I was also torn between suffering in the rough and cycling toward traffic, which was deemed improper not only by tour standards but across most, if not all, state laws. Riding against traffic also created a serious potential for oncoming cars to cross into the other lane putting the riders following proper road etiquette at risk.

It didn't take long for the staff to pull Hopper over and it was not a pleasant conversation. In the end his compliance would be a condition of continuing with the tour. As a group we discussed it officially in route rap and in private amongst the riders in the hotel hallways. It sucked a lot to be on the rough road but it was required to be safe. Comfort was secondary and I can assure you I was anything but comfortable. Hopper continued all the way to Boston and after today there was nothing much said about his going rogue.

Over the next twenty miles, the clouds and rain would give way to sunshine, raising the temperature into the mid–eighties and accentuating the ninety percent humidity. The roads also improved but were still nothing to brag about. I could deal with the occasional pothole or crack as long as the washboard roads didn't return. My wrists and teeth were still traumatized by the miles of pounding.

We passed through the town of DeLand, Illinois, and I was hoping for something interesting to photograph in the town of no more than six hundred people. Since I lived in a town by the same name back in Florida, it would have been appropriate to capture an image of an impressive monument or building bearing the name. There wasn't anything at all but straight marginally passable roads and corn. About the best I could find was the little green standard issue DOT town sign posted beside a cornfield. No creativity at all. No water tower, no billboards, nothing. No wonder they don't have more than six hundred people living there. They don't promote the town. I stopped anyway, if for no other reason than to show people back home the lack of effort and this tiny sign. A quick click of the camera and I moving again with less than twenty–five miles left in the day's ride to Champaign.

We crossed the second of four railroad tracks sixty–eight miles into the ride. According to the cue sheet this set of tracks had the potential to be slick and they demanded a rider's full attention. I myself had not experienced a fall on the railroad tracks but those who did usually did not fare so well. The more angled the tracks, the wetter the conditions, and the older the intersection increases the ability for the tracks to reach out and take down a rider. My fear was taking a spill on the tracks and then getting pitched into traffic.

I crossed perpendicular to the tracks at a reduced speed, pedals level, and my butt off the seat. These tracks did not have the modern rubber surface which provides the smoothest and safest conditions for crossing on a bike. It was old asphalt, uneven and broken with loose gravel. It was very dicey. The only thing it had going for it, or for me, was the tracks were perpendicular to the road direction. "Easy peasy" as Tracy likes to say.

After fourteen miles and many climbs along relatively straight sections of road I was tired, maybe more careless, and definitely more vulnerable to road and traffic conditions. I had already looked ahead on the cue sheet knowing I was about to cross a pair of sharp angled railroad tracks. It was time to focus and follow the rules of crossing to the letter. As I arrived the tracks put me in a bad situation. The rails from my right slanted inward and intersected at a very sharp angle with the rough, gravel encrusted broken road. Either I swing out into traffic to get positioned perpendicular to the rails or I get off the bike. There was plenty of traffic and there was no way I could go out to the centerline as needed. I did the smart thing instead. I slowed and dismounted for the first set. Only one set to go.

A few blocks ahead I met the same conditions, but I had a healthy gap in traffic courtesy of a truck behind me attempting to make a turn across oncoming traffic to a side road. I was clear to take the lane and gingerly rolled across the tracks into loose gravel that almost took me down. Sometimes being clipped into the pedals makes me wonder if their efficiency outweighs the risk of falling. I caught up to a few riders at the light and we were now deep into the city proper.

A few quick turns over the next three miles on a mix of bustling four lanes and a pair of quaint neighborhood roads and we would be in the final stretch. Tired and ready to get off the bike, I had the Drury Inn in sight as I pedaled along the now very busy Market Street. It was nearly five thirty, very late compared to our normal arrival times, but considering the long three hour rain delay, somehow I was okay with it. Traffic was heavy through the last few miles as we found ourselves right in the middle of rush hour on a Tuesday evening.

The last obstacle was the I–74 Highway overpass and then coming down the other side to cross four lanes of traffic to get into the left turn lane. It was the wrong day to mix all of those hurdles together and expect a smile from our fellow motorists. Not everyone made the maneuvers with grace. Some riders drew the ire of motorists who obviously had no clue we were on as much a mission to get to the hotel as they were to get home. In hindsight I think it would be best to stay in the right lane, take the right turn and look to make a 180 degree change of direction as soon as safely possible, and then patiently wait at the light to cross to the hotel. Yeah we should have all done that. One or two riders were smart and did so, but no horns honked in their honor to welcome their arrival. I don't think those riders noticed either.

I went through the normal post ride routine of peeling off the gloves, helmet, and head sock followed by a wash of the bike. She was a dirty mess from the road debris picked up over the day's ride in the rain. I didn't think twice about hosing off my legs and shoes. I wanted to shed the road scum in the parking lot before going into the lobby. It didn't go without a bit of coaxing, I didn't like touching it with my hands, but I cleaned up pretty good. Even enduring the cold water was well worth leaving the bits and pieces of the dead worms and their associates outside.

The talk in the parking lot was about riders who fell at the railroad tracks. Two riders went down hard and suffered lots of scrapes and bruises. Someone said one of those riders was Pat and Vikki's daughter. What was supposed to be a fun experience riding with mom and dad went awry just three miles shy of the finish line. If I learned anything about cycling on this trip it would be railroad crossings are neither forgiving nor to be taken lightly. When in doubt, get off the bike.

So with this news to put a damper on an already dampened day, I continued with my post ride activities. This usually included a poke of the head into the back of the truck to check on Trevor or Tracy, maybe grab a packet of soap if needed, and a quick word or two about the ride. But today there would be no head poking in the truck; all hands were busy scurrying about the hotel trying to wrap up the day and keep tabs on those injured. The vans were still out presumably ushering in the last of the riders

Usually I go into the hotel as soon as I arrive and sign–in at the counter. Not today. I lingered for a while talking to others outside. Time didn't seem to matter today. Eventually I added my name to the sign-in sheet as per the CrossRoads rules. My bike was in no need of maintenance or adjustments so I didn't fill out a repair ticket for Rick or Tom. Besides tomorrow was a rest day and neither of those guys deserved to be tinkering on any more bikes today than absolutely necessary. I'm sure they would have their hands full with all of the normal rider issues that seem to follow a day of climbing or rain. It's never the cyclist who needs an adjustment. Just ask any rider.

I clicked through the bike computer records and jotted down the riding stats in my notebook—88.08 miles, six hours thirty–two minutes of riding time, average speed of 13.4 and a maximum speed of 28.4 miles per hour. From start to finish I was in my cycling gear for nearly ten hours.

A hot shower brought me back closer to normal. I quickly dried off and dressed in the cold of the room. Sometimes the air conditioner can work too well. I figured a quick reorganization of my gear was in order. I sorted and reorganized the contents of my two bags as I had done many times during the trip. It's amazing how you think you've optimized your storage only to realize a few days later you can't find a darn thing. Maybe by Boston I'll have figured this luggage thing out. One thing I was beginning to notice is the bags are getting harder to close. So either my nifty rolling and zip locking of shirts, shorts, and socks was becoming unruly or I was collecting too much stuff. A shipment back home would be in order and tomorrow would be the day to get it done.

I had earned a well–deserved rest day and the Drury Inn was a fine place to do as little as possible. We hadn't had a day off since Abilene, Kansas which seemed like ages ago, even if only a week's time had passed. When I checked in I got drink tickets and an invite to what amounted to a free meal down in the lobby. The only catch was I needed to get down there before seven o'clock. I left my bags on the bed with the intention of possibly reorganizing them again. Maybe a beer or two will help me optimize. Maybe I'll throw out some things I haven't used or used just a little. I only had about fifteen minutes left to enjoy the free spread so I zipped downstairs to enjoy the best free buffet they have to offer. The fact it is the only one hasn't yet sunk in.

As a sign of true transparency, my tally of beers consumed before dinner was five. Every plastic cup of beer was well–earned and liquid refreshment went a long way to replenishing the carbs my body needed.

Day 33: Champaign (Rest Day)

Champaign enjoys a healthy college town vibe with seventy–four thousand plus living in the city. The University of Illinois and Parkland College account for the academic draw to the city which is also home to a number of well–known technology startup companies. The area is often referred to as the hub of the *Silicon Prairie*. Companies such as DOW Chemical, Caterpillar, IBM, and many other Fortune 500 companies have offices in the town and its economy is growing.

The city is also culturally rich featuring a variety of museums including the Museum of Natural History, the World Heritage Museum, the Krannert Art Museum, the Orpheum Children's Science Museum, and the Champaign County Historical Museum. Anything from Egyptian to modern art can be found here. If I had a few more days I would explore a bit more than the immediate area of the Drury Inn which is just about two to three miles out of the downtown center.

My focus for the day is to rest and recover enough for the next stretch of riding to Erie, Pennsylvania. I also need to do laundry, decorate my helmet for tomorrow's helmet contest, postcards and letters need to be written, journals attended to, not to mention shipping stuff back home to lighten my bags and make room for new finds along the way. So it doesn't appear today is going to be so much of a rest day as it is a day to get caught up.

I stopped planning and forced myself up out of bed. A quick shower, a pass through the hotel breakfast buffet, a quick read of the local paper and the USA Today to figure out what is going on in the world, and then off to Walmart to scope out the helmet bling options. The Walmart was just across the road and through a large expansive parking lot so it didn't take long to complete the mission. I wasn't too inspired by the supplies so I opted for a simple and subdued helmet design. Another creative opportunity missed. Kathy opted for some water pistols and I saw a few others gathering some interesting materials for the contest. Walmart's craft department was doing a brisk business with CrossRoads riders.

Back at the hotel I picked through my bags and decided to jettison one of my two bike chains, a few items of clothing, brochures and other miscellaneous stuff I collected over the past few weeks. A few pounds lighter and with more room in the bags I was ready to find a box and mail my package home. Next on the list was to do laundry. And while the wash was in progress I could work on the postcards. It wouldn't be long before I'm hungry so I had already planned to make a stop at Culver's, a local eatery right across the street. Things were coming together nicely. Not much rest happening though.

The dryer stopped spinning; I folded and rolled my clothes, vacuum sealed the t–shirts and socks then packed my bags to be ready for tomorrow. I grabbed my homebound box, dropped it at the FedEx store, and made a beeline to Culver's for lunch. An excellent burger and fries with a tasty frozen custard and I was good to go. I took time for a nap, worked on my journals, and put the bling to the helmet. My day ended early following another round at the hotel dinner buffet. Plenty of lively discussions with Duffey, Big Mike, Gray and a few others, but there would be no beers for me tonight. After chatting with Clark it was lights out for the night. As I drifted off I realized I would have only one more rest day in Erie, Pennsylvania to break up the next fourteen days of riding. We'll be in Boston soon. Me and my forty plus close friends.

Day 34: Champaign to Crawfordsville, Indiana. (80 miles)

There were days on the tour where staff would cut loose, Margaret might put on a colorful wig, Tracy her Ninja headband and Clark his Groucho Marks glasses and mustached nose. Clark always got a laugh from the riders with his get up. In these moments his normally reserved manner would be cashed in for a more animated self. I could tell he enjoyed it too. And that brings us to this morning—Dress–up Helmet Day!

I wasn't too inspired when decorating my helmet yesterday but now, seeing the other rider's creativity, I sure wish I'd put some effort into it. There were balloons, streamers, party hats, some face paint, either a chicken or a duck, I wasn't quite sure which was secured to a helmet. Kathy had her water pistols pointing outward from the helmet slots like a pair of horns. It was wildly entertaining for those of us on tour and made the Drury's normal clientele give us a double take. After all we were jazzed up in spandex with Walmart jewelry wrapped around our noggins looking like a cast of lunatics; what else could they do? It was awesome.

We posed for photos, we pointed, and we laughed. Group shots had a mysterious boa slung across shoulders; there were moments of extreme bonding and joy all captured on film. Gray managed to get a few snippets of it on video. Our age did not prevent us from being totally committed to goofing off. After several minutes we settled back down, finished pumping tires, and checked we had all the required gear in our bike bags and jersey pockets. Long distance riding requires a bit of seriousness from each one of us.

It was a CamelBak day. Earlier this morning I topped it off with ice from the hallway machine and filled the remaining void with tap water. I checked my shoelaces, made one last pit stop in the men's room, and stood in the cycling audience at the back of the truck awaiting Tracy's departing words. I strapped on the CamelBak and quickly felt the cold, the wet, and the weight. In the midst of securing my helmet and cinching up my gloves the call to depart was given and we proceeded to roll out in some semblance of order, with balloons and shiny streamers fluttering in the wind.

I passed riders with American flags fixed to their helmets, words scribbled across notecards like tiny billboards taped haphazardly just above the ears, and then me with the minimalist approach likely drawing the least attention and wind resistance. One rider had something rather large made of newspaper standing up like a stalk or a tall horn; it wouldn't last a mile before it collapsed and flew off. The drag on the neck would be absurd. We were all ridiculous and that was the point.

Today's cue sheet was a long one; six full quadrants. The words *CAUTION: RRX*, and *EXTREME CAUTION*, both in bold print could not be missed. The first set of train tracks would come early, a pair of them just shy of two miles out from the hotel.

We worked our way through traffic with lots of glances back to the cue sheet. It was busy; a tenth mile here then turn, a mile turn, half mile RRX, another half mile and turn again. It was hard to be serious on helmet day but I eventually forgot about everything except navigating and staying on course.

We rode close together because of the congestion leaving Champaign. It was hard to pass and if a slower rider was in front you waited until traffic provided an ample break so it could be done safely. The breaks did not come often enough for some riders. They needed to ride fast and if they couldn't they bucked and braked, standing on the pedals in search of a window of opportunity to shoot forward. Like wild horses.

Traffic for a Thursday was probably normal but it felt like it was excessive. There was little room for everyone, no bike lane, a tall curb, cars randomly parked by the sidewalk, their side mirrors projecting outward in our space. We were at the biking equivalent of DEFCON 3 and teetering on a two. Both my hands were tight on the bars, eyes scanning for obstacles and standing traffic ahead.

Stoplights collected us in packs; a few riders would attempt to dodge around the masses as the light switched to green inviting a few honks from the rushing machines. This would continue through several lights until the riders found their place in the flow. I thought it was smarter to stay in line and not expose myself to a fender as cars accelerated past.

As we crossed our first set of train tracks and made our way along Neil Street toward University the intensity amped up even more. Pedestrian traffic accumulating at the corners, buses, and bicyclists on the sidewalk created additional distractions. Intersections were at odd angles, the distance across the exchanges were long. The streets narrowed and there was neither a bike lane nor a shoulder to seek refuge. My handle bar mounted mirror seemed awfully close to traffic. I thought about pulling it in.

At Main Street traffic switched to one–way favoring our direction but it seemed to narrow even more; still two lanes of moving traffic and breaks in the sidewalk to provide curbside parking. I had to watch for car doors and people stepping out between cars mid–block. I was not alone in having to deal with the assorted curbside obstacles. At least it was shaded, the roads decent, and the curbing and drainage grates easy to see. Making the left onto University was sketchy but doable. All of the riders in my proximity were now safely pointed east, but my state of alertness remained high.

Approaching Lincoln Avenue was an angled train crossing slicing right through the intersection. It was tighter than a forty–five, maybe closer to sixty degrees and in the traffic it was a pretty daunting sight. Lucky for us the tracks had what is best described as an asphalt sidewalk extension. It enabled riders to exit away from traffic parallel to the tracks maybe ten feet into the pedestrian sidewalk where it was possible to safely negotiate the proper right angle to cross the rails. Those of us who made this maneuver did a quick right, left, and right back into traffic. Those who didn't happened to be very lucky.

We were moving with two lanes of traffic a foot off the curb. An inviting sidewalk beckoned me to cross over at the first opportunity. It would have been nice to get out of traffic but the walkers can be even more unpredictable. Not to mention we'd be breaking the law like some of the uneducated local riders pedaling around those walking.

I expected to see more manhole covers and drainage grates but none were in the road. I did hit a few potholes and cracks and even by seeing them well in advance they still jarred me. I couldn't easily slow or swerve for every obstacle so instead I'd jerk the front wheel up or shift my weight rearward to minimize the shock.

Block after block the road opened up, buildings moved back from the traffic, and green space filled the voids. A sign for Urbana Business District marked a noticeable change. The sidewalks ended, a narrow shoulder appeared and I leaned right and turned onto SR–150E. The shoulder was no longer separated by a stripe but at least it was wide providing ample room for the single lane of auto traffic to pass without it being right on us.

To my right a sign read "Home of Miss America 2003." *It must be the corn that makes beautiful people*, I thought. A stand of dense shade trees clustered to my right and hundreds of acres of corn covered everything to my left. Traffic dropped off the farther I rode. The terrain was flat, the road was getting better. Occasionally a shoulder opened up and provided a safe zone to which riders gravitated. If the signs were correct, nine miles ahead I would find St. Joseph. The pavement did not waver left or right, not even the slightest. If traffic were lighter it would be perfect for sitting tall in the seat and to let both arms have a break from the bars. Maybe a bit farther ahead I would do just that.

On the left and close to the road a cluster of farm structures, houses, and even an old weathered wooden church stood alongside dozens of shade trees. The church had to be abandoned; it showed more raw wood than paint. The structures quickly disappeared as my view opened wide to fields of corn and soy beans warming in the brief flashes of sun as it peeked through the clouds.

I passed Fulls Siding Elevator on the south corner of SR–150 and a county road that headed south. It looked like a Russian rocket with several cylindrical columns packed tightly around an even taller rectangular core. Doors and piping and brackets adorned the discolored concrete tower. It was stained by water and rust, aged by the sun and elements, yet it dominated the wider silvery metal holding tanks. A lattice of pipes ran from a platform above the tower and down like spider legs to the smaller tanks. A series of catwalks at varying levels wrapped around the rearmost part of the elevator and across to the top of the largest holding tank. A pair of large diameter pipes extended vertically from the ground up to the platform where all the other pipes connected. A round grain shoot exited the tower thirty feet above the ground, the pipe angling down and toward an open grain trailer, its end bent and hanging precariously a few feet above. I noticed the details in this elevator. Maybe because it was so close to the road, or maybe I just needed a place for my mind to wander and it presented itself. It was interesting to look at.

Green fields with distant farm buildings dotted the landscape until I reached the flat bridge crossing the muddy Salt Fork River and pedaled into the village of St. Joseph. It was clean and prosperous, with less than five percent of the 3,334 residents living below the poverty line. In my assessment there was a healthy mix of local and franchised businesses. A beautiful brick United Methodist Church and a modest collection of well–maintained older homes surrounded by mowed lawns and mature shade trees lined the route. In town I saw a sign, "Home of Mrs. Illinois 2004." I wonder if she knows Miss America 2003 from Champaign.

Exiting the village the road took a series of *S* turns to elevate over a set of train tracks thirty feet below. After the downhill glide the road ran straight east all the way to Ogden. The view of green fields continued. Ogden was much like St. Joe except the homes appeared newer. More ranch styled homes from the '60s and '70s where the homes in St. Joe were from the post war boom a few decades earlier. It was home to 767 people, about a quarter the size of St. Joe.

We rode through the villages of Fithian and Muncie population: five hundred and 151 respectively. Fithian was named after Dr. William Fithian, a friend of Abraham Lincoln, who was rumored to stay at Fithian's farm often during the mid–nineteenth century. I unknowingly rode past the farm a mile west of the village. From the turn of the century up to the Great Depression Fithian was a center for livestock and grain trade.

Like most other villages and towns in this area Fithian had a grain elevator towering high above the other structures. The shape of the Fithian facility was different. A short row of five metal silos all connected with an enclosed metal catwalk across their domes stood by a row of five taller concrete silos maybe a hundred feet tall. The last part of the complex was a metal corrugated rectangle reaching a height of seven stories. It was connected to the discolored silos with piping and walkways. As I looked back at the concrete sections I realized they were not round but a series of three curved shapes pressed together into a single shape, like a string of beads. It was possible they were separated inside but outside they were a single mass of concrete. I don't see many of these structures back in Florida though I am sure they exist.

Next up was the village of Oakwood, population: 1,539. Most of the riders pulled into the convenience store for a bio break and a quick chat with Tracy who had the Crossroads van tucked in by the cemetery on the far side of the parking lot. A quick estimate of the headstones and I'd say about half the population of Oakwood is looking up. No disrespect intended. We had twenty–eight miles complete and about fifty to go. In another hour we would reach the SAG in Meade Park, but that doesn't happen until the end of the third quadrant on our cue sheet. I've got about fifteen more instructions to execute before I get there.

Oakwood does have a few noteworthy people including professional baseball catcher, Darren Fletcher and actress, Angela Watson, known for her role as Karen Foster in the hit TV series, *Step by Step* that ran from 1991 until 1998; a total of 159 episodes for those keeping score. And before the baseball fans get excited about scores, Fletcher played for four major league franchises including the Dodgers, Phillies, Expos, and Blue Jays. During his career spanning 1989 into mid 2002 his performance resulted in 124 home runs, 583 RBIs, 377 runs, and a .269 batting average. He was also a member of the All Star Team in 1994.

The skies were overcast since leaving the Drury. Temperatures warmer, somewhere in the low seventies and a breeze was off to the right and behind me. Conditions were ideal for riding except for the humidity. The optimist in me said it could be ninety degrees and raining so everything has to be kept in perspective. Our route took a right turn at Batestown Road, then up and over the incline crossing the Interstate, and through a mix of homes and businesses until we joined the frontage road on the south side of Route 150. A series of quick turns described in the cue sheet and we crossed over Route 150 and entered Ellsworth Park on a nice downhill glide.

We were greeted by an empty baseball field to our right, thirty yards beyond the lawn on our left was a slow flowing river. Directly ahead a series of speedbumps blended into the road and held our attention until we found the narrow wooden pedestrian bridge to cross the Vermilion River. A few riders missed the bridge and circled back joining Betty and I at the entry to the wooden crossover. We hydrated and snapped a few photos on the bridge, and then we arched down to the path on the far side making our way up and out of the wooded tranquil park and into the Danville traffic. Crossing Gilbert Street was challenging, the intersection had five lanes of traffic and several sweeping lanes on either side entering or exiting Main Street. It was like a small cloverleaf intersection, but more of a cluster. It made the angled twin train crossing that followed seem easy.

I seldom roll past a Dairy Queen but the SAG was less than two miles ahead. I gave it a second thought and for a moment I was close to crossing traffic and giving in to the call of a frosty treat but I stuck close to the riders in front of me and found the SAG a few minutes later in Meade Park.

Occasionally the clouds would let sunlight pass through providing a brief glimpse of the blue above. The temperature would rise and fall just a few degrees as the beams of light would spotlight the ground and then pull back into the clouds. The rider conversation was lively and focused on the next border crossing a few miles ahead.

We were now in a proper city, not one of the villages we rolled through earlier in the day. Danville, founded in 1827 is home to a diverse population of 33,553 people. Whites account for seventy percent, African Americans twenty–four percent, Latinos four percent, and within the remaining two percent are Asians, Native Americans, Pacific Islanders, and a few other races.

Geographically the city lies 120 miles south of Chicago and ninety miles west of Indianapolis. Looking at the maps it hadn't occurred to me I was so far north. It's too far to detour but it's a darn shame we don't roll through Chicago. At least we will go to Indy tomorrow.

The city is a major rail hub with at least four different tracks entering town from all sides. CSX Transportation, Norfolk Southern Railway, and the Kankakee, Beaverville and Southern Railroad operate rail lines that pass through Danville. Thankfully all of the riders were able to navigate across the tracks today. Heading into Champaign two days earlier we didn't have such good fortune.

The region was important for coal mining from the 1850s to the 1940s using a technique called open pit mining that was first practiced in the area. The city gained further notoriety after the underlying coal formation in eastern Illinois and western Indiana was named the "Danville Member" paying tribute to where it was discovered. With the closing of the mines and factories Danville's economy suffered and the population dwindled down from a high of 42,570 in 1970. Today, more than thirteen percent of the population still lives below the poverty line.

Over the years several open mines were converted into lakes, creating fishing and recreational opportunities. One of those includes the lake at Kickapoo State Recreation Area just a few miles east of Oakwood. A second lake west of Danville can be found in the Kennekuk Cove County Park.

The city does have a long list of notable people who were either born or grew up here including actors Gene Hackman, Donald O'Connor, Dick Van Dyke and his Brother Jerry. With such a cast of characters it should be easy to sell movie tickets.

I flipped the cue sheet and tucked it back into the plastic sleeve attached to the bars. The fourth quadrant details were clear; right turn out of the SAG and the state line into Indiana, "Crossroads of America" would be found 2.7 miles ahead. We exited much the way we arrived. Betty in front of me, Ron, Kathy, Gray, Lynn, Geoff and a few others ahead of her. The miles went fast on the flat roads and soon we were off the bikes posing and sprinkling sand. Not at the actual border sign, but a few hundred yards into Indiana where they had a more substantial welcome sign. Corn was the backdrop, there were no rivers or bridges or other defining boundaries between the two states. The corn green and tall masked the border. If not for the small green

DOT sign at the official boundary we would have missed it. Well until we saw the big photo op sign just inside the state. During our dance the skies brighten. Good pictures would be taken today.

The terrain became a bit more varied but the roads remained nearly flat. We annexed Indiana Highway 63, snaked our way through woods and fields past marshy areas; the road elevated and protected by guardrails. We pedaled in the safety of a generous shoulder on the General David M. Shoup Memorial Bridge crossing the wide chocolate colored Wabash River twenty feet below. Once on the other side we had arrived in Covington, population: 2,597.

Following the details on the cue, I made a quick right at the Catholic Church down a tree lined street followed by a left onto Liberty just past the Fountain County Court House. The half mile on Liberty took us past a thriving downtown commercial district, the buildings colorful and varied in architecture. At the transition to the residential area the sidewalks were replaced with imposing shade trees providing intermittent protection from the warmth above. We passed a cemetery and a local grocery mart, more houses and a plaza of small businesses with a 1960s feel. We turned at the blinking light and continued on SR–136.

Gentle rolling hills along stands of shade trees were in contrast to our exit out of Champaign. I didn't mind the shoulder dropped off to gravel as the traffic was light and the road in good shape. The only exception was the confining guardrails leading to the bridge at Graham Creek, but I didn't have to share the crossing with traffic and moments later my gravel shoulder companion returned.

The view from the winding road alternated between shade trees and fields; pedaling was easy, fluid, and smooth. I did my best to stay current with hydration but I honestly think if I had an alarm I'd do a much better job. Snacking wasn't a problem. If food was in my pocket I'd find it, and probably eat whatever it was sooner than I needed it.

Veedersburg was an older town strung out along SR–136. Entering from the west I passed old framed houses beneath stands of trees matching their age. I was pedaling up more than down but it was still easy. Somewhere in the day I would find 1,100 feet of climbing and I hope it's just sprinkled in and not saved for the end of the day.

On a downhill grade I saw the core of the town. It was stubby brick and painted commercial buildings, some a bit rough, a bit worn, with plenty of paved parking to compliment the aged buildings. The space between buildings and road separated by a modest sidewalk, cars parked on both sides of the street constricting the riding space but it felt safe. I enjoyed looking at the old signs and the change of architectural design every thirty feet. Some of the buildings were connected like town homes, each a different color, a different style. Some with porches, others with large windows, a few with extravagant cornice details, but almost all were flat roofed structures with a western feel. It was not as pristine as Covington but it didn't have to be. It felt more blue collar and comfortable. I'd suspect most of the 2,251 people here would fit that image but I'm happy to continue rolling the downhill right out of town without knowing for sure.

I sat up tall in the seat and extended my arms straight out like a cross. I coasted for a few hundred feet, shifting my body to steer straight, my wrists happy for the break. I leaned forward and with one hand before the other I gripped the bar and resumed proper control of the bike.

Still coasting I dipped under the cover of shade trees and over Coal Creek North Fork. As the woods continued I could feel the temperature drop. I broke from the shade and started to climb. For the next few minutes I was riding past a separate commercial area marking the eastern extents of Veedersburg. I came to a stop at a blinking light and flipped the cue sheet to the fifth quadrant. Twenty miles to go and it is getting warmer, the clouds forming, and it might even rain. Even if it does it would take a lot to dampen the enjoyment of my ride today. There were still traces of tailwinds to be enjoyed as I press on.

The next five miles were a continuation of the glorious scenery experienced over the last few hours. There were sections with trees encroaching on the road and other areas where the ground dropped off and guardrails appeared, but I could not have enjoyed the ride more. Occasional conversation took place as riders advanced and retreated, but in a ride like today the focus was on taking in the surroundings, smelling the grass, the hint of flowers in bloom, and even the occasional unpleasant smell of unfortunate animals that were unsuccessful at negotiating traffic.

With dense trees to my right and farmland covering the left landscape I came upon the most interesting sign on the trip since the "You Are Now Beyond Hope" sign back in the Arizona desert. This simple two post sign standing at the gateway to the town of Hillsboro, Indiana read "Home Of 600 Happy People And A Few Sore Heads." I couldn't help but laugh. I definitely needed to take a picture as it would be hard to convince a normal person a town would actually have the nerve to put up such a sign. Everyone including the sore heads knows who they are talking about. If it were me I wouldn't be too happy, but then again I could always defect from the few and join the masses. All you gotta do is smile.

As I made my way through town I was hoping to find a sign with an arrow pointing to the house with the sore heads, but none was found. The humor was not going to get that personal. What I did find was some bicycle humor. On the left side of the street at the corner of Main and Water is a brick building, the Myers Dinner Theatre. On the wall mounted eye level are five old rusty bikes, the touring style, a bit fancy with fenders and baskets and other details. I think they are all pointed the same way I'm riding but I'm not positive. I sense another trip may be necessary to confirm and report back with an update.

Just beyond the Myers building the tin porched brick buildings resembled what I imagined as a 1950s version of a western town from the old cowboy movies. Updating the wood planks with bricks, wood shakes with corrugated metal, and old creaky boards with concrete walkways. At least they fit my version in the moment as I peddled by.

At the exit of town several riders were on the opposite side of the street and though I shouldn't have been surprised, there was another matching sign greeting people entering from the east. Again I stopped to snap a picture of this one. The lighting was perfect and they did a nice job on the landscaping surrounding the sign.

I did a little investigating later on and discovered the town of Hillsboro never had six hundred people, ever! The current population is 509 and it peaked at 561 back in 1980. I guess it means if you are a happy person they have vacancies.

Elevation gain is a funny thing. It's a measure of the incremental climbing and it pays no respect to the incremental drops. It's possible to finish at an elevation lower than where you start yet still gain elevation. It is not the difference between the starting and ending elevation alone. Nobody tracks the elevation loss because you don't have to do any work to go down a hill. And it's the work that relates back to elevation gain and why it's so important. But not all elevation gain is the same. Climbing a steep mountain 1,100 feet up seems much harder than the elevation gains I'm experiencing today. Yet at the end of the day they are technically the same. I don't feel like I'm climbing but I do know Crawfordsville is a 190 feet higher than Danville. So within the small climbs, on the gradual and almost unnoticeable slopes, I need only find another nine hundred feet to complete the day. Your mileage and elevation gain may vary.

I crossed into Waynestown which resembled a mix of several towns before. The modest homes on the entry and exit, the quirky western style downtown with brick facades and weathered paint. The marker said 929 people live in the town but I find the number excessive.

Everywhere I looked fields of corn carried all the way to the horizon. I imagined a clear blue sky to contrast the green but this afternoon I would see only a partial clearing of the clouds. I could feel it getting warmer the more the sun was able to shine through. Between the fields I rolled through the woods and over Black Creek which was almost completely obstructed by trees. Signs for Crawfordsville stood just out of the right of way. Betty was far enough ahead where she would briefly disappear around the corners and reappear on the straights. She usually rode stronger as the day progressed. I tended to run the same pace throughout the day.

On a downhill grade lined with dense trees the sign for Road 125 appeared. My mileage was running a bit over and even though I was anticipating the turn it still surprised me. I was hard on the brakes and came to a stop. After a few cars passed I dodged across the highway and found myself on a narrow rolling rural road. The elevation changes were more pronounced than along the busy road I just exited. A few turns later I descended down a short quick hill to a stoplight; Highway 231 stretched right and left before me. A sign indicated the downtown of Crawfordsville was to my right just over a half mile.

As I waited I flipped the cue sheet and scanned the remaining two lines of instructions; both straight, both 0.7 miles. With the green I hurried across and angled left finding the shoulder of Highway 231. In front of me was a sweeping right–hand bend and for good measure I climbed the entire curve. It felt like more than the half mile it was, steeper than anything I enjoyed earlier. I had a wide shoulder to ride along the two lanes of noisy traffic moving in my direction. I was working hard after reaching what I thought was the top of the hill. It wasn't flat. I was still, ever so slightly, climbing. A case of the false flats had me. So I pushed and pushed to keep a respectful pace. I scanned the view to see if the road leveled off and maybe catch a glimpse of another rider.

A quarter mile ahead I saw a bike turn right. I couldn't tell who. They had found the hotel and exited the highway. As I pedaled closer the pylon sign with the green and white *H* came into view and I focused on the sign until I saw the break in the grass, the asphalt drive that would guide me as I coasted the last moments of the ride.

When I stepped off the bike it was eighty–five degrees in the shade of the portico at the Holiday Inn. My shirt was wet and stuck to my back thanks to the contact from the CamelBak. I had covered 80.83 miles in five hours eight minutes; a solid 15.7 miles per hour, and I felt good, maybe even great. Back in Florida my best was in the low fifteen miles per hour range so I'm getting faster and stronger as I go. I still had plenty of water but it did me no good if I didn't drink it. It actually became excess weight, a reminder to me to better manage my resources as I ride.

My day was blessed with overcast skies and a solid tail wind that carried me through my eighth border crossing and into the ninth of fifteen states I would pedal. It also helped me reach 31.2 miles per hour at some point. Statistically speaking it was perfect, maybe one of the best days on the tour. I hope our ride tomorrow into Indianapolis is as much fun. I know it will be just as humid.

I had a checklist of things to do today once I wiped down my bike. Laundry, writing, and organizing for tomorrow were at the top of the list. Dinner as well as breakfast in the morning would be in the hotel so I did not have to chance the weather. Storm clouds quickly formed and I was sure as it darkened the skies would unleash the rain. It may have rained in the area but the luck of CrossRoads was with us today and we stayed dry. Everyone I spoke with at dinner enjoyed the ride and had no mechanical issues. Rick would have little mechanic work to keep him this afternoon.

I enjoy learning about the cities and towns I pedal through and those I call home for the night. It gives me the chance to get to know America in a personal way and doing so at the speed my bike allows. Crawfordsville is a town I had heard of but knew nothing about. Tonight I learned the town is much bigger than what I saw. When I arrived I skirted the northwest extents and missed the bulk of this city that is home to 15,512 people.

Crawfordsville has an interesting history that would be good material for a game show. It is home to the Wabash College, one of only three remaining all–male liberal arts colleges in the country with a student body of nine hundred. The college has been in existence since November 1832.

The city is the home of the world's first thin–slab casting mini–mill; a steel manufacturing plant that recycles scrap steel using an electric arc–furnace. Manufacturing continues to be the primary employer in Crawfordsville but most of the workers are not employed by the companies directly, instead they are employed by Manpower, a staffing operation, which enables companies to reduce the risk of having direct employees.

Notable people from Crawfordsville include James W. Marshall, the man responsible for setting off the California Gold Rush, Will Shortz, the New York Times puzzle writer, Howdy Wilcox, winner of the 1919 Indy 500, James Brian Hellwig, professional wrestler better known as *The Ultimate Warrior*, and Joseph P. Allen, mission specialist on the first fully operational flight of the space shuttle in 1982. I consider this a pretty diverse list of talent.

It doesn't matter the size of the town, everywhere you look across this country you find something and someone of interest. I am excited to discover tomorrow and then every tomorrow thereafter. If there is anything I have learned from this trip it is I don't know much about this country, but I can change that, and I will change that with each day I ride. With each new town there is a new discovery; the possibilities as wide as the smile on my face. Crawfordsville, check!

Day 35: Crawfordsville to Indianapolis (62 miles)

With low miles and relatively easy terrain we would delay our departure from Crawfordsville until eight thirty. A late start didn't prevent Clark from getting up early; he had plenty to do in preparation for our ride. He was up and out well before six o'clock to tend to important matters like food preparation for forty plus. He wasn't making breakfast but he was meeting with the hotel staff that had the responsibility to make it.

Detailed instructions on when and how many pitchers of water were to be placed on the table; the coordination of the staff to begin seating riders, making sure plenty of the right food would be available, items hot or cold as required. They had a practice run the night before with dinner but the morning crew were all likely new faces to CrossRoads. Under Clark's direction the hotel kitchen and wait staff would become an extension of CrossRoads. The shoes to fill were big and Clark was just the guy to make sure they performed.

For five weeks I watched the CrossRoads magic unfold. It wasn't always easy and it wasn't without its challenges but in front of the curtain it looked like it was. Rooming with Clark I saw the effort and the preparation required, the attention to detail, and rigor involved. I also saw a commitment to deliver only the best, to not let the CrossRoads brand be tarnished in anyway. A level of respect for the leader of the band was evident. And the effort was delivered with passion and a desire to go beyond the expectations of the customer. It was hard work yet it was not work to Clark. You don't see this kind of commitment often. I was fortunate enough to have the view I did. It made me appreciate what I grew accustomed to as the benchmark of service; and the CrossRoads team made it look easy.

Besides breakfast Clark had to prepare the collection of CrossRoads equipment for stowage in the truck. The map I saw everyday as I arrived in the hotel lobby, the easel it was mounted on, the sign–in clipboard, repair tickets, the lost and found bins, and everything else that needed to be mobile had to be returned to its traveling space. Pumps needed to be stationed under the portico, powdered soap needed to be available, rags, and tubes, and tires for last minute changes pulled from the truck on request. And this was just Clark's checklist. Margaret and the rest of the team had similarly sized efforts. And I hadn't even mentioned the replenishing of the water, ice, and Gatorade for the orange coolers in the back of each van.

So much goes on behind the scenes that without skill and efficiency the staff would never rest. But beyond the ability was the caring, and it was the caring the staff delivered day after day. That's the experience I remember. It could be a case study in customer service for any business to learn from.

At quarter past eight we assembled under the cover of the portico, bags placed on the pavement in pairs, Trevor coordinating the selection and sequence of our personal items going into the truck. Clark, Rick, and Margaret provided the heavy lifting. It was all routine and orderly.

Tracy spoke to us from her perch, the wooden deck of the box truck. She recognized rider successes, called out the name of the rider, sometimes two, who would be the first to depart, and then she provided additional details about the ride into Indy. Her nominee could be celebrating a birthday, some other personal milestone, or her choice could be totally random. Everyone listened hoping it would be them but we always applauded after the rider was identified. I had a two percent chance it could be my day, but I would not be the one leading us out, not today. We had more riders than riding days. If everyone got a turn to lead from the hotel Tracy would have to call more than one rider on at least a few days.

Tracy then turned her attention to the clock and began calling groups to follow the leader out. We departed mostly by riding speed, the slower first, me in the middle group, and the faster riders filing out last. Sometimes she grouped us by riding partners or roommates. I'm not sure if she gave it much thought or made her decision in the moment but it didn't matter. Within ten minutes all riders signed out and the staff was left at the hotel to button everything up and join us on the road.

We would negotiate 1,200 feet of elevation gain over a shorter ride than yesterday but I expected a similar experience. I planned on a causal, almost lazy day on the bike where I could poke about at maybe fourteen to fifteen miles an hour. Maybe I'd stop at the creeks and listen to the water as it moves beneath the road. Maybe I would take a few more pictures, or maybe I would just stop more often and take in the views and try to burn the images into my mind. I would not constrict the day to a well–defined plan. In fact I didn't have any plan other than to just ride the cue sheet and let the rest happen on its own.

It was comfortable, the temperature not yet reaching seventy degrees; the breeze was just beginning to stir, and the haze of the morning was lifting to reveal clear skies. There was no need for a jacket or leg warmers. At least not for me.

Hopper did have his full sunblock riding whites on as he did every day. The only skin he exposed was where his fingers exited the gloves and a small oval, maybe six inches across, surrounding his nose, his shades protecting his eyes. He was serious about protecting his skin and I'm sure it was much warmer to ride in long wear.

Other riders favored wearing fewer clothes, some with tank tops exposing their shoulders, and a few riders like Kathy and Ben pushing their recumbent pedals with sandals. I think Peter Crowell was also in that camp because the reclined position was compatible with the sandal styled footwear. I preferred the full protection of standard cycling shoes, my feet fully wrapped with a sturdy layer of leather in case I took a spill. I remember Ben injured his toe much earlier in the trip and he may have even lost the nail on his big toe. Yupp, I'll ride with my closed toed shoes.

The cue sheet was full on both sides. Some of the most complicated instructions we have yet encountered. Most of the turns were less than a mile apart, only two greater than five miles. Each quadrant averages nine lines and these lines described what would happen over approximately a ten mile distance. The eighth quadrant provided instructions to a Velodrome. I found something I must see for sure. It's my only required stop I'll pursue after reaching Indianapolis.

I–74 was to our right a quarter mile as we exited the hotel. We turned left back toward the direction of town and took full advantage of the long sweeping descent we climbed the day before. I sailed right through the green light near the bottom and began my climb up and over the long concrete bridge with Sugar Creek below. To the right I could see the shimmer of the water, an almost black–green color as it flowed over the rocks and reflected the sun. The water was low, the sun dried gravel and tan dirt banks looked more like a beach separating the water from woods. It was a long way down, maybe sixty feet or more. Across traffic over the concrete retaining wall, an old brick power plant or factory of some type was framed in a cluster of shade trees. The speed limit was thirty miles per hour but I was not a threat to break it. I ground the pedals and stayed to the far right of the shoulder in the company of other riders.

Getting across Washington into the turn lane took some doing. This is where riding in a group helps. One rider near the back of my little group moved over a lane signaling the cars behind of our intent to turn. The action worked and all riders in front now had a motorist providing a bit of cover for us. We jumped one lane then the next and finally bunched up in the safety of the turn lane and waited for the green. We rolled through a commercial district of mostly short brick buildings and then carefully crossed the angled train tracks called out on the cue sheet. The tracks were framed in old wooden planks that can be slippery in the morning and they were. A slow approach with a turn left of the bars to square up with the rails and the crossing was behind us.

Our route continued on the undulating road in need of repaving. Large vintage houses with wraparound porches stood on simple green plots of grass, the sidewalks cracked and overrun by weeds and grass in many places. The road bent to the right and at Turtle Park I followed those in front of me onto SR–136 east. For the next ten miles I would not have to refer to the cue sheet. New Ross was my destination.

The population of Crawfordsville slipped away, houses and commercial structures tapered off, rural areas of green filled in on all sides. The road narrowed and curled about the trees and rolling hills, the lines on the edge of the road let me know where the gravel and grass started but I would have to share the road with whatever traffic the morning presented.

This stretch of the ride was heavily wooded, and where there weren't trees, there was corn, and when the corn gave way I passed homes set back from the road on acres of mowed grass with landscaping of evergreens, post and rail fences, and even a few rocks. I noticed the color and texture of the trees were more diverse around the houses but almost identical in the wooded clusters along the route.

The breeze was behind me, just enough to give a soft push and cause the corn to dance. I could hear the stiff leaves of corn as they moved and rustled against each other. It was a low roar; it had a course texture to it, like white noise to mask unpleasant sounds.

Birds were active, calling out and giving away their location. Some flew across the road in plain view while others stayed safely within the protection of the trees. Song birds, crows, and when I passed animal remains on the road, a predator could be found circling or standing nearby.

The forest of trees made a softer sound as their leaves fluttered, small branches bending and flexing. The sun shimmered through the dark canopy down to the road, my sunglasses filtered most of the distraction but it added an artistic quality to everything it touched.

Close to the road were drop–offs calling for safety rails and others not so dramatic that rolled into a ditch or under a thick cover of thorns and bushes. I had no plans of testing either obstacle and kept scanning the scenery and enjoying the ride. The occasional car or small truck would announce its approach and quickly pass. I pedaled over Walnut Creek, a small cut with a trickle of water moving across the brown mud. There were farms with red barns and white driveway gates, field fencing separating horses from the road, and mailboxes of all sizes and shapes dotting the road's edge.

The rural ride gave way briefly to the unincorporated place called Mace. A pair of tiny brick buildings, a small wood–framed pavilion sheltering a dozen unpainted picnic tables, a white steeple extending skyward from the United Methodist Church, and a few small houses with American flags displayed proudly were at its core. A few more houses peppered the road and I was back into the rolling green countryside.

Periodically the fields would be interrupted by the occasional house and at one point I noticed a large weeping willow standing on a slight grade in front of a big colonial. It was unusual to see these away from water but I also observed a cluster of thick reeds in the ditch spreading outward toward the tree. It was wet ground, able to support the thirsty demands of the willow. After white birch trees, the weeping willow is my favorite. The long dangling branches offer shade and if you grab a handful of the vine–like limbs you can swing from them. My grandfather had plenty of both trees on his eastern Pennsylvania property where I would visit as a small boy and that's why they are my favorites.

Across a set of angled railroad tracks omitted from the cue and I was in New Ross. The town was well–worn with an old grain elevator marking its center. I saw agricultural buildings, a small convenience mart, and a handful of cross streets defining the town of 339 people before I exited. I stayed parallel to the rail line until crossing Big Raccoon Creek. From this point the road and rails angled apart until we met up again in Jamestown a few miles ahead.

The welcome sign for Jamestown was the same arched design and likely built by the same person who constructed the sign for New Ross. The town was longer and more residential than commercial; the dominant colors were white, gray, and brick. American flags were plentiful and swayed slowly in the breeze. At First Street a white picket fence and a vine covered arbor framed the sidewalk leading back to a house. At the intersection with Park, another picnic pavilion and a few storefronts tucked into an early century brick building. A few more blocks of commerce and I leaned left at the blinking light quickly finding the rail line at the gated crossing. I was safely over another set of tracks and looking for my next turn.

I stopped to flip my cue sheet, took a pull of water, and broke off a piece of the Clif bar to get me to the SAG. Then I continued through winding relatively flat roads except for the crossover at I–74. A left at a church and a quick right found me crossing Big Walnut Creek marked only by an old concrete wall and then I passed Main Edlin Ditch. Neither required more than a two foot pipe to let the small amount of water flow underneath. I found the right turn onto SR–39 and followed it through farms and expansive stands of corn. I crossed over an unnamed creek that was more worthy of a name than the ones prior and then to my right a white post and plank fence lined the road defining one of the larger farms. I turned left onto 1075 and tracked along the road as it bent at right angles around the fields, over the ditches of Pound and Ross, and then I reached the end of the quadrant on the cue sheet. To my delight I flipped to the third section and found the SAG at Gentry Farm was just a few power poles away.

I angled into the drive and found a patch of grass to lay down my bike. Gloves and helmet were off as was my bandana. It was hot, pushing eighty and very humid. By now the skies had cleared off all but a few wisps of clouds. I wiped my brow and walked into the conversation. Our hosts let Tracy set up under the shade tree and fluids became the primary draw. I topped off my bottles and set about picking snacks for the rest of the ride; Pop–Tarts and a granola along with a whole banana to make sure I didn't cramp. Then I grazed on the fresh fruit, and more carbs to replace what I had burned.

The size of our group was evident; the scattered bikes covered most of the lawn in front and alongside the house. A few bikes leaned on fence posts and tree trunks. Riders continued to filter in but not many were leaving. A few were enjoying the shade from the comfort of folding lounge chairs as others sat or stood in the grass. There was no hurry as we had only thirty miles more to ride and it was just shy of eleven o'clock.

Our hosts were generous enough to invite us in and let us use their restroom. As much as I appreciated the privacy of not having to pee alongside the road, it was the ladies who were the most thankful. We took turns waiting on the small wooden porch talking about the ride, and then one by one a rider would step out the door and another would step in.

Inside the house was a small but modest kitchen and sitting room. It was not cluttered with store bought excess but it was adorned with family pictures and keepsakes. There was a sense of family and pride, of community and a neighborly spirit. The furniture had patterned prints long out of style but they were clean and comfortable. Quilts and other handmade artifacts were a testament to patience and craft. In those few minutes talking to the Gentry's I gained a bit of an understanding for the effort it takes to run a farm, but their hard work does not deter them from inviting in dozens of strangers so they can experience their hospitality. We were guests but strangers no more.

My body was beginning to adjust to being off the bike so it was time to go. I retrieved my gear and turned my bike in the direction of the road and started to pedal. I backtracked the way I came until I saw a break in the corn and angled right. Big Mike, Duffey, Paul, Kathy, and several others were in my general area. We would get strung out but I always had at least one of them in sight. Two if it were Duffey or Big Mike as they stayed within earshot of each other.

I enjoyed the quirky names I encountered on my ride including the West Fork White Lick Creek I crossed over before making the right onto County Road 500. The roads that followed became less traveled, often with no cars passing by for a few miles. In these sections riders rode in tandem socializing without worry. In more than one section I was off the bars sitting tall in the seat and bantering right back. If I could go back twenty-five years it would be like my days pedaling the backroads of central New Jersey. Not a care about cars and traffic, not a care in the world.

I quickly ran out of instructions and the cue sheet needed to be flipped again. As long as one of the group riders was on the current page it was okay if I was a bit late flipping mine over. I was a few steps into quad four before I synced back up.

The numbered roads were a bit confusing. They repeated several times with the only difference being a directional letter in front and behind the number. When we crossed 900E it was actually running north and south, not east and west as I assumed. The proper designation was N County Road 900E; the leading letter indicated it was a north running road. I can only speculate the E at the end stands for being to the east of some central marker. Just as long as I don't get lost, I'll be fine with whatever names they use.

I passed over School Branch Creek and made my way to Raceway Road and headed north. The climb became more noticeable, the road narrowed, and the trees encroached tighter to the asphalt. Across Hook Creek and a left onto Traders Lane I was climbing again up and over I–65, the traffic building and flowing quickly on the four–lane twenty–five feet below.

At the bottom I turned onto Lafayette and had the benefit of a dedicated bike lane with four lanes of moderate post–lunchtime traffic to my left. Off to my right I could see I–65 as I crossed the bridge over Eagle Creek. I was climbing more than gliding in search of my next turn. I could see it ahead, a left across traffic was Lakeside Drive. Without the benefit of a turn lane or a light I was forced to stop on the right side of the road and wait for a crossing opportunity. I didn't wait long, an opening safe enough to get me through presented itself and I was happily riding a narrow tree canopied road that carried me through a park–like setting with even more climbing.

Without a stripe dividing traffic the pavement appeared suitable for a single lane rather than two–directional traffic. It was tight when cars approached and I pedaled with one eye ahead and the other on the instructions positioned over the handle bar stem. Blind lefts and rights, tree branches within reach, and I'm hoping no cars would come flying around the bark clad chicanes to steal my path. I saw water and zipped across the narrow ribbon dividing the eastern portion of Traders Point Lake from the rest. The road narrowed and ducked under low branches until it ended at a stop sign on the busy 71st Street.

I took a moment to breathe and to flip the page once more. Less than thirteen miles remained and I still had three quadrants full of instructions. I rolled east but the one lane quickly became two, then three. The transition from a narrow path to a full–on highway took less than two hundred yards. I was under the I–465 mega beltway which must have been two hundred feet wide and I crushed the pedals through traffic lights to avoid stopping. I remained cautious of the cars merging into my lane.

I felt relief when I leaned right onto Corporate the wide asphalt traded for a more manageable two–lane through a professional park. A curb without a shoulder was the best I could hope for over the next mile, but traffic was more forgiving until I come to a stop at 62nd Street. A few riders gathered waiting to cross so I took a pull of water and finished the remains of the Pop–Tart I had been working on since leaving the SAG. I was down to a granola bar; my banana long gone.

Once I made the left I found a bike lane to go with the increase in traffic. From there the turns and signs became a blur, my head bobbing up and down between the road and my guide. Soon I was deep into a residential neighborhood, over creeks, past a golf course, and at mile 56.9 I optioned for the velodrome and flipped the cue to the eighth quad for the series of quick turns that would have me guessing if I were on course or completely lost.

I scampered out of the safety of the neighborhoods and found my way across the busy 38th Street over I–65 and by way of a generous downhill I coasted to the entrance of the Lake Sullivan Sports Complex and found the Major Taylor Velodrome. I approached the crossing gate on the east side and peered out over the concrete track, the short straights banked nine degrees, the turns a full twenty–eight. A lap would cover 364.55 yards or 1,093.65 feet. I'm not sure if it was measured from the bottom, the top or somewhere in between. It didn't matter; I was going to give it a try.

I rolled over the top lip and stayed along the outside wall. My pace was slow, maybe eight miles an hour, if that. The banking on the straights required me to lean right and turn slightly up hill to maintain a straight line. I wasn't comfortable staying at the top in the turns so as I approached the increased banking I dropped to the lower third and continued around the sweeping corner. I continued around another full lap and then decided to shed some of the extra gear to see how fast I could go. Back in Florida on a hot day I was able to push myself just over thirty–one miles an hour on a flat straight road before I hit my max cadence in top gear. I was hoping to better that on the banking.

I turned into the infield and began removing my tire pump, bike bag, water bottles, even my flag pole and the Three Stooges. Everything I could easily remove including my granola bar in my jersey pocket was set in a pile on the ground. I took a pull of Gatorade and was as ready as I could be. Only a few other riders optioned for the velodrome detour. They staggered in as I took to the track.

I pedaled in mid–gear slowly working my way up to the middle lane. My thought was to make a few laps to get the feel of the track and then accelerate into the turn from the top lane and drop off the banking on exit. I found a comfortable cadence and stared heads down at the digital readout and the track. My speed fluctuated between twenty and twenty–two miles an hour over four laps so I declared it good enough, I was ready to go fast before my legs stopped working completely.

With the courage to climb the two–and–a–half–story banking I got up to top speed near the outer rail. Once there I looked down through the left handlebar and saw the bottom apron twenty feet down. I felt like I was on a ledge. The view to my right was the racing surface. I could almost reach out and touch the concrete. I was riding a wall in the turns, the sound of the tire slipping against the slope made me think the bike could wash out from under me if I slowed the pace, so I didn't.

The banking tested me mentally as much as it did physically. As I passed the middle of the back straight I was in top gear, my feet moving the pedals faster and faster. Nearly touching the top rail I entered the corner and I gave it everything I had. My feet pumped, the force of my arms against the bars caused the bike to lean left and right, I stayed at the top down the straightaway feeling the elevation drop and then climb as I reached the opposite turn. It took great effort to keep pace as if I were climbing the entire circuit. My heart was racing and I continued to pedal until there was nothing else to give. I rounded the north turn and with only the slightest twitch of the bars I went left diving down and rocketing toward the bottom lane in a *bonsai* move.

The acceleration was instant, I was falling. A perfect execution would earn a boost from the banking; a bad one could fold the front wheel in a pancake maneuver and send me face first to the concrete. Body tensed, my grip tight on the bars, I stopped pedaling only when I reached the bottom. It felt like my heart would explode as I relaxed on the flat apron coasting half way around before leaning into the infield. It was brutal, exhilarating, and scary all at the same time.

My heartrate was nearly 180 and it took a few minutes before it came back within the desired range. I sucked down Gatorade and water in between hard fast breathes. I stood straddling the bike my head resting on my forearms as they lay crossed on the handlebars. I had my feet far apart and I was reasonably sure I would not fall over. I was dripping in sweat and my eyes burned from the salt.

I was sure I was fast. When I checked my computer to see the max speed to my surprise I was not. I managed only a disappointing twenty–seven miles per hour. I figured it was the heat or the miles I had already pedaled, that held me back, but inside there was real disappointment. No time or energy for another attempt.

While I reinstalled the parts on my bike riders circled the track in much the same progression I went through. The results were also very similar. The velodrome is a monster but I'm glad I tried it out. I was beginning to feel okay about my speed on the track. I now have a benchmark to shoot for if I ever return.

I slowly rode out of the park complex through the maze of turns and precautions called out on the cue sheet. The entire way to the Marten House Hotel on 86th Street I was dripping of sweat and sapped almost completely of energy. There was no fanfare on arrival except for a shout out from Trevor and Tracy as they worked from inside the open box of the truck. When I finally stopped and dismounted the bike I saw riders much fresher than I; they had not gone to the *Drome* nor did they have the story to go with it. The extra effort was worth it. After I cleaned up and was back into street clothes I felt recharged. It's funny how a shower and getting out of the cycling outfit can do that.

My detour and the laps around the velodrome raised my mileage from sixty–two to 70.64 for the day. I had a solid performance in the mid–fifteen mile per hour range, but I must admit the last few miles to the hotel stole away some of the performance. I was in the seat for five hours two minutes and hit a maximum speed of 29.7 miles per hour according to my computer display. No mechanical issues, no broken bones, no scrapes, and no real close calls to make note of in my journal entries. I would write only good things today, including a respectable performance on the banks of the velodrome.

Don Hardin, one of the riders injured on our first day in California, drove up from Louisville, Kentucky to meet everyone. He was in good spirits and said his shoulder was doing much better. His doctor cleared him to get back on the bike so he is planning on making another cross country attempt with CrossRoads next year.

A group of us decided to go check out the famed Indianapolis Motor Speedway across town so we piled into a van and off we went. The Formula One racing series was running the road course on Sunday so we thought we would check out the grand atmosphere, maybe see the drivers practice, and get a chance to see the yard of bricks at the start finish line. It was sunny and hot, a lower class of formula cars was on the track and we saw sons of former drivers trying to earn their way into a professional career.

The formula cars are the most sophisticated and technologically advanced open wheel cars on the planet. The engines while relatively small turn more than five times the rpm's of street cars giving them tremendous power for their size. They can go around a corner as if on a rail thanks to the aerodynamic body that literally sucks the car to the ground. They are fascinating machines to watch. I did see the yard of bricks, I was in awe of the crowds, and my only disappointment was come Sunday I'd be pedaling to Marysville, Ohio and not sitting in the speedway club.

In years past Crossroads detoured to the speedway and riders were allowed to pedal around the two and a half mile oval. While it would have been cool to say I rode around the Brickyard I was happy to see the racing instead. Since the Formula One series races only about fifteen times a year and most of those races are outside the United States, this could possibly be the only time I ever see the cars in person. It was a day of fun and excitement that will be hard to beat.

After returning to the hotel and enjoying dinner on property the day was still not done. Several people decided to watch the cycling races at the velodrome. Tonight was a club night of racing featuring riders of various ages and skill level. Earlier in the day I struggled to go just a few laps over twenty but these hearty souls could speed around the track at twenty–five to thirty miles per hour in races lasting eight to sixty laps. I was quite impressed watching as many as twenty competitors pedaling inches apart without a single incident. And they did it on bikes with only a single fixed drive wheel and no brakes.

The objective was to make the bike as light as possible so they didn't have any bar wrap or other non–essential items attached. The fixed gear meant they would start very slowly, pedals barely turning and they could not coast. It was just like the old tricycles we had as kids. The rider became one with the bike and if calamity unfolded in front there was no way to brake to slow down. Focus and commitment required along with a set of strong lungs and legs.

The racing was a rolling chess match, not a contest of pure speed. Races usually started slow, the laps clicked off; the crowd anticipating the tight pack would produce a breakout rider who would set off the scramble to the finish. At the one–to–go bell riders hammered the pedals and dove down the banking to pass. They raced three or more wide crossing the finish line, inches separating first through fifth. It was exciting and dangerous. Then the riders would complete a slow lap waving to the cheers of the crowd. It was a fantastic evening even though the winds picked up with some healthy gusts that played havoc on the racers. Storms were around the greater metro area but by eight thirty we were back under scatters clouds, calm winds, and the temperature a comfortable seventy–one degrees.

The velodrome opened in 1982 and was named after Marshall Walter "Major" Taylor; an American track cyclist who began his amateur career as a teenager in Indianapolis. He would go on to become a professional racer in 1896 and at the age of eighteen he would win the sprint event at the 1899 world track championships in Montreal, Quebec, Canada to become the first African American to achieve the level of world champion. At the time, he was the highest paid athlete in the world.

Taylor was the American sprint champion in 1899 and 1900, and he would race across the globe until retiring at the age of thirty–two. He was inducted into the United States Bicycling Hall of Fame ninety years after winning the world championship. In retirement, Taylor wrote his autobiography titled *The Fastest Bicycle Rider in the World*. A first edition 1928 hard copy will set you back 1,950 dollars.

Over the years the velodrome played host to national and international competitions including the 1987 Pan American Games and the USA Cycling's Collegiate Track National Championships in 2003. It is a wonderful facility to spectate and to compete on. I just wish I had the legs of the riders who could pedal at speed lap after lap and then come back later and race another event.

Tomorrow my sights are set for Richmond, Indiana some eighty plus miles away. The climbing will be about five hundred feet more than today with slightly cooler temperatures and overcast skies. I'm sure traffic getting out of this city of more than 797,000 people will be more of a challenge than when we arrived. In less than ten hours I will know for sure.

Day 36: Indianapolis to Richmond (84 miles)

Momentum, habit, and perseverance are three words familiar, if not rooted in every cyclist's mind. Without them you are not a cyclist. You could only say you ride a bike. Getting up every day and doing the same thing over and over on a trip like this becomes habit. You need to get out of bed and do all those things required to get ready without thinking, and by day thirty–six you are doing just that. Your mind and body are on autopilot as you emerge from the depths of sleep, deeper than any other I have experienced. Through the day the body is taxed and to recover it needs to find that remote place of sleep. I draw no comparisons to "Waking the Dead" because they have no scheduled stop in Richmond this afternoon.

Momentum is continued rhythmic success; a ball team on a hot streak, becoming stronger and more confident with each game played. It is the same for me as I look at the cue sheets and stare down the challenges of heading east. I made it through the desert, the Rocky's, and the Great Plains. I made it through the heat, the pain, and the monotony. I'm stronger and more confident I can overcome whatever is before me. I have momentum on my side and I'm going to need it as I begin a five–day stretch of near century rides, each day more climbing, stair–stepping to nearly three thousand feet en route to Wooster and then only slightly less climbing from there the following day to Niles.

I will need to persevere, to grind and grunt out the slow climbs in my lowest gear, in the high heat and humidity in the stagnant air. I will leak sweat like I'm in a sauna and I'll have to get my mind focused, distracted if necessary, to keep the thoughts of doubt and quitting from taking hold. This is all on me and while intensely physical, I believe and I have been told many times by Clark it is more mental than anything else. I've got to get my head around it. I need to ignore the slow–motion advance of the odometer. I'll need to watch my heartrate and I'll need to drink plenty of water and Gatorade. I may even dip into the salt tablets that were so critical to getting across the desert. I need to persevere. I need to if I want to arrive at the beach in Boston whole and victorious.

These three words have become rote to me since the early days of preparing for this journey. There are other words like see, feel, experience, and enjoy. Maybe even savor. While habit, momentum, and perseverance are the words that will get me through, it's the other words, the sensory, tactile, experiential, and immersive, they are the reason, the purpose of such an endeavor. It is the *Why* and I imagine my harvest of the personal and emotional rewards will overflow in abundance. But unlike fruit they will not spoil, they will not wither. They will continue to ripen with age and bloom eternal so long as I can remember. Maybe this is what people mean when they say, "Heaven on Earth." I will know when I reach my destination, but for now I must soak in the journey one day, one mile, one moment at a time.

My cue sheet was a respectable four quad draft with warnings for risky railroad crossings reserved for the second and third quadrants. The morning presented itself as cool with steady winds coming out of the north. It would be a day of buffeting from the left as the strong crosswinds would push and pulse to drive me closer to the ditch. My job would be to tack into the wind as much as needed, to react quickly and adjust should the wind pause so I don't turn into traffic. It's a balancing act a cyclist learns to manage just like everyone learns how to walk over uneven ground. It's a back of the mind subconscious activity which is fortunate because I have better things to do than actively manage the subtle twitches of the handlebars.

As I warmed up in the first ten miles the cue kept me going straight on 86th Street. Traffic was much the same as I found coming into Indianapolis. It was early rush hour chaos, three lanes each going east and west. I felt exposed to the sleepy drivers, the angry ones, the drivers running late with kids screaming in the back, and those trying to multi–task. I assumed that to be true but I could not be sure as the situation didn't lend itself to pleasantries and introductions. I'd prefer they keep an eye out for me and not try to occupy the little bit of pavement I ride on while hugging a six inch curb of concrete that has me boxed in. Maybe I'm a bit selfish on the bike but I have no room for anyone trying to hitch a ride or force me over when I have no exit option to yield to them. To be honest the sidewalk is looking pretty appealing right now but I'm unable to transition to it even if I decided to take the option.

I was nervous with each storm drain I encountered. Where traffic allowed I moved left a foot and then quickly returned to the curb. Most of the drains were slotted perpendicular to my direction but even a crack in the grate could stick the front wheel and I'd be vaulted over the bars. It's not as bad as it sounds until it is.

I've vaulted over the bars a few times in my cycling life and one more time is one more too many. I hate it, and it leaves you at the mercy of the ground you hit, but I ride anyway. I do so because the thrill and independence of riding is worth the risk the rider should be able to mitigate. Be careless and you get hurt. Rarely, but sometimes you get hurt even if you are cautious and do everything right. That's life and I'd rather live it than watch from the sidelines. Even if it bites me in the ass, I'm going to live in the lane out with the cars because that is what I have to do to get back to the calm of the rural roads that are somewhere ahead. It's the usual cyclist's experience in a busy city. You have to block it out but you can't ignore it; if you do the bite could be unforgiving.

The excitement spiked as I rolled under I–69 where traffic expanded briefly to a full six lanes going in my direction. Cars and trucks exiting to the right and left, I wanted to stay against the curb but the right lane was turning. I had to move left one lane and ride the white stripe with inches between my body and a bad ending if anyone forgot their place. In the busiest of the morning drive, fear and apprehension became exhilaration and a heightened sense of awareness. And I thought there was no room for dialing up the excitement, yet there it was, a thirteen on a ten scale. It was strange that a smile replaced any trace of fear that was on my face. I got this.

I cleared the mass of traffic and the road necked down to a single lane separated by a bright double yellow line. Gone were the curbing and sidewalk, the flat concrete with the rhythmic expansion joints replaced with smooth black asphalt. Flat was out and incremental rolling terrain was in. The white stripe I was hugging was the last of the usable surface available; beyond were loose bits of gravel and ground. I could touch the overgrowth if I didn't mind a stiff branch of thorns. I clung to the bars and followed the trail of colorful jerseys and waving orange flags marking the cyclists in front of me.

On a sweeping woodsy downhill bending right the pesky curb returned. The elevation dropped quickly and I accelerated well beyond twenty, cars and small trucks in a steady stream alongside me had my focus. I had one eye laser sighting the road a dozen yards ahead, the other twitching between the one inch square mirror, my digital speed display, and farther down the road where an intersection was coming into view. And just my luck there was a traffic light controlling the wide intersection.

I was hoping it would stay green to keep my speed. I had to be ready should it turn yellow and I needed to stop. And right at the critical point, right when I thought I would make it, the hard pedaling was for naught as the amber light lit up and I was hard on the brakes shedding precious momentum. Before I stopped I downshifted then unclipped from the pedals. Other riders came to a stop behind me and after a few quick adjustments and flexing of hands I was pedaling across Sargent Road. I used the last bit of downhill available to gain momentum before I climbed the other side.

I enjoyed a brief shoulder of good asphalt to the right of the stripe but it was gone a half mile later as I neared the crest of the hill. The trees moved away from the road, traffic gradually eased, and I was able to enjoy the view of brick vintage '70s homes surrounded by rambling acres of lawn and ornamental trees. If I had to exit the road it would be easy and safe; if I tumbled the landing soft.

Before I knew it, and as the cue sheet predicted, I was screaming down a hill and heading toward a repeat of a broad intersection, traffic light waiting at the bottom to challenge me. I lost again but not without giving it a respectable try.

On the other side I crossed over Fall Creek, a rather interesting yet simple architectural design of concrete spanned two hundred feet flat and true, the low walls allowed me a clear view of the brown water below. The canopy of trees tightened around the road, the occasional section of guardrail raised my pulse, and I didn't seem to pay much attention to the inclines I was on. Without thinking I was crushing the pedals to keep a respectable pace.

I was in and out of the trees as the scenery wavered from forest to rolling well–maintained lots. Under the trees, debris such as small gravel and vehicle residue could easily blend in. Wearing shades makes these hazards even harder to detect but I was rolling straight so even contact with a bolt or a stone would likely startle me at best. I did pinch out a few stones from under my tires but other than that I was enjoying this stretch of road.

It smelled different under the canopy of trees than it did in the open; more organic, more subtle, and a bit cooler. Riding past the fields the smells were more pungent, a grassy sour mixed with the delicate floral fragrance of the blooms doing their best to attract bees and ensure their species. The scents of life spread over the rising warm petro–based odor lifting from the asphalt were also in play. There was an abundant bouquet to be enjoyed with each breath.

I turned right on Sunnyside and began a thirty mile stretch without services available. The CrossRoads vans would be my only support until I reached the SAG at mile 41.7, the halfway point in the ride.

With each mile the traffic dissolved further and the greenery became more enjoyable. Quiet would come, I would hear only the wind and the mechanical sounds of the bike. I shifted when needed and could easily tell if I was a half notch off on the chain guides. A soft tap and the metal on metal chatter would cease. Birds and the sounds of leaves and tree branches dancing about filled in the background tones; the many reasons why riding is such a beautiful experience.

I had all but forgotten the intensity of the first few miles this morning as I was going deeper and deeper into the cycling zone. I had flipped my cue sheet as I rode and was looking for the first of several railroad crossings to negotiate. I found it on a slight incline where the woods transitioned into plowed fields planted with rows of green stalks of corn. The tracks were skewed to the direction I was traveling coming from my right cutting across and ahead toward my left. Two sets of tracks were framed with rubber mats on either side and between the rails. Had it been wet these mats could be as slippery as the smooth rails themselves. I carefully leaned left to move to the middle of the road and then banked back to the right to cross square to the rails. Successive bumps as my wheels found the narrow voids between road and rails and I was safely over the obstacles with a cautionary red octagon growing just ahead.

A quick left at the stop sign and I was back on an undivided four lane heading toward the small business district of McCordsville, Indiana, population: 1225. I pedaled by a sign for Tim's Bakery but I saw only a trio of small pastel colored wooden shed–like buildings on the corner of Hanna Street. A block later I rolled past the typical convenience store gas station with the massive roof over the pumps supported by a few steel columns in the center. The ones you see getting twisted to the ground when a hurricane or a tornado blasts through. The ones they put up everywhere across America if they can squeeze it in.

Land available signs dot the fields, new asphalt and recent strip centers indicate growth is coming. This stretch of road affords a proper shoulder even if the asphalt is worn and cracked. I'm happy to have some room to move about and avoid the grit and rusty hardware left behind by the mainstream traffic.

Just ahead a cornfield on my right marks the turn onto East 234. I head off in the direction of New Castle thirty–one miles beyond according to the sign. I leave behind the generous shoulder I was so happy to see, but now I feel safer in the lane.

If the world were perfect cyclists would enjoy traffic free downhill roads no matter which way they traveled, temperatures topping off at seventy degrees under clear blue skies, and of course tailwinds. Today I would say I did well on the wish list. The temperature was just under the ideal, skies were clear and blue, and traffic was light. The wind, though not at my back, was fluttering around ten and steady from the north; predictable and easy to manage as I was pointed due east.

To my left and right were sprawling farms with framed white houses, silos, and barns for animals and equipment. There were sheds and small structures of various shapes, post rail fences and even a few wagon wheels surrounded by modest plots of flowers offering beauty to those traveling past.

Farmers come from generations of farmers. Few would have the resources or gumption to become a farmer if they weren't brought up in it. It is one of the toughest, most demanding of all occupations; a twenty–four by seven job that is truly full–time. As tough as it is to be a farmer they still exist and here in Indiana there are plenty. I have no doubt that on these acres of waving green the same family has been caring for crops and cattle for generations. The stories they could tell if I took the time to stop and if they had the time. I might have to settle for a wave to the man in the passing tractor as he hustles equipment between fields. His grin or grimace the only sign of happiness or frustration.

I grew up around farms and even worked on one for a summer or two. Farming is in the blood, not something decided on one day as a career. As much as I loved being on farms as a boy I could never be a farmer. I don't have the personal metal to do what they do. They have my respect and I'm thankful they chose to work the land. I'll be content playing hobby gardener on weekends.

As I rode along I noticed a shimmer at the base of the corn; standing water. In some places the ground was saturated mud and in other tracts several acres were in shallow pools of water, flooded from the heavy rains earlier in the week. Too much or too little rain can ruin the yield, if not the entire harvest. I can only hope the weather remains favorable and the water recedes. I'm rooting for the farmer.

I reached Kennard, population: 461, after an hour and twenty minutes of riding due east through rolling terrain of corn and farm structures. SR–234 made a right angle turn north through the downtown consisting of modest wood–framed houses dating back fifty years or more. Most were painted white with generous front porches not more than thirty feet from the road. Gathering places for people to sit outside and converse across the quiet street. The town had the lay back vibe going for it. The trees, mature and full provided ample shade and appeal to the properties.

In front of the few businesses the ground was covered in old asphalt but near the houses narrow sidewalks, broken and in the process of being reclaimed by the vegetation, held guard as did patches of gravel for car parking right up against the white stripe of the road. Potholes and standing water found sanctuary in the gravel. I rode in the middle of the lane because I could.

It would have been nice to talk to the people enjoying the morning from the shade of their porch but on this Saturday the porches were as vacant as the road. It was too nice not to be outside so I assumed everyone was working or out at one of the bigger towns looking for something to do. If I were not on the bike a tall glass of unsweetened tea on ice and a good book would have kept me on the porch.

A few blocks later I exited back into the waving green fields and into a mild headwind for two miles before flipping the cue sheet at the bend in the road. After the turn I was back on an eastern heading and looking at the third quad of the cue. I was happy to see the SAG was just another three miles ahead.

Pedaling at a comfortable pace I let the rustling of the corn sing to me as I breathed in the aroma of its new growth. Even when green the wide flat leaves hanging off the stalks create a wood textured sound as they brush and entangle together. It sounds course and rough and loud. It has a relaxing quality to it like the sound of water running over rocks, or the ocean crashing on the beach.

I rolled into the SAG happy. For the next fifteen minutes the routine I learned over the past thirty–six days was repeated in every detail. The lively conversations, the washing of hands, the taking turns topping off fluids, and enjoying the gastronomical spread Margaret prepared. Tracy was at this stop for a few minutes talking with Margaret and a few riders before she headed off in the direction of the hotel. Gone with a smile but not before she cheered on the late arrivers. I finished my grazing, checked my tires, and was back on the road.

Climbing over the rolling hills and enjoying the glide on the far side became the routine heading toward New Castle. I passed by more small farms, one on the right with a disc tilling attachment and an old dump truck sitting close to the road, a bright yellow backhoe parked on the grass next to the small weathered barn, and a stack of logs as large as telephone poles lay in the dirt out near the corn field. Disorder or logically organized, I could not tell.

I crossed over Duck Creek where the tree line intersected a dip in the road. I could feel the incline beyond as the effort required for keeping pace increased. The road meandered slightly left and right past rusting fenced corrals of small goats, large homesteads of earth–tone brick ranch designs, purposely planted evergreen trees, decades of attention and care evident under their multi–story tall branches and wide girth. Acres of deep green freshly mowed lawn filled in between the structures and corn providing the pleasant tell–tail smell of sour grass. It was eastern Indiana revealing itself for my enjoyment.

I approached the western edge of New Castle and was greeted by a cluster of industrial steel and brick buildings; some had been around since the boom of manufacturing. The old multi–pane window glass held in place with cracked and failing putty, the designs reminiscent of the aluminum and brass foundries I was familiar with back in New Jersey. In the background were the older buildings where men would sweat and physical labor drove production. The exterior paint long–faded revealed a rusty patina that told their age. In front the newer and better kept office space extended toward the road. Fresh paint and modern details suggested thriving office activities were happening inside.

I bumped over an old train crossing no longer providing service. Past Carter Lumber I rode the downhill on a generous shoulder that seemed to appear when needed. The small green New Castle sign stood to my right as I pedaled forward, traffic building. Over Big Blue River which wasn't really so big and across the busy intersection of SR–3. I was now into the throws of the community of New Castle, population: 17,780.

The plan was to go straight for the next twelve miles but road construction threw me and my companion riders a curve. Orange cones, detour signs, and plenty of construction activity were scattered across dozens of city blocks. Most of the work involved underground piping and utilities, creating some challenges for my skinny tires as they negotiated over the bits of dirt and loose gravel strewn across the road. I didn't count the number of turns but was thankful between the abundance of detour signage and having sight of other cyclists I was able to navigate through all of the disruption and make it safely through without incident. It also gave me something to mention in my journal to share with friends back home.

Besides the road crew markers, the CrossRoads team used good judgement and plenty of miniature orange flags and fluorescent paint to let the riders know the route had been evaluated and was safe for us to travel on. The attention to detail under Tracy's watch is amazing yet when executed with such skill it is almost undetectable. As if I never knew there was something I should be worried about. I like that, and right now I like it a whole lot.

I crossed over several more railroad tracks and by applying the appropriate safety crossing techniques they quickly faded. New Castle was much larger than expected, the historic business district dominated by brick and concrete showcasing Italianate, Classic Revival, and Commercial styles of architecture is well kept and inviting. It was named after a city in New York State located along the Hudson River and it's also the county seat for Henry County. This means the courthouse and a variety of other government buildings make up part of the urban landscape.

The road shoulder afforded to me at the entrance to town was swallowed up by sidewalks. I remained out in the road confined by the curbing and the steady flow of traffic. No one honked their horn and I had enough space to negotiate the drainage grates and roadway imperfections. All the congestion, construction detours, and urban experience were part of this great ride. Though I prefer the wide open and consistency in the directions I welcome the exposure to the unexpected.

New Castle was settled in 1822 and sits at an elevation of 1,070 feet above sea level. Its claim to fame is the New Castle Fieldhouse, the largest high school gymnasium in the world. The city is also home to the Indiana Basketball Hall of Fame. The Hall honors men and women associated with high school, college, and professional basketball in Indiana. The Hoosier's love their basketball. Some say they are fanatical about the sport.

Agriculture is the mainstay in the area but in the past it was a manufacturing center for the production of sheet iron and steel production, automobiles, caskets, clothing, bridges, pianos, furniture, handles, shovels, lathes, bricks, and flour. In the historic district the S. P. Jannings and Sons Handle Factory and the Coca–Cola

Bottling Building still stand as proud examples of the city's manufacturing past. And another tidbit of information you won't find in the tourism highlights is the population of inmates at the New Castle Correctional Facility. I don't know how many people call the place home but the facility just north of the city can accommodate up to 3,500.

The railroad crossing at mile 48.1 had all the makings of a bike hazard. The rails angled the pavement much the same as a merge lane would intersect. The asphalt, broken and missing large chunks leading right up against the rails were like bear paws ready to swipe the narrow bike tires right out from under an unprepared rider. No rubber mats or wooden boards were present to ease the transitions across the iron lines and it was easy to see how a slight bobble to the left could drop the front wheel down into the narrow void. Should that happen the bars would snap left, the rider would vault up and over the front wheel, and ground contact would be guaranteed. There would be no witnesses to the fall, just acres and acres of corn standing as their leaves rustle as if to applaud your efforts. I gave the corn no satisfaction.

Over the next nine miles leading into Hagerstown I crossed over Mud Run and Flatrock River, I rode past the Millstone, Batson, and Bat Run Drains, and then I pedaled over Symonds, Bear, Brick, and Nertle Creeks. Most were narrow trenches requiring the least of bridgework to cross. All had interesting names that caught my attention. I can only guess some of the names described geological features, others described creatures found nearby, and the remaining waterway monikers were a tribute to people with some connection to the area. There is plenty of time to think about the mundane and obscure as I pedal in the vicinity of fifteen miles an hour through the roadway sideshow of endless corn and telephone power poles.

Midway between New Castle and Hagerstown I passed a small sign for Wilbur Wright's birthplace and museum. An arrow pointed left three miles. A trio of power poles later I crossed South Wilbur Wright Road, the gateway to the historic landmark. It was just a simple intersection, a pair of stop signs controlling traffic approaching SR–38 with stands of corn on three corners and an old farmhouse to my right. In my mind I imagined the crude bicycles and airplanes the Wright Brothers had built. I wondered, besides the pavement and power poles, if the area looked much different on April 16, 1867 when Wilbur was born just up the road. And were either of the roads in existence at that time?

Around the bend and with increased attention on the road I came upon Hagerstown, a little village of 1,890 inhabitants, located in Jefferson Township on the eastern edge of Wayne County, Indiana. It was the last bit of the Hoosier state before rolling into Buckeye territory. And boy does this town have a lot of interesting things to offer. Maybe more than any I rode through yet.

Named after Hagerstown, Maryland, this little metro reminded me of Kennard for all of the white houses with their expansive covered front porches. Well preserved examples of ornate woodwork detail of crown molding, shake siding, and multiple layers of millwork. Several houses were equipped with fancy posts and handrails, and what some refer to as gingerbread garnishing. My attention was drawn to the gables and openings the architect had labored over in design and craftsmen faithfully executed the vision into a place for generations to call home. These homes were right out of a Norman Rockwell painting; appealing, inviting, and a welcome visual detour from the corn.

Hagerstown also reminded me of New Castle for the clean brickwork and attractive architecture I found in the business sector. The post office appeared to be cut limestone, sturdy in appearance, rectangular stone columns separating vertical expanses of glass, a balcony over the entry doors. The design was classic and symmetrical, a pair of engraved medallions were centered above west and east end windows, a wide set of stone steps, maybe sixty feet across, provided a pathway from sidewalk to the double doors. It looked like a modest and miniaturized version of what would be found in the financial district of New York City.

I also took note of a wall mural on a pharmacy building across from the post office. It was a painting of a young couple huddled over a small round table, two straws sharing a single beverage. The image was a mid–

century courtship captured by the artist; the colors bright, the scene happy. It was the only mural I found in the town that had plenty of space for more.

I passed places with interesting names. Places like Welliver's, now known as Willie & Red's Smorgasbord, and another place, The Old Mill, called out for a look in the window to see what was going on behind the brick façade.

On the corner of Perry Street I found the Main Street Antique Mall occupying the first floor of an Italianate style brick building framed with a cast iron storefront. This ornate and well–preserved three–story building is home to the historic Hagerstown I.O.O.F. Hall, the Independent Order of Odd Fellows.

The name begged for a measure of post ride investigation. I learned the organization was founded in Baltimore, Maryland by a Thomas Wildley on April 26th, 1819 and its roots trace back to 1700s England. The organization's purpose is to visit the sick, relieve the distressed, bury the dead, and educate the orphan. And though I never heard about them before, the I.O.O.F has more than six hundred thousand members attending more than ten thousand lodges in twenty–six countries.

As an early career engineer I've always been interested in the people who create the things that have made my life easier. I found in Hagerstown a story about a man who has impacted not only my life, but the life of everyone who has ever ridden in an automobile. Ralph Teetor, a well–known and respected inventor, born in Hagerstown, created a little device called cruise control. Only the steering wheel and car radio are better known.

What's more amazing is Teetor was blind, having lost his sight at an early age, yet he didn't let his lack of sight hinder his creativity. He founded a research and development company called TEDCO to further his ideas. Eventually the company would give birth to Tedco Toys, an education and science toy manufacturer that would continue to impact the lives of budding engineers and scientists.

If as a child you played with a gyroscope it probably came from Tedco Toys, the world's largest maker of those spinning devices. They have an interesting and extensive line of products covering just about everything of interest to the inquisitive mind. The company is located just four blocks south of Main Street and is run by Teetor's daughter Marjorie.

Abbott's Candy Store, founded by William C. Abbott in the early 1890s is a prime attraction in Hagerstown offering tours and viewing of the candy making process. It's even noted on the Indiana State maps. The pink and white trimmed sweet shop sits one block south of SR–38 between Plum and Perry Streets. Caramel is their specialty, but they also make a variety of chocolates and peanut brittle. Had I only known before I pedaled across Perry Street.

Art, science, architecture, and candy; this town checked all the boxes on my list of interesting things. And this is only the tip of what Hagerstown is about. I bet if I continued to look for more I'd never make it out of town.

And if I hadn't mentioned it yet, I did not learn all the granular details from the seat of the bike. Many would be discovered while reviewing my journals and the writings of fellow riders, and by researching countless websites about all of the places I rode through. I think the details add to the story and make it a better record of the experience. And when the time comes to retrace this cross country ride I will use what I have written as my travel companion. I hope it can serve others in the same capacity.

It had been an hour since the SAG so it was time to find a place for some relief. A few blocks later a convenience store answered my call and I was back on the bike pedaling through the tree lined residential extents of SR–38E, East Main Street, at least until I break back out into the open country.

I pedaled over the mild rolling climbs and the almost undetectable valleys. I had plenty of time to look around, to count power poles, and to stare at the digital displays of my bike computers and heart rate monitor.

I did it all with some cadence, just a quick glance, not wanting to lock my eyes on the odometer because when I did it would hold back on me as if I weren't moving at all.

My purpose was out in the fields, in the distance down the road where everything converges, the intersection of sky and ground together with the scent of life and the sound of the wind. Somehow I have to etch the experience deep into the recesses of my brain for future recall. Images properly filed away would become part of my mental box of photos to be sorted through and enjoyed whenever I wanted them.

I was closing in on twenty miles to the hotel; my rear was beginning to let me know I should give it a rest. I popped up off the seat more frequently and gave each hand a break from the bars, making sure to shake out the stiffness building up in my wrists and fingers. I flexed my shoulders and arched my back looking to release the accumulation of tension built up from riding in my biker pose. With traffic sparse and the pavement decent I paid as much attention to my body as it was calling for.

As I stretched I continued to look around and absorb. I crossed over Whitewater River then the creeks of Ocer, Martindale, and Morgan. I crossed an impressive span over the Greens Fork River, the widest waterway of the day, and on the other side of the bridge I discovered a small town of the same name. At an elevation of 1,010 feet and a population of 371, Greens Fork measures less than a thousand feet in any direction. It's a tidy, compact town with a family diner, a fire station, and a pair of churches; a United Methodist and a Christian church. On my right I passed Maple Street and a few hundred feet later I was deep into the corn once more.

Fifteen minutes later I made a right turn onto Centerville Road. A few of my peers had shot right past the heavily wooded corner and were now circling back thanks to the shouts from the group.

Just off the side of the road, the lower twelve feet of a forked tree trunk stood. Someone had carved a collection of animals and birds into the broken extents and hollows of the tree. It was quite impressive with an owl, fox, raccoon, squirrel, and a few other figures all watching us ride past.

The third quadrant of the cue sheet ended when I crossed over a rough set of railroad tracks. Though it was equipped with striped crossing gates designed to drop over the road when a train approaches, the equipment saw no action besides a few dozen bicycles and the occasional car.

I stopped just long enough to flip to the last quad and a smile immediately formed on my face. A Dairy Queen, number twenty–three since leaving Los Angeles to be precise, was just one mile ahead. I had to pedal my way up to the gravel entry but it was not much of a challenge.

With bikes parked our group wandered inside to find more riders still enjoying their DQ break. Greetings and playful banter were in full swing. Orders were placed and tables found, service was quick so we didn't have long to wait. Within minutes a grilled cheese sandwich and drink sat in front of me. The buttery golden toast activated my taste buds, the hot gooey American cheese burned just a bit, and I slowed my pace to enjoy it. I got up and ordered a medium soft–serve chocolate cone and then engaged in more conversation. No rush to get back on the bikes. We had less than an hour to pedal to the Holiday Inn.

When I mounted my bike both my belly and butt were happy, but my legs were not interested in pedaling. It took a bit of coaxing to hang with the other riders as we sailed the gentle slope after crossing over I–70.

On the outskirts of Centerville I found sidewalks extending out to the corn fields. The ribbon of concrete continued past small houses and into the downtown business center. As I pedaled over Crown Creek I couldn't help but feel conflicted. On one hand it was odd to see sidewalks so far out into the country, but on the other hand, it gave a welcome feel to this place 2,500 people call home.

The town is known as the "City of Arches" and their tagline, "Through the Archways of Time," is a reference to a series of events that started in the 1820s. Centerville's Main Street was once so busy the town leaders made a decision to narrow the street from one hundred to sixty–five feet. This created additional frontage for development and business expansion. Those with street front property built onto the front of their businesses and incorporated arches to allow access to the original properties behind.

Many of these arches built between 1823 and 1836 are in good repair and are central to Centerville's Archway Days held every August. The five important arches clustered around Main Street and Morton Avenue includes Backenstoes Archway, Dill Archway, Shortridge Archway, Lantz Archway, and Malone Archway.

Centerville is also home to Wayne County's original log courthouse. This is the only original log courthouse still standing in the old northwest territory. It had been relocated behind the Mansion House on the north side of Main Street between 1st and 2nd Streets from the defunct town of Salisbury which was a few miles east. The log courthouse is open during special city events and upon request.

Centerville has three places of worship including two Baptist and a Christian Church. On Main Street you'll find the Brown Jug Tavern, the U. S. Post Office, which has been operating since 1818, and the town library which still bears the scars from the War of 1873; a feud between Richmond and Centerville over the location of the county seat.

It seems the people of Centerville were not happy about Richmond becoming the county seat. The story goes something like this. When the new courthouse in Richmond was complete the books and records were to be transferred from the Centerville Courthouse. As the wagons were loaded and ready to leave they found the gates locked and chained with guards standing around them. The books were taken back into the courthouse to keep them secured. A guard from Richmond was stationed with the records to prevent the locals from taking them.

Someone got the bright idea to use *Black Betty,* the town cannon used to fire salutes on Independence Day to go on the offensive. The cannon was taken to the blacksmith shop, loaded with iron scraps, then wheeled down to the courthouse and pointed at the front door. They demanded the guard come out but when he refused they fired the cannon and blew the door off its hinges. When the locals rushed in the guard fled. The following day soldiers came in, the records moved to Richmond, and Centerville ceased to be the county seat.

The holes from the cannon shot can still be seen in the brick over the front door of what is now the Center Township Library. I'm sure it was a serious situation at the time but it seems funny looking back.

Centerville is 98.48 percent white, females outnumber males one hundred to eighty–four, the per capita income of the town is a paltry 15,526 dollars, and 6.7 percent of the population live below the poverty line. Not a town rich in ethnic diversity nor is it a boomtown for women looking for a man. In fact for women eighteen and older the women outnumber men one hundred to seventy–seven. If you are a guy looking for a woman Centerville may be your town.

I turned left onto Main Street and pedaled through historic buildings looming large along the route. I passed through a pleasant residential area, then I exited town a few blocks later. The section of highway connecting Centerville to Richmond was known as National Road, part of the first road built by the federal government, and for the first mile it continued to be flat and favorable. To my right, the edge of the road would alternate between curb and ample shoulder. Maybe ample was too optimistic, as it disappeared for long stretches without warning.

The curbs would bring me uncomfortably close to the edge of the auto lane with no room for error. I was extra alert in those sections. I had to be.

After I crossed Salisbury Road the worn pavement pitched upward and I began to labor my way up on the narrow shoulder between cars and sections of steel guardrail. When the railing ended I was passing by used car lots, sheds and pagoda's for sale, a rotation of quick marts and gas stations, fast food joints, and all of the other necessary businesses that backfill between towns. At the larger shopping plazas it was pawn shops, auto parts, chain pharmacy's, and box stores favoring the dollar variety.

Then I realized I was no longer on a two lane road. I was pinned between the curb and two lanes of building traffic hustling in both directions; a center lane for left turns across oncoming traffic was the only divide between opposing traffic. *When did this happen?*, I thought to myself.

The storm drains I swerved around were now coming at me every fifty yards, some with cracks parallel to my wheels that I needed to avoid. Conditions were going downhill in the final miles.

At least the scenery was improving. I crossed a long level concrete deck bridge over a no–name creek dividing a large expanse of green lawns; a well–manicured cemetery and park. The park turned out to be Earlham College but it was much more interesting and inviting than the business lots with cars entering and exiting the road in front of me.

The green lawns receded and I was heading over the East Fork Whitewater River. I was several stories about the water; the tree tops barely cleared the sides of the bridge. I now had to take back what I said earlier. This is by far the widest river I am crossing today.

On the far side of the bridge I saw what looked like a massive four–story stone castle. It was the new courthouse that replaced the one in Centerville as the county seat of Wayne County. If the people of Centerville could have seen this building they would never have put the match to their three pound cannon in 1873. The building was designed by James. W. McLaughlin of Cincinnati and it's recognized as one of the most notable buildings in the city.

I got my relief as I crossed 2nd Street, the road narrowed and became one–way east, traffic dissipated. When I rolled to a stop at 18th Street I had just three miles and series of lefts and rights to negotiate before getting off the bike for the day. The route was a series of rolling hills increasing in scale as I rode. The last stretch was back on the busy East Main Street, four lanes of fun and plenty of traffic. Near the hotel the lanes parted and a proper grass median filled the void. I saw the hotel and made the turn into the parking lot.

Happy, excited, relieved. I felt many things but nothing was as exciting as getting a special delivery from home. Inside the box were fresh–baked brownies made by my two daughters. It was a perfect way to end the day and to enjoy the Father's Day weekend.

I shared my spoils with my friends and soon the brownies were gone. But I still have the card they wrote me along with the memories from the day.

During route rap we watched a video of the Habitat for Humanity cross country cycle tour from Connecticut to San Francisco. Jordan Heitz, daughter of our tallest rider Mike, was in the video. She fell crossing a bridge and broke her elbow, but eventually continued. I knew how she felt; making it all the way is such a powerful force. Even being hurt, drained, sick, or plain worn out cannot stop you. The strength within you didn't know existed takes over and what only can be described as a miracle occurs. Then you look back at what you accomplished and you all but cry. The only way to properly understand the experience is to go through it. Words and pictures can only give a hint of the experience. It is an experience that happens within, a wonderful life altering experience. Many teared up; it was a moving video we were fortunate to see.

I did the usual post–ride chores and in my writing I captured the final thoughts about Richmond. The city sits at an elevation of 966 feet and hosts a population of 39,124. It was settled by the Quakers in 1806 and the highest point in Indiana, 1,257 feet, is nearby. You wouldn't notice the high point on the ridge if it weren't marked. It's pretty flat out in this part of the state.

Richmond has been known by many names including, the Mummy Capital of Indiana, the Lawn Mower Capital, and Rose City; each with an interesting story to support the moniker. The city is recognized as the location of the first projected motion picture on June 6, 1894. Charles Francis Jenkins filmed a vaudeville entertainer performing a dance and projected the movie onto a wall at his cousin's jewelry store. He later patented what he called the Phantoscope. And the world wrongly remembers Thomas Edison as the creator of motion pictures. Edison just made it popular.

For you cycling performance diehards I remembered to record the details from my bike computer before zeroing out the memory. I was in the seat for five hours forty–eight minutes averaging 14.4 miles per hour over the 84.03 miles. I topped out at 26.9 miles per hour. Not too fast, but still a solid performance. I'm not sure how much I'll benefit from recording this data, but I'll analyze it after the trip and make that determination. Good night Richmond. Tomorrow I cross into Ohio, my tenth state and the final century ride on this tour.

Day 37: Richmond to Marysville, Ohio (107 miles)

The morning welcomed us with temperatures in the mid–sixties, the sky was overcast but I figured it would break some time mid–morning. Once it did the temperatures would climb so making the most of the cloud cover would be important.

The cue sheet called for 103 miles but with detours, slight errors in the computer calibration, and maybe some excessive swerving thrown in on my part for good measure, the actual recorded distance would likely be a few miles higher. Along the route there would be 1,600 feet of climbing and the challenge of staying organized given the day's cue sheet was a full eight quadrants.

In the southwest you could ride for a hundred miles with just a pair of instructions, but not in Ohio. Little towns would come frequently, navigating around fields and farms would require close attention to the few street signs, which were supplemented by orange paint and tiny flag markers strategically placed by Tracy and her team. If you get off track here the local instructions would likely include looking for the biggest oak tree near a field of cows, or just over the big hill by the creek. You don't want to get lost in Ohio.

Exiting the hotel we briefly used Route 40 to make our way onto the back roads. A weed–filled ditch, both deep and wide, separated the crowned road from the weathered posts strung together with rusting wire fence. And beyond the fence stands of rugged shade trees and fields of wild–grass would fill in wherever proper crop fields could not.

The rolling aged tarmac was familiar to me. Along the edges it revealed several seasons of past applications of what is known as chip–seal; a thin spray of sticky tar covered with tiny shards of gray granite stone. It's most bike–friendly by mid–summer and it was at its prime for us today. If I rode on a fresh chip–sealed road in the spring the narrow tires would spit out the granite shards making it uncomfortably rough and easy to slip and fall. I might even cut a tire. It would be most treacherous at the edge of the road and in the intersections where the loose gravel accumulates. In the late summer the tar rises up and when warm it adheres itself to the tires making it sticky as a strip of fly paper. But if the tar is wet it becomes slick like ice.

On this Sunday morning the traffic was non–existent and riding where car tires smoothed the surface was a welcome opportunity. Loose gravel was present and extra caution was taken when transitioning from one road to the next. The distinct pinch and ping sound of gravel bits being forced out from under the tires could be heard up and down the line of bicycles. Less frequently I would hear the metallic sound that followed as a shard of rock ricocheted off a bike.

Woodside Drive led to Gravel Pit Road where an angled set of train tracks became the first obstacle to negotiate. Cyclist's maneuvered the rails in a snake–like fashion, first left then right to cross squarely to the rails. I took my turn, bounced over and continued on to the stop sign for the turn onto SR–121.

Most state crossings happened on a busier highway with a billboard sized sign. They also happened deeper into the ride. This morning less than three miles from the start, nearly twenty of us were taking turns posing and trading cameras in front of this small Ohio sign perched over the ditch, a stand of trees forming the backdrop. There would be nothing memorable, no grand river or cityscape, nothing except for the sign and our smiles.

Rider's took out their California beach sand and sprinkled just a bit to ward off any bad luck. To forget was to put your tires at risk of going flat later in the day. Superstitious or not, peer pressure would make you break out the tiny canister of sand and dust the ground with it if you didn't do it on your own. The stop lasted just a few minutes. The churn of riders leaving and arriving was interesting to watch because there was little space around the sign. It had the assembly line feel to it. Riders inched forward straddling their mounts, handing over cameras until their turn came and they were in front of the sign. A few clicks, then they moved again, eventually advancing to the role of picture taker.

I left Indiana behind with Betty, Kathy, Greg, and Geoff under the canopy of shade heading north into Preble County on New Paris Road. A few turns later we were in the village of New Paris, Ohio, population: 1,623. Besides corn, New Paris is known as the place where Benjamin Hanby wrote the Christmas carol *"Up On The House Top"* back in 1864. Lesser known is that Grayson L. Kirk, past president of Columbia University, advisor to the State Department, and a man instrumental in the formation of the United Nations, was briefly the principal of New Paris High School. The village was platted in 1817 and its name traces back to Paris, Kentucky.

In the center of Paris our route turned north. As we exited town we passed houses and business structures clustered close to the road. Their proximity allowed us a close view of the details. Their appearance was weathered and worn, and if buildings could be tired this is how I would describe the look. A few graceful turns later our group pedaled past a series of small grain storage tanks at a farming co–op and then an empty community baseball field came into view. Maybe later in the evening, people will come out, a game will be played, and it will be more like *The Field of Dreams* then a quiet square patch of dirt framed by grass and fencing. Beyond the ballfield were corn fields; with lots and lots of corn.

We continued on the quiet two–lanes of SR–121 for the next fourteen miles. I noticed we crossed back and forth over sections of the East Fork Whitewater River by way of the common and flat concrete structures. The road had a few kinks in it but mostly it was straight with long shallow climbs and downhills. The funny thing is I could feel the resistance of the climb but not the free–wheeling gravity assistance I would have hoped for as I dropped elevation. Maybe I was getting it, just couldn't appreciate it.

Along the expanses of corn, the power poles seemed much farther apart. It could have been an illusion, but I doubt it. Days before I remember paying attention to the spacing of the poles. It's not like I have a habit of studying them, it was more of a diversion of the mind; just something to do. But here in Ohio the spacing was definitely more. Maybe they save a few extra dollars per mile, maybe the wires are lighter. If I counted the number of poles in a mile I might have been able to estimate the distance and tell if I was right. But without the prior day's estimates, doing anything today would be meaningless. I decided to forget about the poles and look beyond for other things to ponder.

Hundreds of yards out to my left and right the contours of the ground were definitely more pronounced than the topology of the road. Farmers might prefer the ground flat, but they have no real reason to contour the earth in order to use it.

Building roads is a different story. High spots are shaved down and the dirt is pushed into the lower areas making the roads as level as cost and effort allow. It makes driving safer and more enjoyable. The cycling benefit is an easier day on the bike.

I remember the old road going to Las Vegas, New Mexico that paralleled the new highway. It tracked very closely with the extreme changes in the greater terrain. It was the road we cheered and cursed depending if we were struggling up or screaming down. The new highway, not two hundred feet away, had benefited from the current mindset that flatter is better. I would look over many times, especially when I was struggling in my low gears climbing in the heat, wishing I was on the flatter road. Today I was on the better road.

The quicker riders who started behind us began appearing in the mirror and then with a few bits of chatter passed by at just a tick more than the speed we were carrying. The recumbent bikes of Peter, Gary, Ben, and Hopper would make their way past, some paired up with others and some enjoying the day on their own. Gary and Hopper would glide by with a minimum of conversation but Peter would bring the party to you. It was always a pleasure for Peter to come into the riding circle. His booming voice married with his New Hampshire speak made you smile no matter the circumstances. He always spoke, he always laughed, and he always cared. Most days he talked about things like green Slime in the tires to prevent flats and his power plant and sawmill his boys back home kept running. He also talked about airplanes and his winter house in Ocala not more than an hour away from my home.

Other riders with a more serious bent sped past, heads down, the conversation limited to calls of "On your left!" and a few cryptic pace line instructions. They would disappear as fast as they approached, and chances are we would not see them again until the SAG or much later at the hotel. Some days I can appreciate riding fast, but most days I want to enjoy the ride. I don't want to be staring at the few inches between bike tires to get the most out of a slipstream. I can only focus like that if I am trying to outrace a storm.

We talked amongst ourselves up and down our little group as we rotated forward and back to improve the conversation. At times we would ride side to side but it would be brief, just to reposition in the line. It was comforting to have people who neither pressed you to go faster nor slowed your pace. We enjoyed the company but also had no obligation to speak just to entertain each other.

Rider's approaching became easy to identify, some with unique riding stances, others with their colorful style, some by size, and some like Gray because of his fenders. Paul had his baggy shorts, Dick rode with his knees pointing outward, and Kim always had Gordon in tow trying to keep up. We all had some unique visual cue to identify us to the rest of the group. It was important both to our safety and our socialization. It gave us some ground for conversation where none might have existed. It made us the group we would remember always as XC04.

We rode through New Madison, population: 847, which was platted in 1817 and named after James Madison, the fourth President of the United States. Like most small mid–western towns and villages, it conformed to the narrative of modest white houses and brick commercial buildings lining its downtown core. Leaving town a small soft–serve place call the Snack Shop caught my eye. It was always time for ice cream but having grown accustomed to regular stops at Dairy Queen plus the few unique places like Culver's Custards, this little roadside stop would not be part of my dairy fix. Not by choice, they just weren't open at eight thirty in the morning.

Our route continued through more rural expanses of corn where the speed limit topped out at fifty–five. I was hovering happily somewhere in the fifteen to seventeen mile per hour range. We passed signs for Hollansburg: population: 220 and Arcanum: population: 2,096. A few miles later we passed a small chicken farm and then approaching from the south we skirted by the eastern edge of Wayne Lakes, population: 696.

This area of west central Ohio is mostly flat with shallow river valleys, but Wayne Lakes has a series of gravel rock hill formations covering a thick limestone base. Some of these hills are steep for the area measuring as much as thirty to sixty feet above grade. In geologic terms these formations are referred to as kame (gravel hills) or esker (ridge of stratified sand and gravel). They are remnants of the glacier deposits during the last ice age. In the early settlement days this area was also known as the Hills of Judea. Surrounding the gravel deposits are peat bogs three to four feet thick.

Also common to the area, based on the Report of the Geological Survey of Columbus, Ohio dated 1878, are seven species of Oaks, Sugar Maple, Slippery Elm, Beech Black Walnut, Shagbark Hickory, Buckeye, Trembling Aspen, Mulberries, Flowering Dogwood, Crabapple, Honey Locust and Pawpaw. Back in Florida my knowledge of Oak trees was limited to Water, Live, and Laurel.

After rolling through the winding back roads over Dividing Branch, twice over Poplar Ditch, then McQuay Ditch, and Greenville Creek, we stopped briefly to flip the cue sheet. We continued over another span of Greenville Creek before crossing the wide Stillwater River into Covington, population: 2,590. We were at an elevation of 932 feet, in the township of Newberry located in Miami County, but more importantly, we were at our first of two SAG stops for the day.

The conversation this morning was about the enjoyable slight tail–crosswind out of the south–southwest helping to push us to the SAG and to some special treats Kathy provided. A surprise box of Cinnabuns and doughnuts covered the fold–out tables along with Margaret's standard spread, which was anything but standard. I was so excited to get a hunk of the gooey sweets I struggled to get my gloves off to sanitize my hands. There was plenty for everyone to enjoy.

We were now forty–two miles into the ride and no part of me was unhappy. I cleaned the last bit of sticky off my fingers then went back to forage on the other food. A half–banana, a few cups of Gatorade, and a Clif bar and I was ready to go burn off what I had consumed. The good thing about riding day after day is you can eat just about anything you want. I think I burned off the Cinnabun after an hour on the hills.

Covington was platted in 1816 and in the early days it went by the names of Friendship, Newberry, and Stillwater. Every October they celebrate the annual Fort Rowdy Gathering, a tribute to the village's origin as the fort of that name.

In 1989 there was a SITCOM television show by the name of "The People Next Door" which was set in Covington. The show about an imaginative cartoonist and his family was a dismal failure and was cancelled after just five episodes aired. The show starred Jeffery Jones whose more memorable credits include Edward Rooney in Ferris Bueller's Day Off and his co–star Mary Gross, best known for her appearances on "Saturday Night Live."

Coming into the town I thought it was a bit sketchy. The nicest place on High Street was the Moore Funeral Home but when I exited the SAG and began riding down Walnut Street I changed my opinion, in fact the farther I rode the nicer and more impressive it became. I still think High Street has some work to do but you folks on Walnut, you are all right. I'd hang with you on those front porches.

Leaving Covington proper I rode the narrow guardrail clad bridge across the Great Miami River, named for the Miami Native American people who lived in the area. The bridge had quite a bit of space between posts and the rails actually were wider than the road surface. I thought it was possible, but highly unlikely for a bicyclist to drop a wheel off the bridge surface, slip under the rail, and into the water some fifteen feet below. I just pedaled faster and focused on getting across to the other side.

In a little over an hour we disposed of the fourth quadrant instructions. At the stop sign for Paris Jackson Road cue sheets were flipped and our route tracked due north to St. Paris. The first few blocks of town were mostly cobble stone brick with asphalt used to bring it to full width. The homes were larger, nicer, and sat on well–manicured lots complete with mature shade trees trimmed by people who knew what they were doing. I like the look of the brick streets but they were rough on the body and the bike. It didn't take long and all of the brick was consumed by asphalt and the ride improved.

The downtown of St. Paris was lined with brick and limestone block buildings, well–kept like the homes leading in. As I approached Main Street, I noticed just under the roofline on one building the name "Buckeye Block." As I expanded my view I realized the brickwork was dimensional and ornate, the windows wrapped with spectacular stone details, and the cornice work was equally amazing. Not just on one building, but on all of them. If I hadn't looked up I would not have realized the architectural excellence. For a town of 2,038 people this was quite impressive.

Sitting at an elevation of 1,207 feet, St. Paris was 275 feet higher than the SAG stop in Covington. I realized I had done a fair amount of climbing in those twenty–five miles yet it didn't feel like I had. I pedaled a few blocks past Main Street, passing more impressive homes, porches large, steps wide, stone retaining walls pointed and proud. Beyond those homes, the lots increased in size while the houses became more modest. I was completely out of the town, nothing but rural road ahead.

We added Ron Atkinson and a few others to our company and quickly learned he was from St. Paris, Ohio. Shortly after we saw people ahead waving us down. It was a few of Ron's friends. They set up a refreshment stop for us with water, soda, cookies, and strawberries. As much as we enjoyed the food and drinks, it was the kindness they extended to us that we will remember. It was as if we were part of St. Paris like Ron. At least they made me feel a connection.

About ten miles farther down the road more friends of Ron had a table with slices of watermelon waiting for us under the shade trees. Several young children with balloons were yelling for us to stop, and even though we weren't hungry, we could not pass by without thanking them for their efforts.

I did find room for a slice, and the kids had us all signing our autographs on special cards they made to commemorate the event. I signed each one and added a smile face as well. What a day it was. As I left more riders were arriving. They were treated like celebrities too and did their part signing and thanking the kids who did so much for us.

More climbing balanced with satisfying glides down smooth grades entertained and added to the quality of the day's ride. The countryside was amazing, the corn ever–present. It was good to have a group to navigate with because the turns were many, the signs few and well–hidden, and my attention was focused on the beauty around me. I followed the group over the train tracks called out on the cue sheet. The routine was well rehearsed and we moved on without incident. Those tracks were pretty nasty, there were boards against the rails, big chunks of wood missing, and what was there was weathered and rotted.

The water crossings continued, some hidden by trees and overgrowth, others clearly visible. In order they were Nettle Creek, Anderson Creek, and then the Mad River. I could imagine it being some wild rushing rapid filled flow but it was actually quite tame and more accurately described as a stream.

I turned onto SR–296 and the SAG came into view. There were only two hours or thirty miles remaining in the ride so I was able to enjoy the time there sharing in the banter with everyone. The talk was about the two mini–SAG's hosted by Ron's friends and of the fun everyone was having. It was a good day. I kept thinking and saying it out load. I don't say it often on a long ride, and definitely not on a normal century, but today it was.

There were no proper facilities at the SAG but there was plenty of natural cover across the road. I took my turn answering nature's call then regrouped with my peers and began chipping away at the final few quads on the cue sheet. We crossed another rough set of train tracks that paralleled the Simon Kenton Trail, a paved and gravel bike trail part of the Miami Valley Trails System. Then we crossed an unnamed ditch followed by Kings Creek before jogging over SR–68. A few miles later we turned north again and ran parallel with a huge expanse of Soy. I was beginning to think they grew nothing besides corn out here but they do have some diversity in crops. Soy was short enough you could see way beyond the field edges. It didn't rustle or make noise like the corn but it did show the wave motions from the wind like a green body of water. And like the corn, if you were at the end of a row you could see the lines of green all tidy and straight.

We crossed Main Street in the village of Woodstock, population: 312 and kept on going east. On the corner was a small convenience store, bags of ice in outside coolers, and a small overhang to grab some shade if needed. Two corners had brick buildings; one was the Woodstock Bar & Grill and the other was the Woodstock Municipal Building. The remaining corner was a vacant grass lot.

The last twenty miles, Betty, Geoff, Greg and I rode together, talking about the ride, the hospitality of Ron's friends, and a new dessert combination where a slice of strawberry is placed on an open–face Oreo cookie. It may sound strange, but Oreos and strawberries are a wonderful treat.

I was now in the seventh quad of the cue and getting pretty close to ten miles remaining. Three Mile Creek passed beneath us as did Buck Run. We continued riding the rural two–lane until the stoplight at Route 4. As we crossed with the green a small sign for Marysville marked the edge of our destination. Cornfields stood to the right, a large water tower nestled in the middle of the green. Residential expansion was to our left, mostly ranch–style homes on acreage, lawns cut and trees trimmed. Evidence of the city could be found in the storm drains twenty feet off the road, in the swales and the fire hydrants standing guard close by dressed in blue with red removable caps.

The speed limit was twenty–five but it was still more than I could muster. The painted stripe marked the edge of the weed and gravel but as shoulders go this provided a safe way out should someone give me reason to exit the pavement. A bit farther up on the left was a white rail fence surrounding a small pond and a more welcoming sign for Marysville with the tag line, "Where the Grass is Greener." More fenced ponds and appealing landscape continued as we followed Collins Avenue.

We made the left onto Maple Street at the Corner Deli then the right onto Fifth Street. It was tight in traffic but I could see the callout for Dairy Queen at the bottom of the cue. Approaching the *Y* intersection I had the hotel option to the left and the Dairy Queen to the right. It was no decision at all. I followed the line of cyclists to get some ice cream. It was DQ number twenty–four but I missed a few of them along the way. We talked until the ice cream was gone and then made our way to the hotel a mile farther up on Delaware Avenue.

Dinner would be a free night and breakfast would be a trip to Bob Evans on the far side of US–33. After cleaning my bike and showering I was on duty for laundry, something Kathy and I decided early on in the tour we would share. The good thing is it cut the chore in half and it was easy to tell our clothes apart. You didn't want someone else wearing your underwear do you?

The Amherst was a two building configuration with the laundry near the breezeway. The line was not too long, mostly the fast riders who were taking advantage of their early arrival. I put my name on the list and decided to hang around and talk with those in front of me. About two hours later and with this chore out of the way I prepped my gear for the ride to Wooster. I wrote all of the journal entries and filled out a few post cards. Then I realized I had lost an hour as I was now on Eastern Standard Time once more.

I went out for dinner with a couple of riders and then back at the hotel I talked with Clark about his day. It was much longer than mine. Not everyone was moving as quickly so he was on the road until the last of the riders rolled into the hotel. I had covered 107 miles in seven hours five minutes which is pretty close to 15.3 miles per hour. Not fast, but respectable considering when I first started training I was happy to average fourteen miles an hour on a ten mile ride. I topped out at thirty–one miles per hour on the downhills. It was another fantastic day on the bike thanks to a cold front holding temperatures down in the low seventies. Tomorrow we'll ride almost as far, but the climbing will be nearly three thousand feet, twice what we had today. Fingers crossed for more of the same weather and luck.

Before turning the page on Marysville I recorded some of the more interesting facts about the city located twenty miles northwest of Columbus. From 1990 to 2000, the population of Marysville expanded by a staggering sixty–five percent and the census report recorded 15,942 were then living within its borders. Today the population is estimated to be more than eighteen thousand.

The city enjoys a healthy economy anchored by companies including Honda Motors, which builds motorcycles and the popular Accord compact autos at two manufacturing facilities, and the Scotts Miracle–Gro Company, the largest producer in the world of horticulture products. Two other notable operations include food manufacturer, Nestle, which has an R & D center here, and tire and rubber company, Goodyear.

The racial makeup for Marysville is 90.4 percent White, 4.5 percent African American, 2.3 percent Asian, with all other races reporting less than one percent each. There are nearly three women for every two men in the city which is consistent with other towns I pedaled through over the past few days. The per capita income is more than twenty–three thousand dollars and less than six percent live below the poverty line.

The city holds many annual events including the All Ohio Balloon Festival in August and the Covered Bridge Festival in September. For those wanting to see extraordinary architecture, Marysville has examples of Frank Lloyd Wright's Prairie style, Victorian, Classic, Italianate, Dutch Colonial Revival, American Foursquare, and others sprinkled throughout the city. There are also plenty of parks and leisure options to explore in Marysville. And as the sign says coming into town, "Welcome to Marysville, where the grass is greener."

Day 38: Marysville to Wooster (100 miles)

Having moved the clocks forward last night the alarm blared uncomfortably early. Clark was first into the shower and then it was my turn to wash off the night and put on the riding gear. First stop was Bob Evans for breakfast. It would have been a bit far to walk so with a small ensemble of riders I rode my bike retracing the route under US–33 until the restaurant came into view.

Coffee was the first thing I looked for followed by what I call the businessmen's breakfast consisting of two eggs over medium, toast, hash browns, and bacon. It's hard to go wrong with this combination and while filling, it still allows me to ride reasonably well through the morning hours. I was done eating minutes after the plate was set in front of me. A second cup of black coffee washed down the last traces of breakfast. Then I was back on the bike to sweep the hotel room making sure all of my personal items were accounted for and properly stowed.

After staging bags and pumping tires we stood waiting for Tracy to set the day in motion. On her call, rider's signed out and left the parking lot in roughly groups of three's and fours. The tandems had a pretty good day yesterday riding most of the distance far in front of me. With the increased elevation today I expect to see more of the Kahrl's and the Reeve's. I also expect to see Kathy riding closer to my usual cycling mates.

We set out for another near–century day under cloudy skies and temperatures in the low sixties. Our traveling road show would exit the city toward the northeast into more of the hilly and rural terrain we experienced coming into Marysville.

I was released mid–pack and quickly set to work warming up my legs. Betty was in her usual forward position and in front of her were Geoff, Greg, and Lynn. Behind me were several riders looking to jockey their way forward. Not a mile out from the hotel and people are getting antsy to move farther up through the pack. They'd have to pace themselves with the early Monday morning traffic.

US–36 was a narrow weathered two–lane divided only by faded yellow striping. The shoulder was crumbing just a foot off the white line, deep cracks filled with tar, scribbled randomly across the road. In some places big chunks of asphalt were broken away creating a hazard if you strayed to the right of the white paint. The grassy shoulder was relatively flat and I was sure if I needed to, I could safely ride off the pavement.

Traffic was busy in both directions. I had one eye in the mirror and one on the action directly ahead. There would be little time for looking around until I got farther out from Marysville. Steel guardrail emerged from the ground and extended along the sides of an old concrete deck bridge spanning an unnamed creek. I stayed right on the paint to avoid the unfriendly shoulder near the railing, cars yielding and giving us room was a much appreciated gesture. Ahead I could see rider's turning left having found Mackan Road. I slowed behind Betty and one by one we timed our turn as traffic allowed.

After joining Mackan we had the road to ourselves. It was amazing how different it felt and how quickly the speed demons seized the opportunity to rocket past. Pat, Gene, Kim, and Gordon and others were the first to go by. Then it was Peter on his recumbent leading a few others.

We alternated between rights and lefts, crossing low boggy flats and climbing up and over the rolling ground between cornfields and stands of trees. The roads would dead end at a stop sign and *T* as described on the cue, and we'd turn according to the directions or at times rely on the riders ahead to guide us. We crossed drainage ditches and saw more of those guardrails rise up out of the ground and conform to the road keeping us from riding off into the wet ground a few feet below.

Barbed wire strung between wooden posts defined the boundaries of farms and fields. Everything was green unless it was brown, or wet. Barns and structures painted white were fading and weathered, but they had a postcard quality to them.

Some of the hills were steep, at least compared to what we had seen recently. My legs were coming around but it was still work to turn the pedals and keep pace.

The small signs marking the roads were often hidden behind low hanging tree branches or bushes making the turns tricky to find. Mistaking a *right* for a *left* on the instructions would also send you well out of your way.

After about ten miles, we were hit with an unexpected rain shower that would be with us for the next two hours. I did not have my rain jacket in my bike bag, so I became wet, cold, and uncomfortable. About the only thing you could do to stay warm was to pedal faster and ride harder, which we did.

We shot down a hill and scrubbed off all of our speed for the stop sign at SR–257. My wet brakes decided to squeal in protest until I planted my foot on the ground and checked to see if it was clear to cross. We continued on over the Scioto River on a double span iron arched truss bridge, and then north parallel with the river. The road here was much smoother. It was a hot tar asphalt blend, not the chip–seal we just came off of. A sharp corner turned us and we were now tracking east.

The wet roads began spitting a thin spray onto the lower part of my bike and onto my legs. Bits of sand and dirt and whatever else was on the road had been transferred to me and the bike. I was not alone in this as I could see the spray coming off of the rider's wheels in front of me. Betty's rear tire put out a spray several feet high.

It never rained hard and I never had to worry about puddles, but it was a consistently pissy kind of rain, a cold rain where the chill penetrated deep under my skin. It was a rain I would be obligated to respond to later at the hotel. A good washing of the bike, a sink cleanse of my riding outfit, and plenty of newspaper to soak the dampness out of my riding shoes. It was extra work but it is part of the experience.

The first signs of traffic returned as did the density of houses and other structures. Soon we were in the outer extents of Delaware, a fairly large city with a population estimated at 29,047. We rode with traffic on Central, past Troy Road, and then dipped underneath a rusting steel train bridge with a clearance of twelve feet seven inches marked on a yellow cautionary sign.

Densely packed two story homes, all in excellent condition and likely built before World War II, were clustered under shade trees. The curbing was erratic and crumbled, drainage grates and potholes needed to be avoided. The road itself was wet and slick. Traffic lights were frequent as were hydrants and parking meters.

The road bumped up, then dropped down for a long glide into a widened exchange carrying us under the busy Columbus Pike and across the Olentangy River. We crossed over dozens of streets through more pre–war residential neighborhoods, over train tracks, and through older commercial zones. It was like a high–speed movie unfolding, accelerated by the traffic, the rain, and the need to avoid all of the obstacles the city put before us.

I was riding through the Historic Northwest Neighborhood, which boasts more than five hundred homes and carriage houses listed on the National Register of Historic Places. Inclusion in the registry means each house is worthy of preservation for local, state, and national significance in American history and architecture. And I was wrong about the timing of construction. My post–ride research revealed the houses dated back much farther. The oldest built in 1826, is a Federal style and there are early examples of Craftsman and French Eclectic styles dating back to 1915 and 1930 respectively.

The area includes Gothic Revival, Italianate, Second Empire, Folk Victorian, Stick, Queen Anne, Richardsonian Romanesque, Shingle, Prairie, Mission Tudor, and Colonial Revival styles. I'm a fan of architecture but my design vocabulary is nowhere near as broad as the list of styles identified in this neighborhood alone. If I could take another loop through maybe I'd spend more time looking at the houses and not so much on the faults in the right of way.

We came to a stop at another busy intersection. At the green we hustled with traffic onto the four–lane of Williams and then navigated traffic to position ourselves in the left lane to turn onto RT–521. Not everyone was successful at moving gracefully over but they all made it and we waited again for a car to trip the turn light. Once through the light the intensity dialed back down and I was looking to turn to the next quadrant of the cue sheet.

Many of the roads were rural so paint striping was unnecessary. Few cars travel the roads and as narrow as they were, adding a stripe might have made the lane narrower than a car. Besides it takes a lot of paint to get good coverage and few would fault the little townships for being good stewards of the people's money. I will admit some sections of the roads were approaching the width of private drives but without traffic to share it with I could only speculate.

Surrounded by farm fields and greenery I passed under yet another concrete train overpass. It was unusually narrow hugging tight to the road. The sidewalls were old and crumbling, overspray of graffiti randomly applied. It was not marked with any clearance heights but it was not very tall. As I approached I thought I could reach up and touch the underside but as I sailed through the narrow structure I realized my estimate was a bit off.

There would be more small creeks like Big Run and West Branch Alum to ramble over, farms to observe, and the sound of rain to be heard as it pelted the corn. The roads bent to conform to the terrain and property boundaries, over the creeks and around stands of trees.

We rode the likes of Bowtown and Old State where fences and mailboxes encroached into the right of way and huge trees, with roots breaking through the pavement, stood uncomfortably close. There were cars parked in the grass just feet off the road, and just three paces back, small, mostly white houses crowded in. Around a right hand bend was a large arched roof barn covered in rusting silver tin. The sound of rain rhythmically tapping its surface resonated with a soft cymbal quality.

We moved beneath thick canopies of shade trees casting shadows over the road and then we were expelled into the open, back in contact with the rain and the view of corn reaching outward a thousand feet to our left and right. Where the road ran straight beyond its dips and heaves in the mid–range, it almost disappeared in the distance, getting lost in the perspective and haze of the rain. Our route turned right onto SR–229, the corner marked with waist–high white laced flowering weeds and a few small abandoned structures decomposing under the trees.

The condition of the roads improved but the climbing became more noticeable. Long straight sections only accentuated the elevation changes and I did not like having the inclined view in front of me. At least the rain was letting up.

By the time I crossed up and over US–71 the rain dissipated and I started to dry out. Not having to deal with the rain, my frame of mind was shifting and I was beginning to accept, but still not yet enjoy tackling the steeper grades. And it was a good thing too. In route rap the night before we talked about the climbing and we understood most of the 2,850 feet would come in the last thirty miles.

By the time we arrived at the SAG in the village of Marengo, population: 342, the roads were mostly dry and only my feet were damp. I checked my tires and picked little bits of stone from the treads. There were lots of cuts and tread wear but nothing to impede my ride. After topping off with snacks and fluids I mounted my bike and rode through the rest of the village.

At the corner I stopped briefly to flip my cue sheet then hopped back on the saddle pedaling quickly to rejoin the group. It's amazing how far behind I could fall even when stopping for just a minute. It did feel good to get up off the saddle and push the pedals. It felt good to know I had the strength to catch up.

Big Walnut and Mill Creek came and went; we passed soy fields and a few large cattle farms. In a field to the right was an industrial grain elevator, the largest I'd seen in days. The round squatty cylinders connected by a maze of piping stood oddly in the middle of a field. As I continued to pedal closer I realized it was part of an even bigger commercial agricultural operation right along the road. Huge storage barns and smaller silos stood between me and the elevator, a fleet of pickup trucks and heavy equipment sat idle in the gravel lot.

The farther I rode the more I noticed the change in the farming preferences. Soy beans were becoming the norm over corn. I also notice the trees were covering more ground. The tree lines and clusters were growing into forested tracts of land. After climbing a stretch of rollers I followed the line of bikes down the cascading hills past an old red barn perched up on a hill overlooking the corn and soy separated by the road. Ahead the turn onto 314 North where another set of hills stair–stepped up into the distance.

This section of the ride, even with the long straights teasing with hills, was enjoyable. The wooded canopy let light flicker through the leaves and it was peaceful and relatively traffic free. There were dips in the road so deep I could not see the bottom until I was close. The illusion of perspective made even the shallow drops look deep. There was a stretch of road beyond Prospect Mt. Vernon where it climbed straight for over a mile. I dropped a few gears and scrubbed off some speed. Even after it flattened back out it still felt like I was climbing. It could have been the distant hills holding my attention, confusing and frustrating, but never out of sight.

More changes came with every turn. The road bent around the hills, each one larger and more sculpted by the mile. On a sharp downhill we sailed by a pasture of grazing horses, the ground heaving and ripped creating long narrow trenches as if a big claw had contoured them. The corn and soy fields were no longer smooth rolling expanses. They had transformed. There were large swells in the middle of the fields rising up and other areas plunging down like a roller coaster. It was quite interesting to see but the changes extended to the road I was on.

On a curved section of road I crossed over the Kokosing River into Chesterville, a village of just less than two hundred in Morrow County. Near the corner for East Sandusky Street stood a blue wooden structure painted with red and white bands around the upper floor. Gaudy it was, but Chesterville likely has no ordinance against it. And based on the condition of the other buildings standing in its proximity, the patriotic structure actually was better maintained.

Ten miles later we reached the fringes of Fredericktown, population: 2,454. Stately old homes sat on big lots, the trees full and balanced. Overall the village made a positive impression, one of people who cared for their homes and their neighbors. Over the next few blocks the road inclined up and we found Main Street, our turn to the left.

The main drag was more of a working zone, rough and ragged in need of a facelift. It was not as nice as what we first saw entering town. Fortunately the road pitched downward giving us a boost past the rows of brick and framed buildings, around an odd jog in the pavement past grain silos that appeared to be right in the middle of where the road should have been. Named after Frederick, Maryland, the most notable person from the village is an actor named Luke Perry.

This part of Ohio is Amish country, and exiting Fredericktown I caught up to a horse and buggy. I followed it for a quarter–mile, missing the fresh road apples the horse dropped on the pavement.

As I came up alongside the buggy, I saw a young father, his wife, and a little girl about three years old. I spoke briefly to the man to make sure I could pass by the horse without spooking him. He gave me the nod to go ahead. Soon the horse and buggy were in the distance.

I wondered about the simple yet hard life the Amish pursue. Everything is by way of nature, physical labor or animal power. Some may say they are lucky to be so happy with so little, but I believe they have much more than material things we accumulate; it's about family, friends, beliefs, and character. In the Amish community, these things seldom change, which may explain how they are able to sustain their lifestyle from one generation to the next.

There were fields of corn planted close to the road towering over my head. The corn created a green canyon staying with us as we meandered along Ankneytown Road over Isaacs Run, though heavily wooded areas and over Toby Run.

After the sixty mile mark the ground folded up on both sides. The farms and fields elevated up and we remained in what was becoming the valley floor. We were climbing but not as quickly as the land mass to the right. It was a small mountain standing not much more than two hundred feet.

As we pedaled the road cut into the left side of the ridge. We were now looking down at the valley floor some forty feet below with the wooded range getting taller on the south side. Farther up we passed an abandoned framed house, windows missing, paint faded, leaving only a whitewash memory on the planks. It was partially covered by tall weeds and tree branches, not sure if it wanted to be seen. A few scattered ranch homes and metal buildings dotted the hills leading into the village of Butler, population: 925.

The site was settled because of the fertile ground and abundance of wild game, but before adopting the name Butler, the area was known to the Delaware Indians as Helltown. If you have time to stop and eat there are three places on South Main Street including Whiffletree, Ducky's Pub & Grill, and the Five Points Drive–In. With the SAG just another thirty minutes up the road I'm inclined to see what Margaret has in store for us instead of pulling up a seat and weighing myself down before the real climbing begins.

I rounded a few corners, crossed over Smoky Run and near the bottom of a fast descent I found the turn for Butler Newville. This road was well–used, patchy in places, potholes in others. It followed the contours of the stream under heavy cover of tall shade trees. The road bucked and turned, there were few cars or trucks to worry about.

On Bunker Hill we exited to the left and climbed our way up the winding trail, alongside the forested hills to our left, corn in the lower valley to our right. Deer crossed the road ahead, leaping out of the field and disappearing into the cover of the heavy underbrush. A sign showed tight turns ahead and a speed limit of fifteen miles an hour. If it weren't for the incline I might actually have a chance at speeding. Around the narrow turns a section of guardrail was strategically placed to keep cars from dropping down into the corn. Over Possum Run we rode and then made the right to rejoin SR–95. The sun had been ducking in and out of the passing clouds for the better part of an hour, a white haze still hung close to the horizon.

This section of road was so heavily covered it appeared dark through my sunglasses. I thought about pulling them off but then the trees would fold back and the light would find its way to the road. Miles of trees, the occasional light breaking through, all the while we were climbing. Climbing steadily up long inclines with limited shoulders and increasing traffic passing at speed just two feet off my left. A sign for Pleasant Hill Lake Park stood by the road.

I could hear the whine of the tires getting louder, the pitch higher as they approached. I'd check the mirror but I didn't need to. The sound told me what I needed to know; how far back, how fast, if it were a car or a truck. Under the trees the sound was more intense, it echoed, and was more dramatic. The big trucks grunted and bellowed, their diesel engines blared loudly over the tire whine. In the last few seconds the volume would peak, and then a rush of wind and dust buffeted the bike as the vehicle passed. In its wake the air would be sucked back in filling the void behind it. Not quite as strong at the passing blast of air but more dangerous. The wake of large trucks could pull you into the lane and into the path of trailing vehicles. You had to be ready to compensate, you didn't want to be surprised.

After working our way up we finally enjoyed a healthy downhill treat before crossing over the bridge spanning Black Fork Mohican River and climbing the last thousand feet to the SAG. A few blocks south was the village of Perrysville, population: 780. It's a popular location for camping, canoeing, and eco–tourism but I would not be exploring any of it today.

My reward was Margaret's cakey treats and fresh fruit. I ate half a banana and put another half in my jersey pocket along with another Clif bar. Other riders were stocking up on *Goo* and a variety of energy boosters. Honey and vanilla flavors seemed to be pretty popular. Gatorade was a must; a few salt tablets were dug out of the bag and washed down to avoid muscle cramping.

The unknown of the last twenty miles was both concerning and exhilarating. We hadn't climbed this much since the tough ride to Kirksville. As more riders came into the SAG we assembled our band and made final adjustments to leave. A few last bits of chatter and well–wishes and we were off to Wooster.

Exiting the SAG we continued on SR–95. It was a straight, steep climb just shy of a mile to the top. A broken shoulder was our path, the occasional guardrail sat just beyond. The ground to the right pitched upward covered with grass and a few houses cutting into the grade, basements exposed only on the road side. The left side of the SR–95 was more erratic. In places the forest rose up, and in others, nothing but the tops of trees beyond the guardrail.

Pedaling was slow and labored. It was even steeper than what we had covered this morning. It was also noticeably warmer. I wasn't sure if it was getting hot or if my effort to climb was heating me up. Regardless, the sweat dripped from my brow and down my back. The air was heavy, the sky blue above, patches of clouds scattered about. There was no shade on the climb, the heat radiated off the asphalt; the slight breeze at my back did little to help. Between the sounds of passing cars I heard only the mechanical objections of my bike. Creaking and straining as my feet pushed the pedals stressing the chain to turn the rear gears. I was breathing heavy and my pulse was soaring. I thought to myself, *This is work!*

A few riders stopped to rest on the climb. I've done it before, but while it gives you the momentary relief, getting clipped back into the pedals on a steep climb is difficult. It also steals away more energy then what would have been used if I didn't stop. I kept my head down and moved forward at a rather slow tempo.

As our line of bikes crested the hill we saw before us a remarkable downhill run. It was nearly straight, stair–stepping down and much longer than the climb. We flew past freshly cut fields, round bales of hay scattered randomly waiting to be collected. I shifted into my tallest gear but it wasn't enough to keep up with my speed. I did what everyone else was doing and just relaxed enjoying the glide. The fast moving wind dried the sweat providing a cooling effect. This was the payoff and I sailed well beyond thirty miles an hour around and down a slight bend until rumble strips and a stop sign reigned me in.

Across the intersection were road crews and detour signs. Then the questions came to my mind, "Has CrossRoads checked and marked the safest route? Is it better to follow the detour or can we continue through?" We saw riders ahead of us beyond the barriers so we followed. The road crews did not try to stop us and soon we were rolling over Honey Creek, climbing and descending one rippled mass after another.

The hills blocked the wind making it very uncomfortable on the slow climbs, but the downhills were fast, long, and sufficient to recover for the next effort. Over and over, climbing as much as twelve percent grades and descending down their twin. The views were spectacular from the top of each hill. Nothing but cornfields, cut hay, and trees against the nearly white horizon.

I passed a sign for McKay then rolled to a stop at the crossroads of SR–60 with the rest of the group. We angled up and over SR–60 past a magnificent log cabin and began yet another climb. Part way up a yellow sign, a symbol of a horse and buggy painted in black was just beyond the ditch. Near the top, bearded men in matching uniforms were cutting logs into finished lumber at a post–and–beam operation called Hochstetler Milling. More hills were climbed, a small cemetery followed by simple farmhouses filled in the greenery providing something besides the natural scenery to look at.

Another sign, this one of a box truck on a downward triangle let us know we were in for a high speed descent. We zoomed into the unincorporated area of Mohicanville and out the other side. We were fast until the road bent up requiring effort on our part to move forward. It was beginning to wear on me. The hills just didn't seem to end. I began checking my odometer more frequently.

We continued a downhill run over the Mohican River and Muddy Fork before climbing past another horse and buggy sign followed by a sign letting us know we were leaving Ashland and entering Wayne County. Close to the road between a tiny farmhouse and barn was a young Amish boy busy hanging a "bunnies for sale" sign. We rode through the unincorporated area of Funk, descending past the Funk Country Store. A few bikes were at the store as we went by but that didn't sway us to stop. We would learn later not stopping was a blunder on our part. Phil and Barb described for us at dinner an eclectic shop full of antiques, limited groceries, a display case full of assorted candies, and an ice cream freezer also full of cool treats. A trip back in time to the '30s or '40s Phil added. They talked to the owner about a fold–up scooter on display in the window. It was manufactured during World War II and used by the owner's disabled daughter for several years after. Old and well–used it still ran.

We crossed Kiser Ditch and the wide marshy flats of the Funk Bottoms Wildlife Area. From here we enjoyed more bike–friendly roads to carry us the final eight miles to the western edge of Wooster. I was tired but appreciating the gentle rolling and smooth road. At SR–3 I paused for the light then crossed over. Several more quick directional changes noted on the cue sheet followed. There were a few bolded instructions about railroad tracks and merging traffic, but they were all quickly dealt with and we arrived at the Amerihost Inn, our home for the night after logging a full hundred miles. It was an unexpected *century* added to the list of milestones defining this trip. I endured seven hours two minutes in the saddle averaging 14.3 miles per hour with a maximum speed of 36.2. These were the last bits of cycling statistics that I would enter into my notebook before clearing the bike computer memory in preparation for tomorrow's ride. I would wash my bike and then step into the shower in my cycling gear to wash the morning road grit away. Some might call it lazy but I'm leaning toward efficiency.

The temperature peaked at seventy–three degrees by mid–afternoon and the sky never did fully burn off the haze. To be honest it felt much hotter pedaling on the hills but it sure was humid. Back in street clothes I felt better; I could feel the slight breeze. I walked up the busy road to find postcards. In an old store full of local flare I found what I needed and put the cards along with three little tea cups on the counter by the register. The cups were travel keepsakes for my wife and daughters. Each cup had their middle name written on them. And before the inevitable question of why not their first name, I have an explanation. It's more common to find Joan, and Joy, and Marie, than it is to find Donna, Nicole, and Janel. It was that simple and I wanted consistency. Besides their middle names are as beautiful as their first, and as beautiful as they are to me. See, I said it was simple.

Dinner was full of discussion about the agony of the climbs, but most of the emphasis was on the excitement of the free–wheeling downhills. Our group had its speed demons and today they had the opportunity to fly. With bellies full we disbursed into smaller groups and then eventually back to our rooms to prepare for tomorrow's ride to Niles. Clark and I talked about the day and he read to me his installment from this day a year earlier. It was always good to get his perspective of the ride. Though the weather was different, mostly it was hotter and windier; his experience helped me to better appreciate the journey I was undertaking.

Wooster is a city of more than twenty–five thousand people and they are picky about how you pronounce the name. It's "WUHS–tuhr" not "WOO–ster."

The city sits at an elevation of 950 feet above sea level located on the banks of Killbuck Creek. It was named for Gen. David Wooster, a high ranking general in the Revolutionary War who was mortally wounded in the Battle of Ridgefield while trying to stop a British advance.

It's home to several corporate headquarters spanning the food, industrial, and automotive markets. And until the end of 2003, Wooster was also home to the corporate headquarters of Rubbermaid. It was the largest employer of 1,400 at the time when it closed and moved to Atlanta, Georgia as part of the acquisition and consolidation process when Newell bought Rubbermaid. A sad ending to a company first founded in Wooster back in 1920 as Wooster Rubber, the maker of toy balloons.

Later in the evening the clouds moved in, stealing what little sun remained. The local news reported scattered showers throughout the area, but the temperatures remained in the low seventies even after dark. When the lights finally went out sleep came fast, my rest had been well–earned.

Day 39: Wooster to Niles (95 miles)

When I stepped outside and headed toward the Country Kitchen the skies were overcast and heavy, as if rain could drop at any moment. The humidity was hovering near one–hundred percent making the cool temperatures seem much hotter. It was sixty–two degrees according to the early weather report. There was no breeze yet, but eventually the wind would stir. In the morning report the weatherman called for mid–day winds between ten and fifteen. Fortunately they would come out of the west, at our backs and not in the face.

For the third day in a row both sides of the cue sheet were full and to no surprise there was the bold print warning of rough railroad tracks. It was the usual drill in this part of the mid–west. There will be lots of climbing, nearly 2,600 feet of it, just a few hundred less than yesterday. I considered the ninety–three miles of pedaling to Niles just an estimate, because most days my bike computer logs a few extra for me. Since actual mileage may vary and yesterday I was spotted a full two extra miles, my money is on ninety–four, maybe ninety–five by the time I dismount at our destination.

Our hotel in Wooster was a mile east of town on the far side of the Ohio Short Line Railroad tracks. Our first objective would be to backtrack toward Liberty Street, find Beall and exit to the north. Even with our large group we managed to not create any situations. Along the route the roads were level and in good condition, the traffic respectful, but my legs were mush. I needed close to ten miles to be in full stride so I settled into the seat, looked around, and observed what the town offered.

We pedaled through the College of Wooster, a private liberal arts school with nearly two thousand undergraduates attending. It was an impressive campus covering several blocks. Following the procession of cyclists I began my workout in earnest turning onto the streets of Cleveland, then Portage, and Black Orrville adjusting my heading into an easterly direction before getting ejected completely out of the busy metro area.

Traffic was brisk, most of it heading toward town. The roads were in good shape but the shoulder was barely a foot wide. Nobody was stepping out of line as we followed the slight dips and inclines, bikes a few lengths apart as if bunching up offered some protection. We remained in a loose formation until Apple Creek and once we made the turn, cars were few.

My legs were coming around as I banked the turn at the cemetery. It was a swift downhill, not too steep, but it was fast. A pair of oncoming cars passed without incident. Conditions were best described as rural, roads tracing the edges of the fields, no painted lines, and no shoulder. In the absence of traffic to restrain them, riders were now confident and comfortable to begin jockeying forward.

The crowned road ramped up to the railroad tracks and I pedaled carefully across and accelerated down the other side. Both sets were rough, just as described on the cue sheet. Our climbing began first with small, short hills, but they progressed from there. Soon they were turning into the rollers reminiscent of yesterday morning's ride.

Through the midst of fields and trees we crossed over the creeks of Sugar and Little Chippewa. There were rural home sites with large brick houses sitting on acres of manicured lawns, fir trees accentuating the landscape. Fields of corn alternated with the residential tracts. Miles later on a long downhill stretch framed by rambling expanses of corn the uphill turn onto Coal Bank came into view. Coal Bank was a workout running straight for a few miles, but it still was small compared to what would follow.

We rode past dairy farms, including a huge commercial operation where three thousand head of cattle were milked three times a day. This building was well–designed with large windows allowing visitors to view the milking process. They thought enough to integrate eco–tourism into their operation, which might help them win public favor should the area expand its residential footprint.

At this same facility, industrial sized cow–manure holding pits served as staging areas for the bovine waste. A tractor–trailer sat in front of one of the four three–sided cement structures. I would estimate it measured fifty feet wide, two hundred feet long and fifteen feet high. The manure mounded up several feet above the walls, and the ripe odor had no trouble reaching us. We held our breath nearly two hundred feet away as we put the piles behind us.

After the first sixteen miles I was now into the third quadrant of the cue. Thirty minutes later riders were strung out; even the group I rode with was stretching farther and farther apart. All the fast riders seemed to have passed. I was riding solo but within sight of others.

The roads we traveled carried moderate traffic. Most cars were moving faster than the posted speed limit of forty–five miles an hour. They could appear suddenly around a bend or from beyond the next hill. The sound of the cars did not travel well out in the corn.

Conversation would come when we stopped at the cross roads but in between there was little chatter. It wasn't until we reached the edge of Canal Fulton, population: 5,228, that much was said between me, Betty and the others in our group.

Originally platted on May 16, 1826 as Fulton, the village was later renamed Canal Fulton just six years later. The name was most likely attributed to a local Pioneer, Ben Fulton.

Canal Fulton is on the Ohio & Erie Canal system connecting Lake Erie to the Ohio River. These waterways had an important role in the expansion of Ohio since their construction was first authorized by the state's legislature in 1822. Twenty–five years later Ohio was managing over a thousand miles of canals enabling the movement of agricultural and industrial products to expand and support growth. In addition to their commercial value, the canals have more recently been used for recreation and to help manage storm water.

We crossed over the Tuscarawas River onto streets bricked with old cobblestone and found the bakery Tracy kindly put on the cue. After a quick pastry stop we returned to Market Street and continued vibrating and chattering up the stone road. The pace was slow but the architecture of the town provided a distraction. We turned onto Cherry and continued to climb up and out of the business center and into the older, more modest residential blocks of town. Soon we were back in the thick of rural Ohio.

The roads tracked the contour of the surroundings. I struggled up long grades but enjoyed the rest coming back down. We turned north and then back east at the next intersection. We crossed Nimisila Creek and pedaled through long stretches of heavily wooded back roads that deposited us in the clear onto Wales Avenue.

The next few turns got us around the busy area surrounding the Akron–Canton Airport. Beyond the fence was a large grass berm. It was the runway elevated above the bordering property. It was a long climb skirting the south side of the airport but the shoulder was wide, even if it was littered with gravel. After pausing for the light on Frank Avenue I accelerated down and past the headquarters for the Timken Bearing Corporation, then shot under US–77. Across Pittsburg Avenue at the Mt. Bethel Church of the Brethren we came to a stop. It was SAG number one of two for the day.

I let my bike rest in the grass near the edge of the cemetery and then went about my normal SAG activities. More riders pulled in and soon we had an animated gathering of spandex covered people. Pods of three or four gathered and fell apart, changing partners and reforming like a crude square dance routine. We must appear odd to those watching from outside the group. To those within the group the behavior was ordinary. Inside the group it was normal to adjust your private parts and down a cup of Gatorade while in conversation with others about blisters and bottom rash.

To those passing by we were likely ill–mannered, maybe even offensive. We fit in with each other but not always with the surrounding public. You could be embarrassed or you could laugh; and within our group we chose to laugh. We meant no harm to the outsiders; in fact we barely noticed them when we were in the midst of cyclist conversation.

After replenishing my fluids and supplies I walked over to my bike, and went about re–applying chamois butter to the places requiring it. I didn't even think to look around. The thought of someone unfamiliar with the practice—shocked at seeing me hunched over, arm nearly elbow deep into my shorts—had never crossed my mind. For thirty–nine days this has been my normal.

The route exited to the right from the church and the area quickly transitioned from commercial to residential. In a few miles it was rural once more. The climbing continued but the short and steep was replaced by long shallow inclines. I could feel the grade but not really see it unless the road was fairly straight. Then it was visible. In the distance the hills were larger, more exaggerated than the roadway. There were homesteads on hills and in the valleys, the view was postcard perfect. I stopped and took a few snapshots.

Out in the country I noticed things homeowners do that is not as common in the more congested areas. For one, they plant fir trees, and not just a few. They use the trees as property markers, as adornments to their driveways, and as central features to their front yards. Fir trees offer no shade, at least not directly under them, but they are excellent wind breaks and require little maintenance once they are established. But they do grow into tall and wide dark green living cones.

The other thing I noticed are the driveway monuments; the short, stocky pillars of brick and stone standing to the left and right of driveways. Some are ornate with ironwork details, while others incorporate lights to keep drivers from hitting the monuments in the dark. No fencing extends off the pillars and they provide no security to the property. I don't have the answer for why these things stand out to me but I have plenty of time to ponder them as I pedal.

On William Penn I passed the well–manicured Seven Hills Golf Course and then on Edison I pass another called Sable Creek. Edison continued through unincorporated Marlboro, a little pass–through with the feel of a place more suited for the 1960s. The route took me past small ponds and over ditches, past old weathered barns, fenced pastures with horses grazing, marshy lowlands, and thick canopies of trees. Conditions were perfect for cycling, though a bit less traffic would have been a bonus. The climbing had become tame and enjoyable. I was moving more swiftly then I had in days thanks in part to the wind steadily increasing, now solidly at my back.

I skirted the northern fringe of Alliance, population: 23,253 and navigated my way onto 225 headed north. Though I didn't see it, Alliance is home to Glamorgan Castle; a massive structure designed by architect, Willard Hirsh and built of Vermont limestone in 1905 by Col. William Henry Morgan. The footprint of the building measures 185 feet by 115 feet with three levels sitting atop a full basement. The construction of the building is as interesting as the final structure. Morgan sent Hirsh to Europe to study and draw the plans.

When the plans were finished, Hirsh sent them to a quarry in Barre, Vermont where the stone was cut and numbered, and then transported to Alliance by way of ninety–six rail cars. Under the thick marble veneer was a structure of steel weighing more than one hundred tons. It was built at a cost of four hundred thousand dollars but in 1939 it sold for only twenty–five thousand. Morgan is credited with inventing the overhead traveling crane used within the steel industry.

The interior of the castle was equally spectacular. Rooms were decorated in a variety of styles including Italian Renaissance, French Empire, Louis XV, Elizabethan and Japanese. For entertainment there were bowling alleys, a billiards room, and a swimming pool in the basement. Today the castle is home to the Alliance City School district's central administrative offices. Tours are by appointment and only on Friday afternoons from one to two o'clock.

Alliance is also referred to as the Carnation City in reference to the state flower, the Scarlett Carnation first cultivated by Dr. Levi L. Lamborn in 1866. Other notable people from Alliance include football great, Len Dawson and Herman Carr, a physicist and pioneer in magnetic resonance imaging. If you've fallen off a bike you're familiar with the MRI.

It was seventy degrees and hazy, the heavy clouds moved off during the last hour revealing patches of blue, the sun bright, casting defined shadows. It would be like this most of the day, the haze in control of the sky above.

Rolling and winding along the asphalt highway I passed some of the finest examples of rural America. I was equally fortunate to be experiencing it under the most ideal of conditions. It was beautiful. And if I seem to repeat these comments as the day goes by it is only to drive the point home.

Over the Mahoning River through endless stands of trees and open fields I tracked north with a cross breeze playing to my left. I crossed over Deer Creek Reservoir on a narrow five hundred foot long strip of land just wide enough for the road. The shoulder was wide, mostly gravel, until I crossed the short bridge affording me a smooth concrete lane. The view was impressive, the rippling water shimmered in the sun, and the muddy banks were flat and wide, tapering off from the water until consumed by vegetation.

I was in the rural area known as Atwater. Most of it flat lowlands with marshy tall–reed vegetation just off the road. Farther back, expansive fields of rich dark soil full of the early summer crops continued to a forest backdrop. Old barns dotted the fields; a few had been ignored and were in various stages of collapse. It felt rustic and postcard perfect.

In the lulls between the increasing traffic there was a quiet sense of peace, a calm that I enjoyed as I pedaled. I hadn't been paying much attention to the mileage or riders around me. None were close but they were still in my view. In places the road rose up in a series of shallow ripples but most of the climbing had passed.

Through a wooded stand of trees, the un–mowed grass bordering the road bent and danced under the power of the breeze. Before turning east I saw more failing barns and the remains of old silos yielding to the fields of corn. Farm equipment and personal effects were scattered about in the fields, some had been idle for a long time.

At the corner of 224E I got my first clue of what to expect next, a sign with the words, "Truck Entrance" marked the beginning of a bumpy and tense section of riding. The volume of traffic was a mental concern but the narrow washboard and gravel dusted shoulder was unfit for my narrow tires. Beyond the riding shoulder there were potholes and rocks, mud and standing water. There were also strands of guardrails I didn't like because they gave me no escape from an out–of–control vehicle. *Just when I was having one of the best days on the bike,* I thought to myself.

I was focused on traffic noise and the loose stones in my path. The vibrations resonating through the bars and the seat were taking their toll after four hours of pedaling bliss. The dump trucks and tractor trailers speed by uncomfortably close, the air pushing and pulling and spraying me with a blast of road grit stinging my legs. I didn't like it and I swore often, mostly out loud.

The scenery was still beautiful but I was too distracted to enjoy it. Ironically the name of the road was Waterloo. I hope there would be no defeat farther down the road.

I chattered my way over Willow Creek and past clustered reeds rising out of the wet marsh. Farm fields were separated by a few houses and commercial operations. I came upon a *circle* as it is called in New Jersey. Others know it as a round–about, but unlike a normal circle where cars continuously merge, Deerfield Township Square had a stop sign gumming up the process. After carefully picking my way through traffic I reached the SAG in the parking lot of a little store called Mike's Circle Grocery. I was in the township of Deerfield in Warren County. Their moto is "Choose Deerfield" but I say, *Fix the roads first!*

There was much discussion about the route. Gary, a second–timer on the cross country ride, had expressed his displeasure with the rough road conditions and questionable traffic risk. He wanted off the road and wanted a better, less–stressful route. Unfortunately this was the best option available. Other routes would have been longer and likely as rough. According to the cue sheet we had another ten miles on 224E and as it played out, we would endure the same stress but with slightly improved road conditions the entire distance.

Along the way I rode over Berlin Lake on a much more bike friendly shoulder that was both wide and smooth. The half–mile thin strip of land and bridge provided momentary relief, the breeze was much stronger over the water, and I was pushed swiftly forward and into Berlin Center, an unincorporated area located in Mahoning County.

They say the definition of insanity is doing the same thing over and over but expecting a different outcome. Yet here I am getting up each day and riding my bike. The outcome is the same; I go east, at some point I experience hot foot, my butt hurts and I end up at a different hotel in a new town.

Friends question my stubbornness, or as I like to call it determination. Is it insane to do this day after day for seven weeks? I guess it depends on your perspective. To an outsider it may be their conclusion but to me and the rest of the pedaling herd we would take the other side of the debate. And our actions are proof of our commitment; for better or for worse. One reason is we have more at stake than those watching us from home or along the route. Our watchers still go to work; they take breaks and return to the comfort of their homes each night. We have to get to Boston. We have a celebration to attend on the beach at Revere, the ending and the beginning of our journey. Besides the hotels want us to move our two wheeled traveling circus down the road and not over stay our welcome. They don't quite understand us either.

You can say we are no different, we ride our bike like it's our temporary job, we take breaks along the roadside, and return to a hotel, albeit a different one each night. I might even accept that if you can show me a four inch wide office chair, a desk sitting just inches off a busy freeway, rain soaking your body, the spray hitting you straight in the face and your legs in constant motion else you fall of the seat. I would give you credit for that.

So is my repetitive grind insanity? I say no, and here's why. Each day I experience something different; inner reflection, scenic observation, people of all walks and type. The weather changes, the wind fluctuates the road conditions shift, and some days I ride stronger. I suffer much and I find reason to savor every moment. Each blink of my eyes captures a mental snapshot of my experience; as different from moment to moment as it is from day to day. No part of this journey is the same. Each day is a unique gift for me to enjoy or suffer through as I choose. The pain tapers off as I get stronger and more conditioned. The satisfaction grows as I build my story of adventure and accomplishment with brushes of near misses and glimpses of some awesome sites while I share in the richness of the life experiences and observations of my peers. It would be insanity not to do this. Just ask anyone who is with me.

The busy traffic just off my left shoulder reminds me I need to spend a bit more effort focusing on the road before me instead of pondering the contrasting points of view that if debated to conclusion would likely end in a stalemate. It's not insanity but it does take a little bit of crazy to do this. And I'll admit to being a bit of crazy.

A quick blink and my eyes dart back to the digital displays between my clenched hands on the bars. Even with the road vibration I can see my heartrate and it's pushing 134 beats per minute. Interesting how it seems to run lower when I'm lost in thought. The other readouts tell me a slew of details but collectively they are telling me to pick up the pace and to work a bit harder. Push, push, push, like little task masters trying to whip me into shape and to be the rider I can be. I'll be happy with incremental improvement. When I reach my destination at the end of today's ride I look forward to turning my little antagonists off, but between now and then we'll work together doing our little dance to the sound of pedals turning and the hum of traffic our only music.

At Ellsworth the route turned north and for the next eight miles we rode through a turnstile of dense stands of trees, fields growing wild and others with corn, and crowded little intersections full of human activity. I passed the first of two Dairy Queens in favor of stopping at the second another ten miles farther ahead. Orange–flagged bikes told me there were fellow riders inside.

The wet lowlands continued as we crossed the North Jackson Ditch and Morrison Run before finding our turn at Gladstone. We disposed of the last set of train tracks marked on the cue and crossed over Clemens Ditch as the road became rough, the scenery more rural.

For a short distance we were out of the busy traffic and able to begin regrouping nearer each other. I could feel the tempo of the ride winding down as we moved through a dense forest of mature trees and broke out into the open on a narrow elevated strip crossing through a swamp full of dead tree trunks. The swamp gave way to a wide body of water more than a thousand feet across. It was the Meander Creek Reservoir and without much traffic we rode the low and flat concrete bridge to the other side.

We broke out of yet another wooded area past a growing number of houses and old buildings before reaching Mineral Ridge, population: 3,900, and our left onto Main Street. We passed churches and old two–story framed apartment buildings, shake–sided cottages, and an assortment of local businesses. We pedaled by the quick–mart and gas station, a pizza joint, a small fire station, and a used car lot. It could have been any small town in Ohio.

The road twisted and turned then ducked through a damp concrete arch supporting a train line above. We had reached Niles. I saw a sign declaring President William McKinley was born here, and across the street at the Niles Ironworks, a twenty–five–foot–tall rusty welded scrap metal structure of a steelworker towered above the landscape.

A short climb up and over the bridge spanning the Mahoning River I found another Dairy Queen on the tour. While in line an older lady was struggling to assemble the money for her order and before I could think my hand was out covering the total. Through her thick glasses, I could see this woman was special. And by the grace of God one simple act of kindness rewarded both of us.

After crossing under another train overpass and across the bridge at Mosquito Creek I rode the final three miles to the Fairfield Inn enjoying several blocks of impressive and meticulously restored homes. It was a happy ending after a rough mid–day on a very challenging road.

In the sun the heat rising off the asphalt made it feel much hotter than the high seventies. I was starting to bake. I hurried my post–ride activities and was in street clothes within the hour.

At route rap Tracy talked about the road conditions. Not everyone was happy about riding on the busy roadways, but no incidents were reported. It was time to move on and talk about tomorrow's ride. Tracy described the ride to Erie as having much less climbing, somewhere near 1,200 feet total, with slightly less mileage than we had today. She also talked about a diner near the Pennsylvania border known for making the best root beer floats and shaved turkey sandwiches. Maybe because I was hungry, or maybe because I like root beer floats, but no matter Tracy had my attention.

In the evening our hungry herd walked the better part of a quarter mile to enjoy the Country Buffet. We all ate too much, but we enjoyed it. The walk back to the Fairfield was slower but the conversation was lively. There was more talk about the rough roads and the burgers a few riders enjoyed at a sketchy restaurant mid–ride. I usually didn't eat much besides the SAG food, not wanting to overdo it and get tired legs while my stomach is trying to process the meal. Others didn't have a problem with eating a full meal and getting back on the bike.

Niles sits at an elevation of 879 feet and is home to 20,226 people. The city is known for its ethnic diversity, including a large Italian–American community. The median family income is 76,704 dollars, but nearly ten percent of the population remains below the poverty level. The racial makeup includes ninety–three percent White, 3.5 percent African American, and less than one percent each for Native Americans, Asians, and other races.

The city was founded in 1806 by James Heaton, the owner of one of the first iron–ore processing plants in Ohio. Heaton is also credited with producing the first bar of iron in the state. Originally named Heaton's Furnace, the name was eventually changed to Nilestown in 1843 after newspaper editor Hezekiah Niles before it was shortened to Niles early in the nineteenth–century.

My mileage estimate was close to the actual. The bike computer displayed 95.16 miles and I averaged 14.4 miles an hour with six hours thirty–five minutes in contact with the seat. As a bonus I saw my maximum speed of 33.6 miles per hour flash by as I clicked through the riding stats.

Tomorrow we will see the last of Ohio and cross into Pennsylvania, our eleventh state. Then after a day of rest in Erie, we will have only seven more days of riding to reach Boston. I find this difficult to imagine. It's exciting but sad. I don't want this to end.

Day 40: Niles to Erie, Pennsylvania (93 miles)

Breakfast was across the other side of Niles Cortland Road, uphill and about a quarter mile from the Fairfield. It was a brisk walk in the cool morning, a few clouds lingered. The bulk of our four–dozen riders arrived in a continuous stream, nearly overwhelming the morning staff. Previous group experience suggested panic would ensue with the order taking stalling or becoming so fouled up I wished I were at a breakfast buffet alone. But the staff of the Niles Perkins was on it, prompted by the CrossRoads staff in the required breakfast combat detail. Large groups require hustle, but our group, well; it was difficult to prepare for.

Immediately pots of coffee, followed by pitchers of juice and water hit the tables in quick succession, the ordering commenced with vigor. Requests were detailed in small installments and sent to the kitchen as the next sets of orders were written down. Yet even with the speed and efficiency of the staff it was almost impossible to keep everyone happy. But try they did. The flurry went on for a solid fifteen minutes until the last order was taken. Hot plates full of food came out in a steady flow and soon everyone had plenty to keep them quiet.

And as the last of the forks fell to the plates, the final swallows of coffee gulped down, and the rider's vacated the restaurant, I'm sure the staff locked the doors and poured their own cup of liquid recovery, maybe cut into a slice of pie, glad we'd not be back anytime soon.

It has been interesting over the past six weeks people watching within our group, but at no point was it as entertaining as when these hungry cyclists were anxious to eat. Having come from a large family I'm pretty easy about the food I'm served and the time it takes to get to me, but in this group not everyone comes to the table with the same experience.

Carrying a full belly of food back to the hotel was made easy by way of our downhill route. I joked around with Paul and chatted up with several others as we took turns topping off the air in our tires and making final preparations to leave.

As the first rider rolled from the lot we had officially started our seventh consecutive day of pedaling, but the next day would be our rest day in Erie. The thought of being off the bike tomorrow has an exciting appeal to it. I pondered what I would do with those twenty–four hours, but nothing came to me. I might do laundry, but I was certain I would do some sightseeing; exactly what it would be I did not know.

The skies were clear with temperatures hovering near fifty degrees as we made our way out of town on East Market. The riding conditions mirrored our efforts leaving Wooster; a brisk flow of morning traffic and narrow roads climbing out of commercial zones, into residential neighborhoods, and finally out into the rural extents of eastern Ohio. I balanced thoughts of the rest day with holding a steady and straight course at the edge of pavement and grass.

For a light day of climbing it began right away; Market was a climb, several more followed that had me struggling. I felt good leaving the hotel but the fatigue of riding nearly 550 miles the past six days caught me early. Riders ahead of me had stretched out by the time we made our way around the north end of the Youngstown–Warren Regional Airport. Fast riders passed and quickly disappeared. I had visions of being the last one to Erie.

As we moved east and north I got a brief rest on a nearly flat and straight stretch of Ridge Road. It was enjoyable, there was little car traffic, and I was able to fix my stare so far ahead I could see riders disappear into the horizon. I wondered how far ahead they were and if I could catch up to them. Then I remembered having similar thoughts on the way to Tucumcari. At least out west my legs weren't like jelly and I could ride harder for thirty minutes or more. And that's what it takes if I were to catch a rider at the edge of the horizon. It was not going to happen now so I stayed the course, pedaling below fifteen miles per hour according to my computer.

There would be long stretches of corn and soy, small ranch estates on manicured acres, and full blown farms with barns and tool sheds, tractors, and various attachments for working the land. Along the road were mailboxes standing straight on wood posts and old wagon wheels propped up marking the entrance to driveways. Power poles sat farther back from the road, many standing deep in the corn. Concrete drainage pipes undermined several driveways where the ditch was present, but most of the shoulder was grassy and flat. I could easily ride off and return but I would avoid doing that.

I saw much that needed work besides the road. There were delinquent barns covered in a mix of faded paint and rusted patina, roof panels bent, a few missing, and side walls leaning at various angles. Few were straight, most were precariously favoring one side with vines and overgrowth clinging and climbing. I wasn't sure if the vines were holding the buildings up or slowing pulling them to the ground.

There was one small structure with a tree rising up out of it, branches extending outward in all directions, the roof laying in pieces on the ground. There were the occasional dead trees, leafless and missing all but the thick members and the main trunk, the bark gone, the exposed wood a weathered gray. Against the backdrop of corn these failing man–made structures and broken trees called out to be seen, to be captured in pictures so they would not be forgotten.

The roads in this area formed a grid; North to South and West to East. Nearly every half mile I cross a road similar to the one I am on. Over this stretch Ridge had the right of way and the crossroad traffic would yield. The names of the roads likely linked to members of the community from decades back. I crossed the likes of Davis Peck and Gardner Barclay then turned right onto Kinsman followed by a left onto SR–193.

On the right a small cemetery, headstones modest and weathered, many of the smaller tablet shaped stones leaning. The black stains of mold, the chips and erosion of details told me they had been there a long time.

For miles I would enjoy the quiet expanses of corn, the occasional encounter with animals moving through the patchy grass, views of barns and tall silos, fences of planks and posts and wire tracing property boundaries. Crows flew over the trees and disappeared into the corn.

There were interesting vintage estate–sized homes, painted white, and decorated with ornate trim. They sat close to the road protected by shade trees. Farther back sat the more recently constructed ranch–style houses, some brick others painted, but they lacked the character of the older models. Empty crossroads would come and go. The frequent rough patches were negotiated to take the least shock. I checked the cue sheet and monitored my displays but my attention was away from the bike.

In Williamsfield I joined RT–322 east, a church and a small local restaurant fading behind me. I enjoyed better pavement at the price of more frequent and faster moving traffic. I encountered railroad crossings and more pronounced climbs. With each climb I was rewarded with a friendly descent, some longer and more generous than I had expected. I was still moving slower than I liked but I was not alone. Others were riding slower too. I normally get up to speed within ten to fifteen miles, but today I passed the thirty–mile mark with legs still feeling like oatmeal. The climbing was less than previous days, so I knew my body just needed a day off.

Over the next several miles the roads saw less traffic. I passed stands of wildflowers reaching up out of the ditch and rode past yet another small and peaceful cemetery. The riding was good, the route enjoyable.

I rolled through Amish farms, the houses easily identified; there were no strands of wire connecting to the power grid. Hanging on the corded clothesline were their basic blue, black, and white clothes dancing and drying in the breeze. There were children standing still, arms down, a horse–drawn carriage idle behind them. Their faces offered no expression, they didn't speak nor did they gesture, not even a slight wave as I slipped quietly by. It was a window into another world for them as well as for me. I continued and passed more of the same in between the fields of corn and wild grass pastures.

Occasionally I would see dairy farms and cows. Massive were these black and white familiar beasts standing amongst the green and the dirt. A cluster stood close to the road, I saw one peering at me from behind the safety of the field fencing. As I pedaled a guttural tone came from my lungs, *Mooooo!* A few looked up at me but the rest concentrated on tearing and chewing the patches of green grass. My call went unanswered.

There would be more barnyard scenes, horses pacing behind fenced corrals, goats playing and climbing on stacks of wood and hay bales. A line of baby ducks followed their mother heading to the puddles near the ditch. If it wasn't the rolling terrain or the beautiful sky it was the impromptu barnyard show providing the entertainment. The price of admission was to pedal. It's amazing how much more you notice when you can't pedal very fast.

At a vacant lot on the corner of US–6 I found riders congregating at the SAG. My legs were finally coming around so I chose to top–off my bottles, grab a banana and head out. Before I left I heard Margaret telling others not to miss the diner in Conneaut. The next ten miles ran nearly straight north, the road only bending and yielding for stubborn creeks and thick stands of trees. The roads could certainly be better but the traffic could be worse.

The sun was bright out in the open and through areas of wooded canopies; dark shadows were cast on the road. Yet in the shadows, as the trees moved in the breeze the rays of light poked through. The light shimmered and danced, moving about like fireflies. It was mesmerizing and magical and it had my eyes searching to balance the light. Clouds were few and the temperature steadily climbing. It was still favoring the cool side of seventy making it comfortable to ride.

Aside from the bumps and potholes these roads are enablers of deep thought. But they could also make you feel lost and alone. I find it relaxing and somewhat meditating, my mind wandering to places I hadn't thought possible outside of a deep sleep. It doesn't mean I'm not paying attention; I am very much in control. But I am also more in tune with what is around me.

I hear the whispers of the wind, the movement of the grass, and the fluttering of the leaves. I hear the birds and the buzz of the occasional bee. I also hear the noise I generate as I turn the pedals and force the narrow tires to adhere and release from the rough textures of the weathered chip–seal road. The more you tune in the easier it is to pick out the individual sounds. It's like finding the one instrument you favor as the band plays; picking the sound apart until only notes of a single instrument reaches your ears. I said it can be meditating.

Before I knew it I was twenty miles farther down the road, a green sign pointing left to Conneaut at the corner of SR–84 and 7N. On Center Road I found a slight uphill grade and a tractor dealer. Kubota and New Holland were his equipment brands of choice. If you had a few acres and time on your hands you'd definitely need at least one tractor and a few attachments. Nothing too big, just something with a bucket and plow blade to smooth out the gravel drive, maybe a root rake to tear up the garden. Out here a simple lawn mower would not do.

Still heading north I reached a straight climb more than a half mile long that carried me over West Branch Conneaut Creek. The water was way down below the road surface, maybe thirty or forty feet. This was a tough climb and at the end I was searching for the next direction on the cue sheet.

The road expanded into a full–blown highway, lanes divided by a grass strip, until I was over I–90 and speeding along a wonderful downhill. I would cross over the West Branch twice more but not before climbing to Conneaut where detour signs would have us zig–zagging and crossing over dirt and gravel in construction zones.

The signs and cones routed us down to the creek near the Old Main Street Bridge. We tracked along a makeshift asphalt road and were slammed with an unexpected steep climb back up to SR–20. Several of the riders couldn't downshift fast enough and ended up unclipping and pushing their bike up the hill. I was a bit more fortunate having enough leg power to make it to the top, but I might have been better off walking. It was steep yet short, but a mother it was. This detour would definitely be bonus mileage for the day and it did offer a spectacular view of the creek and the new bridge nearly thirty feet above.

My weary legs carried me to the White Turkey Drive–In, an old–style outdoor eatery open from Mother's Day to Labor Day. It had large wood panels hinged at the top to open like wings revealing the serving area in the center. The building was painted white and trimmed in red. A bright red roof topped by a red, white, and blue sign, the words, "White Turkey Drive–In and Root Beer" in bold print. Stools were placed along the three–sided counter. I parked my bike in the back and took a seat. New Jersey had similar seasonal outdoor places to eat. The common thread was the root beer.

So here I sit just past noon on a Wednesday appreciating the good company and perfect weather getting ready to enjoy the best root–beer float and a chili–dog set before me. I was planning on a turkey sandwich, but one sniff of the grilled dogs and I was committed. It was everything I had hoped for, the root beer mixing with the melting scoop of vanilla ice cream was a drink from the Gods. This was the best eating experience I've had in a long time, and not just on this tour. It was nothing fancy, just damn good food. I have not had a root beer in decades but this fizzy sweet drink brought back the memories. I washed down the hot dog while others devoured their shaved turkey sandwich and I thought to myself, *Why have you deprived yourself of root beer you idiot?* But I had no answer. I just kept drinking and vowed to not wait so long before enjoying this interestingly sweet beverage again.

I spoke to the owner and bought a shirt as a souvenir. I was getting close to the end of the trip so I could start accumulating keepsakes from the ride. This shirt would be one of them.

Conneaut is a city of 12,627 and they pronounced it, "KAHN–ee–AHT." But my brain kept telling my lips to say "KAH–know." The popular regional summer destination sits on the waters of Lake Erie in the northeastern–most corner of Ohio, their motto, "Ohio's Sharpest Corner." Points of interest include the Conneaut Lighthouse, which overlooks seven miles of shoreline and the Conneaut Historic Railroad Museum in the middle of town.

A half–mile east on RT–20 we sprinkled west–coast sand at the border and captured the smiles of our tenth state line crossing. In Pennsylvania we're immediately greeted by a pair of large hills in a heavily wooded area before it flattened out for the last thirty miles going into Erie. At Turkey Creek Route 20 branched left onto SR–5E.

I passed through vineyards and Christmas tree farms, the route followed the winding road climbing up and sailing down the rail line overpass by Erie Bluffs State Park. Over Elk Creek I passed the sign for the Borough of Lake City. I saw newly planted corn as traffic began to build at Avonia. Along a few peaks I was able to catch a glimpse of the lake. Nothing encouraged me to stop for a photo, but it did incent me to pedal hoping for a better view.

Past the Erie Airport I turned left onto Peninsula Drive and rode the downhill to the waters of Lake Erie. I continued riding the coastline until I found Presque Isle State Park. Close to the water the ride was relaxing, the breeze much stronger than on RT–5. I was impressed with the blue water and how it turned an emerald–green in the shallow areas. Canada was thirty miles out but I saw nothing except water vanishing into the horizon.

I talked to several beachgoers, and it seems this area is frequented by campers wanting to pitch a tent right near the water. I remember camping in my back yard as a young boy in New Jersey and I suspect it would be fun to do it again. Maybe I'll return to the beaches of Lake Erie and find myself a spot in the sand.

Before I backtracked I took a photo of the surf, a lifeguard tower and a few people in the breaking waves were in frame. I pedaled uphill past the amusement park and picked up 5E toward Erie for the final five miles.

Through a string of commercial zones bordering dense neighborhoods I made my way toward the heart of Erie. I tracked along State Street stopping at several lights, slowly increasing my elevation until I reached 10th Street and the Avalon Hotel. It was an older yet grand facility and I was excited about the prospects of a day off in the middle of so much activity. An old movie theatre was just across the street, a robust array of small businesses extended outward from there.

The city of Erie is clean and alive. I learned they have a Maritime Museum, a planetarium, and many architecturally interesting religious buildings. They also have a minor–league baseball team called the Seawolves, which play in Jerry Uht Park just two blocks from the hotel.

A group of us went to the night game to watch the Seawolves play the Portland Seadogs. The Wolves were a Double–*A* division operating under the Detroit Tigers affiliation. Their logo was a pirate–wolf face over crossed bats in the pirate appropriate colors of black, red, and gray. The game was exciting, maybe the best I've ever attended. I sat with Clark and Peter, and we cheered the visiting *Dogs* to a come–from–behind win in the final inning. It was a full nine innings of hustling "no–name" players trying to get their break and advance to the major leagues. During the game I saw one player hit the ball so hard it screamed as it disappeared into the sky, then found the top edge of the outfield wall. The ball ricocheted back into play and I was witness to my first ever infield home run since Little League.

Between innings the mascots took to the field for some shenanigans. C. Wolf and his mascot buddies, Paws and the three sausages named Kenny Kielbasa, Herbie Hot Dog, and Santino the Italian Sausage ran around entertaining the crowd. Of course the sausages were sponsored by the Erie–based Smith's Provision Company as we learned over the PA announcement.

At only eight dollars for seats three rows behind the Seadog's dugout, this evening at the park could not be beat. When the game finished the temperatures were dipping into the low sixties, the stars were out and there was barely a breeze. There would be another game tomorrow and riding the excitement of tonight's game I just may go again.

Erie is home to 103,717 but because of its steady population decline it has slipped to number four of the state's largest cities behind Philadelphia, Pittsburgh, and Allentown. The city sits at an elevation of 650 feet and has been called by several names including, "Gem City" because of its sparkling lake and "Flagship City" for being the home port of Oliver Hazard Perry's flagship *Niagara*. The oldest lighthouse on the Great Lakes, Land Lighthouse, is located two hundred feet from the water's edge on Lighthouse Street.

I racked up a total of 92.84 miles with the detours and my excursion to Presque Isle. As for the rest of the numbers my tally for the day was six hours thirty–three minutes of pedal time averaging 14.1 miles per hour with a top speed of 30.1. Now if the computer could learn to measure food taste and riding quality. It's just a thought. I'll explore more tomorrow but given today's weather it is hard to imagine Erie is one of the top ten snowiest places in the United States averaging just less than seventy–nine inches a year.

Day 41: Erie, Pa. (Rest Day)

The skies were clear with a light breeze from the north. With temperatures expected to peak in the low seventies I put on my sneakers and headed out the doors of the Avalon. I turned left and at the end of the block I headed north on State Street toward the waterfront. Along the walk I passed the local FM station. The soundproof production rooms were on the ground floor of a tall granite clad building, picture windows providing a view of the DJ's, mouths moving and arms waving around. Other people stopped to watch the radio hosts jabber–jaw into the microphones while they worked the controls on the console. A Rock station sign was hanging on the wall.

As I continued the mile trek down to Liberty Park, I glanced at the cars crowding the streets and a steady flow of people moving swiftly in the crosswalks. In the middle of the sidewalk stood a large frog–structure painted in wild colors. It was one of several I would see around town, part of the Erie Art Museum's 2004 project to raise money.

Ahead a narrow slice of water between the tall buildings came into view and it didn't take long before I was up a flight of steps and leaning on the railing at Dobbins Landing looking across the bay to Presque Isle State Park. The 3,200 acre peninsula is popular for bird watching with sightings of more than 423 different species reported. Besides the road to the Park a water taxi makes hourly runs from Dobbins. A few CrossRoads riders made the trip but I stayed on land.

Bicentennial Tower resembles a steel girder lighthouse with an upper level observation platform 138 feet above the ground. I was standing on the lower level platform seventeen feet above grade, but for a few dollars you can climb the 210 steps to the top and enjoy an unobstructed view of the port area. And for those who care, the top of the flagpole is 187 feet up.

If you are hungry, Rum Runner's Cove and Smugglers' Wharf were just a few steps away, lines for lunch starting to form. I looked at the menus and found one of my favorites, Crab Cakes, at the Wharf.

Heading back toward land, a marina with a mix of cabin cruisers and sailboats occupied the right and a small fleet of charter boats rocking in the water were to my left. The walkways were wide wooden planks and appeared new. Landscaping ran the length of the boardwalks on both sides.

I took the time to tour the Erie Maritime Museum and the U.S. brig Niagara. The Niagara is a reproduction of the relief flagship Commodore Oliver Hazard Perry used in a major naval battle of the War of 1812. With a few modifications to meet current training–ship requirements, it is as close to the original as possible. The boat smelled of wood and a salty dampness. The heavy ropes had their own smell, something close to burlap. Below deck the ceilings were low and the space tight. It was dark and I could tell I would not have been a sailor on this ship.

Inside the museum is a reconstruction of the mid–ship section of Niagara's sister ship, the Lawrence, complete with mast, spars and rigging. A portion of the Lawrence replica was fired upon with live ammunition from the current Niagara's own carronades. This innovative and unprecedented "live fire" exhibit vividly recreates the damage inflicted upon the ships during the battle of Lake Erie. It must have been frightening to be on those old ships as cannons fired, not knowing if the next ball of lead would punch a hole through the wood like the splintered replica on display.

I learned a few interesting facts about the people, the area's natural resources, and Erie's storied manufacturing past. Ann B. Davis, Alice from *The Brady Bunch* TV show, calls Erie, Pennsylvania home. In the 1920s Erie was a major summer resort city with more than four million people each year coming to enjoy the beaches and cool waters off Presque Isle. And the name Presque Ilse in French means peninsula or loosely "almost an island." At one time Erie was the largest freshwater commercial fishing port in the world. The city is home to the largest U.S. locomotive manufacturer and back in 1844, the Navy's first iron warship, the USS Michigan, was built here.

I worked my way back toward the hotel and then over to Jerry Uht Park for an afternoon ballgame. It was hot in the sun, the game exciting, but not as much as it was under the lights. No infield home–runs and no come from behind win. The Wolves would finish the season with a record of eighty wins and sixty–two losses, good enough for second place in their division.

The hot dogs at the ballpark were a primer for a later afternoon lunch and some quality time back at the hotel for writing about the past week. It felt good to be off the bike and walking around in my White Turkey t–shirt and cargo shorts instead of spandex.

The demographics of Erie are worth mentioning. The racial makeup includes seventy–five percent White, twenty percent African American, seven percent Hispanic, and just fewer than two percent Asian. The median household income is 28,387 dollars with nineteen percent of the population living below the poverty line. Most of the residents are from European descent and the Catholic Church claims the greatest number of members. Since the mid–1990s the International Institute of Erie has been helping in the resettlement of refugees from Bosnia, Eritrea, Ghana, Iraq, Kosovo, Liberia, Nepal, Somalia, Sudan, the Soviet Union, and Vietnam. The area is rich in cultural festivals and unique community events. Something for everyone I guess you could say.

Pondering the small towns

Today I had time to reflect back and think about the small towns and the people who live in them. These are my thoughts:

Moments; the time it takes for the bike to slide out from under you, the time it takes to become friends, the time it takes to roll through a crossroads town along your coast to coast journey. All can make a lasting impression on your life.

The first two are fairly obvious but the significance of slipping through a town, a village, or even a hamlet measured in less than a few blocks can easily be missed. What seems like a little bit of nothing, a nowhere town, and in some instances a "no name" place with unmarked roads, is an opportunity for discovery. After all someone lives there and it would be reasonable to assume they do so because they like it. It's home, a safe place, a community in which people belong. It's a place of birth and death and a whole lot of living between these extremes.

The first at bat on a little league ball field, the first high school dance, the place where someone planted their first tree and dreamed about the future while remembering their past. It's a place of love, of strong values, and of memories; lots and lots of memories. But we often pass through with our focus on our destination and not the journey and we miss the stories of these places. And it's these stories that can increase the richness of our own story about our journey we make as we pedal from the Pacific east to the Atlantic. What we are doing is as much about the in between as it is about the start and the finish. Each town, each day becomes a chapter in our story, our life, and our memories. It will forever be a part of us; it may even define us, or allow us to discover who we are.

It's easy to dismiss these pass–through zones because they hold no history for us, no relatives, nothing to bind us in any way to them. To pay them any mind would also require effort on our part which might seem to be in short supply as we focus on the physical and mental challenges. We might even find them out of alignment with our personal preferences.

But if we take the time to talk to those who call these places home we may find they would think the same about us. "What's not to like about this place," they might say. Crime may be non–existent, traffic obviously is not an issue, a slower pace most certainly prevails, and stress, if there is any at all, is not an inhibitor to enjoying life.

I took the time to speak with Carmen in Wilhoit, Arizona, George Clark in Abilene, Kansas and others along the way but certainly less people than I should have spoken to. To those I spoke with but have since forgotten their names it's my loss; the details they added to the richness of my experience are gone. I should have paid better attention along the way and I should have written more down instead of trusting it to memory. Maybe this is a lesson for me when I have conversations with people going forward.

I asked what keeps them in place and why these communities are so special and important to them. The reasons they gave were varied but generally followed the same theme; it was where they felt they belonged and where they were happiest. Imagine that; just like I would say about my town. What was unexpected for me was the degree of their attachment for home. I guess the reason it surprises me really shouldn't. My values and memories are from someplace else and they are equally deep. Why would I expect anything less from someone else about their preferred place?

And several years later I would add the following entry:

After my crossing I felt compelled to retrace my route and learn something about these towns. What I found was amazing. Each town seemed to have their own interesting and unique historical past. They were the birthplace of successful business professionals and presidents, hideouts for legendary fugitives, home to sacred burial grounds, the setting for major motion pictures, home of "one of a kind" museums and notable people who have done amazing things. Had I known more about each of these places before I passed through I might have been in awe instead of in a hurry. Everyplace has a story, everyplace is unique, and everyplace is important to someone. They are the many stitches that make up the fabric of this country and they tell an interesting story. We just have to want to know it for ourselves.

Day 42: Erie to Hamburg, New York (78 miles)

Looking out the window from several floors up, I took in the view of the early morning. It was crappy, the sky dark and full of clouds. The window glass was cold to the touch. A drizzly pissing kind of morning waited for me somewhere outside. The weatherman was not able to pinpoint exactly when or where I would find bad weather, but he knew I would find it.

I got in the shower and turned up the heat. *Maybe I can stand in the shower long enough to take some heat with me*, I thought. Like that was going to happen. I would be cold before I finished topping off the air in my tires. Of that I am certain. I would put on my best rain riding gear which consisted of my yellow jersey and my lightweight Tyvek jacket. The rest of my wet–gear was the same stuff I wear every day. All–weather gear I guess you could say.

For breakfast I stayed in my street clothes and took the elevator down to a private banquet room the staff of the Avalon set up for our group. It was a bit dim, mood lighting for breakfast. I would have preferred bright lights and a toasty warm room.

None of the excitement we had when we arrived in Erie remained. The mood was somber, most riders were quiet but there was plenty to eat so I made sure I loaded up on the hot foods and plenty of coffee. Back in my room, I scanned the landscape one more time and carefully balanced my bags and bike through the door toward the elevator to make a single trip down.

The cue sheet instructions only filled three quadrants, short by comparison to what I had been working with the last few days, but the mileage was still a full effort at just under eighty miles into Hamburg. Factor in the rain and it would feel much longer. I would only need to pull the cue sheet out of the plastic sleeve twice to flip it over so getting it wet should be the least of my worries. I had added an extra pair of inflator cartridges to my rack mounted bag because bad weather seemed to increase the number of flats. I've been lucky so far but I'm neither very lucky nor a gambler so it made sense to be prepared. Besides if I got a flat I didn't want to resort to the hand pump to inflate the tire.

I had changed my front tire a few days earlier so I had good rubber and reasonable tread for these narrow tires to find some grip. I'd hope for textured roads and not the smooth asphalt. And while I might feel the vibrations more through the bike it would improve the grip. On a dry road I would have wanted just the opposite surface. My rear tire was scarred and worn having made it this far. I was determined to ride it all the way to Boston, but I had a fresh one should this tire fail.

Several riders changed their tires and chain midway into the ride. Others did not consider the preventive measures opting to get everything out of their components and tires riding to failure. I was in the "Get the most out of it" camp until I studied the tire one evening and began to question my judgement about riding a front tire looking like it could come apart from all the splits and cuts in its carcass. A rear tire I would ride to failure but not the front.

In the first four miles I exhausted all of the first quad instructions except for the last. I would get a reprieve until mile fifteen before I would have to flip my instructions.

With such a large pack of riders it was difficult to stay together through the endless city traffic lights. Even under ideal conditions our string of riders covered nearly two blocks. The lights sliced our group into smaller pods stretching us even farther. I watched from a few rows deep as a dozen more advanced beyond the light and disappeared into the next block. The same was happening at a light farther back behind me.

Restarting was a slow process, having to wait for the person in front to get clipped in and moving forward. Each rider in succession would have an added delay making it difficult for several riders to get through the intersection on a single sequence of the light. For groups of more than six or seven rows deep it was almost assured you would take at least a second light cycle to clear the intersection.

Highway 5 would track along Lake Erie providing views enhanced by the slow speeds I traveled. Outside the city and the villages the road was noticeably smoother and the shoulders wider. Two lanes became four for a brief stretch and while traffic was busy it tapered off to a manageable flow. I felt safer and more comfortable with the extra lane as it gave cars and trucks room to move left providing the proper clearance as they passed. Not all of the cars moved over but with the shoulder they didn't need to. It was more of a gesture of courtesy demonstrated by those who recognize how vulnerable a cyclist is in the proximity of traffic.

Within the first thirty minutes it started to rain. I zipped up my Tyvek jacket to ward off the drops but it would do more to keep in the heat then to keep me dry. The fabric was an ingenious design consisting of very tiny holes to allow sweat to escape. Without the holes I would overheat even in cold weather. The holes also let water in.

I pedaled through traffic, rain coming down and water spitting up off the narrow tires. Cars passed shedding a spray of water, their tires splashing through the puddles ejecting even more water in my direction.

The road had a glassy sheen reflecting back the overcast sky and my sunglasses did little more than protect my eyes from the water. While I needed the glasses, they actually made it appear darker adding an element of risk I did not need.

Along RT–5E I stopped for few lights, but when I did it meant braking and unclipping. I had close calls getting my favored left foot unclipped before I stopped. A few times I had to hurriedly unclip the right as my balance shifted and I nearly toppled over toward the ditch. The clips were great for keeping my feet in the proper pedal position but if I didn't release my shoes fast enough they could ruin my day, leaving me bruised, or even broken.

I fell a few times in Florida as I was learning about the clips, how tight they should be, and the time it takes to release and extend my foot as I stopped. On the occasions I realized I could not release in time, at least I was smart enough to avoid catching myself with an extended arm. That would be a sure way to break a wrist or do more damage. I would fall like a fainting goat, the bike tilting over with my hands on the bars, body straight up and the impact with the ground taken from hip to shoulder in a single thud. It hurt every time I did it and each time I was lucky nothing except my ego was broken. Bruises were another story as my blackened hip and shoulder were proof of.

No part of me was dry by the time I cleared the eastern extents of Erie. I was completely soaked, my feet, legs, and hands would remain numb for the duration of the ride. All I could do was pedal faster to generate heat into my extremities.

I would run the jacket zipper down to release the accumulating core heat but I could do little about the water accumulating in the sleeves. It was a mix of sweat and rain water that found its way in. It was unpleasant to think about. Eventually I figured I could pull the elastic at the wrist and point my arm down releasing the water. I did that often, never enjoying the feeling of warm water draining, my arms uncomfortably warm and the rest of my body cold.

Today I was not a Pluviophile, which means a lover of rain; someone who finds joy and peace of mind during rainy days. Maybe it was the cold or maybe a rainy day is best enjoyed from the cover of a porch with a hot coffee and a thick blanket.

Traffic thinned as the miles clicked slowly by. My digital displays were difficult to read through the wrinkled, wet plastic bag they were enveloped in. The drops of water running across my tinted lenses and the fact the prescription was good for distance only didn't help. More water found its way through the open slots of my helmet and into my eyes. A shower cap might have been a good option today.

Less than thirty minutes beyond the North East Historic District I exited the Commonwealth of Pennsylvania and entered the Empire State. The rain continued to fall but it would not prevent the sprinkling of sand and photos in front of the New York sign. Besides Tracy was there making sure we didn't anger the cycling fairies. We took turns shuffling cameras and bikes into the grass and getting positioned under the big green sign. Some of the cameras flashed in the dim light and most joined in for group photos to accelerate the border crossing activities. This was our 11th state–line crossing; just a few more to go as the tour winds down.

I checked the rubber bands on my traveling partners, the Three Stooges, and realized they were in need of a change if I were to avoid losing them. They were part of my childhood when this cross country dream was concocted so it only made sense to include them. Just plastic and fabric finger puppets, but they were part of my story. They were an icebreaker in conversations and a reason to smile when I looked behind me. With the boys I was never alone on the road.

The temperatures were still in the low fifties, but the wind and rain off Lake Erie made it seem much cooler. I could see the lake to the north, the blue of the water disappearing into the clouds and rain in the distance. The highway afforded several photo opportunities, including a fifty to sixty–foot–high cliff overlooking the lake. I stopped and snapped a few pictures. Our route was never more than a half mile away from the water but at times it was not more than a few feet beyond the guardrail.

The sound of traffic was muffled by the rain and heavy air but it did not prevent me from enjoying the scenery. I passed small cemeteries and rode through several miles of vineyards that covered all available land on both sides of the road. I also remember passing the Penn–Shore Winery, which according to its sign, was part of the wine–sampling trail. The road followed the contour of the surrounding land and I pedaled hard when needed and coasted where I could.

My pedaling took me to the north of Ripley, population: 2,500 and then over the Hamlet of Forsyth before bypassing the town of Westfield, population: five thousand. The economy of this area is driven by agriculture, most of it dependent on the Concord grapes growing in the vineyards. Even in the wet it's beautiful.

Back in 1897, Charles Welch moved his grape juice operation to Westfield from New Jersey to take advantage of the ideal climate for growing the fruit. Today the region is noted for growing grapes for both wine and grape juice. The area has twenty buildings listed on the National Register of Historic Places including the Barcelona Lighthouse.

I rode over the Chautauqua Creek and into the Hamlet of Barcelona encountering the first traffic light for RT–394 in the rain. Slowing and stopping in the wet were dicey at best. Tire traction was minimal and the cycling shoes with their hard–sole bottoms and exposed cleats offered no grip.

Through the intersections and dips in the road standing water was to be avoided. It might only be a shallow puddle but it could also mask a deep and treacherous pothole. You couldn't tell until you hit it and then it was too late. My attention was divided across the wet road, the busy flow of traffic, and my riding peers. Staying upright all the way to Hamburg was my goal for the day.

On my left was Barcelona Lighthouse, a definite stop for pictures as several other riders were already off their bikes on the side of the road. The lighthouse, built in 1829 has a conical tower with a keeper's cottage attached. The structure was built out of local fieldstone and was significant because it was the first lighthouse in the world powered by natural gas. The lighthouse provided navigation for boats on Lake Eric and overlooked the little Barcelona Harbor. Just beyond the lighthouse was Daniel Reed Memorial Pier. In the lot was more of our group pausing to drink and take in some protein. I pulled in for a few minutes to do the same before remounting the bike and continuing down the highway.

The area is dotted with more hamlets, little population clusters smaller than villages, too small to report on population or much else besides a locally known intersection or historical landmark. I like the terms Hamlet and Village. They have a comfortable community air and maybe even a trace of romance. They suggest a setting of old homes and mature trees, expansive fields, and country quiet. A view of the valley with a barn in the distance and rolling planted fields beyond. It's what I imagine and on this section of road it's my reality. It is wet, but it is my reality.

Another ten miles I rode in the rain crossing over Bournes Creek and past the falls. The route ambled through winding wooded forest over rolling hills and gentle climbs. I pedaled close to the shores of Lake Erie and back into the woods once more before I landed at the SAG. It was a soggy stop but after almost forty miles it was good to dismount, socialize, and eat again. I took advantage of the restroom break making sure to try and warm up my hands. It didn't help much, my fingers maintained a bit of the curve from the bars, and the skin was swollen and wrinkled.

I twisted my gloves to extract the water but putting them back on was still a challenge. My head sock was next to twist but it yielded little, and it was a mistake to take it off as it cooled quickly making it even more uncomfortable to put back on. I liken it to putting on a damp bathing suit, nothing feels right about it.

My feet were cold and I'm sure they were pruned up like my hands, maybe worse. My calves and thighs were a few shades whiter than normal and covered in tiny goose bumps as they attempted to cause me to shiver some warmth back into them. Standing around was not helping so I was back on the bike heading toward Dunkirk.

The city of Dunkirk was first settled in 1805 but did not incorporate until 1880. In the early 1900s it served as a minor railroad hub and steamship port on Lake Erie. Since the 1960s the population has been shrinking from a high of 18,205 to less than thirteen thousand people today. The drop in steel manufacturing has been the primary driver of this continued contraction.

The per capita income for Dunkirk is only 15,482 dollars leaving a population of more than twenty–two percent below the poverty line. The racial makeup for the city includes sixty–six percent White, five percent African American, and less than half a percent each for Asian, Pacific Islander, and Native Americans. Nine percent were from other races and Latinos accounted for almost twenty–seven percent of the population. This is the highest concentration of Latinos I recall outside of places in the southwest and Dodge City, Kansas. The city sits at an elevation of 617 feet above sea level and is home to the Dunkirk Lighthouse at Point Gratiot which still stands today.

Out of Dunkirk, but still on SR–5E, I crossed over Beaver Creek and passed by Eagle Bay. Through the trees I could see Lake Erie peeking in and out as the road ran close to the water.

At Silver Creek I crossed under an old cement rail bridge and through the old yet well–kept village of 2,896 inhabitants. On the third weekend of September every year the village hosts a Festival of the Grapes featuring a parade, live music and grape stomping. This has been going on since 1968.

A baseball pitcher by the name of Howard "Bob" Ehmke is Silver Creek's best–known resident. Ehmke was the hero of the 1929 World Series, striking out thirteen Chicago Cubs batters in the first game of the series for the Philadelphia Athletics. His record would stand until 1953.

I made the left onto Howard Street, stopped for a minute to flip the cue sheet for the last time, and proceeded to climb a long sweeping right–hander out of the village. SR–5E blended back into SR–20E and I would follow this road climbing up long inclines through mostly forested country until reaching Hamburg. Fortunately the rain let up but it was still cold and I was a long way from being dry.

Over the miles I was no longer entertained by the continuous view of trees with traffic whizzing just off to my left. The road was mostly straight so my only responsibly was to pedal and keep an eye on other riders so I didn't go off course. I finally got a bit of a break as I passed a cemetery on a nice little downhill run near North Evans. At Shadagee Road I crossed a bridge spanning a deep gorge with a sheer rock wall on the far side. Trees clung precariously close to the edge of what looked to be shale layers of brown and gray rock. I was across the bridge and climbing again but at least I enjoyed something different.

The traffic and the density of civilization grew as I continued the gradual climbing to Camp Road. I turned right at the sign for RT–75 and even though I had access to an unused sidewalk I opted to stay on the tarmac and pedal with the two lanes of traffic moving in my direction. Another quick turn at Commerce and I was at the Comfort Inn and Suites.

I didn't recall the final elevation gain but it was something north of 1,500 feet. Not bad considering the mix of miles and the rain. I set about cleaning my filthy bike of all the grit and road trash that clung to it. In the later stages of the ride the dirt had dried and was resisting my efforts to wash it off the frame. After cleaning I inspected the tires and found six to seven glass shards and a piece of radial–tire wire firmly embedded. Fortunately, I did not experience any flats on the road but several other riders had.

Looking back, it was still a good day on the bike. I covered 80.58 miles at an average pace of 14.6 miles an hour. My butt endured five hours twenty–nine minutes of soggy contact with an increasingly intrusive seat. I sailed along at 30.3 miles per hour and while it might have been brief, I did it. I moved the pedals. I made the bike go. The wind and the hills played a part but most of it was me. It was more than a good day. It was a great, wet, cold day.

I'm another day closer to finishing the journey, and after taking a piping hot shower, I'm finally warm. I believe it was also the first time in forty–two days my roommate, Clark, and I both wanted the heat on full.

I skipped the CrossRoads dinner opting to meet friends I had worked with years earlier. Dirk and Dave both live in the Hamburg area so they swung by the hotel and we headed to one of their local haunts to enjoy chicken wings and beer while we filled in the gaps since we last saw each other. It was a few hours well–spent.

Back at the hotel I learned several riders also skipped dinner to go to Niagara Falls an hour north. They had some good stories about their adventure. Many who went had never seen the "Falls" before. As the lobby gathering was breaking up, I stepped outside to take in the last bit of the evening. It was pleasant, the temperature had come down from the high of sixty–three degrees and the skies remained mostly cloudy.

I closed the book on the ride adding in a few details about Hamburg. The town has a population of 56,936 and was named after the city of Hamburg in Germany. The town motto is, "The Town that Friendship Built" and when it was first settled in 1805 it was known as Barkerville. The per capita income is 21,943 dollars and less than five percent of the population lives below the poverty line. Hamburg sits at an elevation of 732 feet and from a demographic perspective it is nearly ninety–eight percent White with only fractions of a percentage for all other races.

Notable people from Hamburg include Pulitzer Prize winning editorial cartoonist, Tom Toles, the infamous E. Howard Hunt, author, CIA Agent and Watergate conspirator, and retired NFL quarterback, Jim Kubiak. Just a short ride up the road is the city of Buffalo, home to the Anchor Bar where Buffalo wings originated back in 1964. Years earlier I was lucky enough to enjoy the wings they prepared at the "Anchor."

Tomorrow we climb 3,200 feet, twice what we did today, and our ride will be approximately ninety–six miles. If we have drier and warmer conditions, it should be a spectacular day.

Day 43: Hamburg to Canandaigua (94 miles)

The calm of twilight was rudely interrupted by siren sounds emanating from the cheap hotel alarm clock radio. Clark got to it first with a forceful slap to the *off* button and silence was restored to the room.

Like every day before I unwillingly left behind a deep sleep, warm covers, and fragments of dreams that dissolved without a trace. Slowly my mind was regaining control of the body as I made my way back into the light of reality. I unintentionally flexed my ankles and flirted with a calf muscle cramp but it quickly retreated as I relaxed my legs. It was another prodding to get me out of bed.

Clark found the push button on the nightstand lamp filling the room with a glow that quickly tapered off as it reached the ubiquitous beige textured wallpaper. My eyes, clouded with a thin film of morning haze, took a few blinks, but it was enough to jumpstart the clearing process. In the dim light I was able to make out shapes and some detail; enough to get my bearings but not much more until I put on my glasses.

With Clark being on staff and having to prep the vehicles and collect items like the map, easel, sign–in sheets from the lobby, and put out the tire pumps, he was always the first to put feet to floor. I took advantage and pulled the covers up and tried to drift back to sleep but my mind began running through its daily checklist making it almost as annoying as that alarm clock. I held back a few minutes and finally rolled out of bed and started assembling my riding outfit. The daily ritual of prepping for another day on the bike had begun.

I showered, dressed, and checked my stock I would carry in my bike bag. It was most of the usual stuff; spare tubes, a multi–tool, tire levers, CO2 cartridges, a small inflator, and then the assorted personal care items. Things like SPF 50 suntan lotion, triple ointment, band aids, and chamois lube. There was more in the bag for emergencies like zip ties, zip lock bags, my cell phone, and my wallet. I managed to add about five extra pounds to the overall riding weight with the supplies in the bag. It was as close to the sweet spot of having what I needed but keeping the weight to a minimum as I felt I could get. On most days I didn't need anything out of the bag, but if I were stranded along the road without a critical item I would not be very happy.

I stepped out of the room and headed down to the lobby where I met a group of riders on their way over to the Bob Evans for breakfast. We were getting a later start this morning so breakfast was moved back to seven thirty. We usually rode out of the hotel at this time but today we would delay an hour.

Breakfast was a cup of coffee accompanied by eggs over medium, hash browns, crispy bacon, and a side of buttered wheat toast topped with strawberry jelly. Just enough to get me to the first SAG about thirty miles into the morning ride. I made an interesting personal observation—I never have strawberry jelly at home but I seem to gravitate to it when I am dining out for breakfast. Most of the riders were sitting down when I arrived. Not sure if they were naturally punctual or if on tour they thought they might miss out if they weren't early for breakfast.

It was always good to see our group fill a place in the morning though I don't think it was always appreciated by the serving crew and kitchen staff. Ken and Gayle sat nearby; I was at the table with Gray, Kathy, and Greg. Behind me it was Big Mike, Duffey, and a few others. It didn't really matter who you sat with. Everyone was friendly and had something of interest to talk about and it reminded me of being back in high school. At this point of the cross country ride it was like spring of senior year. With breakfast complete it was a short downhill walk back to the hotel to put the day on the bike in motion.

Tracy moved the CrossRoads truck to the front of the hotel and in fifteen minutes the bags were loaded, tires pumped, helmets secured, then riders signed out and we officially were on our way to Canandaigua.

As we rolled out under cold, partly cloudy conditions, I thought about the 3,200 feet of climbing ahead. Fortunately, we would enjoy another day of healthy tail winds on our ninety–four–mile ride to Canandaigua, and the hills were mostly rollers instead of long steep climbs.

The ride took us through quaint neighborhoods of brick and board clad homes under full canopies of shade trees, the light piercing through in places, and traffic both light and kind as if they were accustomed to cyclists riding in the lane. We rode through traffic lights and turned at streets named Legion and Armor Dells. At points along the route we would break out into the open where houses sat farther from the road on acreage and the trees gave way to impressive lawns and fields. A few miles later we would be returned to the close quarters of more residential town blocks.

I was in the cycling zone; perfect weather, body in fluid motion with the bike, and my mind able to wander; only minimal attention was needed to keep moving safely east. There was no thought of the effort to pedal, no signs of bike shorts wedging uncomfortably under my weight, or the tingling of nerves in my wrists threatening to go numb with each road induced tremor passing up through the handlebars.

Did it look as effortless to those who might have caught a glimpse of me riding by? I doubt it. They probably didn't even see me. I was as common as any guy on a bike they've seen so many times before. I was all but invisible as I quietly moved in and out of their periphery.

About an hour into the ride we joined a section of Route 20A that took us to a roundabout full of well–manicured flowers and a white pole with the American flag hoisted twenty feet above in its center. This was the village of Aurora. I stopped briefly in the shade to flip my cue sheet and then continued. I took the first right off the circle past Reed's Wine and Spirits and there I saw the first of the CrossRoads vans sitting in the parking lot making sure all of the riders were moving along at a respectable pace. Seeing the support team gave reason to smile and to appreciate how well riders were looked after through the entire ride.

I continued riding east on US–16—locally known as Main Street—enjoying the dedicated bike lane running for blocks away from the roundabout. When the bike lane ended a well–marked three foot wide shoulder afforded a safe zone between the curb and traffic. I passed by a large stone church on the right and a more modest white clapboard church set back from the road on the left. On the corner of South Grove Street was a large fortress–like stone structure complete with a rounded tower and stone wall separating it from the sidewalk. It was impressive and well maintained.

Minutes later I was out of town, the road markings reverted back to Route 20A east, and Main Street was lost again in my mirror. I was looking ahead on the cue sheet for the next turn—Two Rod Road. After pedaling under a highway overpass I rode through miles of rural tree lined country.

I accelerated down a long descent flanked with steel guardrails on both sides. I saw what should be the turn ahead, a blinking light and a Mobil station on the left. It was Two Rod Road. I checked my mirror and oncoming traffic, slid across to the left turn lane and completed the transition heading north toward Porterville.

Farm fields, old farm houses, and barns paralleled the rolling road as I made my way forward. Lynn and Greg were just up ahead but I could see no other riders. There were sections of guardrail close to the shoulder where the ground would drop off, a stand of trees following along the road with intermittent breaks and just a few crossings to negotiate. Porterville turned out to be the intersection of Two Rod where County Road 402 dead ended into it. About the only unique thing I saw was a cluster of evergreen trees, some blue in color and others a dark green, spreading out over a few hundred yards and then tapering off farther north.

I passed an eatery called Kodiak Jacks and noticed the road had its fair share of tar painted over the random cracks. With the temperatures on the cool side the tar did not stick to my tires yet it did a good job masking the defects and providing smooth cover. I have no reason to complain as this state has done a great job keeping the roads in cycling friendly order.

Marilla was another crossroads town with a country store on one side of Two Rod and a little eatery in an old two–story wooden house on the other. Across a creek and I started to look for the next turn onto Clinton Street. Actually it was called out on the Route 354E marker I saw a hundred yards from the turn.

Talk about rural. There was plenty of room for future commercialization of this crossroads area. I stopped and checked the next section of the cue sheet; only six more miles to go to the SAG. I took a long pull of Gatorade and chased it down with a short sip of water. This was the first drink I took since breakfast. I returned the water bottle to its cage and clipped back into the pedals in search of the SAG.

The scenery flipped from fields, farms, fields, and more fields through this stretch. As I made my way along the peaceful journey I felt down on power and was becoming a bit sluggish. I crossed over Cayuga Creek and just beyond it was my left turn toward Alden. Less than three miles up Exchange Street the cue sheet warned of rough railroad tracks.

I saw signs ahead as I crossed another small creek. Just before the tracks on the left was The Whistle Stop banquet and catering business. They had a weathered sign of an old steam engine and in front of this was a miniature wooden train about fifteen feet long complete with a few cars and a caboose all perched two feet above the ground on its own set of tracks. It was all well landscaped and gave me reason to stop and take a picture. These are the unique images to be recorded and shared with others.

I mounted up and carefully approached the railroad crossing without issue. A tenth mile more Exchange came to an end as it ran into Route 20 east. I turned right. The breakfast I filled up on had been used up in the first thirty miles so I was happy to see the SAG up ahead at the Mobil gas station.

I parked my bike, removed my gloves and helmet, then walked over to the van to sign in and fuel up on banana, strawberries, and cakey snacks. I hadn't used much of the water or Gatorade from my bottles so I made a point to top them off for the next leg of the ride. It got me thinking that falling behind on hydration may have contributed to my sluggishness. To catch back up I drank three paper cups of Gatorade from the Van cooler and readied my gear. I noticed the difference within the first five minutes of riding and I was feeling strong again.

I would ride straight east on Route 20 for the next thirty miles through Darien, Alexander, LeRoy, and Caledonia before crossing the railroad tracks highlighted on the cue sheet. These were a bit ragged and slightly angled which is what makes the tracks risky for a rider. Approaching the tracks at a right angle is critical to keep from hooking your wheel and going down. Through this stretch there was corn, a few barns and farms with a sprinkle of private homes and commercial businesses. There was no question farming is vital in this part of New York, and corn is the mainstay of the economy.

In the open with the tail wind I was able to reach thirty miles per hour on the flats and exceed thirty–eight miles per hour on the downhill grades. I was giddy like a little kid on his first downhill run.

Route 20 intersected and combined with Route 5 at a blinking light and my ride continued along an easterly trajectory on what was now Route 20. I crossed a long concrete flat bridge over the Genesee River on the outskirts of the village of Avon where the second SAG would be found.

It was a slight climb into the town center past older framed houses and businesses but I still had the wind pressing firmly at my back and the incline posed no real challenge. Safely over another set of railroad tracks I pedaled into a series of multi–story brick buildings surrounding a large roundabout forming the heart of Avon. I had arrived and needed only to negotiate a quarter of the roundabout to pull into the fire station parking lot where Margaret was ready to serve the afternoon snacks and replenish our fluids.

Things were going well sixty–eight miles into the ride. I found a bit of real estate to park my bike and took advantage of the fire station hospitality for a well needed nature call. The pause also gave me a chance to butter up the undercarriage for the final twenty–six miles.

I usually avoid having a normal meal during my riding but today was different; I thought conditions would allow me the indulgence. Before finding lunch I topped off my water bottles, grabbed a few snacks to eat during the last stretch, and started down the sidewalk against the roundabout traffic in search of a sit down meal.

To the right of the fire station was Pizza Land. I do like pizza so I gave it consideration but decided to keep on moving nearer to the road where I entered the roundabout. Just a few doors away I found the Village Restaurant. It was centered in the middle of a three story red brick building to the right of the State Bank of Avon.

Cars were pointed "nose–in" at an odd angle in front with only a few yards of concrete and brick sidewalk as a separation. The front door sat beneath a green canvas barrel canopy and it was flanked on both sides by large commercial picture windows. An inviting wooden bench sat just left of the door. The impression of the eatery was homey and inviting at the same time. I think it was the exterior sign above that really caught my attention. Painted a cool white with bold blue lettering and a coffee cup graphic, all aged by the elements was enough to sway me to walk in.

I found a booth halfway back and to the left then slid into the padded vinyl seat facing away from the windows. Not the way you would sit if you were paranoid but I had Geoff Brown sitting across from me.

A thirty something waitress brought over two menus, asked if we wanted coffee, and placed pre–wrapped silverware on the table. The interior was much older looking than the brick front and sign but it had a reasonable number of diners to put me at ease. I had a sandwich, a side, and an ice tea. It was nothing fancy, just good food at a fair price. We chatted about the ride and traded comments with the waitress; nothing memorable, just random conversation.

The seat was getting more comfortable the longer I sat but after a little over thirty minutes it was time to go. Back at the SAG a new set of riders meandered around. The clouds were now consuming the sky and beginning to take on a more ominous appearance. The temperature was also changing. It was warm when I went into the restaurant, but now it was noticeably cooler.

I did not have my cycling jacket with me so the final push had the potential to a bit uncomfortable. What the weather is going to do was anyone's guess. It was nature's unpredictability in charge.

The winds were still strong and they remained favorable blowing west to east as they had all day. I took in the view of the grassy area inside the roundabout. It was a formal and well–manicured park complete with sidewalks that crisscrossed the grass into nearly equal slices, and there was a pole mounted American flag flying taut in the wind at its highest point. Flowers covered a good portion of the ground adding color and interest. Large trees provided ample shade.

I mounted my bike and rolled out with Paul, Geoff, and a few others strung out in a rag–tag line with no sense of order. We navigated another quarter of the roundabout and then one by one peeled off to the right continuing on Route 20E. Over the next twenty miles the temperature dropped and a un–forecasted storm closed in.

I pulled to the side of the road where it was level and I dug into my bike bag to get a plastic Ziploc bag to cover the bar–mounted computers. Today I would take field action. Had the morning weather forecast called for rain I would have put the bag on before leaving the hotel. I would have also grabbed my cycling jacket and found space for it in the bike bag. Not two minutes later I was back in motion.

In the mirror I could see the storm coming. It was approaching from behind and to the south, the wind advancing it faster than I could sail. Ten miles from the SAG riders were consumed in a heavy downpour working from back to front; west to east. We still had a strong tailwind but it had a new erratic component added to it; the dreaded occasional side gusts. I was chilled to the bone in the freezing rain, jacketless with no supplementary layer to help retain my body heat. At least my computers were dry and readable.

My helmet, like all Road bike models, is well–vented with several long slots running front to back each more than half an inch wide. The slots are intended to let heat out but right now the rain pours into them like funnels directing the water to my head sock. In short order my sock is soaked unable to hold back the rain washing down on all sides of my head. So much ran down my forehead it was like facing into a shower. Just a few notches away from being water boarded on a bike. Things were getting interesting but not in a good way.

The discomfort from the cold rain was nothing compared to the sudden fogging of my sunglasses and water in my eyes reducing visibility to about zero. I could barely see the white line separating the shoulder from the traffic lane, and with all the rain, and the lack of noise because of the strong tailwind I lost my sense of speed. I felt like I was barely moving and was about to put my right foot to the pavement thinking I was going slow enough to come to a stop. That would have been a huge mistake. It wasn't until I wiped my eyes and caught a brief glimpse of the computer display when I realized I was going thirty–four miles per hour.

I've never put a foot down going that fast but I was seeing the results of such a move in my mind. God needs a little extra knee time tonight for keeping watch over this boy.

So here I am speeding in the rain, one hand on the bars, rain masking all the road holes, debris and imperfections, cars speeding by two feet to my left and brakes that don't work; throw in an occasional side gust with the steady burning in my eyes and you have all the ingredients for a nasty bike wreck. Fortunately, I stayed up and avoided all of the traffic.

The last few miles, I tipped my sunglasses down and rode blurry–eyed as the rain dialed back from torrential to a steady but tolerable soaking. I could finally breathe again.

In the air was the smell of ozone and a freshness that often comes after a heavy rain. My legs and lower body were covered in a spray of road grit, slimy bits of things once alive, and pieces of dried grass and flecks of clover. My bike did not fare any better and both would be in need of a heavy cleaning when the ride ended.

Water spray continued to stream off my tires and onto my body. If I leaned or turned the bars left or right the spray would angle out to hit my forearms and it would run down from my elbows to wrists before it dripped back onto the road. My shoes were so wet I could look down and see the water squishing out by the laces as the shoes flexed. At times they made an audible sound that was fitting given the amount of water they had been burdened with.

I don't like having my feet in wet shoes and I make no exception when I'm on a bike. I could feel my toes getting waterlogged. They would be pale wrinkled digits by the time I get them out of the socks and into the free air. Drying the shoes will be important because I won't do well riding if I have to start with wet feet.

The rain tapered off to a drizzle and eventually stopped completely. My upper body began to dry as I rode on through the New York countryside. My lower body and my back were not so lucky. There was so much water lying on the road it provided a steady supply of wetness splashing up off the tires. I was hoping the sun would poke out and help return conditions to a more normal state.

I caught sight of a sign "Canandaigua Business District and Lake Resort Area" on a long downhill glide so I knew my turn was just ahead. I passed the Route 5E sign and approached the fork in the road where I would roll off to the right toward the resort area. The road had a slight grade to it causing me to work a bit harder to keep speed as the wind was no longer at my back. It was now coming from my right side as I rode more south than east. Both sides of the road had berms tapering up into thick stands of trees but they flattened out in short order and the trees thinned out too as I continued.

It didn't take long and the sun did indeed come out. It warmed up quickly, or at least it felt like it was as I began to dry. The water on the road reduced to dampness and only a few shallow puddles remained. Eventually dry patches appeared and the asphalt began to turn a few shades lighter as it dried. My shoes still wet I continued to move down the road. As I dried I could feel the grit and goo on my legs. I looked a few times but I couldn't do much about it. The tops of my shoes also had their fair share of sand and residue sitting on them. I assume I'll find more of the same inside my shoes and socks when they finally get removed.

I crossed over NY–21at a traffic light and continued straight toward the end of my ride. The road started a long wide left hand sweeper and oncoming traffic now had two lanes to work with. I was descending again but ever so slightly. The road came back in line with the tailwind which was now just a shadow of what it had been but after riding just shy of a century I was not one to complain.

Along Route 5E I noticed several large patches of gravel rocks, the size of softballs on both sides of the road. The rocks were on the berms just across the drainage ditches from the pavement. Not something put there by man but it looked odd and out of place.

Safety rails came into play and I was crossing over County Road 16 still riding the downhill. The road bent slightly to the right and I could now see water; it was Canandaigua Lake. Buildings, signs, and more intersections came into view and I was now riding on the flats and counting down the minutes.

A pickup truck pulling an open trailer with a racecar on it passed on my left about a mile shy of the hotel. I didn't notice the number painted on the doors because it was fifty yards past before I realized it was a racecar. I can tell you it was painted black if that matters. It was a "dirt car" common in this part of the country which meant it had a narrowed tin body, no front fenders or windshield, and big wide tires with deep treads cut across at an angle to grab traction in the dirt.

I knew Canandaigua had a half–mile dirt track, or at least there was a track by that name. I watched the rig disappear in the distance about half a mile ahead. I thought I might ask around at the hotel if the track happened to be nearby and if they could provide any details about the racing. If the track was close by, and if the rain didn't wash out the night, I might just get a chance to take in my second evening of racing on the tour. I was thinking back to Dodge City, Kansas where I was able to catch the racing on their dirt track but rain abruptly ended the entertainment before it had really gotten started. Maybe tonight will be different.

Anyway there would be lots to do when I get to the hotel; bike cleaning, sink washing of my gear, cleaning and drying of my shoes, then route rap, dinner, and the prepping of tomorrow's riding outfit.

I remember using newspaper stuffed into my shoes to dry them out just a few days back so before I get to the hotel I better think about stopping to pick up a local publication to serve as the wick for my footwear. Lucky me I was close to the Parkway strip mall so I ducked right into the parking lot to look for a paper. I found a local newspaper supplement with just enough pages to fill the shoes. With the paper in hand I mounted the bike, meandered through the lot back to the Route 5E, and was on my way down the last half mile where I would turn left into the Econo Lodge Muir Lakes. It was a fancy name for a basic hotel sitting two hundred yards back from the highway.

I did a basic cleaning and mechanical check of the bike then I hosed it off using the water from the hotel faucet. A gentle wipe–down with some old towels the staff had set out for us finished the task. With the bike cleaning done I was ready to move to the next item on my to–do list which was sink laundry and a body cleaning.

The lobby was small and it was cold because I was still wet and the air conditioning was working overtime. I was given my key, verbal directions to the room, and traded quick conversation with the lady working the front counter. Since the hotel was only two floors it was an easy trek up the steps and down the hall to the room facing the rear of the hotel.

In standard CrossRoads style I opened the room door, the air conditioning was turned way down low, and the curtains were pulled wide open letting in the light. Out the window was a pond surrounded by a mowed lawn. Behind the pond was a stand of trees separating the hotel property from a field of wild grass. A water view at least.

My bags were set on the end of the bed near the window as I came in so I rolled my bike to the far side of the room and turned it around facing the window with the chain nearest the wall. Still wearing my shoes, helmet, gloves, and all my clothes, I stepped right into a piping hot shower. Piece by piece starting with the helmet and then my shoes, I rinsed each item and set them in the back of the tub. I made sure I rinsed all of the road grit off my legs before I peeled off the shorts and socks. Then I rinsed those items and gave them a thorough twist to get out the bulk of the water.

I gave myself a full body scrub and soaped up a second time because I still felt gritty. My feet were slow to let out the cold and they were wrinkled from the wet ride. I picked up my shoes again and took out the liners and flooded them with more water. Satisfied there was nothing else to wash out I shut off the water and repeated the twisting of clothes to get even more water out. I stepped out, grabbed a towel, and dried off.

I dug through my bag and pulled out a fresh pair of underwear, my black cargo shorts, and my prized blue CrossRoads t–shirt. Soon I was all decked out in street clothes complete with a pair of socks and my white New Balance sneakers. I went back into the bathroom and did a more thorough washing of my cycling clothes. I set my damp socks on the air conditioner housing and used my bike frame as a hanger for the rest of my gear. The shoes were stuffed with newspaper less the liners and set upside down directly over the blowing air conditioning vent. I'd change the paper before going to bed. I also hung my helmet and heartrate monitor strap on the bike handlebars like I did at the end of each ride.

I wrote down the details of the day in my journals and started to plan what I would do before route rap. It was now late in the afternoon, route rap would be coming up soon and then I heard a sound out the window; it was the sound of race cars and they were not far away. I hurried down to the lobby and sure enough the lady said the Canandaigua Fairgrounds were only a mile away by road, maybe a half mile directly behind the hotel.

Clark's wife had joined the tour and she had a car. Clark was kind enough to offer the use of the car so long as I was careful with it. I was thrilled. Tom Jelmyer and Dick Duffey heard the sounds too and wanted to go so we set a plan to catch some dirt track racing after we ate. Just a few hours should be plenty to watch.

Across the highway from the Econo Lodge was a Wegman's Grocery store where riders were getting their film developed at the One Hour lab. Several raved about Wegman's but I've never heard of it. They were supposed to be a high–end grocer complete with their own food court. It sounded cool and the riders I talked with liked it. A few said they were going back over after dinner to do more exploring and maybe check out the lake behind it.

Route rap was one of celebration for the day's ride; some folks laughing about the rain, there was talk of wet shoes and the ride to Syracuse tomorrow. Tracy shushed us so she could detail what to expect. It would be nearly thirty miles shorter and a thousand feet less climbing then we had today. She gave us the chance to comment and ask questions and then we were off to the Ponderosa for dinner.

As always feeding the herd was a daily event. The staff did their best to accommodate us and tonight they were on their game. They had us spread out at tables and booths, the orders quickly went back to the kitchen, and after getting our drinks the food started coming out. I heard few complaints and saw lots of clean plates. We would be back here tomorrow for breakfast at seven thirty for another late morning start. I hope the morning shift will be as prepared.

There was one item on the checklist to address tonight; the stock car racing at the dirt track. I got the car key from Clark and rounded up Tom and Dick. Conditions were favorable so we headed out in shorts and t–shirts.

It was just over a mile away and directions were simple—left out of the hotel, a quarter mile, left at the light, one mile left into the fairgrounds property. I parked the car and then we made our way to the ticket booth; a little wooden shack painted white with the admission priced according to age. Ten dollars each and we were headed to the bleachers running parallel to the main straight away.

We sat up about twelve rows, just a few shy of the top, and soon the stands were completely full. They love their racing here in Canandaigua.

The track was shaped like a paper clip. The turns were tight and along the back and left end of the speedway they did not have a fence. If drivers were out of control they had ample room to drive off and slow down until they recover. The racecars and support equipment were all parked in what was called, "the pits" about three hundred feet outside the left end turns. The pits were full and we arrived as the last practice sessions were taking place. The only seating was along the front stretch. And we were between the flag stand and turn one which was to our right. The track was equipped with concrete sections forming a wall between the stands and the muddy racing surface. Behind the concrete wall was a chain link fence wired to a series of vertical poles providing additional protection from cars and parts should they attempt to fly off the track.

The announcer was behind and above us with some other officials in what looked like an enclosed shed with picture windows to see the on–track action. They played the national anthem, the announcer called the drivers to line up, and it got really noisy again. We watched for about two hours, maybe more. It had gotten dark and the track lights were now illuminating the racing. There were spills, and fender benders, and some close racing. I couldn't hear the announcer well enough so the drivers remain unknown to me but we had a good time. We decided it was getting a bit cool for shorts and t–shirts so we packed it in and headed to the car for the short hop back to the hotel. I reversed the directions and in less than five minutes we were parked and walking into the hotel.

No riders were strolling around the hotel; they were all smartly in bed getting ready for the ride to Syracuse in the morning. I was up the stairs and in my room after saying goodnight to Tom and Dick. I changed the newspaper in my shoes, set the clock, and readied for bed. I was surprised my cycling shoes were almost dry so I happily re–stuffed them with crumpled newspaper and returned them to the vent of the air conditioner. There was nothing left to do except turn out the lights and drift off. A cyclist counts his stats, not sheep—94.2 miles, six hours, 15.7 miles per hour average, and a crazy 38.3 maximum speed rolled through my mind as I burrowed my head into the pillow and pulled the covers tight. I could still hear the stock cars rumbling from the track. It was the last sound I would hear until the buzzer in the morning brought me back.

Day 44: Canandaigua to Syracuse (70 miles)

Mild temperatures and tail winds gave us another good start for the day. The ride to Syracuse would be short, so our departure time moved back an hour to eight–thirty. Breakfast was a hike on foot so a few riders opted to pedal their bikes the half mile each way. I walked. My normal breakfast routine with the riders was much like any day before. A typical country style spread of scrambled eggs, bacon, and toast, lots of coffee, juice, and water. A few riders ate heavy with pancakes and French toast while others, a bit more health conscious, worked on their oatmeal and yogurt. It was like the forty some odd days before.

When traveling with such a group you forget how odd you look to the average diners. Spandex padded shorts, vented jerseys, head socks, and some with leggings. We looked like a freakish cast of dancers trading grace and balance for depends under garment protection. People looked at us but didn't want to be like us. And we were okay with that. We had our own "cool" going on.

Full of breakfast comfort I was back up in the room finishing my preparations for the ride. At about 8:20 a.m., Tom J. came up to the room and told me the other riders had just left. *What the heck?* A sense of semi–panic settled in. I felt I needed to be with the group and they would soon be an easy two to three miles down the road.

So with a ten minute head start, I would really have to push hard to catch them. I zipped my bags, grabbed my bike, and hurried all my gear down the stairs. Even with the recessed mountain bike cleats, moving fast on foot was a bit sketchy. I made my way out the hotel lobby door and to the back of the CrossRoads box truck. Trevor took possession of my carry–on bags and stowed them in back with the rest of the rider bags. I quickly checked my tires, clipped my helmet and slipped into my gloves.

With a stroke of the pen I signed out and was pedaling toward the main road heading east once again. I was back on Route 20E where I had finished the day before. Traffic was steady, the shoulder narrow, and my legs would take some time to warm up. I pushed up gentle climbs and enjoyed the shallow drops but kept the pressure on the pedals. I rode past farm equipment retailers, car dealerships, antique shops, and a variety of other distractions. Old houses with cars parked in gravel drives and others askew in the grass; some homes well cared for and others showing signs of neglect. This was rural highway riding at its best; nothing but a ribbon of pavement, two lanes of traffic from one small town to another through the countryside.

The sound of the wind, the road, and the cars drowned out the ticks and clicks from my bike as I shifted the chain across the cog of gears. I could feel my breathing as I worked but stayed safely within my comfort zone. My legs were sluggish but warming up quickly. I needed them to catch the pack.

I had come a long way since LA, not just in miles but in strength and endurance. I was tanned, toned, and one with the bike. I know this ride will come to an end but for now I'm going to keep my mind on the rhythm of the pedals, the beauty beyond the road, and the carefree feeling that only riding a bike for days on end can bring. A boy on his bike enjoying the wind in his face and the freedom that comes with it. I wish my girls Janel and Nicole could see the smile filling my face right now. I hope in their life they get to be a kid for a second time, or maybe even a third. That would be one of my many wishes for them.

I think about those following my progress through the end of day phone calls, the post cards, and the newspaper articles I've been writing each week. I wonder what they are thinking. I think back to Abilene

Kansas and the phone conversation I had with my friend Kathy who I worked with back in Florida. She was inspired and I was humbled. I was living life like the few who dared to dream. I liked being on this side of life, not bound to a desk, logging time, and dreaming of a "someday" adventure. In and out my mind goes as I push myself to be faster in search of the riders ahead.

I'm deep into New York and this epic trip is about to become one of the biggest checks on this boy's bucket list. I have enjoyed all of the country but upstate New York to me is God's finest work. I'm immersed in lush green foliage, fields of wild flowers, meandering rivers, and all of this against some of the bluest skies to be seen. At my pace I can drink it all in and create the mental images I hope will stay with me throughout the rest of my life. A thought came to mind; how do you explain a trip like this to someone who has never done anything as unusual? This is certainly not normal yet I would argue it should be. How will I convey the emotions, the challenges, and the joys? I know I'll tear up when I try to explain it so maybe those listening will see through the shaky delivery and grasp what I have to say and what I've been through. Or they may not. They may need to go on their own adventure. Then we can share our stories, the feelings, the pains, the joys, the fears, and the tears. More than the words; yes it was more than the words.

It has been a roller coaster ride in many ways; climbing and coasting, roasting in the sun, and freezing in the rain, chased by dogs, spooked by careless drivers, rattled by divots and debris in the road. Riding hurt, feeling strong, being old and feeling young. Alone facing a relentless headwind and being with friends tapping the brake levers because the tailwinds make you uncomfortably fast. Tired and cramping, energetic like a wild horse, bored at times but never at a loss for the beauty was all around me. In and out of focus, my attention drifted from the now to places in my mind. It has been everything and nothing I expected. It was pure joy. I was a kid again.

Staying hydrated and carb loaded even in today's ride is important so I took pulls on my water bottle and nibbled on the Clif bars and a banana I was toting in my jersey pocket. I began to drop into a longer and steeper descent revealing a large body of water ahead. This was a change from the expanses of green fields and trees so my attention to the surroundings became sharper. Signage indicated Route 20, which was also Highway 5 through this part of New York. In Geneva proper it was known as Hamilton Street.

The road angled to the left as the small town of Geneva grew before me. I say small because Geneva is just shy of three thousand people and it sits right on the northern end of a lake; Seneca Lake to be precise, yet some maps just call it Finger Lakes. One of the many north–south cuts through the countryside created by southbound glacial migrations more than twenty–two thousand years ago leaving behind smooth exposed land and deep trenches of water. On my right was Long Pier and as I pressed forward still enjoying the downhill grade I crossed over East Castle Street and had an even closer view of the lake a hundred yards to my right. Hamilton gave way to Lake Front Drive and the road began to flatten out. Pedaling was now required to keep any momentum at all. Running parallel to the highway was a rail line to the left and a narrow ribbon of parkland wedged in between me and the lake. One sign said Lakefront Park and another sign said Seneca Lake State Park. They were both beckoning me to stop but I was still lagging behind and wanted to join the company of other riders instead of riding in solitude.

For the next three miles I rode with the lake to my right. Geneva gave way to fields and marsh as Route 20 continued on an east–northeast heading along the meandering Cayuga Seneca Canal Trail. Route 20 took on another new name, Waterloo Geneva Road, as I worked my way toward Waterloo, the birthplace of Memorial Day.

So many little towns across America lay claim to some piece of history and in 1866 Waterloo would claim hers. The following words cast in raised bronze on a blue background of a historical marker just outside of Waterloo are a testament to its history.

On May 5, 1866 the residents of Waterloo held the first complete community–wide observance of Memorial Day. They dedicated the entire day to honoring the Civil War dead in a solemn and patriotic manner. Throughout the village, flags draped in mourning flew at half–mast. Ladies prepared wreaths and bouquets for each veteran's grave. Businesses closed, and veterans, civic organizations and townspeople marched to the strains of martial music to the village cemeteries. There with reverent prayers and patriotic ceremonies the tradition of Memorial Day was born.

Henry C. Wells, a prominent citizen, first proposed the idea for a day completely devoted to honoring the Civil War dead. General John B. Murray, the Seneca County Clerk who had commanded the 148th New York Infantry Regiment in the war, quickly advanced the thought and marshalled community support. Since that year, Waterloo has annually observed Memorial Day. New York, in 1873, became the first state to proclaim Memorial Day, or Decoration Day, as it was originally called, a public holiday.

In May 1966, a joint resolution by the United States Congress and a proclamation by President Lyndon B. Johnson officially recognized Waterloo as the birthplace of Memorial Day.

Waterloo incorporated April 9, 1824 and again on May 5, 1866. It's a typical rural upstate New York community with a population fewer than 5,200 and a 97.61 percent white make up; which means it's nearly void of any diversity. Median family income for a family in the village is 65,709 dollars and women out–number men by nearly five to four so single guys take note.

I felt a sense of calm as I rode through the Village of Waterloo. It was a good feeling. It was good to mark a day to remember those lost fighting for our country, even when the fight was amongst our own.

Eastward I go. One pedal revolution after another. The sound of tiny bits of gravel fragments getting pinched out from under my tires firing off in random directions ticking across the asphalt. I'm still in pursuit of the other riders, but enjoying the time alone. No pace line riding to coordinate with, I'm free to ride at my pace whatever it may be.

The four miles past Waterloo kept me within five hundred feet of the Cayuga Seneca Canal, the connector between the two lakes it was named after. I pedaled past convenience stores and Coon's Cans, car dealerships and Kinney Drugs. Small businesses were alive if not thriving in this busy stretch of Highway 5. I suspect it's tourism related. Upstate New York suits me. It's beautiful this time of year and probably the other 364 days I'm not pedaling through it.

As I entered Seneca Falls proper to my left were Avicolli's Pizza and Little Italy, another Italian eatery. Beyond those two as I continued on what was also Fall Street were Parker's Grill and Tap House and the National Women's Hall of Fame.

The Women's Hall is both interesting and historically significant giving reason to pause. The building was an architectural delight; a two story stone block structure of limestone material with twin gothic fluted columns supporting an ornate parapet and a cantilevered overhang. Centered between the columns, an entry, mostly of glass and trimmed in a bright paint to match the tall but narrow window frames to the left and right. Above the door a small row of fixed windows and a proportionally sized cantilevered overhang that tied in with the rest of the architecture. Carved into the stonework just above the windows were the words, "76 FALL ST" marking the location. It was a unique building and in its prior life it was the Seneca Falls Savings Bank. Between the floors flanking the entry, two American flags were proudly displayed. The design was balanced if not completely symmetrical and it looked much older than it probably was. The Hall also stood out from the brick fronted buildings making it easy to find.

While off the bike I did some snooping around to learn about the Hall's history which dated back to 1848 when the Women's Rights Convention was held nearby. The Hall was officially dedicated in 1969 by the people of Seneca Falls with the mission of honoring in perpetuity those women, citizens of the United States of America, whose contributions to the arts, athletics, business, education, government, the humanities, philanthropy and science, have been of the greatest value for the development of their country.

Acceptance into the Hall is a rigorous process. Women are considered based on the changes they created affecting the social, economic or cultural aspects of society, the significant national or global impact and results of change due to their achievement, and the enduring value of their achievements or changes. I've paraphrased a little here but I think I've captured the essence of its purpose. The Hall is near the Women's Rights National Historical Park established at the site in 1848. So if you want to stand on the holy ground you are just a few steps away.

I flipped the cue sheet to the second quadrant and was eyeing the SAG at the 38.5 mile mark another forty–five minutes down the road. Back on the bike I made a quick turn to the left to stay on Route 20. It would be almost seven miles before the next turn so I pedaled and soaked in the scenery. Bending left then right the road made its way around the north end of Cayuga Lake following a lumpy clockwise half–circle through the Montezuma National Wildlife refuge toward Turnpike Road where I would make my next left. It was very quiet and enjoyable with only a few mild elevation changes. The next thirty–six miles would serve up more challenging terrain as we were on track to gain a total of 2,200 feet of climbing for the day.

I executed the turn and was blessed with a smooth and generous shoulder to ride on. The two lanes of traffic were light and drivers courteous as they had been so far since entering the Empire state. Traffic lights were nonexistent with only stop and yield signs to control traffic on the intersecting roads. A slight breeze from behind remained as I continued in a northeast direction.

After bragging on the great roads New York State had served up I caught sight of what I thought was a road patch but I was wrong. It was a deep hole and at the last instant I jerked the bars up sparing the front wheel but planted the rear tire solidly with a jolting thud that resonated right through my tailbone like an electric shock. The tire didn't blow and a quick glance down reassured me the wheel was still intact. I need to learn to "Bunny Hop" these obstacles like Tracy does.

I was humping it up the slight grades and racing the downhills averaging about 18.5 miles per hour when I began to see other riders. Thoughts about conversation would be short lived though as my bike got sluggish at the thirty–five–mile mark and the riders vanished in the distance. Not a problem. Flat tires are an easy fix having changed many for other riders over the last several weeks. When I craned my head down and looked between my legs to catch a glimpse of the rear tire I could see it throb to the side like it had a nervous tick. Definitely not a flat tire but I would have been happier to be out of contention for the "No Flat Tire" money wagered back in Los Angeles. The wheel was bent from the pothole impact and with each rotation the wobble got worse.

Things were getting interesting in a not so good way; the angst of a late start, the pounding of a pothole, and the excitement of seeing riders only to watch them fade before reaching them. I sure didn't need this to turn into a major mechanical failure midway through the ride so I backed off my aggressive pace.

I was no longer thinking about the sights and sounds as much as I was focused on the road ahead and grinding out the next few miles to the SAG. I thought about last night's route rap; mostly the talk of climbing to Syracuse. At nearly a thousand feet less than the ride to Canandaigua it sounded easy but most of the 2,200 feet of elevation gain would happen in the second half of the day. With the ride to Syracuse being almost thirty miles shorter the climbing would also be steeper.

Tailwinds would not be as strong nor would they find their way to my back to push me up the hilly tree–lined windy roads. I'd have to work to get to my destination and I would have to navigate more attentively. The cue sheet had five quadrants and there were many turns and markers less than two–tenths of a mile apart creating just the right opportunity to get off course if but a single detail was not executed properly. It was so much different than yesterday.

One step at a time. One turn of the pedals. Mile by mile. Inch by inch. Wobble, wobble, wobble. It was getting worse, the rim started rubbing on the brake pads; I was slowing down but I could see the riders stopped ahead.

At the SAG, Tracy adjusted out the wobble. With a few turns of the spoke wrench it was almost perfect and my anxiety level settled back to concerns of making all the right turns. I spun the tire once more after putting it back on the bike. There was no rubbing on the brakes and no apparent damage. I'd have Rick or Tom J. take a look at the wheel and put it on a proper truing fixture to make sure it passes their approval.

I fell back into the standard SAG routine of topping off fluids, loading up on carb snacks, chatting and joking with the other riders and telling stories about missed turns, interesting landmarks, flat tires, and things that fell off or were dropped from the bikes. It seemed everyone had a story and a different perspective of the day as it unfolded up to the first SAG.

Once fueled up I was back on the bike and heading toward restrooms eight miles ahead. Where possible the SAG stop is located at a place where conveniences exist but in this part of New York convenience and a logical place for SAG stops do not always intersect.

I had to pee so I was now focused on getting down the road to one of the stores Tracy noted on the cue sheet. Plan *B* was a tree by the roadside. As I pedaled I was constantly catching a glimpse of my mileage readings. Like watching a pot of boiling water the miles seem to go slower when I get fixated on the displays. It was tough to occupy my mind and forget about the digital readouts and I became more obsessed with the process. It's clearly a disorder albeit a harmless one. I also have similar quirks about counting steps between sidewalk cracks. Go figure.

Passing through the town of Sennett I merged onto Route 5E in search of a convenience store. My pace was back up to a healthy seventeen plus on the relatively flat stretch and it wouldn't be long before I reached my destination. I passed the famed Rolling Wheels Raceway dirt track I had read about in the racing papers. It would have been fun to take a closer look but my bladder was in charge, pushing me to go even faster. I arrived in Elbridge and found my relief. Plan *B* was not necessary.

The village of Elbridge and the town surrounding it are named for Elbridge Gerry the fifth Vice President of the United States and one of the signers of the Declaration of Independence. He was paired with James Madison and the two were elected in 1812. Gerry died late in 1814 and while he was instrumental in forging the Bill of Rights, most people are more familiar with the infamous term "Gerrymander" attributed to his controversial redistricting plans giving the Republicans an advantage in the 1811 Massachusetts elections. I wonder how many of the six thousand plus residents know the story?

Route 5E comes to an end turning into Route 174S as I approach the village of Camillus. The cue sheet becomes critical with turns every few tenths of a mile. A left on Newport, a right onto Devoe Road and I'm riding by the Erie Canal Park. Several riders stopped to see the Sims Store Museum and the Steam Engine Exhibit. The Sims Store features exhibits, early photos, and maps of the canal with models of locks, aqueducts and canal boats. The Steam Engine Exhibit has a fully restored, turn–of–the–century steam powered power plant considered "high–tech" a hundred years earlier. The Park also offers more than ten miles of wooded walking trails and boat rides along the Erie Canal. I rolled in but only for a few minutes. I was anxious to get back to the hotel and check my rear wheel in more detail.

Just past the park the climbing kicked in and it would not let up for the remaining ten miles of the ride. Kathy Stevens on her recumbent bike was crawling her way up the hill. It looked formidable, like a wall, as I approached it and it sure felt that way when I was pounding the pedals on the way up.

The Northeast has some of the steepest old roads in the country, built before the days of modern highways and better planning. We would be treated to some of them. Having to climb with only pedal power magnified the difficulty and then the memory exaggerated it even further. For the record an eight percent grade challenges your ability not to swear! Years from now when I tell the story about the climbing it will seem like an exaggeration that can only be accepted as truth if I could put you at the bottom of the same hill.

Lucky for us we didn't have to climb this road to the top. Thompson veered off to the right and appeared to be the easier climb. Only those who missed the turn and grunted their way up Devoe would know for sure. We were treated to several climbs and exhilarating drops along Ninemile Creek until it angled off under the cover of heavy foliage. Then it was more turns and more climbing. Our riding was a balance of pedaling under the cover of shade trees in the quiet rural settings and out in the open with congested traffic and lots of tension. There was a little something for everybody.

Throw in a couple of railroad crossings to make sure you sweat and the next thing you know the seventy mile outing ended at the Hampton Inn at 417 7th North Street; our home for the night. Who's ready to go another fifty miles said no one. My final tally for the day was 69.91 miles, four hours twenty minutes of seat time, an average pace of 15.9 miles an hour and a top speed of 33.6 miles per hour. I also dodged mechanical woes thanks to Tracy and her little spoke wrench.

I needed to shower and get the wrinkles and aches, not to mention the road grime, off of me so I can get into my street clothes and feel human again. It would be laundry night for some but not for me. After having Rick true up my rear wheel on the jig I had other plans.

Kathy invited several of us to a family gathering at her Brother Tom's house not far from the hotel. It was a multi–purpose party that for starters celebrated Tom and his wife Sally's retirement and their upcoming relocation to Florida. In addition they were celebrating Kathy's cross country journey and as good hosts they celebrated our efforts as well. It was also a small family reunion of fifteen relatives and a birthday celebration for the twins.

Somehow we managed to fit nearly a dozen of our group into two cars for the ride over, but before we got out of the cars we were treated to a proper tour of the area. You get enough riders together and one of them is going to know somebody along the way.

Tom and his wife were exceptional hosts. They prepared a full barbeque spread with all the fixings and they welcomed us like family. It was a perfect evening capped off by our singing happy birthday to Chelsea and John, Kathy's twin niece and nephew. What a day it was.

Syracuse tipped the population scales at 146,070 people and it increases to six hundred sixty thousand if you include the greater metro area. What's most interesting is this city has been shrinking since 1950 when its population peaked at 220,583. The city is still the fifth largest in the state and sits at the northeast corner of the Finger Lakes region at an elevation of 380 feet above sea level.

The demographics of Syracuse are wildly more diverse than other cities we have pedaled through in the state. The racial makeup includes fifty–six percent White, 29.5 percent African American, 1.1 percent Native American, and 5.5 percent Asian, with Latinos of any race accounting for 8.3 percent of the population. The per capita income is 19,283 dollars and more than thirty–five percent of the population lives below the poverty line. For those under eighteen the number increases to fifty percent.

About twenty–seven percent of the land area is covered by eight hundred ninety thousand trees. Sugar Maple account for 14.2 percent followed in descending order by Northern white cedar, and European buckhorn. I thought it interesting Syracuse was one of the few cities that counted and identified the trees within their borders.

I found a few other interesting facts worth mentioning. Nearly as many people bike to work (1.2 percent) as those who taxi to work (1.6 percent). Jesuit missionaries visiting the Syracuse region in the mid–1600s reported salty brine springs around the southern end of "Salt Lake," known today as Onondaga Lake. From the 1700s through the early 1900s commercial salt production influenced the city being named after Syracuse,

Sicily in 1847, which at the time was famous for salt mining. The city carries several nicknames including, "The Salt City," "the 'Cuse," and "Emerald City."

Day 45: Syracuse to Little Falls (79 miles)

It was another cool fifties day with overcast skies greeting us as we rolled out of the hotel parking lot in Syracuse. The winds had died down, so we had no tail winds to help and no head winds to fight. We had only 1,500 feet of climbing and less than eighty miles of road to cover.

Our route was a series of downhills with some short climbs mixed in. We worked our way through light morning traffic over rough tracks in an effort to make our way toward the east. I followed the chain of bikes in front of me from Seventh, to Court, then James, and onto Kinne Street before the group made the right on Kirkville.

This part of America is old. Some of the structures date back to the late 1800s and early 1900s. The architecture tells the story of a blue collar city, of basic and simplistic design without the frills. Houses were square, most two–story in height, the roofs gabled with maybe a dormer or two for added space. The windows were tall and narrow, the exterior skinned in clapboard or shakes and white or some other light yet modest color covered it all. These were homes from the post–World War II era we passed through in the first few miles.

Sprinkled in were the older homes built several decades earlier. They were more ornate with large front porches adorned with sturdy round columns and intricate archways and door details painted in colors that contrasted the main color scheme. Some of the older homes incorporated stonework and most had more than one chimney exiting high above the complex roofline. These homes were built by people of means; they were the owners of the businesses, not the rank and file. Yet sitting together they were in harmony.

As we advanced the lots increased in size and the houses increased in scale. Trees and fencing became more common, the overall appearance showed more attention to detail; there was less clutter and better landscaping. The homes were still old but not as old as those neighborhoods we first passed through; the ones nearer to the industrial buildings and small factories. Out here the route took us past the churches of brick and stone, and newer rural homes from the '60s and later. Ranch–style houses on a few acres of land sitting under canopies of shade trees defined the outer edge of East Syracuse. As Kirkville progressed the shoulder became as wide as the car lane. It was smooth and clean making it fun to ride on. My legs were also coming in early; it was a nice complement to the road conditions.

After crossing under US–481 I pedaled through the wooded flats beyond Butternut Creek. The road briefly bent to the north and then back east. I was looking for the turn onto Manlius Road. In the bliss of the western upstate scenery I was so consumed by my surroundings I nearly missed it. The red barn Tracy noted on the cue sheet and the riders ahead kept me on course. I turned left in pursuit of the pack. After the turn the shoulder was not as generous but it was plenty wide given the reduced traffic. I wouldn't be surprised if I were smiling. It was that kind of a morning.

A few quick turns had me cruising through fields of soy and other crops planted on table top smooth expanses of ground. Thick stands of trees framed the acreage defining the ownership boundaries. More trees filled in the distant background. They towered over the fields, varying shades of dark green contrasting with the lighter color of orderly ground hugging crops. Row after row, equally spaced and perpendicular to the road, the plants soaked in the sunlight and pulled life from the ground. It wouldn't be long before the harvest and there may still be time for a second planting.

I spotted a large field wagon in front of a small farm building; flats of what looked to be broccoli were stacked on it as if they just came from the fields. Men were moving the flats into a small arched steel barn surrounded by stacks of wooden crates and scattered weathered pallets.

Across the road a yellow and red trimmed fire hydrant protruded from the ground. It was unusual to see a hydrant sitting by the edge of the road in the middle of rural farmland. The scene could have been from the '70s if it weren't for the late model cars and trucks parked in my view.

There would be more farms and interesting features to catch my attention. I passed a long run of plastic hot–houses used to protect delicate plants. Cabbage or some other bluish–green leafy plants formed rows on my left. As much as I liked the scenery of eastern Ohio, the state of New York is even better. I couldn't ask for more in a ride.

I rode past yellow signs with symbols for deer crossings, pedestrians, school bus stops, and one for a man on a horse. There were signs for crossroads and curves, stops ahead, and speed limit postings. Mailboxes stood in front of houses with names and numbers, a few with fancy scrollwork, others adorned with flowers. There was a continuous stream of manmade artifacts along the road and they offered a diversion from the abundance of green that blanketed the ground. A little visual spice for the green salad bowl I was riding through.

The speed limit was a casual forty–five and I was moving at just a third of that. Leisurely and steady was my pace. I turned the pedals at a slow cadence, my heartrate was below 140 and my breathing was slow and quiet. I counted the power poles and compared the fractions of miles on my computer to see how far apart they stood. With some mental calculations I figured two hundred feet was a good estimate on the long straight roads and somewhat less when the terrain demanded it.

A small barn with its length running parallel to the road stood on a fresh cut lawn. It had never been painted. Nature had aged the vertical plank siding to a deep brown mahogany base, weathered gray streaks and knotholes added texture, the lower two feet were bleached to a light gray. It was straight but old and I guess it had been standing for a hundred years. The big sliding doors were closed but I imagined the thick smell of aged hay and dust inside. Maybe a vintage tractor was parked inside, dull and brown by years of dust, sitting idle, its nose pointing to the doors. And there would be old tools hanging from hooks secured to hand–cut square posts supporting the beams above. If only the doors were open I would have my answer.

Riding through the woods on the quiet Tag Road I shared the pavement with few vehicles aside from a CrossRoads support van and the fleet of cyclists I traveled with. I was in the vicinity of Chittenango, a village of five thousand people. The name Chittenango was derived from the Oneida Indian word for Chittenango Creek meaning "where waters run north." The most notable person from the village is L. Frank Baum, the author of the children's novel, *The Wonderful Wizard of Oz*. I believe everyone has seen the big–screen film adaptation at least once.

As I crossed over Canaseraga Creek, a clearing to the right revealed US–90 running parallel to my route and farther beyond was the village of Chittenango. Striping was not important on these rural roads and neither was a proper shoulder. Even with the old patchy pavement I continued to enjoy the route as it snaked its way through miles of sharp bends before depositing me into the village of Canastota (kan–uh–STO–tuh), population: 4,425.

As I angled to the right onto Main Street I stopped to take in the view to my left. It was a massive white sandstone structure partially covered in ivy. A tall round turret with arched entries and stained glass windows extended up to the top where pointed capped crenellations formed a ring around a pole supporting the American flag. It was Greystone Castle on the corner of 201 North Main Street.

The building was not originally intended to be a castle; it was a replacement to the wood–framed Methodist Episcopal Church which burned down in 1908. Construction began in 1910 with a budget of forty thousand dollars and the building was used as a sanctuary until it closed in the late 1960s. By the 1990s it had deteriorated and was scheduled for demolition but a local contractor, Martin H. Bargabos, purchased and renovated it into the banquet facility it is today. He and his wife Annette named the building Greystone Castle because of its aging color and castle–like features. The building is listed in the National Historic Registry to ensure it remains long into the future.

Canastota was incorporated in 1835 and sits at an elevation of 430 feet on the banks of the Erie Canal. In the late 1800s and early 1900s Italian families immigrated to the area to farm the land. The area is popular for growing onions, and in the past it was known as the "Onion Capital of the World."

The village has been home to the International Boxing Hall of Fame since it was relocated from Madison Square Garden in 1990. Every second weekend in June Canastota hosts the past and current champions with a Sunday parade and an induction ceremony. Just two weeks ago the Hall inducted several boxers, historians, and journalists who contributed to the sport. So the answer to the question of why Canastota was selected is simple. It was to pay tribute to the village that was home to two world champions, Carmen Basilio and Billy Backus. It's located a few blocks north on Peterboro Street.

A quick turn by the canal and I was tracking along the crushed stone Canalway Trail, part of the Old Erie Canal State Park. Along the canal the road was nearly flat with only the slightest hint of rollers. The pedaling was easy and through this section I was able to chat with other riders. The cue sheet called out a left at the sign for Durhamville followed by a right onto Center Street. There would be climbs to clear US–90 followed by another over a wide railroad right of way. A series of climbs followed that matched the contours of the terrain before flattening out at the SAG near Mason's Pond.

As I dismounted my bike I see dozens of riders walking around, snacking, and talking, and taking pictures of the "World's Smallest Church" sitting in the middle of the pond; a Slime green colored water hole in Oneida, New York. The sign near the road described the structure as measuring fifty–one inches by eighty–one inches with seating for two. Built in 1989 the church is non–denominational and the only way to get to it is by boat. Services are available upon request. Of course I took a picture of the sign.

While it might seem hard to believe the ride could get more rural it certainly did. Our route was authentic backroads New York, past overgrown pastures and fences with planks and posts in need of repair. I rode past dozens of planted fields of corn and soy, shade trees forming lines running out from the road like a column of green soldiers. No stripes of paint, no dedicated shoulder, just a ditch with mud and traces of water to keep me on the pavement.

I stopped at the sign for Beacon Light Road and crossed over the dry bed of Stony Creek. Trees close to the road had been cut back, their branches forming a hedge–like wall of green to my left and right. The road had been level for a stretch and ahead it looked like more of the same. And if I hadn't mentioned it, the ride is absolutely fantastic. The joy ride was momentarily interrupted for the stop sign at RT–31 before it continued back into the far reaches of the backcountry.

At Skinner Road the pavement improved and the stripes returned. The shoulder was narrow but traffic was still thin allowing us use of the lane. Our turn for Main Street took us to the town of Westmoreland, home to 6,213 and settled in 1748 by a missionary named James Dean. The buildings were weathered and old, mostly wood–sided and simple in design.

A mile later we were back in the woods crossing Oriskany Creek and climbing hills through the woods dotted with tiny cabins; shed–sized, but with windows and chimneys. They could be summer shacks or hunting cabins, but not full–time residences, though it was all a person really needs.

After a wide open stretch of fields the route returned to the woods and I realized this stand was dominated by birch trees. The white papery–peeling bark and the small leaves are unique and they are my favorite. I fell in love with these playing in my grandfather's yard as a boy and they remind me of him; all good memories.

Tucked inside the town of Whitestown is the village of Whitesboro, home to 3,943 and located on the northern fringe of Utica. It was the next populated area I passed through. Whitesboro has numerous buildings dating back more than a hundred years, and a few have been standing for twice that long. The architecture of the older buildings is impressive. I saw many early 1900s homes with grand porches, thick columns, impressive door and window details, and intricate cornice work. The Whitestown Town Hall dates back to 1807 and is on the National Register of Historic Places.

There is an interesting story about the Whitesboro village seal. In its original design from the early 1900s, founder Hugh White was shown wrestling an Oneida Native American. Though the city officials contended it depicted a friendly match White had won, his hands around the neck of his opponent looked more like he was being choked. After a lawsuit by a Native American group the seal was updated in 1970, White's hands were relocated from the neck down to the shoulders. Even in its current form it still is considered offensive.

Exiting Whitesboro I climbed a rail line overpass and enjoyed a speedy downhill that took me across the Mohawk River and a section of the Erie Canal. River Road had me back in the busy traffic but thanks to the New York road department a lane–wide shoulder became my personal highway.

River Road transitioned into RT–5E and the next hour became an enjoyable opportunity to look across the Mohawk Valley, the wooded mountainsides growing taller, the town of Frankfort briefly in sight across the Mohawk River. I continued pedaling down the road easily traversing the gentle inclines and accelerating on the downward slopes as I went.

At several points along the ride, the route paralleled the main rail line, which runs between Boston and Chicago. I saw the silver Amtrak passenger trains, and several freight and tanker cars pulled behind teams of powerful diesel locomotives.

The rumble of the fast and weighty trains could be felt and the sound of the horn changing as they approached and then receded into the distance was an interesting audible treat. I think I will always enjoy this simple yet practical form of transportation.

I also need to comment on the roads we've enjoyed in the Empire State. From our entry point just west of Barcelona, to the east side of Syracuse, the roads have been smoother with more generous shoulders than anywhere else in our journey.

Most of the riders would agree New York is the most bicycle–friendly state based on our experience over the past few days. In fact, New York unseated Kansas as our *number one* bike–friendly state. At the other extreme are Ohio, Missouri, and Texas. These states have much work to do to get a favorable cyclist review.

With rules about riding with ear buds there wasn't much in the way of music to be heard while on the bike. Except for the quick blast from a car passing by with the windows down or Ken Gregor's audio wonder that dangled from his bike frame. It wasn't often Ken passed by but when he did he didn't linger long. He was a steady rider able to move more swiftly then I could so when our paths crossed it was usually preceded by the welcome sound of Frank Sinatra as if out of the audible mist behind me until his tones were filling my ears with joy. I love Sinatra and I loved it when Ken brought him into my hearing range. But a quick, "Hey Ken!" and a few moments later I was returned to the droning of cars and the sound of wind blowing past my ears. Ken and Frank both farther up the road. For at least a little while after I would recycle the mental impression of "New York, New York" or whatever song was playing at the time through my mind. Not as good as the actual sounds emanating from Ken's bike but good enough that I would play it over and over until it faded out and was gone.

My internal cerebral jukebox kicked in most days when my brain drifted; probably thinking that full attention to the road wasn't necessary. On this ride through scenic New York I wasn't bashful about tuning it in and cranking it up.

I wouldn't admit this to Tracy because she'd probably find a creative way to keep me focused. Anyway, I could turn up the volume pretty loud in my head and course through a musical lineup that included a long medley of country songs and a few rock classics from the '70s; Meat Loaf, Billy Joel, Springsteen, and when I was in the west, a little John Denver. After all, how can you cross the mountains without singing a little "Rocky Mountain High" or amble down a winding rural road and not have "Take Me Home Country Roads" come to mind? When I was feeling a little racy I'd summon up from the depths "Bat Out of Hell" or "You May Be Right (I may be crazy)" and "Born in the USA" would get its fair share of airtime. In between my Rock tune moments were the ballads and stories of losing all your possessions in three minutes or less; Alabama, Travis Tritt, Willie Nelson, Merle Haggard, Ronnie Milsap, and definitely Johnny Cash. My vault was deep with talent and I let the day's experience dictate the playlist. As I retrieved the songs from memory I would turn up the volume and tune out the noises around me. It worked most of the time but it required concentration which meant it took away from other activities.

I don't multi-task. I used to think I did but I only switched really fast and I fooled myself into thinking I did. Multi-tasking is a myth that can get you in trouble on a bike. Kids following along at home forget the last few paragraphs and focus on the road.

I entered Herkimer, a town of just under ten thousand residents, it's one of the older upstate settlements tracing back to 1722. The town was named after General Nicholas Herkimer, a Revolutionary War hero who gained notoriety when his horse was shot out from under him and he continued to direct his men while sitting under a tree. It occurred during the Battle of Oriskany, considered one of the bloodiest battles and a pivotal point of the war.

The town includes a section known as "East Herkimer" separated from the core of the town by the West Canada Creek. And if you go north up the creek you can find clear quartz known throughout the world as "Herkimer Diamonds."

Crossing over the five hundred foot span above the creek provides an unobstructed view to the old stone arch bridge known as the *Herkimer Trolley Bridge*. It was originally built in 1902 by a bridge-builder named Beckwith Quackenbush from across the river in Mohawk.

The trolley provided transportation from Utica to Little Falls as an alternative to horse-drawn wagons. With the popularity of the automobile the Trolley was abandoned in 1933. Trees and other vegetation grow on the remaining eight arches. Nature will slowly take it back to the river below. Man does not need to intervene. As for photos, they do not do this arched monument justice. It must be seen in person to be fully appreciated. I took a few photos so I could share the memories and pushed off.

On the far side of Herkimer a few of us stopped for ice cream at a small roadside stand. It was not a Dairy Queen but they had soft-serve cones that were rich and creamy. It was still partly cloudy and only in the mid-sixties but those conditions never stopped us from enjoying these cool treats.

Six miles later entering into Little Falls the road narrowed and I was treated to houses perched on the steep embankment to my left and an old brick industrial establishment standing three stories tall to my right. Between the first and second floors of brick I could make out the faint traces of the words "Stafford Warehouse Co., Inc." flanked by the words *Trucking* and *Storage* whitewashed in bold block letters.

Beyond the brick building houses clung to the edge of the road on both sides. The houses were deeper than they were wide, their architecture provided clues to their age. Though all were modest some had flat roofs over impressive cornice details while others were topped with steeply pitched roofs of tin and shingles. There was no consistency in the care afforded to these structures. Few were well-maintained, but those that were stood as impressive examples of what could be achieved with a pile of old wood and brick.

I arrived at the Best Western with seventy-nine more miles under my cycling belt, which had been getting smaller as I progressed across the country. A total of five hours fifteen minutes of riding averaging 14.9 miles an hour would be recorded in my journal. I'd also include a maximum speed of 27.8 miles per hour for consistency, but without remembering exactly where it happened I don't think it really means much. And my mileage was actually 78.73, but I was close enough to seventy–nine so I rounded up. At least I'm honest.

I picked up the room key and made my way to the shower. The bike would need nothing from me this evening and it would find its own station of rest alongside the bed.

Back in street clothes I was off for what I hope will be the final laundry trip before arriving in Boston. I walked up the hill to a vintage laundromat, dropped the powered soap in with the clothes, put the coins in the slide, and got busy describing the ride in my journal. Most of the machines were under CrossRoads rider occupation, many lingered and chatted both inside and outside the building. Time passed quickly as my clothes tumble noisily in the machine. Folding and packing took only minutes and I was on my way back to the hotel.

At route rap Tracy posed a challenge to the riders involving a steep climb to the top of the mountain overlooking Little Falls and providing what was described as an amazing view of the Mohawk Valley. I saw no hands go up but in the morning I'm sure someone will bite. It was only sixty–nine miles to Albany with less than 1,300 feet of climbing.

Dinner was buffet style at the hotel and later that evening many of the riders enjoyed a choice of two movies in the Valley Cinema 1 & 2 Theater conveniently located in the basement of the same building. The hotel was old and quirky but it fit well in Little Falls. The lobby was one of the few that could not contain our group; that is until everyone crowded in tight, doing their best imitation of the college phone booth challenge.

Little Falls is home to 5,188 people and it sits at an elevation of 420 feet. I'm not sure exactly where the elevation was officially measured and with the city running from water's edge to mountain top I would accept anything within range of a hundred feet.

The name "Little Falls" comes from a nearby slope of narrow rocks where the water cascades forty–five feet in less than a mile. When it was settled by a German contingent in 1723 it was the westernmost European settlement in the colony of New York. In 1782 the settlement was destroyed by the Iroquois Indians and it would not be resettled until 1790. During the early times it was known as "Rockton" and "Rock City." In 1811 it was officially incorporated as a village.

Everyone knows the "Pledge of Allegiance" but few know the author and Baptist minister, Francis Bellamy once lived in Little Falls. The *Pledge* was first published in 1892 in an American Children's magazine called *The Youth's Companion*. Surprisingly the original pledge did not include the words "under God." They were added later by Congress in 1954 under the encouragement of President Dwight Eisenhower.

The city has several structures listed on the National Register of Historic Places. Included in the register is the Little Falls Historic District that totals 347 buildings. The structures date from the mid–nineteenth– to the early–twentieth–century and include Italianate–style commercial buildings and nineteenth–century residential architectural styles including Federal, Greek Revival, Italianate, Second Empire, Queen Anne, and Colonial Revival. The city needs to be walked to be fully appreciated. And while walking around I'd recommend a stop at the Little Falls Historical Society and Museum located across the street from the Best Western and a frozen treat up the hill on Ann Street at the Stewart's Shop.

Before I close the journal for the night my final thoughts are of Little Falls' bragging rights on the Erie Canal and an author who uses the city as the setting for his novel. Lock 17 of the Erie Canal replaced the three original locks and at forty feet and six inches it has the highest lift elevation of the state's canal system. At the time of construction, it was the highest lift station in the world.

As for the book reference, a new author by the name of Brock Clarke incorporated Little Falls as the backdrop for his debut novel, *The Ordinary White Boy*. Reviewers used words such as "Brilliant" and "Hilarious", "Introspective and Interesting." And who doesn't want to have those words flung about in the books they read? I know I do. Let's give the guy a break and see if he captures the essence of the city and the people of Little Falls.

Tomorrow will be a short day with minimal climbing into Albany, the state capital. Weather permitting; it will be a fun day.

Day 46: Little Falls to Albany (71 miles)

I took the postcards to the front desk and was told they would go out with today's mail. I thought about buying more off the rack in the lobby, but I had faith Albany would have some of their own. It's the capital of the state so postcards shouldn't be too hard for them to keep in stock.

Before parading out of Little Falls we learned Kim, Gordon, and Tom J. took Tracy up on the challenge and rode to the top of the mountain earlier this morning. In their words the valley view was spectacular.

We rolled out the side entrance, coasted downhill to the light and waited for the green. It would be our only glide for the next few miles. There would be no shoulder along the first steep stretch of RT–5E so we took the right lane near the curb, traffic moved left and passed safely by. As we continued laboring over the pedals, our chains taut and our breathing heavy, a wide shoulder opened ahead and as if connected the riders angled right in a single fluid motion.

At the fork for RT–169 a wall of rust colored exposed limestone and shale surged out of the trees to a height of more than twenty feet above the far side of the highway. Cliff–like in appearance, fractured and rough and stained with traces of earthy colors, this stone wall was joined by similar protrusions that framed the road angling to the right. Had I taken the turn it would have led me across the Theodore S. Wind Bridge and over the Mohawk Valley and the river itself. Beyond this junction the stone formed a shallow canyon until the rock receded back into the ground amongst the thick trees a few hundred feet farther up.

Looking down into the gorge I see a different rock, syenite, known locally as "burnt rocks" that form the darker lower cliffs. These cliffs rise up from the ledge where the train rails are perched and dramatically contrast with the rare exposures of dolomite limestone and the thick green vegetation. Below the rails the syenite forms the bottom of the gorge and is referred to as the "bed rock" of the valley. The lower stone resembles granite but contains little or no quartz. It is the product of molten materials that cooled and solidified at considerable depths before erosion exposed it millions of years later.

The climbing continued along a steady incline, the grades not severe but they were taxing. The view from the top revealed the rail lines and river edge, the tops of century old homes showing off their spires and slate roofs, tall chimneys extending skyward from the industrial buildings of Little Falls, and narrow steeples gave away the churches. In the distance the imperfections that may exist were softened and made perfect.

On my left a rising bank of trees were constant, relieved only by brief clearings exposing more rocks farther up the mountain. As I was getting close to the top, the road began to level, the trees to my left were no longer towering over me, and I pedaled with less effort past the sparse houses and the occasional farm.

I was finally over the first climb and was looking forward to the long and easy return to lower elevations. I was not disappointed; the downhills were indeed long and rewarding. At times I thought to temper my speed with a little braking but I was enjoying the rush of the wind too much to let a little fear steel away the excitement. I hit my fastest speed of the day on this descent topping out at 35.6 miles per hour.

On my left an expansive series of short stone walls marked the property where Beardslee Castle was located. The stone and ivy covered structure stood two stories tall; a series of arched windows flanked what appeared to be a massively scaled solid wood door. The stones stacked over the central part of the building formed the shape of a triangle. The structure was elevated on a platform of stone; a small grass courtyard filled in between the walls and the front steps. It was constructed in 1860 as a replica of an Irish castle and it's used today for banquets and fine dining.

This morning I am riding with Kathy and we are talking about the views and the perfect riding conditions. Well, we were after we disposed of the first steep climb. Our bikes are quite different; she rides a lay–back recumbent and enjoys the freedom to ride with clip–in sandals. I ride hunched over on a more traditional road bike and I'd only wear closed toe shoes on a bike. There is a contrast in bike styles and our riding form but we travel the distance at a complimentary pace enjoying the world and each other's company. The two of us have been riding together and socializing throughout the tour, starting on day one when we met in Los Angeles. We were part of the group that rode the *Strand* to test ride our bikes after they were reassembled at the hotel. I also remember dinner with Kathy, Peter, and a few others the night before we met the rest of the gang of forty–eight. We've also been laundry partners which I've described before. She is from Boston and has given me advice on what to see and do when I get there. Kathy is cool, maybe that's why she rides a recumbent.

We traversed a steel girder bridge of two spans over the East Canada Creek which divided Herkimer from Montgomery County. The overhead webbing of the bridge structure cast an interesting series of geometrically shaped shadows across the deck, creating a flickering effect as we rode through. To my right was a similar bridge supporting the rail lines. The creek was not more than twenty feet below, the bed was shallow and full of well–worn rocks and small boulders.

Beyond the bridge in the near–ground was an expansive green space and in the mid–ground, stands of trees revealing the far side of the valley. I caught a glimpse of a few cattle in a field off to my left, and ahead the road lifted and receded like a flag in a gentle breeze. Crum Creek passed under the road and meandered aimlessly off into the field and out of sight. It was picturesque, a sensory treat.

Another hand–stacked wall of rounded stone ran along the left of the road for a distance of three power poles. It stood three feet tall and marked the West St. Johnsville Cemetery perched up on the ridge. I've passed by many cemeteries on this ride and I often wonder about the lives that were lived and the things these people who preceded me were fortunate enough to see. I'm sure most were known to many and loved by those whose lives they touched.

I know I will never rest in the ground, in some cemetery with a stone marker etched with my name and an end–date that is not known to me. I don't want a patch of dirt with a slab of granite being a place people feel the need to go in order to remember me. No not in a cemetery. I'll be turned to ashes and hopefully spread on a grassy hillside overlooking a valley, a river running through it, like where I am riding. In this way the spirt or essence of who I was can enjoy for all eternity the views afforded to me today.

Hiding in the distance was a long, old, multi–arched stone bridge. It stood over the shallow creek abandoned along Highway 5E. Trees reaching twenty feet high grew densely on the old bridge surface and appeared to be doing their part to deteriorate the structure and return it to the earth. I was not sure if it was once used for autos or trains but today it did the best it could to hold itself up. I caught only a glimpse and then it disappeared into the background, few will likely see it as it slowly decays and becomes no more.

Approaching St. Johnsville we encountered a rare sight. It was a pair of horses with their two colts in a field close to the road on our left. One horse was on its back in what appeared to be an attempt to satisfy an itch, much like a dog would. Our presence startled the horse, causing it to quickly leap to its feet, and then all four galloped to the far side of the fenced–in area. Their speed was impressive, but it was the awkwardness of the few day–old colts that really made the moment.

St. Johnsville is a town of 2,567 people and it overlooks the Mohawk River a few hundred yards to the south. The first thing I noticed entering the town was the architecture of the homes. It mirrored the finer properties in Little Falls, the details exquisite, the finishes nearly perfect. The words *ornate* and *gingerbread* come to mind as we pass by what could have been model homes in an upscale community one hundred years earlier.

The brick downtown followed and it was just as impressive. Exiting St. Johnsville I saw more homes but they were not as striking or as tightly clustered, yet they were still drawing my attention.

Just outside of town a cluster of cabins and small buildings stood near the road. It was the Fort Klock Restoration. The site is a living museum that preserves the history of the territory as it was in the middle to later part of the 1700s. The Battle of Klock's Field was fought on October 19, 1780 just to the northwest of this site. It was closed so we continued riding.

Over a tributary to the Mohawk River we moved swiftly along a descending stretch passing by Wagner's Hollow and into Nellistown, a village of just over six hundred overlooking the Mohawk River from an elevation of 367 feet. Across the bridge on the southern banks of the Mohawk was the larger village of Fort Plain, home to 2,288 people and the birthplace of the first black professional baseball player, Bud Fowler.

Our ride continued along RT–5E through the Village of Palatine Bridge where stacked stone walls seemed to be all the rage. On the right stood a beautiful stone church next to an interesting house with a three–story turret. The house was dressed in an impressively dark shade of red contrasting with the brilliant white trim.

Off to our right the rail lines tracing the Mohawk River moved teasingly close to the road and then angled away. Over the miles we were treated to several passenger and freight–laden trains moving up and down the line. The ground would vibrate and the thunderous sounds of weighty locomotives would arrive well in advance of the sightings of the train. The rumble would give way to sounds of metal–on–metal, a grinding and clanging and clattering between the wheels and rails. The couplers connecting the cars would tug and bind adding their own notes as the train grew smaller and smaller until the sound was no more and the mass of railroad iron would vanish. Over and over the trains approached with the blast of a horn and their unmistakable rumble.

Beyond the tracks, the Mohawk River meandered about with clean, almost emerald–green water, and an abundance of shade trees lining her banks. Every couple of miles, we would encounter what looked like an old truss–style rail bridge crossing the river. Each structure had several extensions and platforms reaching down to the water but I could not see their purpose. It wasn't until our first close encounter revealed the structure was in fact a lock and not a bridge as first thought. Once past the lock, we could look back and see the water cascade over the walls in an impressive display of power and volume.

Farther down the road, a large collie charged at our bikes, barking in an unusually deep and strong tone. Kathy was behind me by several hundred feet so I circled back to block the dog from going after her. Her recumbent bike would have made it both difficult and dangerous to deal with the inquisitive canine. Fortunately for us, he was not interested in anything more than protecting his turf.

Over smooth roads with a healthy shoulder we tracked the contours of our surroundings. The road pitched up and settled back down, never too extreme but always changing. There were times we dropped low enough to see the Mohawk running not much below the level of the road. It would pull close leaving just a narrow space for the double sets of rail lines. When we found the valley floor the forest to our left would elevate to heights reminding us just how far up the mountain side we had been.

We crossed the bridge over Cayadutta Creek and entered into the village of Fonda, population: 810. The village was named for Douw Fonda, a Dutch–American settler who was scalped in 1780 during an Indian raid in the Revolutionary War. He probably would have been happy for it to be named after someone else.

The village of Fonda is also home to the Fonda speedway, a half mile dirt track that ran four NASCAR sanctioned races with Junior Johnson winning the first race in 1955, David Pearson winning in 1966, and Richard Petty winning the last two races in 1967 and '68. The track butts up against the Mohawk River and over the years several drivers waded out of the water after their cars climbed up and over the safety fence.

After miles of casual terrain we found our way climbing another long grade. Not quite as long as the one exiting Little Falls but it's still slow and tedious. At the apex of the climb we were delivered to the SAG at a rest area with a view overlooking an expansive meadow and the valley beyond. We communed with the herd that was not in much hurry to leave the comfort of friends and a delicious spread sitting atop the red and white checkered fold–out tables. We grazed until Margaret said we better get rolling. Thirty–three miles had been covered and slightly more than that remained to reach Albany.

A long gradual descent took us out of the SAG and on our way toward Fort Johnson. We passed an impressive stone structure with a sign letting us know we had found the village, but aside from a blinking light and a few other buildings it was hard to imagine 491 people call Fort Johnson home.

Amsterdam quickly followed but we had to climb more than 360 feet in our short trek from Fort Johnson to find our way into the town of more than 5,800. In 1916 it was the birth town of actor Kirk Douglas. Named after the capital of the Netherlands, Amsterdam was first settled in 1715 and incorporated more than a hundred years later. The official elevation is 660 feet above sea level, but I'd like to know how high above the Mohawk River we are right now.

We passed another spillway at Cranes Hollow and stayed tight to the river. On the left the mountain would expose pockets of fractured rock in between the thick stand of trees. Just a peak, and just often enough to keep us looking left every few miles. At times the mountain would move farther away from the road and when it did low grassy meadows would fill in. The wild flowers of purple and long stalks topped by fluffy cattails told of wet marshy ground hidden beneath the green.

We climbed and crossed over the rail lines then passed a sign for Scotia five miles ahead. Twenty minutes later we passed rows of houses on a berm to our left, the driveways cut into the ground were lined with walls of concrete and long straight flights of concrete steps connected the sidewalk to the front porch. The homes were old but interesting. Though they were all similar in design, each of the houses sported features that set them apart from the next. There were gables and dormers, open porches and those that had been winterized. Opposite on the right the homes were much the same but they were level with the pavement.

We rode through the congestion of narrow streets, squeezing by cars parked at the curb, and busy traffic past the fire station and the City–View Church before the roadway opened and the buildings pulled back. On the left the Scotia Collins Park filled my view with green, a small white structure known as the Abraham Glen House stood close to the sidewalk under a cluster of trees. Constructed in the 1730s, it is a rare surviving example of a Dutch Colonial heavy timber frame house. It features a steep–pitched slate shingled roof, dormers, a wraparound porch, and a pair of chimneys. Today it is used as a library for the town of 7,957.

Out of Scotia by way of the Western Gateway Bridge we crossed over the Mohawk River and the Isle of the Cayugas. On the other side was the booming city of Schenectady, population: 63,547. The name "Schenectady" is derived from a Mohawk word meaning "beyond the pines" and it is pronounced "ske–NEK–te–dee."

State Street guided us past wide and busy intersections. Transit buses lined up near the curb kept us out in the thick of the traffic. It was extreme cycling after spending the day in the wide open with a healthy shoulder to find comfort. On the far side of Church Street the road necked down to a single lane each way with on–street parking seeing plenty of customers. It was narrow and sketchy through several blocks of underground construction just to keep it interesting.

The roads were bumpy and full of potholes and patches, construction debris elevated my concern as small shards of stone spit from my tires. I was beginning to retract all of the praise I had poured on the state but I kept pedaling. Through the maze of brick and glass uttering words like Dorothy did as she tapped her heels, and somehow I was through the worst of what the city could dish out. I swerved and climbed the inclined street around Veteran's Park past the court house. Then I climbed the straight stretch until I found a way out of the congestion on Consaul Road. Kathy soldiered up the hills and we made it safely to the paved sanctuary that had us riding through residential neighborhoods sans the curbs, ditches, and traffic. The varying elevations were not an issue.

Schenectady, like Syracuse saw its best years decades ago. The population had peaked in 1930 at 95,692 and when the great depression took hold a steady outflow of manufacturing jobs caused people to leave. Schenectady will need to reinvent itself to stop the exodus and make the area a viable place for growth.

The demographics of Schenectady are even more diverse than Syracuse. Whites account for 59.4 percent, African Americans 24.2 percent, Latinos 14.5 percent, and Asians 2.6 percent. What is telling of the future is the diversity amongst students which include thirty–five percent African American, thirty–two percent White, eighteen percent Hispanic, and fifteen percent Asian. The per capita income for the city is 17,076 dollars and 25.9 percent of the population lives below the poverty line. Religious affiliates include forty–four thousand Catholics, six thousand Muslins, 3,600 Reformed Church, and 2,800 United Methodist members.

The city is the birthplace of actor Mickey Rourke and drag racer Shirley Muldowney. It was also the film location for the movies including, *The Way We Were* starring Barbara Streisand and Robert Redford and *Heart Like a Wheel*, the story of drag racer Shirley Muldowney.

At the Albany International Airport we made a series of turns to get around to the eastern side of the property. As I banked left across traffic into the Super 8 parking lot I had logged 71.18 miles for the day. Most of the distance I enjoyed a solid tailwind, partly sunny skies and cool temperatures through some of the most inspiring scenery in the East. Yesterday was a joy but today was a gift. Heaven on a bike is the only way to describe it. The entire ride lasted four hours forty minutes, but the memories will endure. I averaged 15.5 miles an hour and early in the morning I tipped the speed charts at close to thirty–six miles per hour on a long downhill.

We were seven miles due north of downtown Albany, the capital of the state of New York and home to 96,537 people. The motto I found to be one of the most unusual on the trip. It is but a single word, *Assiduity*, which means constant or close attention to what one is doing. I don't know who comes up with these ridiculous tag lines but I would guess they also have something to do with all of the safety warning labels put on ladders and stepstools.

With the bike cleaned and a hot shower checked off the list it was time for route rap and dining at the all–you–can–eat King Buffet just across the parking lot. After dinner I'll fill out postcards and finish my day's journaling. Then maybe some bedtime stories with Clark about the crossing into Vermont.

Day 47: Albany to Brattleboro, Vermont (80 miles)

Friendly's for breakfast! *Waitress, I'm thinking a big banana split—Okay, coffee and a standard breakfast it is*. It would have been a bad idea anyway with all of the climbing in front of me.

The table conversation revolved around the few days of riding remaining. There was excitement, there was a desire to be finished, but there was also a hint of sadness detected in the conversation. You could hear the emotion in the voices, there was the giddy and jovial, and there was the hint of a crack, a stumble, and a pause between words. You couldn't hide it and you knew others felt it too. We had been through a lot together. We fought headwinds and fixed tires together. We joked and poked and encouraged each other. We picked each other up and we cried together. We bonded. We became part of something about to end and we would need to prepare for that moment. It was the unspoken denial that would be dealt with a few days forward.

The silverware hit the plates for the last time and we left the tables to make our way back to the hotel. Today would be another big day for us, our 12th state line, and our 13th state. We would climb 5,600 feet on roads built over the old trails, steeper and more challenging than the more modern western climbs governed by controlled grades. I imagine the eastern ranges will be like Oak Creek Canyon overlaid with the 148 rollers of Missouri. It will be tough, maybe the toughest yet.

We set out in pursuit of the villages and towns that would line the route to Brattleboro. There would be incredible history, impressive landmarks, and the most climbing of any day on the tour. But first we had to get onto RT–7E and out in traffic.

I decided to wear my sleeved sun–shirt as a windbreaker to start out this cool morning. The temperature had yet to break sixty but it was clear and calm. I expected at some point it would warm up and I could peel it off. The forecast called for temperatures in the high seventies in Brattleboro by midafternoon.

Single file through the first traffic light we hugged the curb over the Adirondack Northway and started climbing in the heavy morning rush toward a popular northeastern traffic management feature known as a rotary. In *Jersey* they call them circles and our British riders know them as roundabouts. Nobody stops; they join the flow into the circle and then peel off in their desired direction. The rotary is pretty effective so long as everyone knows what to do. But there is always the novice, the moving roadblock. Having two lanes of car traffic merging into and out of the hub can get dicey. Adding in dozens of cyclists slowing the pace would only increase the intensity. We provided ample spacing allowing the cars to alternate with the bikes. We slipped through the tricky curves and exited on the far side of the rotary. We lost no one in the first mile and I doubt we created many cycling fans judging by the drivers who honked and gestured as they passed.

On the horizon mountains appeared. We were descending toward the Hudson River, a sign strategically placed at a sprawling cemetery cautioned trucks to use low gear. Through trees and around curves the road pitched more aggressively cutting downward through a channel of earthen embankments, our speed climbing quickly. We shot through man–made canyons of concrete dropping almost three hundred feet into the heart of Watervliet, population: 9,707. It was an old community of houses and corner stores hovering over the sidewalks first settled in 1643.

The traffic lights separated riders and slowed the pace. Cars parked along the sidewalk crowded us as we moved through the busy flow of east–bound traffic. The mountains ahead continued to grow. I was moving swiftly through the intersection of Third Avenue but with the bridge spanning the Hudson in sight I came to an abrupt stop for the light on Second. Riders stacked up behind me, their brakes pads crying out against the rims. If only the lost momentum could have been available for the climb ahead.

On the apex of the long bridge I looked down the Hudson. It was wide and the water shimmered with movement some fifty–five feet below. In the distance the river cut through a flat blanket of green and disappeared against the pale blue of the sky. New York City was some ninety miles beyond the horizon.

My speed quickly increased as the pavement dropped into the commercial center of Troy, population: 48,246. The welcome sign with the words "Founded in 1789" and "Home of Uncle Sam" couldn't be missed. The road ducked down under Russell Sage College and into a darkened tunnel, the potholes, drainage grates, and fractures difficult to see. Beside me a curb and a stripe of white visible only under the dim glow of the lights running above. Just a few hundred feet and I began climbing back into the daylight.

Ferry Street was tree lined, narrow, and one–way. The view in front of me was in stark contrast to the presentation of Troy as I descended off the Congress Street Bridge. I was climbing between aged shops and storefronts, faded white bulletins of block lettering still visible on the brick walls. Then the road wrapped around a few buildings into a clearing of green and rejoined Congress at Prospect Park. Before me was the base of the mountain I first saw as I descended toward the Hudson. It was time to climb. From this point I would leave the congestion of the city and venture into expansive forests and rural villages on narrow crowned roads, with a ditch to my right and few curbs and painted lines.

The early climbing was slowed by road construction, lanes of traffic having to alternate through the narrow work zones. There were three century–old stone churches huddled along the winding roads, brick and stone retaining walls holding back the earth, ornate brownstone rowhomes, and several two– and three–story buildings of brick with shops below and apartments above. This is the charm of the northeast; the old buildings, the complex architecture, the details and spires and wrought iron railings. The brick buildings began thinning out and eventually they gave way to the wood–framed structures painted in white. The stone walls would advance farther up the climb but they too would come to an end as did the sidewalks.

Climbing and climbing into thicker stands of trees there would be brief shelves of near–level road, then the pavement would rise again and disappear around a corner. On the steeper twisting sections the vegetation would yield to exposed walls of rock and on the opposite side of the road would be guardrails preventing us from dropping off into the woods.

We pedaled past St. Mary's Cemetery, followed by a few large estates framed with fir trees and expansive lawns. Up the climbs the sun seldom found us. We stayed deep under the shade of the broad trees enveloping the road. It was a grind having to work hard only to move so slowly. If you wanted the reward you need only look around. It was quiet, there were few cars, and the forest exuded a tranquil quality about it.

Ahead of me riders begin to pull away, accelerating over a long sweeping downhill and speeding across a short steel bridge cutting over the Poesten Kill River. The river twisted and ran parallel to the road for a stretch, the sound of the water spilling over rocks could be heard and for a moment the cascades could be seen through the trees. The water was clear, the rocks forming the dark riverbed visible. It may have been clean enough to drink.

We had reached what is known as the Rensselaer Plateau, the separation from the low, flat Hudson Valley and the Green Mountains. Across the plateau the riding became more forgiving and the terrain gentle. In a flat clearing a field of corn and several smaller vegetable gardens filled in around farm buildings. Houses were tucked in among the trees. We passed the oddly named roads of Birchkill and Moonlawn, and an interesting white–framed Christian church in Eagle Mills. Up and down the hills we rode, in and out of the trees. A sweeping descent brought us to a stop at RT–278 where the CrossRoads van was parked. We had moved higher into the range, but more climbing could be seen. The rolling mounds of green reached higher the farther we traveled. I had been pedaling for more than an hour and I had but twelve miles to show for it. Most of the riders stopped to use the restroom of the convenience store where the van was parked. I stopped as well and took a few minutes to check my tires. No wires and no stone shards were found embedded in the tread.

Tamarac Road climbed more than it dropped, the elevation changes were modest and the views of the lower valley with peaks in the background had riders stopping for pictures. Betty was ahead of me. Beyond her were a handful of others separated by a few lengths to a hundred feet or more. Trailing riders appeared in my mirror. It was comforting to know others were around but it was also nice to enjoy the quiet of the ride.

I was free to listen to the birds, the fields of grass rustling in the breeze, and the wind moving through the trees at the higher elevations. The variety of color and texture of the trees was a visual treat. In some sections the density of the forest created a near nightscape under its canopy. The air was filled with the fragrance of fresh wildflowers and field grasses. It was a day for all the senses. I would chat with Betty when we were looking for landmarks and when we just needed to hear a friendly voice.

My legs were finally warmed up and I began making better time. It wasn't long before I followed the line of riders into a place called Boyntonville. We were back on RT–7E climbing with Pittstown State Forest to our right. It was a rounded dome of endless trees covering most of the view. Boyntonville was little more than a roadway sign. It never materialized into anything besides a few deteriorating houses, a tractor sales business, and a used car lot. Our route descended into a shallow valley through Tibbets State Forest and delivered us to the first of the two SAG stops we would enjoy today.

Besides the usual spread there were donuts. Glazed, filled, powdered, and those covered in icing and sprinkles. If only I could keep this calorie burning potential after the ride is over. After seven weeks of gorging and grazing I've forgotten about the lean smart eating I did to prepare for tour. Relearning to control my appetite might be a more difficult task than pedaling coast to coast. I chased the donut down with a few cups of Gatorade and a whole banana. Then I pocketed a few traveling snacks, topped off the fluids, and looked for Betty.

Out of the SAG we were treated to a long gradual glide crossing over the Hoosick River and we then passed through a town of the same name. What we saw of Hoosick as we crossed South Street were a pair of competing country stores. To the left stood a wood–framed three–story colonial structure named the "Hoosick Country Store" and to the right a single story country–style structure with a tin–roofed porch and a large sign above declaring the place as the "Big Moose Deli & Country Store." The *Moose* was using gorilla marketing to attract visitors, and I mean that literally. An old red flatbed truck was parked on the corner, with statues of a gorilla, a moose, a gnome, and Uncle Sam in the back. Protruding out of the roof of the building was the tail end of an airplane. There were horses, cows, ducks, geese, buffalo, a canoe, a few gnomes, and a turtle on the roof. Nothing was small; in fact much of it was larger than life including a pink pig and comic book hero's Superman and Batman standing on the porch. Gaudy continued around the far side of the building and to be honest if I were to stop there would be no question as to who would get my business.

From Hoosick I climbed up the Taconic Mountains over Browns Brook onto RT–9. It appeared the road I was now on would be more forgiving than the straight climb up RT–279 but I was wrong. This road continued winding up through the mountain without relief. I was grinding slowly, chipping away at the climb when not far ahead I saw a clustering of riders. They had reached the sign for Vermont. I kicked a little harder on the pedals and dismounted when I got close. I joined the celebration and began the state line border routine starting with the sprinkling of sand and then the required photos.

Back on the bike I pushed my way uphill until our group found the Bennington Battle Monument. It's a slender stone tower standing more than three hundred feet tall and constructed out of Sandy Hill Dolomite, a blue–gray Magnesian limestone embedded with fossils. It was completed in 1889 at a cost of one hundred twelve thousand dollars and from the observation windows two hundred feet up, it's possible to see Vermont, New York, and Massachusetts. I took the elevator ride to the observation level and looked out the windows. I tried to imagine what the countryside might have looked like two hundred years earlier. I expect it looked almost the same as it does now with forests and fields of wild grass in every direction.

The monument commemorates the Battle of Bennington which was fought during the American Revolutionary War in August 1777. Led by Brigadier General John Stark, more than 1,400 New Hampshire men reinforced by members of the Green Mountain Boys defeated the two detachments of General John Burgoyne's British Army and prevented the capture of food and weapons stored at the monument site. The actual battle was fought ten miles away in Walloomsac, New York at what is now a National Historic Landmark known as Bennington Battlefield.

Forty miles remained in the ride with the second SAG at the halfway point. Our band of riders rolled off from the monument as other cyclists arrived. I might have been there for only fifteen minutes but I felt refreshed and ready for more climbing. Down Monument Avenue we coasted turning left on Main Street making a quick descent into Bennington. We moved swiftly past the impressive stone Sacred Heart Saint Francis de Sales Church and into the historic district. In those quaint downtown blocks I saw many interesting storefronts offering chocolates, coffees, pastries, and everything else you might desire. They even have cobblers, breweries, Vermont crafts & toys, music shops, and books.

The commercial buildings were of brick and stone, the undersides of the roof garnished with impressive cornices and plaster details. Many of the shops had inviting names carved and gold leafed on signs fixed to their front. Everything was neat and well maintained. As interesting as it was to look around I needed to be mindful of the narrow streets, the cars parked at the curb, and people crossing. Bennington sits at an elevation of 817 feet and is the most populous town in southern Vermont and third largest statewide with 15,737 residents. Ahead of me I could see the Green Mountains that I would soon climb.

We followed the Molly Stark Trail that climbed up through the gap with the mountain peaks rising on both sides. We would continue climbing for the next seven miles over grades as steep as eight percent. I know it doesn't sound like much of an incline but they can make even a strong rider struggle; and for the average guy like me visions of riding the flats into the Midwest headwinds become clear, if not desirable.

Along the climb there would be scenic views of mountains, water cascading white and splashing over wide expanses of rocks, the dull roar echoing through the trees. I saw deer, moose, log cabins, beautiful clear ponds and meandering creeks. The views were breathtaking. Around a very slow bend a small white church and parsonage sat off the road on a bed of grass. Absent was a place to park cars.

For the next few miles into Woodford I would see only trees as I looked up from the inclined floor, I passed a small pull–off with a sign for Green Mountain and smaller signs indicating an entry point to the Appalachian Trail. Beyond this point the road cut through the rock forming a canyon with walls standing more than a hundred feet tall. Trees and vegetation clung precariously to the crevasses. This blind curve with a partial view of another mountain peak left me wondering what was coming next.

Stamford Stream roared beyond the trees as I labored over the pedals, the pavement snaking its way higher and higher, the mountains getting shorter. I began to question the road grade. *This feels much steeper than the eight percent incline I was told about,* I shouted in silence. Had I yelled it out loud no one would have noticed; Betty was already around the next corner.

The bike was creaking from the stress on the chain; I turned the bars left and right as I swerved. My progress slowed even more as my breathing became louder, my heartrate pushed well above 160. Relief on this stretch cannot come soon enough.

I passed by Prospect Mountain Ski Area and the Greenwood Lodge and Campsites as I climbed at the unimpressive speed of five miles an hour. Through the town of Woodward I reached an elevation of 2,165 feet and was still climbing. I passed another modest white church much like the last, sitting on a grassy mound just off the road. It was reported to be the highest church in Vermont. Farther up, a small village of houses and cabins formed a circle around the twenty–five acre water feature known as *Big Pond*. It was amazing and a welcome distraction from the wall of trees that have been taking most of my attention. For a short stretch the pitch of the climb relaxed and then it tightened again testing my will and patience. I kept moving and I kept climbing.

A few more bends and the road began to level out; I could see the top of the crest and my feet began to move faster. I shifted and moved the chain to keep pace but I could see the next climb. I stopped pedaling and coasted as far as it would go. As my speed dropped back into single digits I prepared to settle in for another long grind but the road peaked again and I was over the top and sailing past the junction for RT–100. A sign warned of an eight percent grade for the next two miles. I clung tight to the bars as I passed the gravel truck run–off. Faster and faster before I finally applied some brake to slow below thirty. It was a welcome change but it was also uncomfortable to let the bike scream out of control.

I sailed through Searsburg and Medburyville, past the Deerfield River, down to an elevation of 1,565 and into the charming small town of Wilmington, home to 2,085 people. Little cottage businesses selling a variety of local products dotted the road leading into the central part of town. Wilmington was yet another taste of classic New England albeit a much smaller and more village–like version.

As I crossed over Main Street it marked the end of the joyride and the beginning of more climbing. Just ahead I would find the SAG and I was happy to step off the bike once more. It was pushing the high seventies but the steady breeze out of the west, and the shade of the trees when we had it, made the day feel much cooler.

Exiting the SAG I began the climb up Hogsback Mountain. It started out easy but as I advanced over Beaver Brook and approached Molly Stark State Park it was taunting me. I could have used a larger rear gear as I was struggling to spin the pedals, but I kept on going and it was well worth the effort. Over a distance of less than five miles I had climbed to the top and took in the view from an elevation of 2,409 feet. It was an impressive climb of 844 feet in my book.

I walked out onto the observation deck and stared toward the south. I imagined where the state lines were and I tried to estimate the distance to the horizon. It is said that, under perfect conditions, you could see for a hundred miles. I couldn't image better conditions than this afternoon but I still couldn't say for sure exactly how far I could see or how many states I was looking at.

While at the top of Hogback Mountain, I reflected back on the day. I finally was able to ride with Clark for several miles and I was certain no other day could match this one.

Cautiously I began the descent into Brattleboro, but my luck would take a turn for the worse. Not two miles down from Hogsback as I was screaming through a wooded stretch, a spoke in my rear wheel broke, which caused the rim to wobble. All I heard was the, *plink* of the spoke then the rubbing of the rim against the brake pad. I felt the vibration, it was slight at first, but the situation quickly escalated until the wheel wedged itself against the brake caliper and stopped my progress. A single rider ahead of me disappears into the woods.

I was alone but didn't expect more than a minor delay so I dismounted and removed my gloves. I set about pulling my seat off the bike to retrieve the plastic bag of spare spokes I carried in the frame. I thought I was prepared. I had the bike shop in Florida make six spares. Plenty I thought and it would have been if they were the right size. This is where I learned my bike had three different spoke lengths. The shorter ones go to the rear wheel and I've got half a dozen of the longer front wheel spokes. I was not about to give up on riding every inch of this journey so I had to get creative.

I removed the rear wheel and peeled off the tube and tire. The broken spoke turned out to be two. I removed them and began strategizing the repair. It seems these really cool wheels I bought with my bike have what they call bladed, low–count spokes. Very aerodynamic and lightweight but with nearly a third less connections between the rim and hub there is no tolerance for having even a single spoke break. I was learning a lot about wheels standing by the road.

As I studied the parts I had to work with I realized the aero wheels had clearance for the half–inch–too–long spare spokes and if I could install the retainer nut backwards inside the rim it could pull the wheel back into position. Not the way I would fix it at home, but it would get me through the day. My problem now was I didn't have the tools. This isn't something you plan for so I rooted through the bike bag trying to improvise a way to install and tighten the nut. I struggled. I cursed, I kicked the ground and then I laughed. Not much but I did. I was not willing to accept that I was done. That I couldn't fix the bike and I would not ride every freaking inch, my EFI status gone.

A few minutes later Margaret drove past and when she saw me stranded she pulled over and offered to help. In the van she had a pair of pliers that I tried. At first nothing, they were too bulky to reach into the recesses of the rim properly. She would only give me a few minutes to fix the wheel and then I'd have to put the bike on the rack and take the van into the hotel. I would rather walk and I was not too pleased but I couldn't let Margaret know my frustration. After a few more attempts with the pliers I was finally able to grab the end of the retaining nut with the tip of the pliers without dropping it. A careful twist and the threads engaged. I carefully repositioned the grip and it slowly took hold. The rim began to move as I tensioned the spoke. It was working. I repeated the process with the second replacement spoke.

I set the rim back on the bike to check the progress and when I spun the wheel it cleared the brake pads. It wobbled but it was good enough so I quickly reassembled the parts and aired up the tire. I gave Margaret the pliers and I was moving down the road. I waved in response as she passed by beeping the horn. At that moment I knew what relief felt like. And fortunately for me most of the ride would be downhill.

With patience and the good Lord watching over me I covered the last fifteen miles without further incident. I was cautious but it didn't mean I didn't enjoy the ride. In the five miles between Hogsback and Marlboro I dropped more than 1,200 feet. Over the remaining miles I would give up another 950 feet before arriving in Brattleboro.

As I approached the light on Main Street I could see a small bike shop in a narrow storefront across the intersection. I told the man my story and he was kind enough to custom–make a pair of spokes that would get me to Boston. I stuffed the spokes in the bike bag and took my time covering the last mile and a half to the Holiday Inn.

Outside the lobby entrance Rick was busy adjusting on a bike hanging from his work stand. I let him know what happened and later in the evening he installed the replacement spokes and gave the wheel a proper adjustment on his truing fixture. Watching Rick carefully adjust the spoke tension was like watching a world–class violinist fine–tuning the strings of a precision instrument. When he finished there was no wobble, it was perfectly straight. I would be fine for the last two days of riding.

Today was one of extremes; the climbing, the emotions, the near failure only to comeback and finish. I was still EFI. I may have been the one who rode the bike but it was Margaret and Rick, and the Brattleboro Bicycle Shop who made it possible. Behind every successful person is a team who deserves the credit. My job was easy; all I had to do was to not give up. If things went differently my first visit to Vermont could have easily been my worst day on tour. It ended up being one of the best.

For a town of 12,021, Brattleboro maintains a small village feel. The downtown is compact and wedged in between the steep terrain to the west and the Connecticut River to the east. Candle and coffee shops, art galleries and jewelry boutiques, they have their place on Main Street along with a trio of churches and a farmers market. Dating back to 1753 when Brattleboro was chartered it delivers the authentic New England charm people seek. And at 246 feet above sea level I still have some elevation to shed before I reach the Atlantic.

In my journals I would write about the highs and lows, the slow pace of 12.8 miles an hour, the 79.92 miles traveled, and six hours thirteen minutes of seat time, much of it grinding up hill. But the numbers today were not really important. What I wrote and what I hope to remember is I made it to Brattleboro with help; limping a bent wheel in the final hour. I needed to capture how I felt so I won't forget what this day was for me—A turning point to dig deep, to overcome. Quitting is easy, but pushing forward through the challenges is what makes you, and what makes me. I am better because I almost failed. I needed that personal victory today so that tomorrow I know I have it in me.

Day 48: Brattleboro to Lexington, Massachusetts. (93 miles)

I got up extra early to finish writing postcards. I was winding down having but a few days left to scout out picture cards to share, to write my thoughts of what was behind me, and what was yet ahead. It was a liberating moment, one where I would soon put down the pen on this journey, calling it done, the last shout out to friends and family, the last bit of wit and wisdom, the last sketch of me on my bike pedaling across the margin. There was relief but it also brought a hint of sadness. What became so familiar, almost automatic would become yet another thing I would no longer do.

Today was a short stack of a dozen cards but tomorrow and the day after the final flurry would come. My scratchy printing and script would get even more distorted, a mix of excitement, exhaustion, and my body's uncontrolled shaking driven by emotions washing through me and exiting from hand to paper as I write.

I can't say I'll miss the stress of not being able to find the right postcards, or any cards for that matter. I lost track of the hundreds of cards, the number of addresses written, and who they went to. But in each postcard, in that moment, I thought about the person receiving it. It was a one–off message for them alone. It was my personal expression to someone who cared enough to read it, that's what I remember. In those moments, one card at a time, one life touched, a connection would be made.

There would be a delay in the receipt of the messages and I would not see their expression, but with each one I hoped it would brighten their day, maybe they might feel a bit of what I feel, and if I'm lucky, just maybe they would laugh or tear up. None of the cards left me without some emotion attached. They couldn't. And I'm sure the embedded emotion would find the reader once their eyes were set upon the words.

Writing the cards, sharing the moments was as much of this journey as pedaling. I didn't realize it early in the ride but I see it now. I'm glad I did it, that I shared as much as I could. The writing will remain one of my fondest memories.

I fixed the stamps on the back of the postcards and dropped them at the front desk on my way to breakfast. Then I stepped out to yet another day of perfect cycling weather. The air was fresh as clean sheets drying on the line. It was a bit brisk for this Thursday morning, the first day of July 2004, but the chill would provide some early comfort as I muscle my way out of the valley and into the hills of New Hampshire.

We were heading into Peter Crowell territory and I was looking forward to him pedaling nearby and sharing his impression of the state. I wanted to hear Peter's voice growing in volume as he approaches from behind. I imagine he'll boast about the area in a way as only he can. This is his stage and so far on the tour he hasn't shied away from the spotlight.

Clark also lives nearby in Keene, so I'll look for his guidance on tackling the 3,800 feet of elevation standing between me and my image of Lexington some six or more hours ahead of me. His advice, carefully measured out at the end of each day, has gotten me this far. I'm sure he won't let me falter now.

Many riders were layered up for the sub–fifty degree start but the forecast for later in the day called for heat, maybe even a passing shower. We would be tested for sure. I had my pale yellow and white sun–shirt on giving me both arm protection and a second layer over my core. My thick legs would need to warm up in the morning chill without any help. There would be no leg warmers covering them today.

At Tracy's call we left the parking lot of the hotel, the mood upbeat, happy feet turning the cranks as gears shifted and bikes accelerated back into the heart of Brattleboro. Single file across a concrete deck bridge we rode. I earned a wider shoulder over the water on Putney and quickly moved right as far as the curb would allow. The bike lane narrowed as our two–wheeled procession entered Main Street and eventually it disappeared into curbside parking. I joined the flow of traffic, blending in with the cars and the other bikes sharing the lane through the narrow street. Old brick buildings standing like dominos made it feel even more constricted until we bunched up at the light for our left onto Bridge Street.

With the green I stayed tight with Betty and several others crossing the steel truss expanse over the Connecticut River. It was a full football field long and without a shoulder we rode two–by–two in a pack of about eight taking the full lane. Ahead and behind were similar groups safely managing their way forward. A shorter steel bridge straight ahead called for the same tactic but first we stopped at the official New Hampshire welcome sign with the tag line, "Live Free or Die." Some might interpret the state motto as a threat but it is really a declaration of their independence to be free to manage their own affairs; as it should be in every state.

Later I learned New Hampshire, named by John Mason in 1629 after his home county, Hampshire, in England, was the first colony to declare independence from England on January 5, 1777. Yeah, they earned the right to use "Live Free or Die" as their motto.

Sand was spread, photos were taken. It was the thirteenth time to go through the motions. It was the fourteenth state I've set my wheels in since leaving California. The sign stood behind the guardrail with a marshy expanse beyond the trees, the river and the mountains of New Hampshire formed the backdrop.

Growing traffic and the limited space required efficiency in the border dance. I clicked and smiled then got back on the bike. It was time to climb. The morning motorists were forgiving and the horns remained silent as we cleared the second bridge and followed the river south.

I was treated to panoramic views of the river valley that were stunningly beautiful. The blue sky and dark green forested mountains mirrored against the water in a slightly blurred, soft reflection. The line between real and reflection was almost undetectable yet it added a sense of calm over the entire view.

We were gradually climbing along the narrow shoulder, the road staying close to the water. Beyond the guardrail the grassy ground dropped steeply to the river and to the left, rock walls standing thirty feet high jutted out from the earth. The scenic distractions helped to keep my mind off the effort I was applying to the pedals. I also noticed the riders ahead of me were beginning to stretch farther apart. It was a reminder I should pedal just a bit harder so I don't lag behind.

The road dipped and heaved as it tracked the waterline through the forest. The guardrails came and went. I passed a few lone houses with mowed yards and gravel drives scattered along RT–119. There was no activity this early in the morning aside from the few motorists heading to work and our group of riders pedaling along the shoulder.

At several points the elevation of the road dropped very close to river level affording an intimate view of the water's edge. Without traffic I was able to enjoy the sounds of birds off in the woods and the freedom to look out onto the water for more than a quick glance. I hoped to see a small boat or a fish jump to interrupt the shimmering of the surface but I saw neither. There was no visible movement in the water at all. It offered no ripples or cascades to create sound. It was my quiet companion that meandered through the valley.

The miles were relaxing and the riding easy as I angled away from the Connecticut River and rolled into the town of Hinsdale. On my right a white clapboard church crowded the road and just beyond the left edge of the pavement, a long stacked stone wall three feet tall guided me along the downhill past the VFW and into the compact center of town where the post office and town hall stood.

The Hinsdale post office dates back to 1816 and is the longest continually open U.S. Post Office in the United States. The area is known for the fertile farmland and at one time it was a center of industry for paper manufacturing. It was also home to inventor George A. Long, a machinist, who built a self–propelled steam vehicle in 1875 known as the Long steam tricycle. For his efforts, Mr. Long received one of the nation's earliest automobile patents.

The town proper is home to 1,500 but the official population of Hinsdale, including the surrounding area, is just over four thousand. It was named after Colonel Ebenezer Hinsdale in 1753 when it was chartered. The Colonel was a chaplain from a prominent family in Deerfield.

Older framed and mostly white buildings crowded the road leading out of Hinsdale before tapering off into the wooded background. To the north was the Pisgah State Park, a year round recreational park covering more than twenty–one square miles of forest and trails. Through the trees to the right the fast flowing Ashuelot River, water spilling noisily over the rocks creating a whitewash of turbulence. It was a long running cascade moving in the opposite direction as I climbed toward Ashuelot. I gained 213 feet of elevation in just a few miles.

In the river, boulders the size of cars diverted the water into fast flowing narrow channels making it a challenging place to kayak or canoe. The water was at most two feet deep limiting the ability to swim but it was definitely deep enough for tubing and horseplay.

Ashuelot was little more than a post office and home to less than four hundred, if you included the area beyond the Main Street. It did have one gem I was happy to see; the Ashuelot covered bridge. White wide lattice sides capped with a bright red roof and fancy curved archway details made this bridge unique. Most covered bridges are fully enclosed to protect the supporting structure but this style, known as the Town lattice truss bridge, has an extended roof providing protection to the structure while allowing the sides to be partially open above the handrail level. It also had two covered walkways integrated into the bridge that were outside the structural framework making it safe to walk across while motorists used the bridge. Traffic was limited to three tons and nine feet eight inches of height. It was built in 1864 and is the only river crossing between Ashuelot and Winchester a few miles upstream. The bridge consists of two spans covering a total length of 178 feet and passes over the top of the water by a little more than eleven feet. The uniqueness of the bridge has landed it on the National Register of Historic Places ensuring it will be preserved well into the future.

I stopped and studied the bridge as I delayed my crossing. I'd only seen a few covered bridges and I remember crossing only one in New Jersey. The sunlight had the bridge in partial shade and I waited for a few others to cross as I dug out my camera. A few quick pictures and across the boards I went. The sunlight flickered, the water rushed below and in just a few pedal strokes I emerged into the sunlight. "Stop!" someone shouted. As I paused at the fork in the road, my picture was taken and to this day it is one of my favorites. It would also be the only covered bridge I would cross on tour and the only one of its type I would ever see.

In Winchester, population: 4,258 I pedaled past a series of old framed buildings backing up to the Ashuelot River. The structures appeared to have been built separately then connected over time like some old–time strip center. They were in decent shape but their made–to–fit connections between buildings of varying styles and age drew my attention. To my right were more significant structures including a few religious centers and a multistory brick building home to the Conant Public Library. At the war monument on the corner I followed other riders to the right and we pulled into the post office parking lot for a quick break. Across the street children played under the shade of trees on the Center Church playground. Winchester was also home to the first *Avon Lady* named Persis Foster Eames Albee. That may not mean much to the younger generations, but in my day the Avon Lady was very popular and responsible for most of the beauty products reaching the rural middle class.

The foliage in New Hampshire matched that of Vermont. The stands of the peeling white–barked birch trees a few miles east of Winchester aroused the memories of my early days. As a boy I always knew when I saw birch trees I was getting close to my grandfather's house in eastern Pennsylvania. I love the birch trees and the memories they bring back.

Peter shouted announcing his intention to pull along side of me on a short steep climb. He slowed when we were side to side and he gave me a bit of advice on how to climb. He also told me to expect a more intense workout in the miles to come. We talked like we did earlier in the tour about home and what would come next. He like Clark had done this before. His insight held a lot of weight with me so I listened. We laughed, we talked about his place in Ocala that was not too far from my home and we said we would ride again when he was wintering in Florida. Then he moved forward and the man who had fourteen years and many pounds on me just pedaled away.

Riding from Winchester to Richmond I gained more than six hundred feet of elevation pedaling through dense remote wooded wilderness crossing over the Brickyard and Tilsey Brooks. It was beautiful by day and I saw little vehicle traffic. I wouldn't welcome a flat or any other major bike issue on this stretch since I saw so few riders and motorists. I pedaled through the intersection that was Richmond and rolled through more of the same wooded scenery along the southern edge of the Barden State Wildlife Management Area. I traversed the Rice, Tully, and Kemp Brooks and rode into the town of Fitzwilliam, population: 2,141. I was now riding at an elevation of 1,145 feet above sea level. Fitzwilliam was a postcard town of white plank–sided houses and churches, painted post rail fencing and monuments to wars fought and lives lost. A few quick turns and I was crossing over the busy RT–12 in search of the first SAG of the day another five miles ahead.

A few miles to the north hikers can find Mt. Monadnock. At 3,165 feet it towers over the landscape and is easily the tallest mountain peak in the area. It's nearly a thousand feet higher than any other peak within thirty miles and with the upper third being rocky and bare; it is easy to spot if you know to look for it. The mountain is visited by more than one hundred twenty–five thousand people annually making it the third most hiked mountain in the world behind Tai Shan in China and Mt. Fuji in Japan.

All of the towns I'm riding through have an interesting story. For some it is the origins of the name, for others it is the historical events that took place nearby, or the people who lived there. Many of the towns like Winchester and Richmond were renamed at some point, their names before and after paying tribute to a noted person by name or to their place of origin in England. Winchester was known as Arlington for twenty years beginning 1733 and Richmond was called Sylvester–Canada until 1752.

This part of the northeast is steeped in history dating back nearly four hundred years. Some of the oldest settlements and skirmishes have marked the migration of people from the coastal Atlantic near Boston as they pushed westward into territories that at the time were either unnamed or still in dispute. The space between towns was often the distance a person could travel in a day or less. By today's standards many of the towns in this area seem to run together as they grow and expand filling in the open tracts between them. Modern highways and automobiles bring them even closer. But on the bike at a steady pace of fifteen miles an hour that sense of space still remains.

Since leaving Winchester I have been climbing long steep hills that seemed to be a mile or more in length. They were tough and some were just *sum–bitches*. There were climbs stepping up the mountains, revealing only one section at a time. Just when I thought I was done and ready to celebrate cresting the top I'd have to dig down and do it again.

A few clouds passed over and a brief mist rained down on us but it was only enough to say we rode in the rain. The pavement stayed dry as did my clothes and it was gone as quickly as it came.

On the last incline of a very long staircase climb I attempted to stand up and power my way to the top. This was not a good idea. It sent my heart rate up over 171 beats per minute; I became anaerobic and was unable to catch my breath. I was smarter climbing the next hills and kept my butt glued to the seat.

Ahead and behind me I could hear the shouts of other riders commenting on the aggressive climbs. It was especially tough on the recumbent riders and the two couples on the tandem bikes.

At our first SAG, Clark joked that today was like our final exams. We had everything, including a slight rain shower to cover all conditions experienced on the trip. I focused on climbing and taking in as much scenery as possible. Before long, I was making my fourteenth state–line crossing and the second one for the day. It was the last time to sprinkle sand but I didn't spill it all. I thought I'd save some of it as a keepsake from the ride. I might even spill a little at Revere just to put a little west coast grit into the Atlantic sand.

Once in Massachusetts, I left the big climbs behind and then passed through a section of flat plains and marshlands. To my right just beyond the dull steel guardrail was a large tranquil pond that gave me reason to stop and take pictures. I checked my mirror for traffic, angled across the freshly painted centerline to the left, applied the brakes, unclipped from my pedals, and dropped off the pavement onto the loose gravel. In less than thirty feet I had rolled to a stop by a small weathered rustic cabin. It was a small roadside ice cream stand, or at least that's what the sign said.

I hopped off the bike and turned to fetch my camera out of the rear rack bike bag. Both bag and camera were showing the wear of the trip but neither let me down; continuing to provide dependable service since departing the Pacific Ocean seven weeks earlier. Tomorrow I'll reach the Atlantic; after that the bag and camera can enjoy a well-deserved break.

After rooting around in the bag I grabbed the camera and removed it from the plastic bag. The camera sprung to life and I started focusing on subtle ripples in the water caused by the dance of the slow breeze. The sunlight was off to my left and the sky was clear providing just the right conditions to photograph the pond. There was no traffic, no other cyclists, just the pond beyond the guardrail mirroring the trees and sky and the calming sound of the leaves fluttering, playing in my ears.

I captured what I hoped would be pictures worthy of stopping when I noticed Paul Kvam rounding the corner and heading my way. He was easy to pick out on his bike since he only wore the baggy mountain bike shorts, not the more accepted skin hugging road bike shorts with the unflattering built-in seat pad.

As Paul rolled by I snapped a single picture of him and then went about getting back on the road toward Boston. I would later learn it was a darn good photo; slightly off center, sharp and about what you would expect to find in a cycling magazine. A proud rider on his Bianchi captured in film forever.

Miles later the terrain began to change from wide roads along the flat wetlands to more narrow and fractured rolling contours dark with shade under the canopy of large slow growth trees. Getting cover from the sun made the temperature feel more tolerable but it was still warm in the shade.

Potholes and broken gravel became the norm and care needed to be taken to avoid flats or other undesirable events. There was talk earlier about the lack of sensitivity and an almost aggressiveness by motorists toward cyclists in the area I was quickly approaching. I kept thinking that after so many days and so many miles it would be tragic to have an incident on the last day riding to Boston. Heck, I just escaped a close call riding off of Hogback Mountain yesterday when I popped a few spokes and Margaret nearly scooped me into the van. I am so close to Boston. So close to—*Focus!*, I thought. There will be plenty of time for replaying the last days when you actually get to Revere Beach.

I crossed through the town of Ashby through the Willard Brook State Forest and onto the final SAG of the trip in Townsend. There was excitement; we were in the final stretch. I snacked and joked and with the sun beating down on me I knew it was time to move on.

Over the last forty miles, I rode with Hopper and a fellow called "Boston Bob," who made the crossing last year with Hopper. He decided to join in for the final run to Boston; a kind of reunion ride of sorts that I was learning was a common thing for graduates of the CrossRoads program.

The country roads soon gave way to busy neighborhood streets with traffic that was not conducive for pleasure cycling. In my mind I thought back to events that happened earlier in the ride. There were two places where I came in contact with moving vehicles, one was a car at slow speed, and the other a fast moving tractor trailer nipped my rain jacket as it billowed loosely near my elbow. I didn't speak of either event nor did I mention exactly where the contact happened. I prefer to forget about them both. I didn't fall nor was I injured and by letting it go it allows me to remain comfortable pedaling in the proximity of traffic. As I am doing right now in the middle of this New England crazy congested traffic.

We passed through the towns of Groton, Littleton, Concord, and then Bedford. It was a blur of lights and signs trying to stay on course. It was definitely getting tense on the road and being this close to finishing I wanted no part of a pavement dispute with any of the motorists. There were a few horns honked and a couple of cars aggressively passed with engines racing. I stayed close to the road edge leaving plenty of room and little reason to create any confrontation with drivers who think I was infringing on their road. I find it amazing many people still think bikes belong on the sidewalks.

With my attention on the traffic I missed much of the architecture and the significance of the events that unfolded through this area centuries earlier. This is where America was born, the battles fought, the blood let and people died. I would not be capturing the details of glorious battles won and the significance they had. I would be riding my own battle to get to the hotel. That was my focus. I was on a mission to miss the potholes and drainage grates, avoid the glass, stay clear of the cars, and to not cut a tire. I would leave the final stats about the villages of Massachusetts to those with an affinity for the history. I didn't need to dwell on it in the final miles.

Near the end of the ride, Greg and Geoff joined the group, and we arrived at the hotel without incident. The stream of bikes continued to flow into the parking lot to a chorus of cheers and hoots. The camaraderie was amazing; we celebrated everyone's personal victory as if it were our own. Seven weeks, that's all it took to develop the bond.

I covered 92.84 miles in six hours fifty minutes averaging 13.4 miles an hour. Coming down one of the hills I reached thirty–two miles per hour. It was my last long day on the bike, at least on this tour.

My wife, Donna, pulled into the parking lot moments later with our van decorated with well–wishes much like you would see at a high–school graduation or a wedding. I learned it was the handiwork of my Sister–in–law Kathy. Donna had to drive her van all lettered up like a rolling billboard from Charlotte, North Carolina, to Lexington, Massachusetts. I'm sure she got some crazy looks and a few honks from passing motorists.

Even though we still have twenty miles to ride tomorrow, it feels like the trip is over. Maybe it was seeing my wife and several other riders' spouses and friends that marked an end to our daily routine. Tonight would be different, no recap of the ride from Clark, no need to prep the CamelBak. I felt the impact of what arriving in Lexington meant. Done. Well, almost done. Just a twenty mile parade remained to complete this epic adventure and return to a normal world. I didn't know if I wanted to or if I even could return to what was considered normal. It had been an amazing transforming experience and I felt my days going forward would be anything but normal.

I knew after washing my bike, I would finally shave off my goatee, which had gotten long and bushy. Then on a whim, and Trevor's suggestion, I let Trevor shave my head with the electric shears to mark the end of this event. Ever the clown that T–Rev is, he shaved most of my head leaving three tufts of hair a few inches long giving me an "unfit for public" look. We laughed and he finished the job leaving a buzz–cut causing my ball cap to ride low on my head like it did when I played little league baseball. So much was changing but it was a good change.

Tracy told us in Los Angeles we should shave our heads. Since nobody knew what we looked like at the start of the trip it wouldn't matter, and maybe it would give people a chance to try something without fear of criticism from their circle of friends. Usually heads get shaved at the beginning of the trip, but as best Trevor or I could recall, not a single head was shaved until mine. I just wanted to do my part to keep the string alive. Not thirty minutes later Ron Atkinson asked me why I didn't get my head shaved at the beginning like he did. Oh well, the streak continued regardless of my actions.

Dinner was at Denny's and everyone enjoyed rubbing my stubble, taking pictures and laughing. We were in clusters of eight people at each table, spouses and friends mixed in with the riders. The conversations were loud; introductions were non–stop as if we needed everyone to know the names and stories about our riding friends. We also engaged in discussions about carpooling from the beach. We are only going to pedal to the water and then, after seven weeks in the saddle, we are riding in a car back to the hotel.

Tracy said parking at the beach was limited so Donna offered to shuttle a group of us back. Ken Pope and his wife would be amongst our return passengers. By the end of the night we added a few more people and the details were shared with Tracy so she could confirm all riders and guests were covered. There would be more than a hundred people at the beach and nearly forty bikes to be loaded for the twenty—mile return trip. It would be chaotic, exciting, and fun. We just needed to make sure nobody got left at the beach.

Between the Coasts

We are blessed to have such diversity of nature on display along the ride. There are thousands of miles from the beaches of the west coast to the waters greeting us in Boston; each mile different from the rest. The hot brown sandy desert, the massive fragrant pines in the high country, purple hued mountains capped with snow, green endless seas of grasses and corn, the rolling hills and exposed rocks of all colors and splendor, waterways still and others fast moving, cascading over rocks. Rain, wind, heat, cold, and humidity all adding spice to the experience. I have no favorites. I enjoy it all. I could not have imagined how much I would be moved by what I see as I travel through each day at a pace that ensures a connection to my surroundings.

If I were traveling by car I might be impressed but I would not have the connection. I doubt I will ever forget what I am experiencing. And I doubt I will be able to convey it to others. Words alone, at least those I can muster up, just won't do.

Circumstances in my life aligned making this trip possible. A job lost, a soul wondering for purpose, and a long forgotten dream. Unfortunate events and sadness brought about purpose and joy. I would gladly go through the fears and uncertainty of what led me here again, and again, and again. I am transforming into something and someone much better than who I was before. I like who I am becoming. I am no longer lost.

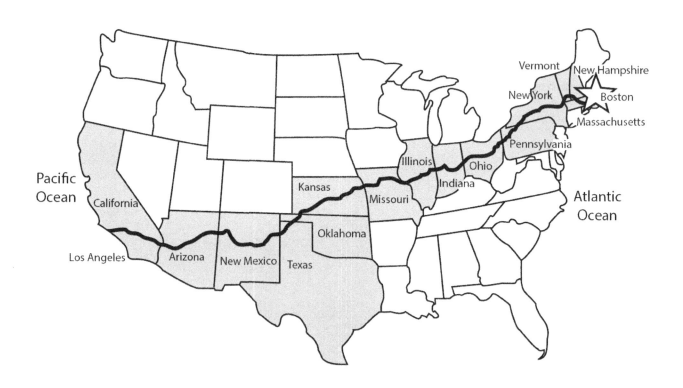

Pacific
Ocean

California

Los Angeles

Arizona

New Mexico

Texas

Oklahoma

Kansas

Missouri

Illinois

Indiana

Ohio

Pennsylvania

New York

Vermont

New Hampshire

Boston

Massachusetts

Atlantic
Ocean

To The Atlantic!

Day 49: Lexington to Revere Beach (Boston – 21 miles)

Morning came and I suited up for the last time. In the mirror was a smaller version of me. I was fit, trim, and tanned. I was also bald thanks to Trevor's handiwork and what some might consider a bad decision made in the moment. My hair would quickly grow back but today was a singular event I needed to embrace. I would need to mentally record all of it, to store it away to be recalled and replayed and shared whenever I wanted or needed it. I think I am ready and my bike is up for the challenge. The *Silver Streak* earned this day as much as I did, and as much as the rest of the riders and their mounts did.

Today was our graduation day, a celebration of the ride and a formality of ceremony we earned. These miles would be important as they are the last of the ride. But they really are nothing more or less than the other miles we had enjoyed, fretted and struggled over, or overcame whatever challenges they presented to us. These could arguably be the least important if you considered the elevation changes, the temperature, or the day's mileage. I think what makes them special is they are the miles allowing us to reflect back on the earlier miles while we are still in the company of those who we've come to know as we journeyed together. I believe this is why these miles will be important.

We assembled in front of the hotel as we always did and went about the business of topping off the air in our tires and making final adjustments to our bikes and personal gear. All of the riders were appropriately outfitted in matching red–white–and–blue CrossRoads jerseys. American flags were waving from the bike poles as they have since California. Under my flag were the Stooges—Moe, Larry, and Curly as they had been since I first assembled my bike in Los Angeles. Where the roads and traffic required we would ride single file but exiting the hotel and the last few miles to the beach we would ride side–by–side in two columns of twenty rolling at a slower than usual pace. It would be an enjoyable twenty mile stretch from Lexington to Revere Beach.

From the deck of the box truck Tracy orchestrated the final instructions and the official start to an anxious crowd. We left in waves to a rousing applause that faded quickly as I took my turn to exit the parking lot. The final day of riding had officially started

Our route would take us through small towns and old neighborhoods. I was surprised at the number of people waving and cheering from their porches and sidewalks. I hadn't expected any but maybe Tracy worked her magic and spread the word we were coming. As if we were important enough to capture their attention even for the few minutes it would take to pass by. It was an opportunity to reflect back on the seven weeks we spent together and to burn into our memories the sights, sounds, and emotions of this wonderful group of like–minded individuals.

We rode the likes of Mystic Valley and Governor's Avenue; then on to Salem, Washington, and Broadway. The names appropriate for the historical area in which we were riding. I paid no attention to the cue sheet because I had dozens of people around me keeping an eye on the route. I just turned and followed the procession in front of me. It freed me up to listen to the sounds around me and to do whatever I needed to keep my head clear.

The last five miles, the pace slowed, the level of chatter dropped and I could feel the change from outward expression to inward reflection taking place. I realized I was almost finished with this fantastic journey and then it hit me. I would likely not enjoy nor endure anything like it again. The thought washed over me like a chill, but not a sad one, one I couldn't quite describe. My legs continued to move the bike forward without instruction. I continued replaying the days in the rain, the days of endless miles and of steep climbs. Even the hard days I was remembering more favorably then I believe they really were. That's the beauty of time. It softens the pain and enhances the joyful moments.

In the final mile we rolled as if in a parade, everyone evenly spaced and lined up in two perfect columns. We stopped for the lights and continued as one. In front and behind our group the CrossRoads vans were there protecting us and ensuring safe passage to the beach. I had the perfect seat right in the middle of the pack. I could feel the excitement building and as I crested the small overpass on Revere I saw it, the Atlantic Ocean. *The Atlantic!* Under cloudy skies it revealed itself and the emotions came on as I followed the group and rolled to the right on Ocean Avenue.

Standing at the turn a large gathering of family and friends awaited us, with signs and balloons, cheering excitedly. If tears could be heard there was a roar building up.

Instead of crossing the road to the beach, our parade of bikes turned south for a quarter of a mile and then reversed direction, paralleling the beach so we could enjoy a long unobstructed view of our destination. Small rays of sunlight shined through the clouds and played off the water, giving it a golden sheen. The salty–scented ocean breeze confirmed we had indeed arrived. In the final hundred yards on Revere Beach Boulevard the pavilion came into view. The crowd that met us at the overpass had hurried over to the pavilion joining an even larger group of people. We could hear the cheering and we turned the pedals for just a few more revolutions before coasting to a full stop.

The sights, sounds, and smells were overpowering, and few could say they weren't caught up in the moment, the emotion, and the finality of our collective accomplishment. We ended as we started, not as forty individual riders, but as one unit, a family of adventurers.

From here, we would disband to points across America and abroad, but in doing so, we would take a small piece of everyone with us. I think back to my high–school graduation and how I felt that day. Happy, sad, wanting for it not to end, at the same time being glad it's over.

I was trading my roommate of seven weeks for my spouse, returning to my job in place of the day–after–day pedaling on the bike. I was giving up staying at different hotels every night for the comfort of my own bed, and I would have to stop eating everything in sight and start watching my diet. This moment was one of tremendous change, a change started long before with a dream of crossing America on a bicycle nearly thirty years earlier. A dream discovered and put into motion by the love of my life who knew better than me that not only could I do this but that I had to do this.

After several minutes of hugs and handshakes it was time to go to the water. We wheeled and carried our time machines through the damp sand and into the surf. Carefully I immersed the front wheel in the water as if to baptize the bike as I did in California. Everyone else did much the same. A few bikes were fully immersed and many were hoisted high in the air. Most of us kept our sunglasses on, which masked the tearing in our eyes, but quivering lips and stuttered speech revealed to all the power of the moment.

After embracing my wife, I wrapped my arms around Betty, my biking partner since Arizona. Few words were said; few were needed; we just held on until we collected ourselves.

Then Kathy popped a bottle of champagne, spraying everyone on the beach, which lightened the moment. Cell phones were dispatched from our bags and calls to family and friends not at the beach were made. I stood ankle–deep in the surf, talking to my mom back in Florida. She had been one of my biggest cheerleaders all through the trip. I could tell she was happy I finished the ride safely.

Candid photos were taken followed by a series of more formal group shots on the steps connecting the pavilion to the beach. As the activities were winding down I took the empty container Tracy provided and filled it up with Atlantic beach sand. This would be my reminder of a journey finished. It would find its place with the Pacific sand becoming my reminder to go after the dream. I stepped off the beach for the final time and carried my bike up the steps to the street.

As the bikes were loaded into the truck and atop the CrossRoads vans, people found their rides and buckled up for the short drive back through Boston to the hotel. Tonight we will have a closing dinner, some awards will be handed out, and it will be an opportunity to say goodbye. I can't believe I rode across the country. But I also wished I'd done it sooner.

At the hotel I recorded the miles and my performance every day for seven weeks. Out of habit and a sense of closure I feel I should include the details covering the final miles to the beach. I pushed the recall button on my bike computer and wrote the following into my journal; 20.73 miles, 12.4 miles per hour average speed, total seat time of one hour thirty–two minutes, and a maximum speed of 28.2 miles per hour. I let out a long slow breathe, my final stats safely recorded to paper. Someday these details may mean something to me, but for now I'm happy to close the book on this part of my cross country housekeeping. Pencil down, my final exam is now over.

And So It Ends

Day 49: The Banquet

The closing to our grand adventure has finally arrived. With family and friends, we assemble in the hotel banquet hall as Tracy and Trevor presided over the group. All of the CrossRoads staff dressed in coordinated colors as they have all tour. This will be the last time I'll likely see the staff, so one by one I focus on them and remember how they helped ensure my success.

Lynn: This gem of a lady from Montana started the trip as a rider going only to Abilene, Kansas. To our surprise and delight, she joined the staff from there and provided an abundance of enthusiasm, which kept us pedaling and smiling.

Tom J: Though not able to attend the banquet, Tom did provide his mechanical expertise when my bike was acting up. He also patiently walked me through the process of disassembling the rear hub and performing all the required maintenance. I also roomed with him for a few nights and have nothing but good things to say about this California custom–bike–shop owner.

Margaret: This wonderful lady from the Florida Panhandle inspired me on many a day when I could pedal no farther. Her cheering and encouragement along the route would fuel me for several more miles of pedaling. I'm not sure how, but it worked.

Rick: When my wheel was bent in New York and I broke spokes in Vermont, this Texan was there to make it right. Had he not been with the CrossRoads staff, my cross–country ride might have ended 113 miles short of Boston.

Trevor: This Canadian with his baggy shorts and cowboy hat was a hoot. Always positive, always joking and doing so with his funny accent considered the norm north of the border. His nickname was "T–Rev," and he seemed to have nicknames for everyone else. I would laugh every time he would call me "Tommy–Tom."

Trevor was in charge of baggage–handling, equipment, logistics, and was second in command on the tour. He was also our barber, specializing in buzz cuts.

Clark: For all but a few days on the tour this man from New Hampshire was my roommate. He successfully made the crossing last year, and most nights he would read the following day's journal entry from his trip to me. Through the Rocky Mountains and especially leading up to the 125–mile Guymon, Oklahoma to Dodge City, Kansas day, his attitude and support helped this flatlander move from fearing failure to embracing success each day. His goal was to do whatever he could for me to achieve my goal— pedaling every freak 'n inch (E.F.I.). My friend Clark and I both succeeded.

Tracy: If lightning, positive energy, and smiles could be combined into human form, it would be this lady. When I spoke with her prior to committing to this tour, I could tell she was passionate, excited, and someone I needed to be around. A single phone call to Tracy moved me from indifference to anticipation of this experience. Throughout this trip, she inspired me, motivated me, and impressed me with how much she could do and how well it could be done. It was detail and perfection with a smile.

Each day along the route, she would pump her fist and yell "Boston!" I looked forward to that each day and responded in kind. It was also more of a motivator than the Dairy Queen stops because she kept the goal of finishing fresh in my mind. To succeed, you must first see yourself as successful. The power of the mind will determine the outcome. She is a gifted lady, and to some degree, I take a part of her energy with me.

Certificates of achievement were handed out by Tracy, and with each one was a story about the rider. Kathy presented the results in the weight–loss pool, and Ben Dudley was the biggest loser, shedding a total of twenty–four pounds.

Ron Atkinson was awarded the tour map in a unanimous decision by the staff for his unwavering determination put forth each day. Six people tied for top honors in the flat–tire pool, and they donated the proceeds to a charity CrossRoads supports.

Eight riders managed to pedal every inch of the trip, and I was happy to be counted amongst the group. While I was glad I accomplished this goal I would be remiss if I didn't advise future riders to focus on enjoying the trip and not pounding out every mile if you are not physically able. A few people pushed beyond their limits and ended up off the bike because of blisters and dehydration. It's not necessary to go EFI for the trip to be a success. With that said, Peter Crowell pulled off the feat for the second year in a row and mentioned something about turning around and riding immediately back to California.

During the evening Ken Gregor shared with us his personal story about life and cycling and how the two are intertwined. I've included his inspirational writing in this book. Under the heading: *The adventures of Tom Sawyer, Huck Finn and Ken Gregor*. It is as he titled it and it is how he would want it to remain. I am amazed at the parallels between Ken's experience and my own. His words encourage me to continue my pursuits in cycling, exploring, in living, and in finding my soul.

It was a graduation in every sense. Smiles, clapping, cheering, tears of joy and sadness. All the emotions you would expect from a life–changing, or, more appropriately, a life–making experience. The emotions of one could be felt by all. We were a family of like–minded road warriors. Nothing can last forever, but in our memories and journals, our fifty days together will live on and hopefully we will continue to share with and inspire others to step out of the comfort zone and live life as it was meant to be experienced.

Day 50: Departure

As it began in California fifty days before, we trickled out of the hotel lobby and back to our lives. Tony Hepburn, the Englishman from the Bahamas, said to me, "You are the first person I met in California, and how fitting you are the last to bid me farewell in Boston." I promised to visit him on my next trip to the Bahamas.

The last person I said goodbye to was Kathy Stevens. She was one of the first people I met in Los Angeles, and we quickly became friends. We shared laundry chores, rode together at times, but always enjoyed each other's company. Her amazing wit and easygoing nature were magnetic, but what inspired me most was her just being there.

In Erie, Pa., she told me she was a cancer survivor two years and counting. Doctors offered little hope except surgery, chemotherapy and medication. Shortly after, she became a rarity, a cancer–free person with a new outlook on life.

No matter how bad a day may be, it is still a day to breathe, love and laugh among the living. Through the tour, she endured mechanical troubles and lost her wallet in Prescott, Arizona. You would never know adversity knocked so hard at her door.

God puts people in your life for a reason, and I think I got the message. As long as you are alive and have your health, how bad can it be? Just be thankful for what you have, and enjoy life. After a long embrace, a few tears and conversation, it was time to go.

My wife, Donna, and I headed for Cambridge to enjoy our first visit to Boston. The weather was perfect and we quickly settled into the hotel and then on to the downtown by way of the subway. We toured most of the historical sites, including the USS Constitution, Boston Commons, the two hundred–year–old cemeteries and the Freedom Trail. We walked all through the city and then into the park to relax.

We learned the Boston Pops were having a dress rehearsal for tomorrow's Fourth of July celebration, so we ventured down to the esplanade by the river to get a seat. We arrived at six o'clock; about three hours before it started, and were able to get into the main grassy area center stage about two hundred feet back. Jennifer Holliday and David Lee Roth were also scheduled to perform with the Pops.

As the skies grew dark, the music began. I had no concept of just how wonderful it would be. When the Pops began playing a medley of patriotic songs, including "God Bless America," "America the Beautiful," "This Is My Country" and others, I could see images in my mind displayed in rapid succession of everything I witnessed the past fifty days.

I not only saw America the beautiful, I lived it, smelled it, tasted it, felt it, and shared it with others. America, every part of it, is beautiful, and God blessed us with it. I am proud of our country and thankful that more than two hundred years ago, ordinary people did extraordinary things to give it life.

Then Jennifer Holliday sang "This Is the Moment." It was like a bow on the best gift you could receive. That moment, in that place, with my wife was an exclamation point on my adventure. As long as I can remember the moment, the sights, sounds, smells, the emotions, I will be a happy man. This experience was more than I imagined. It was more than it was meant to be.

The adventures of Tom Sawyer, Huck Finn and Ken Gregor

At the age of fifty–three and after 12 years of managing the MARTA effort it was time to redirect my energies in a different direction and to seek personal rather than professional endeavors and adventure. So, I purchased a used touring bike, changed modes of transportation, and began cycling. First I started biking in the neighborhood and then across Georgia. Cycling became so infectious, challenging, stimulating, and rewarding that in the pursuit of my own personal "manifest destiny" I ventured from Los Angeles to Atlanta, completed treks down both the East and West Coasts, and journeys in Australia and New Zealand – over 26,000 miles, more than the circumference of the earth at the equator.

During these fascinating trips I discovered not only new lands, marvelous sites, intriguing cultures, and gracious people, but more significantly, I discovered myself and my soul.

While on my longest trip – 3,000 miles and 43 days – it became apparent that we contemporary Americans are similar to old hunting dogs who have been in the house too long. The senses function but they have become dulled, diminished, and even atrophic. After several days of touring my senses became alert and alive. Trees and flowers began to have more fragrance, sounds were heard more acutely, objects were seen with more detail and description and together I was able to touch and feel and sense things more completely and fully. For the first time I began to feel part of the earth not as an observer but as a participant and ultimately discovered the true meaning of the expression "one with nature." There is a richness and beauty in our natural environment which can truly, or perhaps only, be experienced through cycling.

Magic and even mystery are related to tour cycling. I do not know the reasons why, I merely know that it is true. It is magical maybe because a bicycle is more than an extension of one's arms and legs; it is also a furtherance of one's soul.

Cycling provides a natural connection to the world in contrast to other forms of contemporary transportation. In an automobile, for instance, one simply adjusts the internal environment – temperature, radio, and the power seat – to one's preference. On a bicycle one must react differently to the elements since a cyclist is not in a protective shell but rather is part of the wind, rain, sun, and earth.

Maybe it is a result of the fact that one must supply the energy – you are active not passive. Your body is the sole continuous source of energy. Somehow there is something noble, human, and even majestic about a human body providing the power and life to a simple yet magnificent machine.

Or maybe cycling is marvelously nostalgic because we learned to ride as children and now we can revisit our youth.

Although there are many reasons tour cycling is exciting, enlightening, and rewarding, I believe that the most significant factor lies in our soul. Cycling allows us to be reflective, intuitive, imaginative, and full of thought while simultaneously moving through life. A ride frequently starts as a flight from sadness and continues toward the thrill of life. It can enable you to discover the difference between quitting and stopping, it permits the seeking of the unknown, it encourages the discovery of one's self, and it allows your soul to emerge and your spirit soar. Cycling demonstrates that like life itself, the joy is in the journey not in the destination. Cycling enables you to tend to your soul.

And so –
The woods are lovely, dark, and deep,
But I have promises to keep,
And miles to go before I sleep
And miles to go before I sleep.

The benefits of tour cycling not only provide nourishment of the soul but fill one's spirit with adventure. From every trip I have returned with interesting experiences and adventure. To cycle where Caesar Augustus defeated the Gauls and to view the Arc de Triomphe built 2,000 years ago in his honor and to pedal by Waterloo where Napoleon was defeated leaves one in awe. Cycling near Namur, Belgium and visiting an 11th Century abandoned Benedictine Monastery gives one a sense of peace, tranquility, and spirituality. More mundane but still very interesting experiences are also common. While in New Zealand I stayed at a local farmer's house where we watched the dogs gather sheep, learned to sheer the sheep, and spent time exchanging stories over quality New Zealand wine. In the Tuscany region of Italy, during a heavy downpour, I found an ATM machine shelter and took a nap. After the storm cleared I discovered that two of my fellow cyclists had sought shelter in a garage where the owner appeared, invited them into his home, and had his wife prepare a 4-course Italian meal. After dessert the rain ceased, and they were on their way. Getting lost or perhaps a kinder choice of words would be getting misplaced, in a desolate area of England where I chose the wrong road and ended up in a farmland for an hour with the bike tires flipping up sheep and cattle dung on my fashionable jersey was an adventure in itself.

The benefits of cycling are noticeable. My heart rate at rest is in the low forties. I now weigh only three pounds more than when I was thirty. Food and drink do more than satisfy hunger; one begins to view food as a source of fuel and as a result healthier choices are made. Moreover, depending on the terrain one can burn from 300 to 500 calories per hour cycling. My typical tour requires 4 to 6 hours of biking, therefore ice cream, apple pie, wine and other pleasurable foods are not prohibitive along with the nutritional stuff.

Reflections

At the end of the trip I reflected back on two things; the process of how things come to be and a baseball analogy on life. Before I let them slip out of my memory I jotted them down just in case I had the opportunity to share. I think this is one of those times...

This thing we do
by Tom Gray

I wish I could do this,
I want to do this,
I'm going to do this,
I'm doing this,
I've done this,
I'm going to do this again.

And one additional verse:
I'm going to help someone else do this.

Baseball, Life and Dad

My dad loved baseball and was a Little League team manager when I was young. He instilled in me a love for the sport which I am very thankful for. Whenever I get the chance to take in a baseball game I feel like he is sitting right beside me. He believed in letting everyone play no matter how good or bad. Little League was about developing character, not about winning. A few awkward young boys given the chance to play on his team ended up becoming very talented athletes in high school. All they needed was the opportunity to swing the bat, to try and hit the ball. The following baseball analogy sums up for me how my dad viewed life and it's something I'm glad he passed on to me.

"We may not always be successful in the things we attempt, but you can be sure success will always be denied to those who fail to try. It is the opportunity to stand on the ball field and to swing the bat that matters. Whether you hit the ball or not is of little consequence. Let the record show you chose to take the field and in that decision you are already a winner. And you will fear not the opportunity to take the field, to stand at the plate and to swing for the bleachers again and again and again."

On behalf of all those awkward Little League ball players who proudly wore the Yankees uniform, thank you coach!

Endless Thanks To...

Mom: For telling everyone you talked to all about what I was doing. I'm as proud of you as you are of me.

Dad: For riding with me through the eastern extents of Kansas and watching over me the entire journey.

Janet & Mike McKenna: For posting a large map on your restaurant wall and faithfully moving the little plastic bike to keep your patrons "up to date" on where our group was riding.

Kathryn Carlisle: Your prayers kept me safe.

Friends and Family: If you thought I was crazy, an inspiration, a potential roadside memorial, or whatever. If I made you think or wonder then it was good for both of us.

Jimmy Bishop: This ride was our dream. I thought about you along the way and I imagined you pedaling alongside me as we did when we were teenagers back in *Jersey*.

Barb Shepard: Co–Publisher and Editor, *DeLand Beacon* owner and risk taker in allowing me the opportunity to share my story with your readers each week during the trip.

Margery Dykes: *DeLand Beacon* Newsroom Manager–My reviewer, editor and photo selector.

Phil and Barbara Bransky: Co–riders in XC04, for providing a copy of Phil's diary that provided population details and some other interesting back stories I missed.

Ken Gregor: Co–rider XC04, for sharing your personal cycling story titled, *The adventures of Tom Sawyer, Huck Finn and Ken Gregor,* that I needed to include in its entirety exactly as written.

My fellow riders: You provided company, support, and humor each day whether I needed it or not.

Bert & Iris Randolph: For following me, and getting the Hunterdon County Democrat interested in my much–delayed trip. Iris also provided the final proof reading and edits that gave polish to my writing.

Joe Vernon: My friend, your passing just months before I started this adventure was one of the reasons I committed to this trip.

Kristin at Orange Cycle: For working with me to pick the right bike and for continuing to take care of my cycling needs.

The Brattleboro Bike Shop: For custom making a set of replacement spokes to get me the last 113 miles to Boston.

Steve Arseneault: For showing me it shouldn't take years to finish writing a book.

Scott Machetti: For not believing I could do it. I did!

The people I met along the way: You touched me with your stories.

To the young boy who found a passion for reading through my articles in the *Beacon;* your story gave purpose to my writing and made the long nights scribing my notes all the more satisfying.

And I saved the best for last, to Tracy and her staff, without you there would be no celebration. Thank you for changing my life.

Trip Stats:

- 7,275: Feet above sea level: Highest: (Continental Divide, NM)
- $5,999: Trip registration
- 3,495: Total miles (somehow I managed an extra 80 miles)
- $1,900+: Bike cost
- 1,300+: Photos taken
- 400+: postcards sent from the road
- 197: Starting weight before training
- 156: Ending weight in Boston
- 124: Longest ride in miles
- 69: Age of oldest rider
- 57: Average rider age at start
- 55: New friends (48 riders, 7 staff)
- 49: Days on tour, 43 riding and 6 rest days to get back East
- 46: Miles per hour: Fastest downhill speed
- 45: My age during the trip
- 44: Shortest ride in miles (excluding the 20 mile ceremonial ride to the beach in Boston)
- 43 Riding days
- 41: Total pounds dropped (27 in training and 14 on tour)
- 41: Age of youngest rider
- 36: Miles per hour riding with the wind and not pedaling
- 24: Number of Dairy Queens listed on the cue sheets (We actually found more)
- 16: Longest climb in miles
- 15: Number of states cycled in
- 14: Miles riding without pedaling (wind in Palm Springs)
- 14: Feet below sea level: Lowest (Indio, CA)
- 11: Longest descent in miles
- 8: Number of riders EFI (Including me)
- 8: Days with rain
- 7: Most days in a state (Tie: New Mexico and Kansas)
- 6: Century Rides (more than 100 miles in a day)
- 6: Birthdays celebrated on tour
- 6: Rest days
- 5: Hours by jet to go coast–to–coast
- 4: Time zones cycled in
- 4: Tires used
- 4: Tubes used
- 2: Chains used
- 2: Broken spokes
- 2: Back–to–back Century rides
- 1: Bent wheel
- 1: Pair of shoes used
- 1: Tornados observed
- 1: Tornado watches
- 0: Official Flats (though I did have one in a hotel room and one at the Jack Rabbit trading post)
- Biggest issues: Hot foot and saddle sores

Cross Country in Rhyme

A few years ago I lost a friend and co–worker, a wonderful graphic artist and poet. I find this poem he wrote a few years before his passing to be both an accurate description on life and my personal challenge in crossing America by bike. Greg Davis you are deeply missed and I hope you are happy I chose this poem to describe my journey.

Trust
by Greg Davis

Now when we think of things that are,
And wonder how we've come this far,
We pause and think of things gone by,
Recalling how we once asked why.

For now we see what then was dark,
When fear and doubt did cloud our heart,
And thank our God that he saw best,
When we could only see the test.

So may we come to know that time,
Will pull away the clouds that blind,
To teach us then each day to trust,
That he still knows what's best for us.

Daily Poetry to My Daughter Nicole

Every day for you my poet, I write in verse. It is as much a challenge to write in rhyme as pedaling, but I've committed to describe each day to you in the medium you so love. In my words I hope you see the tears, feel the fears, and know the joy of my journey.

Preface to an adventure

A Poem a day,
For my little poet,
After each day's ride,
I want you to know it.

The sites, the sounds,
I'm sure I will like,
As I ride cross country,
Just me and my bike.

Dad

May 15 (Los Angeles)

Excitement and concern,
Two very different emotions,
Meeting new friends is easy,
For the aches and pains there's lotions.

I have packed too much,
But prepared too little,
I guess you could say,
I'm somewhere in the middle.

A thirty–mile tune up ride yesterday,
Venice Beach, Santa Monica Pier, hooray!,
The different people were something to see,
I just wished I had no pain in my knee.
Thinking of you will be the key
Millions of smiles, my little monkey.

May 16 (Manhattan Beach to Riverside)

The pain in my knee is beginning to subside,
Allowing me to ride, ride, ride.

From the surf on the coast,
To the mountains in the east,
We saw dry river beds,
And flowers to say the least.

Eighty miles from sea to here,
They call it Riverside,
But you won't find any water here,

Mountains of dirt with nary a tree,
Ribbons of roadway as steep as can be.

On to the desert tomorrow we ride,
Three days, three hundred miles, but it must be tried,
Indio, California is next on the list,
The windmill farms just can't be missed.

I see your smile,
I'll see you in a while.

May 17 (Riverside to Indio)

Hills, hills, hills,
Nothing but hills,
I'm going the distance,
I'm not gonna stop,
After twenty–eight miles of climbing,
I thought I would drop,
But then we dropped into the canyon,
With wind at our backs in reckless abandon,
For fourteen miles I never did pedal,
Never used the brakes, I didn't meddle,
I hit thirty–six miles per hour on the flats,
And twenty–seven uphill, imagine that.

Past windmill farms and snow–capped peaks,
The smile on my face covered both cheeks,
A taste of the desert is all that we had,
A hundred miles of desert and climbing will be bad.

May 18 (Indio to Blythe)

106 in the desert sun,
Two thousand feet up the mountain I did run,
To Desert Center fifty miles in,
Half way, half way, I said with a grin.

Not a living thing did I see,
Except for a vulture eyeing on me,
Wind to my back,

Water bottle hot,
I poured it over my head,
A thirty–degree drop I got.

A dust devil caught me,
I was covered in dirt,
Gritty I was, my muscles they hurt,
Then it was green, an oasis in sight,
Blythe, Blythe, I'll sleep well tonight!

May 19 (Blythe to Wickenburg)
117 miles through the desert I went,
Not the same desert yesterday I spent,
This one was hilly, uphill for most,
Through abandon towns, not even a ghost.

In towns we saw people and stayed a short
time,
Would best be described frozen fifty years
in time.
Old cars and old trucks all tired and aged,
I even saw wooden wheels off an old stage.

A town called Hope I did pass through,
Two abandon houses and nothing to do,
Then the sign, "You are now beyond
Hope,"
At fifty–seven miles I reached the end of
my rope,
But Charlie was there with ice and a drink,
I was able to go, once I could think.

The second half of the ride I looked all
around,
Painted by God the landscape I found,
After ten hours of riding I am happy to say,
Wickenburg, Wickenburg, I'm here,
hooray!

May 20 (Wickenburg to Prescott)
Mountain, mountain, climb the mountain,
A lot of complaining, a lot of pout 'n,
But what I hear and what I see,
Birds singing and God's great scenery.

Climbing out of Wickenburg was a view,
Of rocks, dried weeds, an old goldmine or
two,
Over the top to Yarnell Pass,
My first sighting of real trees, what a gas!

An old train museum, a farm or two,

I stopped to pet horses, took a picture or
two,
From Skull Valley to Willhoit eight miles I
go,
It looked flat, but it's up hill don't you
know.

Then eighteen miles in the Bradshaw
Range,
I climbed 5,700 feet, the scenery constantly
changed,
Narrow roads without guardrails zig–
zagged all the way,
The views at each turn begged you to stay.

I reached 6,100 feet before I went down,
Burnt forest then lush trees in Prescott I
found,
Tired I was after a long day ride,
Fifty–nine more miles on my backside.

May 21 (Prescott to Cottonwood)
Forty–four miles today was the plan,
The climbs were steep, but I know I can,
Make it to the top of Mingus Peak,
7,023 feet high I smiled cheek to cheek,
We cheered for the others,
It was quite a feat,
After twenty–four miles riding,
We could hop off the seat.

Then downhill we raced into Jerome,
A Cliffside village they proudly called
home,
Lunch on the café porch with a mile high
view,
The red rocks of Sedona and Cottonwood
too!

The remaining miles were scary and fast,
Narrow roads, crosswinds, I hope my
brakes last,
Then I arrive at tonight's resting place,
Yes my monkey that's a smile on my face.

May 22 (Cottonwood to Flagstaff)
A mountain ride,
Before a day of rest,
The red rocks of Sedona,
Mom likes best.

Then we started a ten mile climb,

Steep grades and switchbacks would take
some time,
But today mind and body were working
just right,
And the view from the top was an
awesome sight.

I've seen Oak Creek Canyon,
From low to high,
And now off to the hotel I go,
Bidding Oak Creek Canyon, bye, bye!

May 23 (Flagstaff – Rest Day)

Today for me is a day of rest,
Postcards sent to those I like best,
The others are busy,
There's so much to do,
But I'd rather stay here,
And write poetry to you.

May 24 (Flagstaff to Holbrook)

Off to Holbrook ninety–six miles we ride,
The wind at our backs,
The traffic at our side,
The interstate is flat and fast,
But with all the debris,
Our tires won't last,
Flat after flat, the riders slow down,
But they have flat tire parties,
When they are no longer round.

Past the Petrified Forest and Meteor
Crater,
Down historic Route 66 and then later,
I sat on the Jack Rabbit at the trading post,
But standing on the corner of Winslow
Arizona,
With Eagles music playing I liked most,
Dad's smile is as big as can be,
Thanks to thoughts of little monkey.

May 25 (Holbrook to Gallop)

Today we rode to New Mexico,
With the tailwind we sure did go,
Past dinosaurs and tacky signs,
Several trains running the lines,
All in all it was a good day,
Not a single flat all the way.

I did stop at old Fort Courage,
I was disappointed and discouraged,

It was used as a backdrop for an old TV
show,
Called "F–Troop" long, long ago.

Tomorrow again the highway we ride,
I hope good luck is on my side.

May 26 (Gallop to Grants)

We pedaled for thirty miles,
On bicycles we ride,
Then at the top of the mountain,
We stood on the Continental Divide,
7,245 Feet above sea level,
At the sign we stood for pictures,
Hoping they would hold the camera's level.

To the west the waters drain into the
Pacific Sea,
To the east they flow into the Gulf or the
Atlantic,
It all makes sense to me.

Then we all started joking,
To Boston should be an easy ride,
Because it is all downhill,
Since crossing the Continental Divide.

May 27 (Grants to Albuquerque)

Passing by volcanic fields,
Horses, flowers, each corner yields,
The red rock cliffs tall as towers,
The rolling fields of yellow flowers.

The smell of pollen in the air,
The adobe architecture is everywhere,
This is Albuquerque, what a place,
A ring of mountains surround the space,
The tree lined Rio Grande River I did see,
It was a wonderful day for my bike and me.

May 28 (Albuquerque to Santa Fe)

Climb, climb, climb,
All we did was climb,
4,500 feet up we go,
Very hot and very slow,
My heart raced and my lungs burned,
I gave all I had, the pedals turned.

Then a few steep and long grades,
Coming down scared, hoping my brakes
don't fade,
Sixty–eight miles all the way,

I'm tired, very tired, but in Santa Fe.

May 29 (Santa Fe – Rest Day)

I did my laundry,
And washed my bike,
A day of rest,
Is what I like.

A few hours in old Santa Fe,
The art and jewelry,
Just blew me away.

Many postcards I did write,
I'm sure I'll sleep well tonight.

May 30 (Santa Fe to Las Vegas)

Mountains and wind,
When will it end?,
I didn't brake,
But I did bend.
Speeding down the mountain pass,
Hard on the brakes avoiding the glass,
We finally made it to Las Vegas,
Not the city of lights,
But I'm out of gas.

May 31 (Las Vegas to Tucumcari)

One hundred and ten miles today I did
ride,
Everything hurts, my feet and backside,
The climbs were long,
But the views were great,
At the midday break I ate and ate.

This will be our last night in New Mexico,
Because tomorrow to Texas is where we
go.

I miss you monkey! ☺

June 1 (Tucumcari to Dalhart)

Hot, hills and headwind,
Wondering if we would ever get in,
Ninety–six miles seemed like two times
more,
My butt hurts, my feet are sore.

A thirty mile per hour headwind got in the
way,
And it didn't let up, not one bit all day,
My spinning pedals was all I could see,
Except for some trains that passed by me.

The huge cattle feeder lots I see, oh my,
They have no clue, they don't ask why,
This is the last stop the cows make,
To fatten them up for your next steak.

It's time to rest, it's been a long day,
Tomorrow strong headwinds will be in our
way.

June 2 (Dalhart to Guymon)

Rain, rain go away,
We want it dry when it's day,
Tornado warnings are something new,
They even showed us the storm shelters
too.
124 miles we have to ride,
They call for winds from our side,
I guess it's better than in our face,
When they blow hard you don't go
anyplace.

If we are lucky and God takes pity,
Before it's dark we'll be in Dodge City,
I hope my butt can make it through,
Provided my legs can take it too!

Every inch I plan to ride,
With the Three Stooges at my side.

June 3 (Guymon to Dodge City)

Jack rabbits running left to right,
Tornadoes and storms nowhere in sight,
Wheat fields amber, corn in green,
Nothing else could be seen,
Mile after mile the wind was our foe,
But we had 124 miles of pedaling to go.

Trains would pass and so would time,
We even traveled the "Yellow Brick Road"
for a time,
Signs about Dorothy's house from the
Wizard of Oz,
When we neared we didn't stop, just
paused.

The last twenty miles we made a left turn,
And got the tailwind that we earned,
My longest day sitting on the bike seat,
This is a day I'd rather not repeat.

June 4 (Dodge City – Rest Day)

Today was a day off,
A day of rest,
I think you know,
What I like best,
I found a race track,
Just out of town,
I watched them go,
Round and round

Dad – I miss you monkey!

June 5 (Dodge City to Great Bend)

In 1846 on Pawnee Rock,
If I stood there I'd be in shock,
As buffalo roamed wild and free,
Their numbers made a blackened sea,
Fifteen miles to North and East,
Imagine nothing but wild beast.

That is what a soldier did say,
On a plaque on that rock to this day,
I learned much history,
It was a great day I must say.

To live in the days of the pioneers,
With Indians and buffalo year after year,
Kansas is quite a place,
History and beauty in your face.

June 6 (Great Bend to McPherson)

I may be wrong,
But I think I'm right,
That God Bless America,
Was inspired by the sight,
Of the hills, the corn,
The wheat and the skies,
From Great Bend to McPherson,
Beauty before my eyes,
This was likely the best day yet,
Of all I ride,
This one I'll not forget.

June 7 (McPherson to Abilene)

Hang on tight,
The wind is to your right,
To the left turns the pack,
The wind is at your back,
Uphill, downhill, fast, fast, fast,
You barely pedal,
You pray that it lasts.

Riding like a boy,
On his two wheel toy,
Sailing into town,
Before the wind died down,
It was fun for sure,
And we got ice cream at the store.

June 8 (Abilene – Rest Day)

The Hall of Fame for pups that race,
It was quite an unusual place,
Greyhounds with their legs so long,
On a track is where they belong,
But once retired what do they do?,
Hope to be adopted by me and you.

While standing in this wonderful place,
On my leg, a cold nose and a face,
A dog named "Shige" I got to see,
I wanted to take her home with me,
If in the future I'm doggie bound,
Let it be a retired Greyhound.

*Nicole – Without a sound Shige came up to me
wanting nothing but attention, yet was patient
knowing that it would come.*

June 9 (Abilene to Topeka)

Rain, rain misty rain,
The first we've seen I can't complain,
Emerald hills all about,
Horses, cows, and buffalo are out,
Some ponies and some donkeys too,
A snake I saw one, well maybe two,
All in all it was a good day,
Soggy yes, but I'm now half way.

June 10 (Topeka to St. Joseph)

Rain, rain I should be a duck,
After twenty–five days we ran out of luck,
But it stayed cool,
I ain't no fool,
We had a good day,
Not much else to say,
We arrived in St. Joe,
And tomorrow we go,
Eight–six more,
To Chillicothe.

June 11 (St. Joseph to Chillicothe)

Climb monkey climb,
Uphill takes your time,
Down is fast,

It won't last,
Climb monkey climb.

*Nicole – It was a day of hills. About 100 to 150
hills that were very big and very tough. Tomorrow
we go ten miles less (75 miles) but the hills will be
bigger and there will be more of them. I miss you
monkey!*

Papa.

June 12 (Chillicothe to Kirksville)

Race down the hill,
Boy what a thrill,
One hundred–forty–eight peaks,
They made my knees weak,
I made it over a dozen or so,
The rest I climbed oh so slow.
But the feeling you get,
When you make it with ease,
Sends you sailing down the next,
Riding the breeze.

Though I'm tired,
It was a good day,
The old man on the bike,
Was a young boy today.

June 13 (Kirksville to Quincy)

So long Missouri,
You don't need to worry,
The "Show Me" state,
Was really great,
So long Missouri.

I moo'd at the cows,
They moo'd back,
As if to say good–bye,
Now count the states,
Illinois is number eight,
A fun day for this guy.

June 14 (Quincy to Springfield)

One hundred–eight miles we ride,
Oh my poor tender hide,
The scenery I hardly recall,
But the wind and the hills,
I remember them all,
We've been riding now,
For six days straight,
We ride again tomorrow, then rest,
I cannot wait.

Nicole – I'm a tired monkey…. ☺

June 15 (Springfield to Champaign)

An hour of riding then a storm,
Into a barn to stay dry and warm,
The rain sideways and heavy came,
Thinking tornadoes but none just the same.

A three–hour delay then we go,
Rain, rough roads and headwinds don't you
know,
To a town called DeLand,
A little store, a few houses,
And corn all around, to the left and right,
Five hundred people live here, but few are
in sight.

Finally we arrive in the town of
Champaign,
Legs tired, hungry, my butt was in pain,
Tomorrow we rest for the day,
Then again we pedal, I hope I'm okay.

June 16 (Champaign – Rest Day)

Rest Day,
The Best Day,
Decorate your helmet too,
Not sure what I'm gonna do,
To Wally–World to see,
What ideas they have for me.

June 17 (Champaign to Crawfordsville)

Back on the road for seven straight,
We had a tailwind, we couldn't wait,
The town where Miss America was born,
We rode through it and plenty of corn.

Through Hillsboro where the sign read,
"600 happy people and a few sore heads,"
To Indiana our ninth state,
The end is near, I can't wait.

Tomorrow we ride the Velodrome,
The high banked track where speed
demons roam,
I'll go as fast as I can when it's my turn,
Let the pedals spin,
Let the rubber burn.

June 18 (Crawfordsville to Indianapolis)

I rode my bike on the Velodrome,
A barrel shaped track,
That bikes call home,
Like a wall when you're inside,
I pedaled fast when I ride.

The speed, the walls, my heart raced,
I had a great time at this place,
My body tired, my legs sore,
Twenty–seven miles per hour, not a tick more,
I know I want to ride it again,
I'm not sure if, I'm not sure when.

June 19 (Indianapolis to Richmond)

I rode my bike,
How I like,
Sometimes fast,
Sometimes slow,
Eighty–four miles I rode,
Don't you know.

But the biggest surprise,
Was before my eyes,
Brownies from home,
From mom, Nic and Nel,
When I arrived,
At the hotel,
I'm glad to say,
It's Father's Day!

Thank you monkey!

Nicole – Everyone enjoyed the brownies and you made dad look like a hero. I can't wait to see my monkey!

June 20 (Richmond to Marysville)

Another state line,
Into Ohio makes nine,
It's our tenth state,
And I'm feeling great,
We climbed and we glide,
It was a very good ride,
One hundred–seven miles all told,
But my bike was feeling old,
It squeaked and it clicked,
As if it were sick,
But our mechanic made it right,
So tomorrow will be bright.

June 21 (Marysville to Wooster)

Horse and buggy,
Green apples in the road,
The Amish family riding,
From town with a load,
A little girl of three,
Looked curiously at me,
Wondering why I look so funny,
And have no horse and buggy.

June 22 (Wooster to Niles)

I passed a farm of three thousand cows,
Not a single moo, not any wows,
But I saw a pile of something for sure,
The biggest pile of, yes, manure,
Then to Niles where President McKinley was born,
We left behind the cows, left behind the corn.

Tomorrow to Erie for a day of rest,
….great,
Pennsylvania will be our eleventh state,
It will be flatter and shorter by far,
I've got a week more on the bike,
I can't wait to travel by car.

June 23 (Niles to Erie)

I arrived in Erie,
They say it's mostly dreary,
But the skies were blue,
And the lake was too.
To the ballpark,
Before it was dark,
For a double A baseball game,
Into town the Portland Sea Dogs came,
The game was exciting and it was fun,
One guy even got an infield home run.

I liked it a lot,
I will go more,
You never know what will happen,
Or what's in store.

June 24 (Erie – Rest Day)

Sunny day,
Everything's A.O.K.,
Down to the pier,
Where the air is sweet,
And I got to the water,
By taking State Street,
I visited the tall ships and museum too,

So much to see, so much to do,
Clean and neat and big frogs galore,
Erie, PA has much to explore.

June 25 (Erie to Hamburg)

Riding in the rain,
And my feet are numb,
Just about fifty degrees,
Doesn't it sound a little dumb?

But no other way to get here from there,
If I could only stay warm,
I wouldn't care,
My feet are sloshing in my shoes,
But I can stop whenever I choose,
And that will be when I get there,
Hamburg, New York,
After that I don't care.

June 26 (Hamburg to Canandaigua)

Tailwind, tailwind, tailwind, whoa!,
Tailwind, tailwind, tailwind, go!,
Thirty on the flats, thirty–eight on the hills,
Going so fast, getting the chills,
Then the rain came,
And it wasn't the same,
I couldn't see,
But lucky for me,
I didn't fall,
Not at all.

June 27 (Canandaigua to Syracuse)

Fun day, short day,
Seventy miles of riding day,
My wheel got a wobble,
So I had to hobble,
But then it was fixed,
My ride wasn't nixed,
Thanks to Tracy I can say,
It was another good day.

June 28 (Syracuse to Little Falls)

Trains to the right,
Canals are there too,
Today I had ice cream,
And saw Harry Potter too!

It was an easy day,
That's about all I can say,
Except I did my laundry too,
Does that surprise you?

June 29 (Little Falls to Albany)

Today was my best day,
Better than the rest day,
Tailwinds and cool breeze,
Gliding along the shade trees,
By the river, by the tracks,
The wind blowing at our backs,
Horses, colts and running dogs,
Skunks, birds but no ground hogs,
Much to wonder, much to see,
It was a very good day for me.

June 30 (Albany to Brattleboro)

Today was a big climbing day,
Fifty–eight hundred feet or more, who's to say,
The white bark of Birch trees did I see,
They are quite a pretty tree,
Lakes, ponds and rolling streams,
Cascading over rocks the water gleams,
The smell of flowers, the cool breeze,
Daylight turns to night under the thick trees,
The monument at Bennington,
The little town of Wilmington,
The first marks battle victories,
The second shops of antiques and stories,
Hogsback Mountain's hundred–mile view,
A broken wheel nearly stopped me from getting through,
But into Brattleboro, Vermont I be,
It was now the prettiest day for me.

July 1 (Brattleboro to Lexington)

Like a Billy–goat I go,
Mountain roads like steps up whoa,
How big they are,
Even for a car,
But I made them one,
I made them all,
I didn't stop,
I didn't fall.

Then at the hotel I did see,
A pretty girl who came for me,
With a van all lettered tacky,
You knew it involved your Aunt Kathy,
Then I shaved my beard and had
A baldy cut for dear old dad.

July 2 (Lexington to Revere Beach – Boston)

To the ocean we parade,
What a journey we had made,
This is the end of the trip for me,
As I stand with my bike in the sea,
It's over now, but memories remain,
I will never be the same.

Nicole –

I hope someday you venture out,
To see and do what you dream about.

I love you Nicole......Dad

July 3 (Boston)

I finished,
I did it,
3,495 miles,
A million smiles,
I thought of you along the way,
You were the reason for the smiles.

I'm smiling now, I must be thinking of you.
Dad

A CROSS–COUNTRY CAROL

T'was eight months before crossing the country by bicycle;
Our two wheels would carry us, we don't ride a tricycle.

Our training began for strength and endurance,
Swimming, weight lifting and spinning for added insurance.

Two birthdays we'd celebrate, 65 and 69.
Would we be too old? We knew we'd be fine.

CrossRoads Cycling Adventures would help our endeavor,
It was an experience we longed for, maybe forever.

Los Angeles to Boston, we went all the way.
Over mountains, thru valleys, across deserts, "OY VEY"!!!!

With Tracey and Trevor and Margaret and Clark,
And Rick and Tom helping, they got us in before dark.

Our muscles grew weary, our seats they got sore,
But Lynn's great massages left us ready for more.

After 52 days at the Atlantic we arrived,
There was hugging and kissing; WE HAD SURVIVED!

This is the sum of our great adventure this year,
Season's Greetings to all and to everyone good cheer!

Barb and Phil Bransky

P.S. *We miss you all*

Who I Am: A Daily Note to My Daughter Janel

The idea of describing who I am each day may seem silly on the surface, but I can assure you my daughter's gift to me—her request that I find myself on this trip—was anything but silly. It was insightful, emotional, spiritual, peaceful, a source of strength and some of the most difficult writing I have ever done. Personal letters of love, of hope and dreams to my first born child. I love these daily passages as they allow me to travel back in time and to better plan for the person I wish to become.

When you look inside yourself you will find you—the one only you really know—the good, the bad, with your victories, fears and disappoints, the person you have been, the one you are at that moment, and the one you aspire to be. Writing about it will help you close the gap in being a better person.

We need ways to get ourselves on the right track, to see ourselves as winners before we can succeed, and for me this was part of that effort. I hope there is something in this for you as well. It's also an opportunity to laugh at yourself, and life is too short not to be able to do that.

Thank you Janel. You are the gift I did not deserve.

May 15 (Los Angeles)
Who Am I Today

Well Thursday I felt like the kid going to a new school. I was really excited but did not really know what to expect. Getting into LA and to the hotel was easy. Meeting other riders was easy too. Friday we rode thirty miles on the beach bikeways—called the Strand—through Venice Beach, to the famous Santa Monica Pier, through marinas and past shops and villages. The people were amazing. Beautiful people roller blading, biking and running, and then there were the others. There were street people living by the beach, the foreigners were many—Russians, Orientals, Europeans and Middle Easterners. Some dressed for attention and others just to do it. LA is a melting pot. I'm not sure I like the flavor, but a little taste, just another day, won't hurt.

My knee did act up and I hope it doesn't become the focus of my trip. It's 7:20 a.m. I will be riding the beach again today. It will be crowded—it's Saturday—but the weather will be nice again. Tomorrow we ride seventy–eight miles. Anticipation and fear, but thinking of you! I'm just a new kid in school.

May 16 (Manhattan Beach to Riverside)
Who Am I Today

Today I started out as the anxious man and once I got to Manhattan Pier, dipped my wheel in the ocean and headed east, the twelve year old boy came out. Riding in a group of fifty we quickly began to spread out and find riding buddies. I became confident and rode swiftly and spent some time helping others when they broke down. So I guess for part of the day I was a Shepard, a mechanic and more.

When my riding partner Don clipped my wheel and crashed I was a comforter. As I await word of his condition—they fear a broken collar bone—I am like a parent. Too many hats for me today. I did realize that this is already an amazing journey. Somewhere along the way I will find me and realize what my purpose and plan is…..somewhere between Riverside and Boston. You will be the first to know…….xxxooo…..Daddio!

May 17 (Riverside to Indio)
Who Am I Today

Today I was the determined one. Hill after hill, one mountain climb after another. It was hot and the air was still, but I could not give in. Like the little engine that could I would crest each summit and today I had a special treat. I rode fourteen miles on the flat and uphill without pedaling. I hit thirty–six miles per hour at the windmill farm canyon and was like the little boy who just had his training wheels off for the first time. Scared and excited.

May 18 (Indio to Blythe)
Who Am I Today

Today I was nervous about the long ride. I've not ridden a hundred miles in more than thirty years. Eighteen miles of climbing and another eighty–four on the desert floor we would go. I felt like a champion after climbing the mountain and as the day went on I grew fatigued. All the while it was 106 degrees and I sailed along on a tailwind that was much needed. I was like a survivor at Desert Center, fifty miles from nowhere. I felt more like an old man when the day was done. My feet were on fire and my muscles ached. I am just a survivor from my ride today. Tomorrow it is 115 miles and the mountains will be there. I hope I can say I am the survivor again. It will be the hardest ride. Tomorrow I will also cross into Arizona. I guess I am also a bit of an adventurer.

May 19 (Blythe to Wickenburg)
Who Am I Today

Today I was battered, beaten and worn. More like an old shoe than anything else. It was 117 miles into Wickenburg by the time I arrived, too stubborn to give up I barely survived. Not much fight left in me. The kid in me is gone. This desert drains you like nothing I can describe. My friend Don left the tour today and that kind of got me down. After a shower and something to eat you begin to recover and count yourself lucky for making it all the way. Then before bed it doesn't seem so bad. More lotion and ointments and you are normal again. The little boy begins to smile and the adventure continues.

May 20 (Wickenburg to Prescott)
Who Am I Today

Today I was like the little goat climbing hills all day, but after going through the desert I was plumb wore out. The hills grew long and steep and they never ended. I was alone but it gave me a chance to think. Did I want to be the victor or the quitter? I wanted to win this battle with the mountain. I want to do what I said I would do. So I put away thoughts of giving up, I accepted that I was tired and it would be hard. I also thought how sweet doing what I set out to do would be. The little boy was back and he began to fill me. This was a big day for the man in me.

May 21 (Prescott to Cottonwood)
Who Am I Today

Today I was tired but the boy in me could not wait to climb the highest mountain today. I was not going to be first but the more I climbed the more excited about looking back to the valley I became. After more than an hour I finally made it to the top and the little boy went wild. Yelling and shouting excited as can be. Then the man shed a tear because without the little boy he never would be standing at the peak. Today I am the mountain climber.

May22 (Cottonwood to Flagstaff)
Who Am I Today

Today I was relaxed and confident in myself. I was able to think and plan for the day as my legs moved me up yet another mountain. Since I knew I could make it to the top it gave me the opportunity to enjoy it all the way up. Today I am the determined one.

May 23 (Flagstaff – Rest Day)
Who Am I Today

Today was a rest day and it gave my body a chance to catch up with my confidence. I like who I am and I'm learning more about me and what my purpose in life is. I'm excited about life and my future. I am many people today—The little boy living inside this happy man.

May 24 (Flagstaff to Holbrook)
Who Am I Today

Today I was a team player riding together with another rider to make it safely and quickly across the plains to Holbrook. I was strong and positive and getting across this country on my bike is becoming easier to visualize. It allows me more time to think about my next steps in life. This too is getting easier to visualize. I see more enjoyment and less fear. I see great things ahead.

May 25 (Holbrook to Gallop)
Who Am I Today

Today I am the tire man, stopping to help others fix flats and to provide conversation. When riding alone most of the day I was singing my songs. Just a singing away! I looked forward to crossing my second state line. Another reminder that I am doing this and that I will reach Boston on two wheels. My confidence in myself continues to grow and I feel peaceful and without worry.

May 26 (Gallop to Grants)
Who Am I Today

Today I am the champion as I stand on the continental divide. As the waters flow I'm on the east side, hence the saying, "It's all downhill from here!" I crossed 750 miles of the west from desert to mountain, from extreme heat to freezing cold, windy to dusty. I did it. Now I have another 2,700 miles before me. I can do that too. A hundred miles no longer scares me. I've done more than that two days in a row. Today I am the champion.

May 27 (Grants to Albuquerque)
Who Am I Today

Today I am the happy one. I rode well and saw much beauty. Most of the time I rode with others and it became clear that I am getting stronger in body and in mind. Today I am the happy one.

May 28 (Albuquerque to Santa Fe)
Who Am I Today

Today I am tired of climbing mountains. I no longer want to be a goat. We climbed 4,500 feet and the temperature got very hot and the air was very still among the peaks. It was hard to look at the scenery as you grind your way up at six miles per hour in your lowest gear while your heart races and you are out of breath. I guess today I am the survivor again, but I miss my Nellie! ☺

May 29 (Santa Fe – Rest Day)

Who Am I Today

Today I am the tourist walking the galleries and shops in old Santa Fe. The tourist, that is me today.

May 30 (Santa Fe to Las Vegas)

Who Am I Today

Today I am again the survivor making it through the steep climbs and high winds. I thought I was going to be the wounded as I was nearly blown off my bike. The wind was so strong that even with the brakes on I was rolling at more than thirty–seven miles per hour. Others said they were going almost fifty. Not me, for today I am the survivor.

May 31 (Las Vegas to Tucumcari)

Who Am I Today

Today I was a good sport and a team player. With 110 miles to ride with hills, desert heat and wind in your face you couldn't do it alone. I rode with Greg, Betty and Gray taking turns leading our quartette parade. I was tired and sore but I also climbed to the top of several mountains. Today I'm a good sport.

June 1 (Tucumcari to Dalhart)

Who Am I Today

Today I was a time traveler wishing I were somewhere else besides riding into the strong headwinds in the heat and up the hills. It was a long hard ride, the hardest I think, but the worst parts are my sore butt and feet. Tomorrow we will get more of the same, strong headwinds, heat, but not so many hills. We also ride only seventy–two miles not the ninety–six we did today. I wish I was a real time traveler and without the pains I have today.

June 2 (Dalhart to Guymon)

Who Am I Today

Today I am the optimistic one. We have a bad storm with tornado warnings and high winds expected tomorrow. Still I am optimistic that I will make it to Dodge City, Kansas tomorrow. Even though I never rode 124 miles in one day before, it will be my day to enjoy the spoils. I will do it. I can make it. I will look back on the day and say I won yet another round. One day closer to Boston, just me and my bike. I see it. I feel it. I am the optimistic one.

PS – I miss you more than you could ever know, and it is you that gives me the will and courage to do that which I did not know I could. – Dad

June 3 (Guymon to Dodge City)
Who Am I Today

Today I am standing at the top of a personal mountain. I did it. I did it. With tears in my eyes I am a very happy man. I accomplished so much today that I wasn't sure I could do. It is that feeling that reminds us that anything is possible. If you want it bad enough then go after it. I am standing on the top of the world!

Janel —
Right before I left this morning I saw this message painted on the hotel wall. I wrote it down and carried it with me all day for motivation. I think you'll appreciate the power of the message.

"Far better to dare mighty things, to win glorious victories, though checkered with defeat, than to take rank with those poor souls who neither enjoy much nor suffer much, for theirs is a twilight existence that knows neither victory nor defeat."

Theodore Roosevelt
April 10, 1899

Sing my angel, sing!
- Dad

June 4 (Dodge City – Rest Day)
Who Am I Today

Today I am a race fan. I found a small dirt track just out of town and fit right into the Kansas crowd. I felt like I was far away from the bike tour. I needed a break after 500 miles in five days. I feel much better now. I am a race fan. Are you surprised?

June 5 (Dodge City to Great Bend)
Who Am I Today

Today I feel so small. I stood on Pawnee Rock and looked across the valley knowing that in 1846 Private Jacob S. Robinson described the valley being filled with buffalo like a black sea to the hills. It was an incredible view and difficult to imagine such a mass of living beings covering it completely. Today I feel so small.

I love you Midge.
- Dad

June 6 (Great Bend to McPherson)
Who Am I Today

Today I am the observer impressed with the ribbons of bronze, greens, and browns of the wheat, corn and raw dirt. The ride today was beautiful. I never thought I would find it in Kansas. As I head east, I'm optimistic that even more beauty awaits us. Today and for the next thirty more, I am the observer. ☺

June 7 (McPherson to Abilene)
Who Am I Today

Today I am a glider, not just a rider. A kid, a boy playing Superman. I feel wonderful, riding the wind on a short day made it fun and fast. Today I am a boy playing Superman.

June 8 (Abilene – Rest Day)
Who Am I Today

Today an amazing thing happened that may have changed my mind about pets. I like them, but I look forward to not having to be responsible for them. When I paid a visit to the Greyhound Hall of Fame I met a retired hound named "Shige." She came up behind me and pressed her nose on my leg, made not a sound, then looked at me and won me over; calm, majestic, wanting only a friend, a home. I wish I could take her home. Mom will think I'm crazy, but if I ever have another dog I'd want it to be a Greyhound. Today I'm a boy that remembered how much he likes dogs.

Janel –

Today reminded me how much I miss seeing Lady every day. She is a part of the family and my life that defines me.
- Dad

June 9 (Abilene to Topeka)
Who Am I Today

Today I am half way to my goal. It feels good and I know I can make it. Today it was a rainy 107 miles through the hills, but it was a good day. Rain aside it was good. The emerald green rolling hills with horses, colts, sheep, cows, and buffalo made it a pleasant day. Today I am half way.

June 10 (Topeka to St. Joseph)
Who Am I Today

Today I was like a duck. It was wet, cool, and overcast and I was ready to be soggy. It turned out to be a bit less rainy and I enjoyed the day. Tomorrow it may rain again so I will be the duck.

June 11 (St. Joseph to Chillicothe)
Who Am I Today

Today I am a believer. In the people who care and those who remember. We came to a town today called Maysville. A little like Lake Helen and the people of the town greeted us and they prepared lunch for all the riders. They said it was a big deal when the CrossRoads riders come to town each year. They treated us like family. Today I am a believer in people who care.

June 12 (Chillicothe to Kirksville)
Who Am I Today

Today I was the little boy on his bike screaming recklessly down steep bumpy roads hoping to make it to the top of the next hill. I won just a few times but I tried to get them all. I felt like the little boy Kenny Rogers sings about in his song "The Greatest." Each time I fell short and had to struggle to get to the top, I would see the next hill and race down to win the climb to the top of that one. Today I am the little boy on the bike.

June 13 (Kirksville to Quincy)
Who Am I Today

Today I am a believer in luck. Rain and severe weather were in the forecast along with very high temperatures, but we enjoyed partly cloudy skies, lower temperatures and a tailwind. It was a perfect day of riding. Today I am a believer in luck.

June 14 (Quincy to Springfield)
Who Am I Today

Today I am surprised. Surprised that my feet didn't catch fire and leave me in ashes on the road. Long days are tough days and with hills and winds against you, it tests your will. Today I am surprised and sore.

June 15 (Springfield to Champaign)
Who Am I Today

Today I am tired of wind, the rain, sitting on this seat, and being in pain. They say each day you get stronger, yet more fatigued. You never really recover from the long days. I'm now looking forward to being done. Boston I can't wait. Today I am tired.

June 16 (Champaign – Rest Day)
Who Am I Today

Today I am Mr. Vacation sitting around writing and not riding. It feels good. I'm still sore but at least I'm off the bike. Today I'm Mr. Vacation.

June 17 (Champaign to Crawfordsville)
Who Am I Today

Today I am the happy one who rode the tailwinds into the sun. It was another good day as we crossed the border into Indiana, state number nine. Today I'm the happy one.

June 18 (Crawfordsville to Indianapolis)
Who Am I Today

Today I was Speed Racer. On my bike I took to the Major Taylor Velodrome high banks to see how fast and how brave I could be. The track is so steep the banking looks like walls. At the top it is two and a half stories over the inside apron. You can turn left and it is almost like free–fall. I was able to go just a bit more than twenty–seven miles per hour. I was like a kid. I am Speed Racer.

June 19 (Indianapolis to Richmond)
Who Am I Today

Today I am reminiscing about the trip. I watched a video about another group of riders cycling from Connecticut to San Francisco and they passed through many of the same places I did. The desert and mountain images brought back some strong feelings of near defeat. There were several very teary personal moments. To know it is to do it. I'm not sure how else to describe this feeling. A sense of accomplishment never imagined, sadness because it is coming to an end, the knowing that I will never be the same. Every day after I will know that I can do anything I choose. Success is whatever I want it to be. I will never be the same and I'm happy knowing that.

June 20 (Richmond to Marysville)
Who Am I Today

Today I feel great. I rode strong and climbed well, but most of all I have two wonderful daughters who make me feel like the luckiest dad alive. Father's Day is special and it's ten times better than my birthday because, to me, it is a celebration about the ones I love, my girls.

I love you Nellie!
Today I am the luckiest guy alive.

June 21 (Marysville to Wooster)
Who Am I Today

Today I wonder about the simple life. Seeing the Amish living without so much yet I can't help but think they know something we only search for. Peace, having what you want and wanting what you have. Today I wonder about the simple life.

June 22 (Wooster to Niles)
Who Am I Today

Today another purpose rang true, that every day I do something for someone – friend or stranger, even if it is a simple act. I felt compelled to pay for an older lady's lunch when she had trouble figuring out her money. I just reached across and paid her tab at a Dairy Queen of all places. I felt like God put her there for me to help. I'm sure this is part of my purpose and it makes me feel good.

June 23 (Niles to Erie)
Who Am I Today

Today I was the kid at the ballpark watching the players smack the ball and hopefully show they have what it takes to move up to the big leagues. I forgot how much fun going to a baseball game could be. Today I was just a kid at the ball game.

June 24 (Erie – Rest Day)
Who Am I Today

Today was a day of rest and some fun. I'm just me today recharging my batteries. I went to the pier, the tall ship, the maritime museum and made sure I did my good deed for the day. Today I am just me.

June 25 (Erie to Hamburg)
Who Am I Today

Today I was like a puddle jumper. You know the little guy stomping in the rain puddles making big splashes without a care. I just happened to be doing it on my bike. Unfortunately it got cold and I wanted to go inside to warm up, but I had fifty more miles to ride. So much for the little puddle jumper. ☺

June 26 (Hamburg to Canandaigua)
Who Am I Today

Today I am a flying fish. I was riding with a strong tail wind into a heavy downpour without brakes or the ability to see. Imagine going thirty-four miles per hour wiping your eyes and holding on with one hand into a car wash spray. I'm surprised I didn't fall. Today I am a flying fish.

June 27 (Canandaigua to Syracuse)
Who Am I Today

Today I am thinking about you. No other worries on the road so I had plenty of time to think of you.

June 28th (Syracuse to Little Falls)
Who Am I Today

Today I'm the laundry guy. I'm getting pretty good at it. I guess I'll have to continue doing it at the house when I get home. Just don't tell mom.

June 29 (Little Falls to Albany)
Who Am I Today

Today I was a happy rider with all conditions perfect – cool, sunny, tailwinds…who could ask for more? I even got to do my good deed for the day. Today I am a happy rider.

June 30 (Albany to Brattleboro)
Who Am I Today

Today I am in awe of what beauty I see before me. I can be nothing but humble as I see some of God's greatest works. I am amazed.

July 1 (Brattleboro to Lexington)
Who Am I Today

Today I am excited like a young man seeing his favorite girl. I guess that's because I am. With nothing but ninety miles and several mountains between us I cannot be deterred.

July 2 (Lexington to Revere Beach – Boston)
Who Am I Today

Today I am the graduate. I passed all of my tests and proceeded with my classmates to the beach, the point where we will all leave from and head back out into the world, different then we were before and better for it. Like the tin man I am happy and sad at the same time, but mostly happy. I can do anything. I know I can.

July 3 (Boston)
Who Am I Today

Today I know who I am. I am your inspiration. I am an example of how an ordinary person can do extraordinary things. Anything you want out of life is within your reach. I will always be behind you, even when you don't see me. You see, the past seven weeks no matter how hard days were and how unsure I was about succeeding I always thought of you and then it was okay. If I can do this, my girls can do anything.

After the trip had passed I also come to realize something very important that I want to share with you.

Who am I? – Your mom's best friend. Nothing else matters much. That's who I am. Thank you for giving me this gift of self–discovery. Had you not asked me to find out who I am I may never have found out.

A million kisses for you Janel!

I love you.
- Dad

Notes to My Wife

Donna –

Each day I plan to write you a note about the trip and about us. Though you won't get to read this until it is over, I hope you enjoy my attempts to share the experience with you.

May 15 (Los Angeles)

I think this trip is about you as much as it is about me. You are amazing. That is you. I want to be the same to you. It's 7:25 a.m. and I'm going to go ride to the beach. Yesterday I pedaled thirty miles through Venice, Santa Monica and other little villages along the way. I'm meeting some very interesting people and that will be the highlight of the trip. Unfortunately after twenty miles yesterday my knee started to ache and I'm concerned that it may slow me down. Not what I needed just before we go. I miss you and love you and will count the days until I see you in Boston. You are amazing.

May 16 (Manhattan Beach to Riverside)

After much anticipation and nervousness the ride finally began. A calm came over me that I was really in need of, my legs were working and my knee was without pain. I guess we will make it all 3,415 miles. With thirteen miles left in today's ride my buddy Don took a tumble that put a damper on a near perfect day. I'm still waiting to hear if his shoulder is okay. I wish the ER's could move a bit faster. I feel that he'll be okay and I'll have my riding partner back on the trail with me. Eighty miles down and one day closer to seeing you in Boston.

May 17 (Riverside to Indio)

The beauty of what I saw today moved me. The scenery changed with every mile. Snowcapped peaks, high mountain ranges, Jacaranda trees in blue and cows on the big ranches. I was in awe at the windmill farms and shocked that I could ride fourteen miles on the flats and hills without pedaling at thirty–six miles per hour. I laughed at Palm Springs but gained a respect for the heat of the desert. I want to do it all. I think I can, but no matter what I will do what I can. I will be happy and satisfied with that. I hope you enjoyed the picture of me sitting outside at our hotel in Indio, CA. that Don sent.

May 18 (Indio to Blythe)

I survived today honey! The heat was tough and the mountains tougher. Lucky for me we had a tailwind to get us across. I couldn't wait to finish dinner to give you a call. I miss you and love you. It's late and I'm tired so I'll end this note short. I expect more of the same tomorrow. I just hope we have a tailwind. ☺

May 19 (Blythe to Wickenburg)

Today was a challenge. It was my longest day and wanting to share the victory with you was important. I miss you but I feel you with me every inch of the way. I'm proud that you can handle everything while I'm gone and I have no worries about it one bit.

May 20 (Wickenburg to Prescott)

Today I was battling my ability to make it up these mountains. Even the flats, or what appeared to be flats, were hard. The wind buffeted me from the right and I watched many riders take the "bump" van ride in. My confidence was waning and I was thinking that I bit off more than I could handle. I couldn't accept quitting, not one inch, because the rest of the trip would lose its meaning. So I struggled on and won another battle.

May 21 (Prescott to Cottonwood)

After talking to you last night I felt much better and focused on the view from the top. I climbed like I couldn't before. My legs were no stronger, but my mind was. The climb was enjoyable and the view was sweet. I can do this one day, one mountain at a time. Thank you babe for believing in me.

May22 (Cottonwood to Flagstaff)

Today was a day of winning from the start. The first step was climbing to Sedona and the second part was climbing Oak Creek Canyon. Talking to you in Sedona helped quite a bit and my mind was focused on the last climb. Switchback after switchback, zig–zagging up the mountain. The view was better than I had imagined.

May 23 (Flagstaff – Rest Day)

Today we rested. I thought about you most of the day. I love you and I'm in love with you. These things I am sure of.

xxxooo

May 24 (Flagstaff to Holbrook)

I zoomed across the plains all day without thoughts of failure. My legs were tired but my mind was not. I thought of you a lot along the way.

May 25 (Holbrook to Gallop)

I thought of you often as I rode alone. It may sound strange but I thought about having our wedding vows renewed. Actually going through everything we did not do the first time, a wedding with all of our friends attending. Crazy huh? I love you beyond what I can describe and can't wait to hold you in my arms.

May 26 (Gallop to Grants)

Crossing the Continental Divide I felt that I have achieved a major milestone in this trip and in my life. Through the deserts, the mountains, the miles riding alone, I've learned a lot about myself. If I set my mind to do something, determination will get me through. Having your support has allowed me to stay focused and succeed. You and I, together all things are possible.

May 27 (Grants to Albuquerque)

Today was a mix of natural beauty. I saw horses grazing, red rock cliffs and great expanses of fields of green and yellow flowers. Albuquerque was quite a sight from two miles up outside the city. I crossed the Rio

Grande River and was amazed at the dense trees that line its muddy waters. The architecture was unique with the terra cotta adobe and green accents everywhere. I know how much you like the southwestern style and it reminds me of you—all good thoughts. I love you.

May 28 (Albuquerque to Santa Fe)

Today was a never–ending day of climbing in the heat. We climbed 4,500 feet and at points raced down very steep grades at almost thirty–seven miles per hour with the brakes on full. As much as I have tired of climbing I'd rather go up then have to go down these steep scary hills. I miss you and thought of you often to take my mind off of the laborious climbs.

May 29 (Santa Fe – Rest Day)

Santa Fe was unique. Its architecture, arts, and culture are like no other. Each painting and sculpture of the southeast reminded me how much you enjoy it. And when I think of you I miss you.

May 30 (Santa Fe to Las Vegas)

Today was another taxing day. It was cold, windy, and three thousand feet of climbing. The high altitudes cause you to tire easily; it raises your heart rate and makes it difficult to breathe. I was very busy staying on the bike on the downhill grades fighting strong crosswinds and fatigue while working the brakes. I will be glad to get out of the mountains and leave the wind behind.

May 31 (Las Vegas to Tucumcari)

Today was the second longest distance I rode so far. It was 110 miles climbing a good part of the day, nearly 3,800 feet, and several were very steep including the one they call *The Wall*. It was three quarters of a mile straight up the side of the mountain with rocky cliffs on both sides that blocked the wind. It was very hard and I had to stop twice to get my pulse rate down. It wasn't worth pushing it since I had more than forty miles to go after getting to the top. In the morning it was cold and just a hint of a breeze.

We rode through rolling hills covered with grass and not a tree or a mountain to be seen. After twenty miles we crested a hill and found trees on the other side. The grass gave way to rocky soil and there was a hint of the mountains in the distance. By late morning we rolled through a mountain pass revealing a valley floor about 1,500 feet below. We would speed down the winding roads until we finally reached the hot desert floor. From here on we faced headwinds, high heat, ninety–five degrees or more, and hills. It was a long day but Greg, Betty, Gray and I worked together like a train taking turns cutting through the air. We helped each other battle forward, and of course listened to each other whine. I'm glad we made it.

June 1 (Tucumcari to Dalhart)

Today was a day I hope I don't have to repeat. It was heat, hills, and headwinds not to mention a sore butt and sore feet. I hope tomorrow is better but the forecast calls for the much of the same. All I can think of is how am I going to sit on that seat for six hours tomorrow. I was also happy to talk to you tonight. Leaving voice messages just wasn't right.

June 2 (Dalhart to Guymon)

Today was the day I decided I would make it 124 miles to Dodge City, Kansas tomorrow. Days before I was worried, I wasn't sure, I doubted that I could and was trying to justify not completing this leg of the ride, but I came here not to try, but to do. Tomorrow I will stand in Dodge City proud that I could do what I have never done before. I will then continue one day at a time riding my bike to Boston. Every inch of the way, just me and my bike.

Thank you for believing in me, for caring enough to let me go and to allow me this opportunity to find in me what I've been searching for; the confidence to know I can do anything I set my mind to. Not just to try to do it, but to make my dreams real. You have done and continue to do this for me. You are my dream come true, my love, and my life. With you I can do anything.

June 3 (Guymon to Dodge City)

It was not an easy day at all but I was going to make it. The harder it was the sweeter it would be. I know that and it sure was hard. I thought my butt and my feet were going to quit, but my body and mind worked together to make it all 124 miles with side and head winds and heat in the afternoon. I know I can do anything if I set my mind to it. Thank you for believing in me. I love you.
- T

June 4 (Dodge City – Rest Day)

Today was a good day of rest. After yesterday's long ride I was pretty wiped out. Imagine my luck today getting free passes to the races, a free car to drive there and having a good time. Pinch me I'm dreaming….about you.

June 5 (Dodge City to Great Bend)

Today the weather turned better. We avoided the storms and threats of hail. Side winds turned to tailwinds and we enjoyed eighty–nine miles of good safe riding. I stood on Pawnee Rock and was in awe of what the view was today and imagined what it was like 150 years ago. In 1846 Private Jacob S. Robinson described seeing buffalo in such great numbers that they turned the hillside black. It's hard to imagine as the view goes on for more than fifteen miles in all directions. This was the most memorable part of the day. Even more memorable than going twenty to twenty–three miles per hour for twenty miles with ease. I miss you immensely.

June 6 (Great Bend to McPherson)

Today was a beautiful day of riding through some amazing rolling hills of color. I can't believe the Midwest could be so impressive. Tomorrow's ride will be similar as we go sixty–two miles on our way to Abilene. My legs are getting stronger but my tail end and my feet continue to be the weak links. It was wonderful talking to you today. You sounded so happy and I could almost see you smile. I love you.

June 7 (McPherson to Abilene)

Each day something becomes clearer to me. In the times of solitude on my bike I can take time to dwell on one thought at a time. No deadlines, no rush. I can let a single thought roll around until I am satisfied that I understand what it means, why it came to mind and what I need to do with it. Today I realized something that I should have known a long time ago. You deserve better than I have been. I think it is your time to be with someone who puts you first in all things at all times. No need to worry about me going anywhere. That someone new is still me, yet different.

I've been fortunate to enjoy some life changing opportunities and to a great extent through your support and encouragement. Talking to you tonight knowing you have everything under control gives me peace as well. I'm glad you are fine without me, but also glad that you want me. I admire your independence and I'm drawn toward you. I'm sure it would be easier to take up with someone else instead of waiting for me, but I'm looking forward to making you glad about hanging on to this one. What dreams do you have? What life do you seek? I want to be there to see that everything you want comes to pass. You are wanted and loved.

June 8 (Abilene – Rest Day)

Today at the Greyhound Hall of Fame I met "Shige," a red retired greyhound that won me over. I know what you are thinking, I'm an old softy and you are right. I guess there will always be a place for animals in my heart, and for little kids and you.

June 9 (Abilene to Topeka)

I'm half way today. What a great feeling it is. I can do it rain or shine. Just 1,700 more miles to go.

June 10 (Topeka to St. Joseph)

In the last few miles of Kansas I passed the birthplace of Amelia Earhart. It's amazing that such interesting sights exist on our daily tour routes. Kansas provided excellent roads and considerate drivers, but we found neither on our first day in Missouri. Hopefully the next few days will be better. I know you have a lot on your plate, but don't stress.

June 11 (St. Joseph to Chillicothe)

We have so much to talk about when I see you. Not about the trip but about us. Do you realize I don't know what your favorite color is? How can it be that after knowing you twenty–five years I cannot recall this? There are many things I need to know and that I want to know and want you to know. I'm concerned that I've not listened, paid enough attention, or possibly forgot such things. I need to, I want to know about you.

June 12 (Chillicothe to Kirksville)

I climbed 148 hills but only glided over about a dozen. Somehow I still feel like a winner. Like a little boy racing down a hill as fast as he can without a worry, thinking only about getting to the top of the next hill. My legs are tired, but I'm still the little boy.

June 13 (Kirksville to Quincy)

Today was one of the best for riding. Conditions were not supposed to be good but they were. I enjoyed the tailwinds and smaller rolling hills. Missouri is so beautiful. I never thought it would be so impressive. As nice as it is there are no worries about moving out here. I miss you and can't wait to hold you in my arms again.

June 14 (Quincy to Springfield)

I survived today. That may not sound like a big deal but after seven hours and 108 miles with hills, headwinds, high temperatures and humidity it is a big deal. I'm always surprised that I can walk after a day like today. Tomorrow we go ninety miles and the weather will likely be the same. I hope my butt holds out. I wish I could give you a hug right now.

June 15 (Springfield to Champaign)

I'm tired and sore, looking to finish this ride. Twenty years from now I'll be telling people about the ride, the sore bottom, and the headwinds. Ah the memories. I miss you quite a lot and since I'm closer to Boston than LA I'll not be turning around and heading west. I'm excited knowing that I will see you in two weeks.

June 16 (Champaign – Rest Day)

Today was a rest day but it's not long enough to heal the tender spots. Maybe it will be better by tomorrow; likely not. Anyway we ride seven days straight to Erie and then we take a day off before taking on New York, Connecticut, Vermont, New Hampshire and Massachusetts. The end is near. I can't wait!

June 17 (Champaign to Crawfordsville)

I just wanted you to know that even today, not knowing simple things bug me. Favorite flowers, books, movies, days, and on and on. I bet we could spend all night just talking about how much I don't know about you. I'm pretty sure I know who your favorite guy is, after Robert Redford that is. ☺

-   T

June 18 (Crawfordsville to Indianapolis)

You should have seen me riding in the velodrome. I was like a young boy on a new bike. Wobbly and awkward at first and then with each lap more confident. I rode with everything I had in me to go as fast as I could possibly go; just over twenty–seven miles per hour. I thought I could go faster but I was physically drained. Now I smile with what I was able to do. Just like a little boy.

June 19 (Indianapolis to Richmond)

Today I watched a video of the Habitat for Humanity cross country cycle tour. Jordan Heitz, daughter of our tallest rider Mike was in the video. She fell crossing a bridge (on film) and broke her elbow, but eventually continued. I knew how she felt, that making it all the way is such a powerful force that being hurt, drained, sick, or plain worn out cannot stop you. The strength within that you didn't know existed takes over and what only can be described as a miracle occurs. Then you look back at what you accomplished and you all but cry. The only way to properly understand the experience is to go through it yourself. Words and pictures can only give a hint of the experience. It is an experience that happens within, a wonderful life altering experience.

June 20 (Richmond to Marysville)

What a wonderful day it is. I'm such a lucky dad. I can't believe I'm in my sixth week of riding without a clue of what is going on in the world around me. No worries, no job, no stress, just riding my bike. I remember feeling this way when I was twelve. Only then mom did my laundry, not me. I love you tons….T

June 21 (Marysville to Wooster)

I rode through Amish country today and was amazed at the simple life they live. Much like riding a bike instead of taking a car. They do without the modern conveniences yet they appear content. Many lessons can be learned from them I'm sure. I'm tired. It was a hard day and tomorrow will be more of the same.

June 22 (Wooster to Niles)

I'm counting the days to Boston. I really miss you. We had a good day riding but I'm getting tired and need to get off the bike.

June 23 (Niles to Erie)

We had a great ride to Erie through Amish farms in Ohio and then through little towns with much roadwork going on. We stopped at an open air restaurant called the "White Turkey Drive–In" and enjoyed a root beer float and a chilidog. Then we headed down to Lake Erie which was beautiful. It looked like the Florida panhandle with sand that looked like it came from Myrtle Beach South Carolina. It was very, very pretty.

Later we rode into Erie, which had several very impressive old buildings, churches, and houses. They also had a series of dancing frogs on display all over town. It was different. Later that evening we took in a ball game where we enjoyed a close and exciting battle to the end. The visiting Sea Dogs from Portland Maine won the game and I was reminded how much fun it can be. Tomorrow we rest and in one week I get to collect your hugs.

June 24 (Erie – Rest Day)

I enjoyed the museum, the tall ship, and the pier, but mostly I thought about coming home. Erie gave us beautiful weather today and I think the rest was needed for us to go the next week of riding into Boston. xxxooo

– T

June 25 (Erie to Hamburg)

It was a cold and very wet day on the bike, but I did get to end it on a good note by having dinner with Dirk and Dave from Gartner. It's good when people care enough to stay in touch. Both are people I think highly of. I was happy to talk to you as well. You sounded confident, happy, and strong. I miss you and will see you in a few days.

June 26 (Hamburg to Canandaigua)

Today I should have crashed in the rain. I couldn't see anything and I was flying without brakes. Good thing I couldn't see. I miss you and can't wait to see you.

June 27 (Canandaigua to Syracuse)

Today was a short day of seventy miles. Tailwinds, cool temperatures and sunshine made for a good biking day. In the afternoon several of us were invited to Kathy's Brothers' house for a barbeque cookout. We had a great time. See you soon.

xxxooo

- T

June 28 (Syracuse to Little Falls)

I'm really looking forward to finishing this ride and getting back home. Today I had a good ride then I did the laundry and went to the movies. Tomorrow I'm going to the state capital and then it is just a few more days before I finish. See you soon.

- T

June 29 (Little Falls to Albany)

You're getting closer so I'll keep pedaling east. I can't wait to see you. I thought about you all day.

- T

June 30 (Albany to Brattleboro)

Oh no, my wheel broke! I had to MacGyver it back in shape to get to Vermont. I guess you would have found me anyway.

xxxooo

- T

July 1 (Brattleboro to Lexington)

Yippee! Today I get to see you. Only ninety–two miles and a few more mountains to climb before I reach you in Lexington. See you soon!

xxxooo

- T

July 2 (Lexington to Revere Beach – Boston)

Welcome to my graduation. Now I have to get back to my life. I can assure you I'm better prepared for it now. No fears, no worries.

- Tom

July 3 (Boston)

To my best friend

To my best friend who set me free,
So I could do what was meant for me,
And now that the next chapter of my life has come into view,
My purpose is clear, to do the same for you.

I will do everything I can to give you a happy life,
My best friend, my love, my beautiful wife.

2017 – It Is Written

For some readers you might prefer the word Epilogue. Derived from the French language, a word whose meaning is to provide clarity to the main story, a comment about what has happened. The benefit of writing this book, or at least completing it many years later, is that I know what happened; at least most of it. It's a mix of happy endings and new beginnings, friendships made and the loss of those we were fond of. Possibilities, opportunities, and dreams; they did not end in Boston, they began there. Life did not continue as I planned, it was better and I'd like to share what happened after my cross country experience in 2004.

It has been thirteen years since I made my way across the country from Los Angeles to Boston on my bike. I find it hard to believe it has taken me until now to organize the experience into a single manuscript, this book, considering the core of the writing was complete when the trip ended in Boston. I guess it too became one of those "to–do's" that fell off the list as I rejoined the world of the normal working people. Some might argue I wasn't normal before, but after I knew I would always be the square peg in the round hole world of normality. My plan was to help others cross over to my side.

A lot has happened in the years since 2004. We lost Peter Crowell in 2009 just three days past his 65th birthday. I learned he was enjoying a cycling trip in Nova Scotia with several CrossRoads Alumni at the time. You could say he was doing what he enjoyed in the company of people who loved him. Having been a veteran of the cross country ride in 2004 Peter's insight and guidance helped me achieve what I set out to do. During the winter of 2005 I would have the pleasure of riding again with Peter in Florida on the James A. Van Fleet State Trail that runs twenty–nine miles through some of Florida's most scenic rural landscape. We were immersed in wetlands and wildlife as we cut through Florida's Green Swamp, but what I remembered most was his wit, his friendship, and his sage advice. I enjoyed his company immensely and he will forever remain alive in my memories.

A year later in 2010 we also bid farewell to Phil Bransky who was taken by Leukemia. The news came to me through the XC04 alumni network as it did with Peter. Sadness once again with the loss of Phil yet there was one glimmer of delight. I remembered he sent me a copy of his book he wrote about the trip; more of a manuscript just for other riders to enjoy. Within its pages I read about his favorite moments and highlights he enjoyed with friends on the trip. I felt him in the pages alive and speaking to me. In the loss, that was the happy moment. I would remember Phil through his own words.

We celebrated Phil's 69th birthday during our 2004 tour and I also enjoyed good company and some homemade Danish with Phil and his wife Barb in Albuquerque at the hotel while we fixed a few flat tires. I have a vivid memory of riding with Phil and since he rode without a head sock the top of his head was tan striped where the sunlight would get through the slots in his helmet. Phil was a joy to be around and like Peter I will always remember him smiling and enjoying the company of his friends. Both of these men chose to live life fully and were an inspiration to all who knew them.

Gray Pruitt, one of nicest guys you will ever know was the videographer of our trip capturing our group as we trekked across the country. Compared to Gray's extra activities, my writing and picture taking were easy. He lost all of his edited video late in the trip when his computer hard drive crashed. He could have given up but chose to reedit most of the raw footage again. In the end the video was a huge success and enjoyed by all at the banquet in Boston. Actually it was priceless and I thank him for that. Gray, who was also the only rider who had fenders on his bike, now spends his recreational time scuba diving with his wife Niki. He also faithfully stays in touch via the CrossRoads Alumni email.

In Atlanta at an early spring of 2005 XC04 CrossRoads reunion ride hosted by Gayle and Ken, I bunked with Gray for two nights. It was a seamless continuation of our tour that ended just eight months prior. The only difference is we were exploring the downtown of Atlanta and the Silver Comet Bike Trail just thirteen miles northwest of the city. We also enjoyed seeing Ken's maps of all his cycling adventures. A map of the states and one of the entire world; both heavily marked with lines indicating his two wheeled adventures. Ken spoke about the trips with passion and clarity. It was a moment to remember and one that would prime me for the soon to start XC05 tour.

"Big Mike" Heitz followed up the cross country ride with an even bigger adventure. He cycled from the top of the African continent to the bottom and somewhere in the neighborhood of five thousand miles on dirt, gravel, pavement, and a few places where no roads existed. Using the XC04 alumni network Mike provided photos of himself and his son riding in front of pyramids, through the African plains, and at times riding under the protection of hired armed guards when conditions warranted it. The stories about the riding conditions and what he was able to see were difficult to comprehend yet extremely fascinating.

Dick Duffey, Big Mike's tour sidekick moved to Revere where the tour ends. I would suspect and hope I get to see him when we arrive at the beach. He said he bought a new bike and I'm looking forward to seeing him on it.

Other reunion rides took place, several riders returned to CrossRoads for another trek across the states while others rode the east coast tour from Maine to Florida. Pat and Vikki moved from Orlando to the rural wide open of north Florida, Paul Kvam got married and our beloved bagman, Trevor, graduated from college and is now a practicing attorney in Ontario, Canada. The emails and friendships continue to this day.

During the seven weeks on the tour I grew accustomed to being around the CrossRoads vehicles, the white Isuzu box truck and the white Dodge Caravans. Months later whenever I would be riding my bike the sight of one of these machines would immediately send me back in time and deposit me randomly within the confines of the tour. I would innocently scan the driver's area looking for Trevor or Tracy, Margaret or Clark behind the wheel.

I felt disappointment each time when after not recognizing the driver I would then be quickly returned to the present realizing it was just my subconscious playing a wishful prank. Well maybe not an attempt to fool me as my subconscious as well as conscious awareness wanted it to be possible. It would happen over and over without fail. Withdrawal and depression comes just like Tracy said it would happen. It still happens today more than thirteen years later. That's a powerful stimulus. Some might say it's Pavlovian conditioning but whatever term you try to wrap around it the experience is as real as the quick uptick in my heart rate when it happens and the deflation of my spirit right after. I'm not sure how else to describe it. Maybe it is one of those events that must be experienced to truly understand.

As for me I was able to make good on the notion of going cross country again; several times in fact; 2005, 2010 and for the last two weeks of the trip in 2012—from Indianapolis to Boston. I was part of the CrossRoads team providing support to those making their own personal journey. Some might think once you make such a trek that doing it again would be boring, but you would be wrong and you might be surprised to learn each crossing is a very unique experience. Even if you think you are only helping others realize their personal goals and dreams the reality of the matter is you are reliving the experience in a new and very satisfying way which I cannot describe without extreme emotion. That is why Tracy and her team passionately do what they do.

When Tracy asked me to join her team for the 2005 cross country tour I was ecstatic and humbled at the same time. My thoughts quickly went to my ability to deliver on the service and the promise that is CrossRoads. To be a part of this brand was an honor and something not to be taken lightly.

This type of business succeeds or fails on the word of mouth recommendations riders pass on to future customers. A bad web posting could be fatal. This is an extremely niche business that can only service from twenty–five to just under fifty riders each year. So many factors come into play that impacts the sign–up rates and anything less than glowing recommendations can be tragic. After all, nobody needs to pedal from Los Angeles to Boston; they have to want to do it and they must do it with great vigor.

I'm feeling the pressure of being the best I can be and hoping I meet Tracy's standards of excellence. But then again, she asked me to be on staff for a reason. I guess she liked the way I approached my own tour experience and thought I could help others. I was in.

My job in Florida was in the toilet and I figured I could step away for two months and maybe the issues there would resolve themselves. At the time CrossRoads was still based in Newington, Connecticut and I would be heading up there in advance of the tour to build out the truck and the vans, practice setting up and breaking down the SAG's, take a road test in the box truck to determine my readiness, and to be indoctrinated into the proper CrossRoads etiquette. Think of it as charm school for the cycling staff. There was even a test or two to determine how well I learned.

Having now seen behind the CrossRoads curtain I was even more impressed with the preparation, the training, and pre–trip work Tracy and the team does. Maybe ten times more impressed because I now understood how magic is made. I was working with a team of dedicated individuals with Tracy, Rick, and Margaret returning and I would be assuming Trevor's role as the truck driver and chief baggage handler. Mac, a rider from 2003 and Pat who was a mechanic on prior tours would join the team as well.

The next phase of my journey would be driving the truck as part of the five day CrossRoads caravan from Connecticut with overnights in places like Western Pennsylvania, Topeka, Kansas, Denver, Colorado, and St. George, Utah before watching the sunrise in Las Vegas and settling in for the final day's drive into Los Angeles. The trip with Tracy's Father, Red Leiner, Pat, and Mac was just the beginning of our team building process readying us for the next seven weeks on the road. The trip was a story all by itself; guy talk, car talk, Mac with his dry English whit, and Pat with his own Australian dialect took some getting used to as he spoke in his rather soft tones.

Some might say my career took a bad turn after being a director and vice president for a few companies but I would argue their point. This is the first time my primary goal is customer satisfaction; face to face with no intermediaries. And when you are looking into the eyes of the customer the measure of your efforts is immediate and unavoidable. It is extremely rewarding when you do well. I can't begin to tell you how much happier and fulfilling it is compared to overworking a team of software development professionals to please faceless customers operating with unrealistic budgets, schedules, and insufficient resources. I am now the VP of Tour Satisfaction and proud of it.

The fact my friends and colleague's don't get it makes me smile. They think I only carry bags and drive the truck. Maybe for some I will be an inspiration. At least one said she was envious of me. I was happy to hear this because someday she may step out into a similar situation that for her will be as life changing. And I would be proud to be a catalyst to that happening.

While on staff I fully committed to improving on baggage delivery which I measured in speed, the stability of the interwoven stacking and packing of the bags in the truck, the alignment and perfection of the positioning of the bags on the rider's beds each day and on several occasions positioning the rider identification trinkets as if to welcome the rider's when they entered their hotel room. I guess it warrants some explaining. My job by design was to assign hotel rooms and deliver from the truck the bags of each rider into the appropriate room. Each rider has a unique little item attached to the handle of each of their soft–pack bags. Some had plastic horns or ponies or pistols or even little bugs, but all were unique. It was Tracy's idea to provide a visual cue to associate with each rider. Something easy to remember and to match roommate bag sets. It worked flawlessly and helped me to excel in the delivery process.

Sue had the ponies and I always pointed them toward the door, waiting for their master to arrive. For one couple I would attach toothpicks with little Post–A–Note pennant flags to their trinkets with messages of encouragement and that Boston was near. They loved it. I was able to be extremely creative in something as mundane as baggage delivery. I created interest for me and a fun experience for the riders. I employed this same level of enthusiasm across all of my activities and it was never boring and never a job. I was empowered to delight my customers and I would up the ante each day.

Helping the staff with their activities and taking some of the burden off of Tracy's shoulders was also part of my mission. On many levels I wanted to exceed expectations, to raise the bar, and to make an impression that I deliver excellence. Every day I rose energized and ready to build on the success of the day before. At times I would be a rider coach, a cheerleader, photographer, bike fixer or a Band–Aid applier. I encouraged the shy to go beyond their comfort zone and seize the moment and in the process I became even more comfortable as a source of inspiration. Satisfaction was found in everything I did and with everyone I engaged with. What more could a person ask for in life than to have a genuine feeling of purpose regardless of the details of what they were doing? I certainly could not think of any.

I avoid the use of the word "Work" for my time with CrossRoads because it never was nor did I want to put a damper on my perspective; that what I did was fun. To say I enjoyed my duties would be an understatement. I loved what I did and the way I felt by genuinely pleasing others. As crazy as it sounds for some to understand it is a fact. If I saw my time with CrossRoads as a mere baggage handler or truck driver I would have been bored and a disappointment to our guests. I would venture to guess I would not have made it to Boston with that kind of attitude.

I learned it's possible to make any role satisfying and fulfilling. On tour I became the best truck washer and chief bug remover anyone could hope for. I found excellence in everything; something I rarely experienced in my professional work. I learned people motivated me, not abstracts like schedules and budgets.

I would make a point to take what I learned back with me into my project management duties in the corporate world. I would return enlightened and a beacon to others. I had been changed and I had purpose. And so I don't sound pompous, all of the CrossRoads staff were self–motivated to deliver excellence. It was an exciting and wondrous time.

Did I mention it changed me? The staff, the riders, and Tracy changed me. And I thought my own cross country ride was the event that would redefine me. It was only the start and being on staff was just the second phase of my training to become who I am supposed to be. I look to my future as one of excitement and uncertainty and it's this feeling of the unknown I now embrace with much delight; so unlike the previous version of the person I was. Who would have imagined this would be the result of my experience with CrossRoads. It was not a seven week bicycle ride or a seven week stint as a support member. I cannot stress that enough.

Each spring I get the fever. Just like the final snow melt, the first day in jeans and a t–shirt, the first cut of fresh grass and the sight of birds returning north. I get the fever to go back on tour. It resonates in my gut and my mouth starts to water. My pulse races and I begin to get anxious. I am off in a daze, easily distracted with visions of the CrossRoads vehicles and team in matching uniforms ready to delight the riders; to make their experience more than they could ever imagine.

For most people it is easy to understand the excitement of my personal experience and in their own mind how I would like to relive it again. Yet it was never the intent. I know my first cross country experience can never be replicated nor do I want it be. It was a once in a lifetime experience tied forever with the cyclists, the staff, the weather, and the environmental conditions unique to that period in time. All of the good and the bad as it was scripted by a higher power is how it was intended to happen. I am grateful for that and I long to feel so "in the moment" every day forward.

Sadly few have the imagination or even the desire to comprehend how I can be equally excited about being on staff, giving my all for long hours focused solely on helping others realize their dream. It is nothing like achieving my own personal journey but it is equally rewarding; maybe even more so. By helping others you magnify the success across the number of riders you support. Simple math? I think not. Remember it is about the goals and expectations of the riders and each has a different story; cancer survivors, those riding for a cause, a few coming back from life altering injuries, and others searching for themselves just like me. Each day their collective success was inspiring. Happy was I to say I played a part in their success. It is still difficult for some to grasp I know. I wouldn't have understood it until I had the opportunity to experience it myself.

I shared life stories with the riders and staff. I marveled in their courage and the inspirations that drove them. When we arrived at the beach in Revere, just north of Boston, I felt like a proud parent at my child's graduation. I watched them cry in the company of family, friends, and fellow riders at the finish line of their success. They were in a rare state of emotion, overcome by their own accomplishment. They had done what few others can lay claim to; an accomplishment that makes you weak in the knees and chokes up even the strongest of men. In that moment I too was overcome with emotion as if it were my accomplishment, my reward to be their witness. I'd say you had to be there to understand the moment but I think by this point in my writing you've already figured that out.

In the spring of 2013 Tracy invited me to join as a rider from Los Angeles to St. Joseph, Missouri. Knowing how hard it is to leave a tour I committed to go the distance. I wanted to enjoy the experience on the beach in Boston. I returned to CrossRoads as a rider, not repeating my experience but creating a different one with a new group of people riding all 3,415 miles from Manhattan Pier in Los Angeles to Revere Beach just north of Boston. It was a trip unlike the first back in 2004.

While the first experience was special there was a harmony in the XC13 group that allowed me to experience the trip in a more fulfilling way. My prior riding and staff experience also enabled me to enjoy the trip more, worry less, and to focus on the success of the other riders.

It turns out I am a better coach than a player. I did not ride all the miles nor did I ride every day. I had nothing to prove after doing it all in 2004. I did change dozens of tires, fixed bike chains and cables, taught bike cleaning 101, and stayed with riders who needed to recover before getting back on the bike. When not riding I delivered bags, chaperoned dinners, and drove the CrossRoads van and the truck. I was in the zone on and off the bike. I earned my place as both a rider and a staff member and Tracy's nick name for me became my official tag; "TT or TommyTom." It's a term of endearment of the highest order known to just a few who I shared this experience with.

I was off the bike for five days and on about five more I rode only a portion of the miles planned. We enjoyed favorable weather, reasonable temperatures, a few days of rain, blinding mountain fog, and some challenging headwinds mixed in to make us appreciate the better days. We even dealt with a few detours and freshly paved roads just to keep it interesting.

My decision to go was pretty much made at the last moment and I was neither mentally nor physically ready for the challenge. I was a few months into a lackluster job search after relocating to Charlotte, North Carolina and figured two months away wouldn't matter much. So I came to the tour less than prepared, nursing a list of injuries including my still problematic shoulder, a lower back strain, and my always complaining right knee. My riding regimen was way behind schedule but Tracy suggested I consider the first week of tour as an extension of my training.

During the ride I had some saddle issues and was still recovering from a sprained wrist from my soccer exploits amongst other flaring issues related to my knee and back. I rode the sections I liked as well as the parts that gave me trouble in 2004. I rode in the cold rain, into headwinds; I did century rides and climbed some challenging mountains I did not like. I fell a few times including once while in Abilene with a group of about six riders and twice by myself while climbing to Brattleboro. I bled and I bruised. I wanted the other riders to know I was not doing just the easy parts, but I was also smart enough to know my limits.

To say I was renewed by this second crossing would be an understatement. While it didn't equal the physical feats of the first; I didn't pedal every mile, I enjoyed it in a way I hadn't quite expected. My focus was on those riders around me. The group dynamic and the individual relationships built one–by–one through the many miles at this point in my life created more than I could have envisioned.

I explored more of the towns, I found the largest spur on a rainy morning with my good friend Brick in Abilene, and I fixed Ricky's chain in Kansas and saw him pedal all the way to Boston; every inch of the way. And in Syracuse when I stopped to help a cyclist outside of our tour to change a tire I bonked in the heat and humidity and was in need of rescue myself.

Coming to my aid fifteen miles shy of the hotel was Jan Lewis, my hero of the tour who happened to turn seventy en route to Boston. She shared her electrolyte tablets and water with me and doused my head to cool me down. Without her I would not have made it to the hotel. Those are the moments you remember, not the mile–after–mile grinding while you day–dream down the highway. It is the personal connection and care for and between human beings that mold your memory of such an endeavor.

So many stories, so many experiences, another book or two could be written about them. But this time I left the journals at home, I took but a few photos with my cell phone. I decided to be in the moment, to feel, to share, to listen, to explore what I had missed before. Even if it meant that as my memory slips away the details would be lost and unable to be shared with others. That was okay; in fact it allowed me to be fully immersed in the now, to give my full attention to experience it all. And in Boston it played out as I learned it always does albeit with different characters. Photos taken, cellphones dialed, splashing in the waves, and lots of embraces and tears.

I remember one rider back in Los Angeles who shrugged when I said the scene at the beach in Boston would be an emotional one for him. He shrugged it off again in Indianapolis. To see him in tears standing in the sands of the Atlantic convinced me that he too had been moved beyond expectation. And he did not shy away from allowing me to witness the moment. I told you it is a powerful and emotional experience. Even now as I type these words tears of joy and of hope and of course another opportunity to again be a part of the CrossRoads magic well up in my eyes.

I mentioned several times each trip would be different. The weather is a significant contributor to the experience and while most cyclists would prefer not to ride in the rain, it is usually those days you remember the most. Headwinds are always a spirit crusher but you can't expect tailwinds every day can you? Hot days in the desert and cold days coming out of the mountains all add to the experience and differentiate it from any trip made before. I have witnessed the desert parched and barren in 2004 and the following year saw it in full bloom thanks to generous but unusual spring rains.

The riders themselves greatly impact the quality of the trip and those who gel as a group and treat each day as an adventure come away the most fulfilled. XC13 epitomized what a great group experience could be. In other years some of the riders failed to embrace the human side of the experience and let their competitive and sometimes negative baggage from outside the tour find its way in robbing them of the joy they should have found.

This crossing was so much more than a long endurance bike ride and I felt sad for those who could claim being first to the hotel each day as their only reward. With few photos, few interactions with the locals, and very limited exploring of the towns we passed through, the richness and possibilities of such an adventure escaped them.

And there were one or two riders who complained about the food, the accommodations, the weather, and just about everything else every day. I found them to be toxic to the spirit and enjoyment of the other riders so as much as I could, I chose to avoid their company. Others avoided them as well. They were not changed by the experience and returned to their life of disappointment just as they came to the tour; a waste of money, time, and opportunity.

Cross country cycling is as much a social endeavor as it is a physical challenge. You may also learn for a few of the riders the crossing is a celebration of life, a second chance to drive their personal flag into the top of a mountain after coming back from what could have been a life ending event. These moments usually come late in the trip and riders share them with you as they believe you've shared yourself with them. Even if only for riding alongside them for a day when your companionship is just what they needed to reach the hotel instead of getting off their bike and into a CrossRoads van; something special was shared.

Each year the roads are different, areas in 2004 that were like washboards were tabletop smooth the next year. Some were being worked by large grinders while other roads were receiving a layer of tar and chip–seal as we road on them. New roads were constructed and detours erected causing you to deviate from the prescribed route and at times this became a creative process. An adventure within an adventure

Towns change, new hotels and restaurants go up, and even something as simple as looking left instead of looking right at the same mile marker will cause you to see the trip in a different way. My memory though pretty good deceived me on many occasions and at one point I even followed others off route without realizing it. Being a repeat rider with a cue sheet you'd think it just couldn't happen, but it allowed me to see something different, something new as I backtracked to get back on route.

Another factor is the interaction with those you meet along the journey. Sometimes it is another rider heading west, going it alone and not properly prepared. You provide some information, a drink, a snack and even a warning or two. Or it could be the inquisitive little boy in a small town who asks about the bike you ride and why the tires are so skinny.

For those reasons it is always a joy to make the crossing. It will never be like the first time when you had no idea what was waiting around the corner or over the next hill. And sometimes I think the "not knowing" is a good thing. But in my cross country trips since I have learned it is equally enjoyable even if only through the eyes of someone else doing it for the first time. There is something inspirational about watching strangers in Los Angeles become friends by Boston as they succeed in their mission of traversing this country using only their legs to pedal along the way. In the process they join the small group of people who dared to dream. And speaking of daring to dream, the cross country route goes directly past a small marker with the following quote:

"Happy are those who dream dreams and are ready to pay the price to make them come true." — Leon J. Suenes

And what else have I learned? I learned as I passed through the small towns, some with names quickly forgotten, others bearing names destined to be forever etched in my mind, places I perceived as those to be from not places to live, that it's not the location nor the scenery holding its members; it is the human dynamic, the people who make up the town. Doors wide open, arms spread ready to embrace, giving and welcoming even to oddly dressed strangers on bikes. Who could not want to be a part of this world? Even a simple mind like mine can conclude that great people and a great life could be realized within these communities because of its wonderful and remarkable people.

This is the charm and the love I have for places like Maysville, Missouri. There were other notable places, but Maysville was clearly the most captivating, and its people deserve to be recognized for the openness and hospitality they freely share. They celebrated our arrival as if we were returning home. With homemade jelly sandwiches, lemonade, and freshly baked Danish rolls, we were welcomed home.

This spirit of "Home" could be found everywhere I looked. With my bike as the icebreaker to many friendly conversations I had the opportunity to explore the local happiness and places I could imagine as home. Home I learned, or maybe confirmed, is also not a physical place, it is a state of mind. Happiness and home also existed within my traveling family but this was a place where I knew my time would be temporary within my temporary life on this earth.

I also learned Santa Fe for me was a place of peace and I felt a genuine connection with the earth and maybe something even more powerful there. I was drawn to the silent sirens of the Native American spirit; a hint of the wooden flute still plays softly yet clearly in my mind when I think of Santa Fe. The small and rather plain silver cross hanging from the chain around my neck which I had found the first time through in 2004 also reminds me of Santa Fe. Either through routine, an act of faith, or to continue the good fortunes I have been blessed with in my life, I continue to seek out the artist and buy at least one new cross with each successive tour. I still wear the original and keep the rest at the ready just in case. But it is the original I love. It fits and it fits me. At times when I unconsciously hold it in my fingers, it magically transports me back to the Santa Fe Plaza and the feeling I had when I first found it. It is more than a cross. It is a gateway to good things and good memories; a gift and a connection from the maker to one who cherishes it beyond measure.

I'm sure each of my fellow riders has a place along the tour that moved them deeply. And if it worked out like it did for me, it would likely be a place not a part of their past. It would be something new, unfamiliar, and wonderful; something magic.

Should you endeavor to make the cross country ride yourself, I trust you will find the monument and read those words of Leon J. Suenes etched in the stone. As for me I will start getting anxious every spring and begin to dream about another crossing and how I might find the time away from work to make it happen.

And don't be surprised if you hear me say, "I have decided I no longer want to be an adult…. If anyone needs me I will be on my bike somewhere between LA and Boston." I'm right on the edge. I just have to believe in the young boy.

And you might be thinking about my bike. Did I still have it? What about the dreams of a full carbon frame; did that ever materialize? I'm glad you asked. My time machine, affectionately known as the Silver Streak, that got me across the country in 2004 was in the running for a new red paint scheme before the 2010 tour, but during a routine inspection a frame crack was discovered in the headset area and it was officially retired with more than seven thousand miles on it. Orange Cycle and Specialized replaced the frame with a new warranty product without question. I only had to pay for the labor to transfer the components and perform a tune up. To my surprise the replacement frames only come in bright red and I was ready for the tour after the old components were remounted. And yes it was the exact red I envisioned for sprucing up the bike.

I added a new set of Mavic CXP22 wheels with the frame replacement and the end product was a beautiful like–new looking mount. The original low count bladed spoke wheels, tired and beaten from the rough ride in 2004 now hang in the garage and are used for foul weather rides near home where I can afford to pop a spoke or two and still make it back. I've also changed the rear cassette in the new wheels moving from a 25T to a 28T to spin a bit faster up the hills.

Over the years I scanned eBay for a Specialized Carbon frame as I had decided I would stay with the brand if I could find one that I could justify buying. Unfortunately there was little in the way of deals, mostly frame and forks in the 2,500 dollar range. Then I thought if I buy a new carbon bike for just five hundred dollars more I could use the Allez aluminum framed bike for bad weather and training and save the carbon bike for better weather and longer rides. The problem was I did not have the desire to spend three thousand dollars for the bike and then another five hundred or more to accessorize it. The idea seemed to stall. Then on a whim I scanned eBay late November 2013 and found a red 2006 Roubaix Elite triple in my size. It was less than seven hundred dollars and it looked new. It even had a Power Tap hub on a DT Swiss RR585 wheel. There were a few days left on the auction so I figured it would go for more than two grand. I book marked the auction but figured it would still be too rich for me. On the last day of the auction I came back to the site and it was at 850 dollars so I figured what the heck, if I can put in a bid and get the bike for less than a thousand I'd do it. Sure enough the auction stalled and in the last few minutes I won the bid at just under nine hundred. With shipping I was only eighteen dollars over my budget and it arrived a week later. It was a happy ending for this carbon dreamer.

I traded emails with the seller and found out the bike only had about three hundred road miles on it. He bought it for his girlfriend but the frame size wasn't to her liking and the bike sat until he found and bought another that suited her better. He needed to let the Roubaix go and I was lucky enough to outbid about eight others to make it my own. Sometimes things just work out for the best.

I leave you with a few final thoughts, the first I call "Sunflowers of Kansas" that will hopefully convey the impact the trip had on me that continues until this day. The second are the words to the song, "What a Wonderful World" as sung by Louie Armstrong, which played in my mind on many days. These lyrics are for my daughter's, Janel who to her dad can sing like an angel, and Nicole whose poetry moves me beyond words. They are what I am most proud of in my life and they bring tears of joy to my eyes more times than they can imagine; as they are effortlessly doing right now. And my closing thoughts are about the importance of writing all of this down.

So my advice for you is to find your own defining moment in life and I hope it changes and challenges you to be who you were meant to be. Fair warning, once you experience it you will become restless, and that restlessness will stay with you until you answer the call to pursue the path where you are excited to wake up each day with a sense of urgency and inspiration. It doesn't matter what it is, or where it is. We have but one chance through this life and it would a disappointment if we squander it doing things we don't want to do to please others. Go do and be you!

Sunflowers of Kansas

If you are wondering what it must feel like to have finished such an adventure I cannot be certain. You see, while I may have ended the ride physically, in my mind I am still on the bike. Some days I find myself in Kansas pedaling along on the gentle rolling prairie and on a few occasions I've sped down the mountains and worked my way back up the switchbacks. I'm beginning to think the only way to end this journey is to do it again. Then I might be able to find whatever it is I must have missed, the reason why I cannot get it out of my head. I lived the dream and now I dream about the life. Maybe it never ends. Maybe it's not supposed to. I have many questions and too few answers. Somehow on the bike it all seemed right. Like being a teenager with no worries, living for today and dreaming of all my tomorrows. I choose to live today and for all my tomorrows as well. You should see the Sunflowers in Kansas.

What a Wonderful World

By Bob Thiele (as "George Douglas") and George
David Weiss (Made famous by Louie Armstrong)

I see trees of green, red roses too
I see them bloom for me and you
And I think to myself what a wonderful world.

I see skies of blue and clouds of white
The bright blessed day, the dark sacred night
And I think to myself what a wonderful world.

The colors of the rainbow so pretty in the sky
Are also on the faces of people going by
I see friends shaking hands saying how do you do
They're really saying I love you.

I hear babies crying, I watch them grow
They'll learn much more than I'll never know
And I think to myself what a wonderful world
Yes I think to myself what a wonderful world

The Importance of Writing

The end of the journey was not in Boston as I first envisioned. It came with the last of my thoughts being written and rewritten until I felt all I had experienced passed back through me and into a more lasting record; one that would not be lost or forgotten. Yet I struggled in knowing when to bring this writing to an end—mostly for fear of leaving something out and in letting go—but I sensed I was close. As I felt the weight lift I could feel the peace in its conclusion. I finally let go, I finished. The time to share and to move on had come.

In reflection it took much longer to put my trip into words than it did to ride. I didn't count the hours but I counted the years that passed by as it evolved from my notes and my memories into this final draft. It pays tribute to an adventure taken; my adventure. It is unique but not so unlike the journey of those who made the trek with me in the early summer of 2004.

In my journal I captured the essence of each day's ride, I recorded the temperatures where I could and made some cryptic notes in hopes someday I'd be able to decipher them and organize my thoughts into a more enjoyable and memorable read. In writing and assembling the pieces into this single effort I have been able to continue the journey. I feel the typed words transform into visions of what I experienced, the sounds, the smells, and the emotional connections and at times, the detachment between me and my bike from nature. It moved me at points to tears, it brought a smile to my face, and made me close my eyes and immerse even deeper into its call.

When I started writing I thought it would be easy, I thought it would be quick, but it was neither. I began at the beginning and moved forward through time in parallel with my riding; west to east, beginning to end. There were many interruptions; periods of time where I thought about the trip but did not write, and there were long periods where I did neither. I imposed completion dates—or more accurately the calendar year at the time—I wanted to be done but failed to make any of them. I could not sit and write in some regimented fashion, I had to be inspired, and I required purpose.

This is so out of character for a person whose employment as a project manager requires such discipline, but this was not a job, it was closure of a personal journey. And when I accepted it would finish according to plan, on a timeframe to which I could not force, it began to flow and I began to write more consistently. I could visualize in my mind that I would finish my writing and press *Save* for the final time.

There were days where I was compelled to write with furious purpose as if the thoughts would escape me if I did not act. And it was in these bursts of writing where I was connected and in the moment with those memorable events in 2004; so connected all of my senses told me I was on the bike and not at my computer clicking away on the keys at speed. Through the tears in my eyes I saw the road before me overlaid onto the small white screen filled with words aligned with the visions. Those were indeed special moments.

My inspiration did not remain linear. A thought about a specific event or place would come to mind and I could not ignore it. I deviated from my original intentions, jumped forward and back without a plan—Kansas to Illinois and all the way back to New Mexico—and in doing so I found my writing became more satisfying, I was more consistent and focused.

Eventually I would chronical all of the days and it would become complete. Writing was therapeutic, it was necessary, and it was part of the journey. I learned the only release is to express an emotional experience like this cross country trip in words and to share it with others. So here it is.

Yet the journey came with disappointment. Some of those with whom I would have liked to share this story with are no longer here. Most recently the passing of a wonderful friend and fellow cross country XC13 rider, Brick Susko. And that instilled in me a sense of urgency to finish. My dad preceded my cross country odyssey by four years. I am left to wonder if he could have ever imagined me committing to such a rigorous course. What I would give to be able to share it with him; to read my journey aloud in his presence.

And it is in that spirit I have written in hopes of sharing with my mother who turned 84 this year, my sisters, my brothers, my wife, my daughters, my friends, and now my Grandson, Wiley, the new love of my life, what I experienced. And should I lose my mental faculties in my twilight years, maybe someone will read this story back to me. And whether familiar or not it, may I find some connection, some reason to follow this boy on his bike.

I find comfort in knowing my writing will be a place for me to go when I need a reminder of who I am or at least who I once was. I am ordinary but I was once extraordinary. I lived and this is my reminder. It is my gift to me.

I hope you enjoyed reading about my journey. By chance if you were entertained, maybe laughed or even cheered for me as you turned the pages then I accomplished even more. My message to you is that this cross country venture was more about a personal transformation for me and the bike just happened to be the instrument or more appropriately a vehicle to enable the change to occur. My story may have been more enriching or more insightful for an avid bicyclist, but it wasn't necessary.

There is no way I can possibly express in words my experience in such a way you can consume the writing and fully appreciate what it is like to prepare for and live this seven–week odyssey, to suffer mentally and physically, and to emerge in some sorted victory. I realize that. But most people who will read this will never undertake such a personal journey; they will choose to experience such adventures through the actions of others and that I find to be very disappointing.

To observe is not the same as doing; not close enough to break you and rebuild you into something new. This experience did just that to me. While these words are limited to my writing ability I hope the spirit in which it was written gives you a glimpse into how it felt and how I was changed.

A part of me hopes this might be the spark, the catalyst in your committing to let yourself take the first step to live beyond your daily existence, to dream, to chance failure, to be afraid, but not deterred, because in doing you will be rewarded beyond imagination, and it will become your reality. You will be marked for life in a way only you will fully understand. And you will be changed as I was and you will learn what matters in life will be forever different. You can't avoid it and you will embrace it.

Whether you long to bike or hike, or sing on a stage it doesn't matter. It doesn't have to be epic, it's not the miles, and it is not the size of the audience. It is the dream you nurture into your reality. And for you it will also be beyond words.

Should you embark on a journey of your own I hope you will be compelled to share it, to write about it so it may be a catalyst for others. It doesn't matter if anyone else reads it; it will always be your gift to you.

Humbly I declare this both the end and the beginning. Thank you for allowing me the opportunity to share my story.

Tommy

2 Timothy 4:7
I have fought the good fight, I have finished the race, I have kept the faith.

To learn more about cross country cycling I recommend you conduct a thorough web search on fully supported tours, find people who have made the trip, and get their feedback about the support group and the trip itself. The experience is tied to the organization you partner with and the selection of the right team of people is the most important decision you will make in committing to such an arduous endeavor. My good friend Tracy sold CrossRoads following the completion of the 2017 tour. Since I have no knowledge of the new organization I cannot offer my recommendation. No matter the provider the miles and duration are nearly the same. It will be:

1 trip
49 days
15 states
3,415 miles
Many new friends
A lifetime of memories

Made in the USA
Columbia, SC
04 December 2021